RECCHIONI - MAMMUCARI

ORPHANS

VOLUME ONE
THE BEGINNING

ORPHANS series created by Roberto Recchioni and Emiliano Mammucari

Original lettering by Marina Sanfelice
Original logo created by Paolo Campana
Original book design by Officine Bolzoni with Cosimo Torsoli

English translation by Elena Cecchini and Valeria Gobbato
Localization, layout, and editing by Mike Kennedy

LION™
FORGE

THE
MAGNETIC™
COLLECTION

ISBN: 978-1-942367-17-8
Library of Congress Control Number: 2018931325

Printed in China.

10 9 8 7 6 5 4 3 2 1

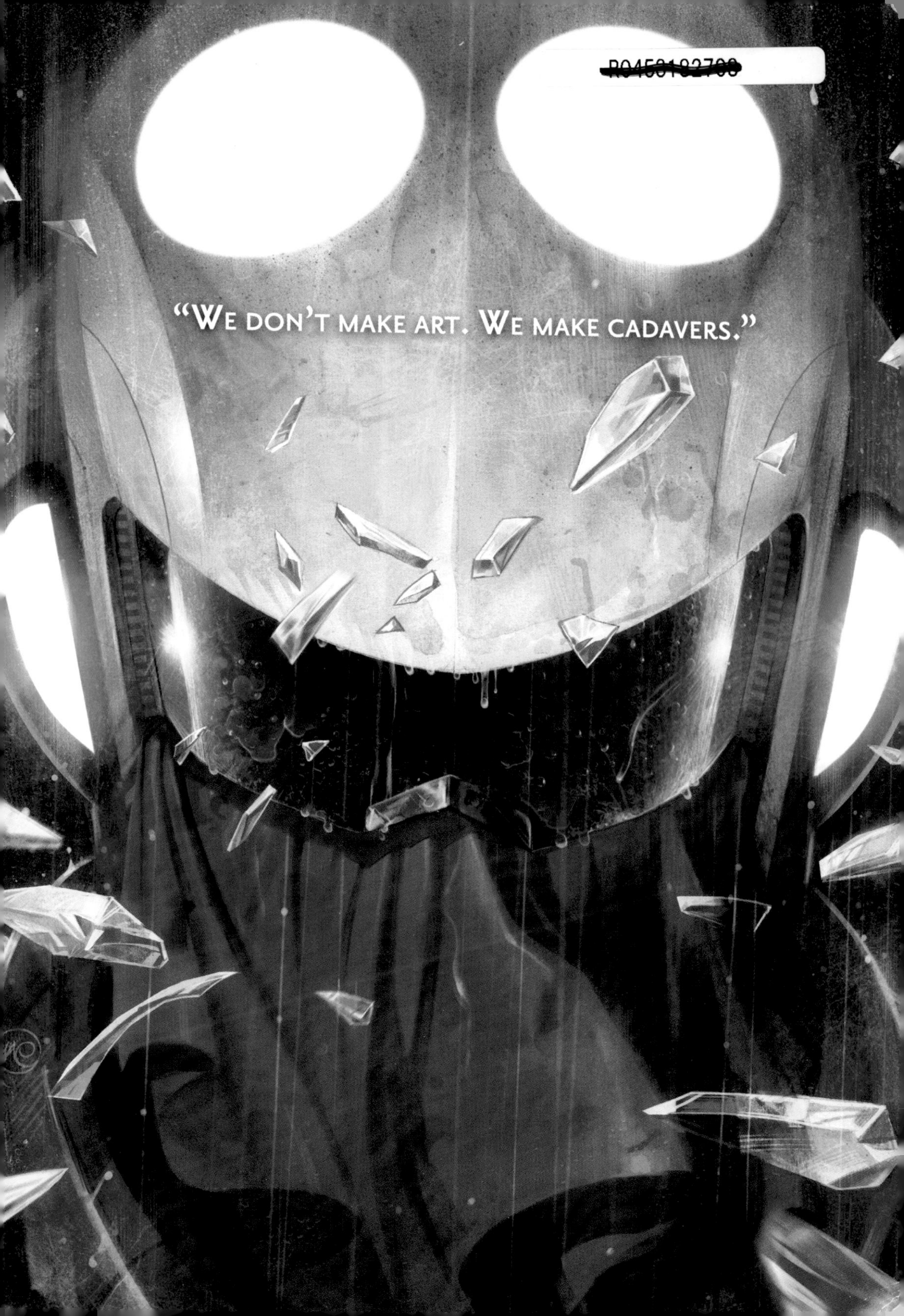
"We don't make art. We make cadavers."

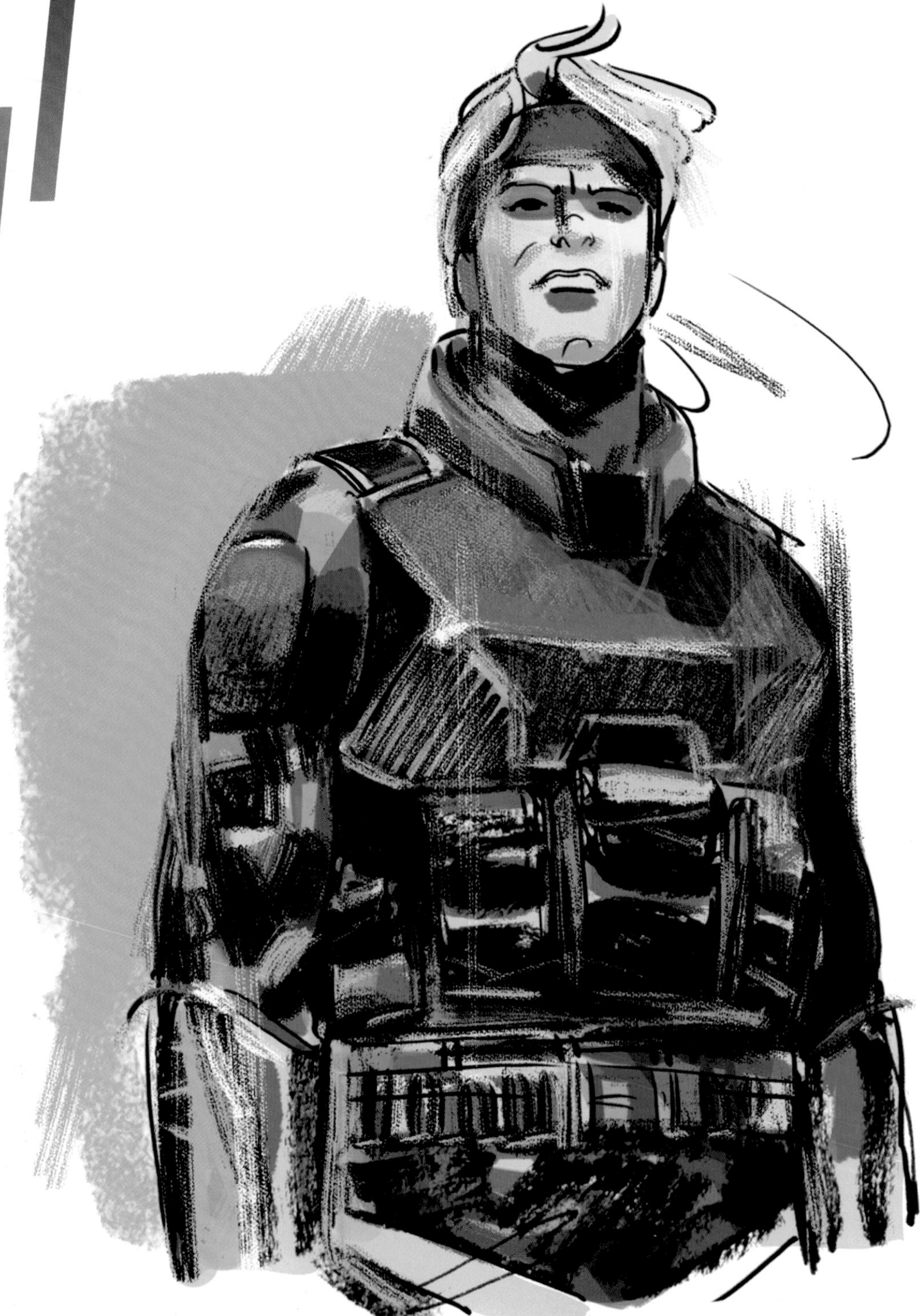

Above: illustration by Gigi Cavenago
Next page: character study by Emiliano Mammucari
Previous page: illustration by Massimo Carnevale

START

In 2013, Sergio Bonelli Editore gave birth to a massive new universe. Helmed by writer Roberto Recchioni and artist Emiliano Mammucari, this new series was to be the first new color comic series for the esteemed company in over sixty years. The team's intention was to motivate a diverse group of artists to create a series unlike the familiar, traditional Italian adventure comics, such as *Nathan Never* and *Dylan Dog*, and to break new ground in visual, dramatic, high-concept storytelling. The result was *Orphans*, a twelve-issue monthly series filled with enough action and pathos to fuel a revolution. And these weren't twenty-two-page American comics — these were ninety-two-page issues, every month, over 1,100 pages total. And that was just considered "season one." The series has since spawned five more "seasons" continuing the tale that begins in this very volume. Like the classic, dramatic sci-fi that inspired it, such as Robert Heinlein's *Starship Troopers*, William Golding's *Lord of the Flies*, military films such as *Full Metal Jacket* and *Aliens*, and even video games such as *Halo*, *Orphans* will draw you into a world that is simultaneously alien and familiar, taking you to places you neither want to visit nor leave once there. So strap yourselves in — you're about to embark on an unforgettable journey.

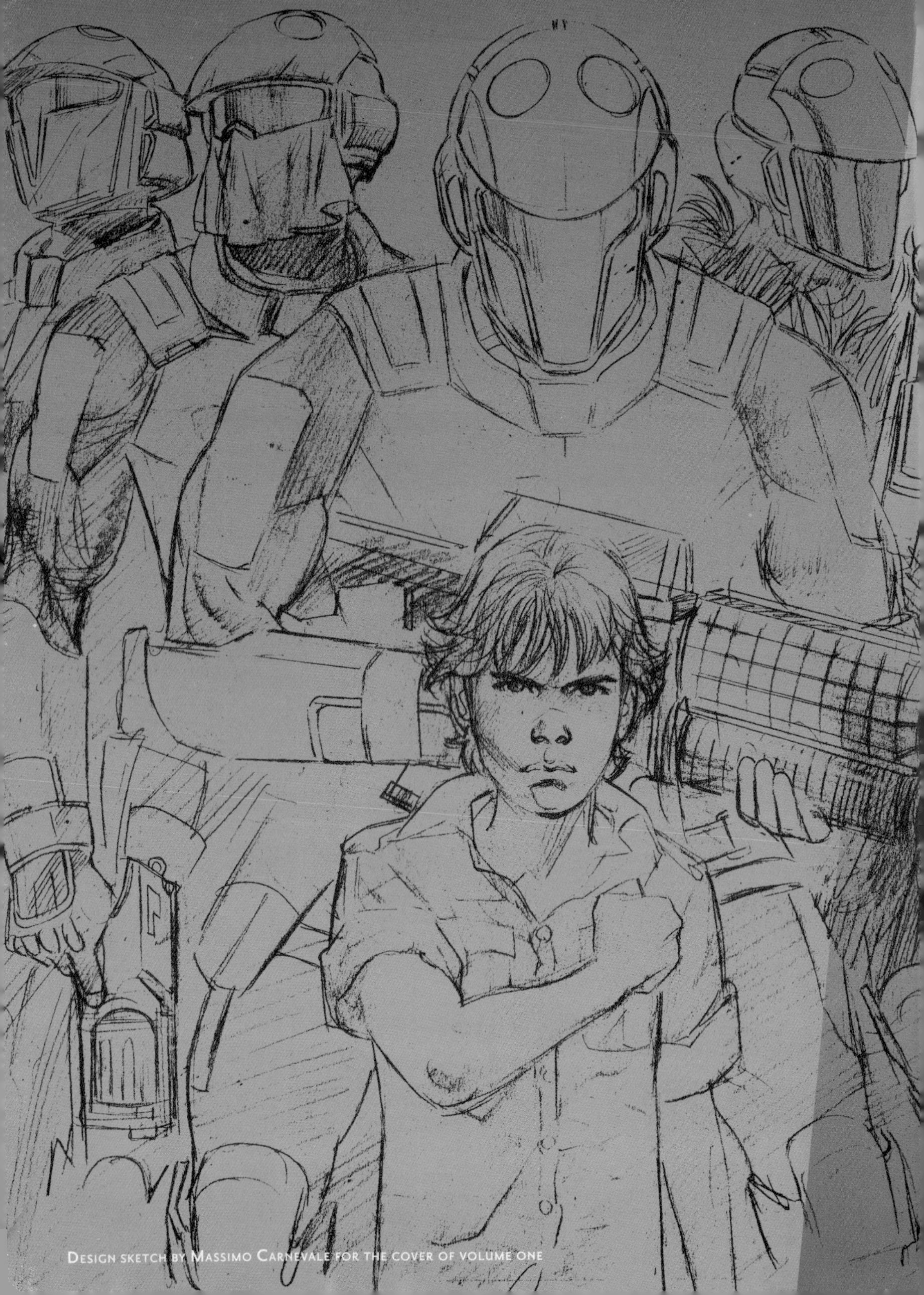

Design sketch by Massimo Carnevale for the cover of volume one

SCARED LITTLE SOLDIERS

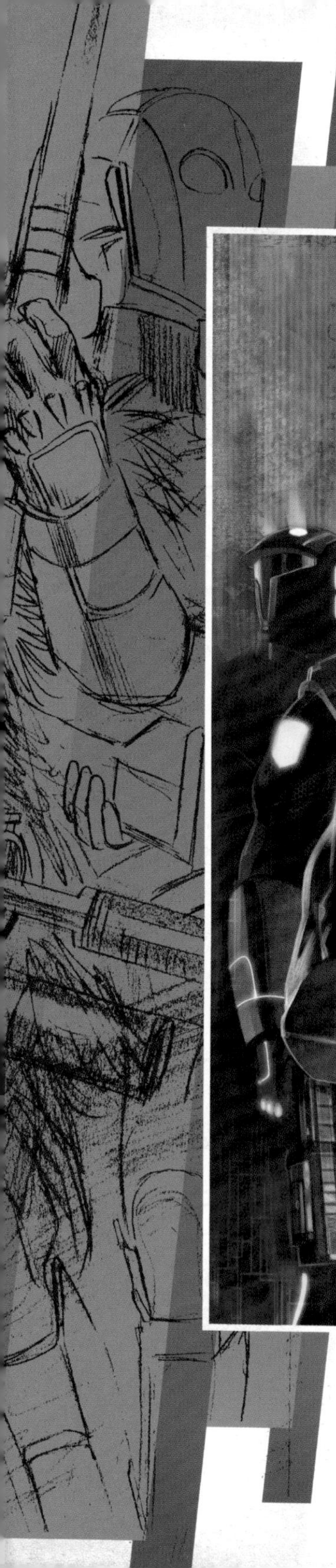

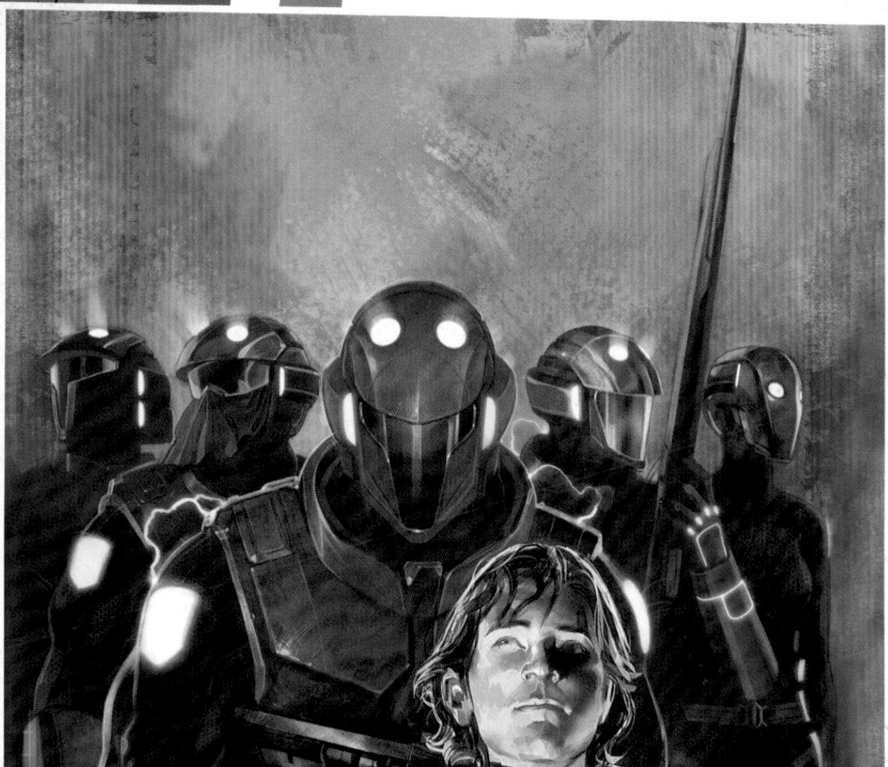

ORPHANS: CHAPTER 1

story: ROBERTO RECCHIONI
art: EMILIANO MAMMUCARI
colors: LORENZO DE FELICI and ANNALISA LEONI
cover: MASSIMO CARNEVALE

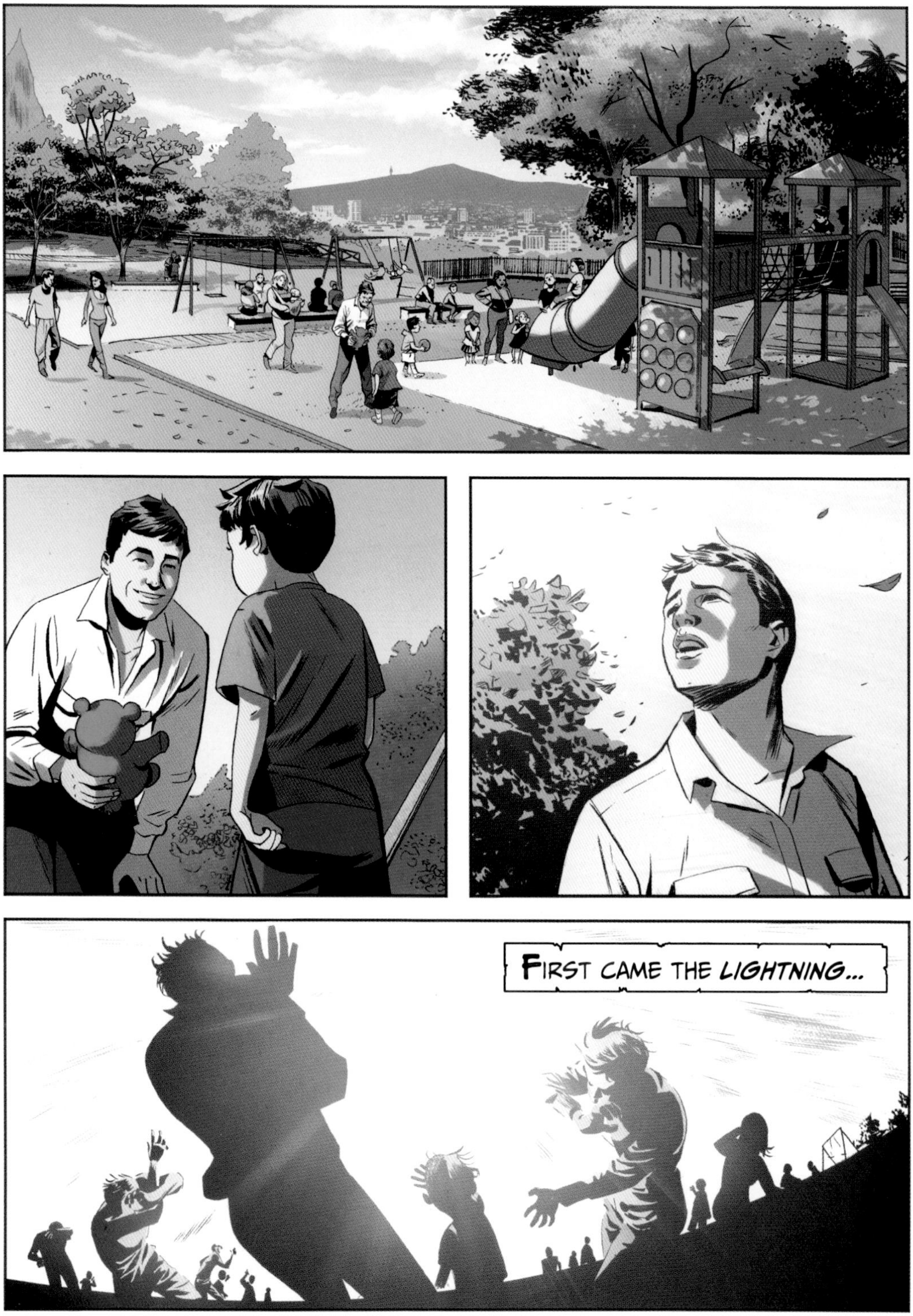
FIRST CAME THE LIGHTNING...

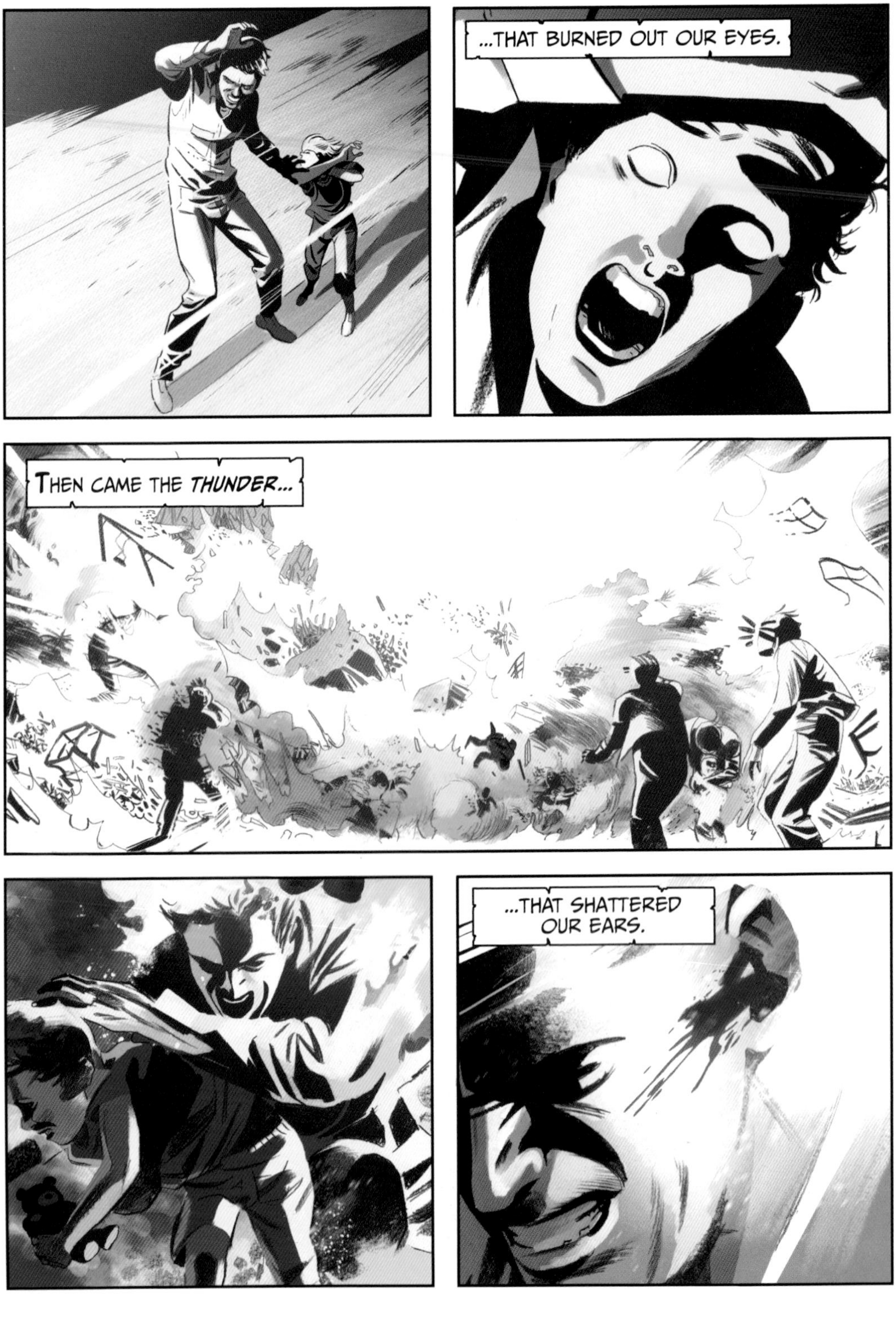
...THAT BURNED OUT OUR EYES.
THEN CAME THE *THUNDER*...
...THAT SHATTERED OUR EARS.

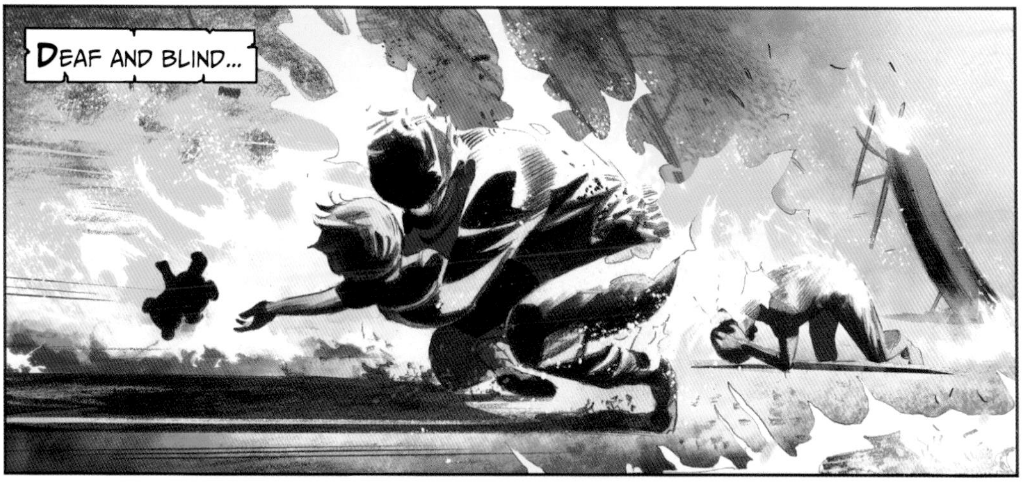
DEAF AND BLIND...

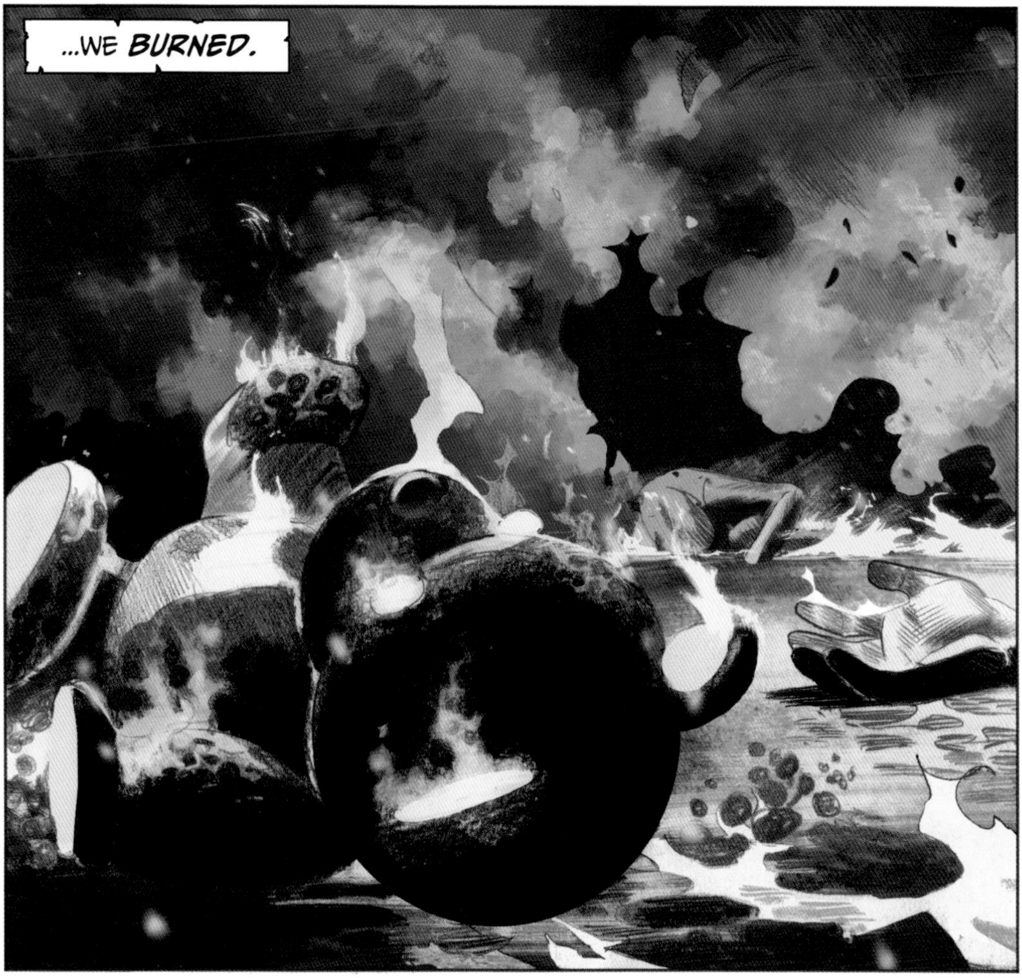
...WE BURNED.

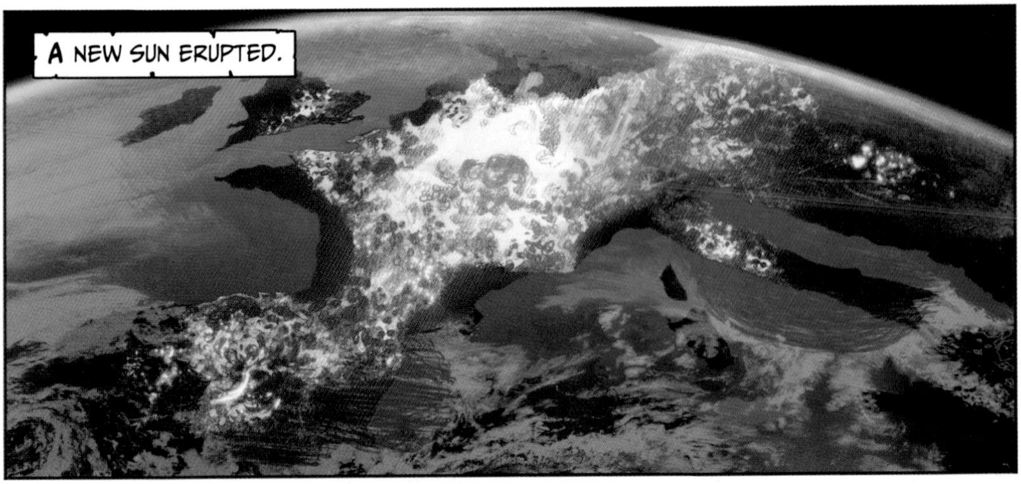
A NEW SUN ERUPTED.

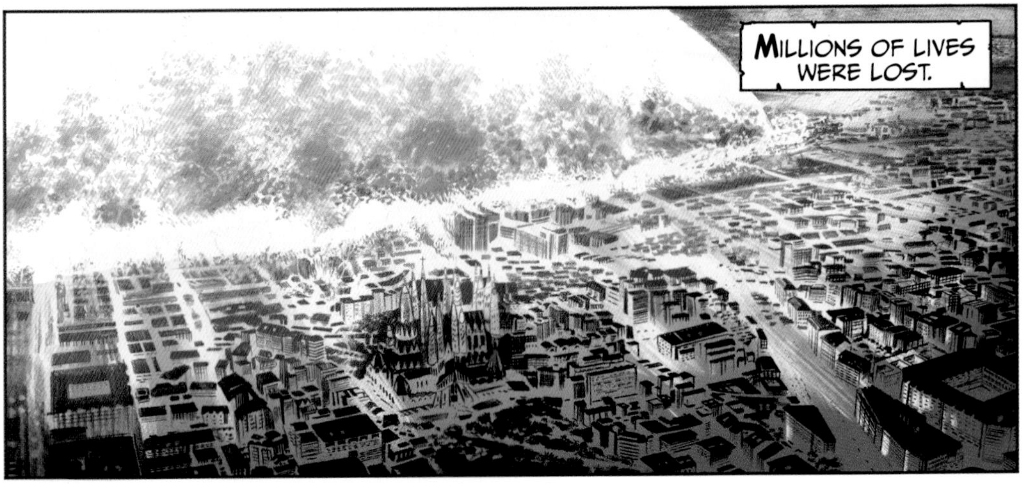
MILLIONS OF LIVES WERE LOST.

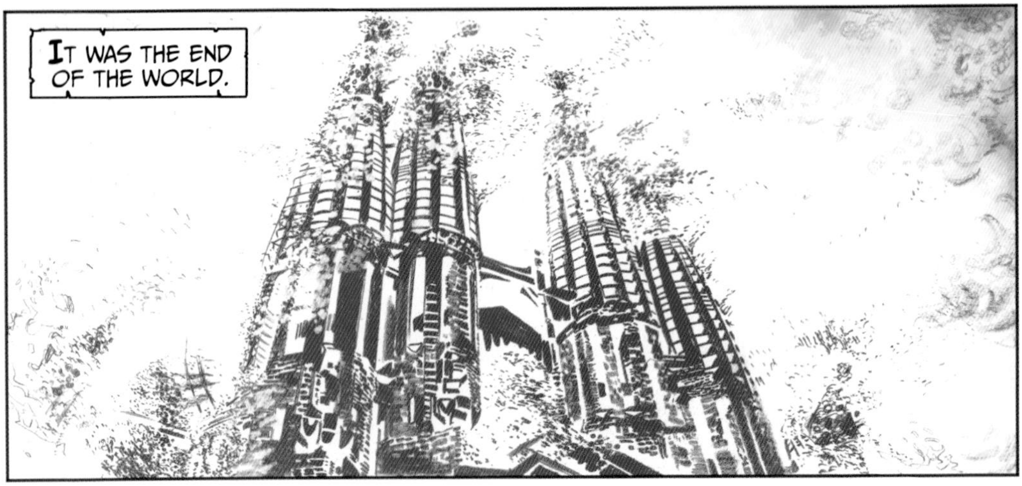
IT WAS THE END OF THE WORLD.

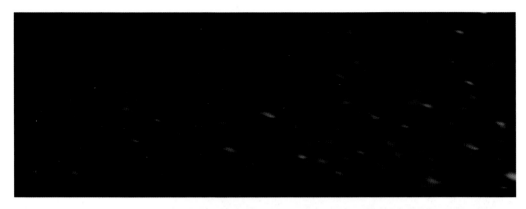

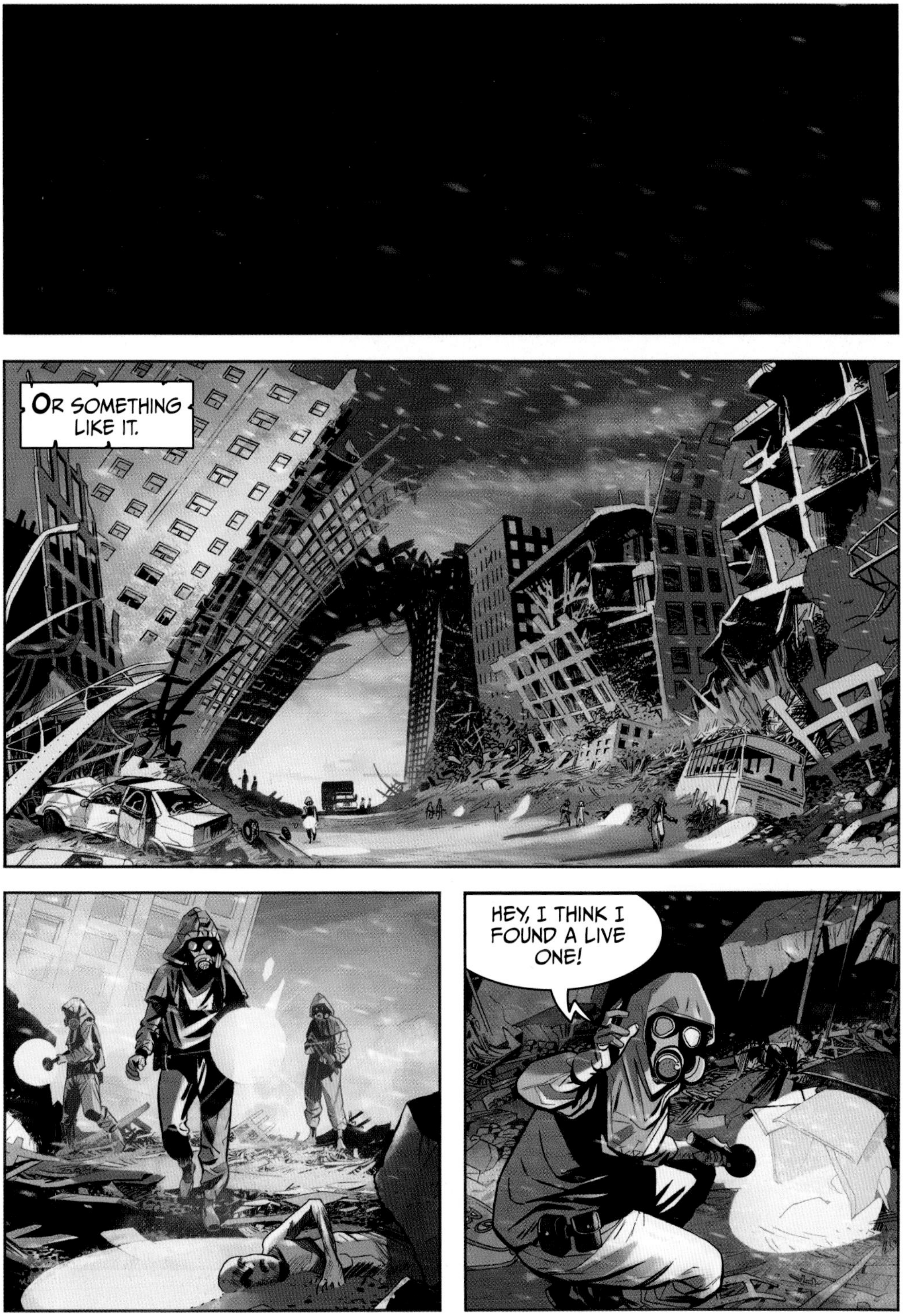
OR SOMETHING LIKE IT.
HEY, I THINK I FOUND A LIVE ONE!

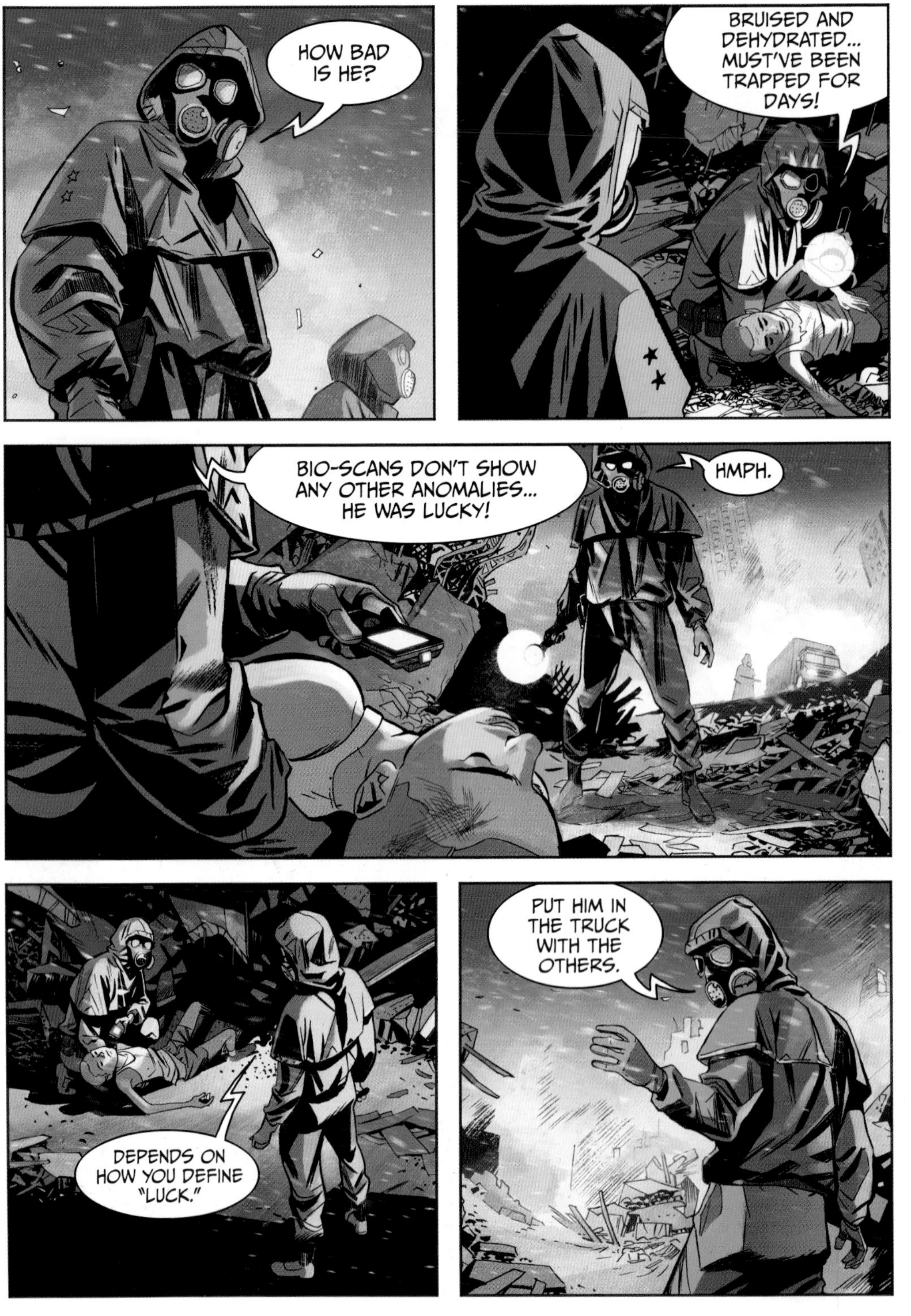
HOW BAD IS HE?
BRUISED AND DEHYDRATED... MUST'VE BEEN TRAPPED FOR DAYS!
BIO-SCANS DON'T SHOW ANY OTHER ANOMALIES... HE WAS LUCKY!
HMPH.
DEPENDS ON HOW YOU DEFINE "LUCK."
PUT HIM IN THE TRUCK WITH THE OTHERS.

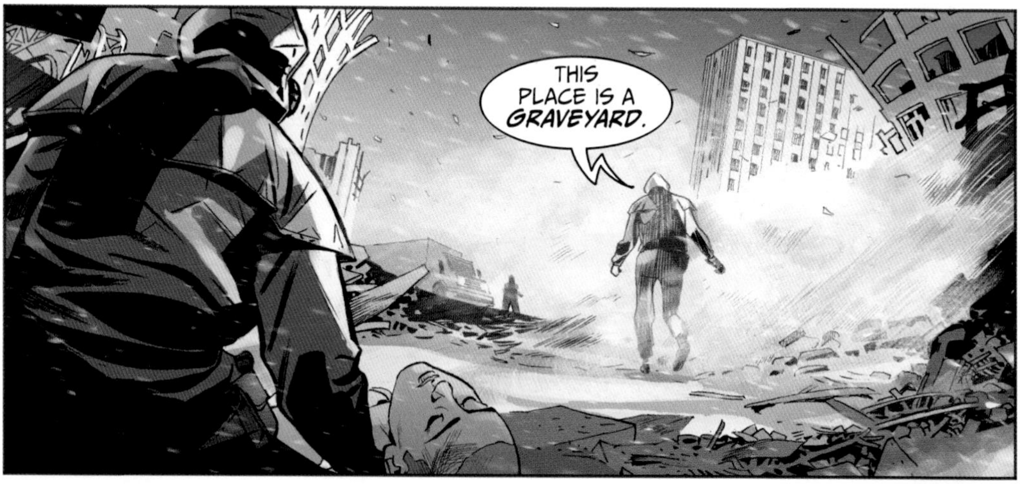
THIS PLACE IS A GRAVEYARD.

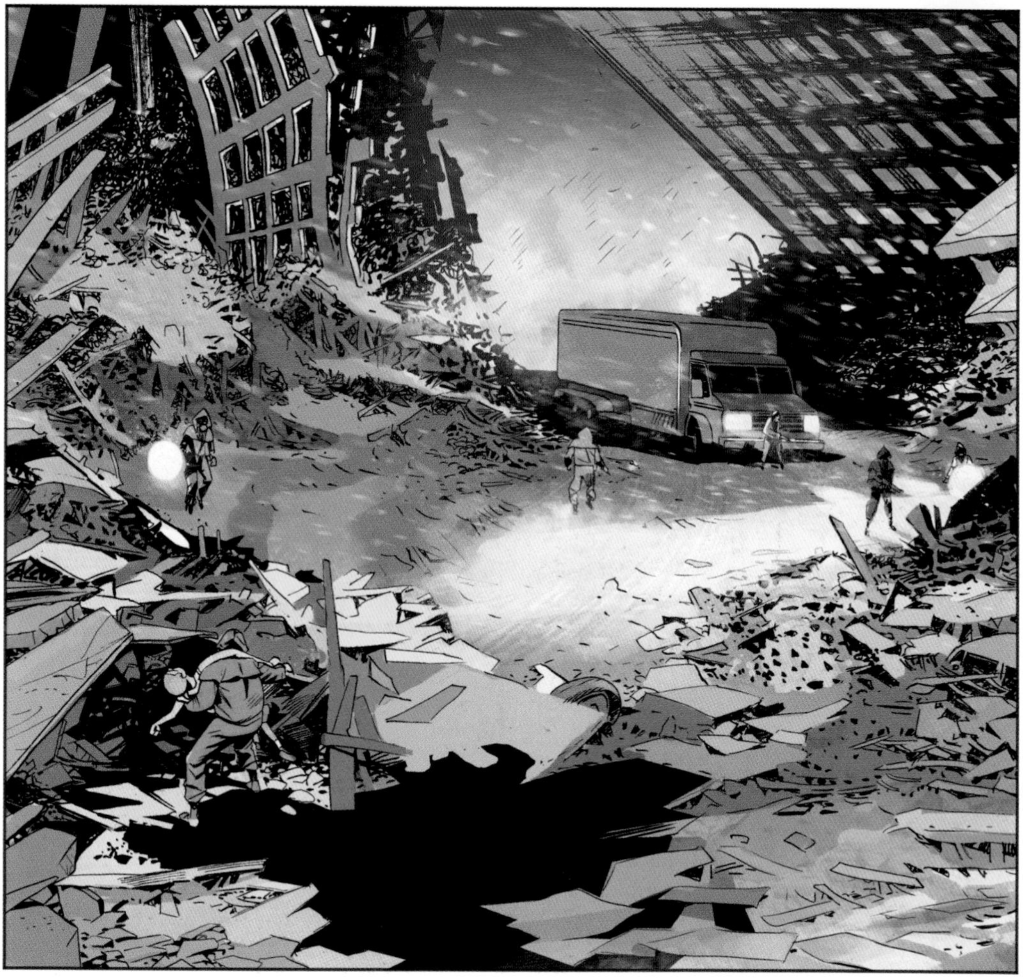

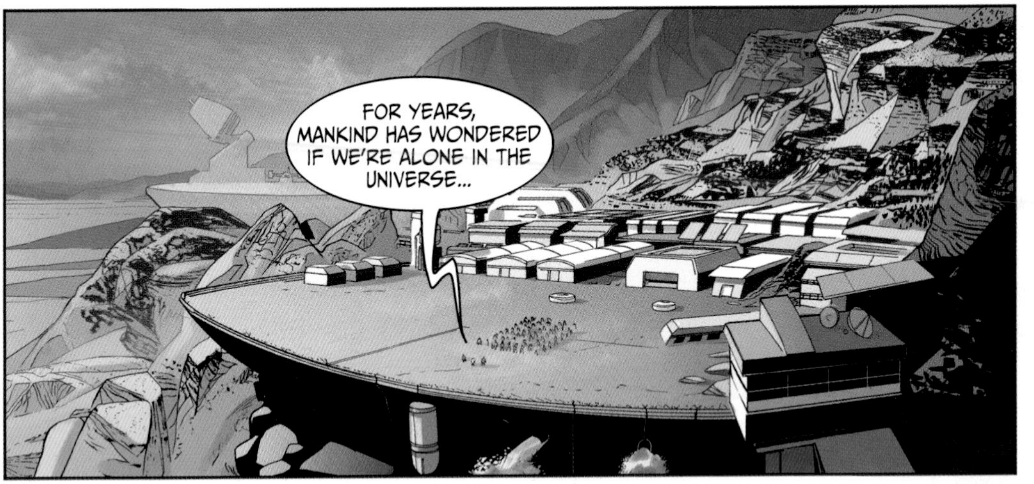
FOR YEARS, MANKIND HAS WONDERED IF WE'RE ALONE IN THE UNIVERSE...

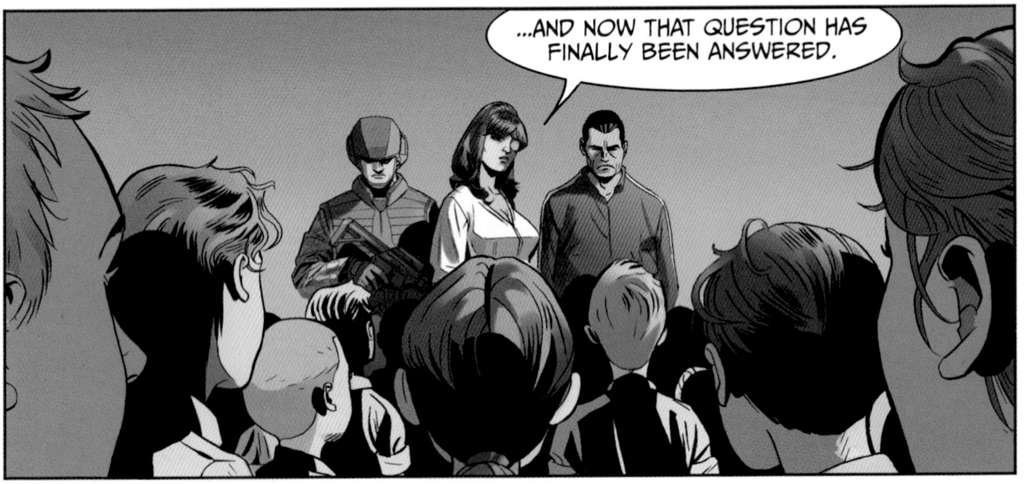
...AND NOW THAT QUESTION HAS FINALLY BEEN ANSWERED.

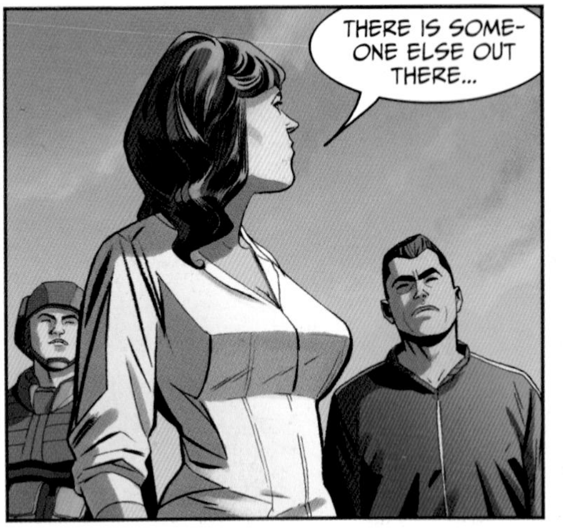
THERE IS SOME-ONE ELSE OUT THERE...

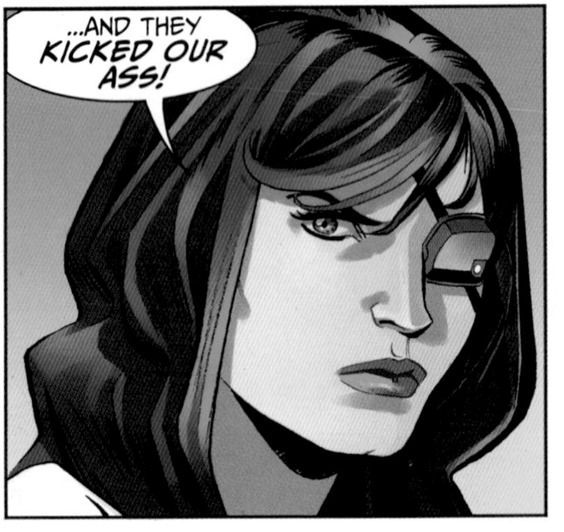
...AND THEY *KICKED OUR ASS!*

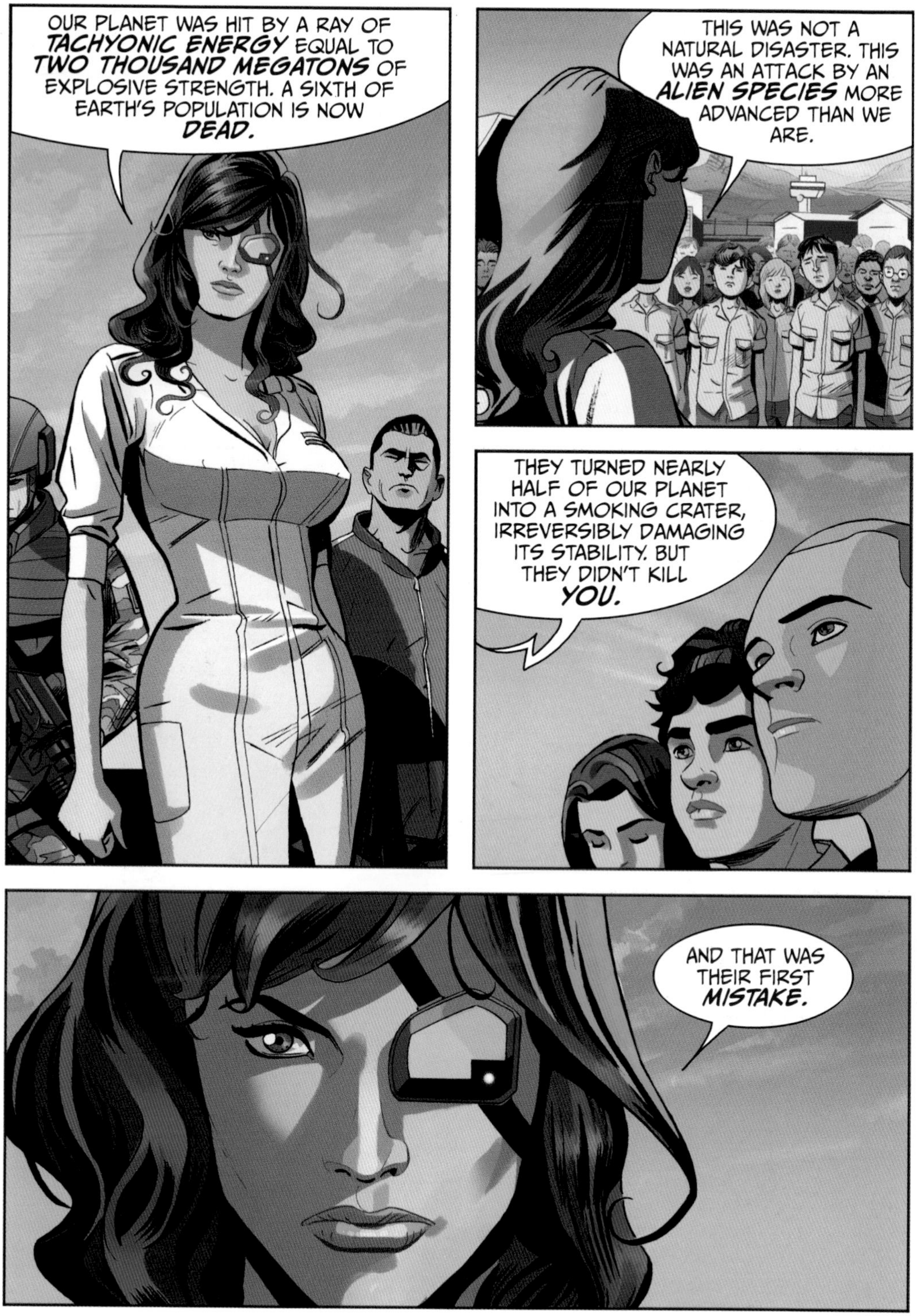
OUR PLANET WAS HIT BY A RAY OF TACHYONIC ENERGY EQUAL TO TWO THOUSAND MEGATONS OF EXPLOSIVE STRENGTH. A SIXTH OF EARTH'S POPULATION IS NOW DEAD.
THIS WAS NOT A NATURAL DISASTER. THIS WAS AN ATTACK BY AN ALIEN SPECIES MORE ADVANCED THAN WE ARE.
THEY TURNED NEARLY HALF OF OUR PLANET INTO A SMOKING CRATER, IRREVERSIBLY DAMAGING ITS STABILITY. BUT THEY DIDN'T KILL YOU.
AND THAT WAS THEIR FIRST MISTAKE.

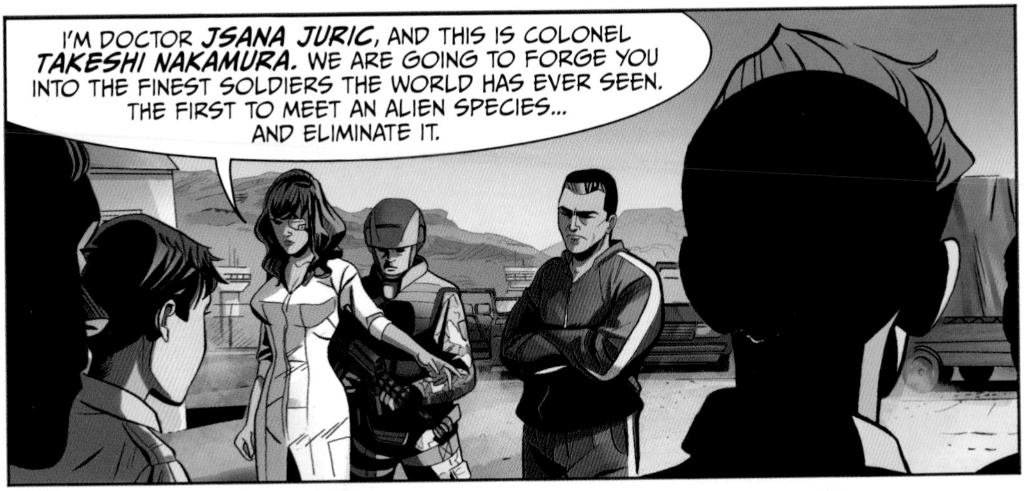
I'M DOCTOR JSANA JURIC, AND THIS IS COLONEL TAKESHI NAKAMURA. WE ARE GOING TO FORGE YOU INTO THE FINEST SOLDIERS THE WORLD HAS EVER SEEN. THE FIRST TO MEET AN ALIEN SPECIES... AND ELIMINATE IT.

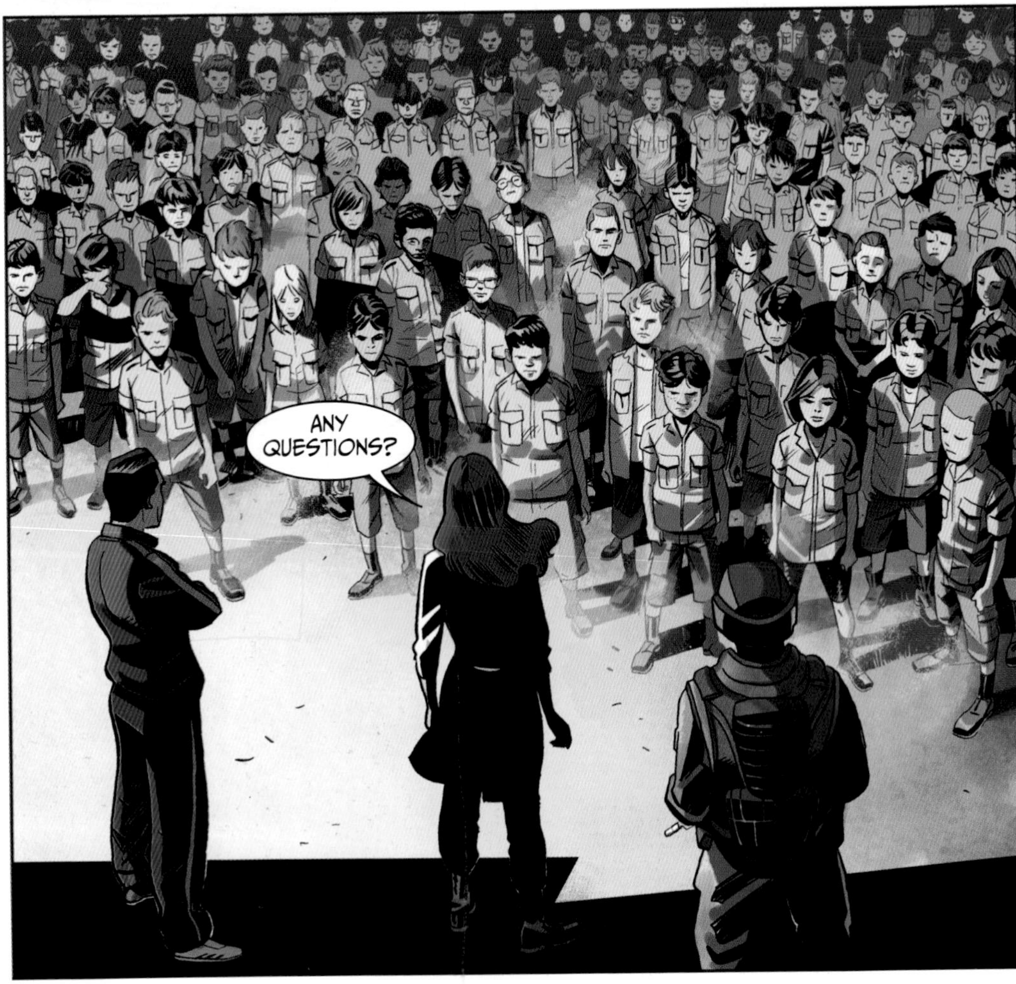
ANY QUESTIONS?

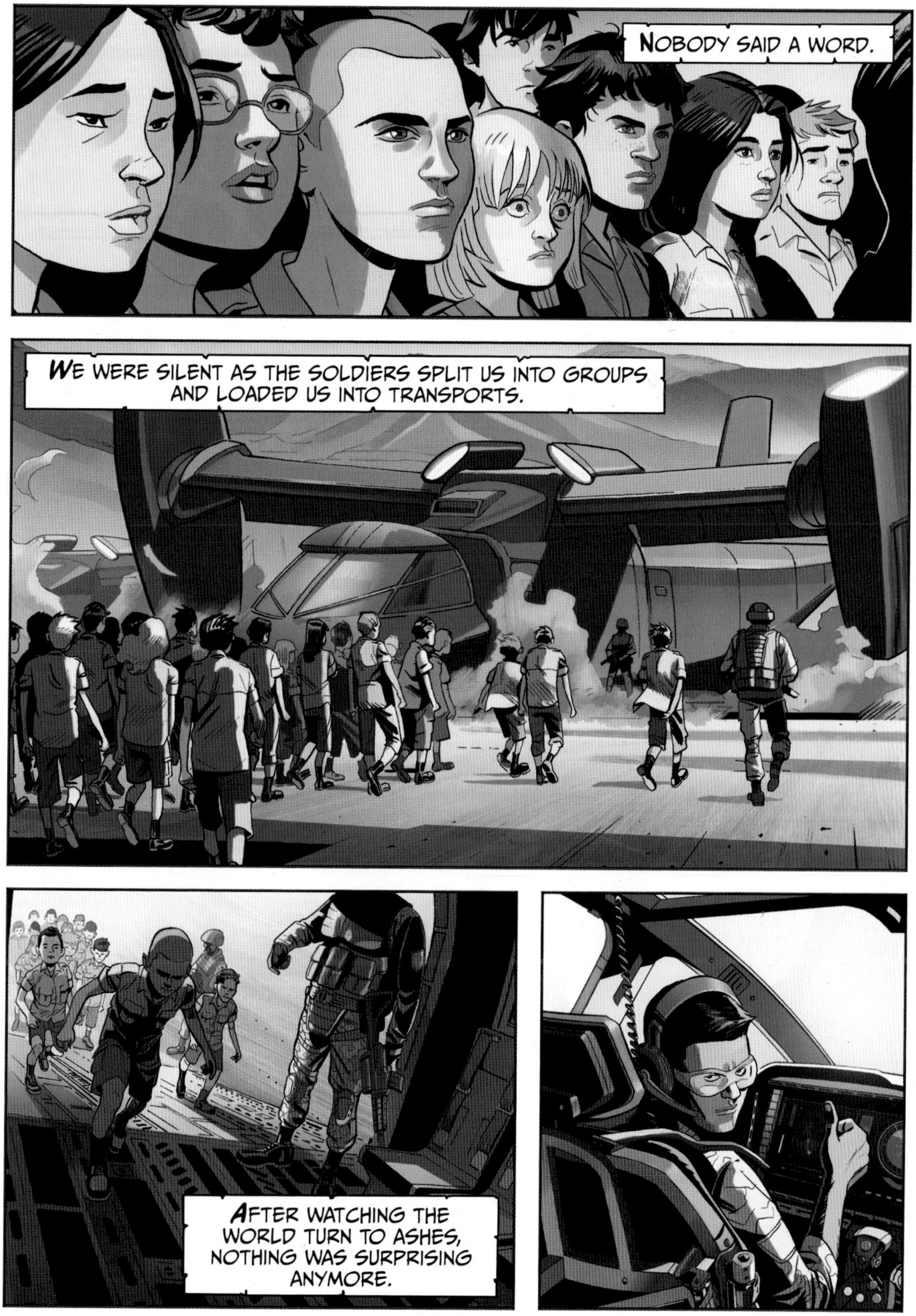
NOBODY SAID A WORD.
WE WERE SILENT AS THE SOLDIERS SPLIT US INTO GROUPS AND LOADED US INTO TRANSPORTS.
AFTER WATCHING THE WORLD TURN TO ASHES, NOTHING WAS SURPRISING ANYMORE.

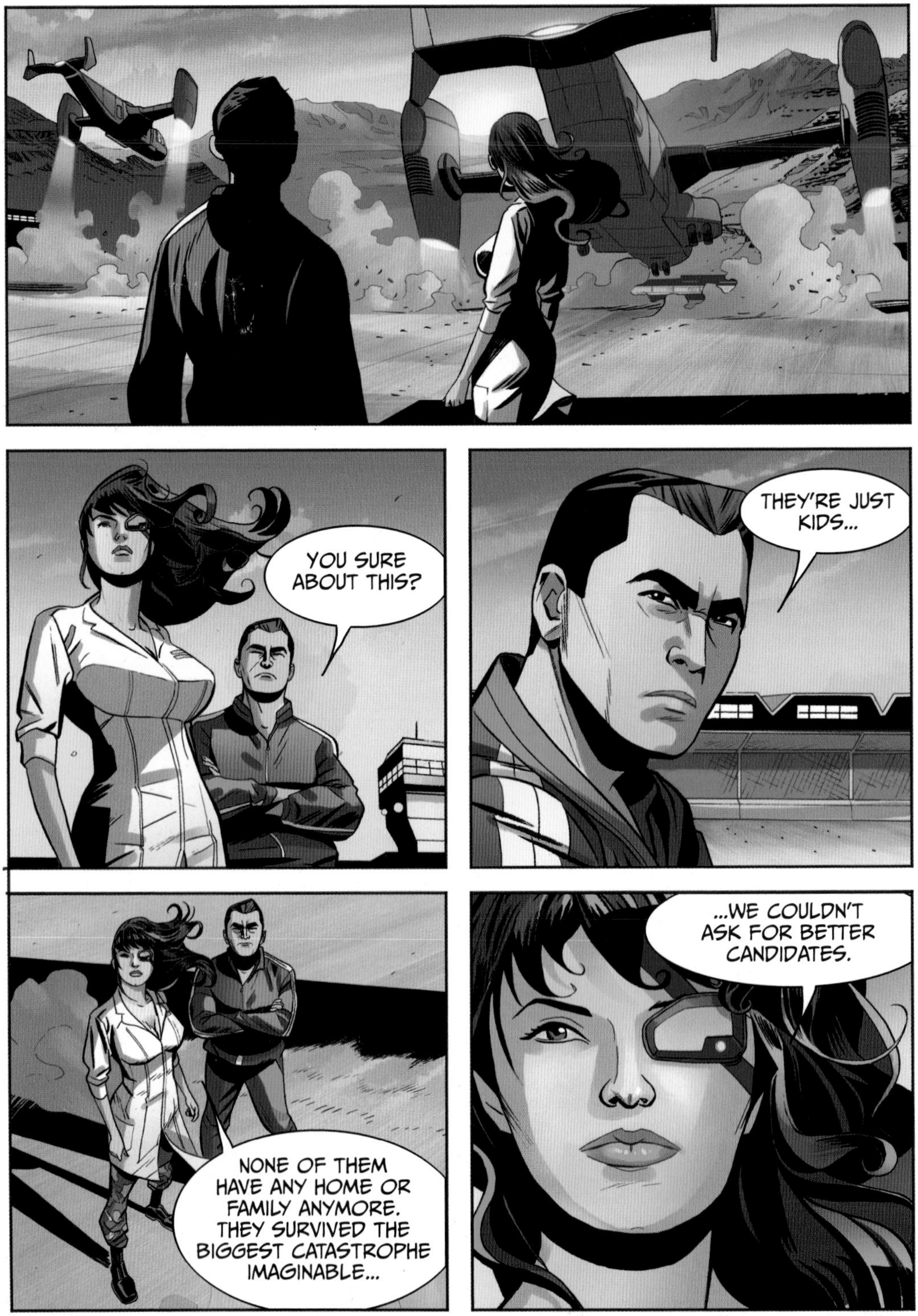
YOU SURE ABOUT THIS?
THEY'RE JUST KIDS...
NONE OF THEM HAVE ANY HOME OR FAMILY ANYMORE. THEY SURVIVED THE BIGGEST CATASTROPHE IMAGINABLE...
...WE COULDN'T ASK FOR BETTER CANDIDATES.

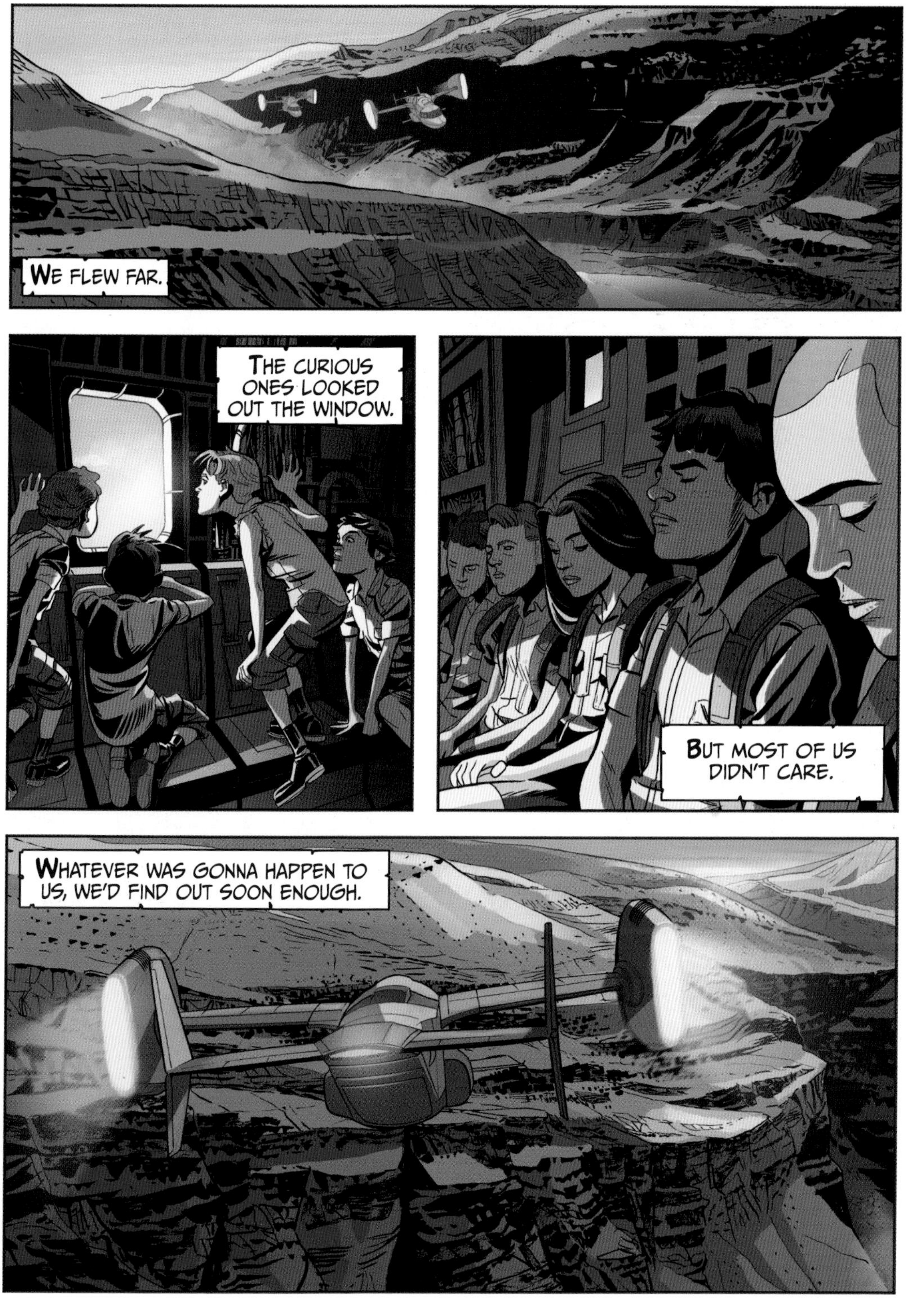
WE FLEW FAR.
THE CURIOUS ONES LOOKED OUT THE WINDOW.
BUT MOST OF US DIDN'T CARE.
WHATEVER WAS GONNA HAPPEN TO US, WE'D FIND OUT SOON ENOUGH.

THE PLANE DIPPED OCCASIONALLY, AND A SOLDIER WOULD FORCE SOME OF US TO JUMP OUT.

C'MON! *MOVE!*

EVEN THEN, WE KEPT PRETTY QUIET.

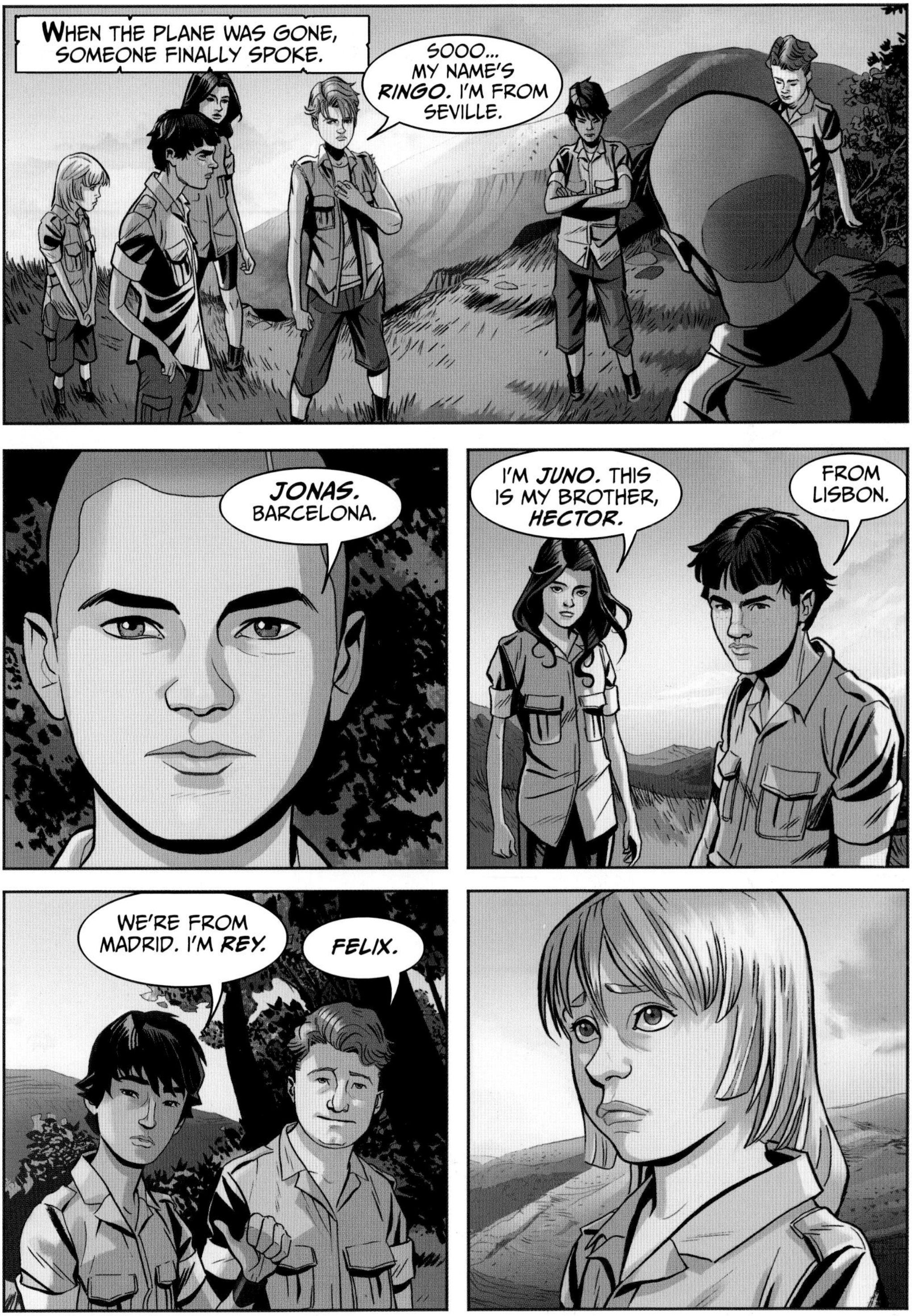
WHEN THE PLANE WAS GONE, SOMEONE FINALLY SPOKE.
SOOO... MY NAME'S RINGO. I'M FROM SEVILLE.
JONAS. BARCELONA.
I'M JUNO. THIS IS MY BROTHER, HECTOR.
FROM LISBON.
WE'RE FROM MADRID. I'M REY.
FELIX.

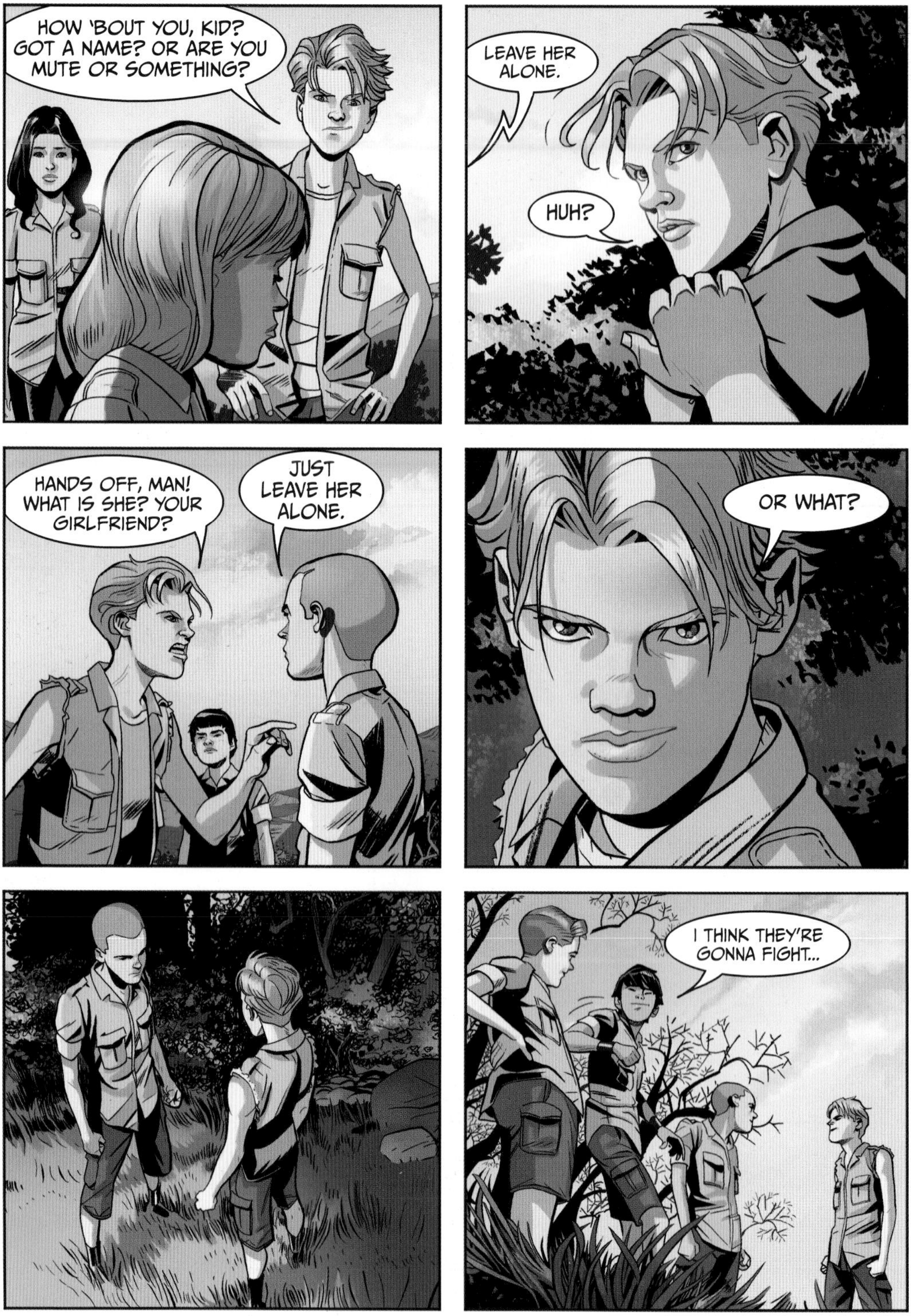
HOW 'BOUT YOU, KID? GOT A NAME? OR ARE YOU MUTE OR SOMETHING?
LEAVE HER ALONE.
HUH?
HANDS OFF, MAN! WHAT IS SHE? YOUR GIRLFRIEND?
JUST LEAVE HER ALONE.
OR WHAT?
I THINK THEY'RE GONNA FIGHT...

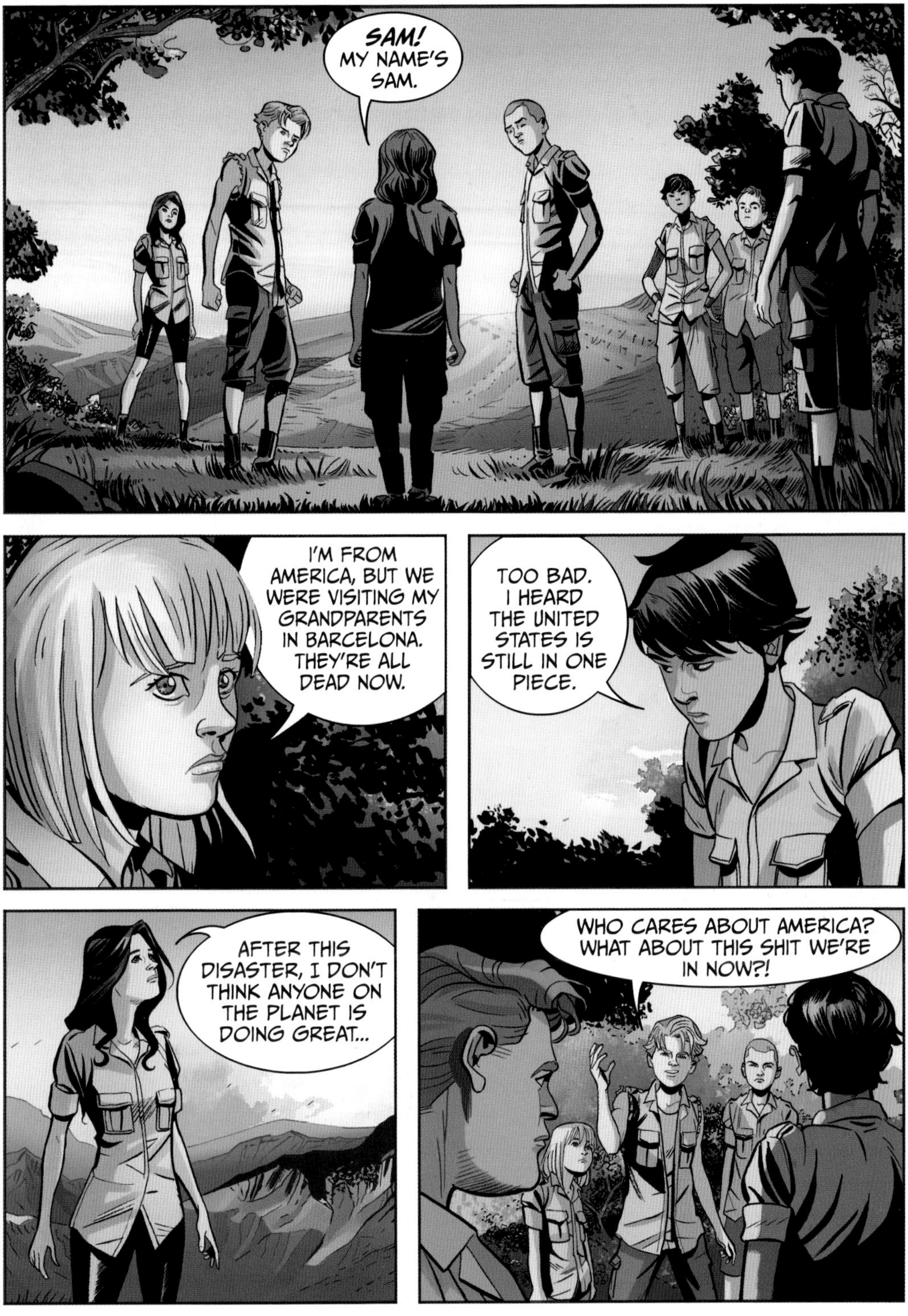
SAM! MY NAME'S SAM.
I'M FROM AMERICA, BUT WE WERE VISITING MY GRANDPARENTS IN BARCELONA. THEY'RE ALL DEAD NOW.
TOO BAD. I HEARD THE UNITED STATES IS STILL IN ONE PIECE.
AFTER THIS DISASTER, I DON'T THINK ANYONE ON THE PLANET IS DOING GREAT...
WHO CARES ABOUT AMERICA? WHAT ABOUT THIS SHIT WE'RE IN NOW?!

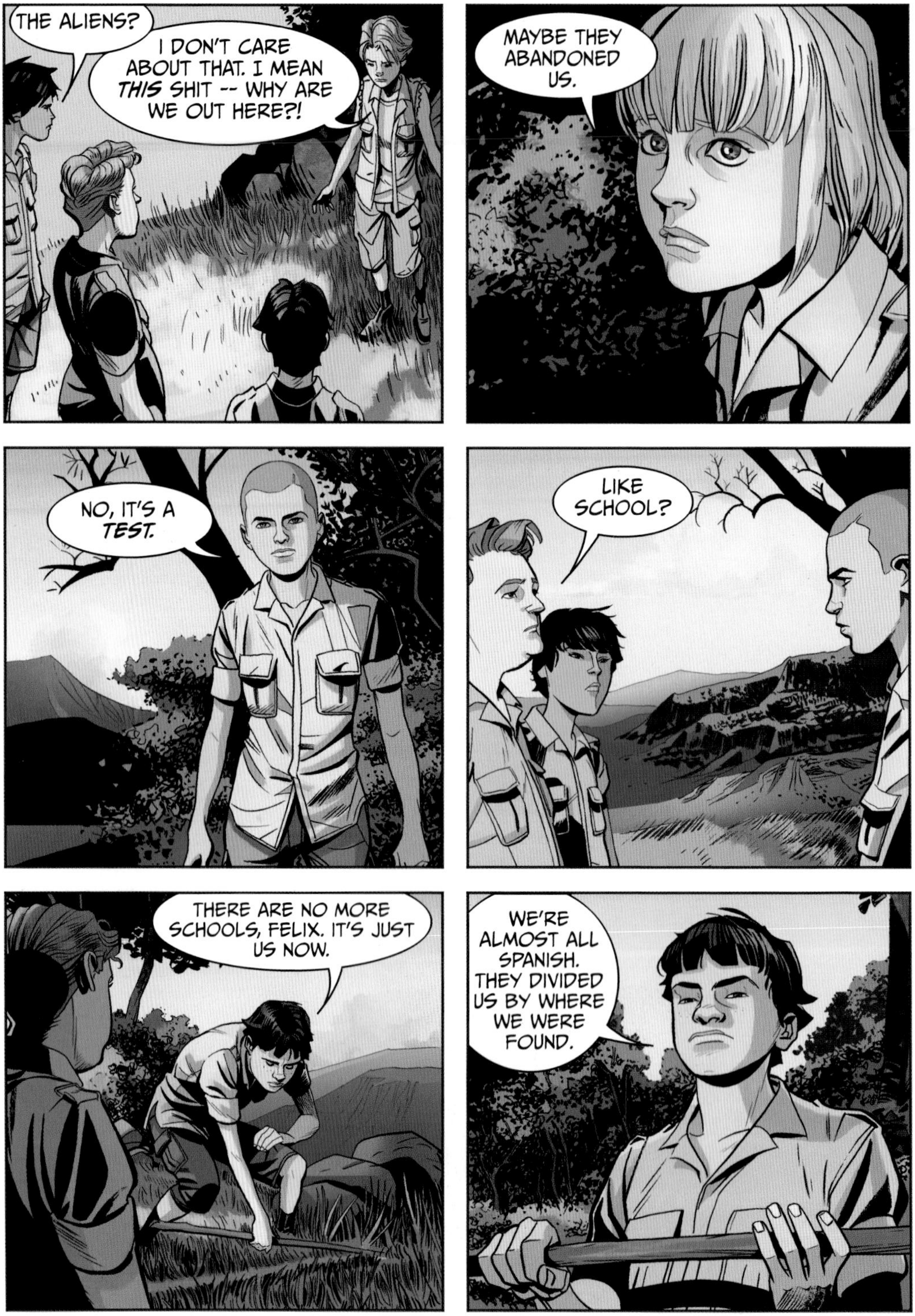
THE ALIENS?
I DON'T CARE ABOUT THAT. I MEAN *THIS* SHIT -- WHY ARE WE OUT HERE?!
MAYBE THEY ABANDONED US.
NO, IT'S A *TEST.*
LIKE SCHOOL?
THERE ARE NO MORE SCHOOLS, FELIX. IT'S JUST US NOW.
WE'RE ALMOST ALL SPANISH. THEY DIVIDED US BY WHERE WE WERE FOUND.

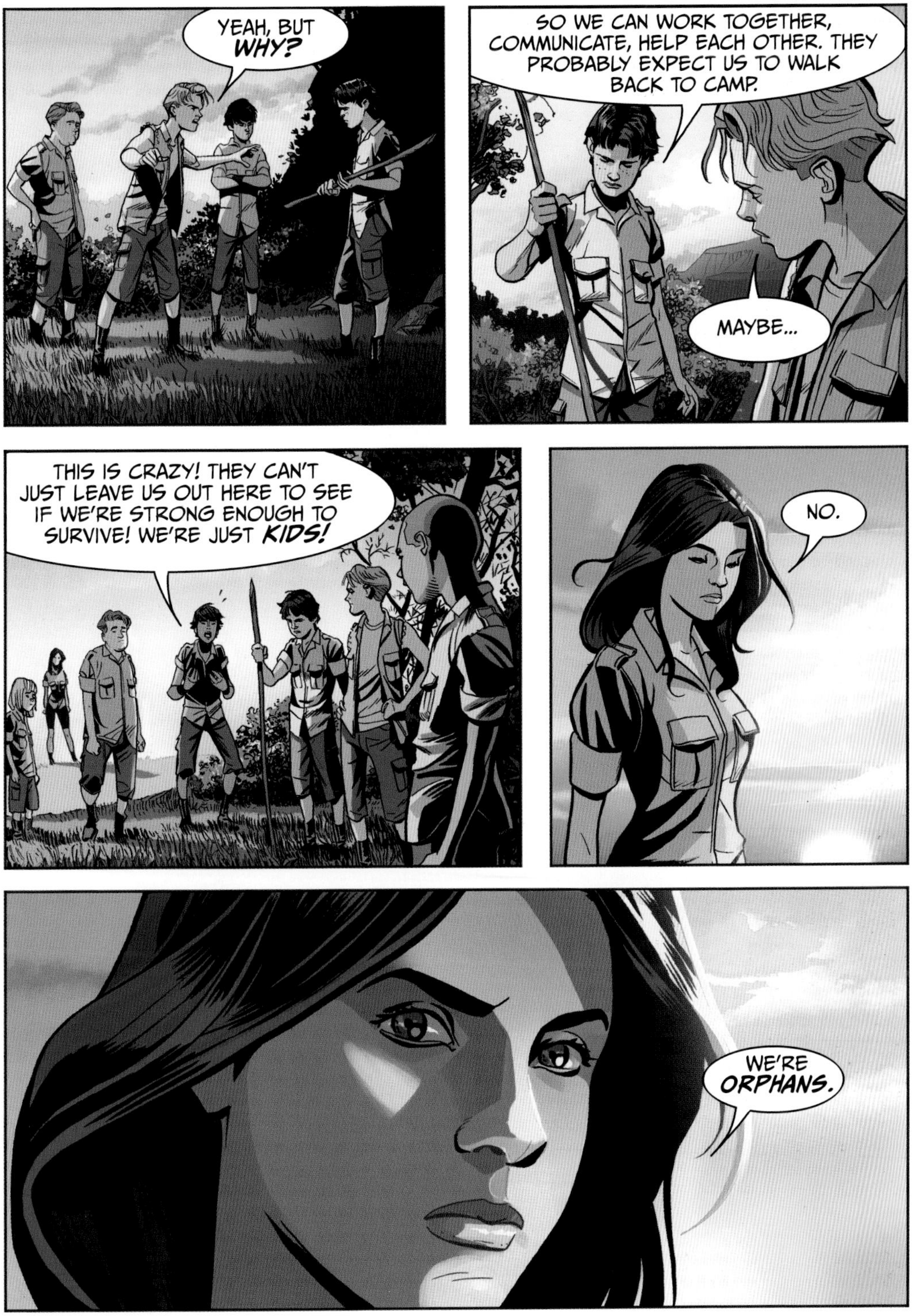
YEAH, BUT WHY?
SO WE CAN WORK TOGETHER, COMMUNICATE, HELP EACH OTHER. THEY PROBABLY EXPECT US TO WALK BACK TO CAMP.
MAYBE...
THIS IS CRAZY! THEY CAN'T JUST LEAVE US OUT HERE TO SEE IF WE'RE STRONG ENOUGH TO SURVIVE! WE'RE JUST KIDS!
NO.
WE'RE ORPHANS.

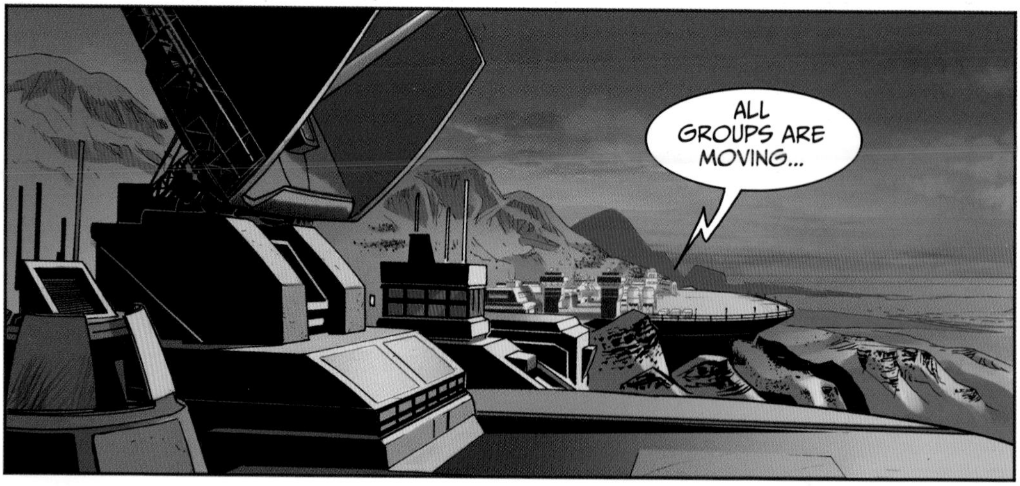
ALL GROUPS ARE MOVING...

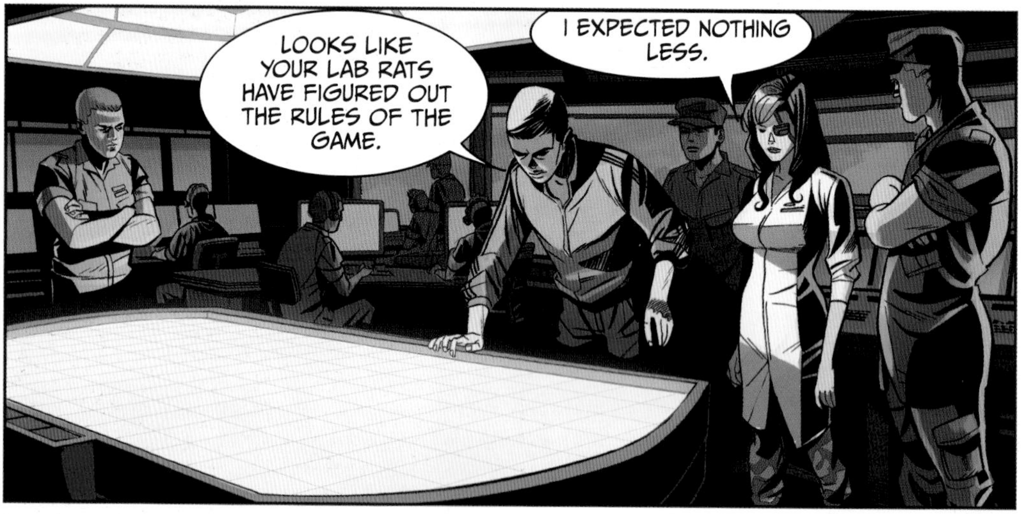
LOOKS LIKE YOUR LAB RATS HAVE FIGURED OUT THE RULES OF THE GAME.
I EXPECTED NOTHING LESS.

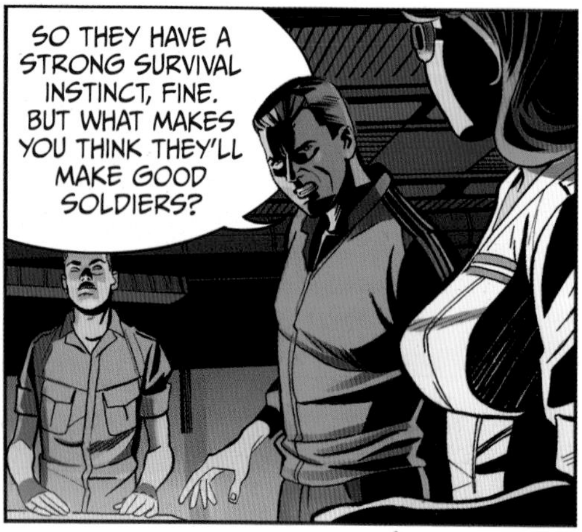
SO THEY HAVE A STRONG SURVIVAL INSTINCT, FINE. BUT WHAT MAKES YOU THINK THEY'LL MAKE GOOD SOLDIERS?

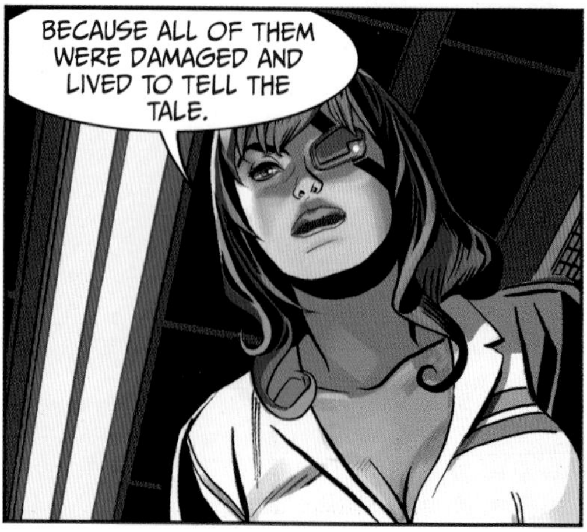
BECAUSE ALL OF THEM WERE DAMAGED AND LIVED TO TELL THE TALE.

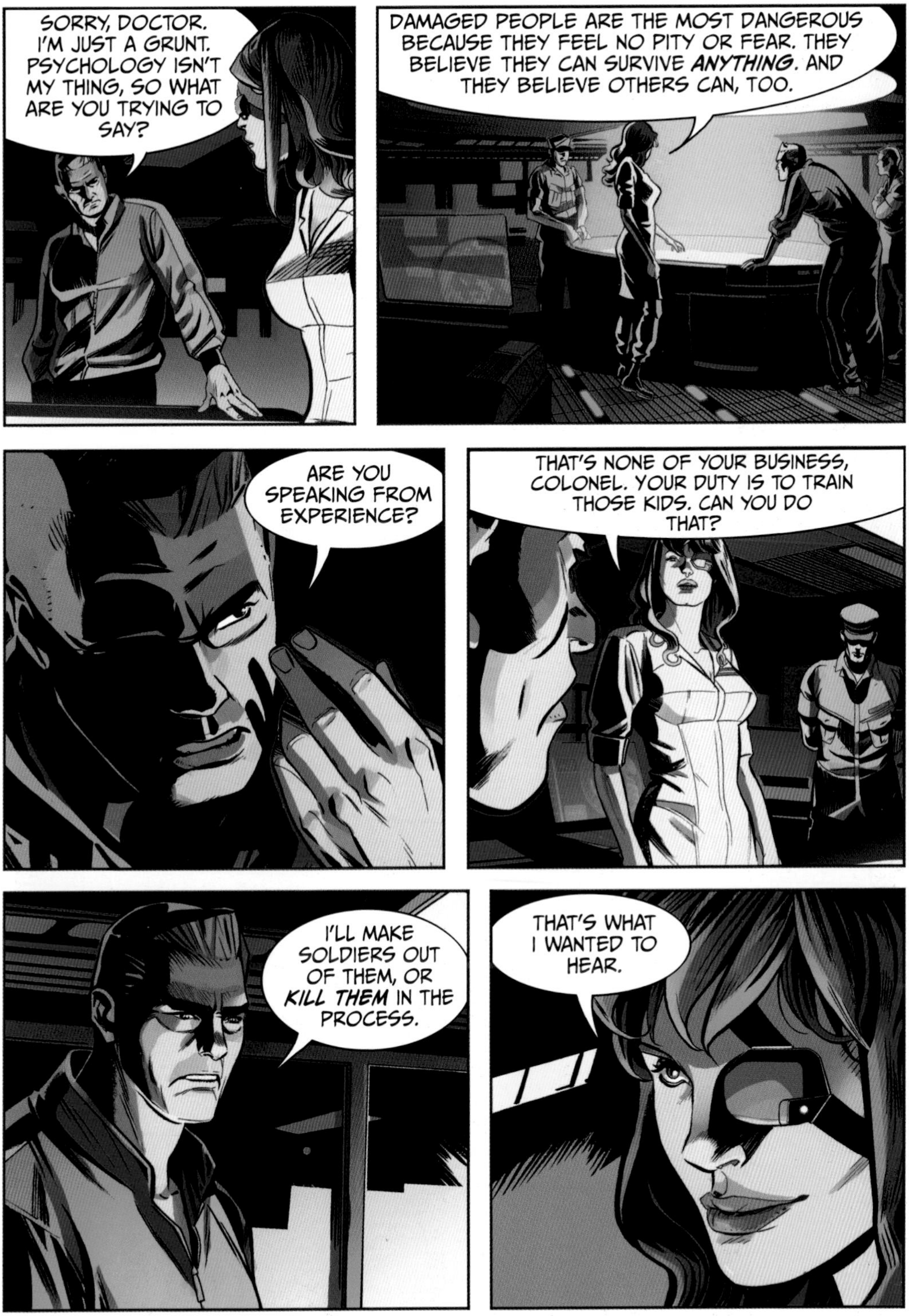
SORRY, DOCTOR. I'M JUST A GRUNT. PSYCHOLOGY ISN'T MY THING, SO WHAT ARE YOU TRYING TO SAY?
DAMAGED PEOPLE ARE THE MOST DANGEROUS BECAUSE THEY FEEL NO PITY OR FEAR. THEY BELIEVE THEY CAN SURVIVE *ANYTHING*. AND THEY BELIEVE OTHERS CAN, TOO.
ARE YOU SPEAKING FROM EXPERIENCE?
THAT'S NONE OF YOUR BUSINESS, COLONEL. YOUR DUTY IS TO TRAIN THOSE KIDS. CAN YOU DO THAT?
I'LL MAKE SOLDIERS OUT OF THEM, OR *KILL THEM* IN THE PROCESS.
THAT'S WHAT I WANTED TO HEAR.

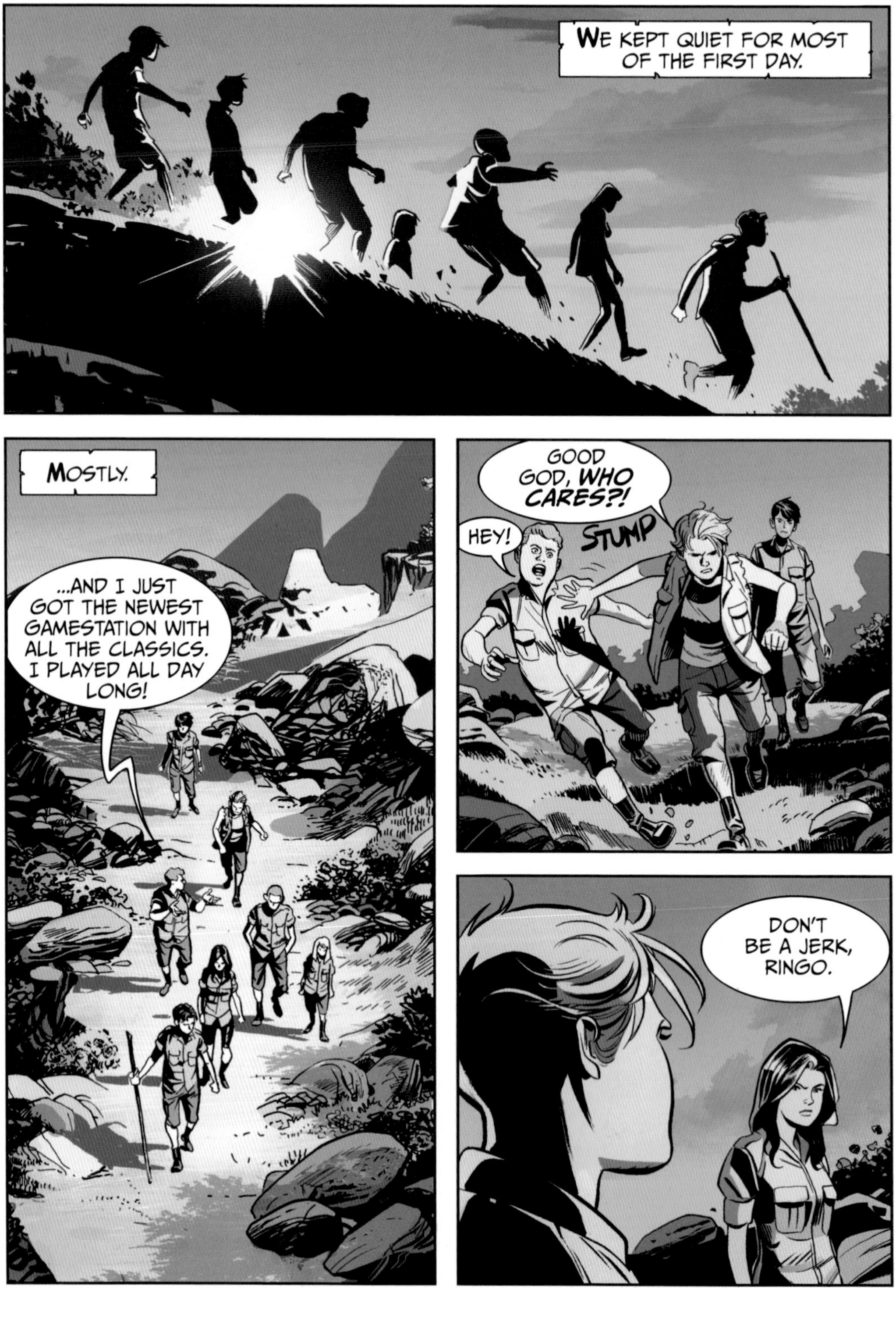
WE KEPT QUIET FOR MOST OF THE FIRST DAY.
MOSTLY.
...AND I JUST GOT THE NEWEST GAMESTATION WITH ALL THE CLASSICS. I PLAYED ALL DAY LONG!
GOOD GOD, WHO CARES?!
HEY!
STUMP
DON'T BE A JERK, RINGO.

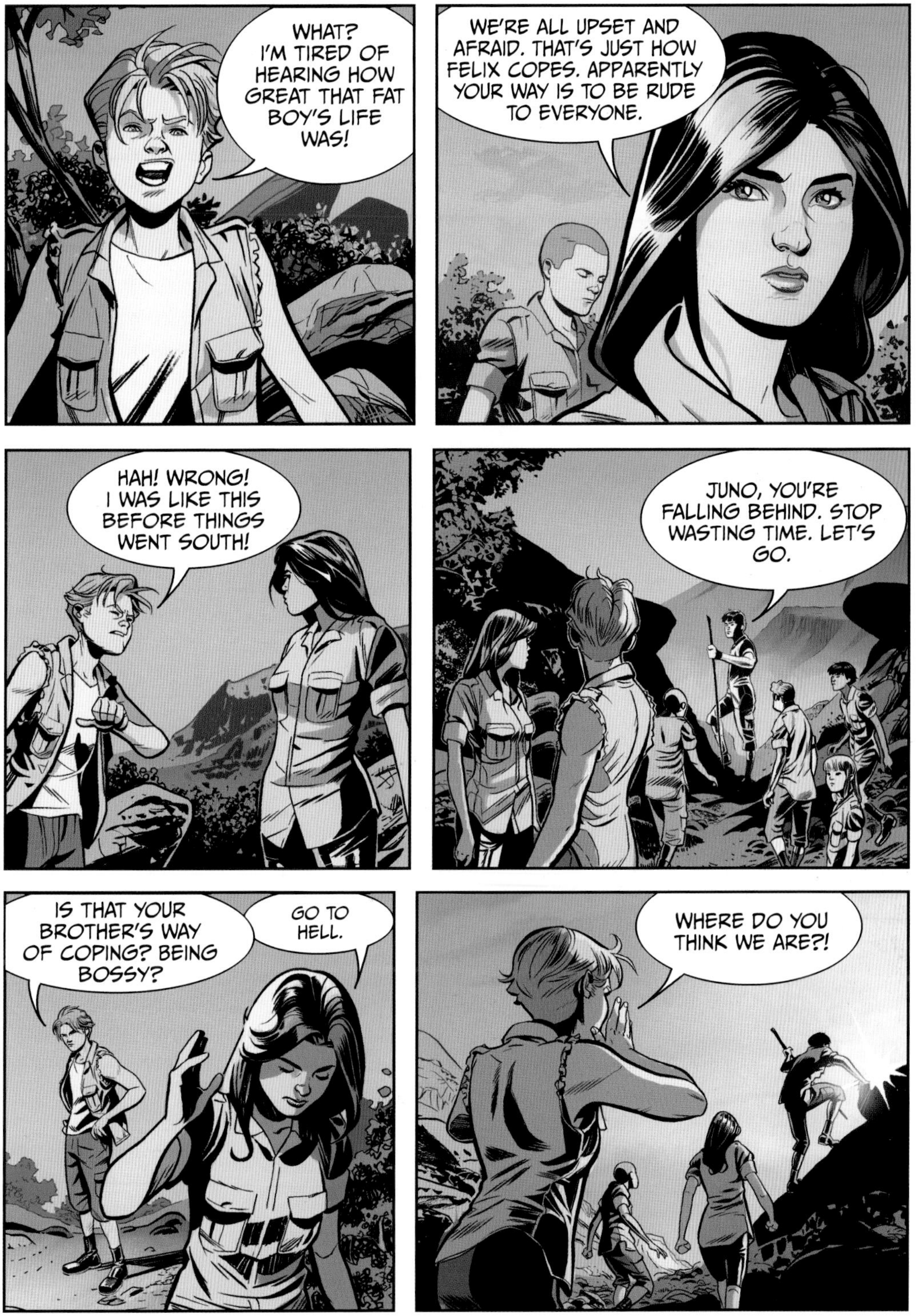
WHAT? I'M TIRED OF HEARING HOW GREAT THAT FAT BOY'S LIFE WAS!
WE'RE ALL UPSET AND AFRAID. THAT'S JUST HOW FELIX COPES. APPARENTLY YOUR WAY IS TO BE RUDE TO EVERYONE.
HAH! WRONG! I WAS LIKE THIS BEFORE THINGS WENT SOUTH!
JUNO, YOU'RE FALLING BEHIND. STOP WASTING TIME. LET'S GO.
IS THAT YOUR BROTHER'S WAY OF COPING? BEING BOSSY?
GO TO HELL.
WHERE DO YOU THINK WE ARE?!

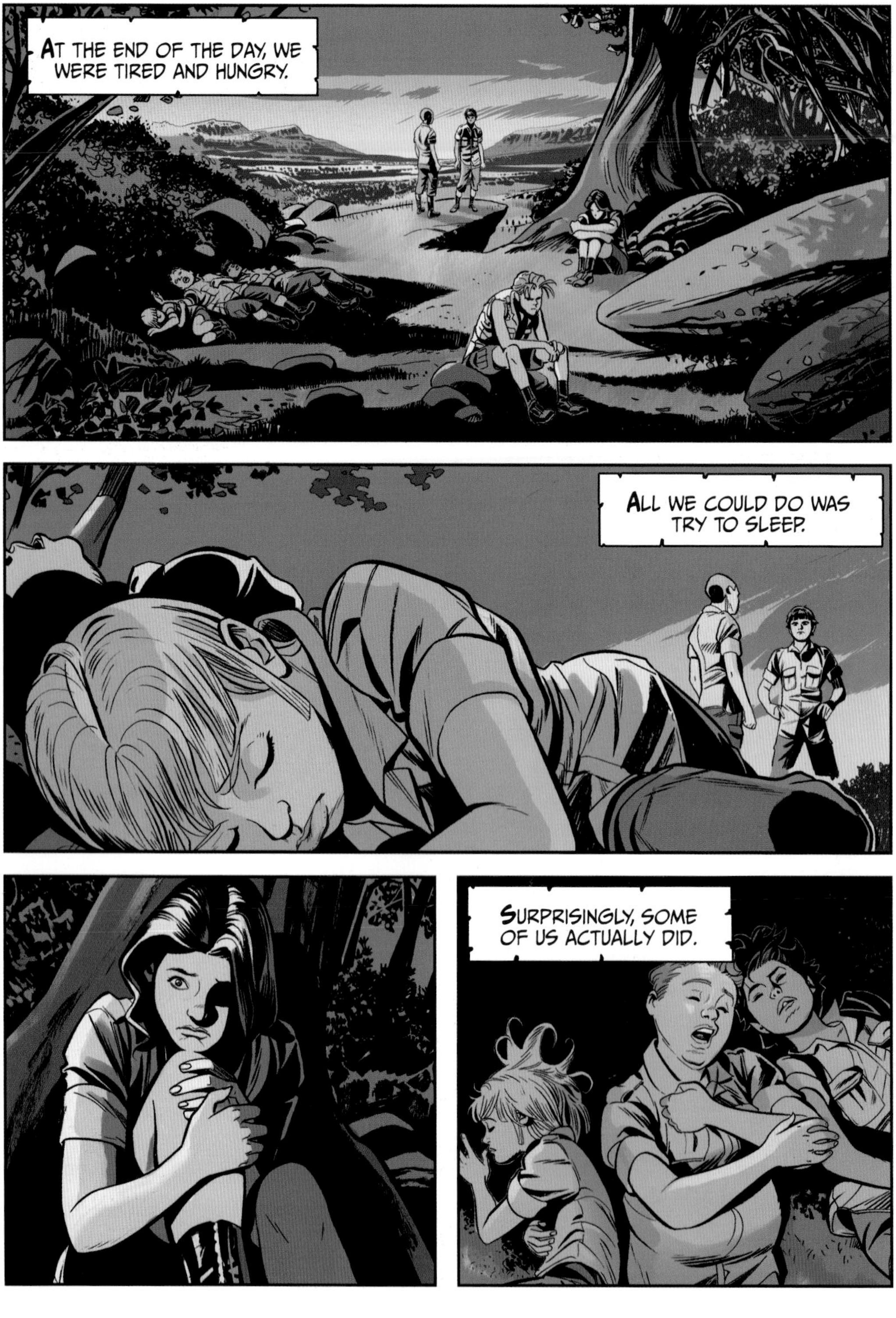
AT THE END OF THE DAY, WE WERE TIRED AND HUNGRY.
ALL WE COULD DO WAS TRY TO SLEEP.
SURPRISINGLY, SOME OF US ACTUALLY DID.

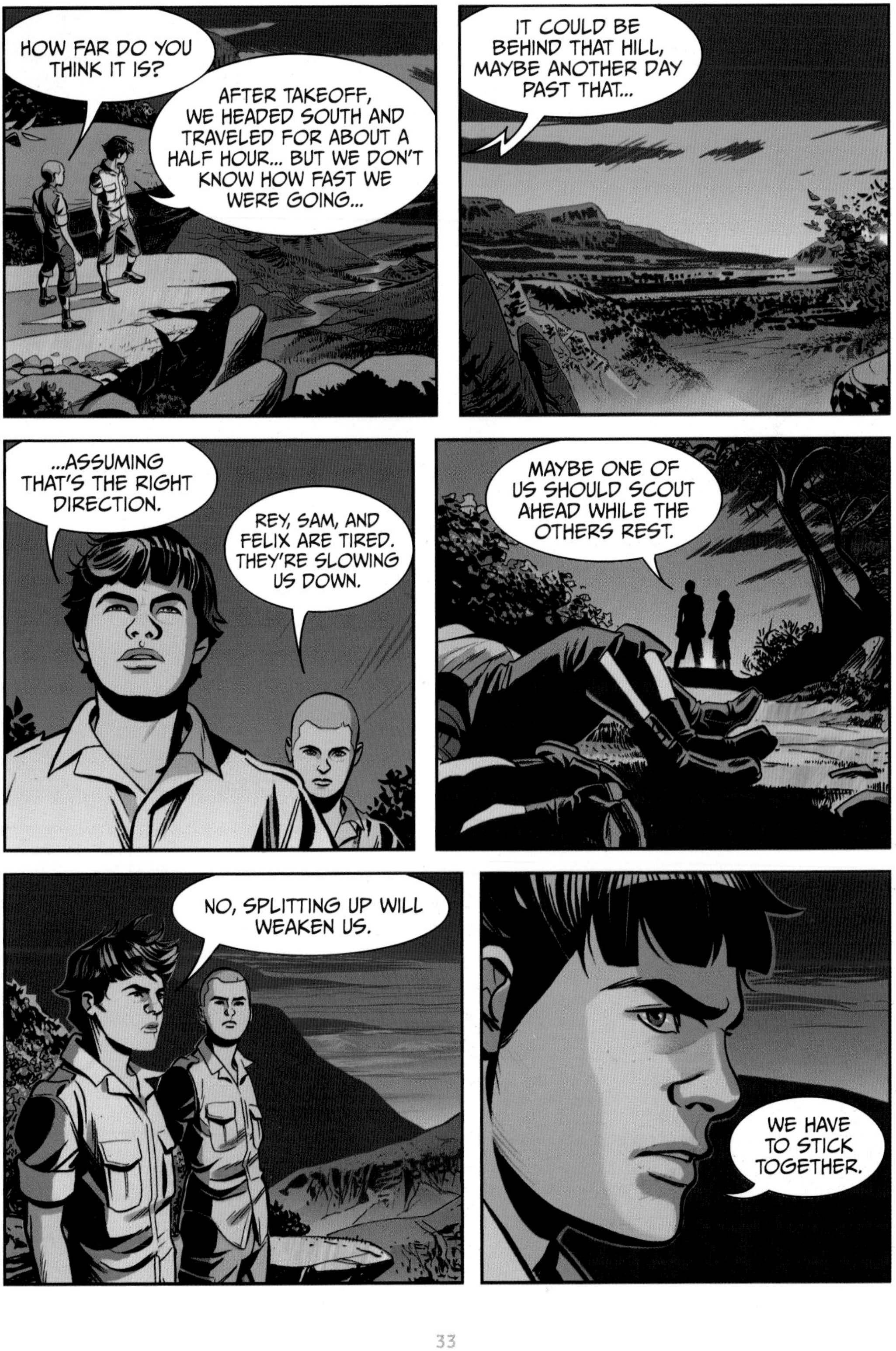
HOW FAR DO YOU THINK IT IS?
AFTER TAKEOFF, WE HEADED SOUTH AND TRAVELED FOR ABOUT A HALF HOUR... BUT WE DON'T KNOW HOW FAST WE WERE GOING...
IT COULD BE BEHIND THAT HILL, MAYBE ANOTHER DAY PAST THAT...
...ASSUMING THAT'S THE RIGHT DIRECTION.
REY, SAM, AND FELIX ARE TIRED. THEY'RE SLOWING US DOWN.
MAYBE ONE OF US SHOULD SCOUT AHEAD WHILE THE OTHERS REST.
NO, SPLITTING UP WILL WEAKEN US.
WE HAVE TO STICK TOGETHER.

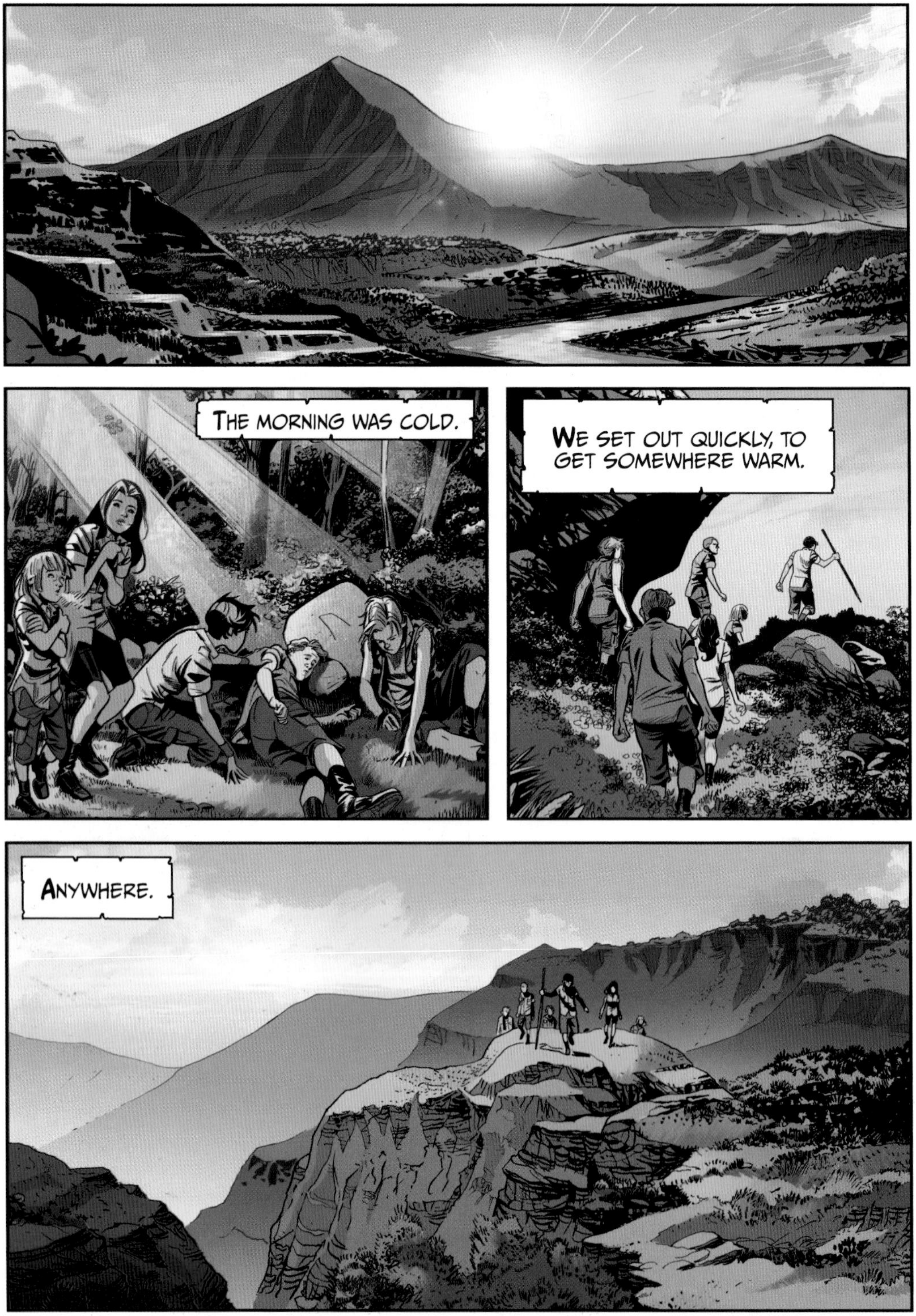
The morning was cold.
We set out quickly, to get somewhere warm.
Anywhere.

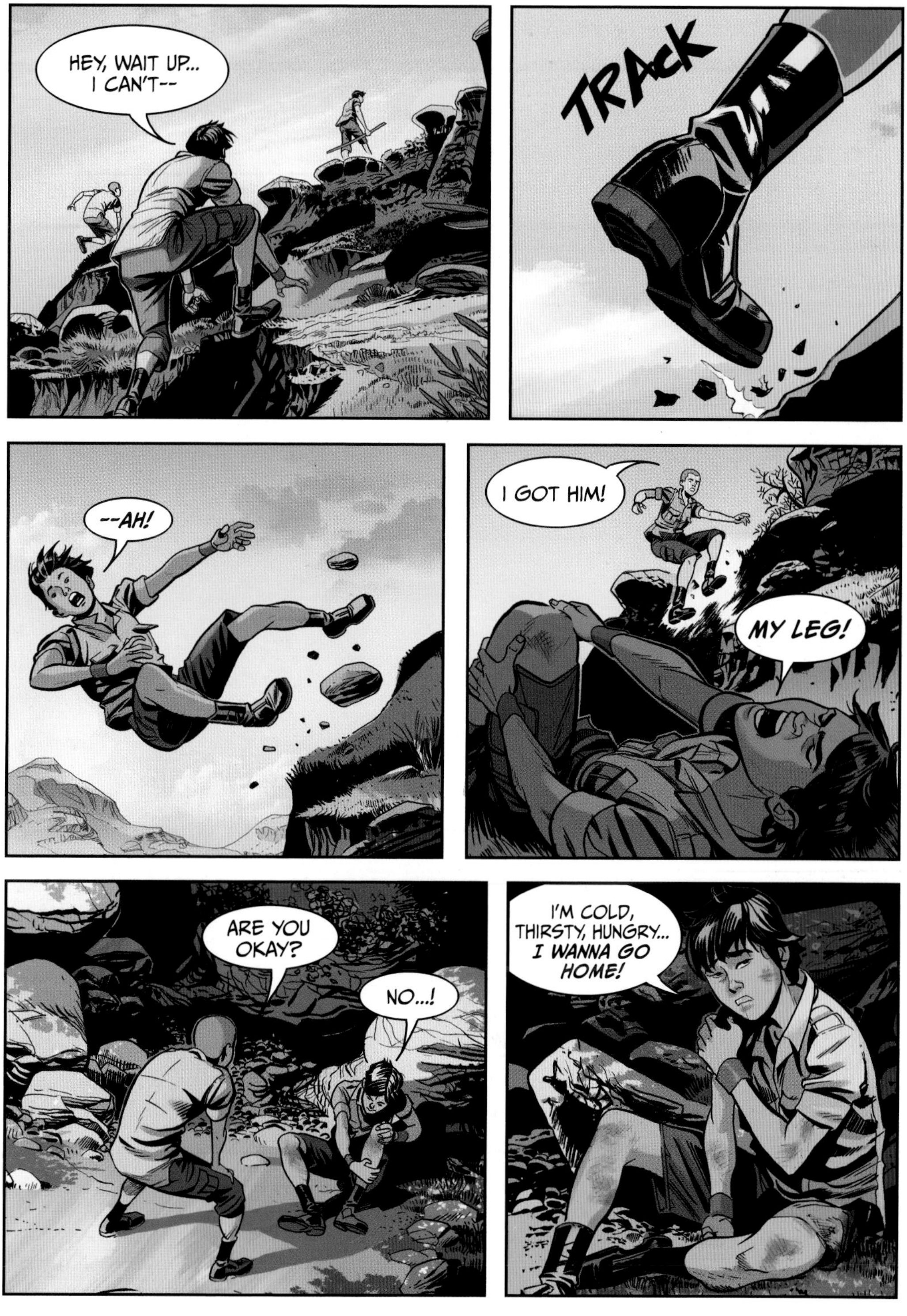
HEY, WAIT UP... I CAN'T--
TRACK
--AH!
I GOT HIM!
MY LEG!
ARE YOU OKAY?
NO...!
I'M COLD, THIRSTY, HUNGRY... I WANNA GO HOME!

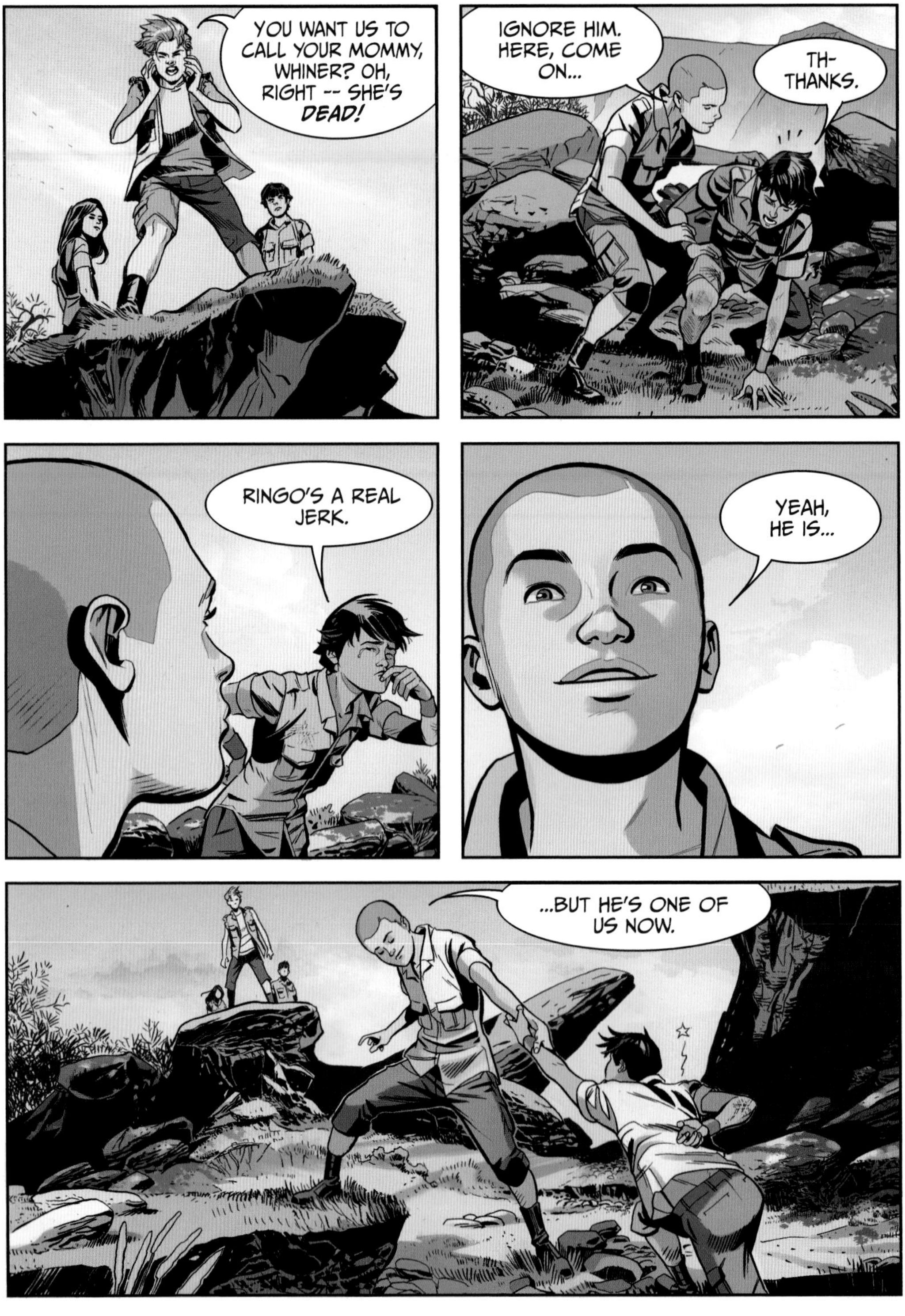
YOU WANT US TO CALL YOUR MOMMY, WHINER? OH, RIGHT -- SHE'S *DEAD!*
IGNORE HIM. HERE, COME ON...
TH- THANKS.
RINGO'S A REAL JERK.
YEAH, HE IS...
...BUT HE'S ONE OF US NOW.

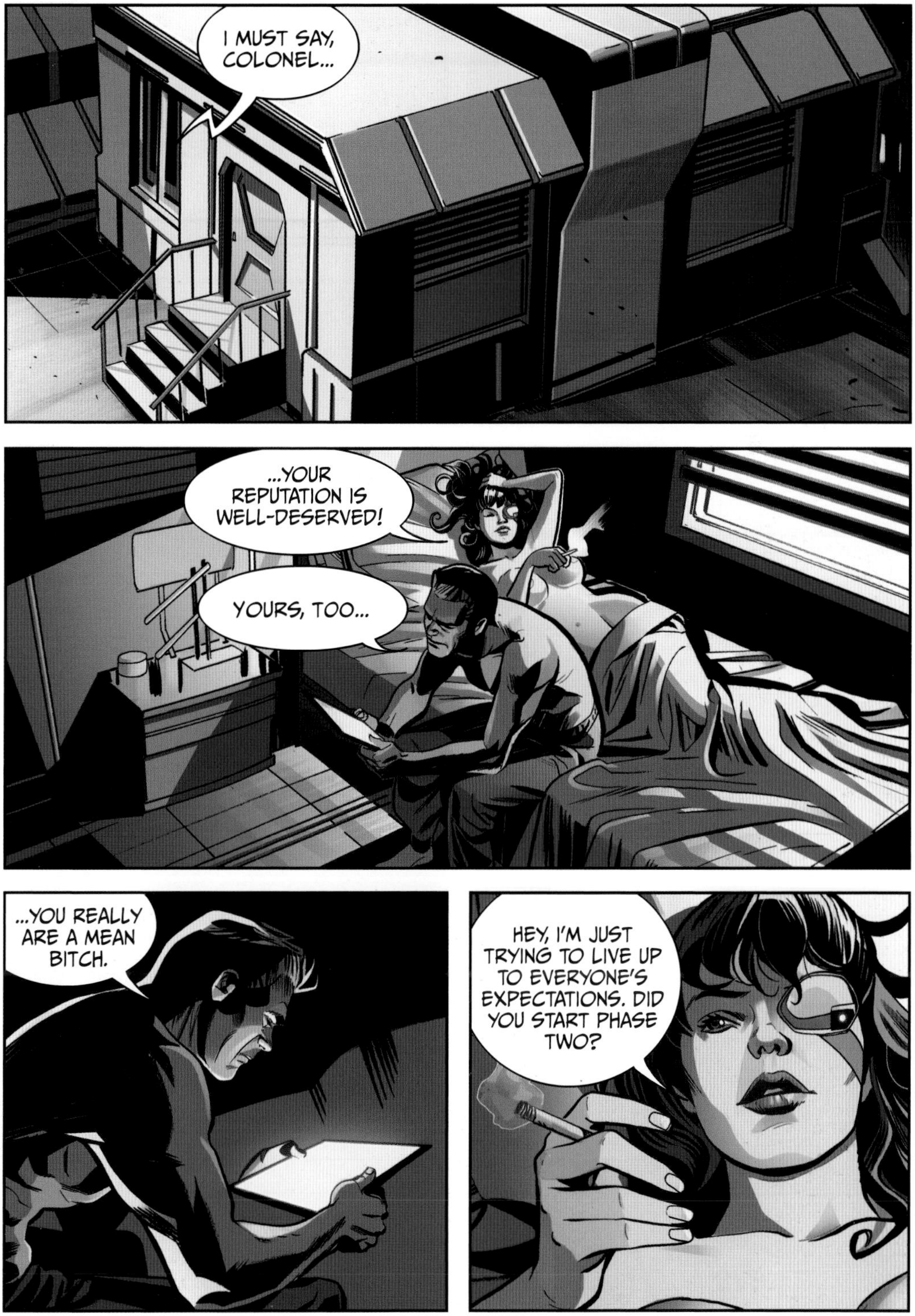
I MUST SAY, COLONEL...
...YOUR REPUTATION IS WELL-DESERVED!
YOURS, TOO...
...YOU REALLY ARE A MEAN BITCH.
HEY, I'M JUST TRYING TO LIVE UP TO EVERYONE'S EXPECTATIONS. DID YOU START PHASE TWO?

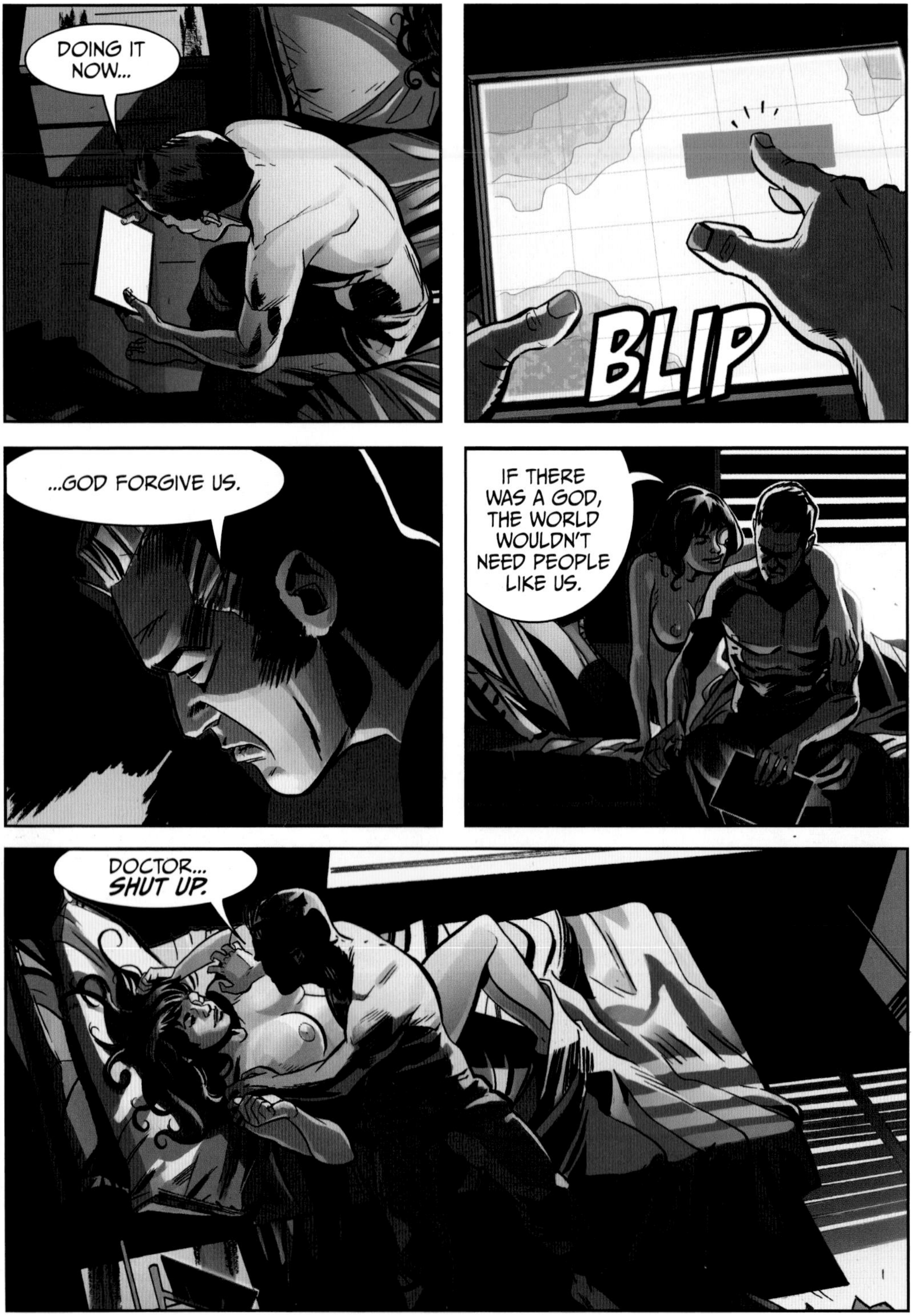
DOING IT NOW...
BLIP
...GOD FORGIVE US.
IF THERE WAS A GOD, THE WORLD WOULDN'T NEED PEOPLE LIKE US.
DOCTOR... SHUT UP.

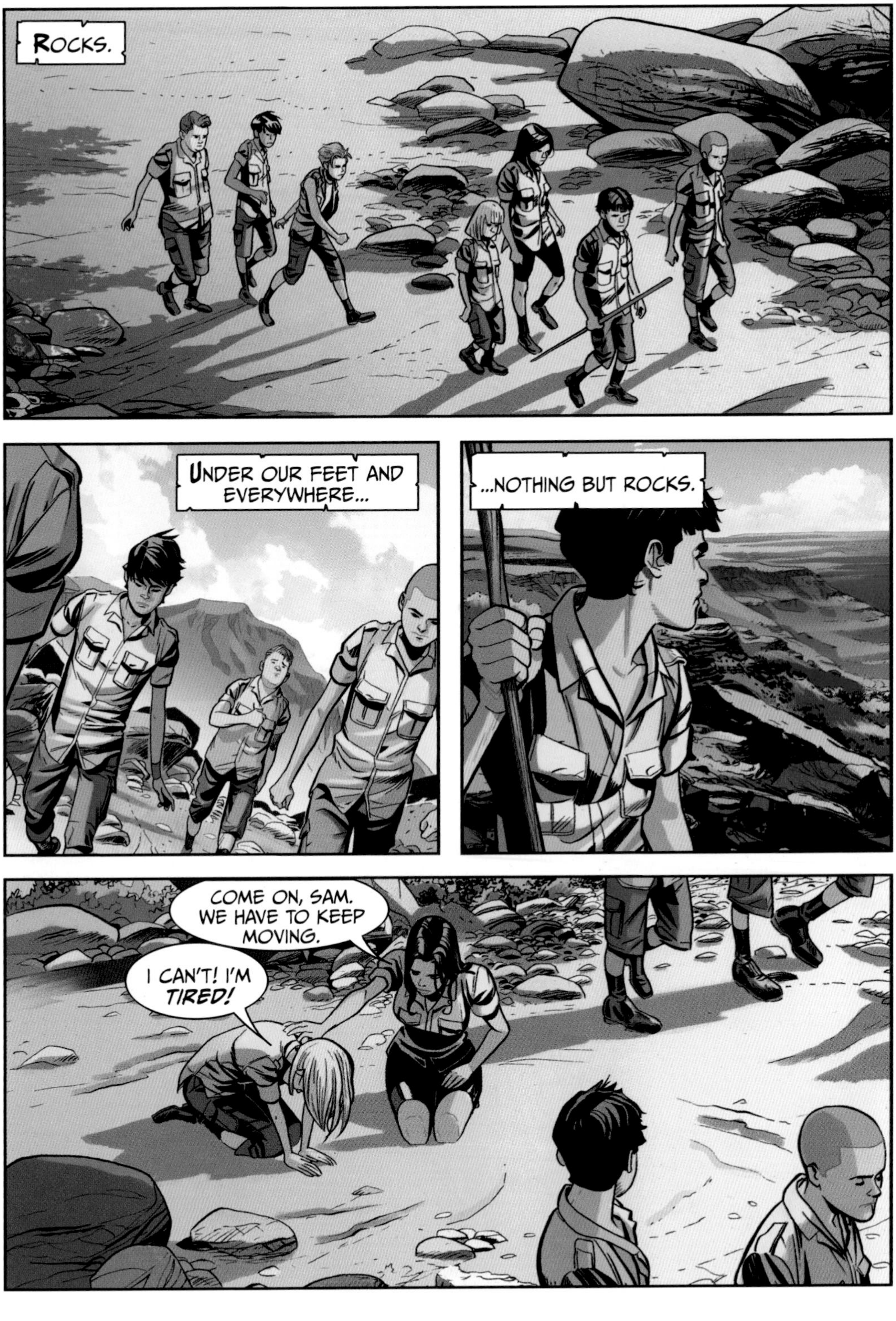
Rocks.
Under our feet and everywhere...
...nothing but rocks.
Come on, Sam. We have to keep moving.
I can't! I'm tired!

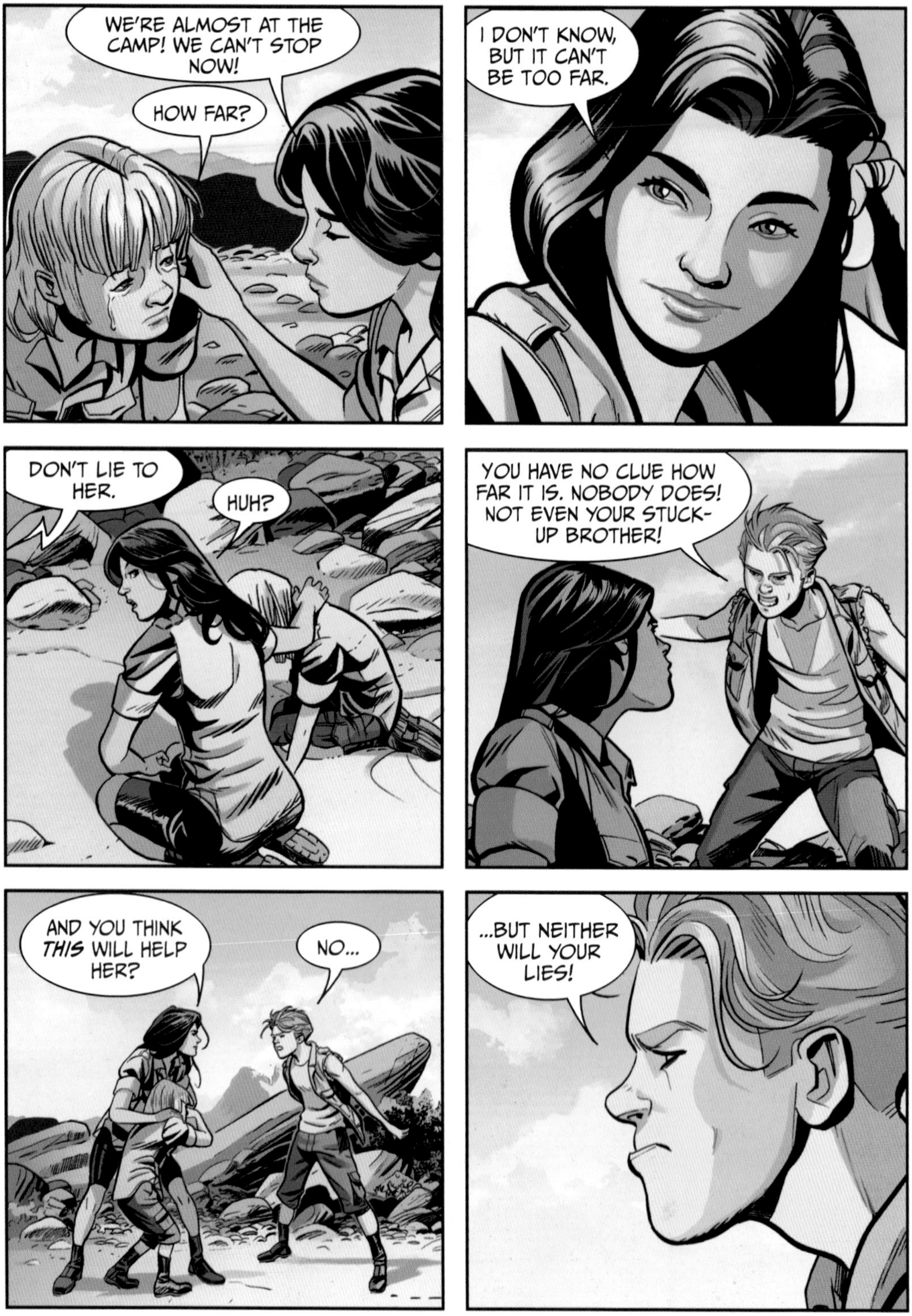
WE'RE ALMOST AT THE CAMP! WE CAN'T STOP NOW!
HOW FAR?
I DON'T KNOW, BUT IT CAN'T BE TOO FAR.
DON'T LIE TO HER.
HUH?
YOU HAVE NO CLUE HOW FAR IT IS. NOBODY DOES! NOT EVEN YOUR STUCK-UP BROTHER!
AND YOU THINK *THIS* WILL HELP HER?
NO...
...BUT NEITHER WILL YOUR LIES!

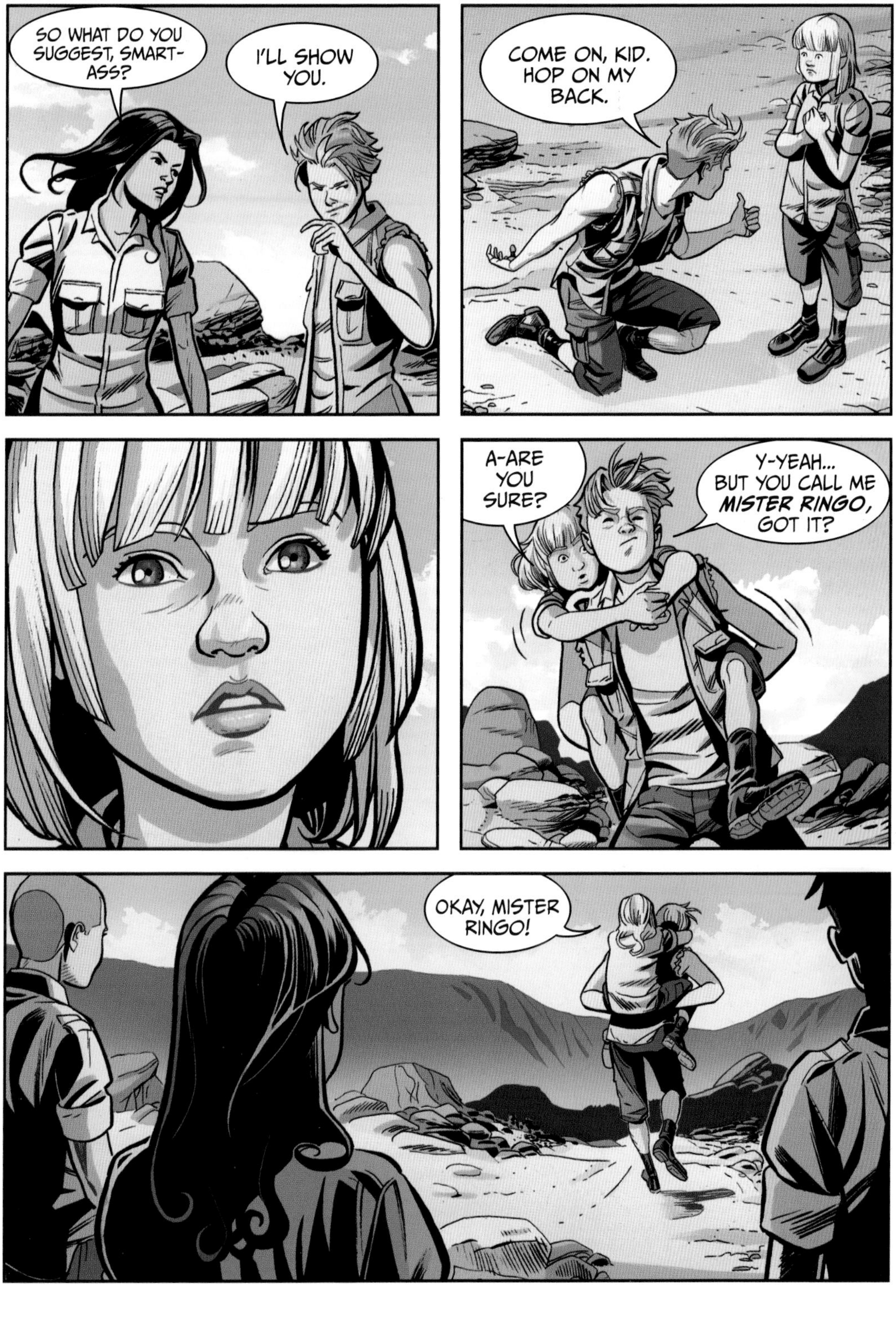
SO WHAT DO YOU SUGGEST, SMART-ASS?
I'LL SHOW YOU.
COME ON, KID. HOP ON MY BACK.
A-ARE YOU SURE?
Y-YEAH... BUT YOU CALL ME *MISTER RINGO*, GOT IT?
OKAY, MISTER RINGO!

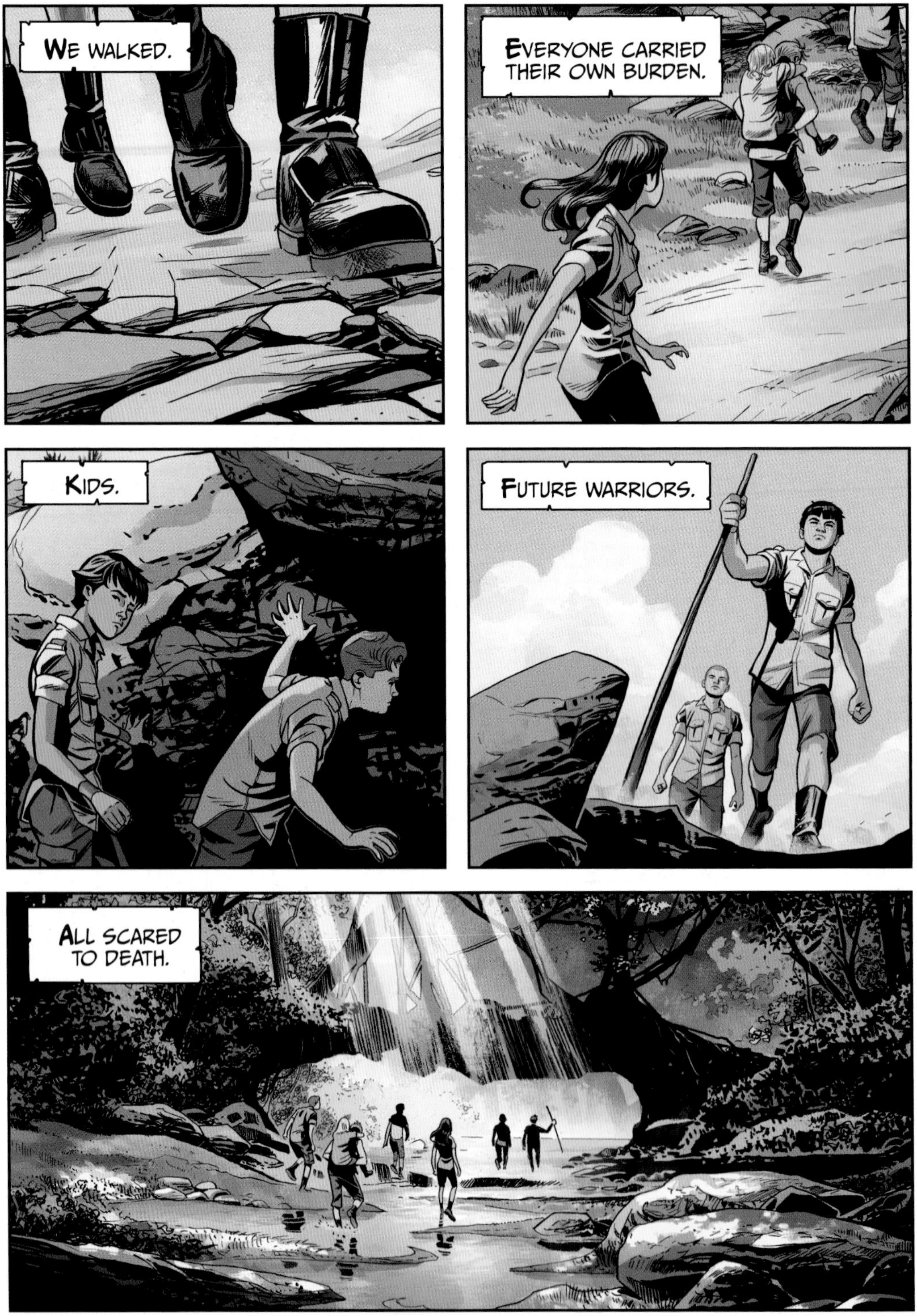
We walked.
Everyone carried their own burden.
Kids.
Future warriors.
All scared to death.

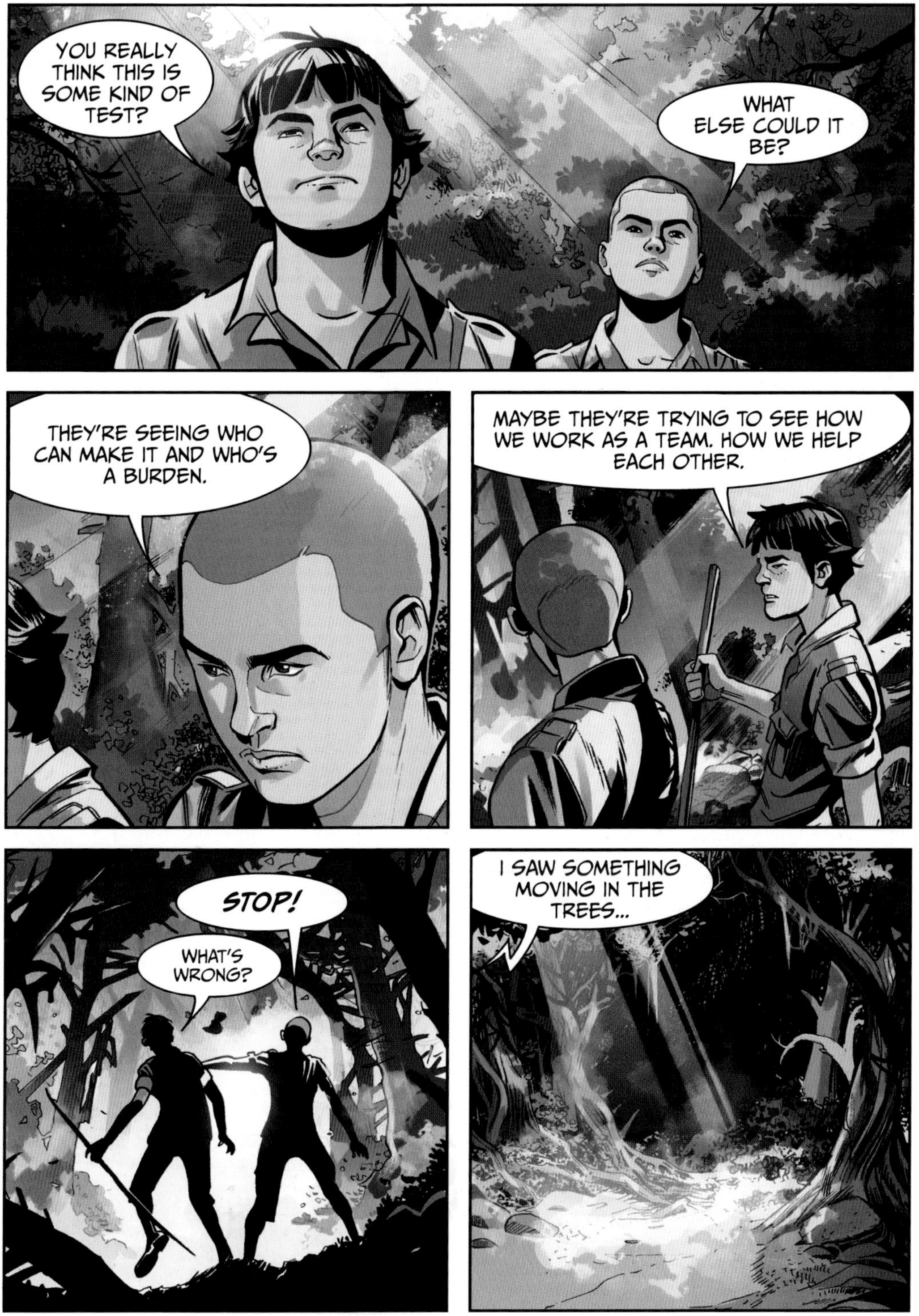
YOU REALLY THINK THIS IS SOME KIND OF TEST?
WHAT ELSE COULD IT BE?
THEY'RE SEEING WHO CAN MAKE IT AND WHO'S A BURDEN.
MAYBE THEY'RE TRYING TO SEE HOW WE WORK AS A TEAM. HOW WE HELP EACH OTHER.
STOP!
WHAT'S WRONG?
I SAW SOMETHING MOVING IN THE TREES...

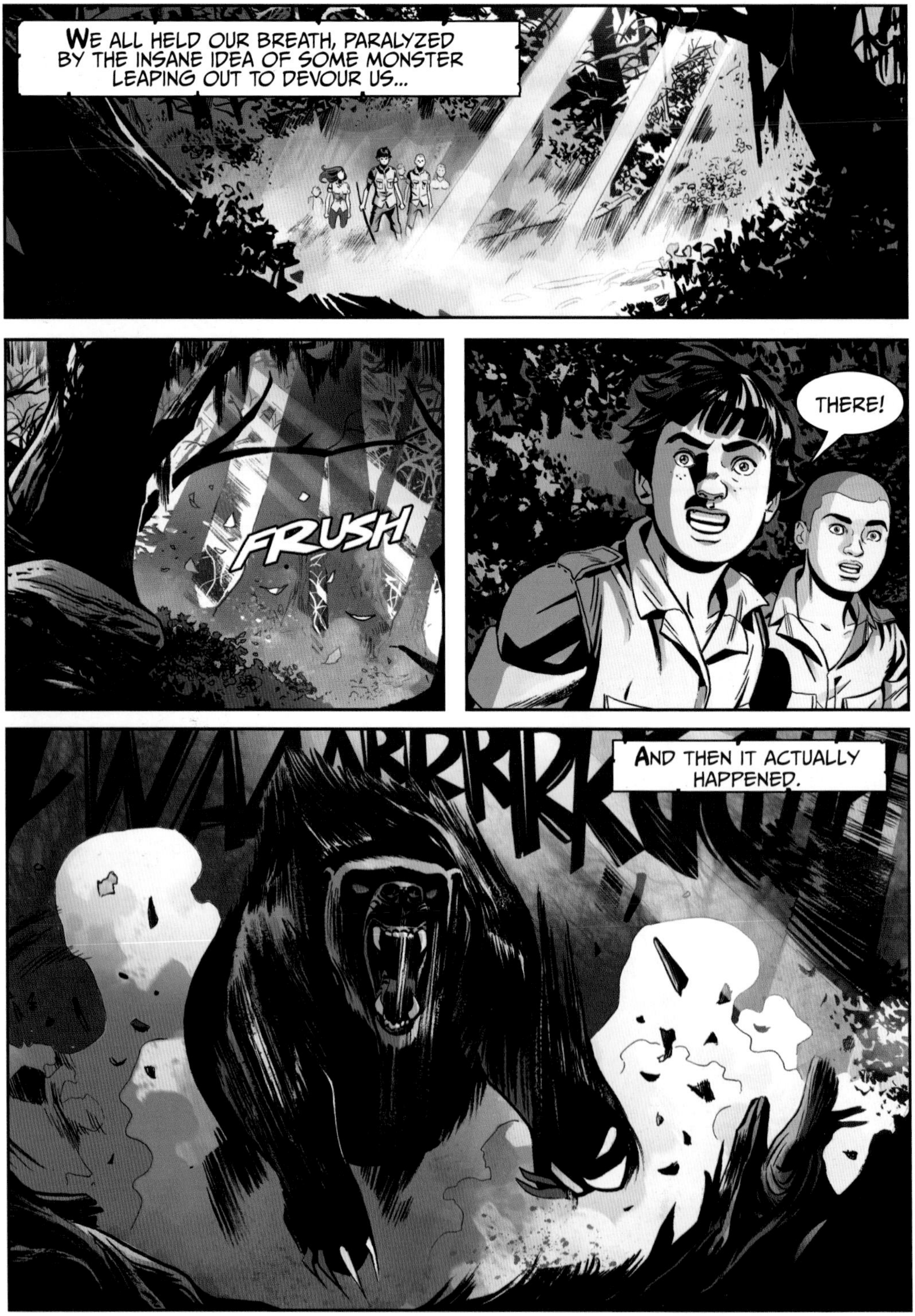
WE ALL HELD OUR BREATH, PARALYZED BY THE INSANE IDEA OF SOME MONSTER LEAPING OUT TO DEVOUR US...
FRUSH
THERE!
AND THEN IT ACTUALLY HAPPENED.

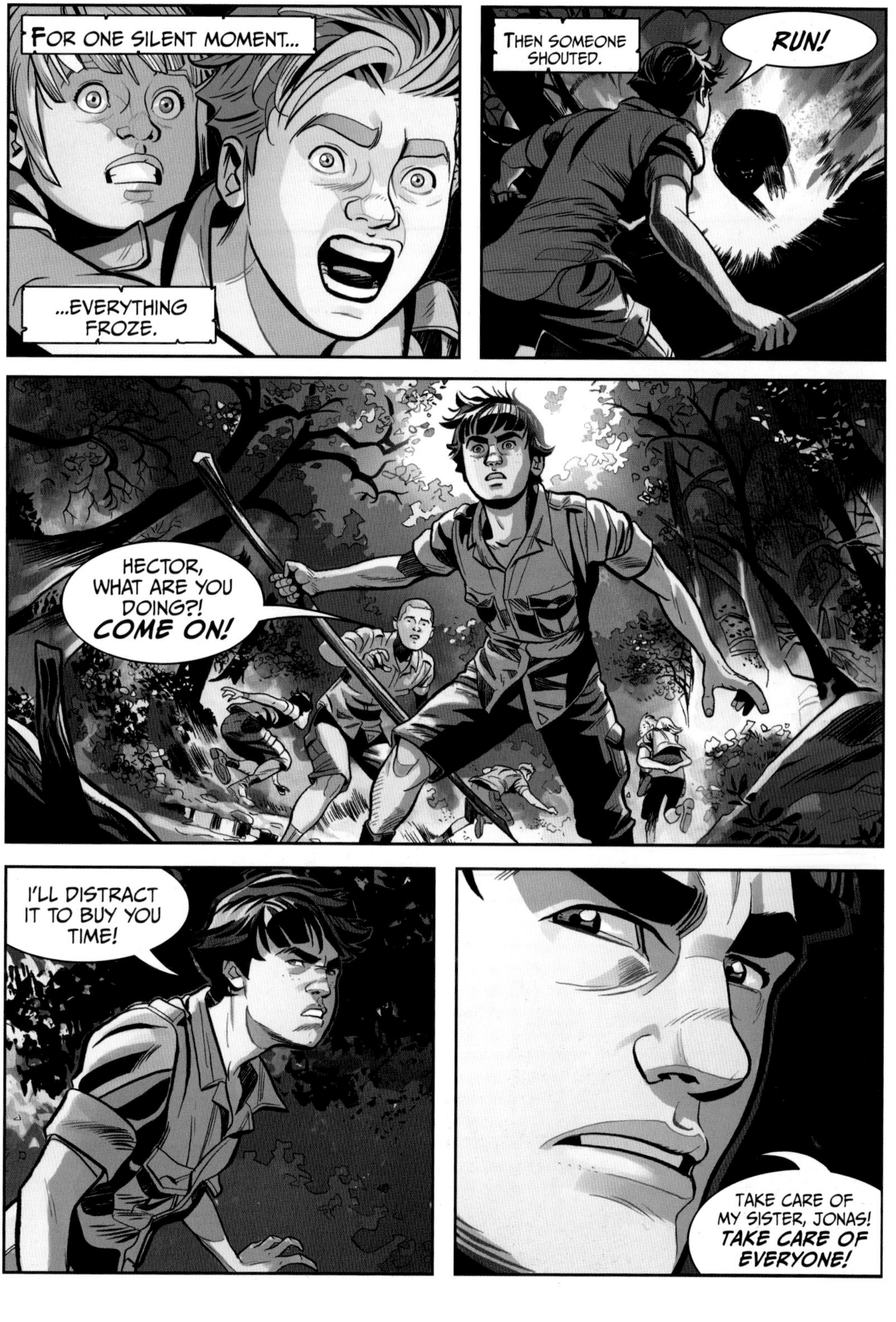

FOR ONE SILENT MOMENT...
...EVERYTHING FROZE.
THEN SOMEONE SHOUTED.
RUN!
HECTOR, WHAT ARE YOU DOING?! COME ON!
I'LL DISTRACT IT TO BUY YOU TIME!
TAKE CARE OF MY SISTER, JONAS! TAKE CARE OF EVERYONE!

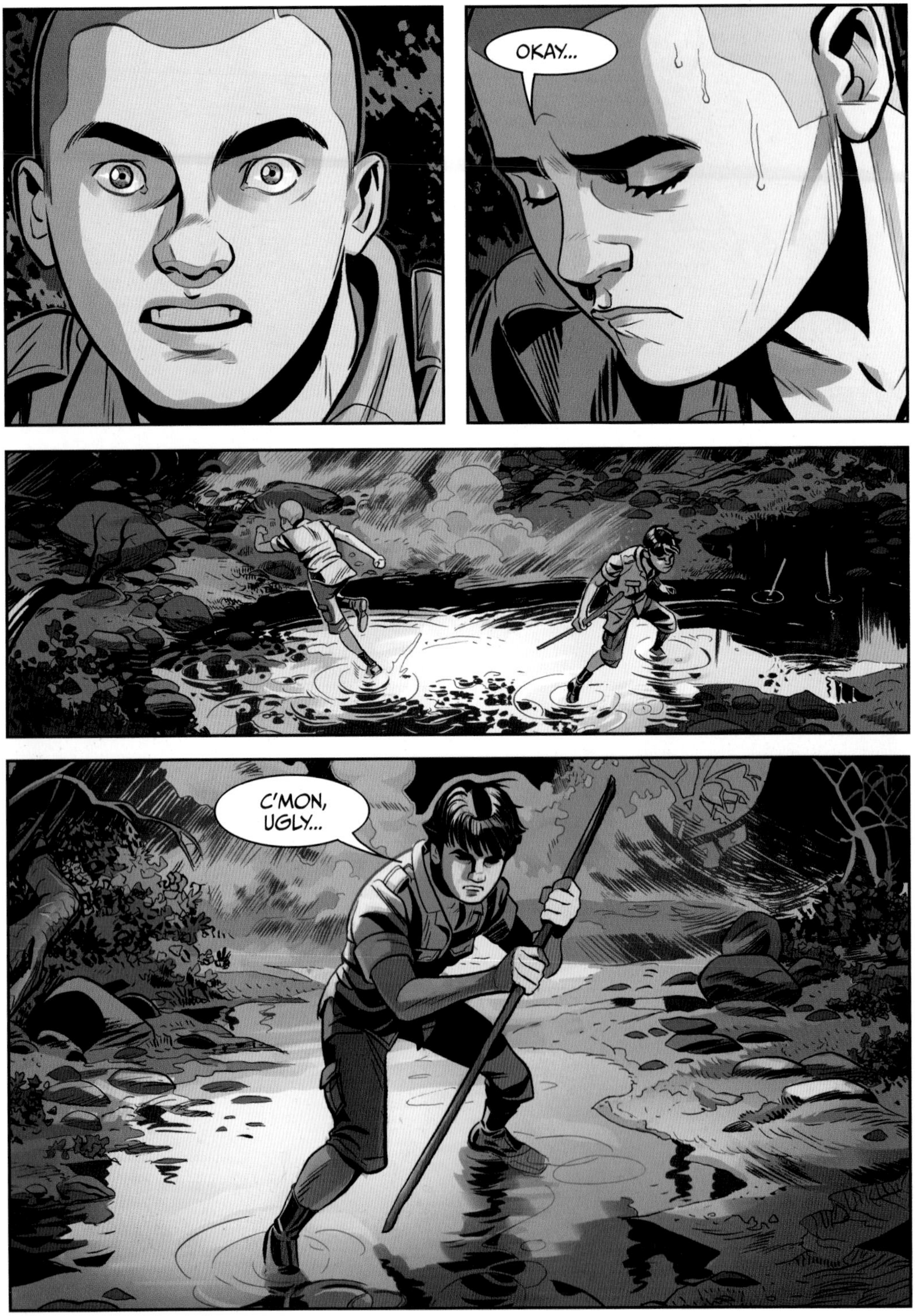
OKAY...
C'MON, UGLY...

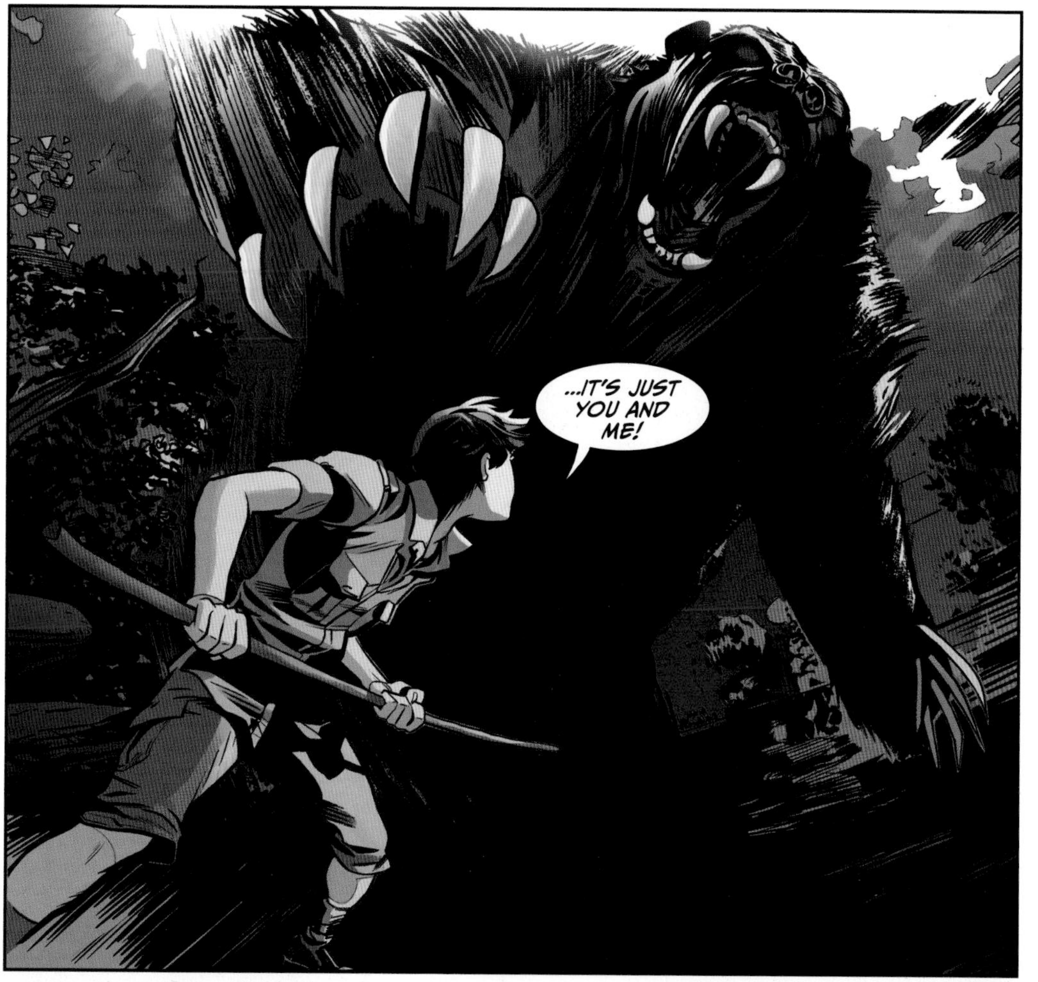
...IT'S JUST YOU AND ME!

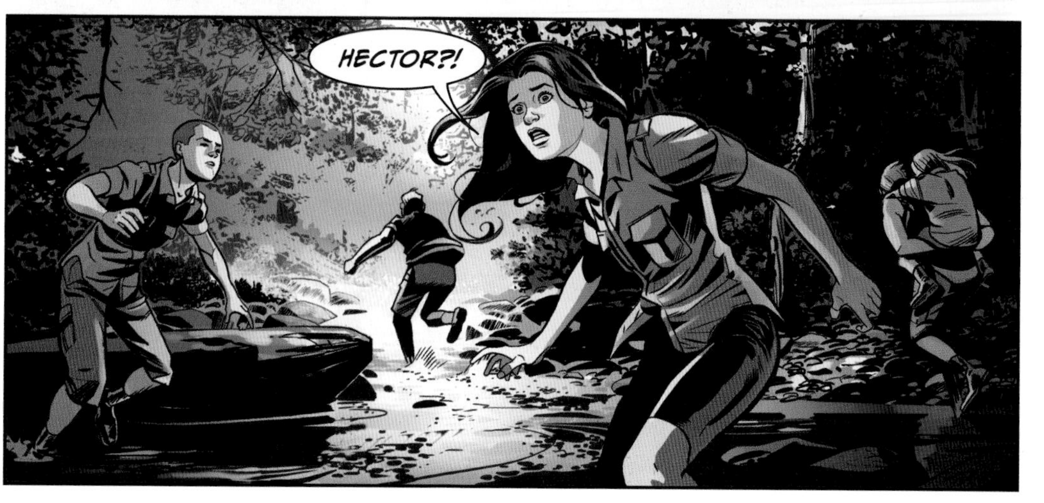
HECTOR?!

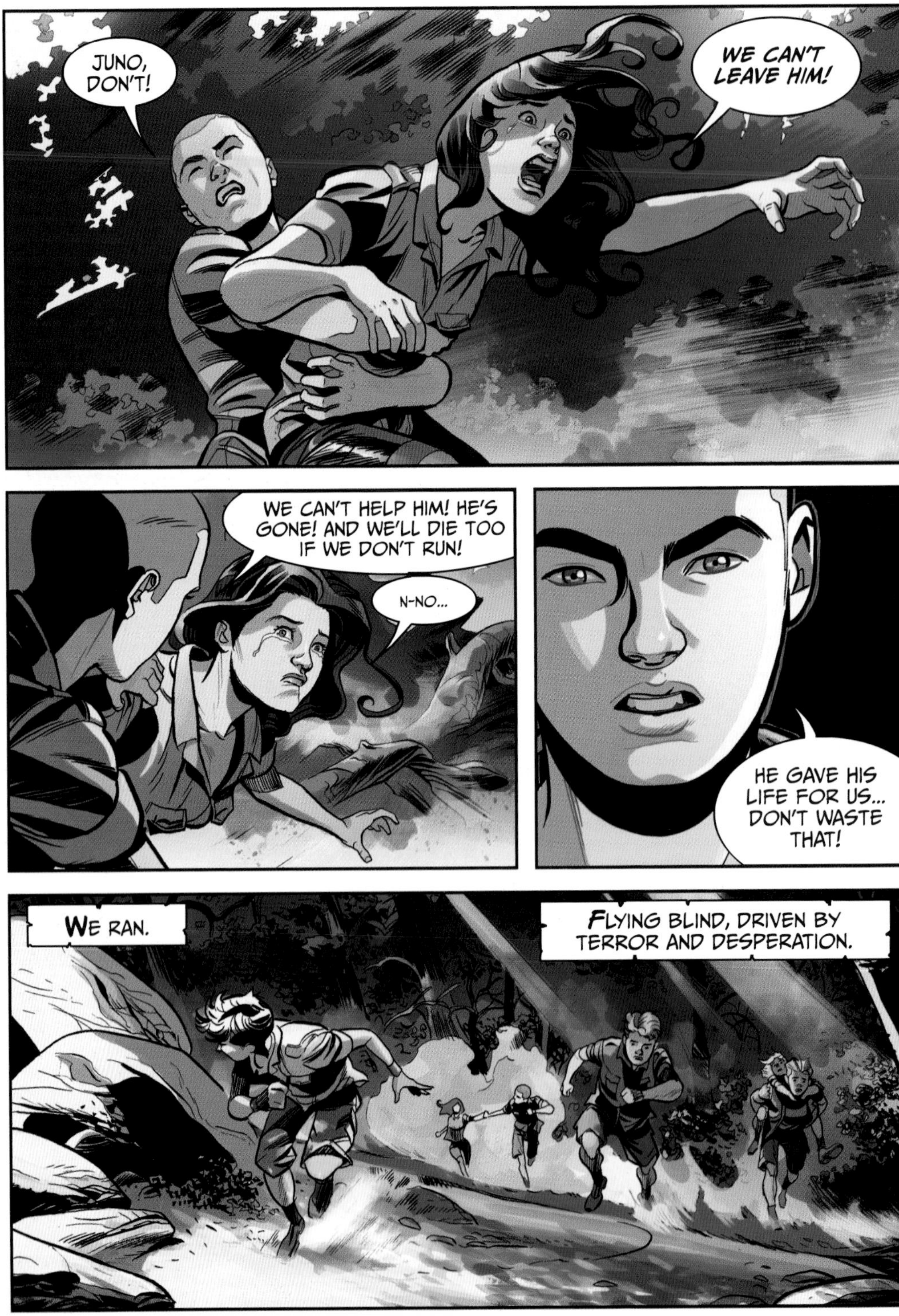
JUNO, DON'T!
WE CAN'T LEAVE HIM!
WE CAN'T HELP HIM! HE'S GONE! AND WE'LL DIE TOO IF WE DON'T RUN!
N-NO...
HE GAVE HIS LIFE FOR US... DON'T WASTE THAT!
WE RAN.
FLYING BLIND, DRIVEN BY TERROR AND DESPERATION.

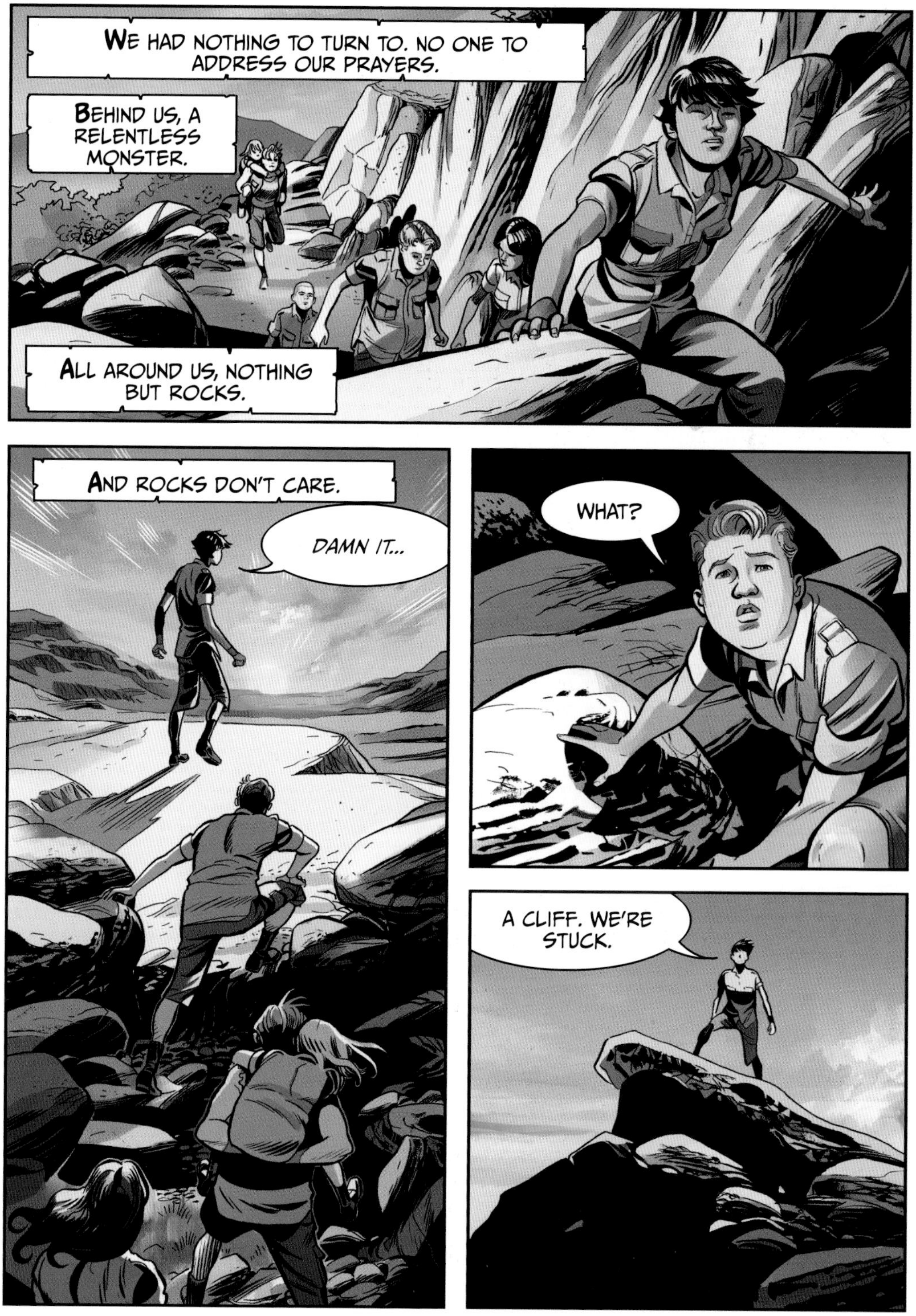
We had nothing to turn to. No one to address our prayers.
Behind us, a relentless monster.
All around us, nothing but rocks.
And rocks don't care.
Damn it...
What?
A cliff. We're stuck.

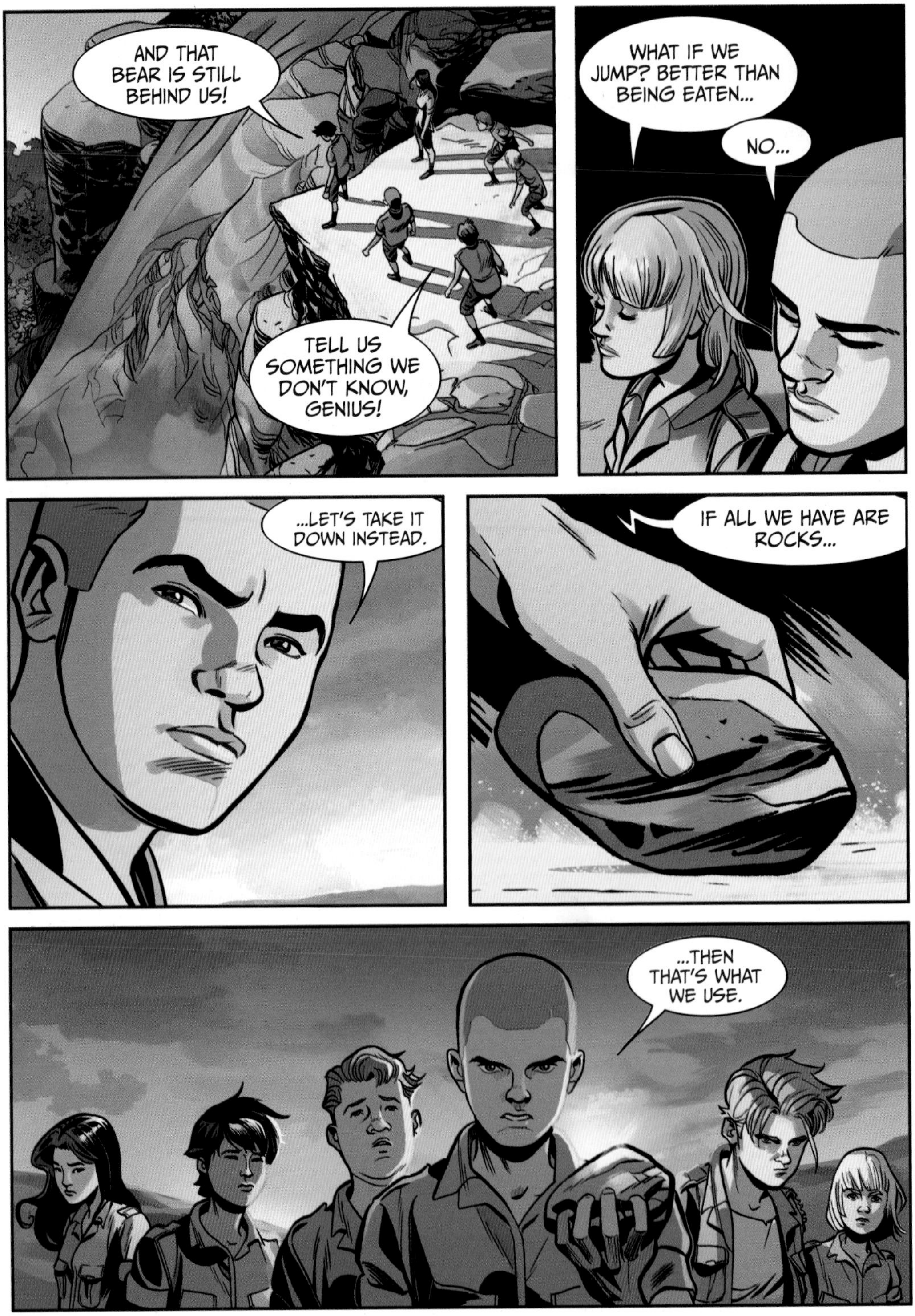
AND THAT BEAR IS STILL BEHIND US!
TELL US SOMETHING WE DON'T KNOW, GENIUS!
WHAT IF WE JUMP? BETTER THAN BEING EATEN...
NO...
...LET'S TAKE IT DOWN INSTEAD.
IF ALL WE HAVE ARE ROCKS...
...THEN THAT'S WHAT WE USE.

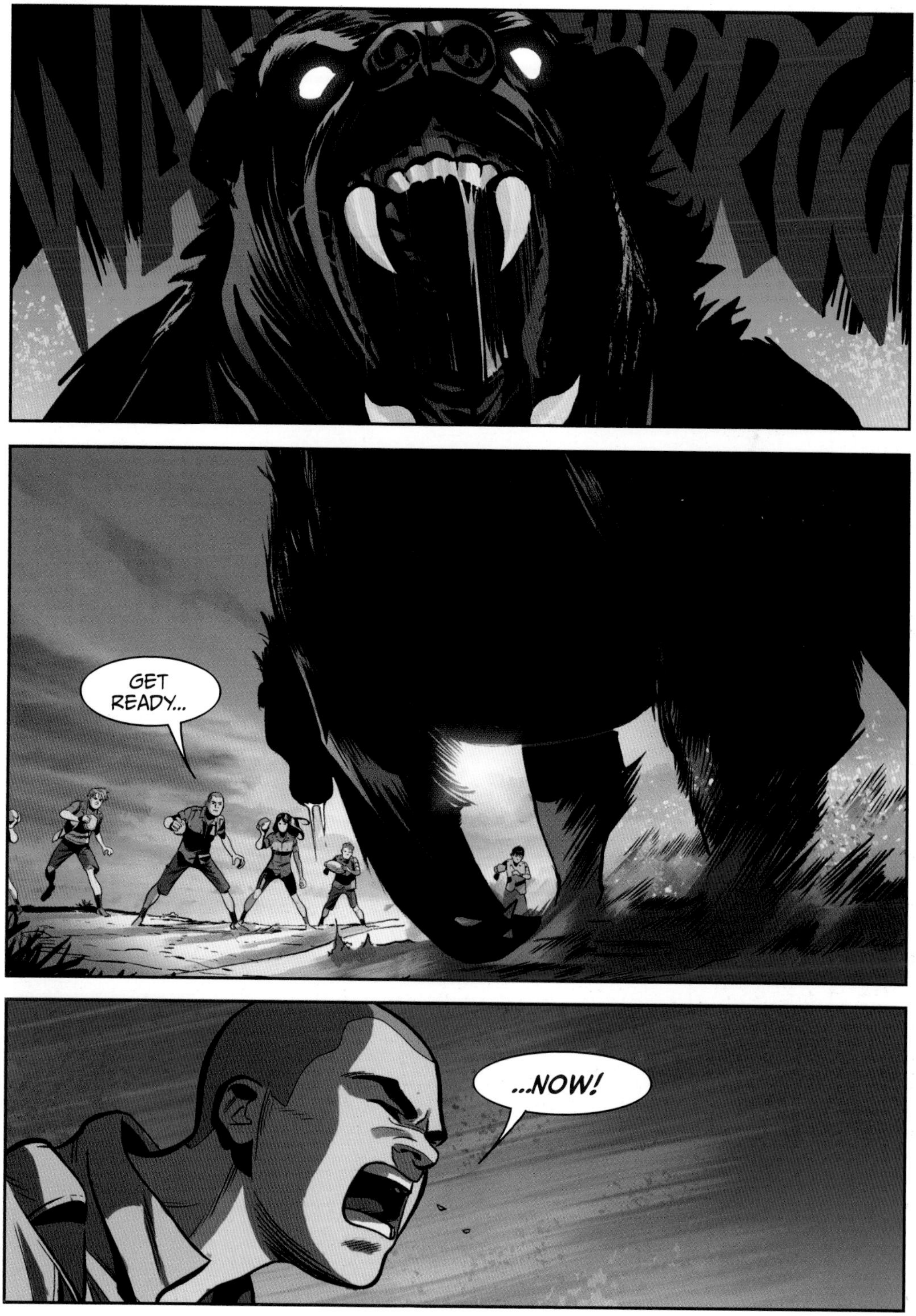
GET READY...
...NOW!

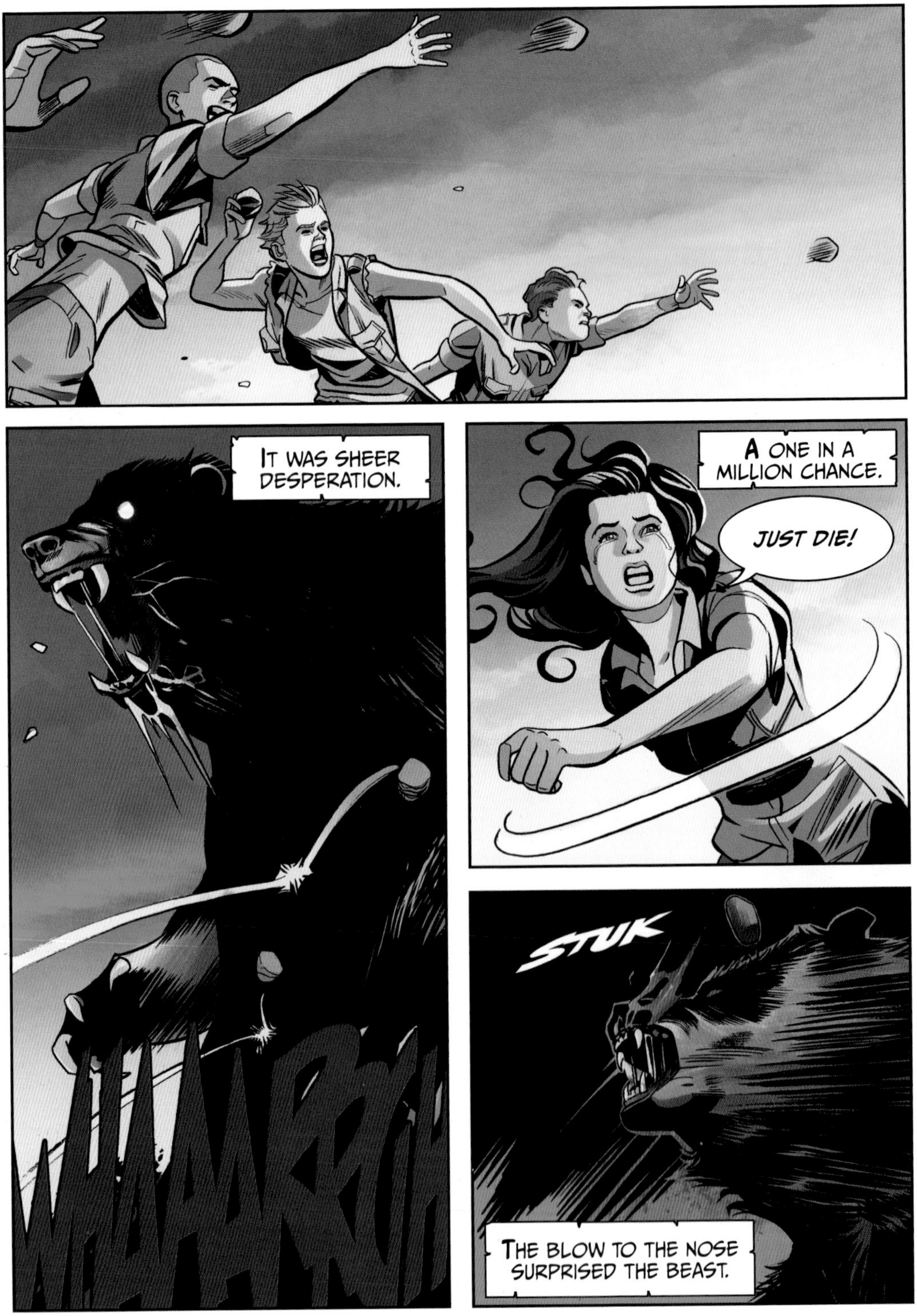
IT WAS SHEER DESPERATION.
A ONE IN A MILLION CHANCE.
JUST DIE!
STUK
THE BLOW TO THE NOSE SURPRISED THE BEAST.

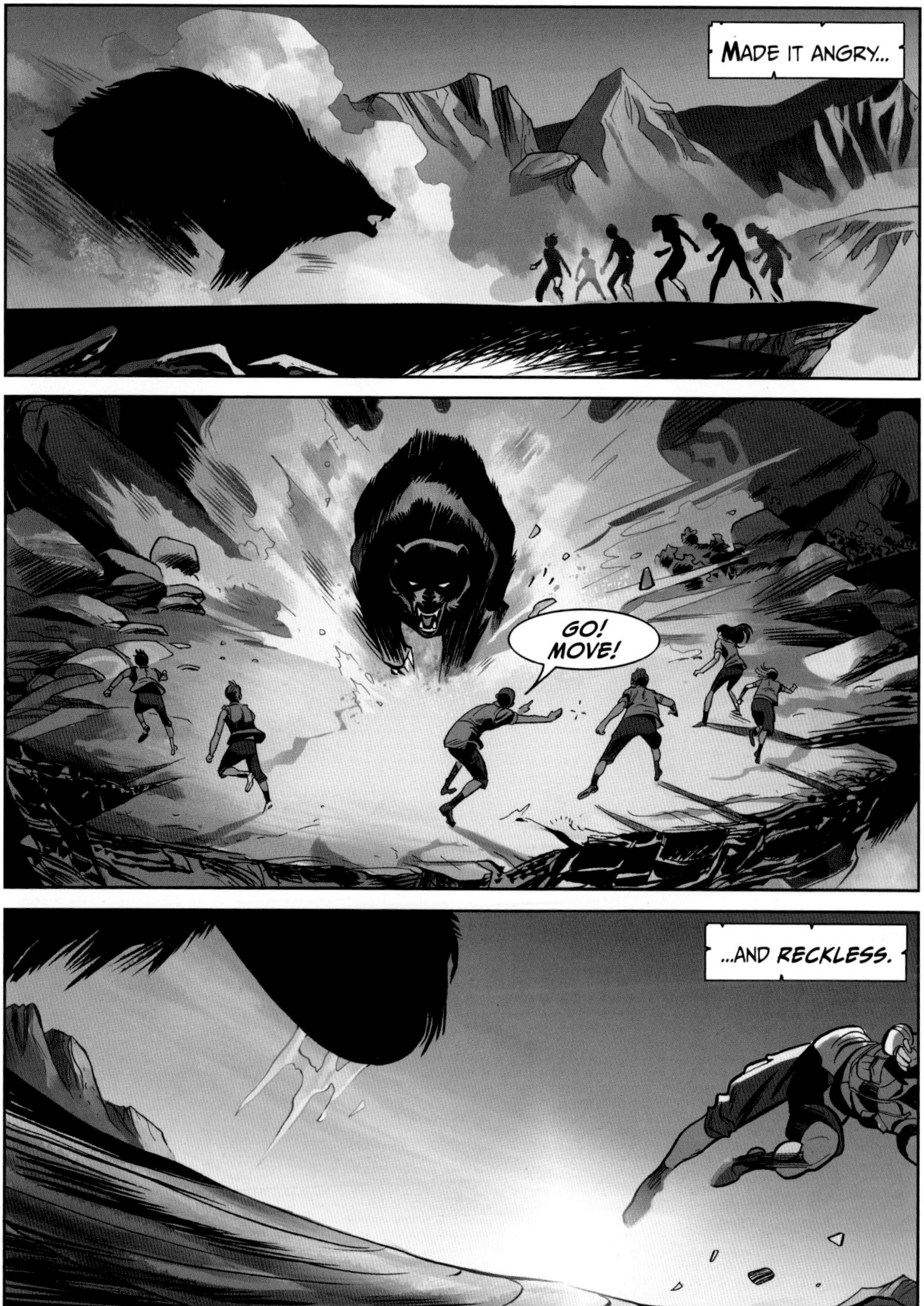
MADE IT ANGRY...
GO! MOVE!
...AND RECKLESS.

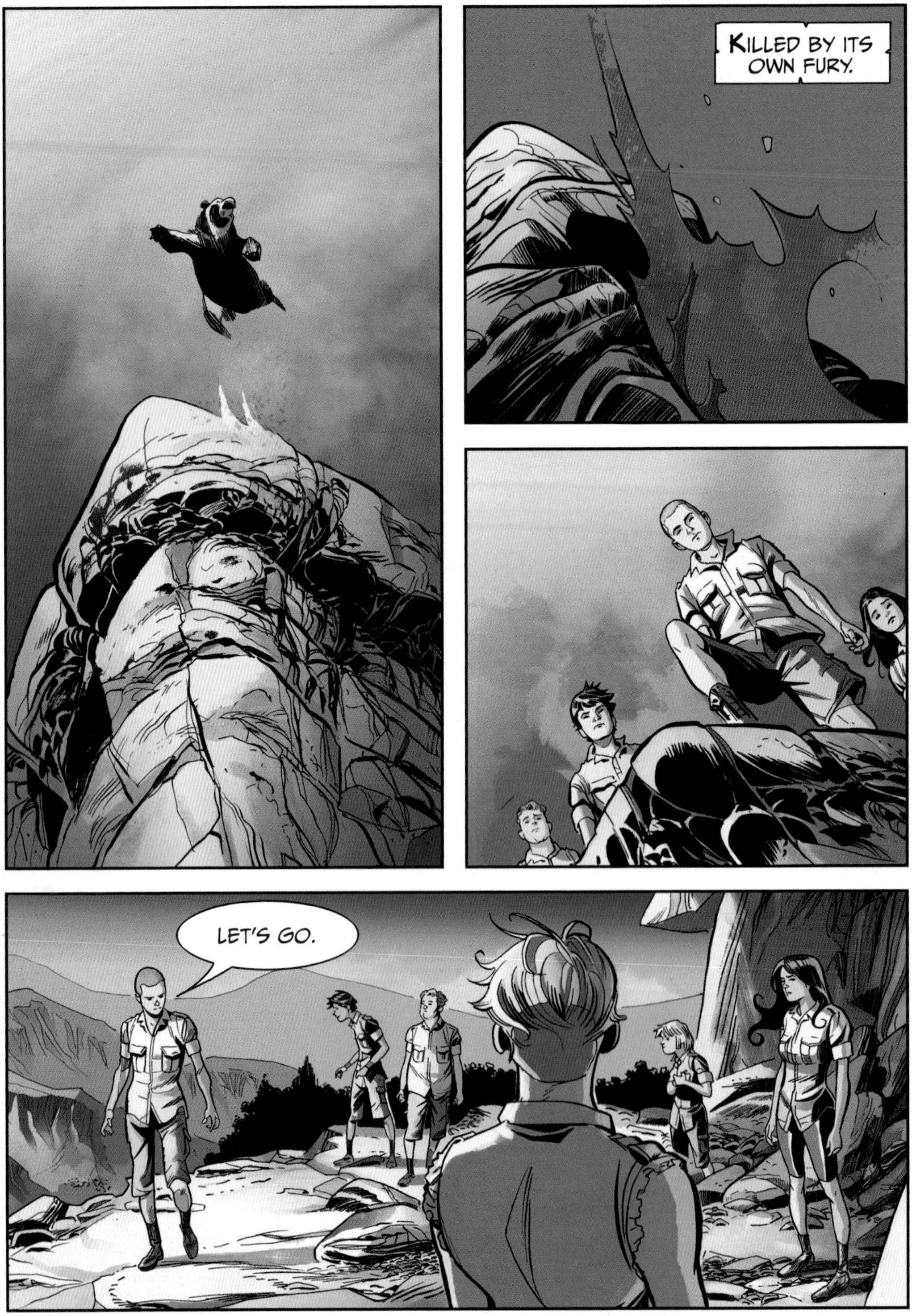
KILLED BY ITS OWN FURY.
LET'S GO.

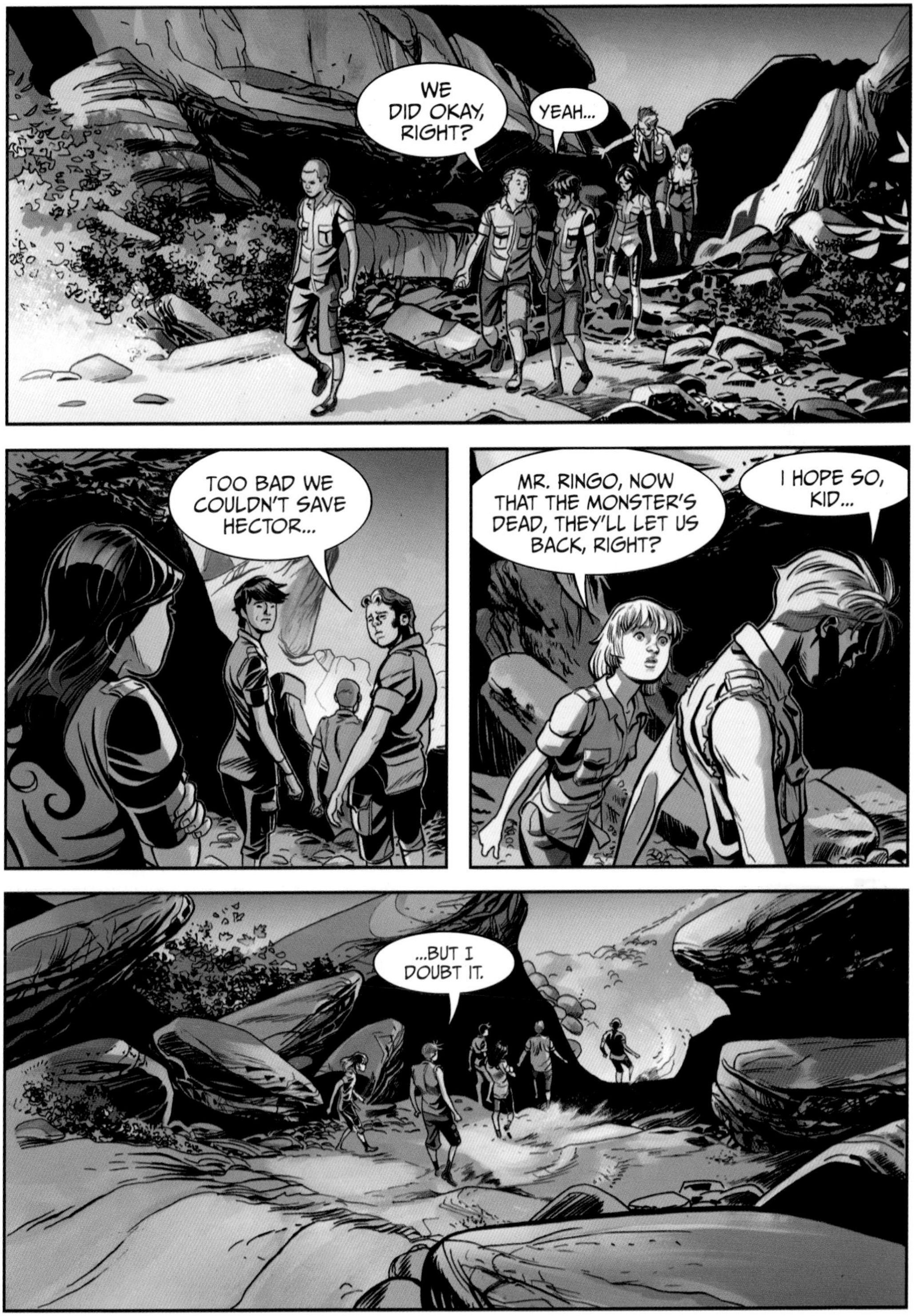
WE DID OKAY, RIGHT?
YEAH...
TOO BAD WE COULDN'T SAVE HECTOR...
MR. RINGO, NOW THAT THE MONSTER'S DEAD, THEY'LL LET US BACK, RIGHT?
I HOPE SO, KID...
...BUT I DOUBT IT.

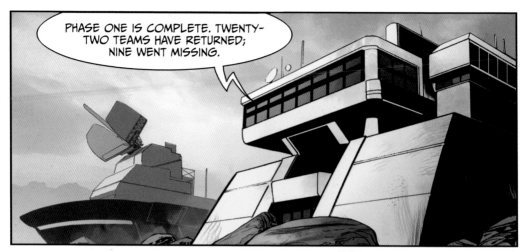

PHASE ONE IS COMPLETE. TWENTY-TWO TEAMS HAVE RETURNED; NINE WENT MISSING.

HERE'S A LIST OF THE MOST PROMISING SURVIVORS.

IMPRESSIVE.

THIS GROUP KILLED A PREDATOR WITH ONLY ONE LOSS...

...THEY MIGHT ACTUALLY MAKE GOOD SOLDIERS AFTER ALL.

MOVE THEM TO THE ADVANCED PROGRAM. YOU'LL TRAIN THEM YOURSELF.

YES, MA'AM.

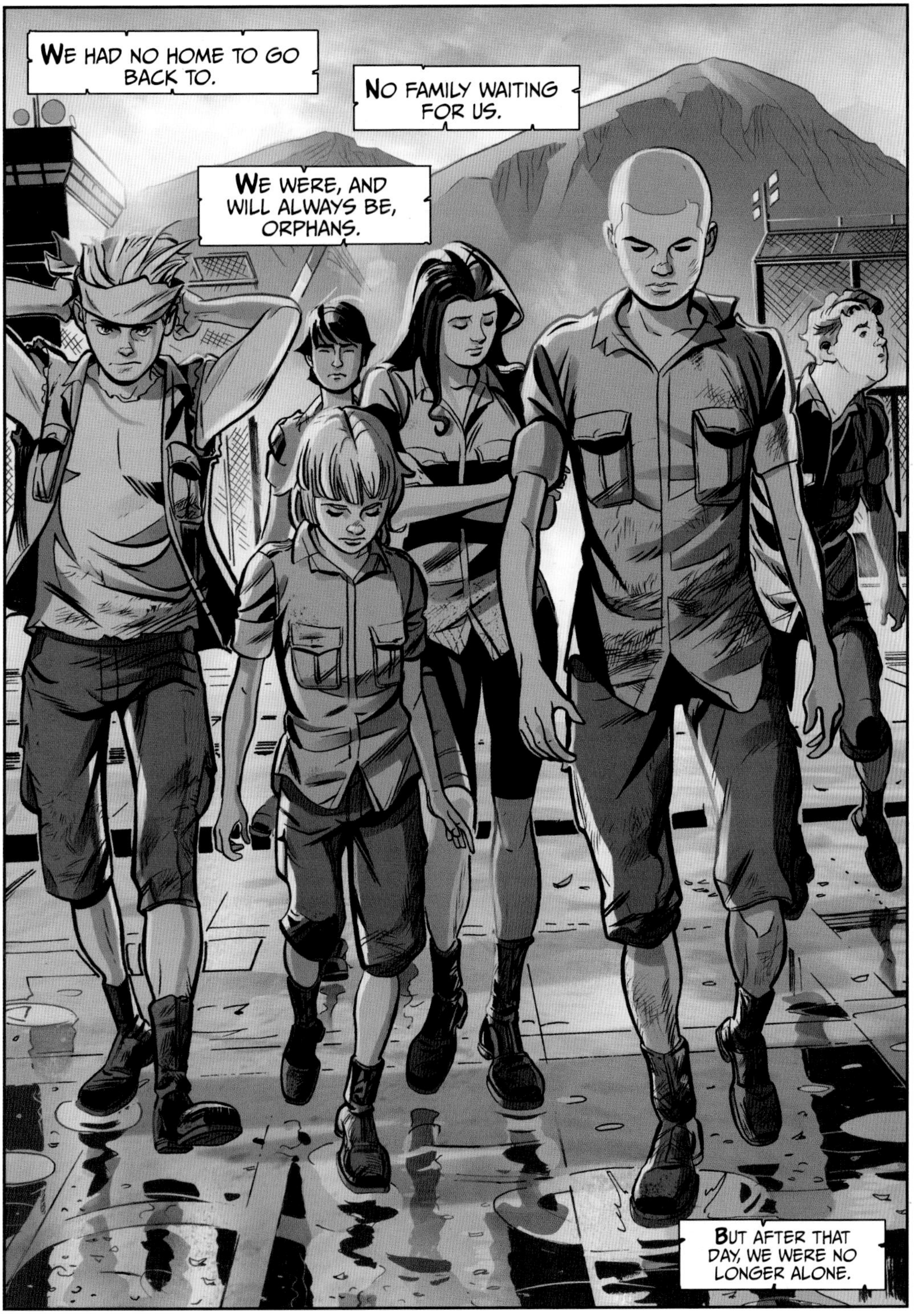
WE HAD NO HOME TO GO BACK TO.
NO FAMILY WAITING FOR US.
WE WERE, AND WILL ALWAYS BE, ORPHANS.
BUT AFTER THAT DAY, WE WERE NO LONGER ALONE.

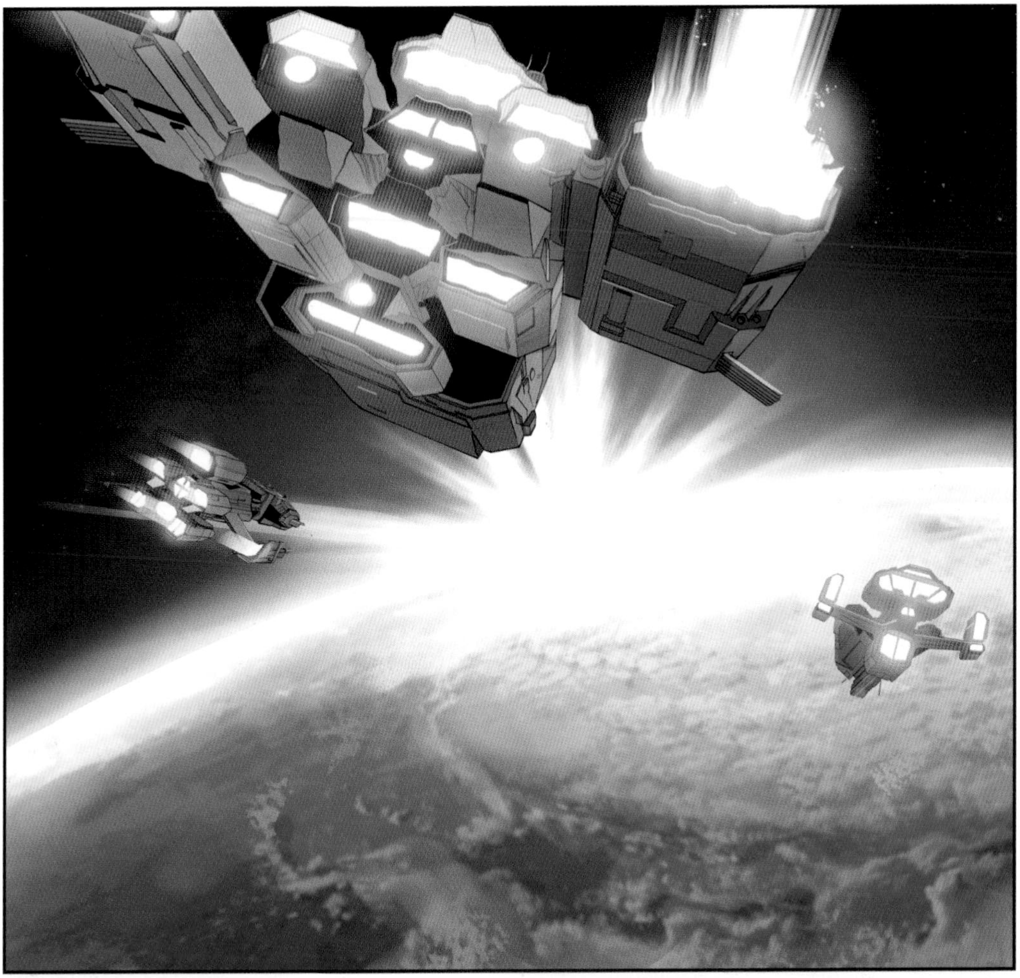

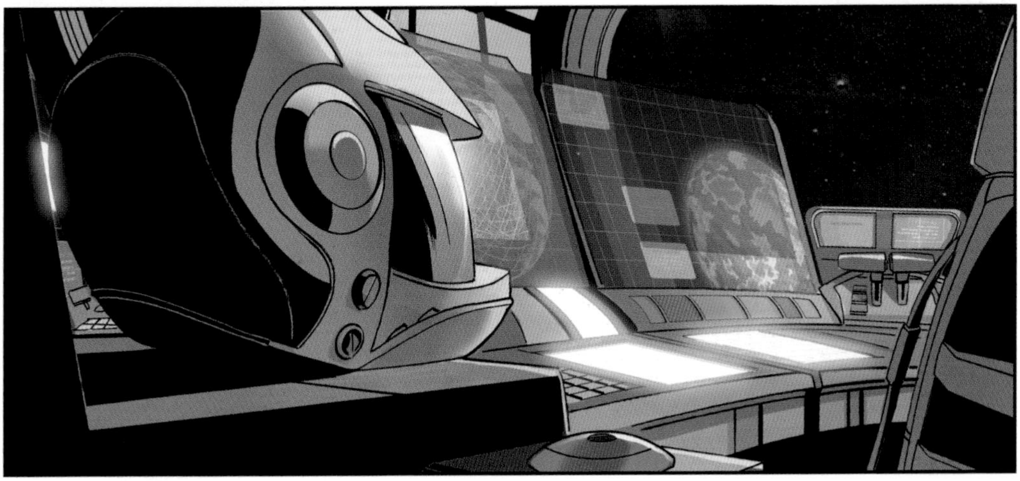

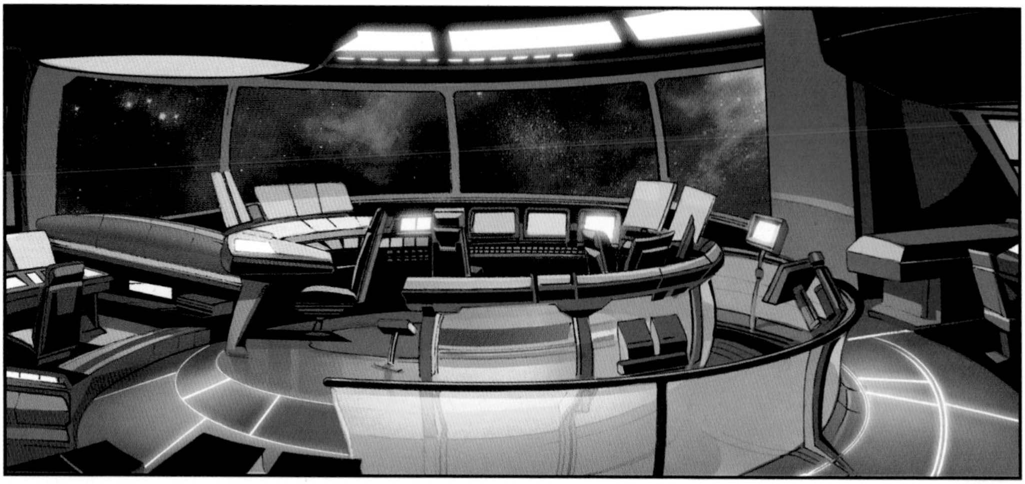

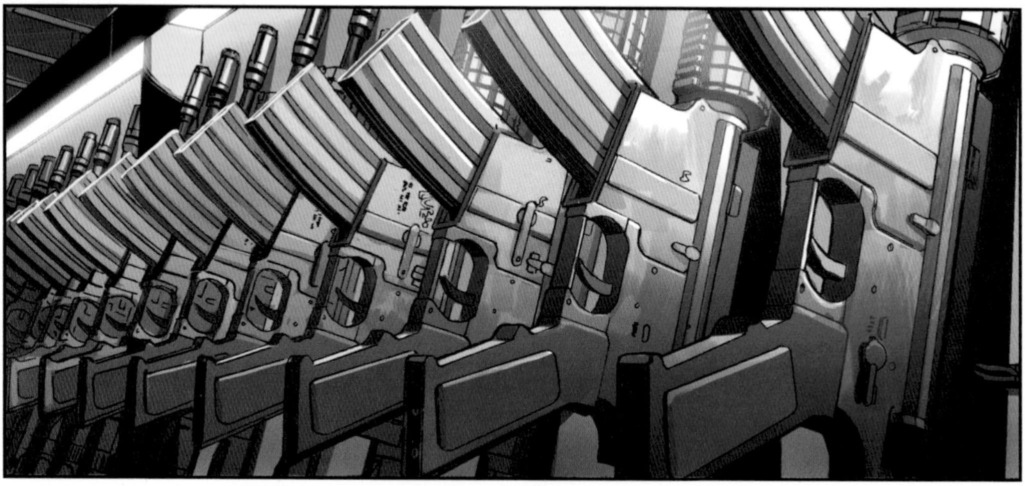

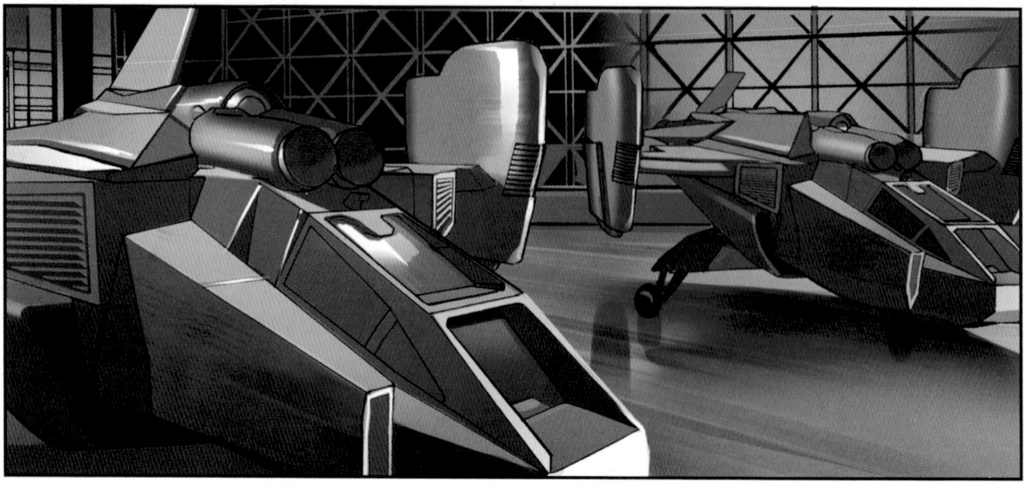

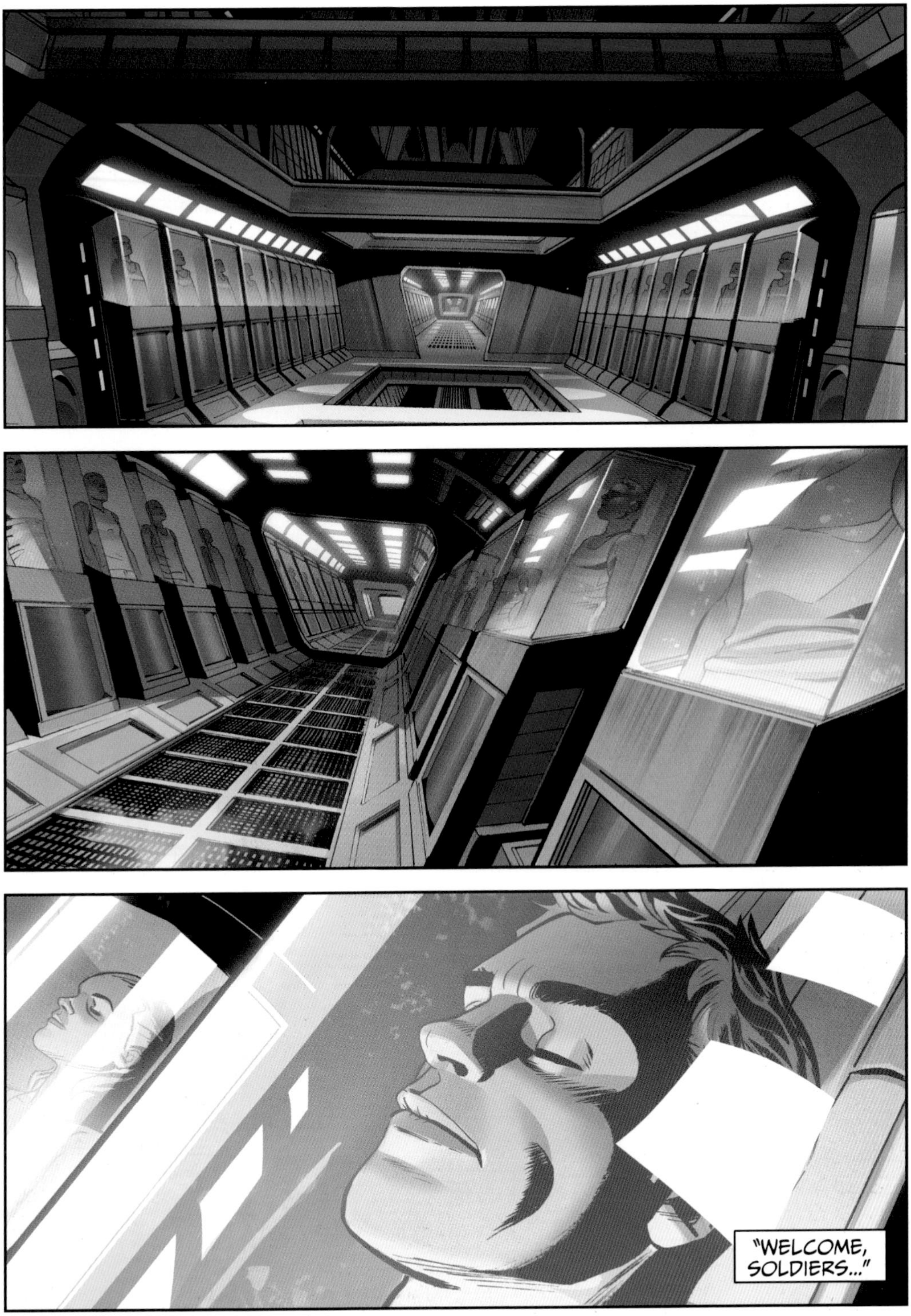
"WELCOME, SOLDIERS..."

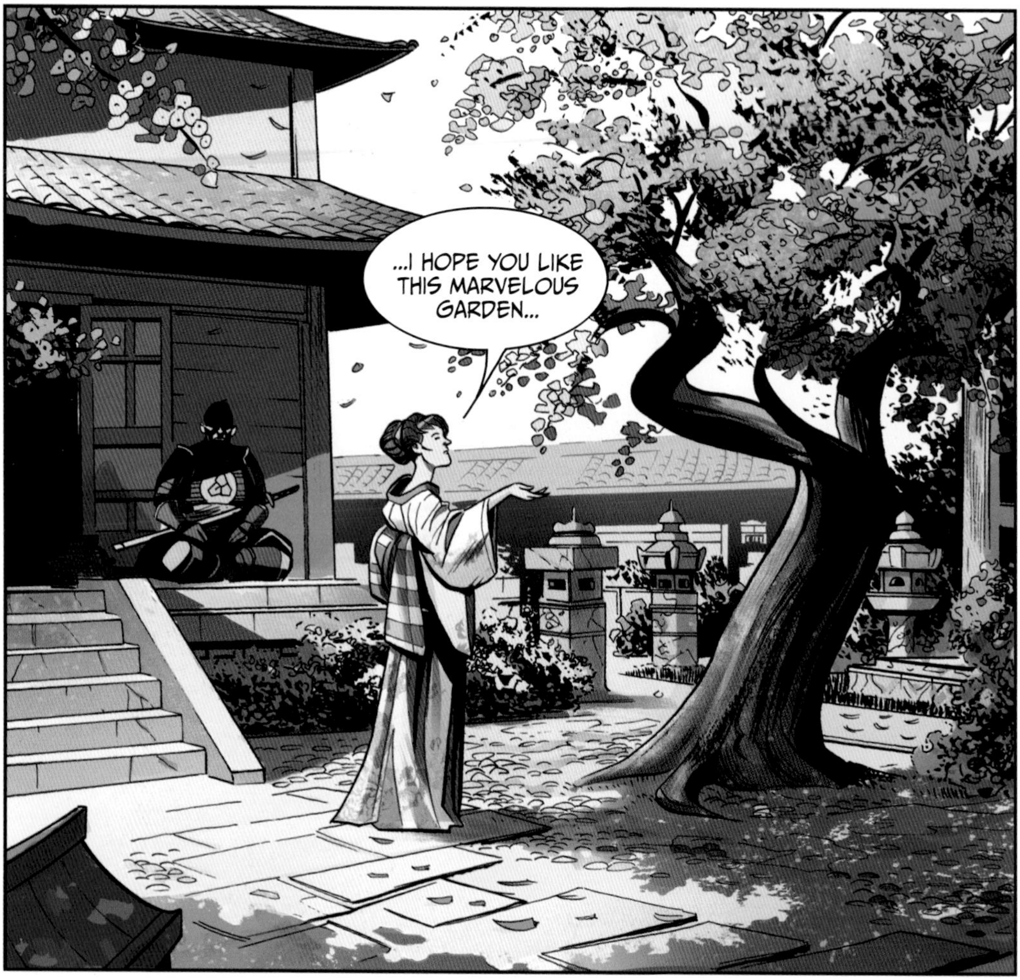
...I HOPE YOU LIKE THIS MARVELOUS GARDEN...

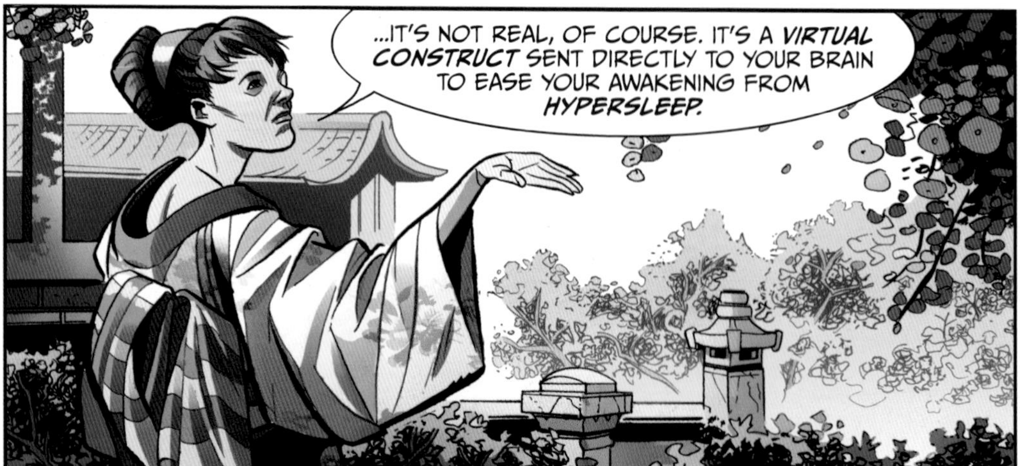
...IT'S NOT REAL, OF COURSE. IT'S A VIRTUAL CONSTRUCT SENT DIRECTLY TO YOUR BRAIN TO EASE YOUR AWAKENING FROM HYPERSLEEP.

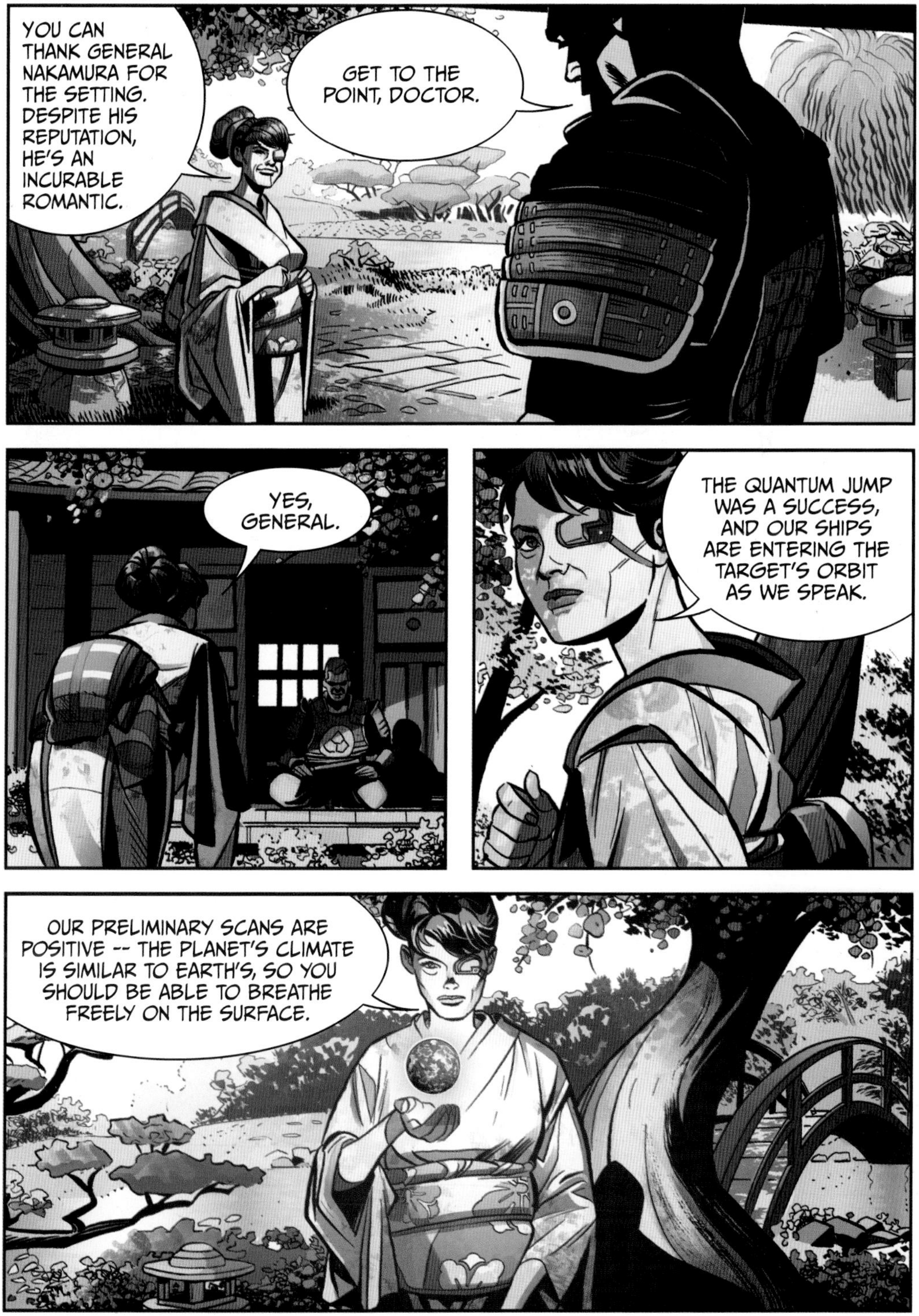
YOU CAN THANK GENERAL NAKAMURA FOR THE SETTING. DESPITE HIS REPUTATION, HE'S AN INCURABLE ROMANTIC.
GET TO THE POINT, DOCTOR.
YES, GENERAL.
THE QUANTUM JUMP WAS A SUCCESS, AND OUR SHIPS ARE ENTERING THE TARGET'S ORBIT AS WE SPEAK.
OUR PRELIMINARY SCANS ARE POSITIVE -- THE PLANET'S CLIMATE IS SIMILAR TO EARTH'S, SO YOU SHOULD BE ABLE TO BREATHE FREELY ON THE SURFACE.

WE DELAYED YOUR AWAKENING TO GIVE OUR MEDICAL STAFF TIME TO SYNTHESIZE A *VACCINE.*

BUT WE'VE ALSO DETECTED A LOW-FREQUENCY *RADIATION* THAT CAN PROVE LETHAL OVER TIME.

YOU WILL FIND ROUTINE DOSAGE AS PART OF YOUR KIT.

IT IS OF CAPITAL IMPORTANCE THAT YOU ADMINISTER AN INJECTION EVERY FORTY-EIGHT HOURS. YOUR LIVES ARE AT STAKE, SOLDIERS.

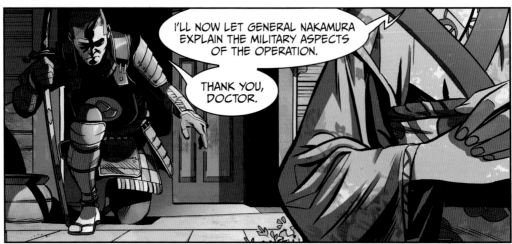

I'LL NOW LET GENERAL NAKAMURA EXPLAIN THE MILITARY ASPECTS OF THE OPERATION.

THANK YOU, DOCTOR.

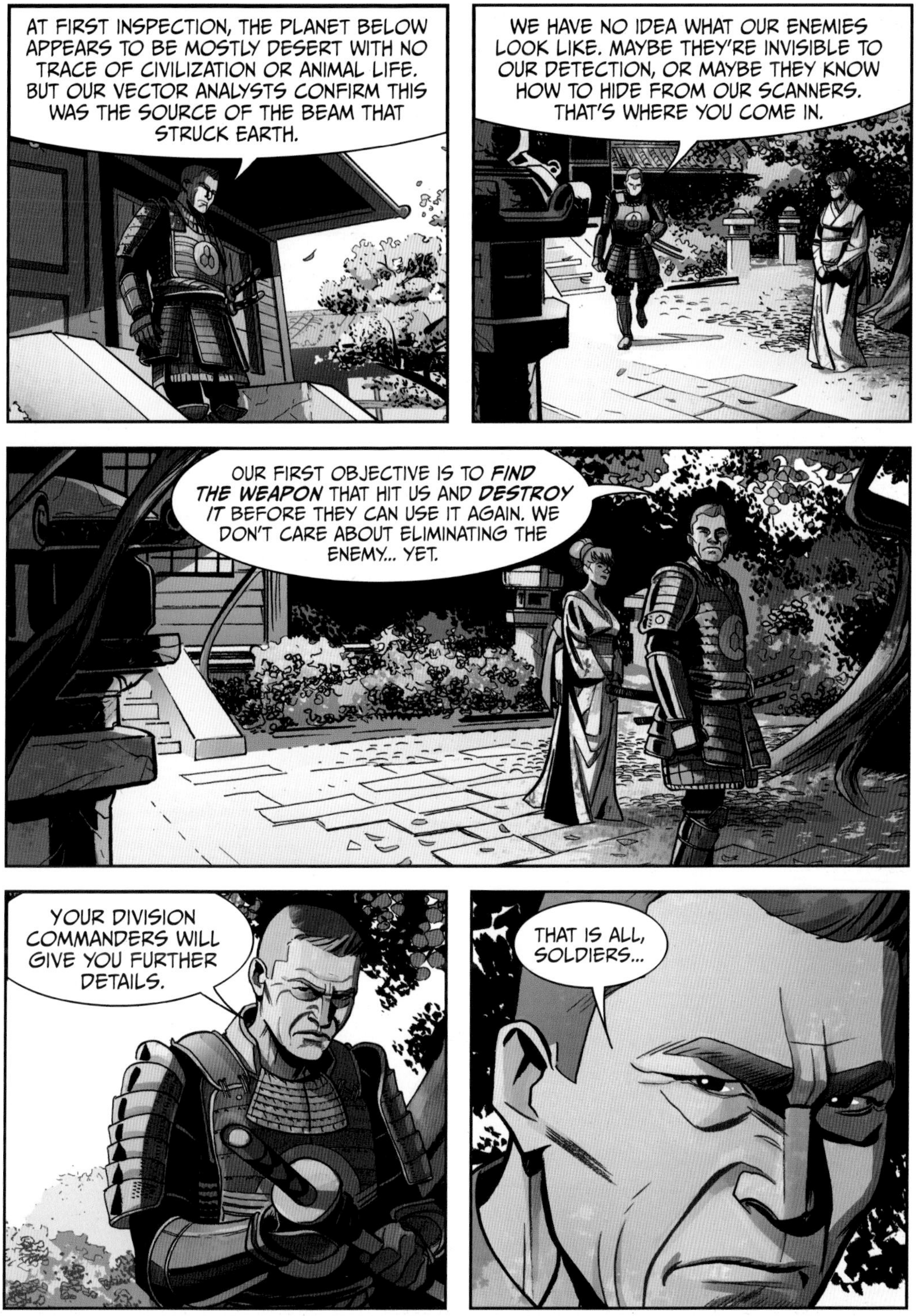
AT FIRST INSPECTION, THE PLANET BELOW APPEARS TO BE MOSTLY DESERT WITH NO TRACE OF CIVILIZATION OR ANIMAL LIFE. BUT OUR VECTOR ANALYSTS CONFIRM THIS WAS THE SOURCE OF THE BEAM THAT STRUCK EARTH.
WE HAVE NO IDEA WHAT OUR ENEMIES LOOK LIKE. MAYBE THEY'RE INVISIBLE TO OUR DETECTION, OR MAYBE THEY KNOW HOW TO HIDE FROM OUR SCANNERS. THAT'S WHERE YOU COME IN.
OUR FIRST OBJECTIVE IS TO ***FIND THE WEAPON*** THAT HIT US AND ***DESTROY IT*** BEFORE THEY CAN USE IT AGAIN. WE DON'T CARE ABOUT ELIMINATING THE ENEMY... YET.
YOUR DIVISION COMMANDERS WILL GIVE YOU FURTHER DETAILS.
THAT IS ALL, SOLDIERS...

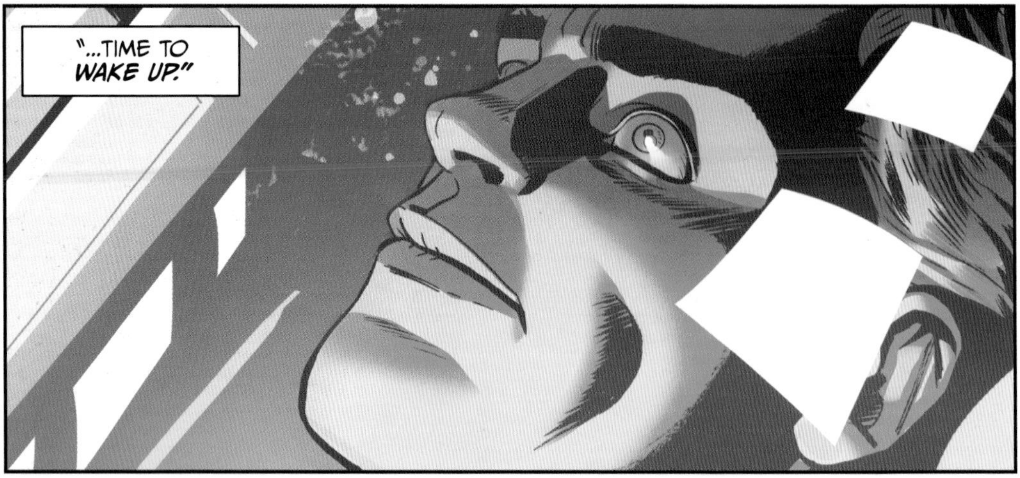
"...TIME TO
WAKE UP."

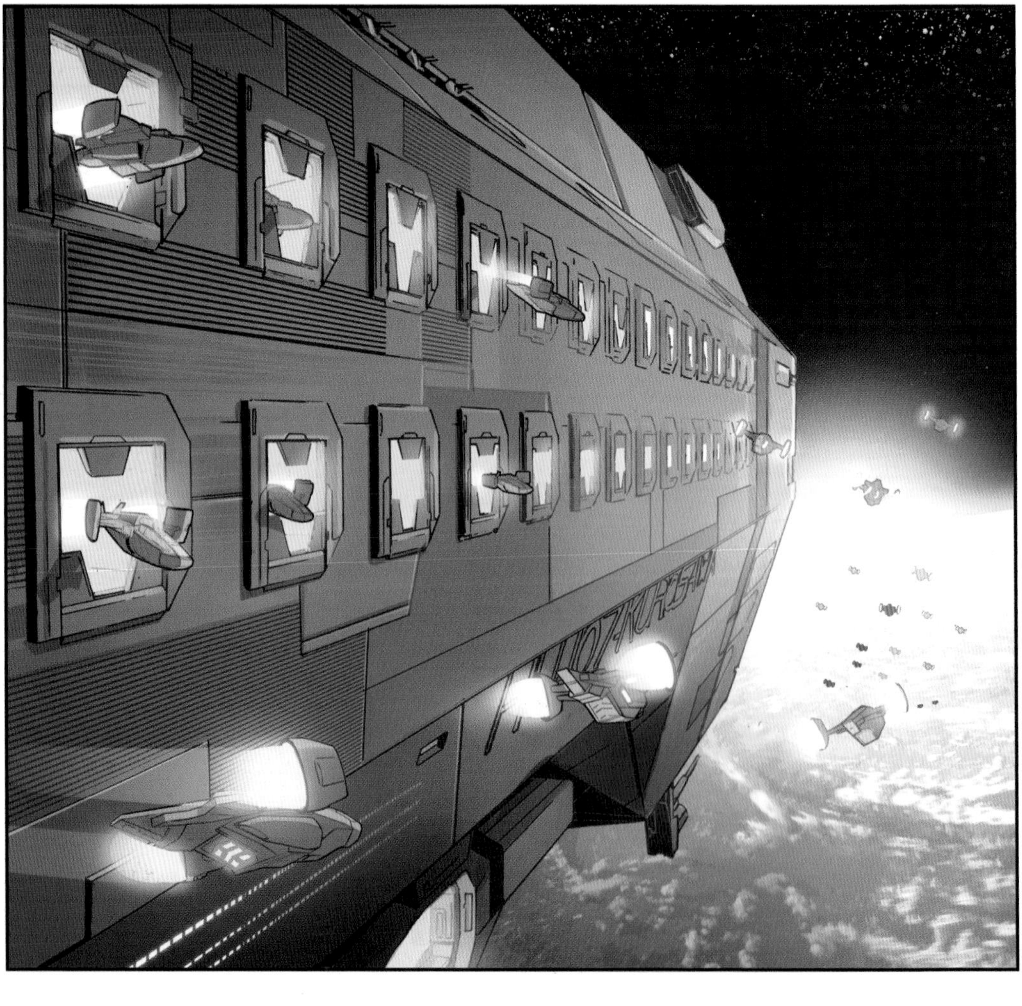

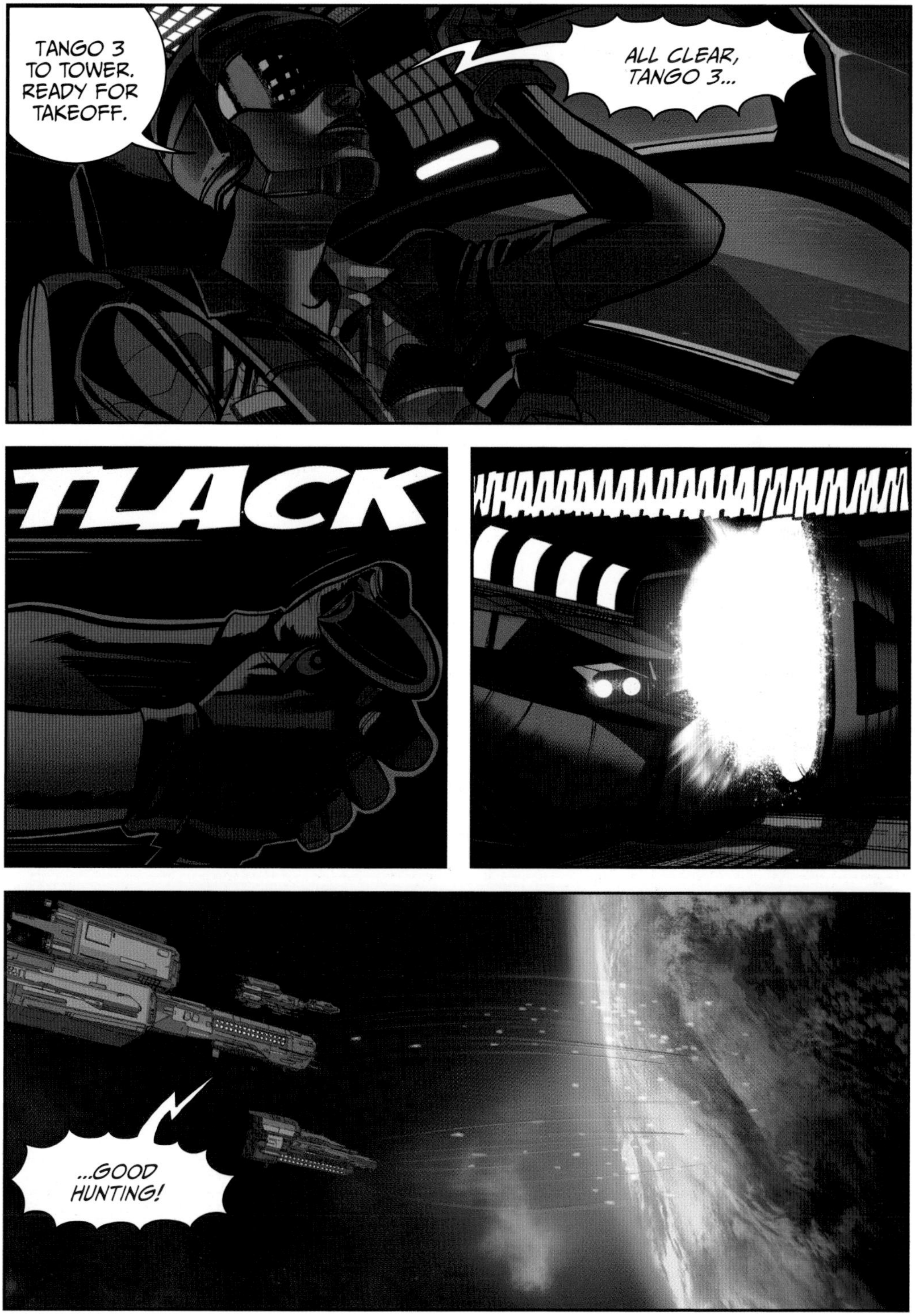
TANGO 3 TO TOWER. READY FOR TAKEOFF.
ALL CLEAR, TANGO 3...
TLACK
WHAAAAAAAAAAAAAAMMMMM
...GOOD HUNTING!

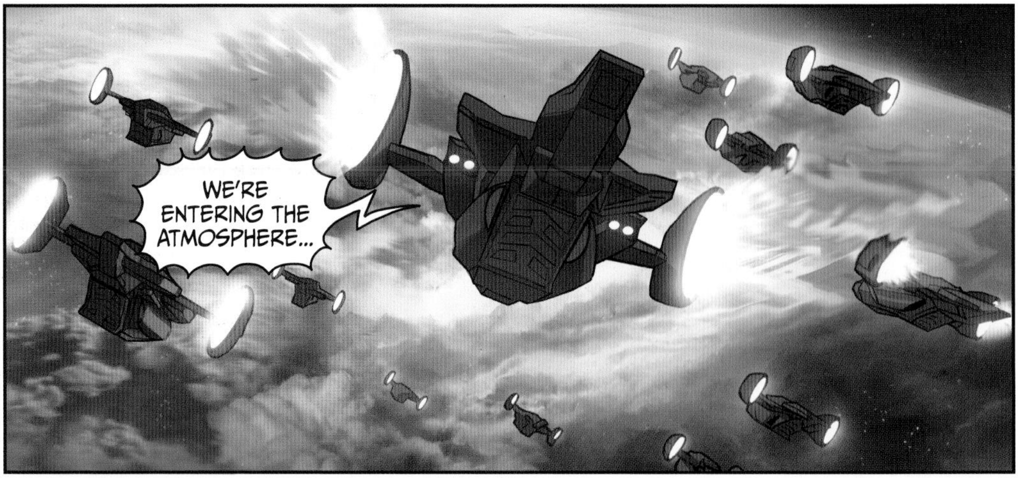
WE'RE ENTERING THE ATMOSPHERE...

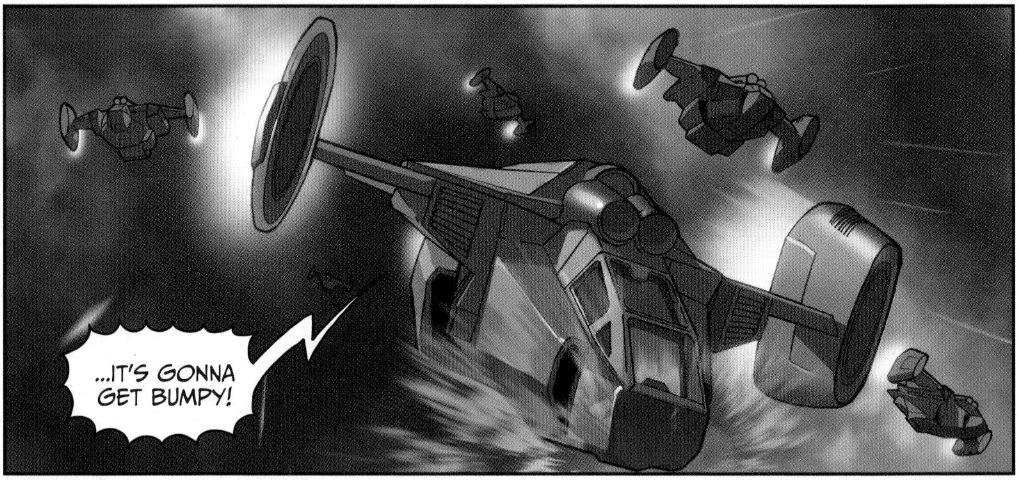
...IT'S GONNA GET BUMPY!

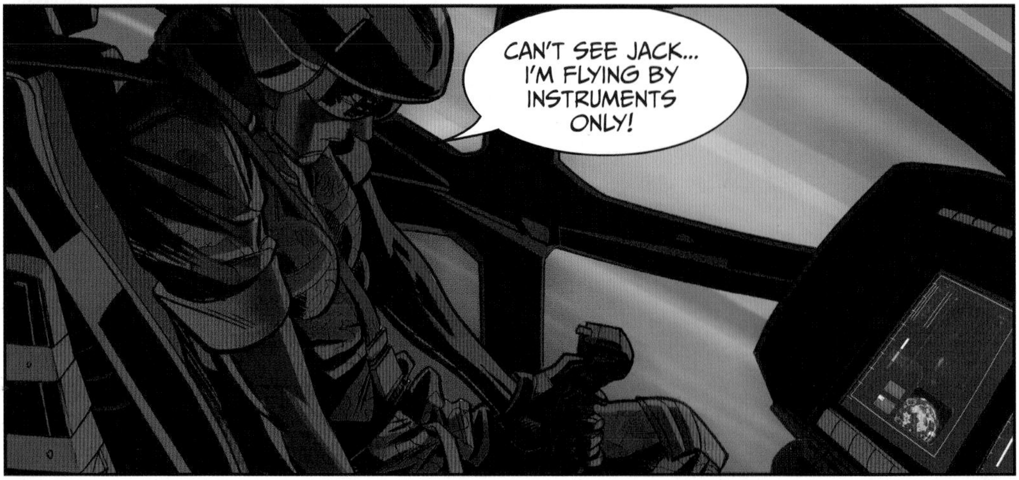
CAN'T SEE JACK... I'M FLYING BY INSTRUMENTS ONLY!

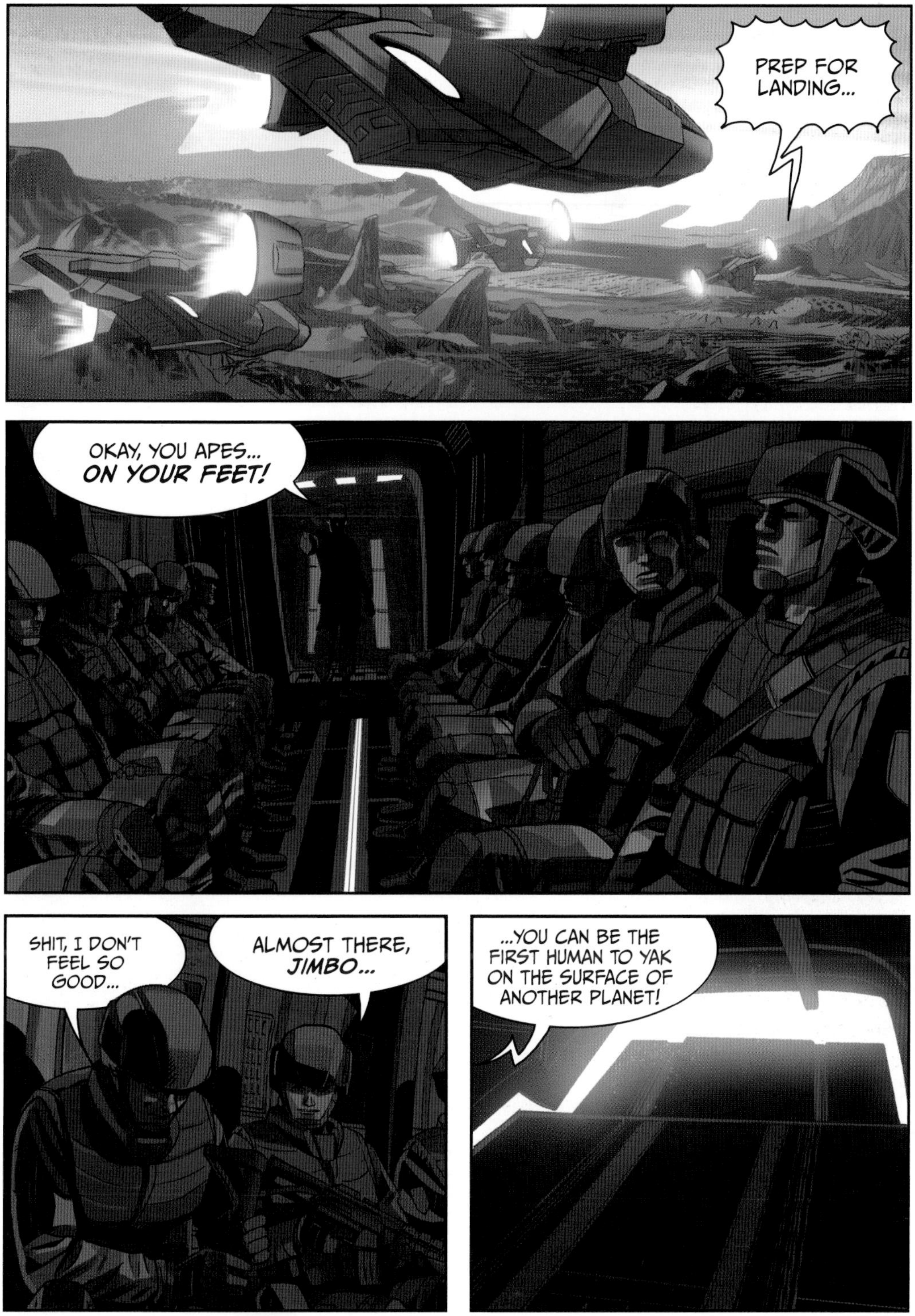
PREP FOR LANDING...
OKAY, YOU APES... ON YOUR FEET!
SHIT, I DON'T FEEL SO GOOD...
ALMOST THERE, JIMBO...
...YOU CAN BE THE FIRST HUMAN TO YAK ON THE SURFACE OF ANOTHER PLANET!

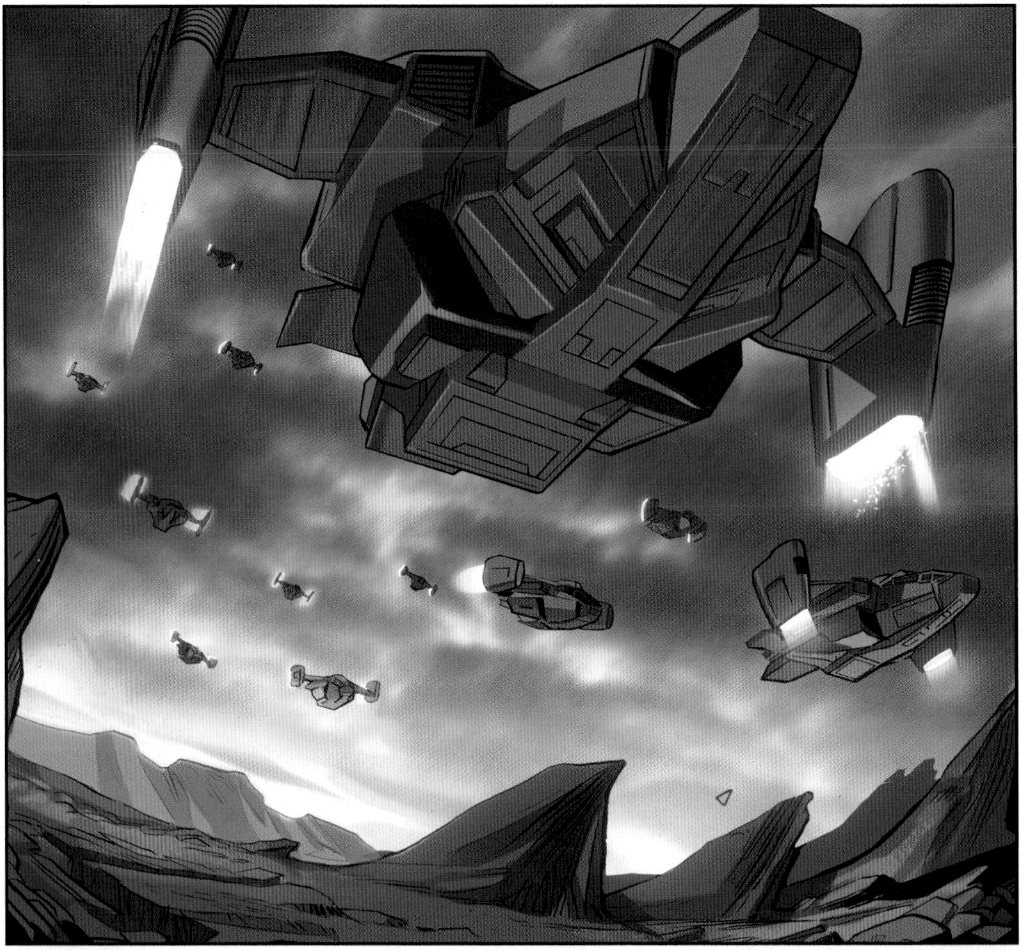

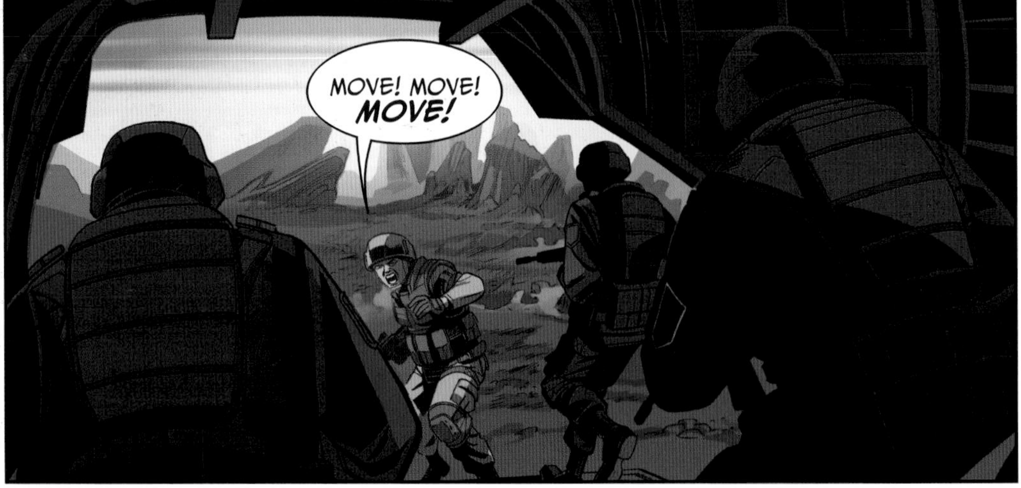
MOVE! MOVE! MOVE!

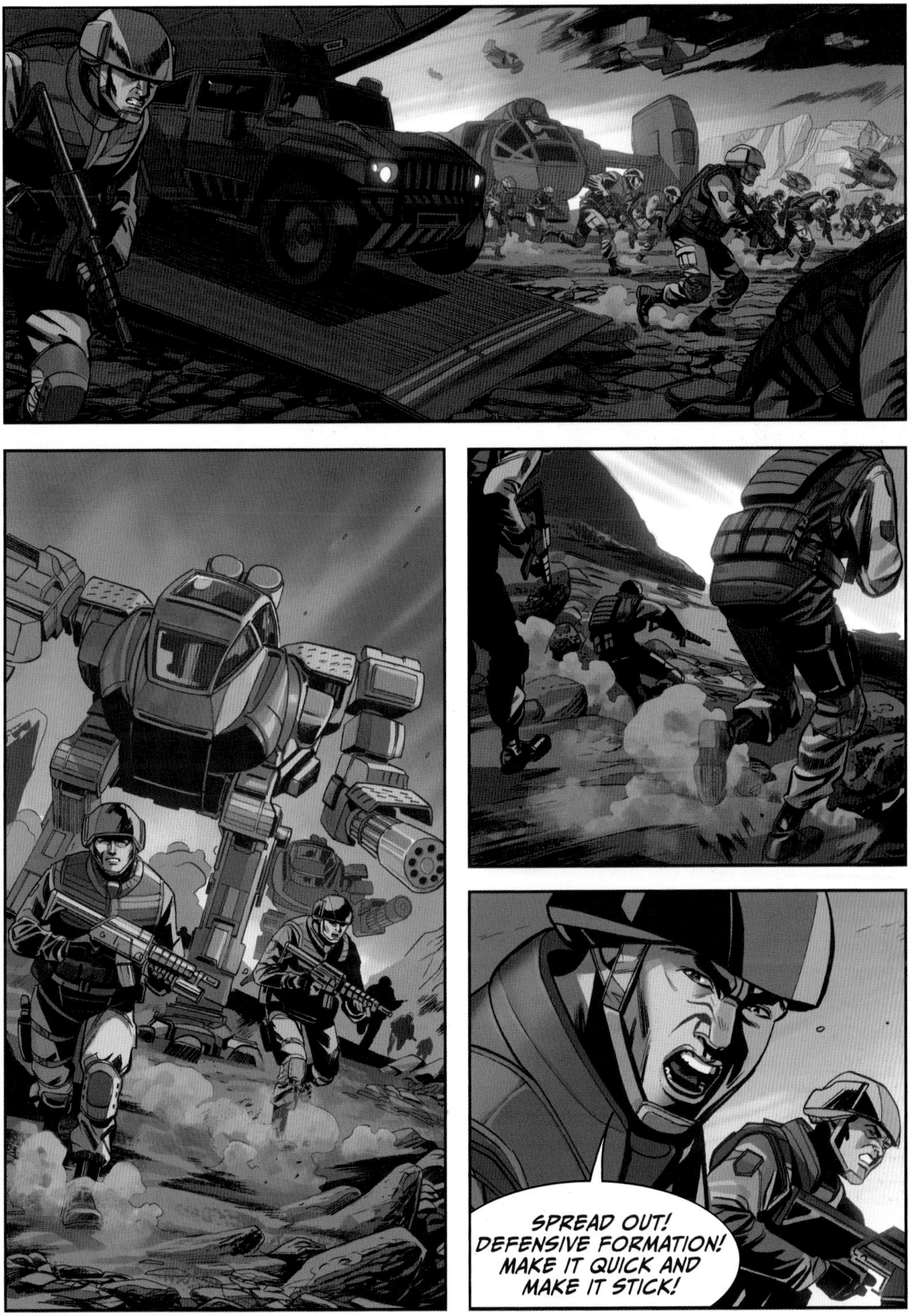
SPREAD OUT!
DEFENSIVE FORMATION!
MAKE IT QUICK AND
MAKE IT STICK!

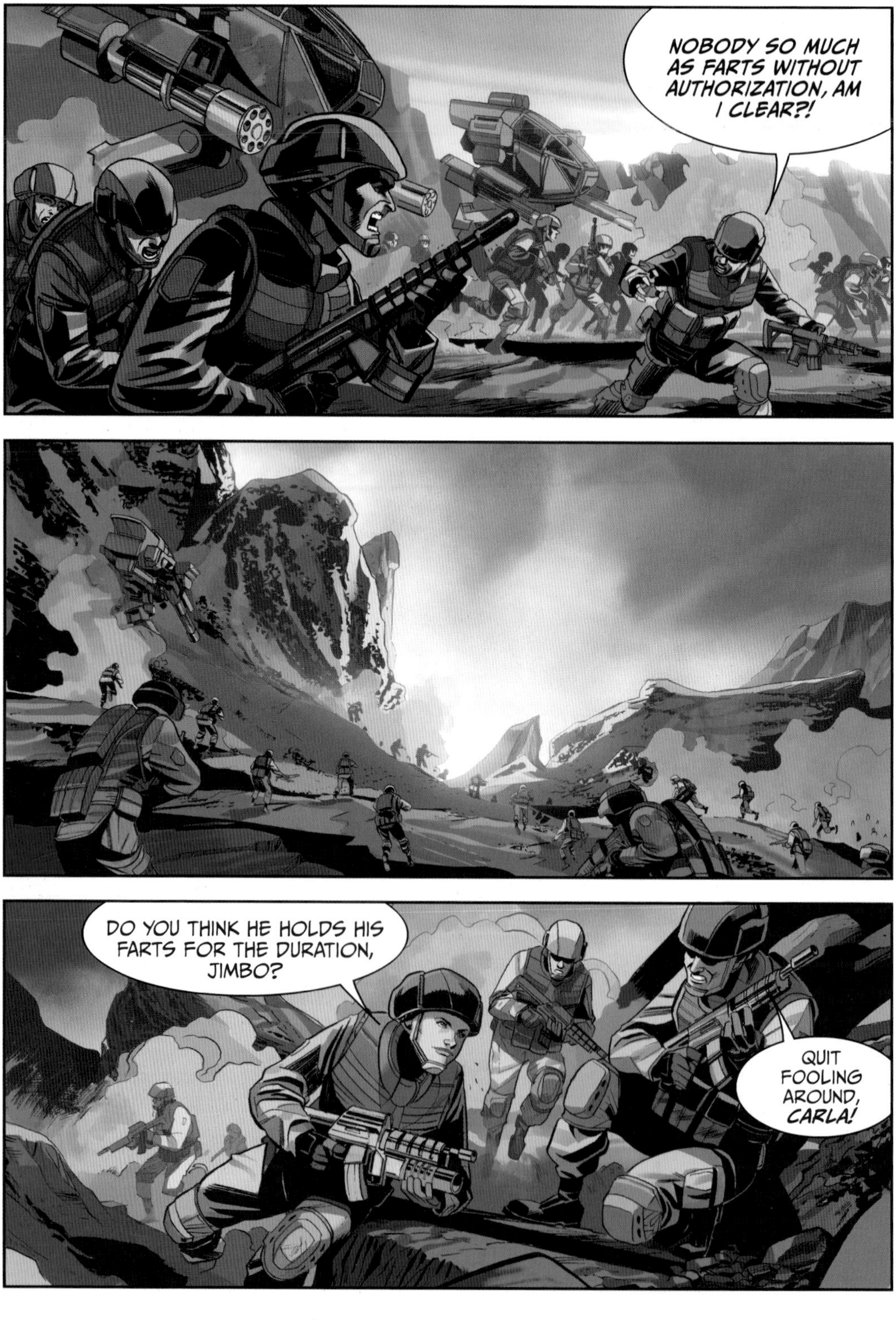
NOBODY SO MUCH AS FARTS WITHOUT AUTHORIZATION, AM I CLEAR?!
DO YOU THINK HE HOLDS HIS FARTS FOR THE DURATION, JIMBO?
QUIT FOOLING AROUND, CARLA!

RELAX! WHAT ARE YOU AFRAID OF? YOU HEARD THE GENERAL, THIS PLACE IS DESERTED...

JUST SHUT UP AND WATCH THE SCANNERS... BE SURE THE AREA'S CLEAR!

THE READINGS HAVEN'T CHANGED IN FIVE MINUTES... NO SIGN OF LIFE BUT US.

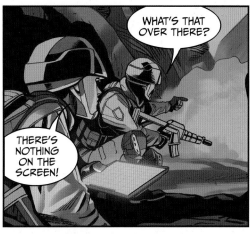

WHAT'S THAT OVER THERE?

THERE'S NOTHING ON THE SCREEN!

OPEN YOUR EYES, DAMN IT!

YOUR EYES CAN DECEIVE YOU... I ONLY TRUST TECHNOLOGY...

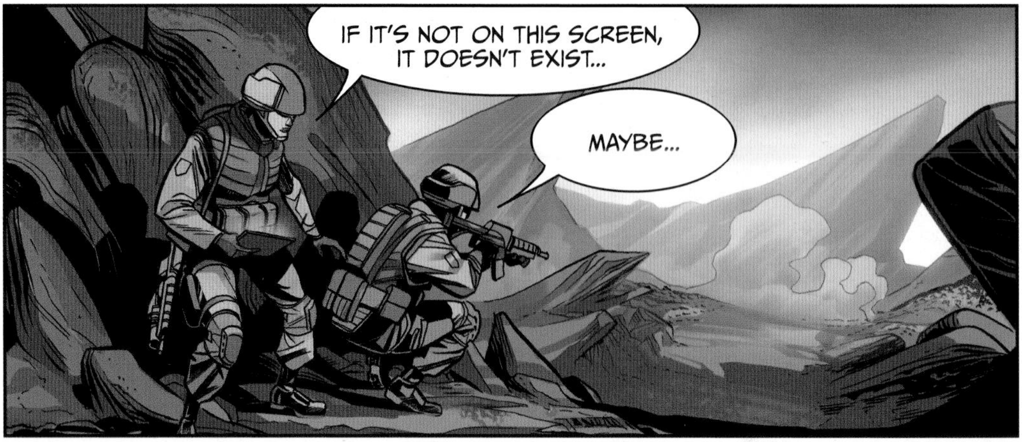
IF IT'S NOT ON THIS SCREEN, IT DOESN'T EXIST...
MAYBE...

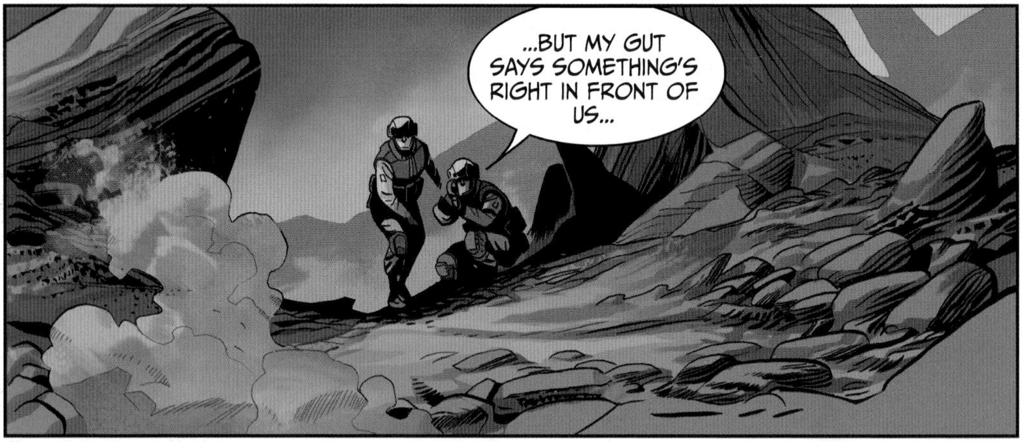
...BUT MY GUT SAYS SOMETHING'S RIGHT IN FRONT OF US...

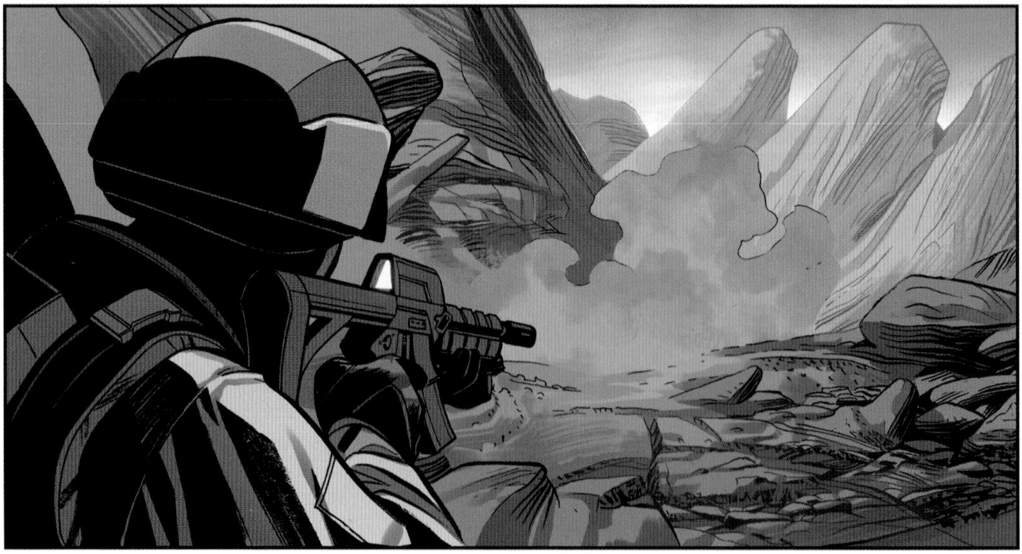

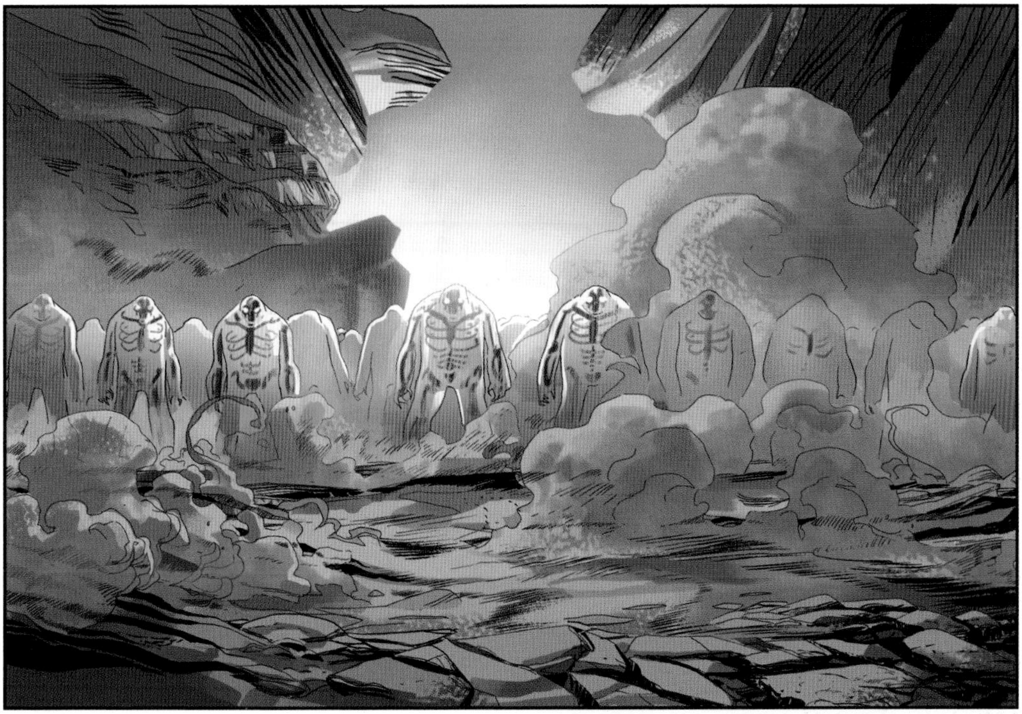

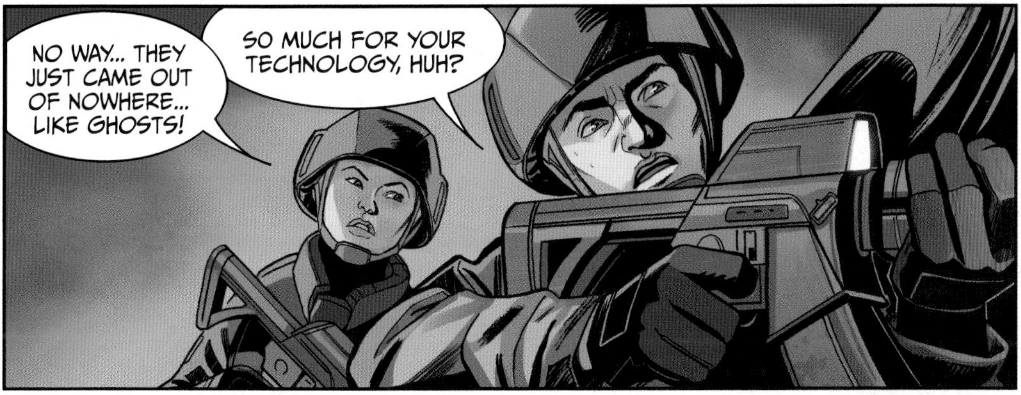
NO WAY... THEY JUST CAME OUT OF NOWHERE... LIKE GHOSTS!
SO MUCH FOR YOUR TECHNOLOGY, HUH?

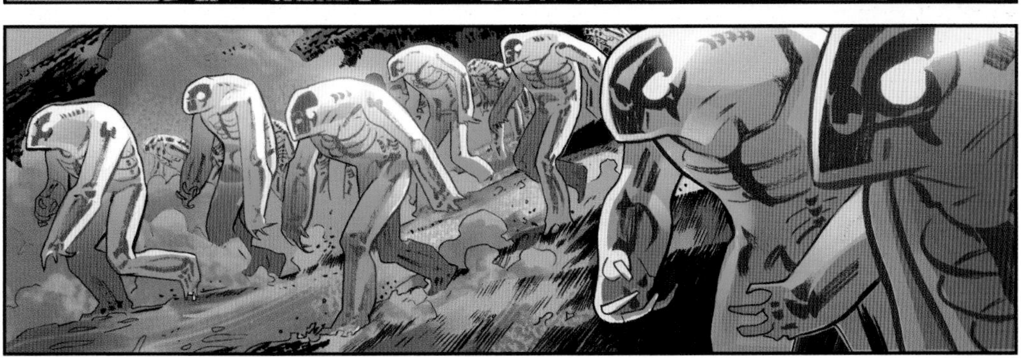

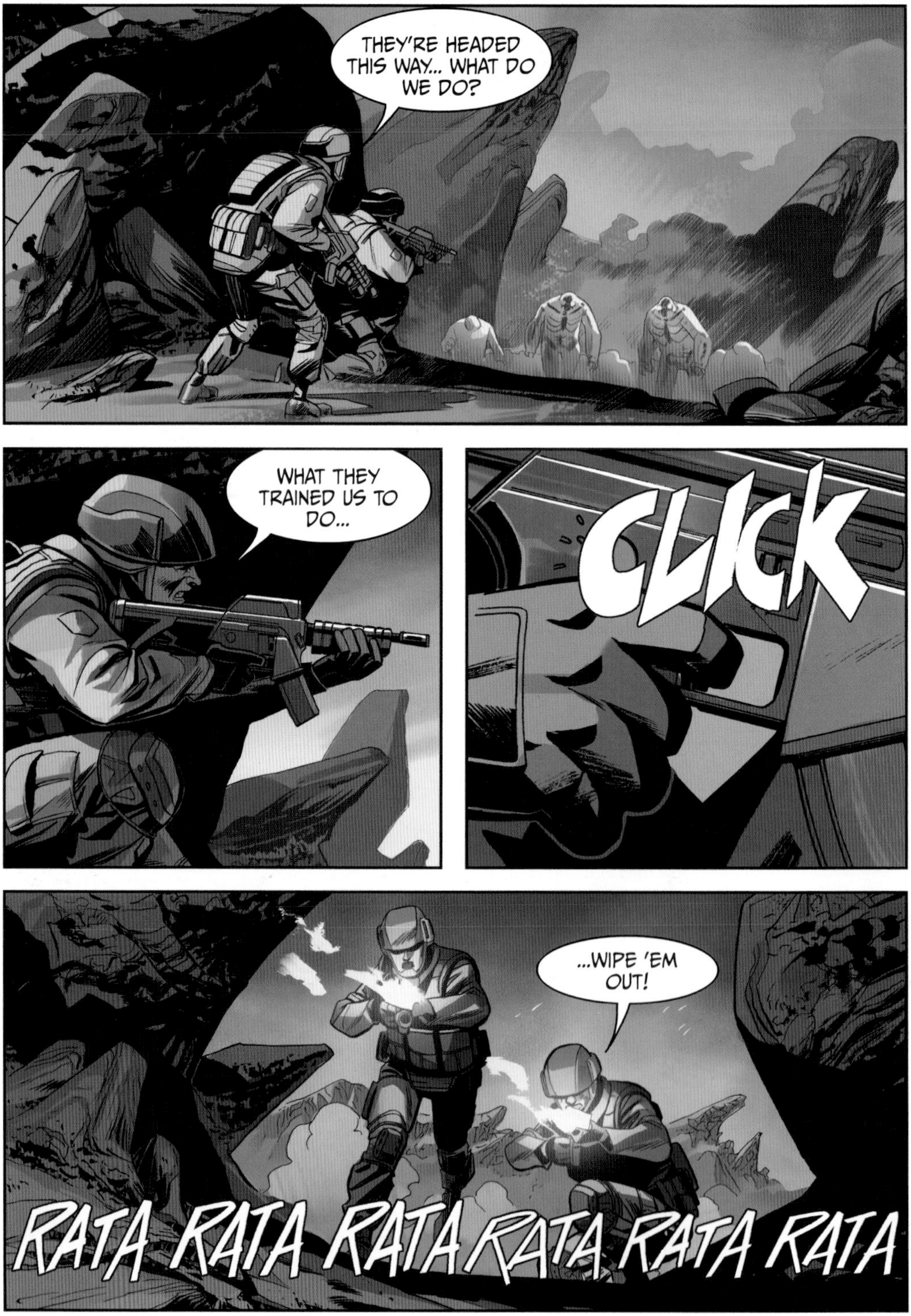
THEY'RE HEADED THIS WAY... WHAT DO WE DO?
WHAT THEY TRAINED US TO DO...
CLICK
...WIPE 'EM OUT!
RATA RATA RATA RATA RATA RATA

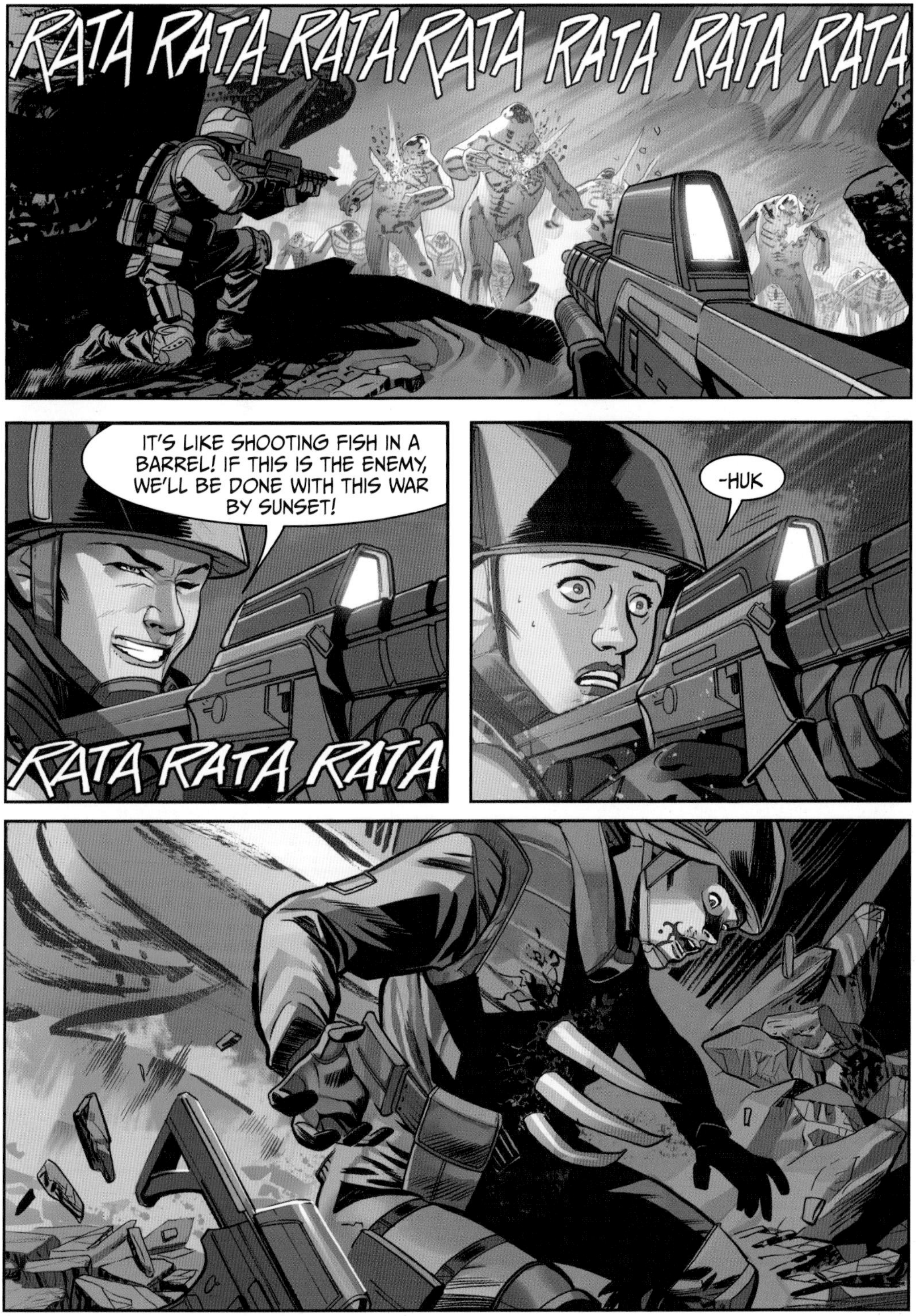
RATA RATA RATA RATA RATA RATA RATA
IT'S LIKE SHOOTING FISH IN A BARREL! IF THIS IS THE ENEMY, WE'LL BE DONE WITH THIS WAR BY SUNSET!
RATA RATA RATA
-HUK

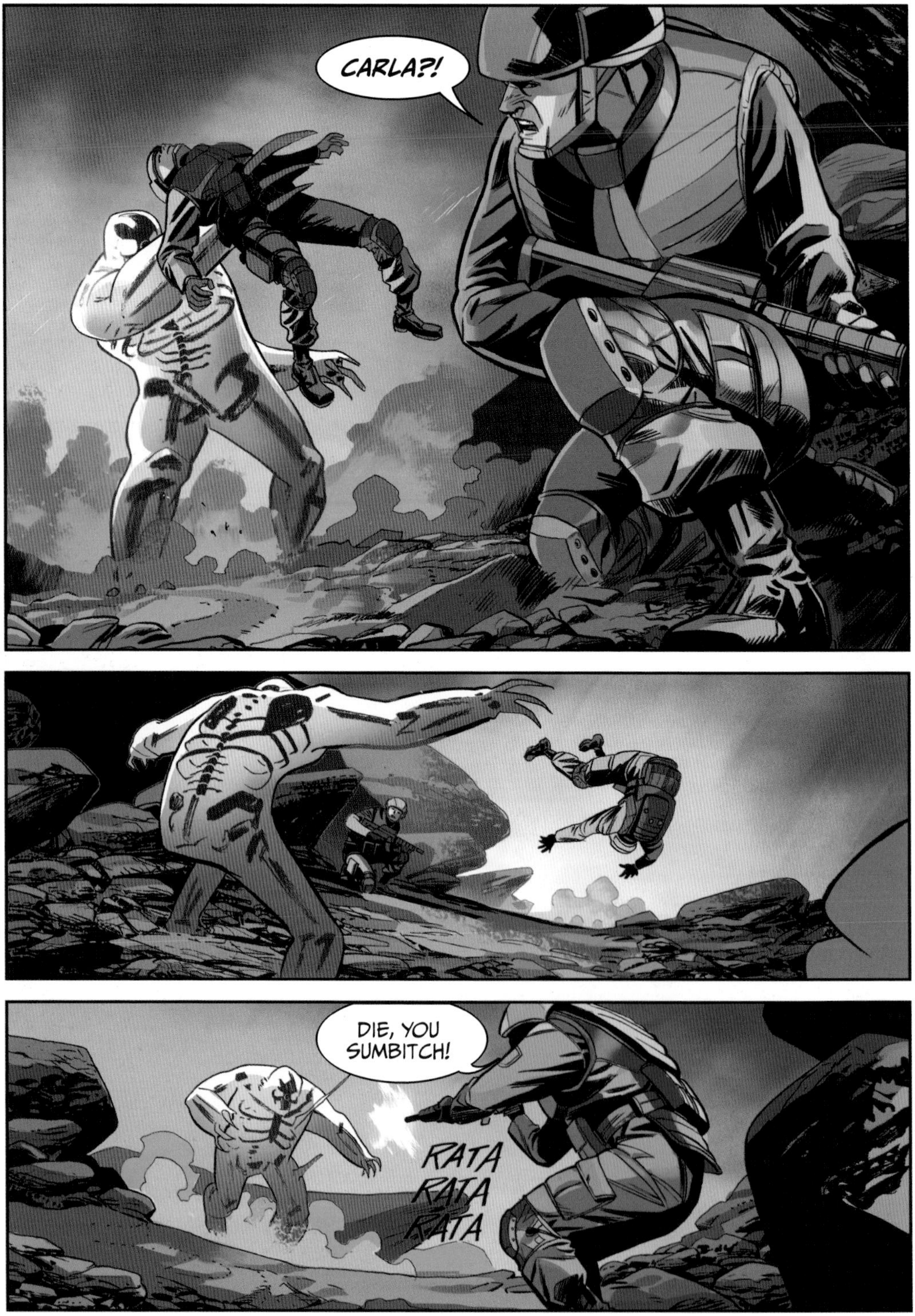
CARLA?!
DIE, YOU SUMBITCH!
RATA
RATA
RATA

CRYSTAL AND ASHES...

...I GOTTA WARN THE OTHERS!

!

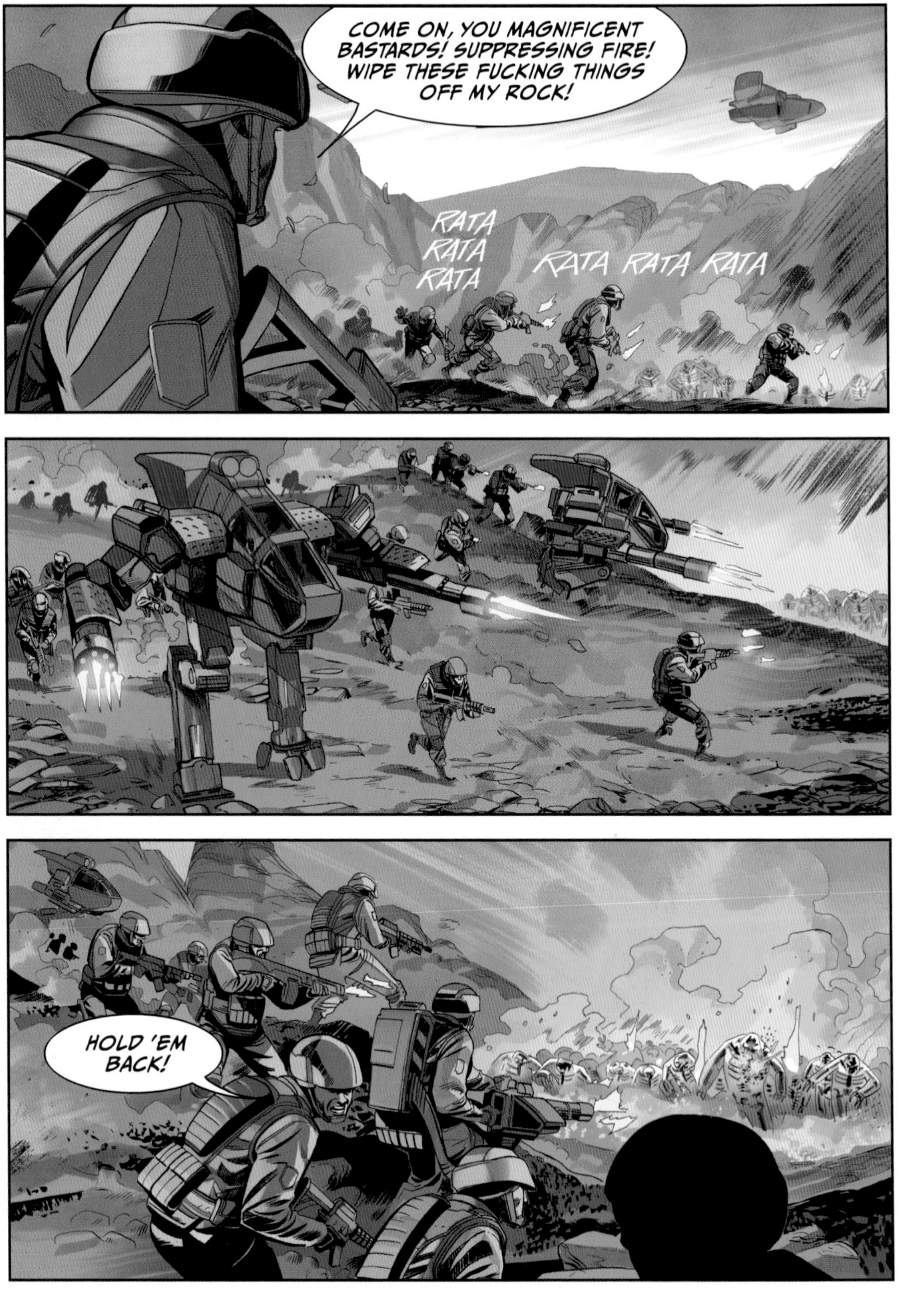
COME ON, YOU MAGNIFICENT BASTARDS! SUPPRESSING FIRE! WIPE THESE FUCKING THINGS OFF MY ROCK!
RATA RATA RATA
RATA RATA RATA
HOLD 'EM BACK!

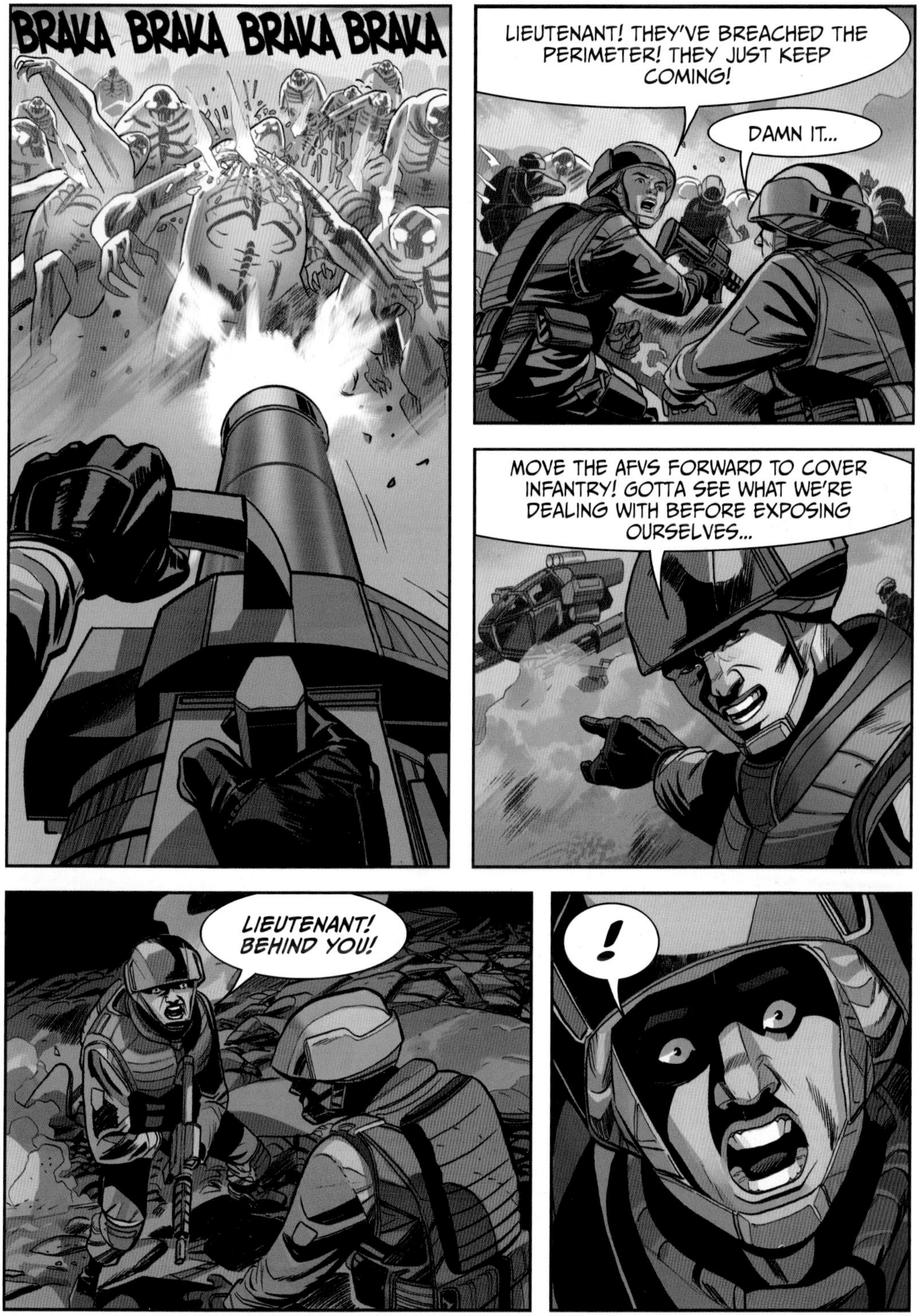
BRAKA BRAKA BRAKA BRAKA
LIEUTENANT! THEY'VE BREACHED THE PERIMETER! THEY JUST KEEP COMING!
DAMN IT...
MOVE THE AFVS FORWARD TO COVER INFANTRY! GOTTA SEE WHAT WE'RE DEALING WITH BEFORE EXPOSING OURSELVES...
LIEUTENANT! BEHIND YOU!
!

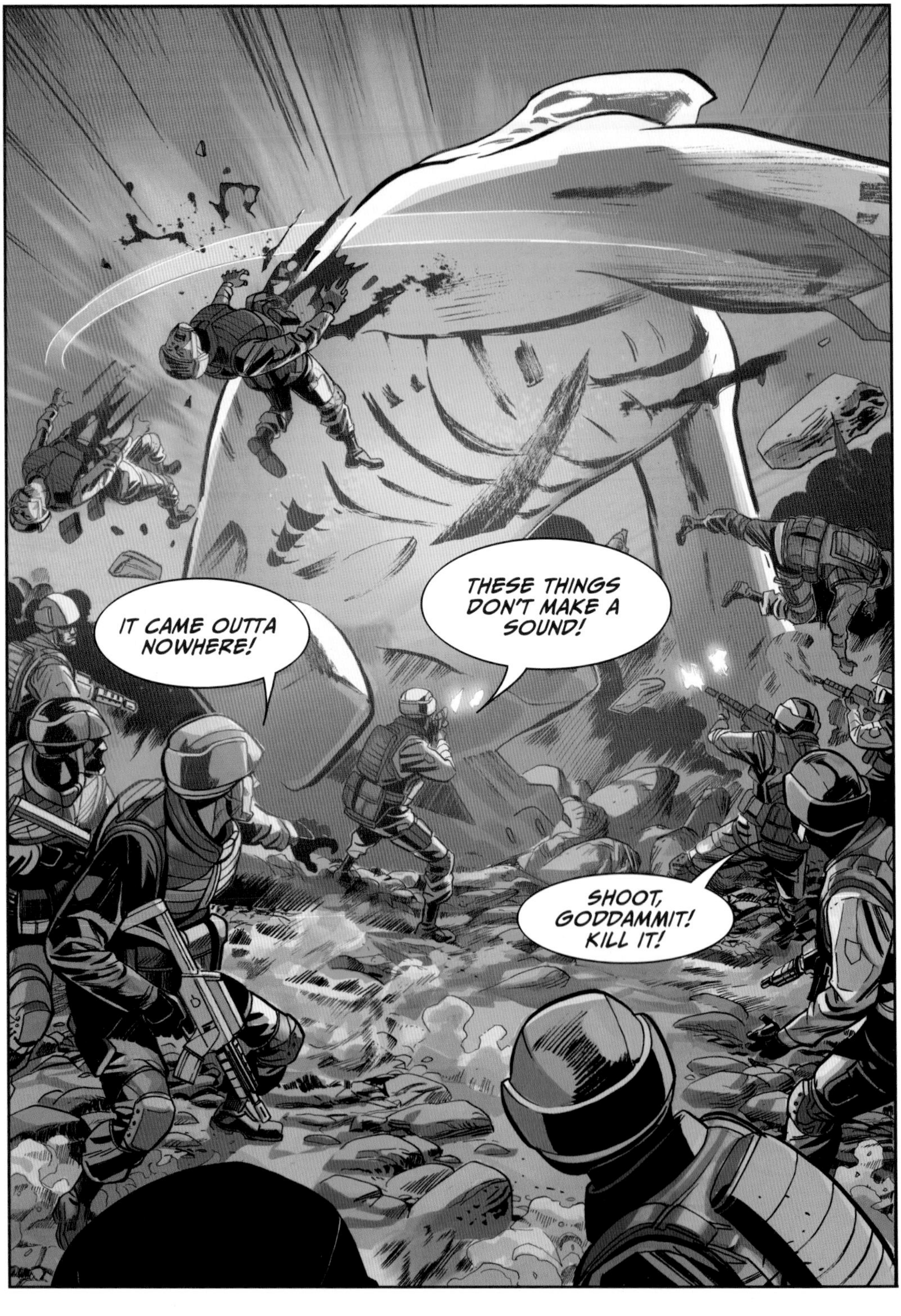
IT CAME OUTTA NOWHERE!
THESE THINGS DON'T MAKE A SOUND!
SHOOT, GODDAMMIT! KILL IT!

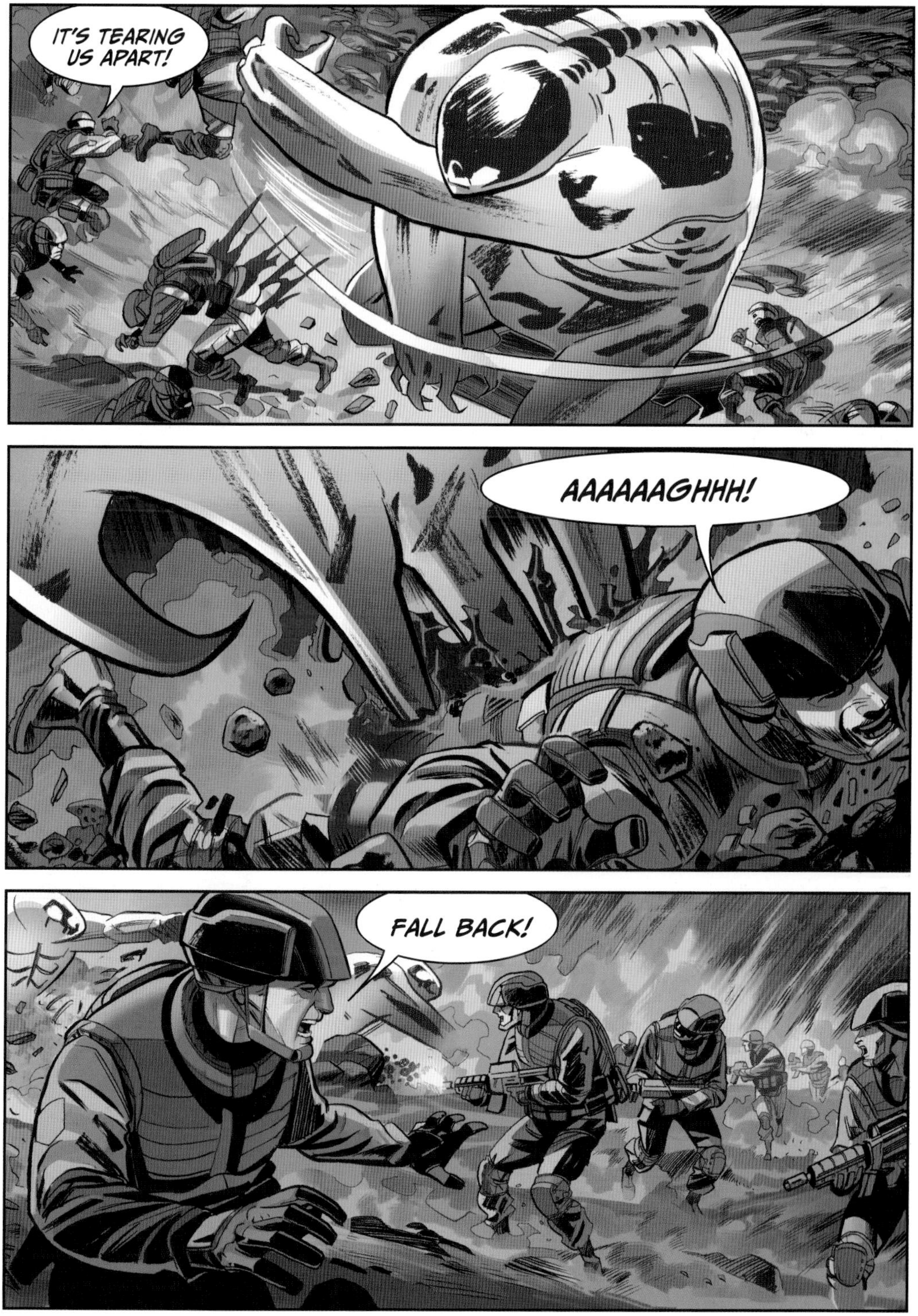
IT'S TEARING US APART!
AAAAAAGHHH!
FALL BACK!

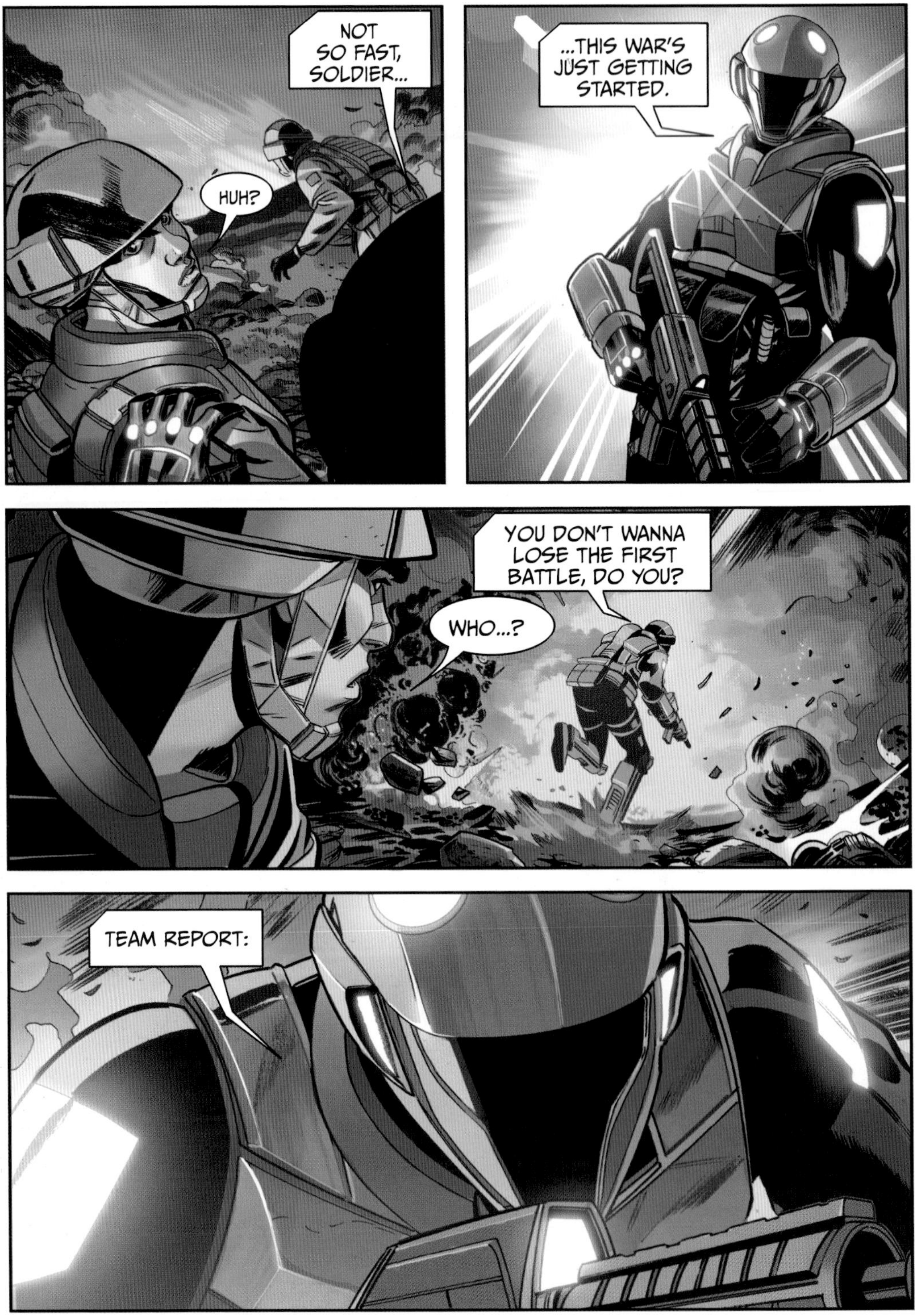
NOT SO FAST, SOLDIER...
HUH?
...THIS WAR'S JUST GETTING STARTED.
YOU DON'T WANNA LOSE THE FIRST BATTLE, DO YOU?
WHO...?
TEAM REPORT:

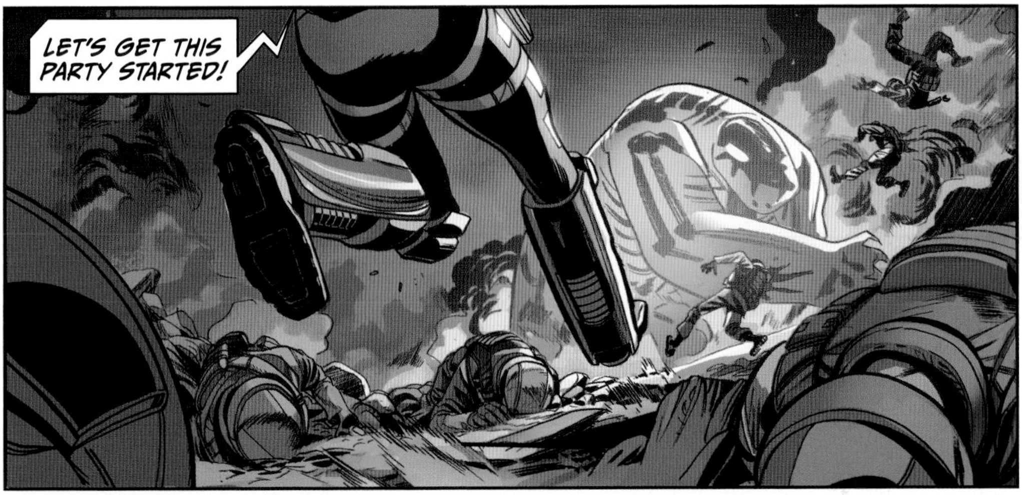
LET'S GET THIS PARTY STARTED!

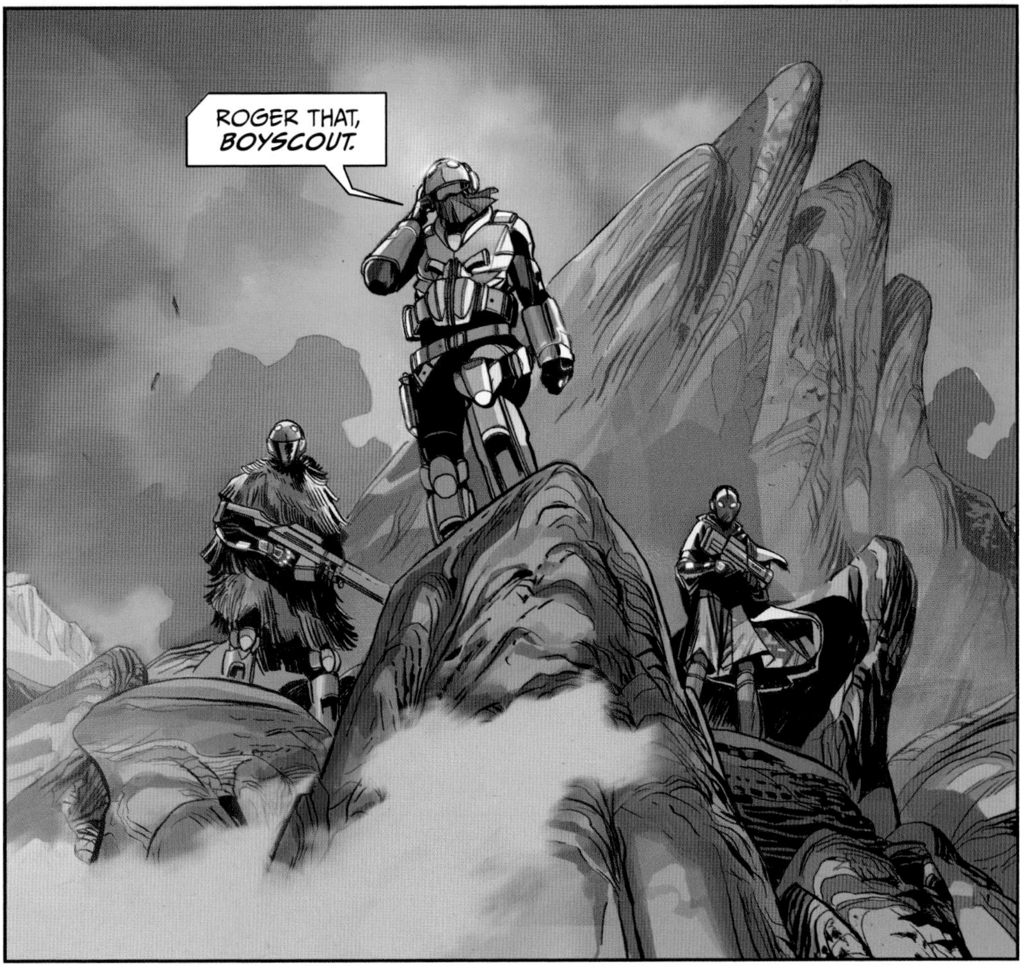
ROGER THAT, *BOYSCOUT.*

THE MOMENT OF TRUTH...
DO YOU REMEMBER RULE
NUMBER ONE?

WE DON'T
MAKE ART...

WWWNNNNNNNNNNNNNNNNNZZZ

...WE MAKE
CADAVERS.

TATLAK

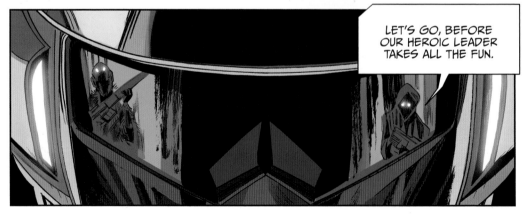

LET'S GO, BEFORE
OUR HEROIC LEADER
TAKES ALL THE FUN.

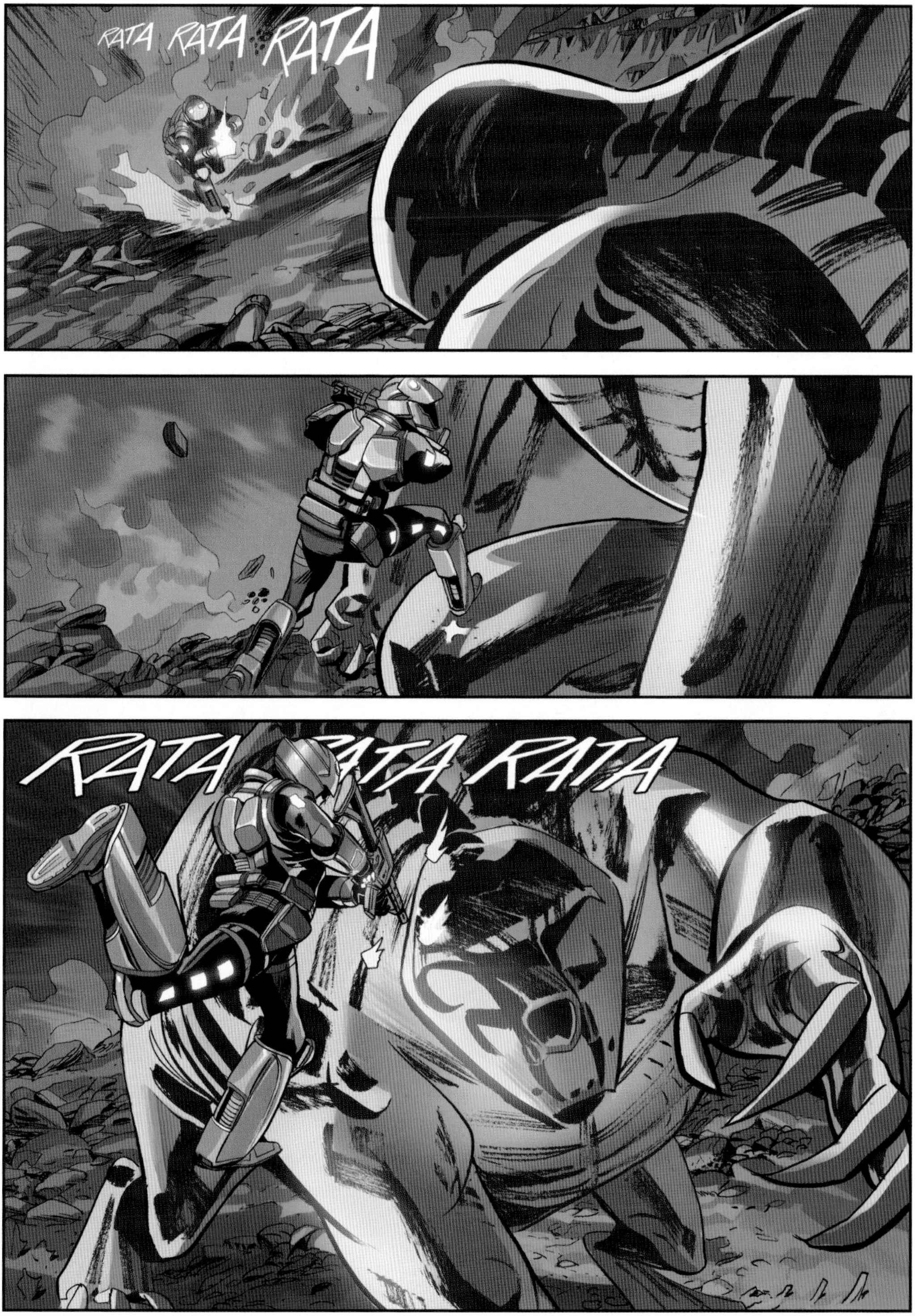
RATA RATA RATA
RATA ATA RATA

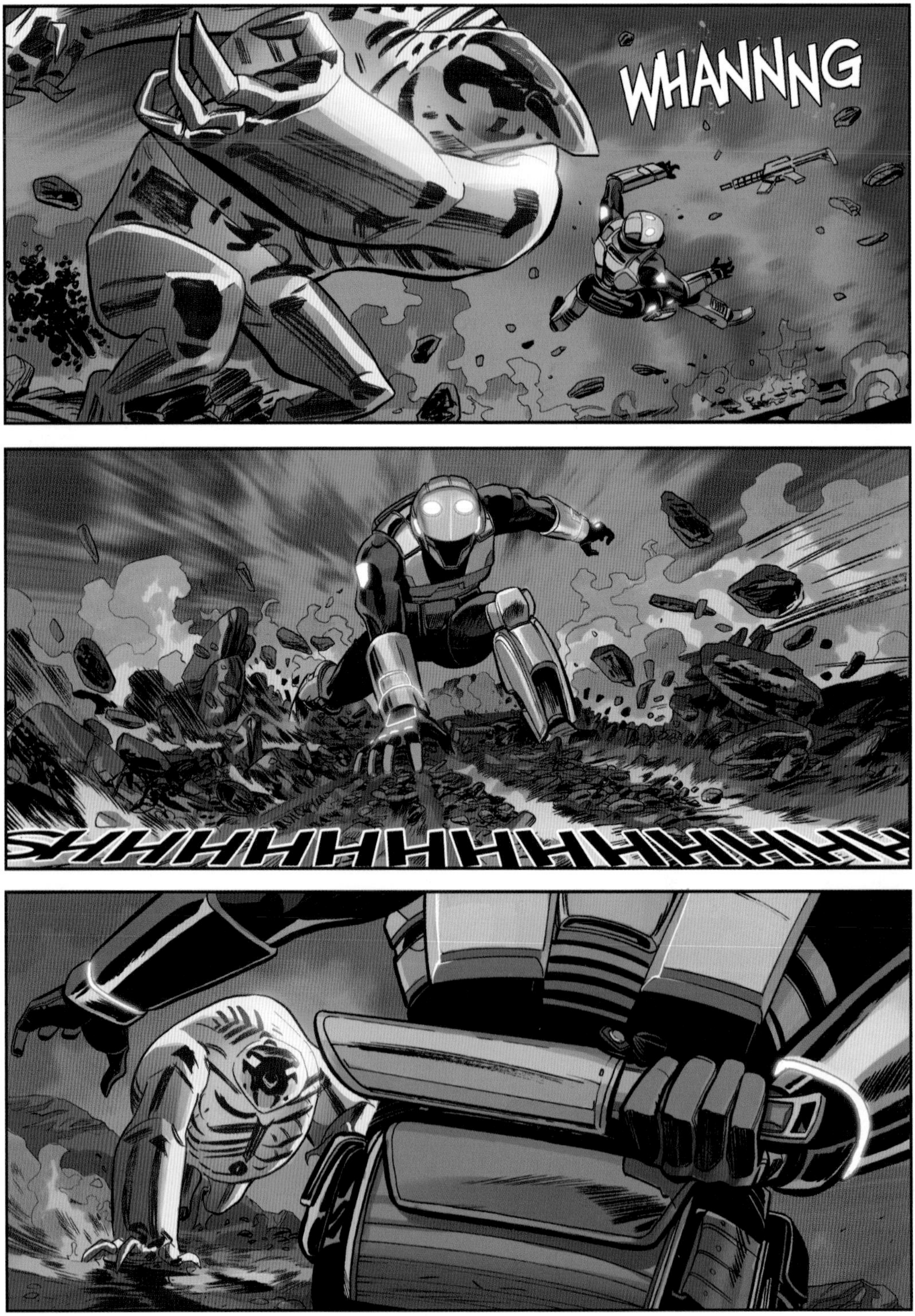
WHANNNG

WOOOOOSHHHHH
STUCK
STRRRAAAAAAAAAAAAPPPPPP

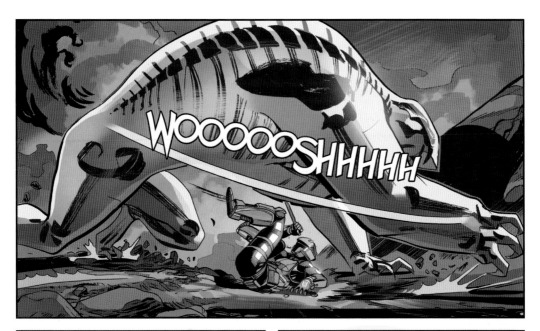

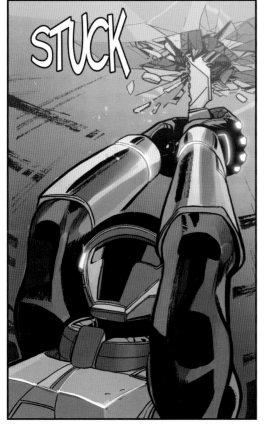

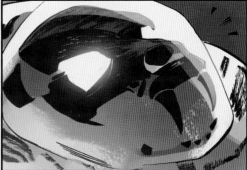

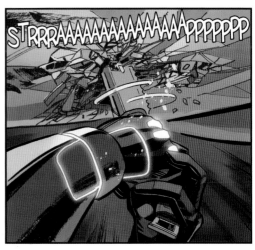

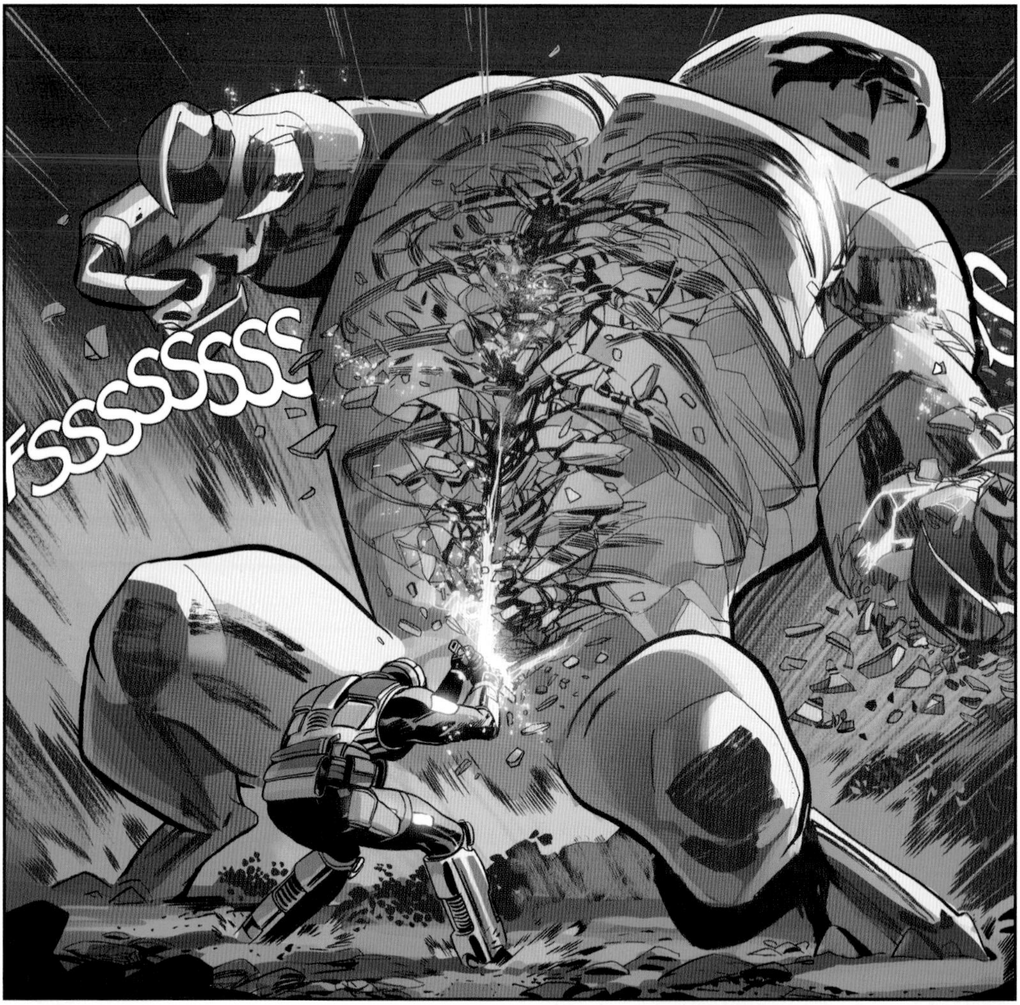
FSSSSSSSS

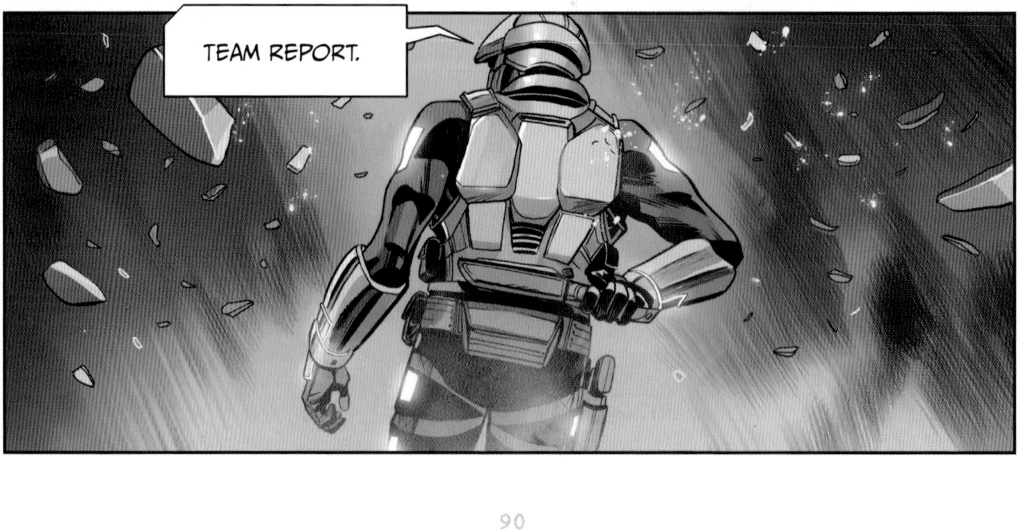
TEAM REPORT.

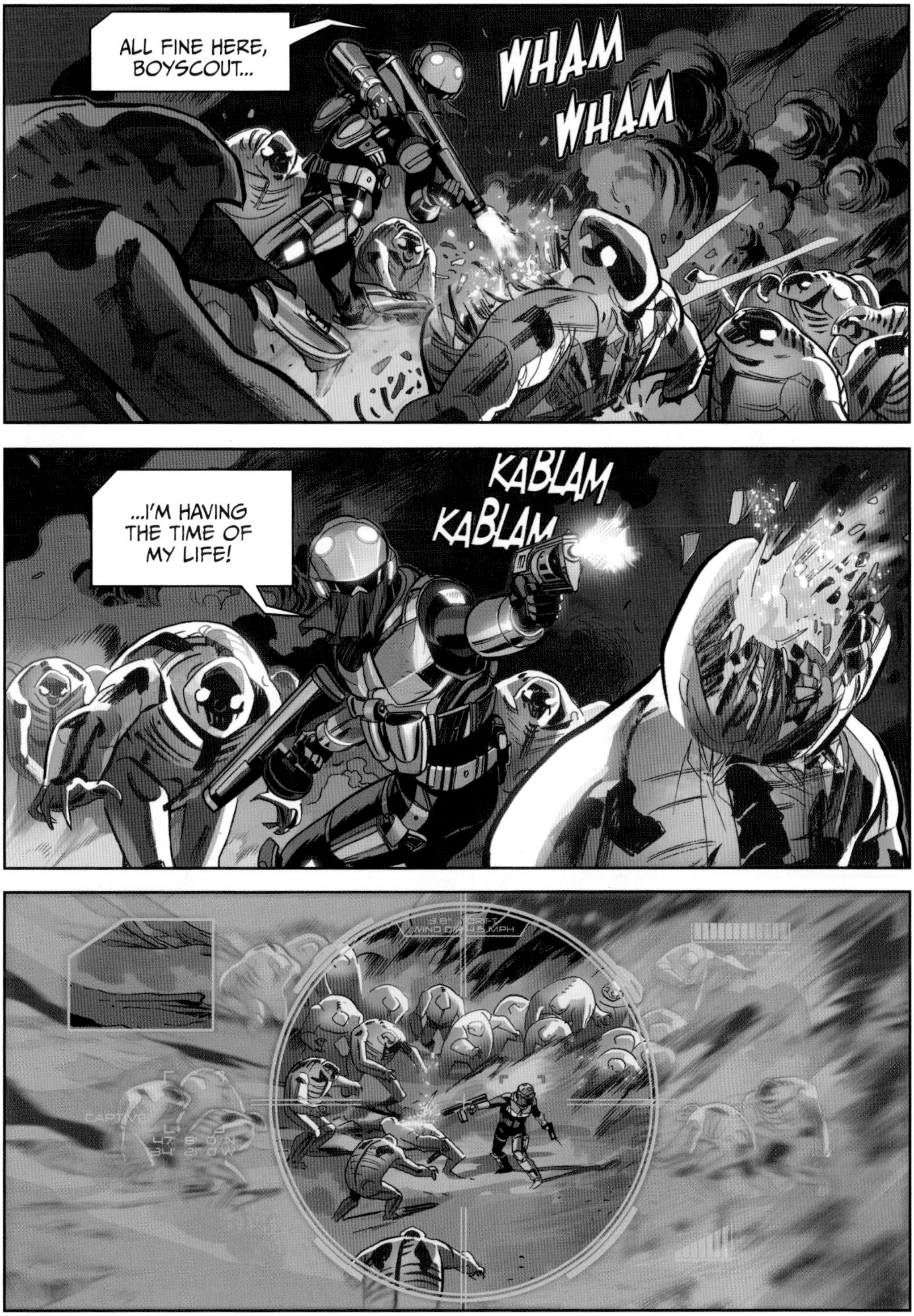
ALL FINE HERE, BOYSCOUT...
WHAM
WHAM
...I'M HAVING THE TIME OF MY LIFE!
KABLAM
KABLAM

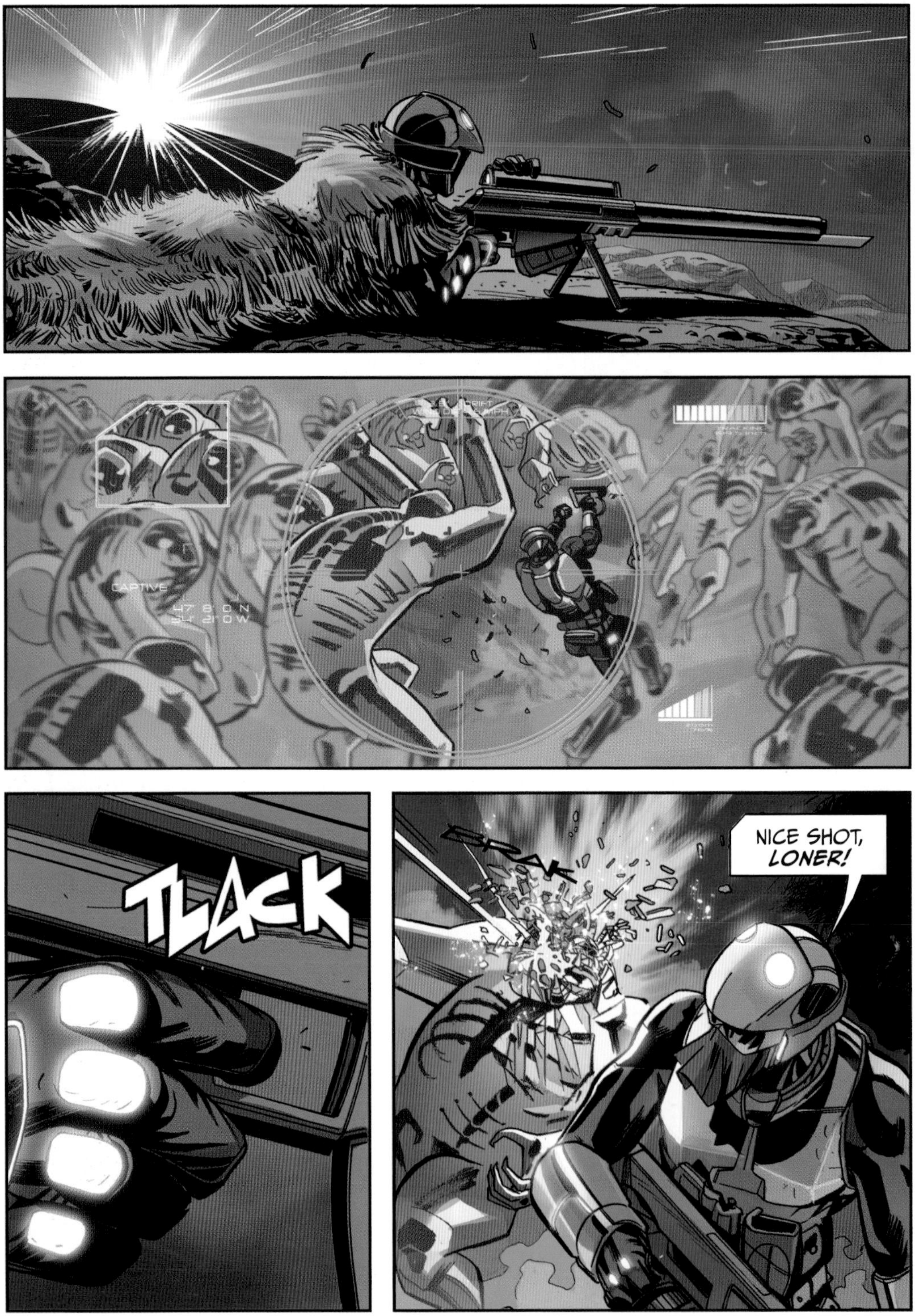
CAPTIVE
47° 8' 0 N
34° 21' 0 W
TLACK
NICE SHOT, LONER!

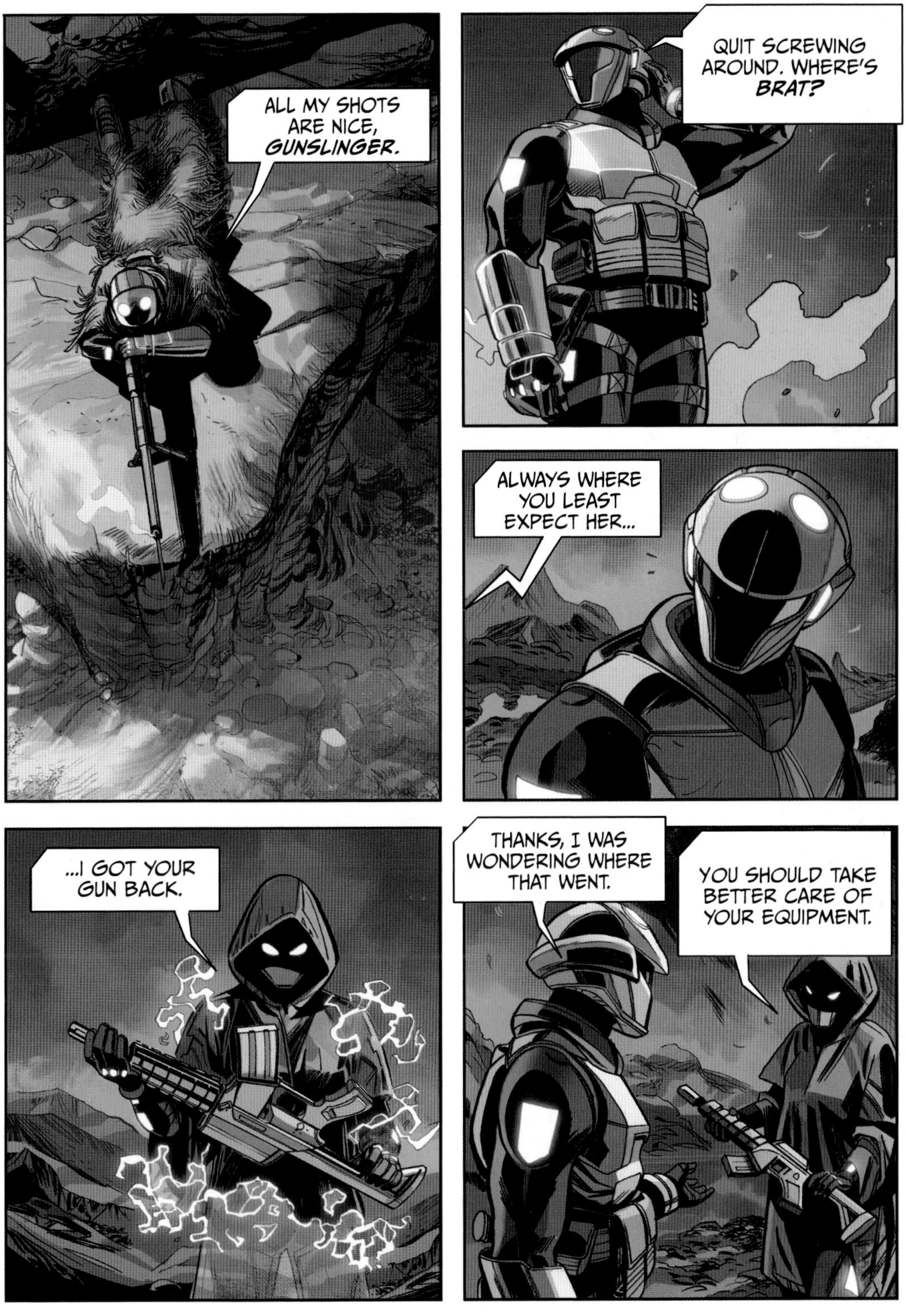
ALL MY SHOTS ARE NICE, GUNSLINGER.
QUIT SCREWING AROUND. WHERE'S BRAT?
ALWAYS WHERE YOU LEAST EXPECT HER...
...I GOT YOUR GUN BACK.
THANKS, I WAS WONDERING WHERE THAT WENT.
YOU SHOULD TAKE BETTER CARE OF YOUR EQUIPMENT.

DON'T GET CHEEKY. GUNSLINGER'S HAVING A BAD INFLUENCE ON YOU!

JUST TRYING TO DO OUR BEST, SIR!

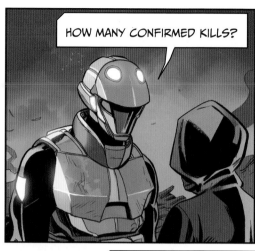

HOW MANY CONFIRMED KILLS?

TWELVE SO FAR. OUR SCOPES ALLOW US TO SEE THEM, BUT THEY CAN'T SEE ME WITH MY CLOAK ACTIVATED.

THE PROBLEM IS IT BURNS UP ENERGY LIKE CRAZY... I'M TAPPED OUT!

THEN I GUESS WE'RE GOING OLD SCHOOL.

NOW YOU'RE TALKIN', BOYSCOUT.

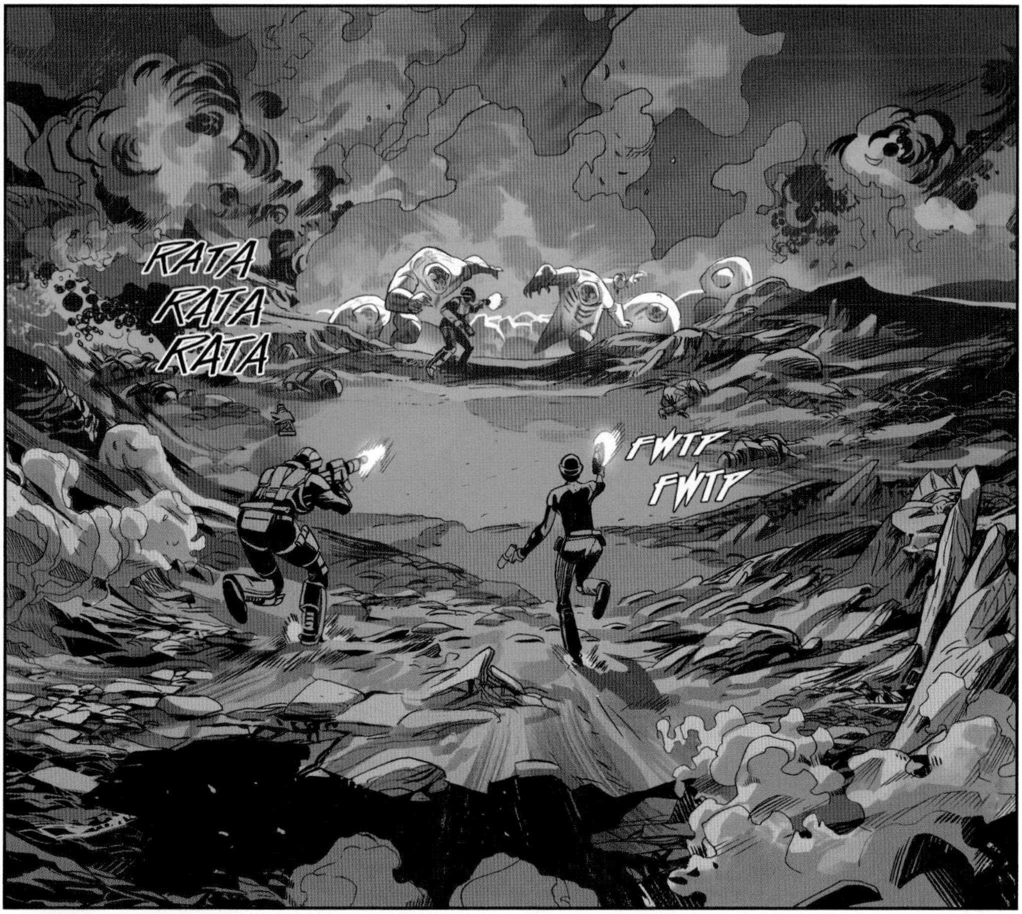
RATA
RATA
RATA
FWTP
FWTP

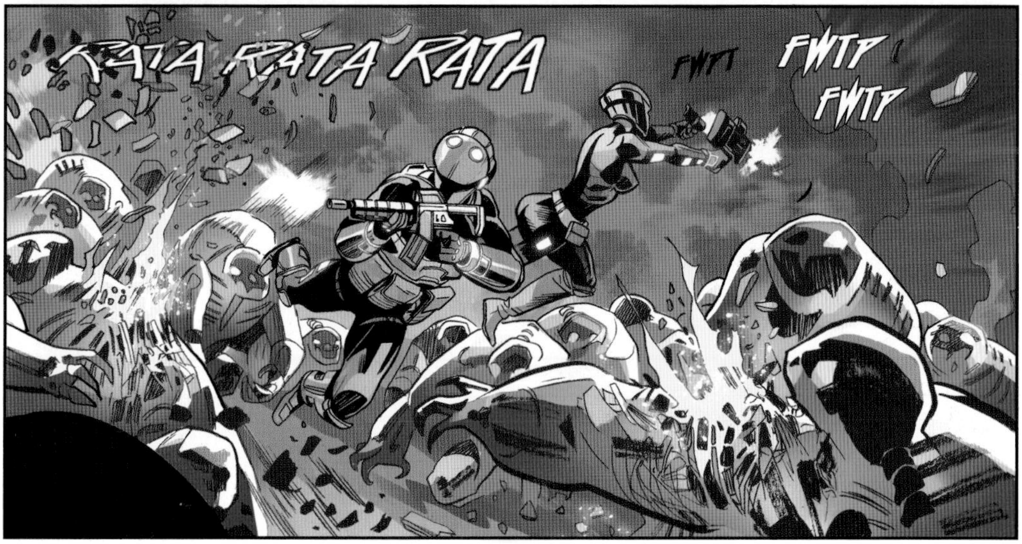
RATA RATA RATA
FWPT
FWTP
FWTP

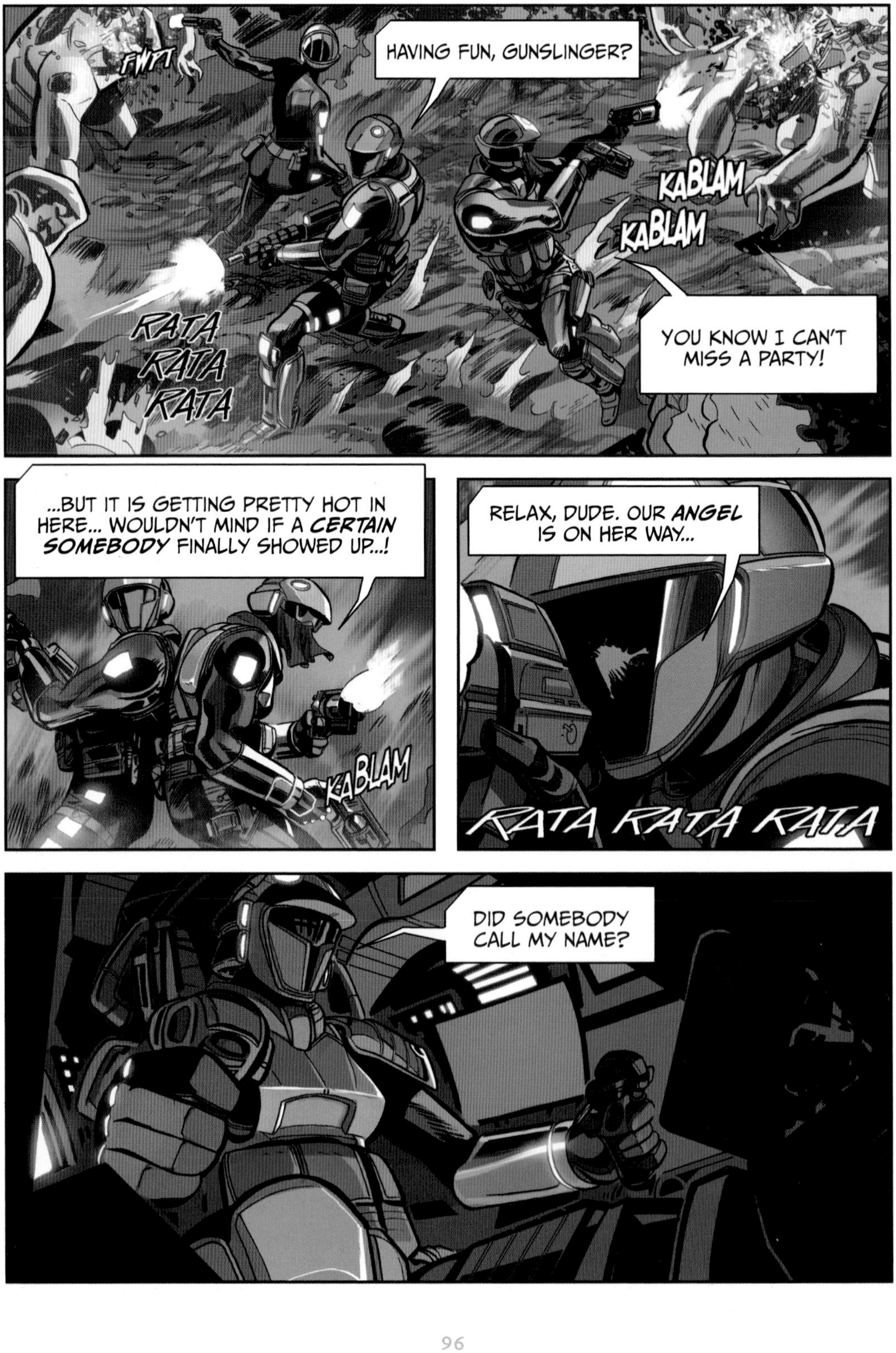
FWPT
HAVING FUN, GUNSLINGER?
KABLAM
KABLAM
RATA RATA RATA
YOU KNOW I CAN'T MISS A PARTY!
...BUT IT IS GETTING PRETTY HOT IN HERE... WOULDN'T MIND IF A *CERTAIN SOMEBODY* FINALLY SHOWED UP...!
KABLAM
RELAX, DUDE. OUR *ANGEL* IS ON HER WAY...
RATA RATA RATA
DID SOMEBODY CALL MY NAME?

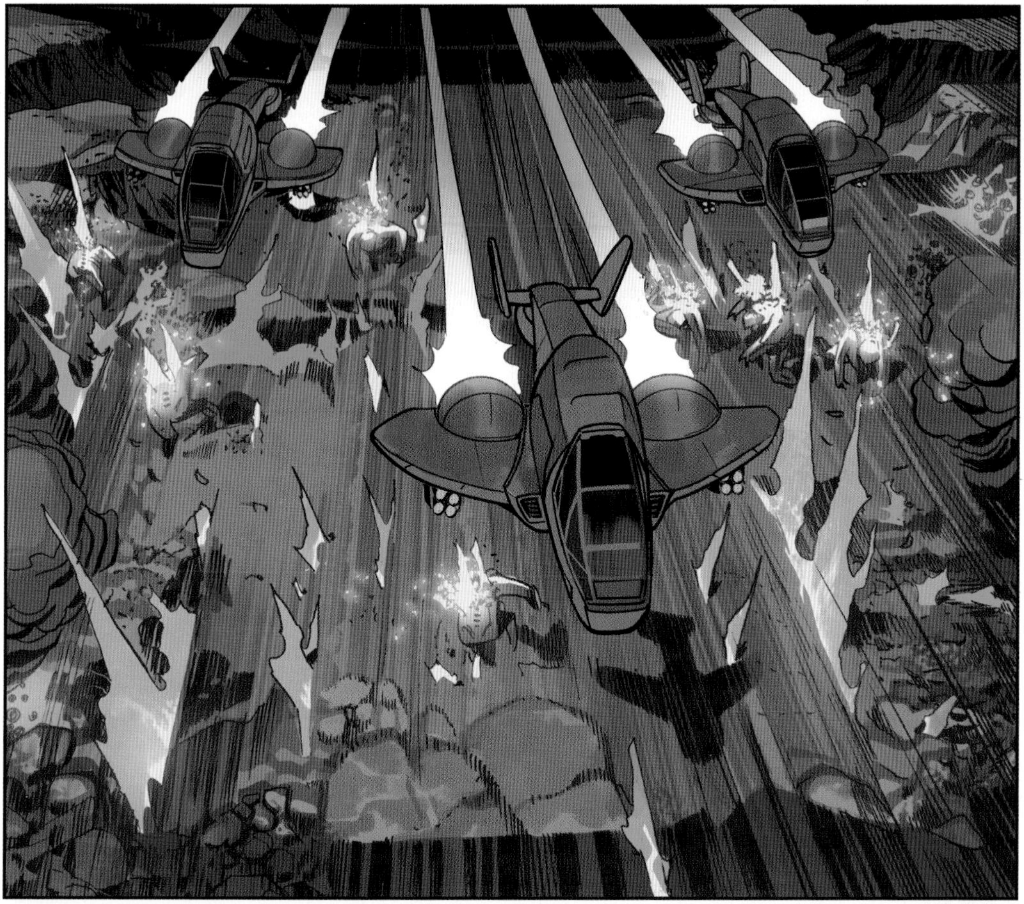

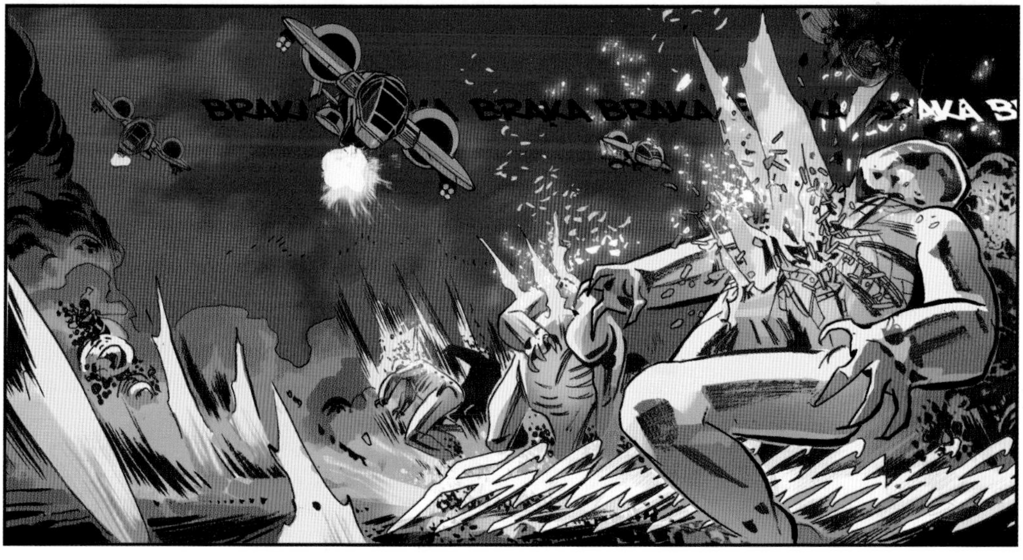
BRAKA BRAKA

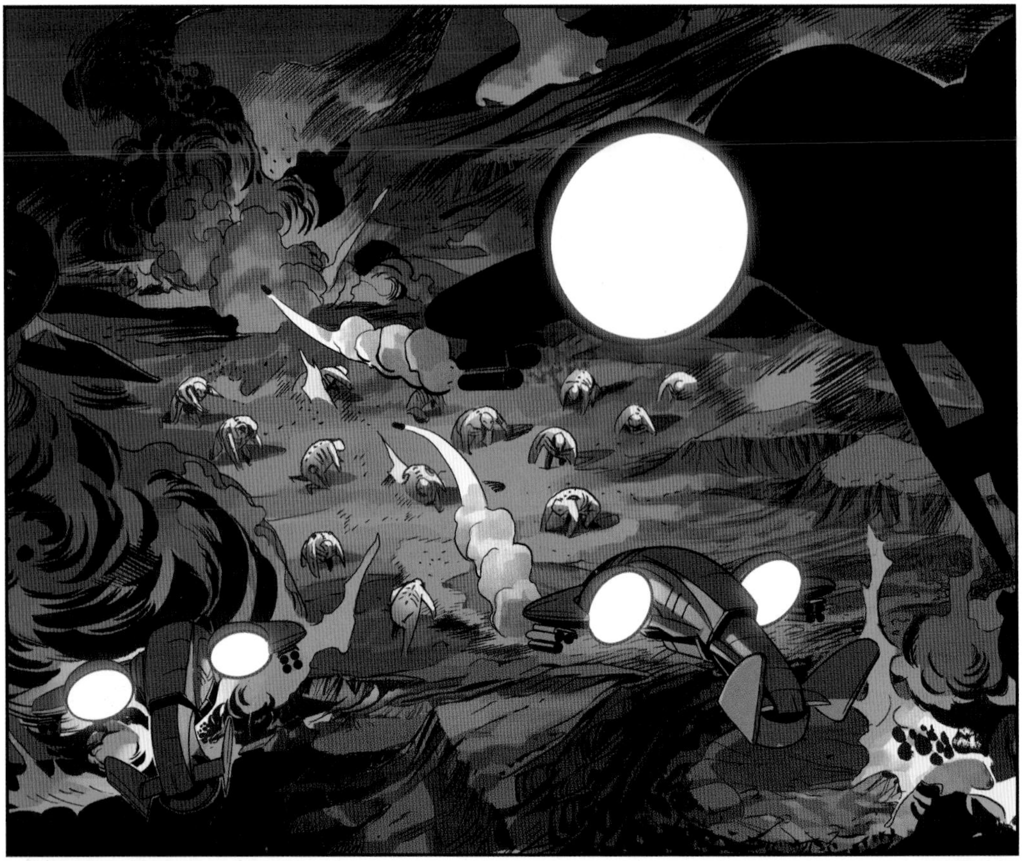

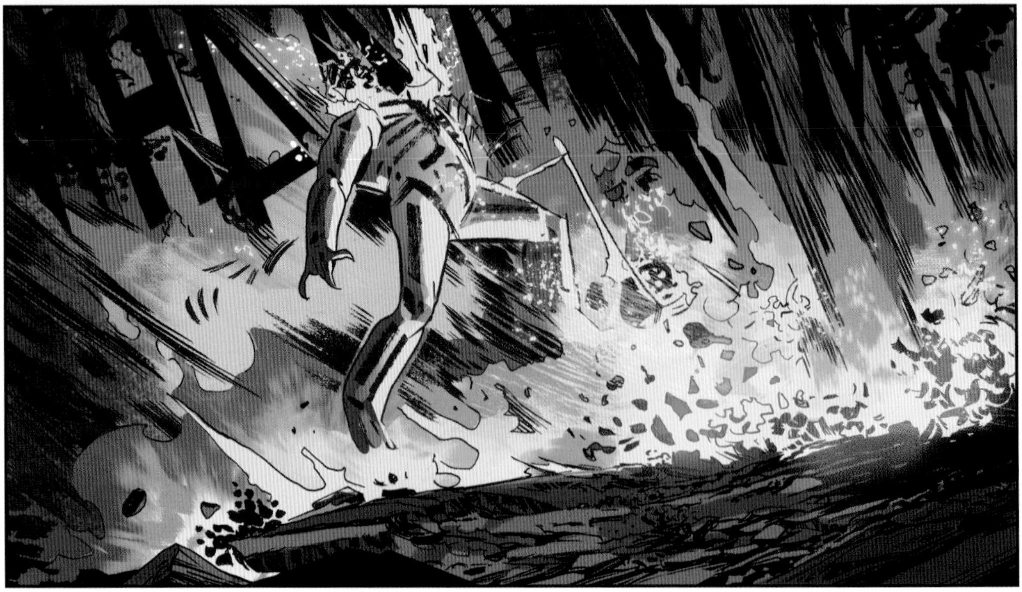

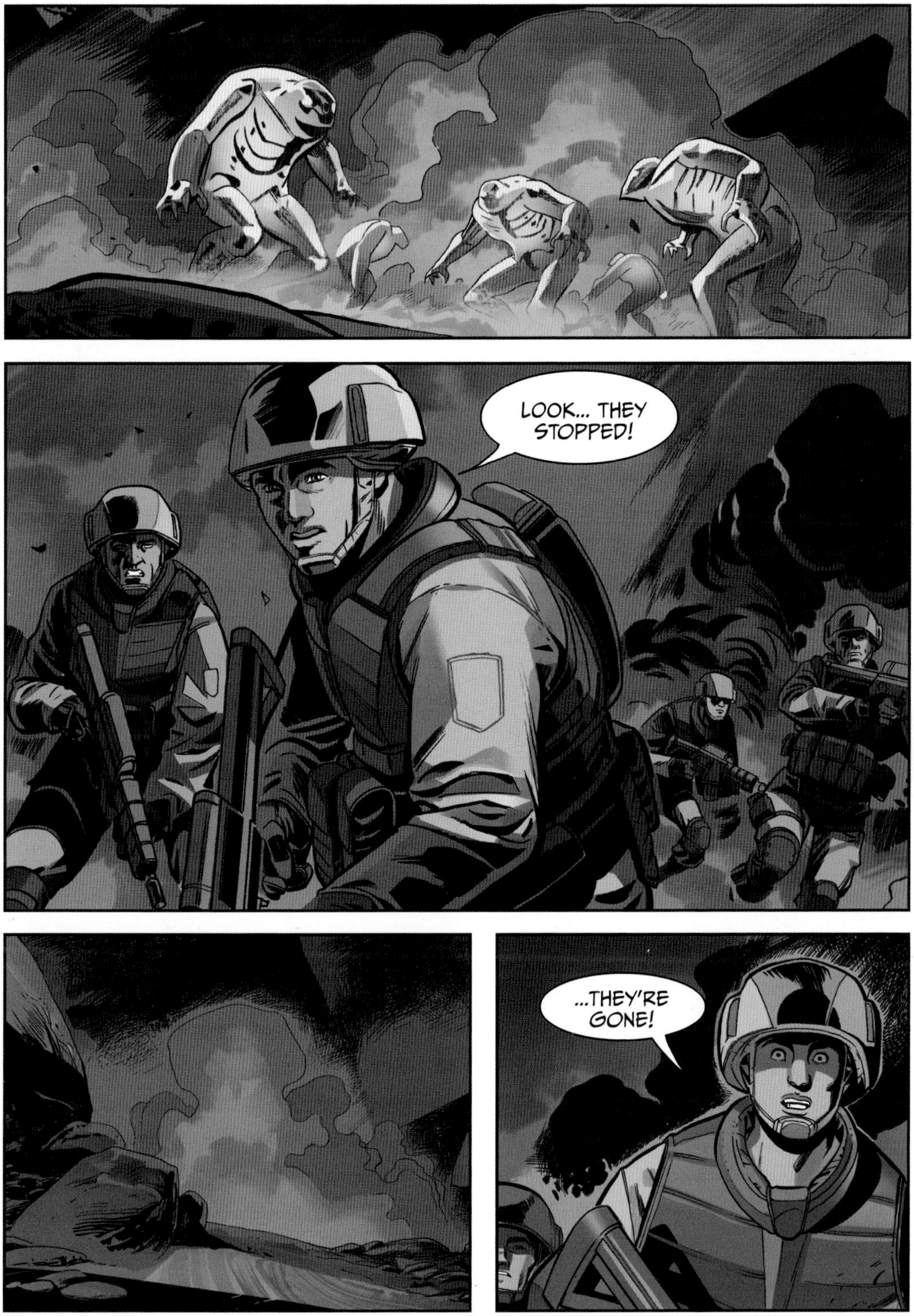
LOOK... THEY STOPPED!
...THEY'RE GONE!

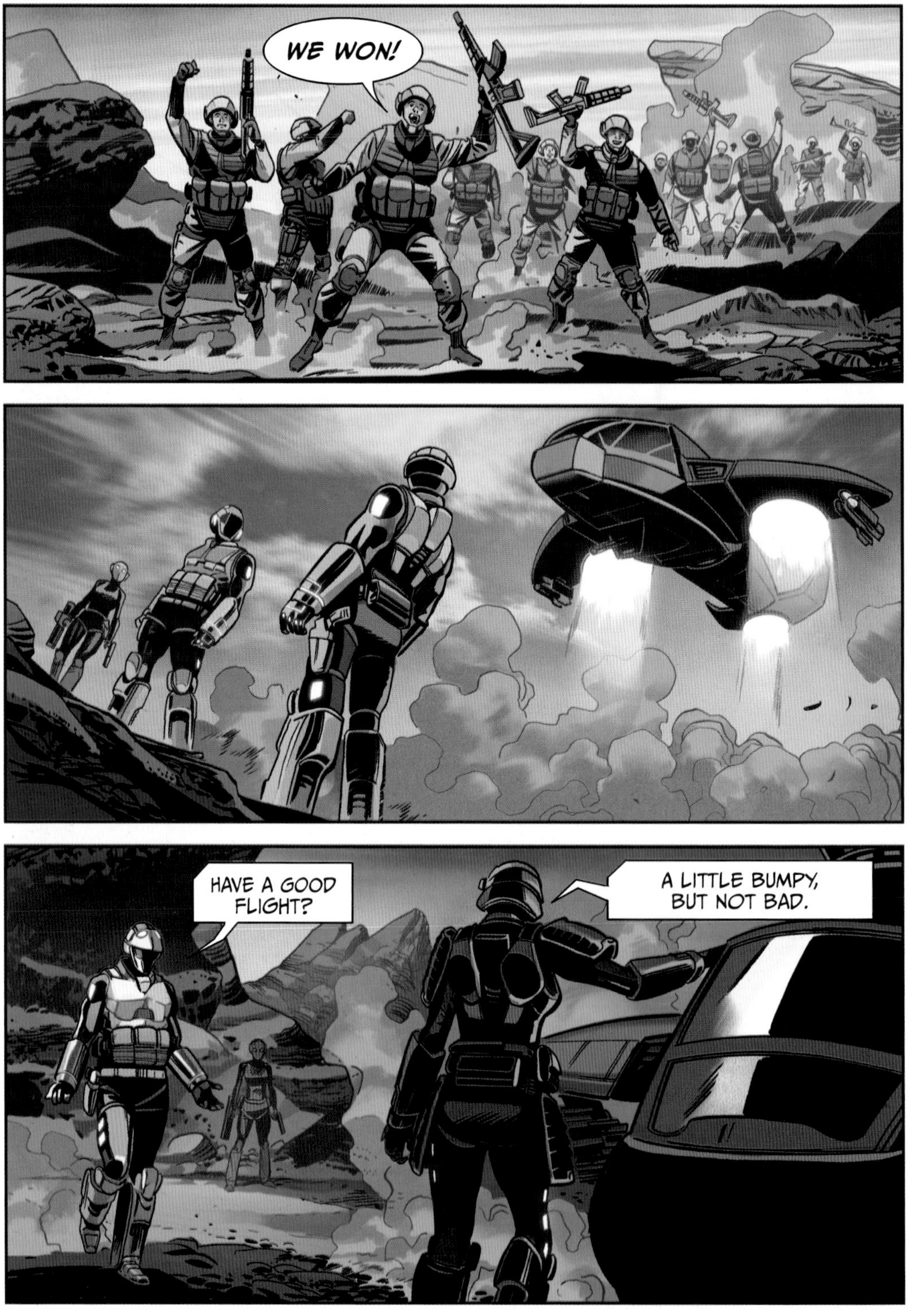
WE WON!
HAVE A GOOD FLIGHT?
A LITTLE BUMPY, BUT NOT BAD.

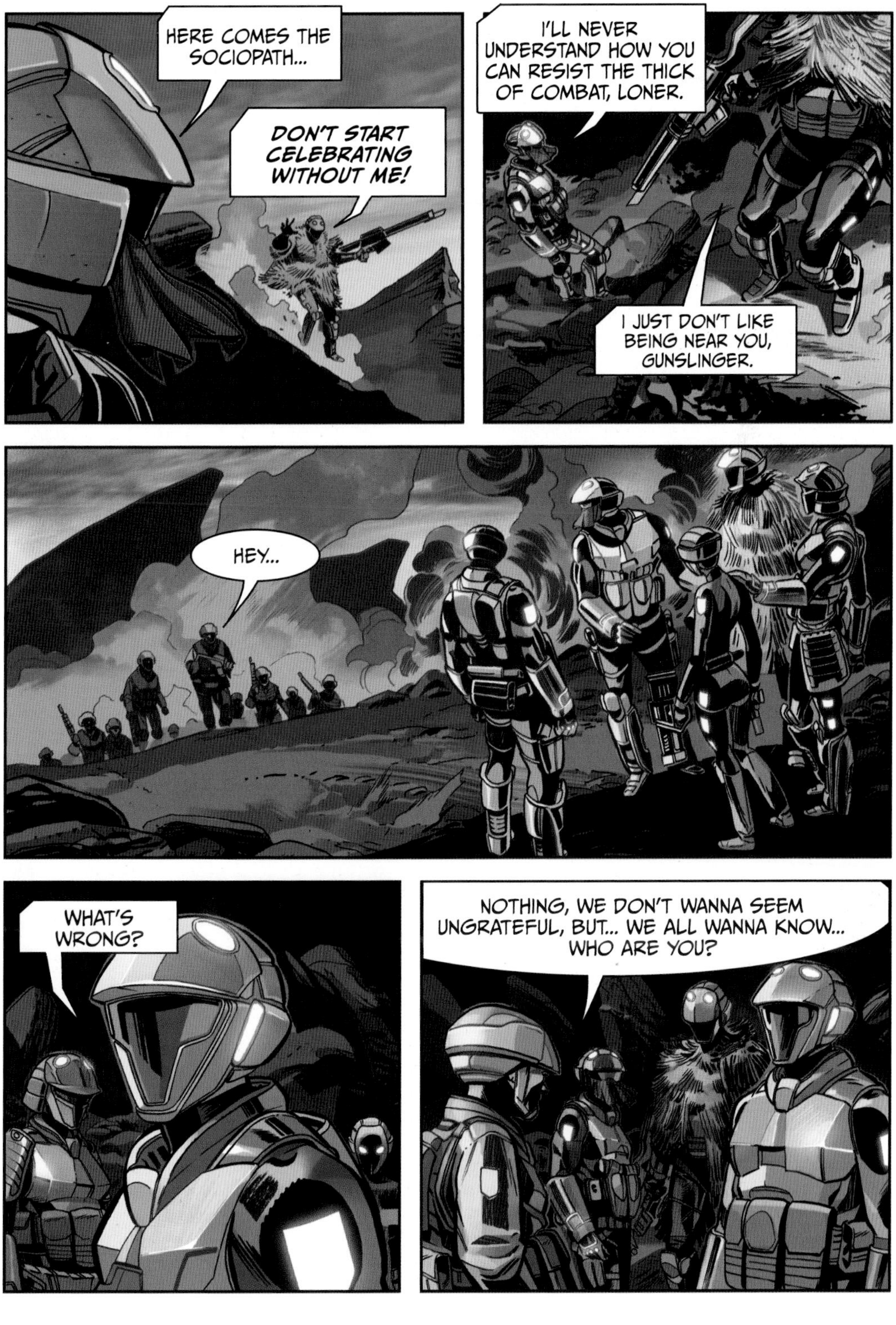
HERE COMES THE SOCIOPATH...
DON'T START CELEBRATING WITHOUT ME!
I'LL NEVER UNDERSTAND HOW YOU CAN RESIST THE THICK OF COMBAT, LONER.
I JUST DON'T LIKE BEING NEAR YOU, GUNSLINGER.
HEY...
WHAT'S WRONG?
NOTHING, WE DON'T WANNA SEEM UNGRATEFUL, BUT... WE ALL WANNA KNOW... WHO ARE YOU?

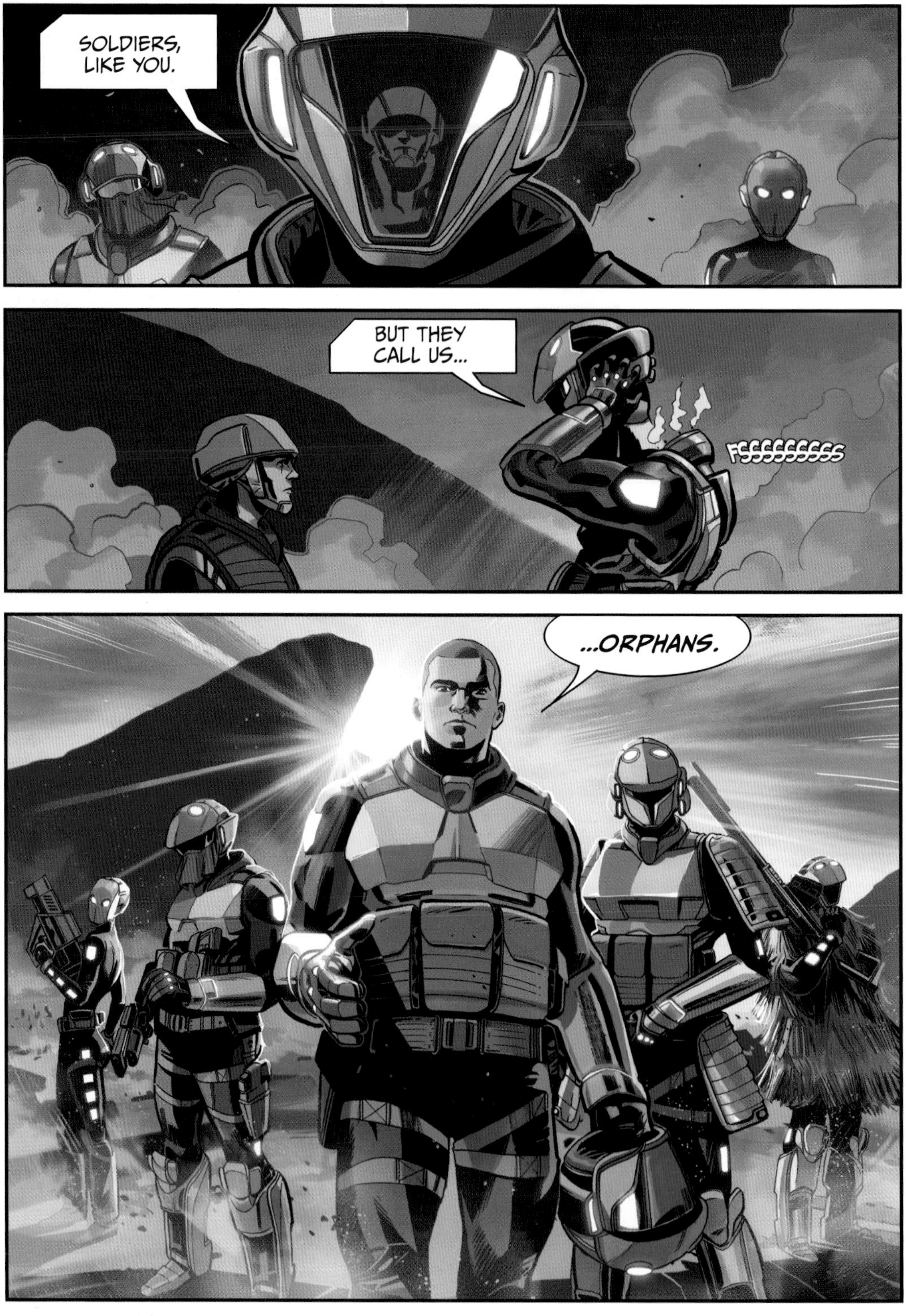
SOLDIERS, LIKE YOU.
BUT THEY CALL US...
FSSSSSSSSS
...ORPHANS.

EMILIANO MAMMUCARI

ARTIST

When and where were you born? Where do you live now?
I was born in Velletri, Castelli Romani, on April 21, 1975. I still live here, in the country.

What sort of artistic education did you have?
I attended a traditional high school, so I had no artistic education whatsoever. After graduating, I enrolled in a comics school and then immediately started working.

Tell us about your previous works, before *Orphans*.
I started with *Povero Pinocchio*, a graphic novel (though at the time they weren't called that) published by Montego. After that, I drew the first episode of the successful series *John Doe* for Eura Editoriale and then started working for Bonelli, specifically on *Napoleone*, *Jan Dix*, *Caravan*, and finally *Orphans*.

When did you start working on *Orphans*, and when did you finish drawing the first chapter?
I started the first issue in 2010 and finished it in 2012. Meanwhile, I was also in charge of developing the visual universe of *Orphans*.

What tools did you use?
Nib, brush, computer.

What was the most difficult scene and which one did you have to redraw more times?
Emotionally speaking, Hector's death. I wanted to convey as much pathos as possible. Technically speaking, however, the scene where humans first land on the planet. It seemed endless!

If you could go back in time, what would you change about this chapter?
I'd extend the scene in the swamp and the flight from the bear — I feel a couple pages more would've helped. Unfortunately, this episode was so full of events that it was physically impossible to extend the scenes.

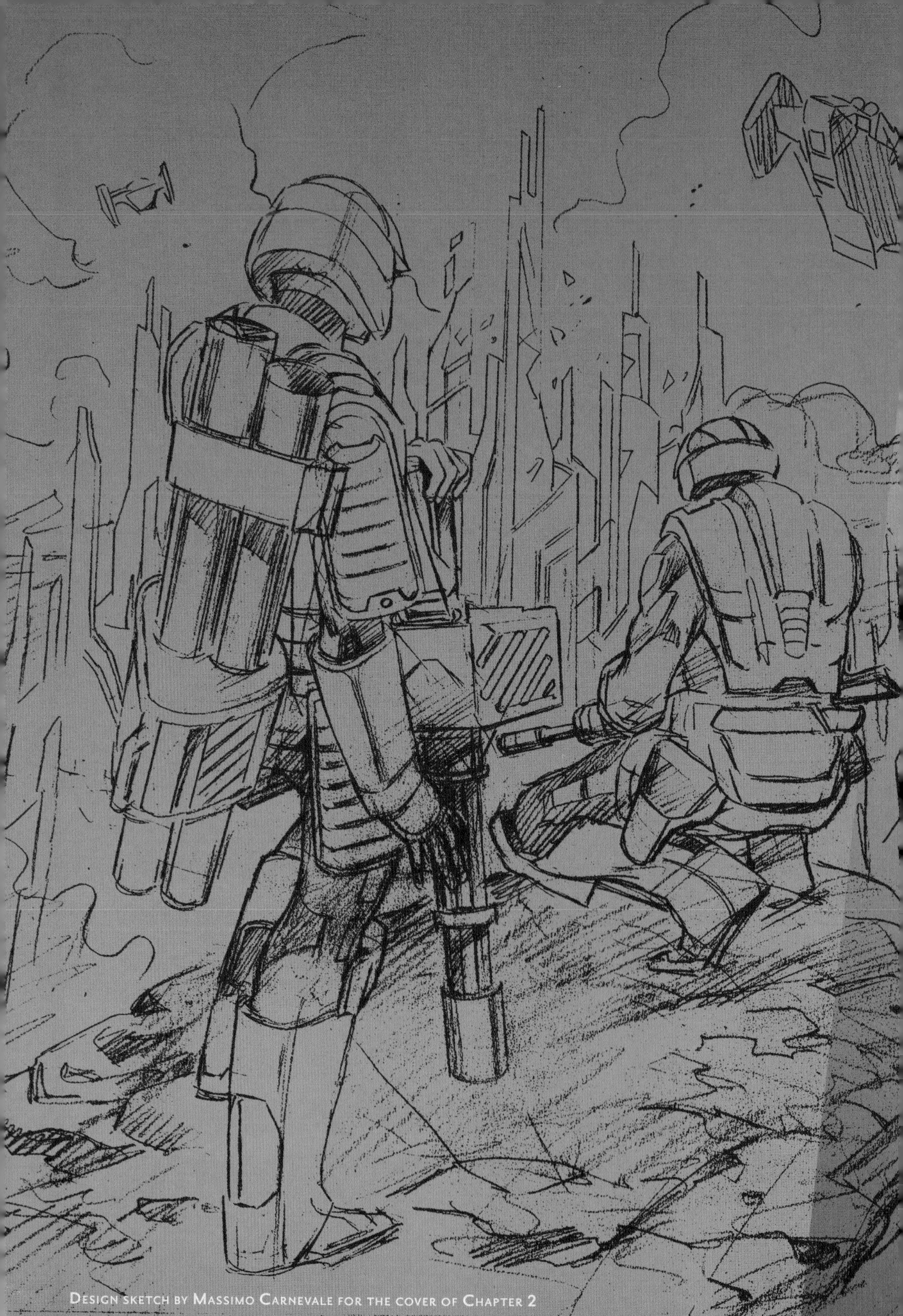

Design sketch by Massimo Carnevale for the cover of Chapter 2

FOR LOVE, NOT HATE

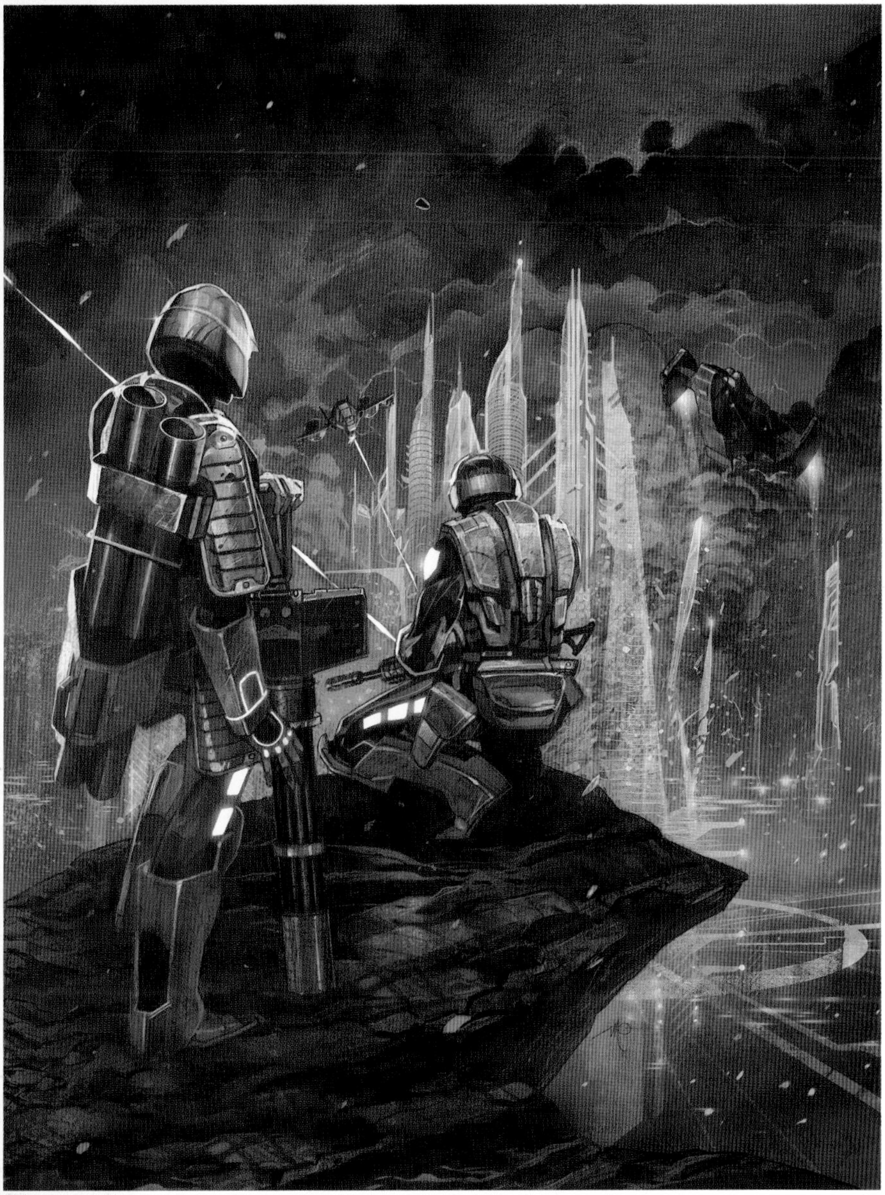

ORPHANS: CHAPTER 2

story: ROBERTO RECCHIONI
art: ALESSANDRO BIGNAMINI
colors: ANNALISA LEONI
cover: MASSIMO CARNEVALE

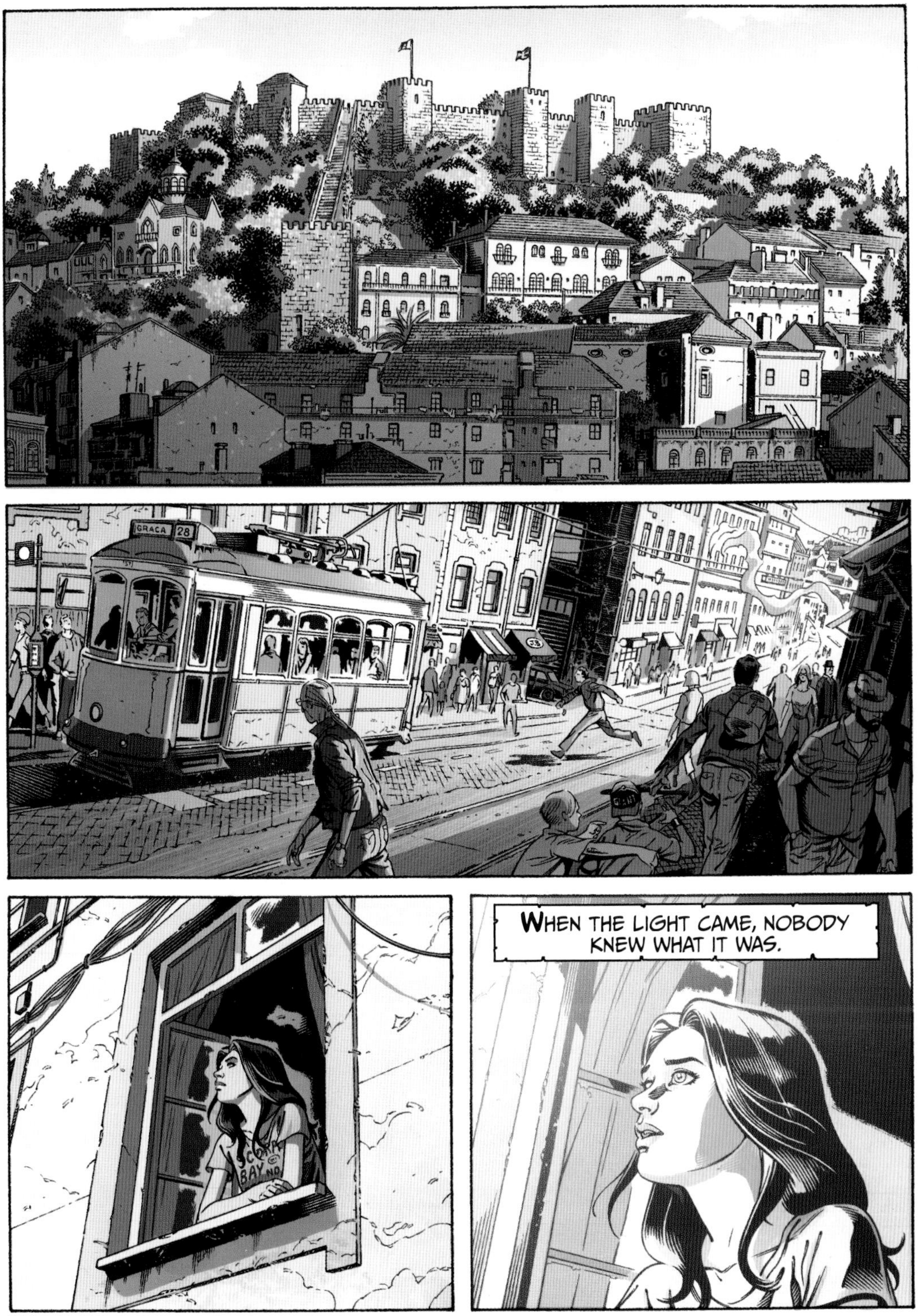
GRACA
28
WHEN THE LIGHT CAME, NOBODY KNEW WHAT IT WAS.

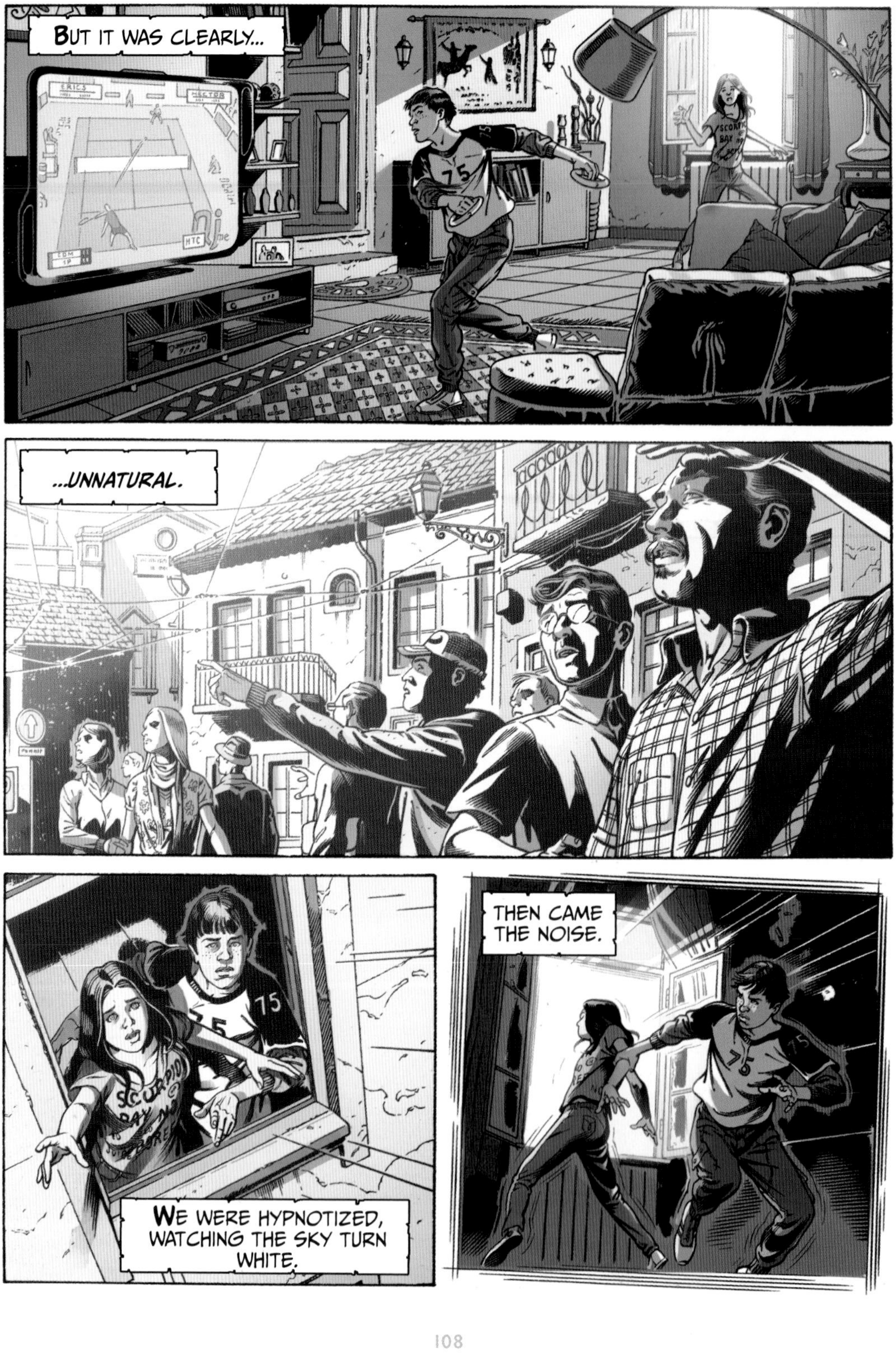
BUT IT WAS CLEARLY...
...UNNATURAL.
WE WERE HYPNOTIZED, WATCHING THE SKY TURN WHITE.
THEN CAME THE NOISE.

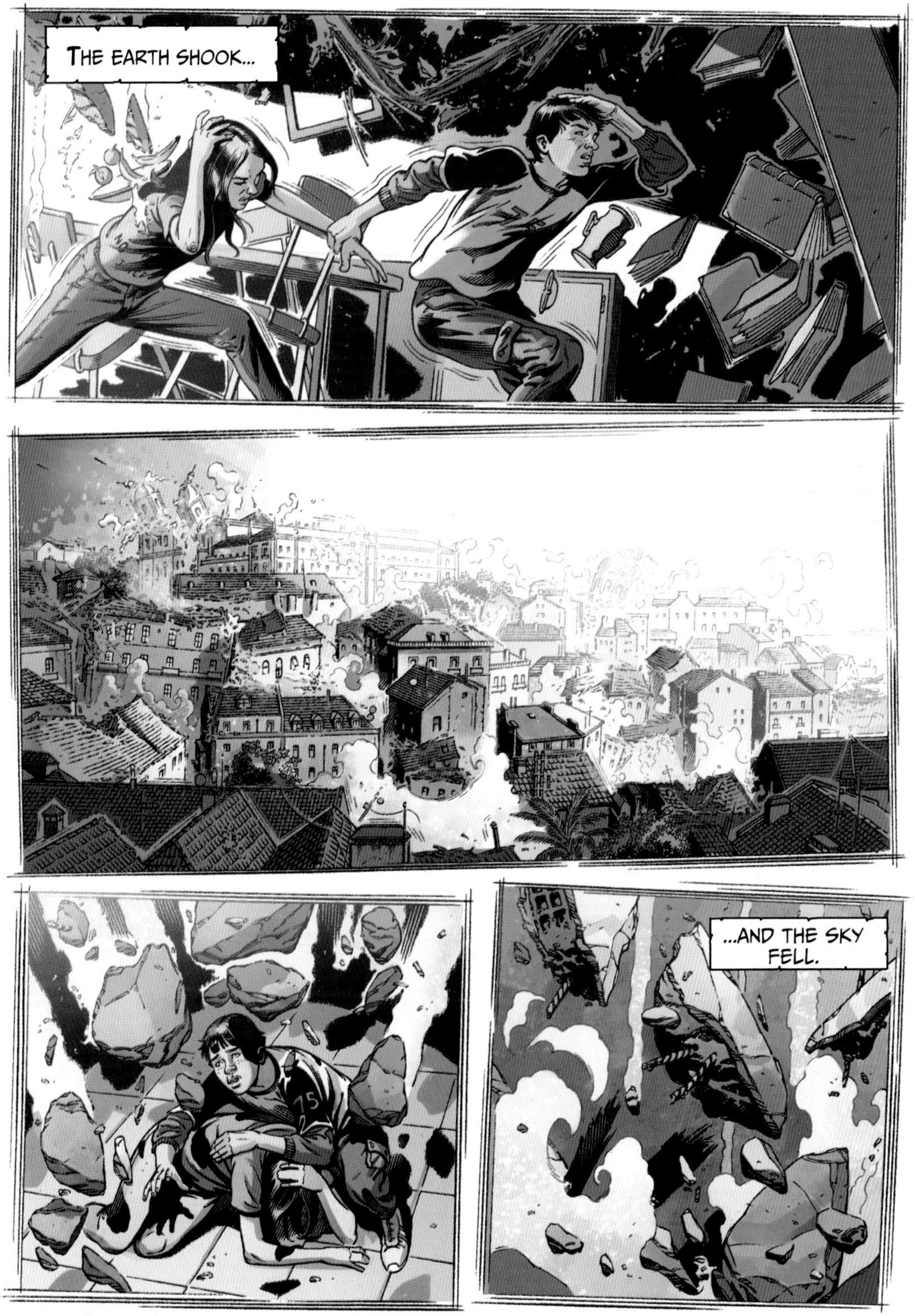
The earth shook...
...and the sky fell.

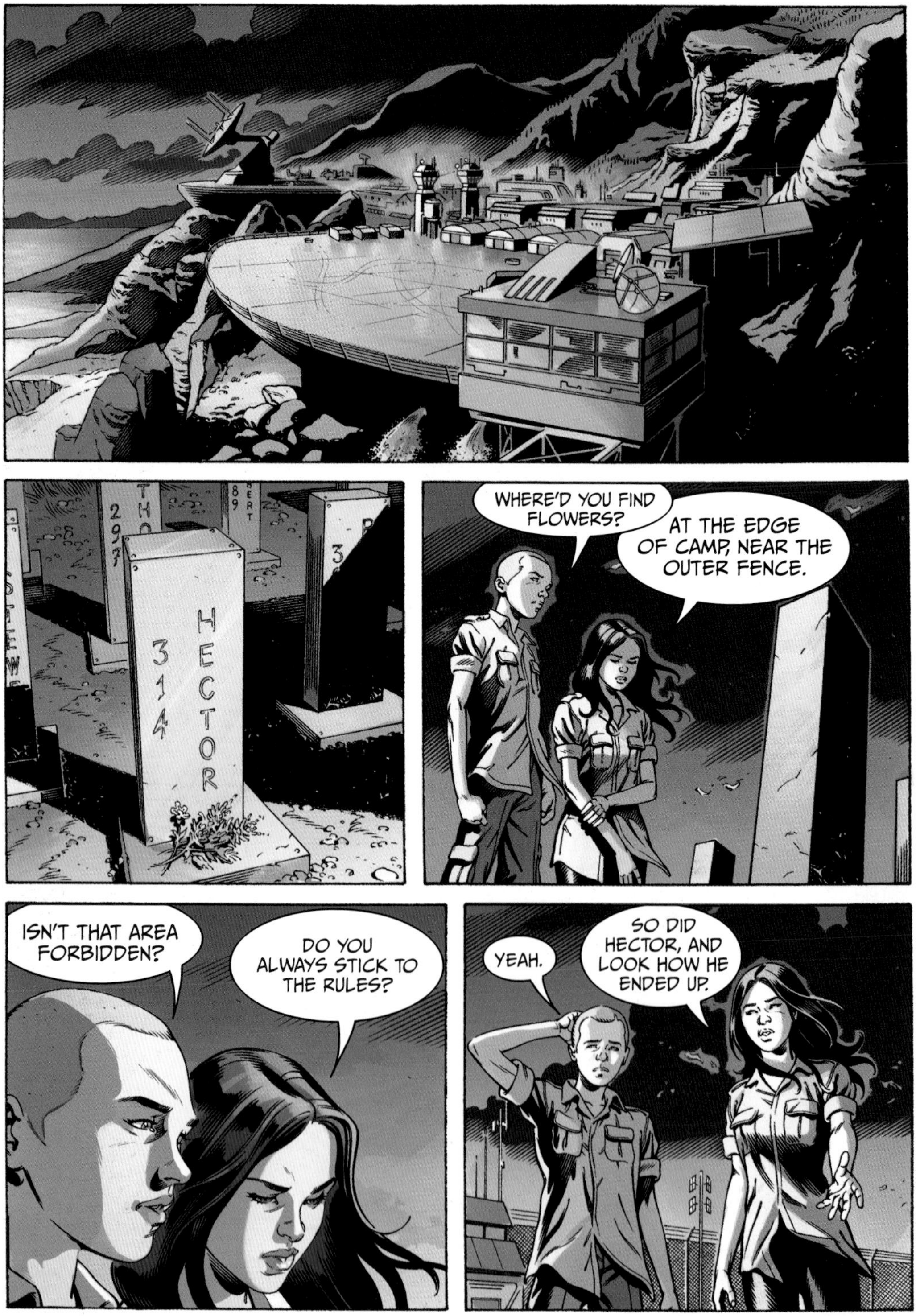
314
HECTOR
WHERE'D YOU FIND FLOWERS?
AT THE EDGE OF CAMP, NEAR THE OUTER FENCE.
ISN'T THAT AREA FORBIDDEN?
DO YOU ALWAYS STICK TO THE RULES?
YEAH.
SO DID HECTOR, AND LOOK HOW HE ENDED UP.

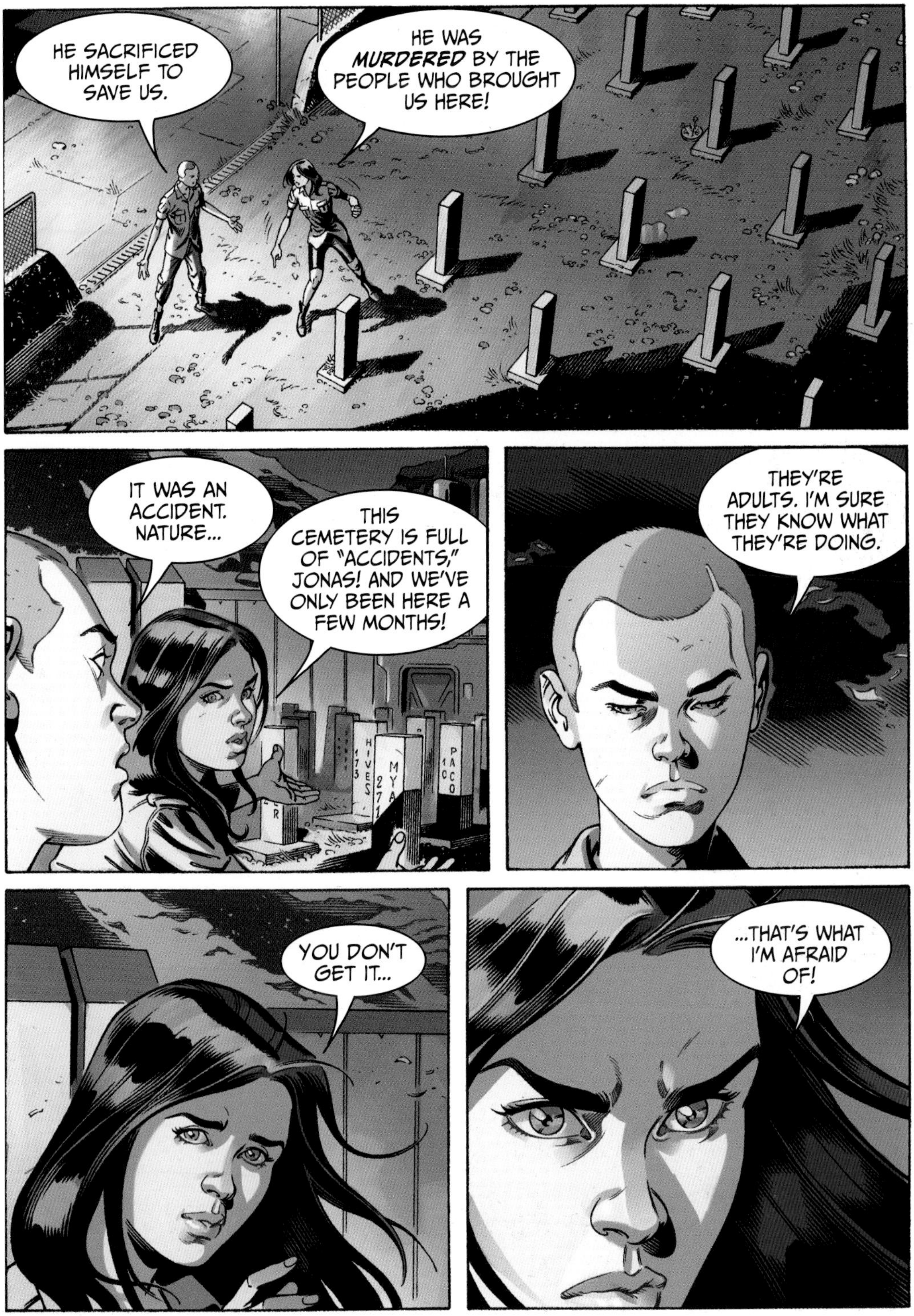
HE SACRIFICED HIMSELF TO SAVE US.
HE WAS *MURDERED* BY THE PEOPLE WHO BROUGHT US HERE!
IT WAS AN ACCIDENT. NATURE...
THIS CEMETERY IS FULL OF "ACCIDENTS," JONAS! AND WE'VE ONLY BEEN HERE A FEW MONTHS!
THEY'RE ADULTS. I'M SURE THEY KNOW WHAT THEY'RE DOING.
YOU DON'T GET IT...
...THAT'S WHAT I'M AFRAID OF!

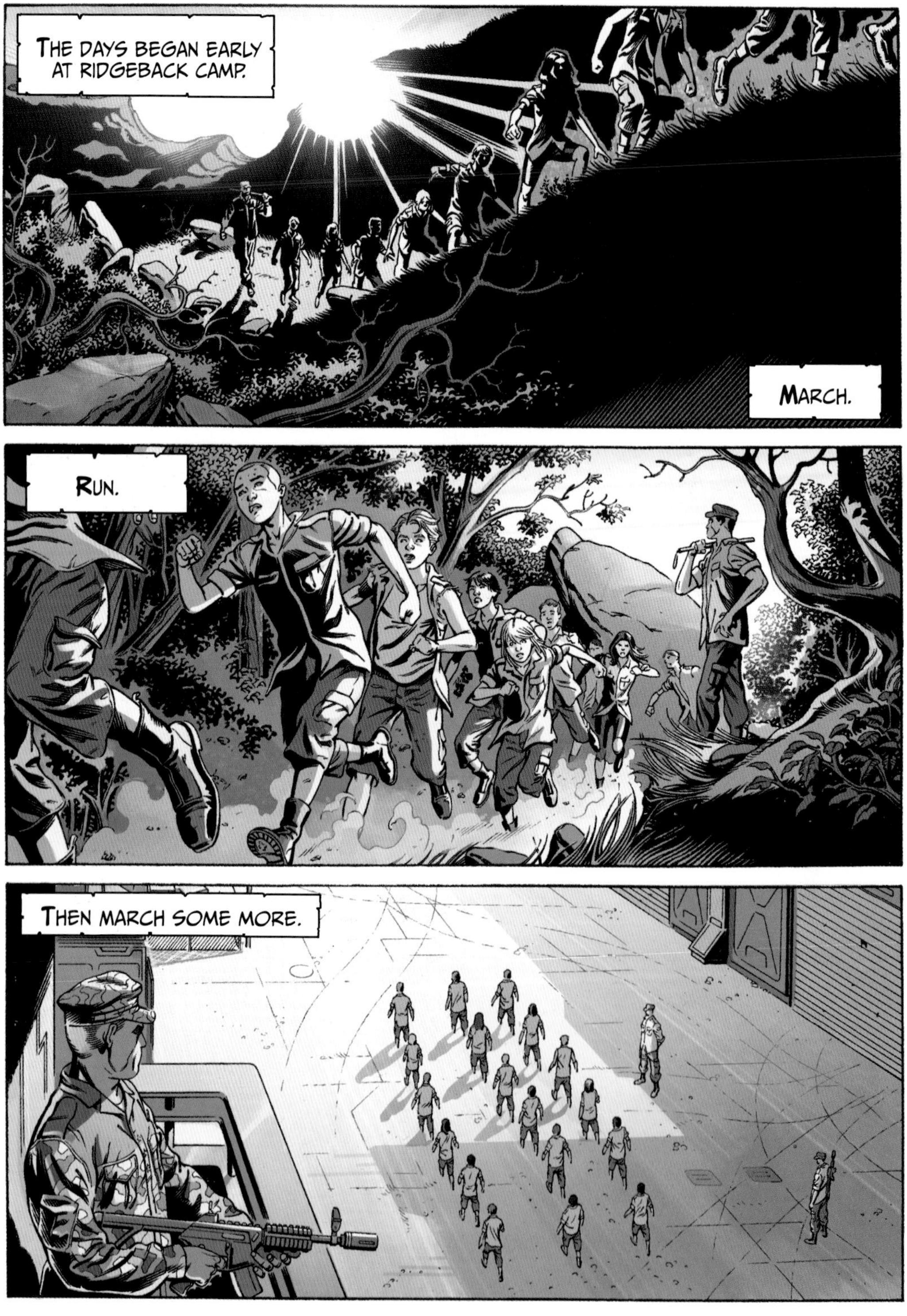
THE DAYS BEGAN EARLY AT RIDGEBACK CAMP.
MARCH.
RUN.
THEN MARCH SOME MORE.

THEN WE'D GO TO CLASS.

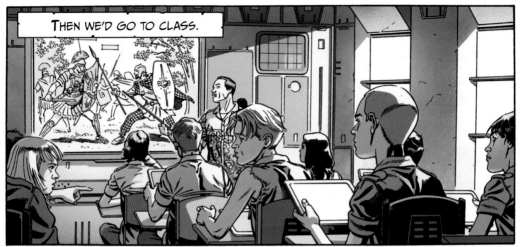

WE'D STUDY MATH, PHYSICS, ANATOMY, AND MILITARY HISTORY.

THE WAY THEY EXPLAINED IT, HISTORY WAS JUST A SERIES OF WARS, ONE AFTER ANOTHER.

WRITTEN BY SOLDIERS.

SOLDIERS LIKE US.

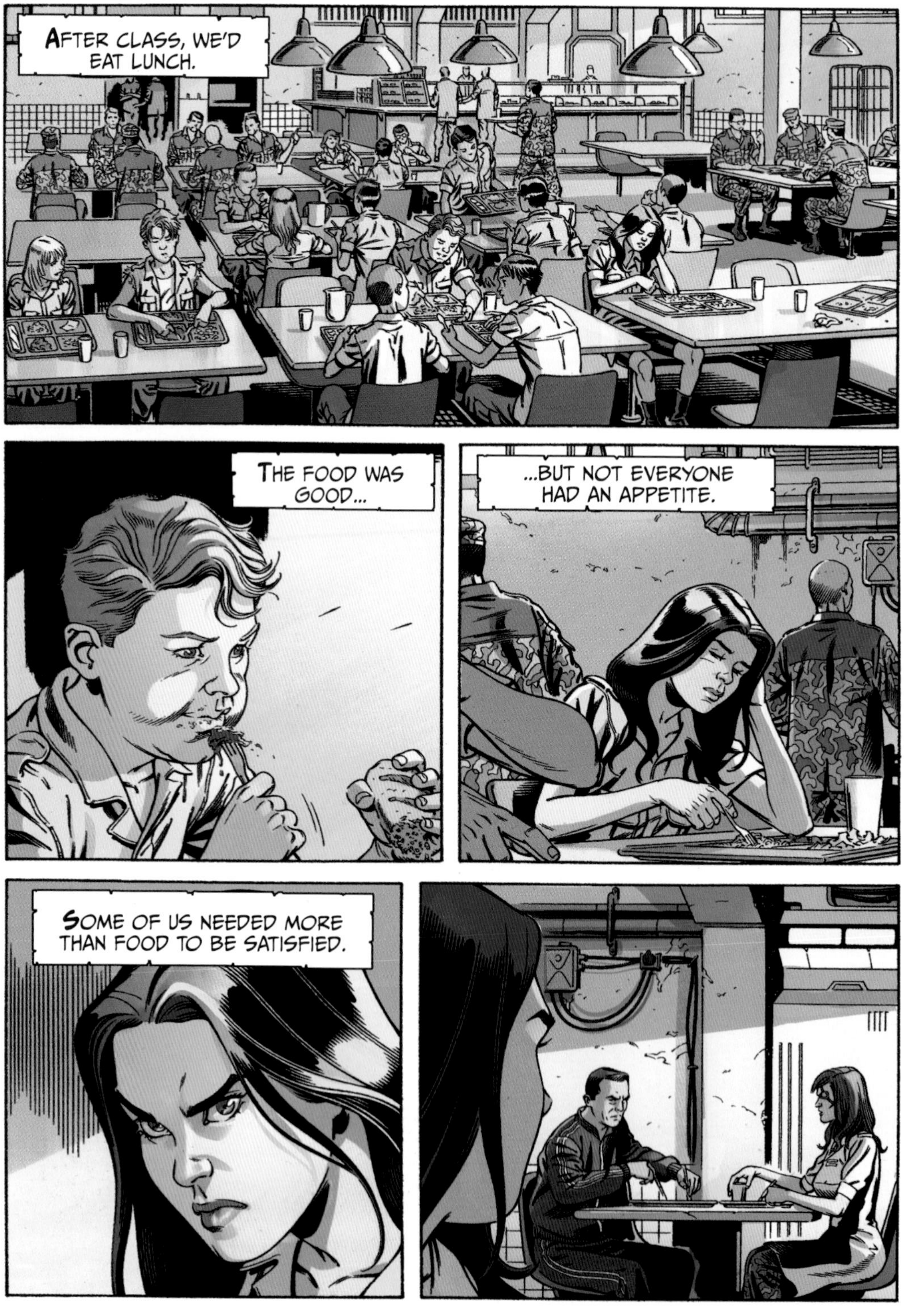
AFTER CLASS, WE'D EAT LUNCH.
THE FOOD WAS GOOD...
...BUT NOT EVERYONE HAD AN APPETITE.
SOME OF US NEEDED MORE THAN FOOD TO BE SATISFIED.

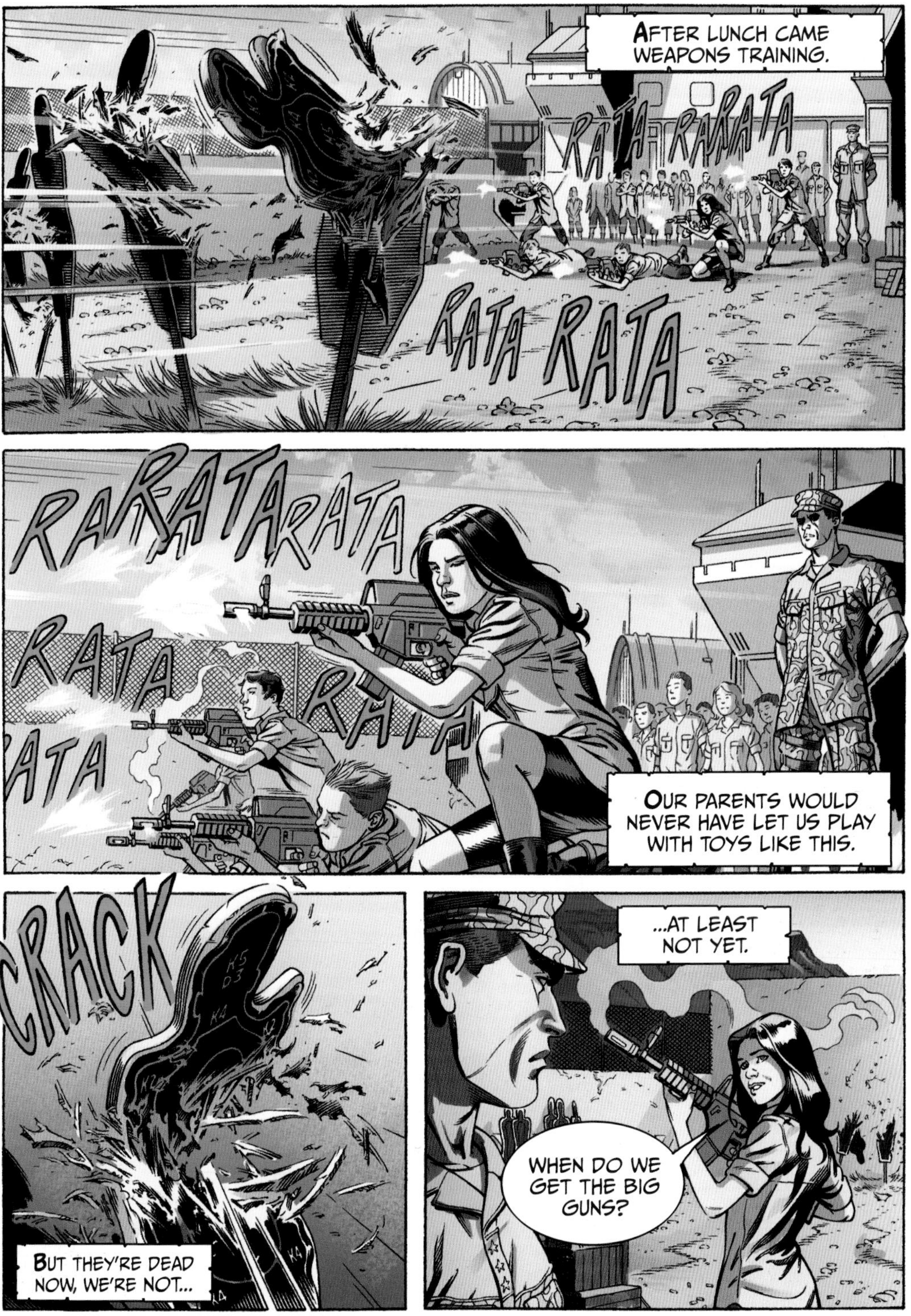
AFTER LUNCH CAME WEAPONS TRAINING.
RATA RARATA
RATA RATA
RARATARATA
RATA
RATA
ATA
OUR PARENTS WOULD NEVER HAVE LET US PLAY WITH TOYS LIKE THIS.
CRACK
BUT THEY'RE DEAD NOW, WE'RE NOT...
...AT LEAST NOT YET.
WHEN DO WE GET THE BIG GUNS?

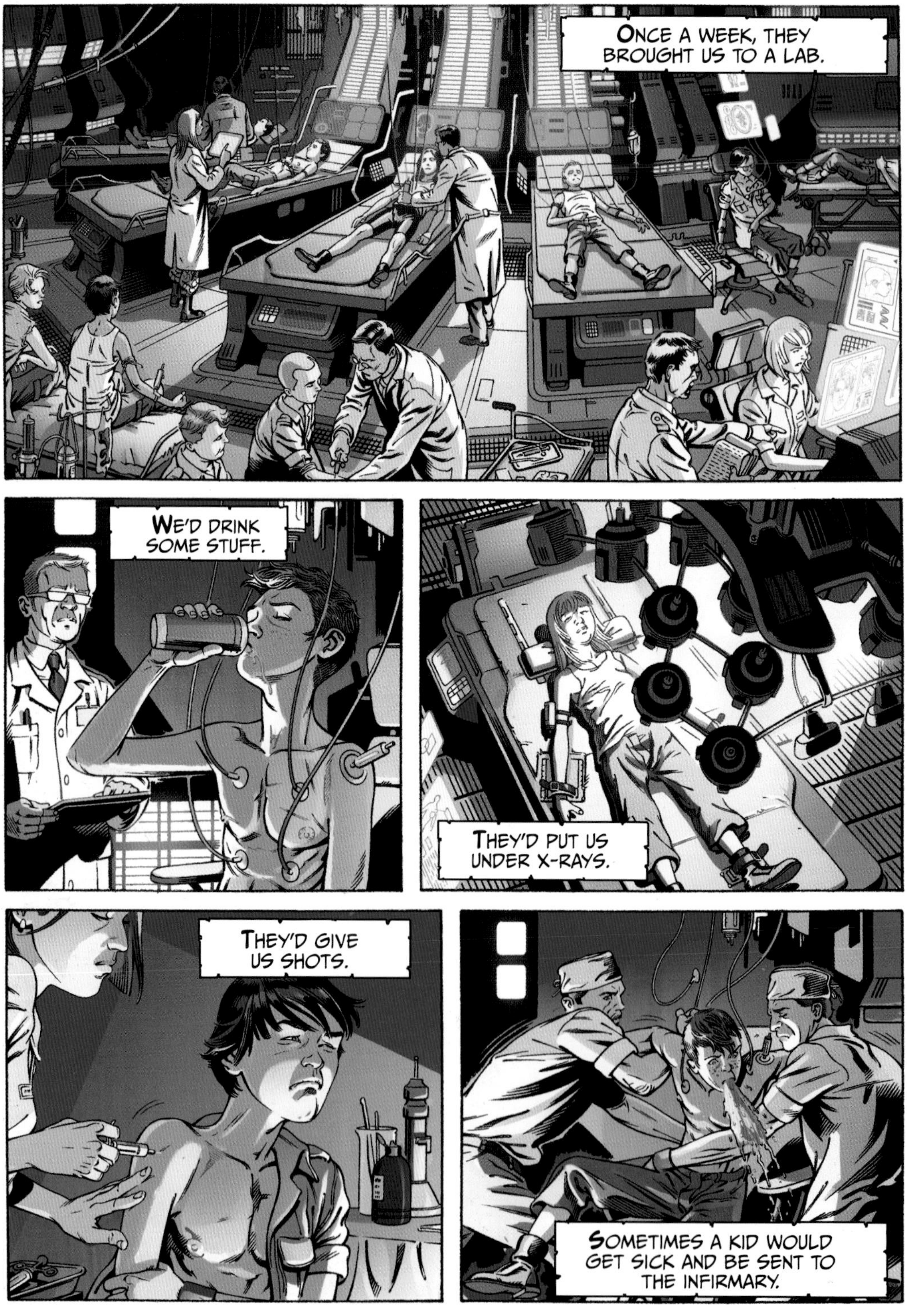
ONCE A WEEK, THEY BROUGHT US TO A LAB.
WE'D DRINK SOME STUFF.
THEY'D PUT US UNDER X-RAYS.
THEY'D GIVE US SHOTS.
SOMETIMES A KID WOULD GET SICK AND BE SENT TO THE INFIRMARY.

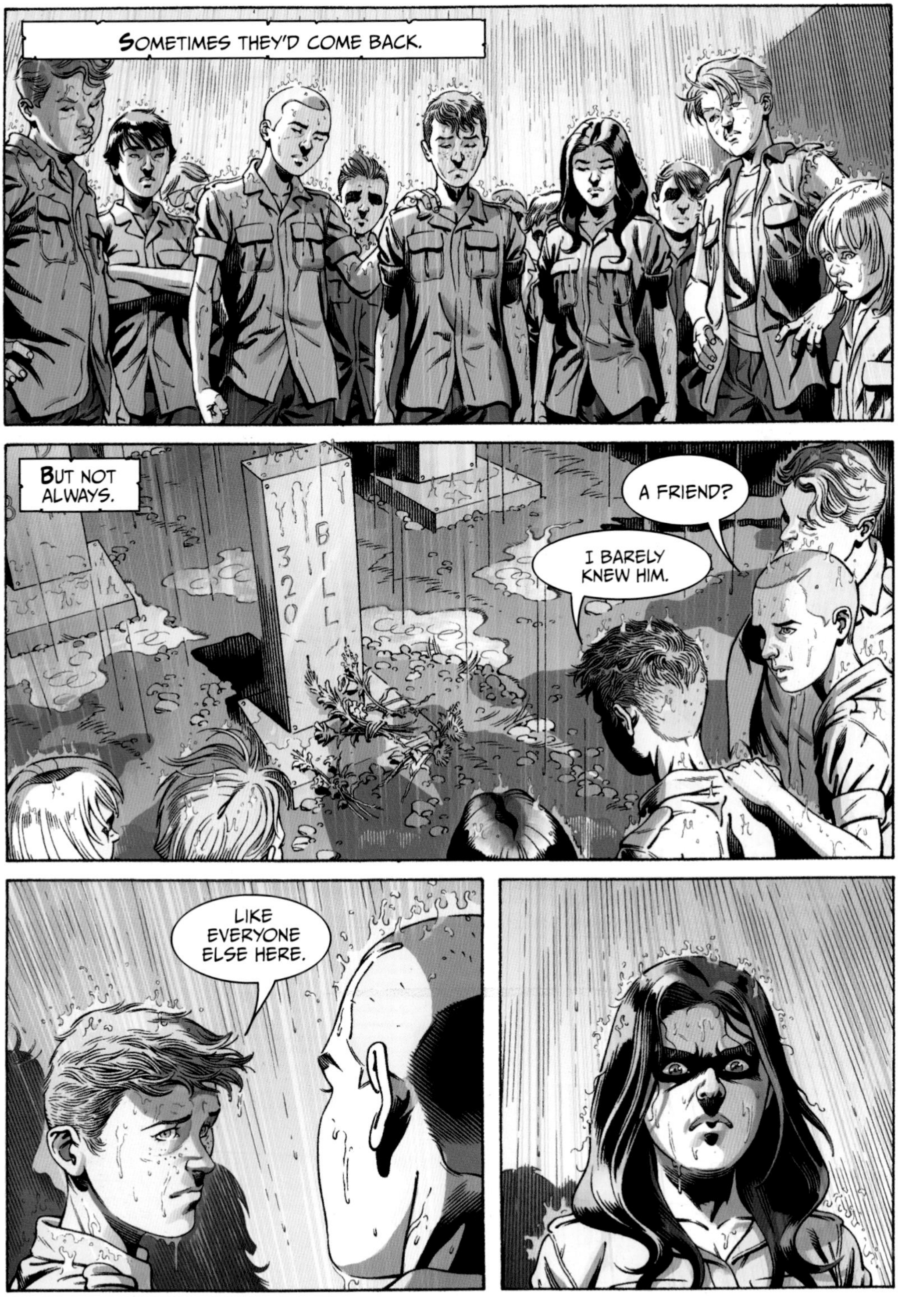
SOMETIMES THEY'D COME BACK.
BUT NOT ALWAYS.
320 BILL
A FRIEND?
I BARELY KNEW HIM.
LIKE EVERYONE ELSE HERE.

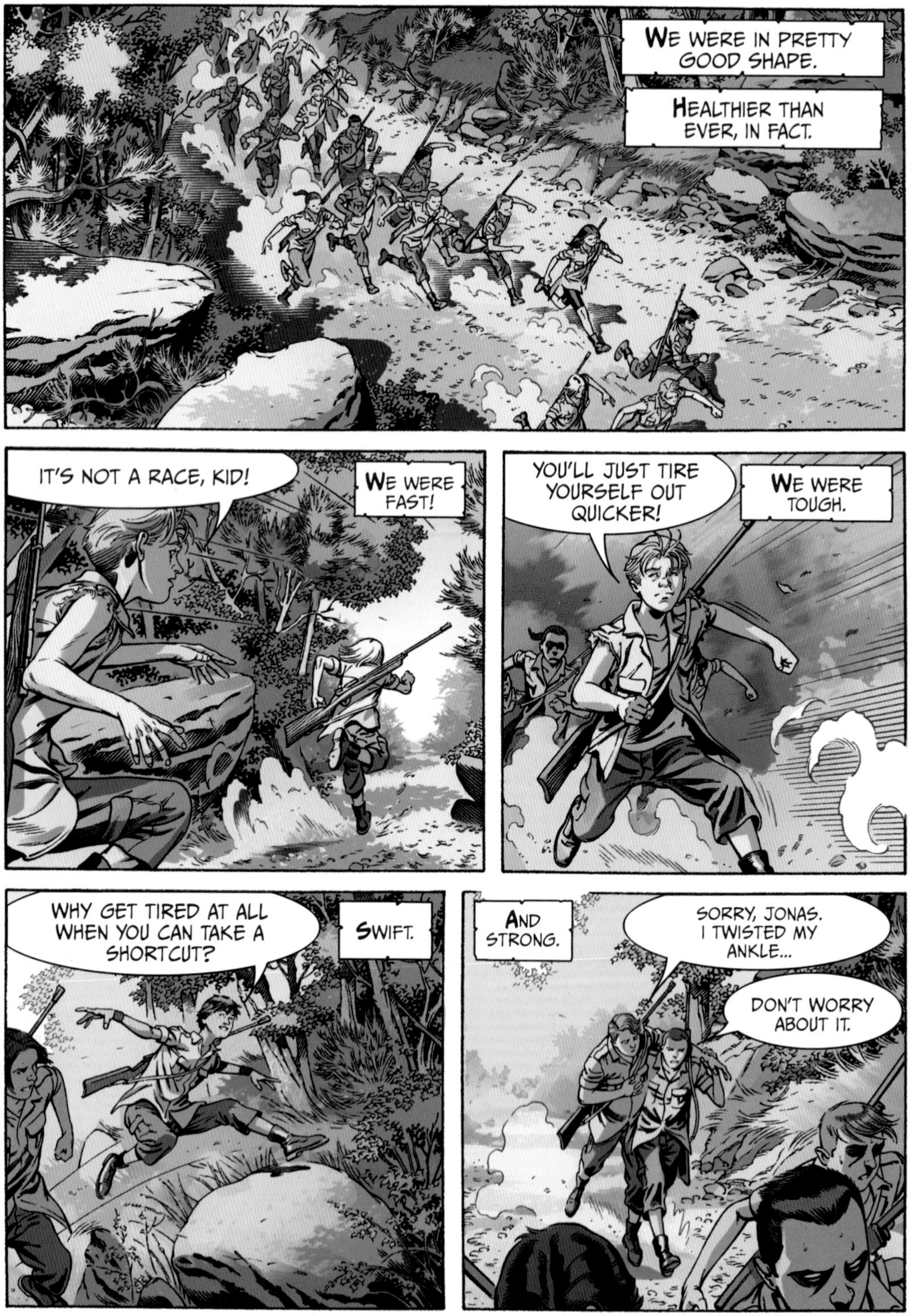
WE WERE IN PRETTY GOOD SHAPE.
HEALTHIER THAN EVER, IN FACT.
IT'S NOT A RACE, KID!
WE WERE FAST!
YOU'LL JUST TIRE YOURSELF OUT QUICKER!
WE WERE TOUGH.
WHY GET TIRED AT ALL WHEN YOU CAN TAKE A SHORTCUT?
SWIFT.
AND STRONG.
SORRY, JONAS. I TWISTED MY ANKLE...
DON'T WORRY ABOUT IT.

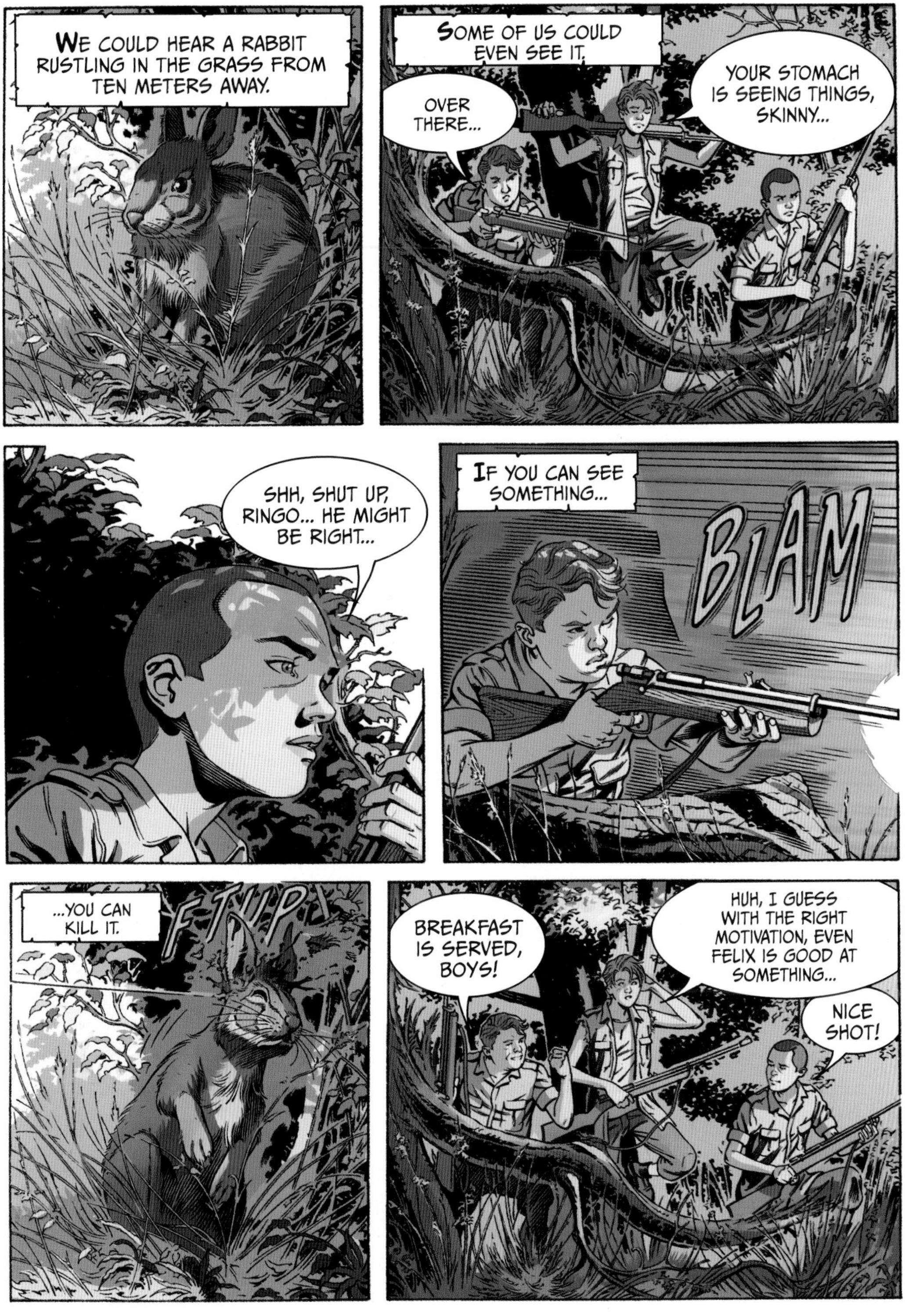
WE COULD HEAR A RABBIT RUSTLING IN THE GRASS FROM TEN METERS AWAY.
SOME OF US COULD EVEN SEE IT.
OVER THERE...
YOUR STOMACH IS SEEING THINGS, SKINNY...
SHH, SHUT UP, RINGO... HE MIGHT BE RIGHT...
IF YOU CAN SEE SOMETHING...
BLAM
...YOU CAN KILL IT.
FTUP
BREAKFAST IS SERVED, BOYS!
HUH, I GUESS WITH THE RIGHT MOTIVATION, EVEN FELIX IS GOOD AT SOMETHING...
NICE SHOT!

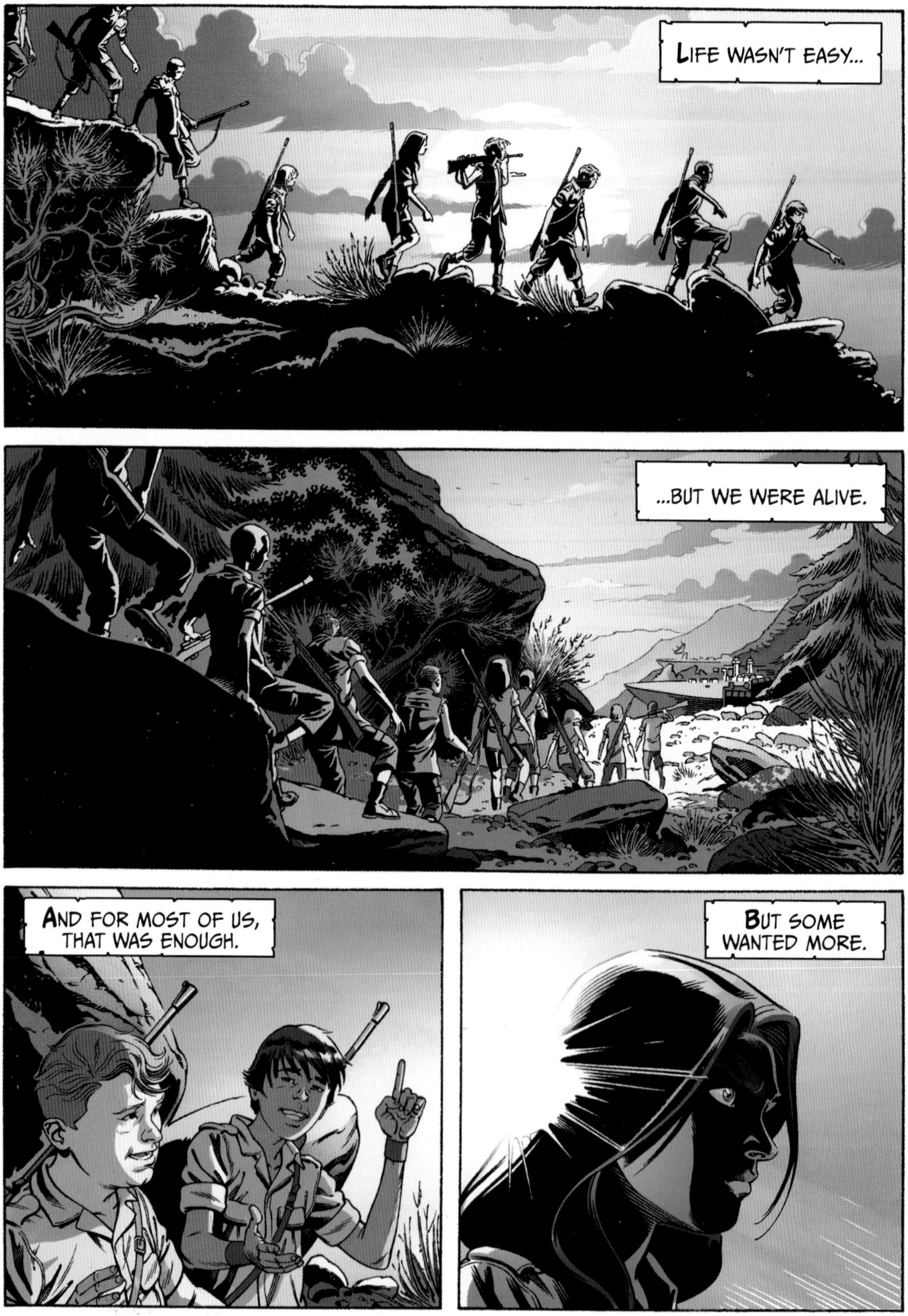
LIFE WASN'T EASY...
...BUT WE WERE ALIVE.
AND FOR MOST OF US, THAT WAS ENOUGH.
BUT SOME WANTED MORE.

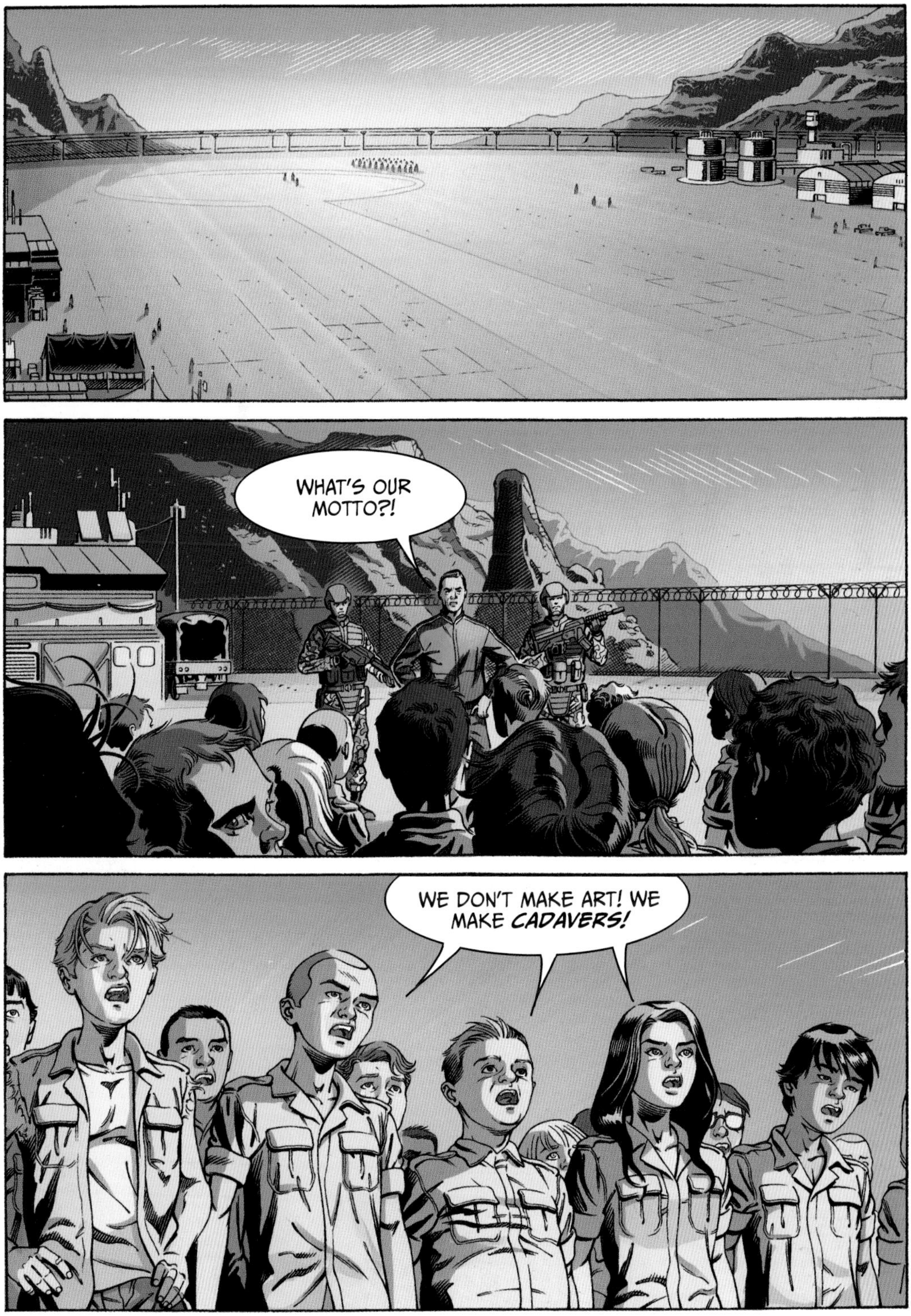
WHAT'S OUR MOTTO?!
WE DON'T MAKE ART! WE MAKE CADAVERS!

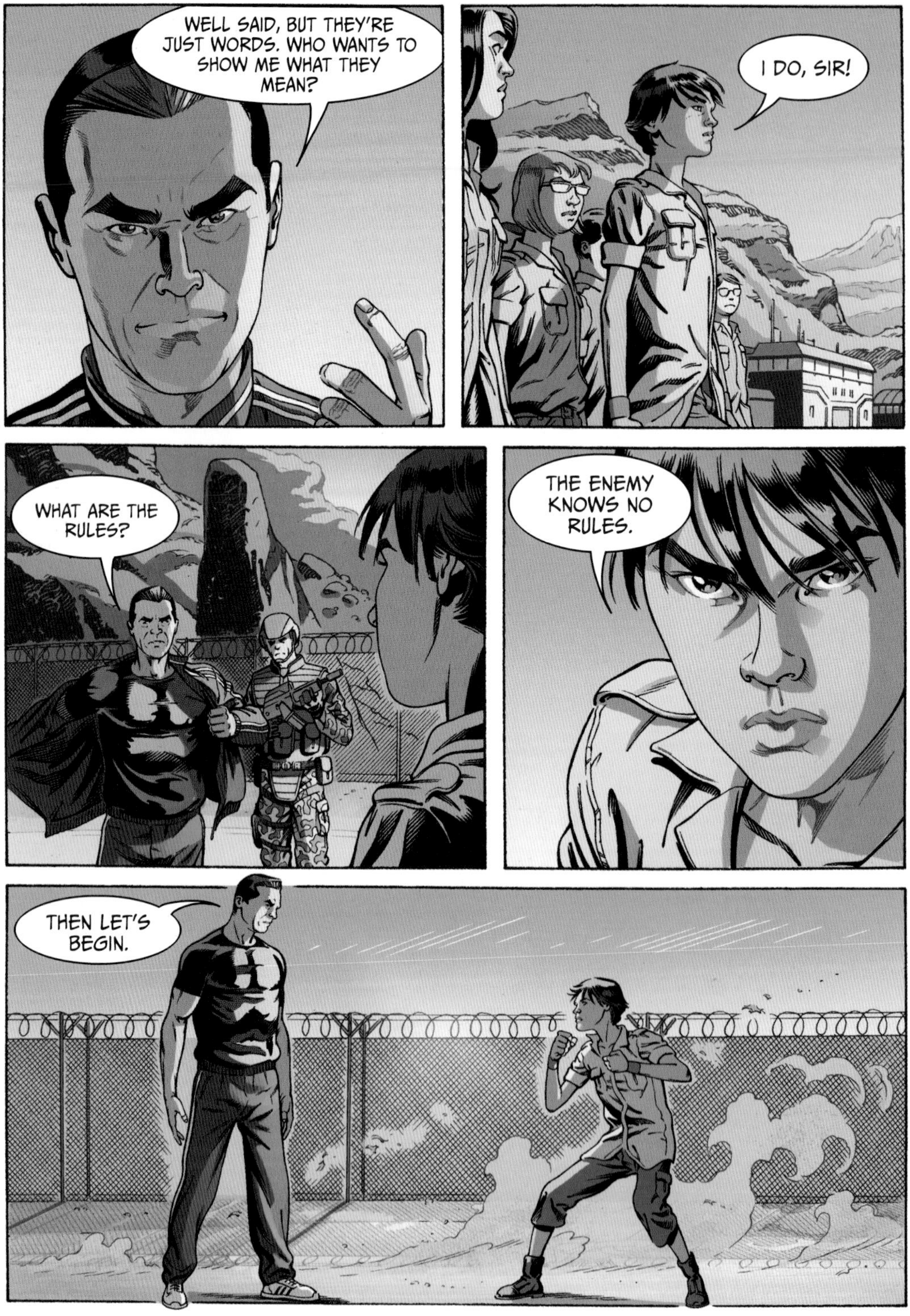
WELL SAID, BUT THEY'RE JUST WORDS. WHO WANTS TO SHOW ME WHAT THEY MEAN?
I DO, SIR!
WHAT ARE THE RULES?
THE ENEMY KNOWS NO RULES.
THEN LET'S BEGIN.

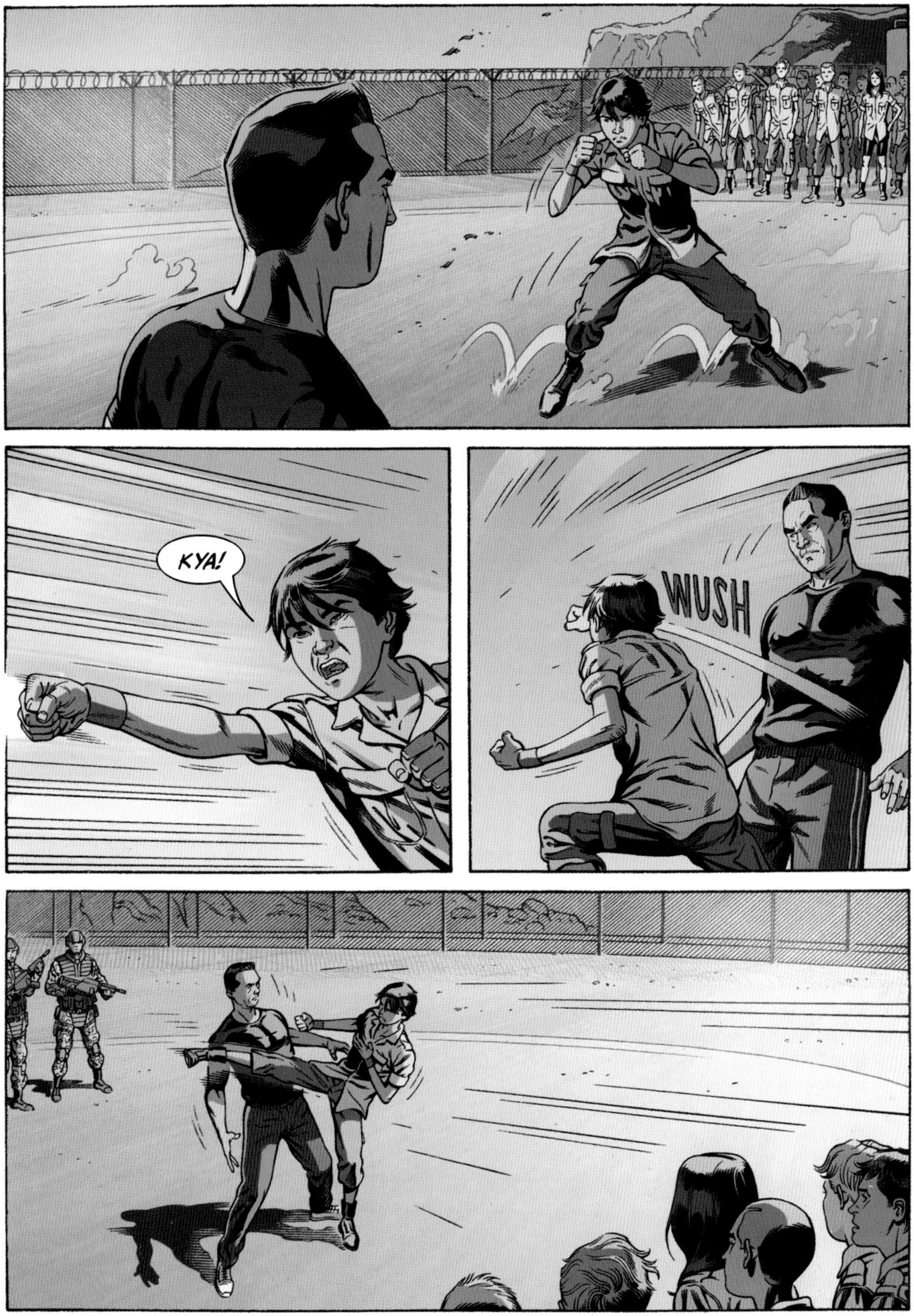
KYA!
WUSH

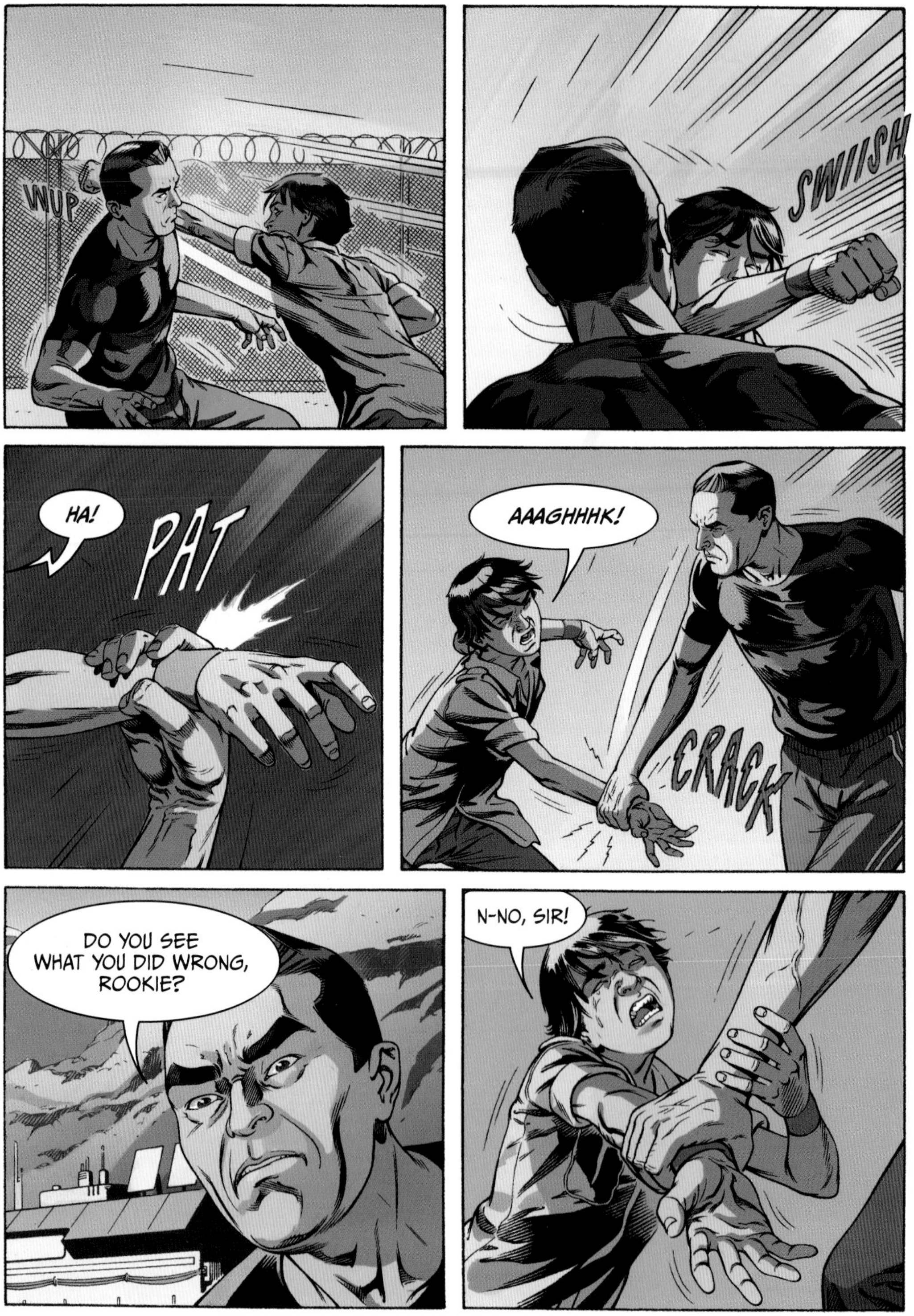
WUP
SWIISH
HA!
PAT
AAAGHHHK!
CRACK
DO YOU SEE WHAT YOU DID WRONG, ROOKIE?
N-NO, SIR!

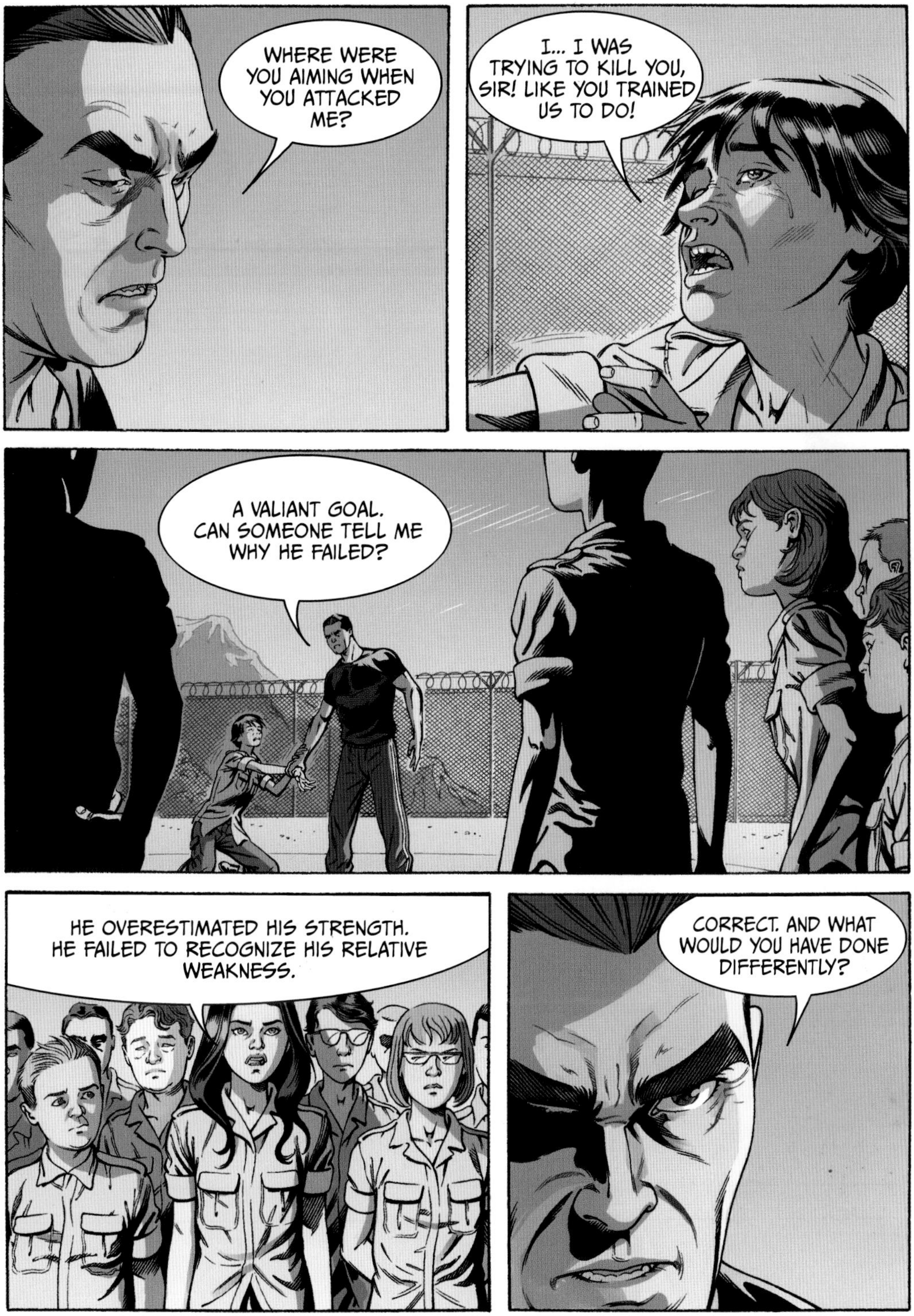
WHERE WERE YOU AIMING WHEN YOU ATTACKED ME?
I... I WAS TRYING TO KILL YOU, SIR! LIKE YOU TRAINED US TO DO!
A VALIANT GOAL. CAN SOMEONE TELL ME WHY HE FAILED?
HE OVERESTIMATED HIS STRENGTH. HE FAILED TO RECOGNIZE HIS RELATIVE WEAKNESS.
CORRECT. AND WHAT WOULD YOU HAVE DONE DIFFERENTLY?

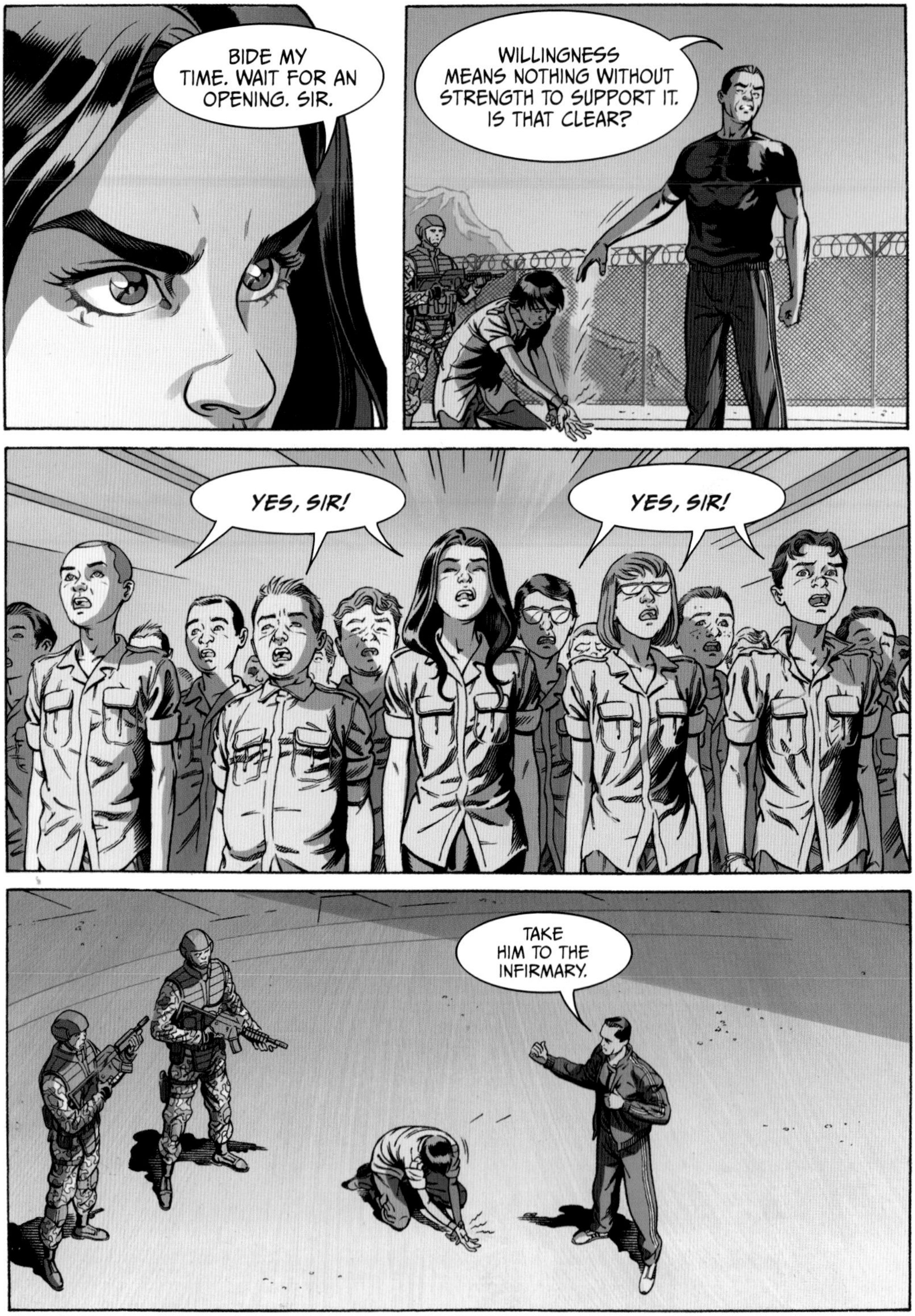
BIDE MY TIME. WAIT FOR AN OPENING. SIR.
WILLINGNESS MEANS NOTHING WITHOUT STRENGTH TO SUPPORT IT. IS THAT CLEAR?
YES, SIR!
YES, SIR!
TAKE HIM TO THE INFIRMARY.

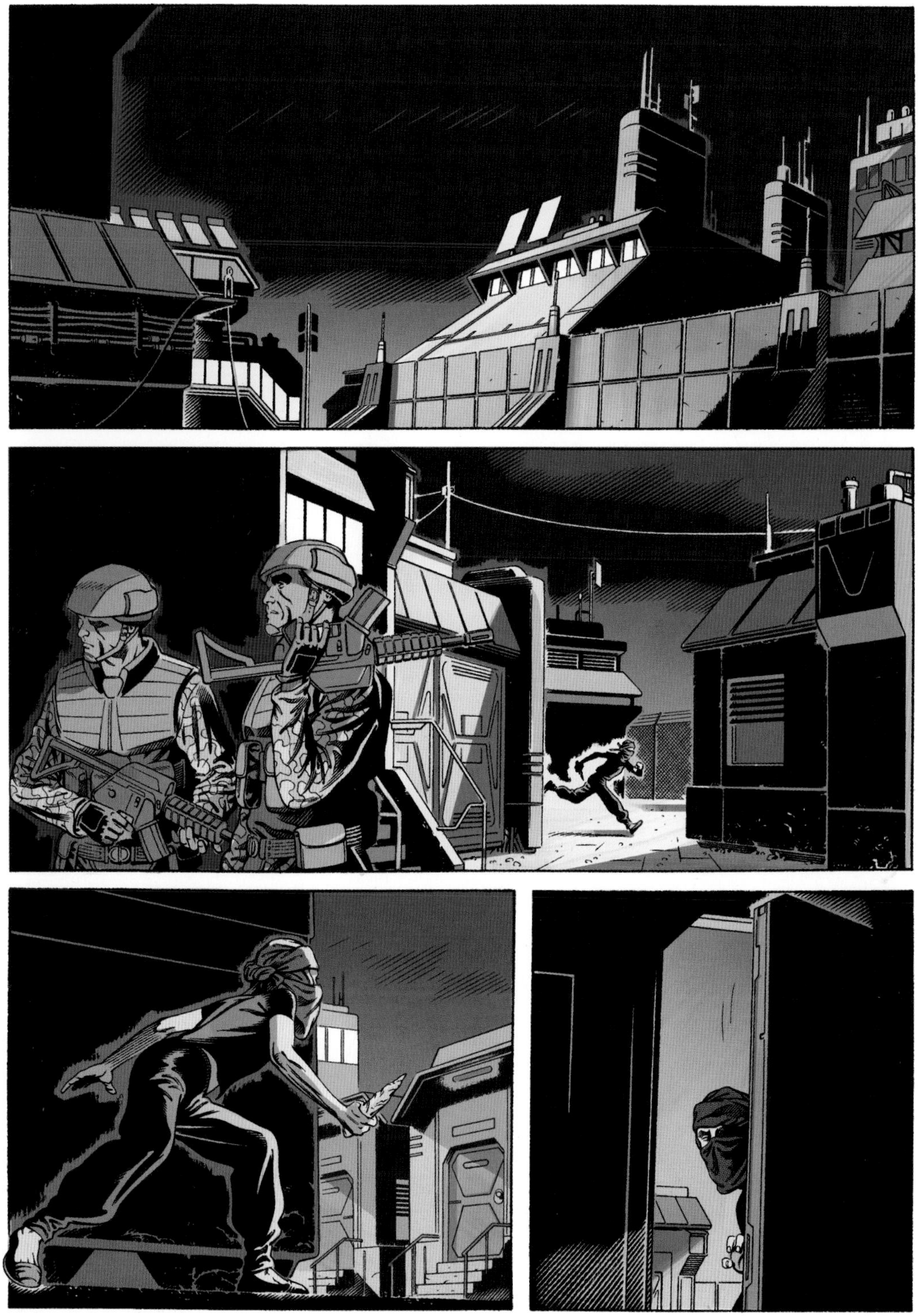

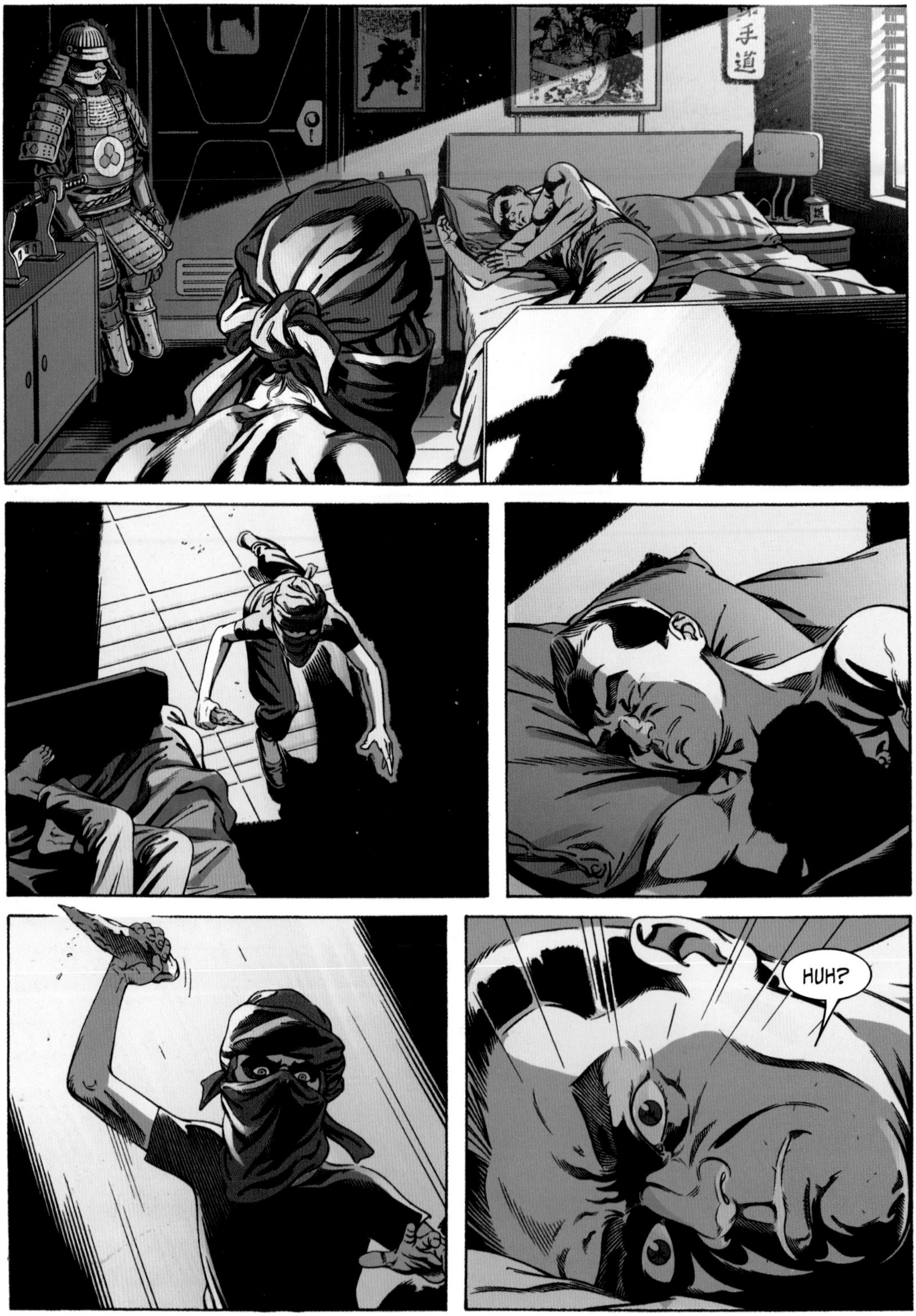
HUH?

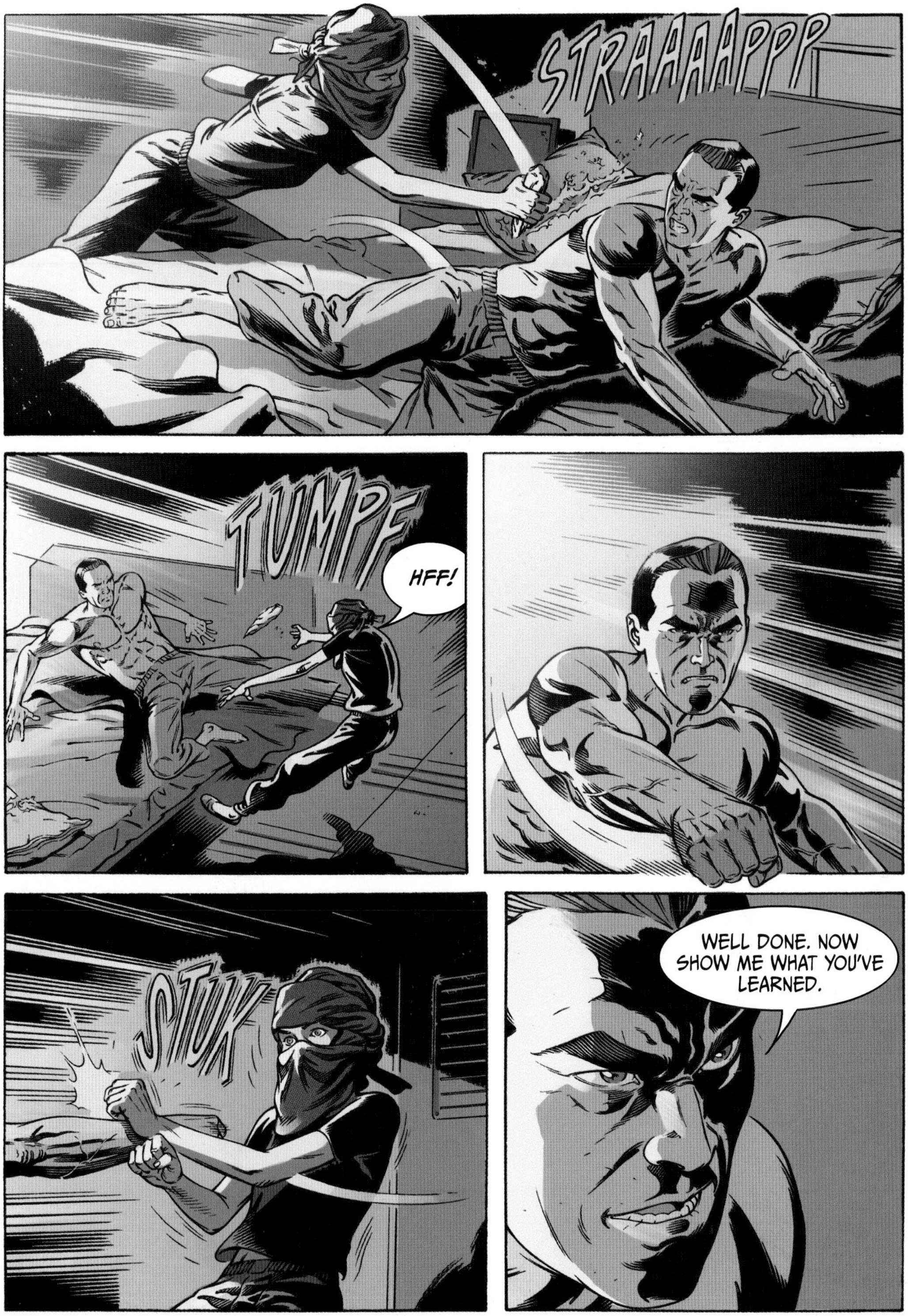
STRAAAAPPP
TUMPF
HFF!
STUK
WELL DONE. NOW SHOW ME WHAT YOU'VE LEARNED.

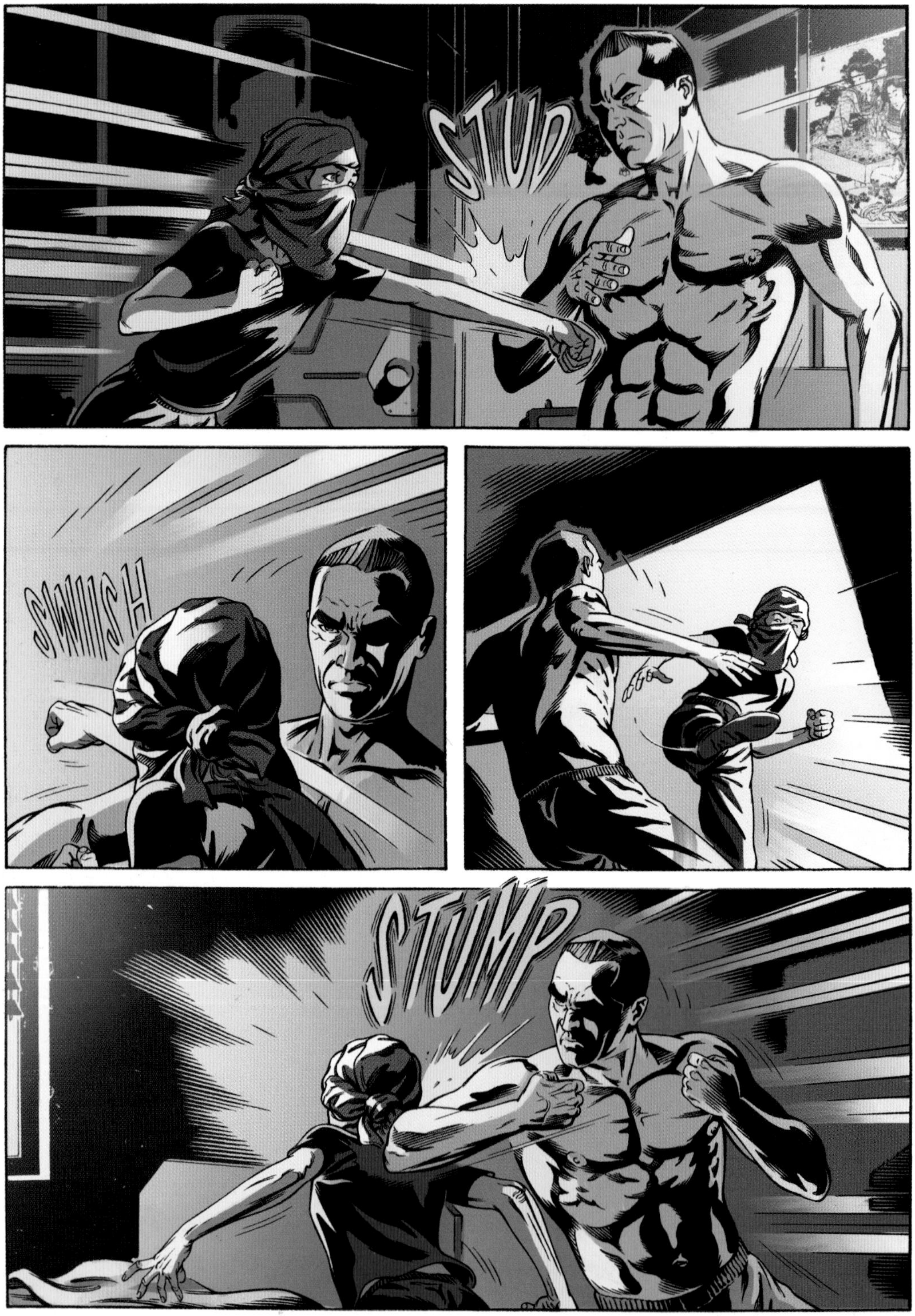
STUD
SWIISH
STUMP

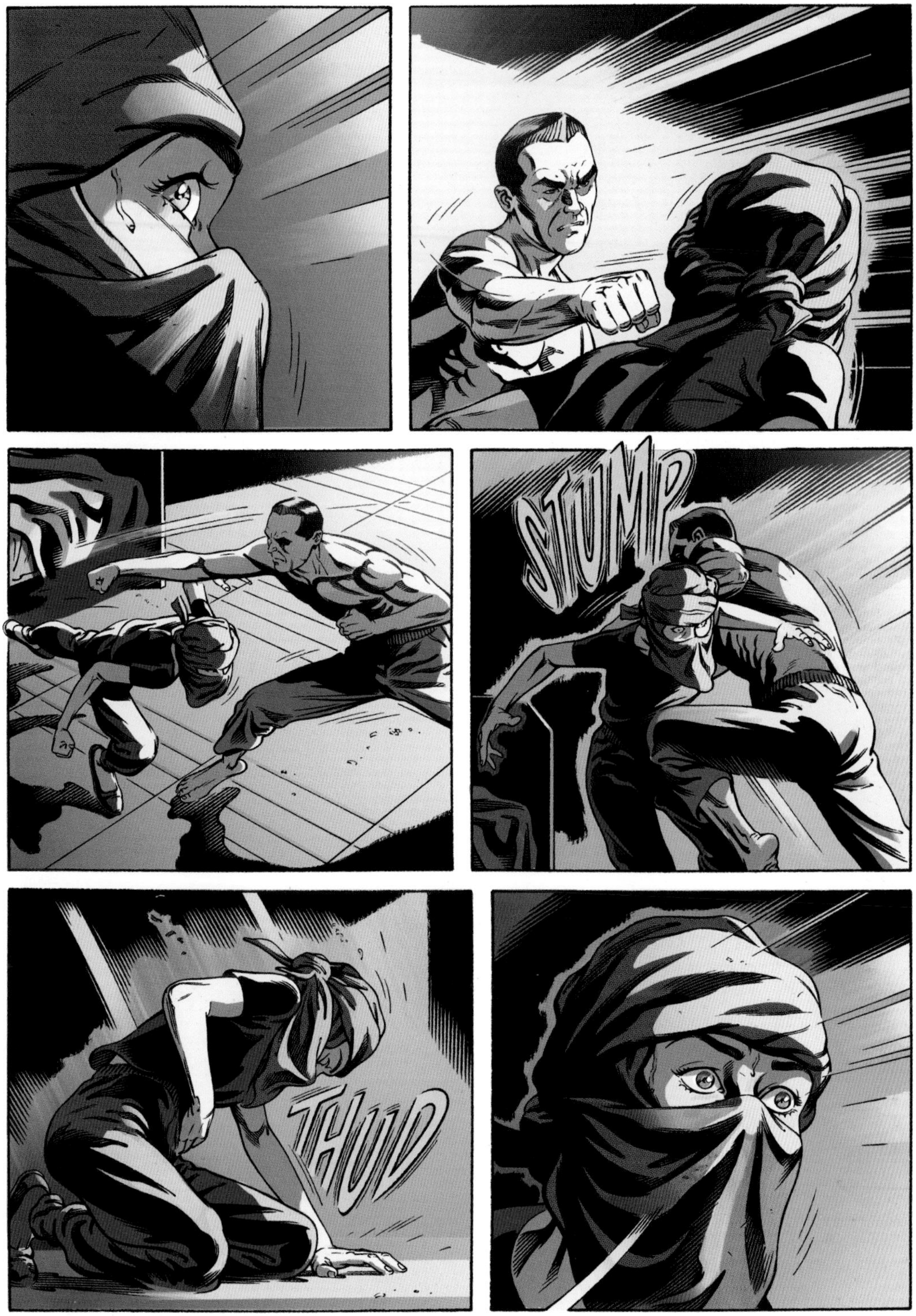
STUMP
THUD

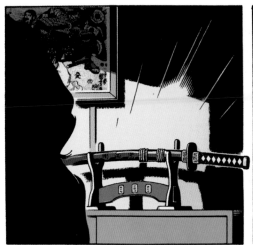

YOU FOUGHT WELL, BUT IT'S OVER.

I HAVE A SWORD!

THAT BLADE IS TOO LONG FOR A SMALL ROOM LIKE THIS...

...AND YOU LOST THE ELEMENT OF SURPRISE. I'D HAVE THE ENTIRE BASE HERE WITH A SINGLE SHOUT.

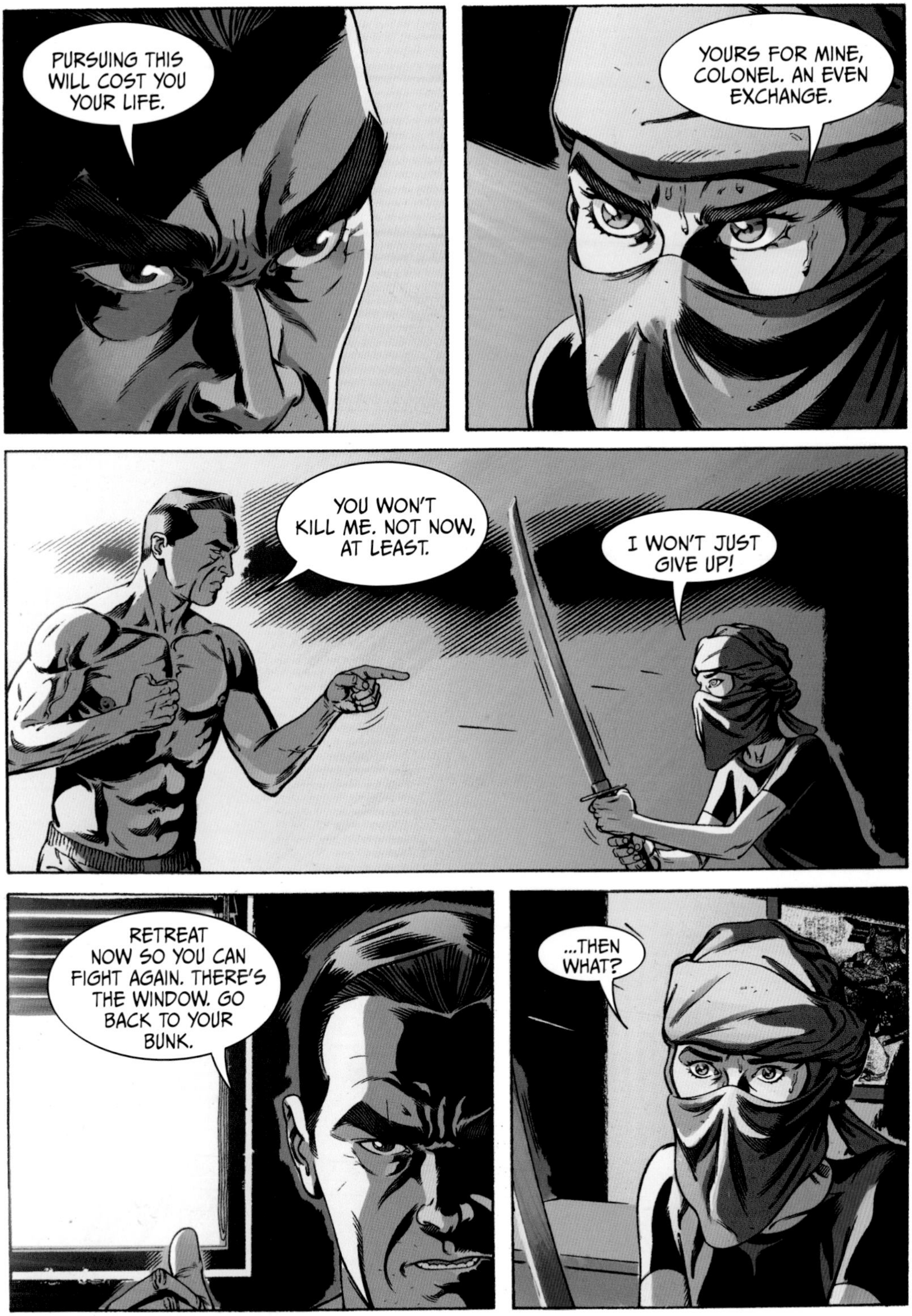
PURSUING THIS WILL COST YOU YOUR LIFE.
YOURS FOR MINE, COLONEL. AN EVEN EXCHANGE.
YOU WON'T KILL ME. NOT NOW, AT LEAST.
I WON'T JUST GIVE UP!
RETREAT NOW SO YOU CAN FIGHT AGAIN. THERE'S THE WINDOW. GO BACK TO YOUR BUNK.
...THEN WHAT?

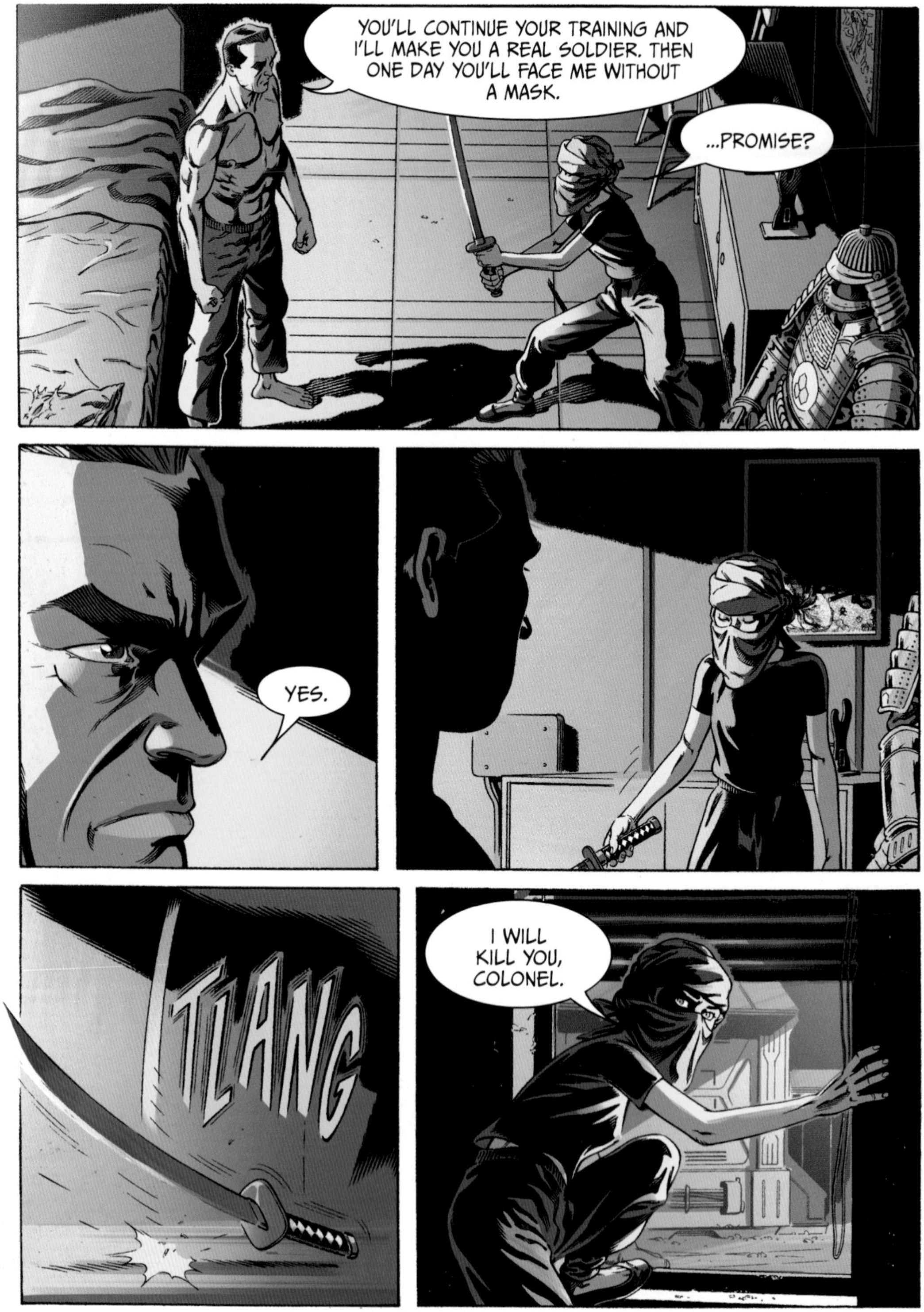
YOU'LL CONTINUE YOUR TRAINING AND I'LL MAKE YOU A REAL SOLDIER. THEN ONE DAY YOU'LL FACE ME WITHOUT A MASK.
...PROMISE?
YES.
TLANG
I WILL KILL YOU, COLONEL.

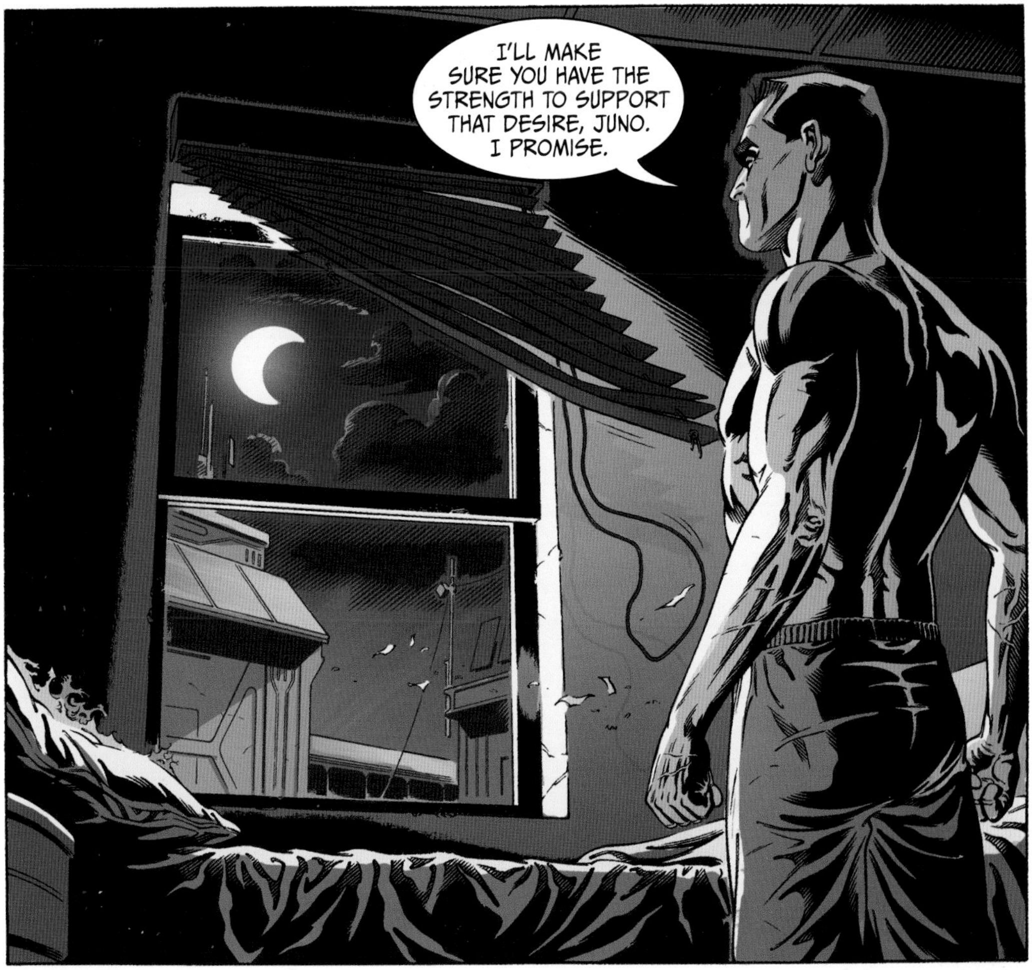
I'LL MAKE SURE YOU HAVE THE STRENGTH TO SUPPORT THAT DESIRE, JUNO. I PROMISE.

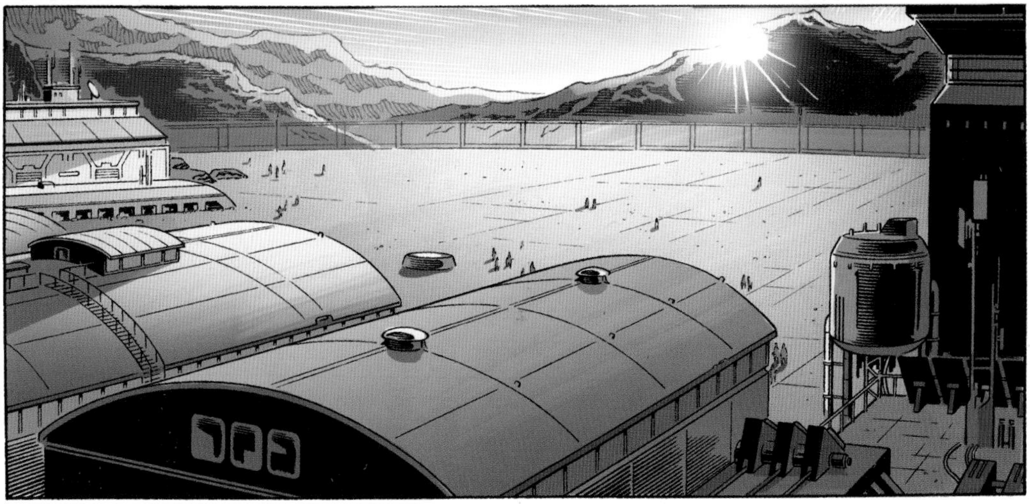

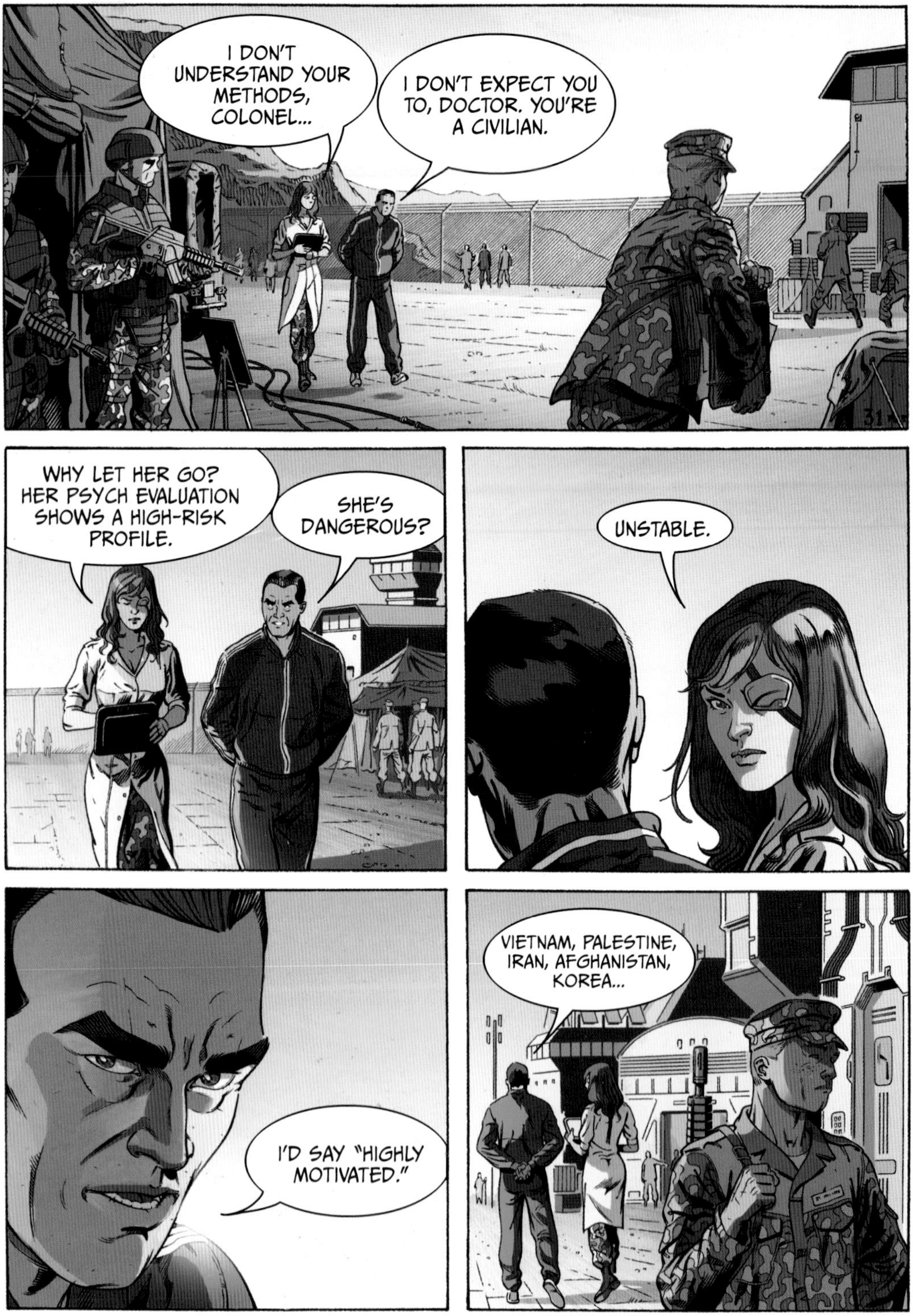
I DON'T UNDERSTAND YOUR METHODS, COLONEL...
I DON'T EXPECT YOU TO, DOCTOR. YOU'RE A CIVILIAN.
WHY LET HER GO? HER PSYCH EVALUATION SHOWS A HIGH-RISK PROFILE.
SHE'S DANGEROUS?
UNSTABLE.
I'D SAY "HIGHLY MOTIVATED."
VIETNAM, PALESTINE, IRAN, AFGHANISTAN, KOREA...

...HISTORY IS FULL OF INVADING ARMIES OF TRAINED SOLDIERS DEFEATED BY GROUPS OF SIMPLE SHEPHERDS AND PEASANTS.

SO?

SIMPLY PUT, THE INVADERS WEREN'T SUFFICIENTLY MOTIVATED AND THE DEFENDERS TOOK IT PERSONALLY...

AND THE NEAR-DESTRUCTION OF OUR PLANET ISN'T PERSONAL ENOUGH?

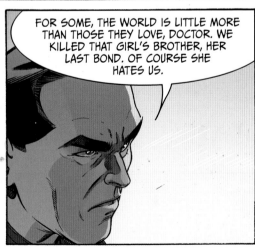

FOR SOME, THE WORLD IS LITTLE MORE THAN THOSE THEY LOVE, DOCTOR. WE KILLED THAT GIRL'S BROTHER, HER LAST BOND. OF COURSE SHE HATES US.

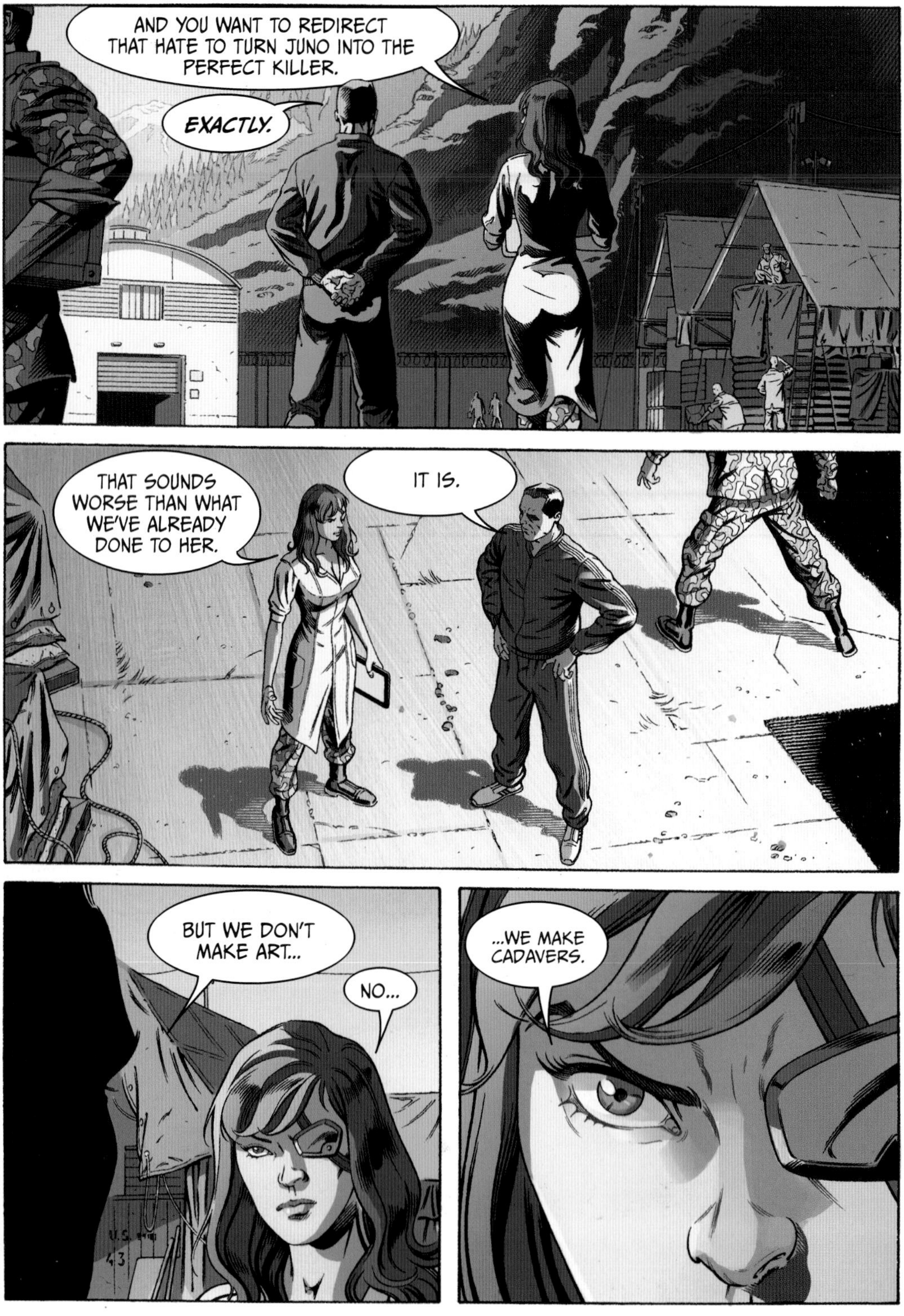
AND YOU WANT TO REDIRECT THAT HATE TO TURN JUNO INTO THE PERFECT KILLER.
EXACTLY.
THAT SOUNDS WORSE THAN WHAT WE'VE ALREADY DONE TO HER.
IT IS.
BUT WE DON'T MAKE ART...
NO...
...WE MAKE CADAVERS.
U.S.
43

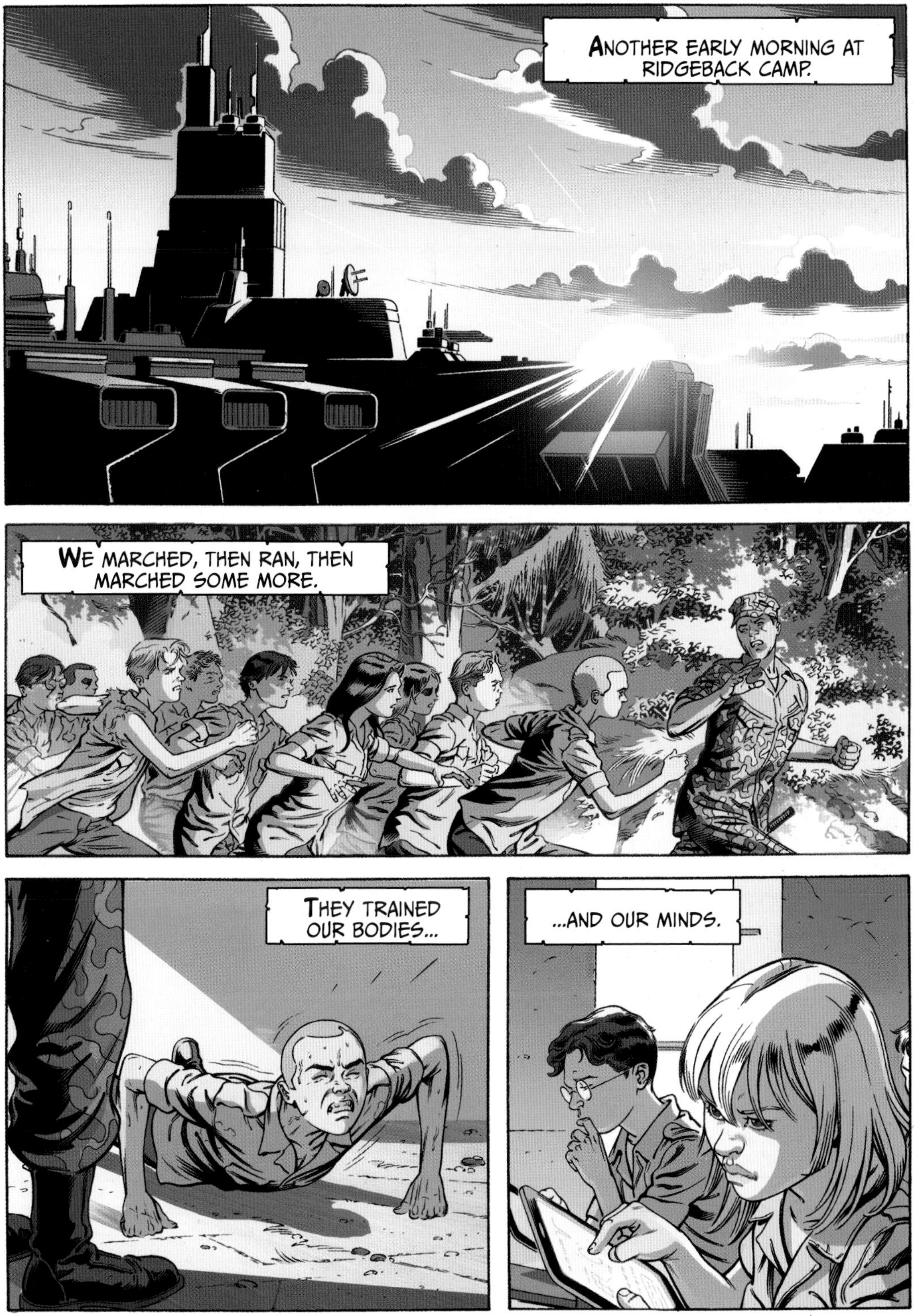
ANOTHER EARLY MORNING AT RIDGEBACK CAMP.
WE MARCHED, THEN RAN, THEN MARCHED SOME MORE.
THEY TRAINED OUR BODIES...
...AND OUR MINDS.

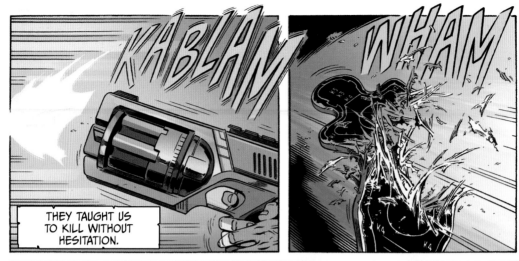

THEY TAUGHT US TO KILL WITHOUT HESITATION.

GOOD JOB.

THERE WERE NO BREAKS.

MOVE, YOU SLACKERS!

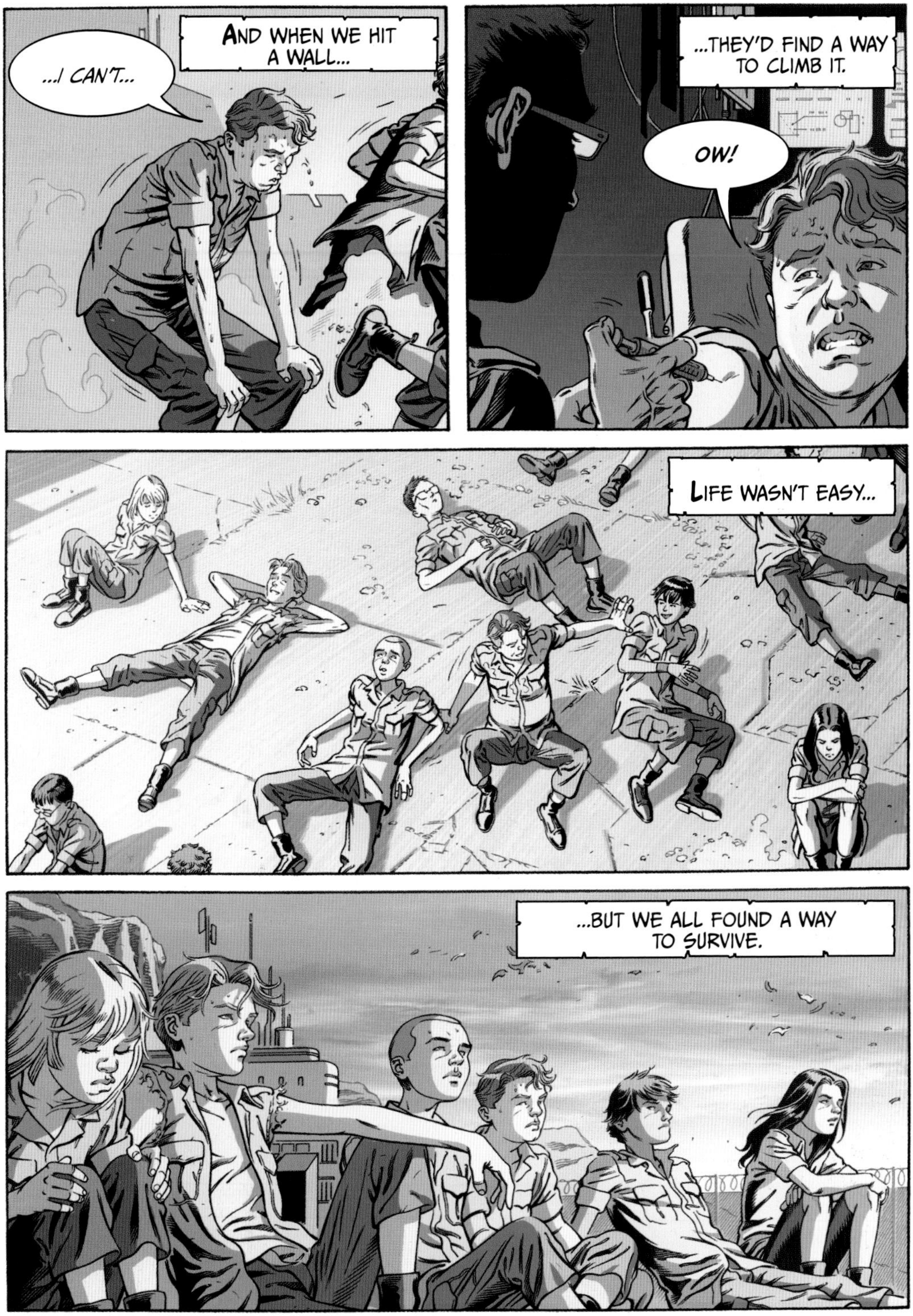
AND WHEN WE HIT A WALL...
...I CAN'T...
...THEY'D FIND A WAY TO CLIMB IT.
OW!
LIFE WASN'T EASY...
...BUT WE ALL FOUND A WAY TO SURVIVE.

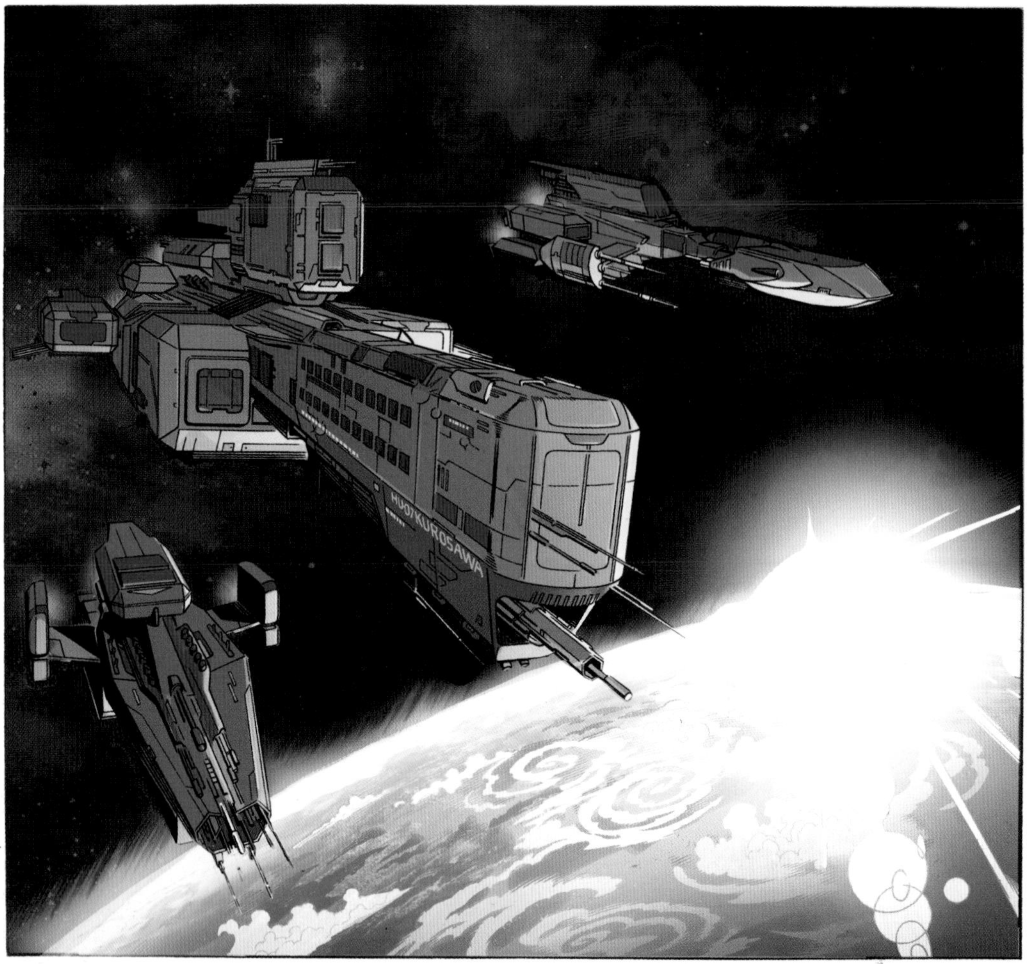
KUROSAWA

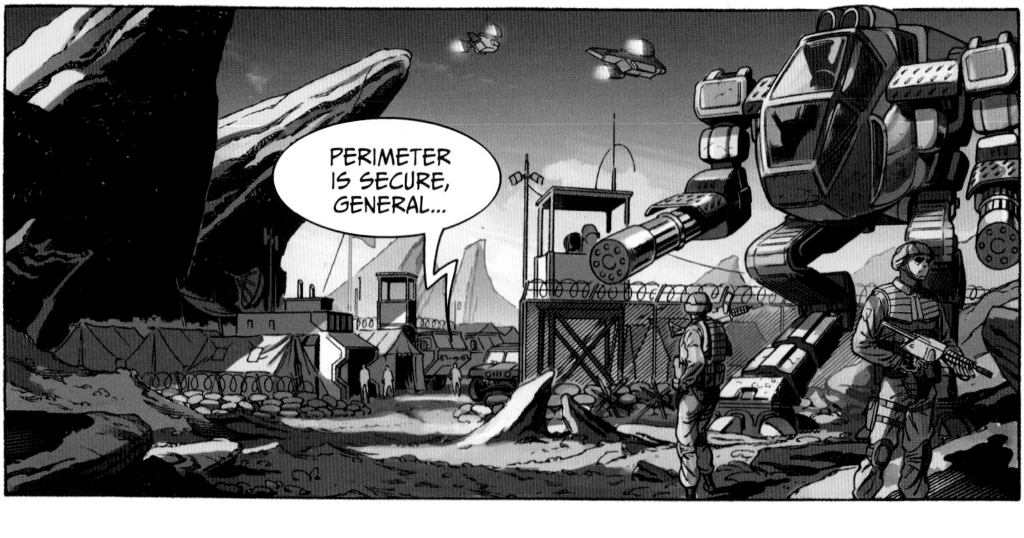
PERIMETER IS SECURE, GENERAL...

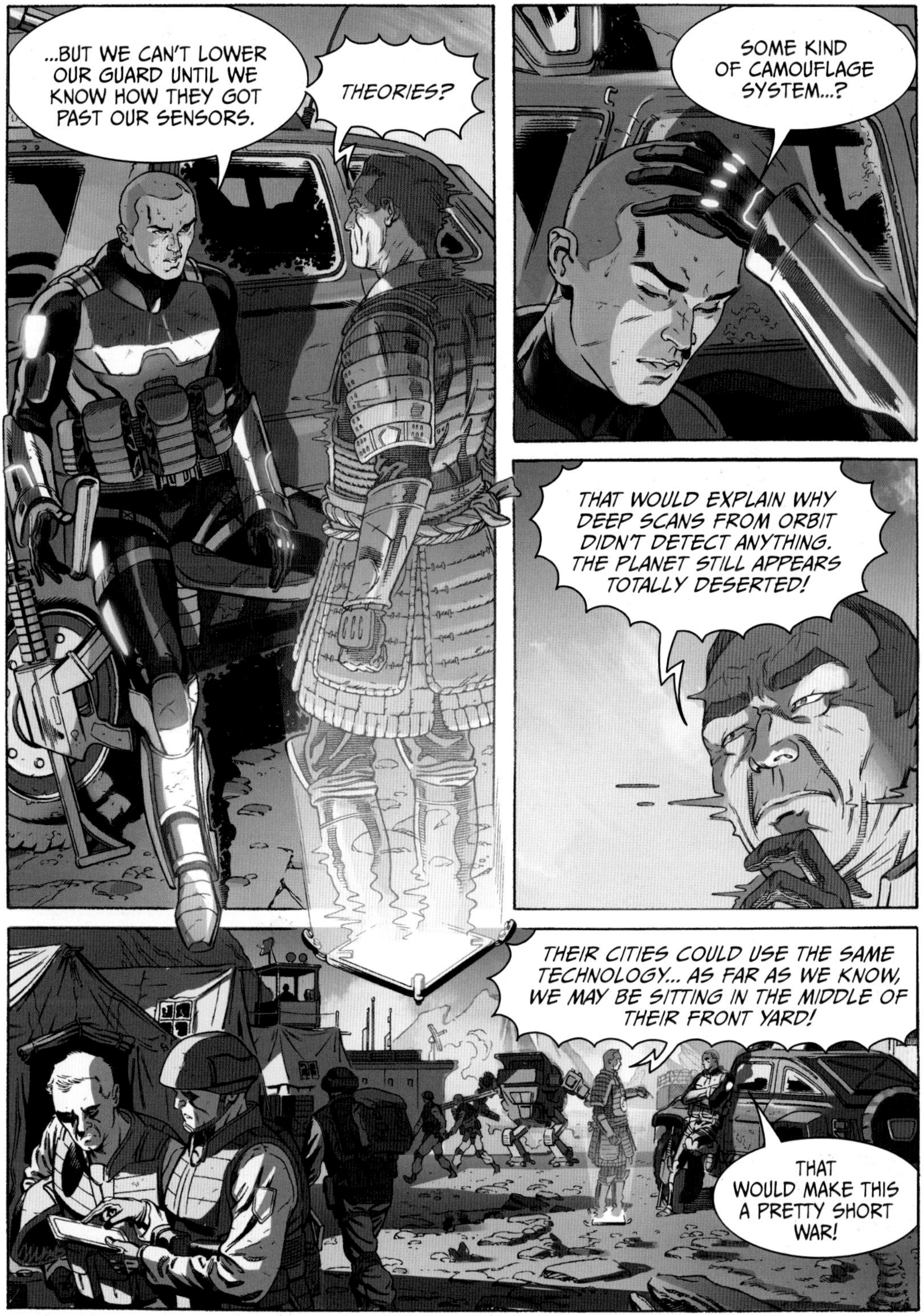
...BUT WE CAN'T LOWER OUR GUARD UNTIL WE KNOW HOW THEY GOT PAST OUR SENSORS.
THEORIES?
SOME KIND OF CAMOUFLAGE SYSTEM...?
THAT WOULD EXPLAIN WHY DEEP SCANS FROM ORBIT DIDN'T DETECT ANYTHING. THE PLANET STILL APPEARS TOTALLY DESERTED!
THEIR CITIES COULD USE THE SAME TECHNOLOGY... AS FAR AS WE KNOW, WE MAY BE SITTING IN THE MIDDLE OF THEIR FRONT YARD!
THAT WOULD MAKE THIS A PRETTY SHORT WAR!

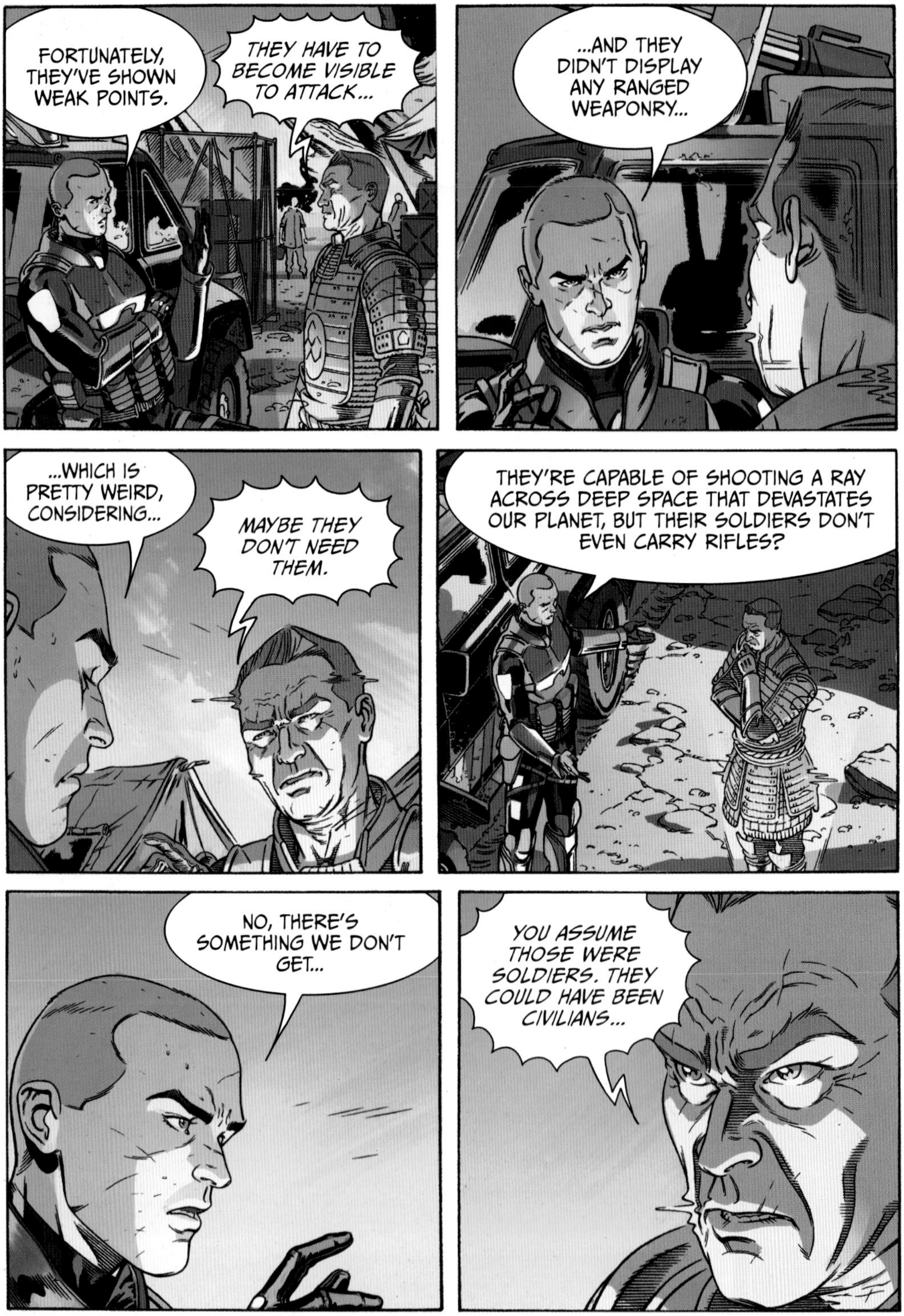
FORTUNATELY, THEY'VE SHOWN WEAK POINTS.
THEY HAVE TO BECOME VISIBLE TO ATTACK...
...AND THEY DIDN'T DISPLAY ANY RANGED WEAPONRY...
...WHICH IS PRETTY WEIRD, CONSIDERING...
MAYBE THEY DON'T NEED THEM.
THEY'RE CAPABLE OF SHOOTING A RAY ACROSS DEEP SPACE THAT DEVASTATES OUR PLANET, BUT THEIR SOLDIERS DON'T EVEN CARRY RIFLES?
NO, THERE'S SOMETHING WE DON'T GET...
YOU ASSUME THOSE WERE SOLDIERS. THEY COULD HAVE BEEN CIVILIANS...

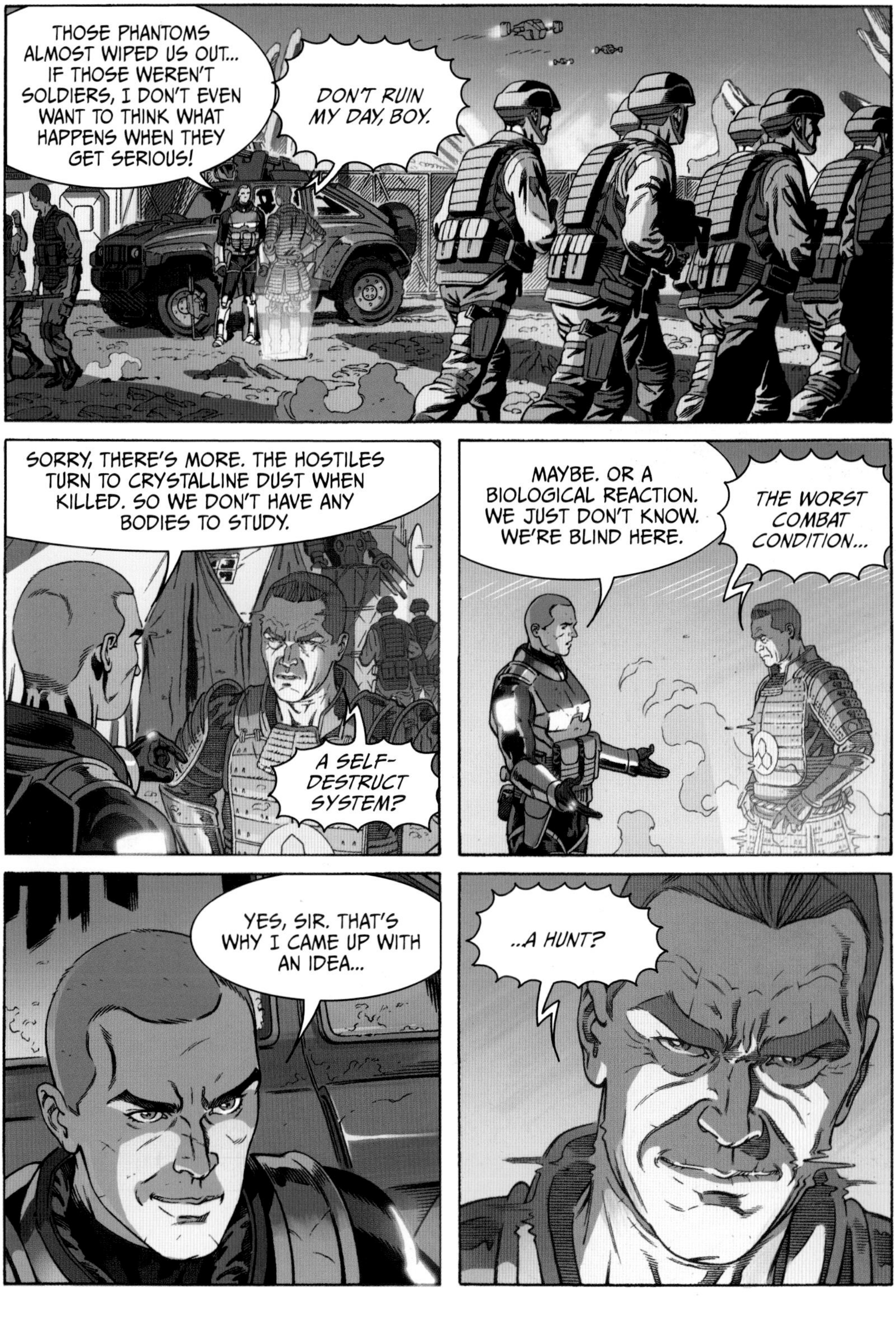
THOSE PHANTOMS ALMOST WIPED US OUT... IF THOSE WEREN'T SOLDIERS, I DON'T EVEN WANT TO THINK WHAT HAPPENS WHEN THEY GET SERIOUS!
DON'T RUIN MY DAY, BOY.
SORRY, THERE'S MORE. THE HOSTILES TURN TO CRYSTALLINE DUST WHEN KILLED. SO WE DON'T HAVE ANY BODIES TO STUDY.
A SELF-DESTRUCT SYSTEM?
MAYBE. OR A BIOLOGICAL REACTION. WE JUST DON'T KNOW. WE'RE BLIND HERE.
THE WORST COMBAT CONDITION...
YES, SIR. THAT'S WHY I CAME UP WITH AN IDEA...
..A HUNT?

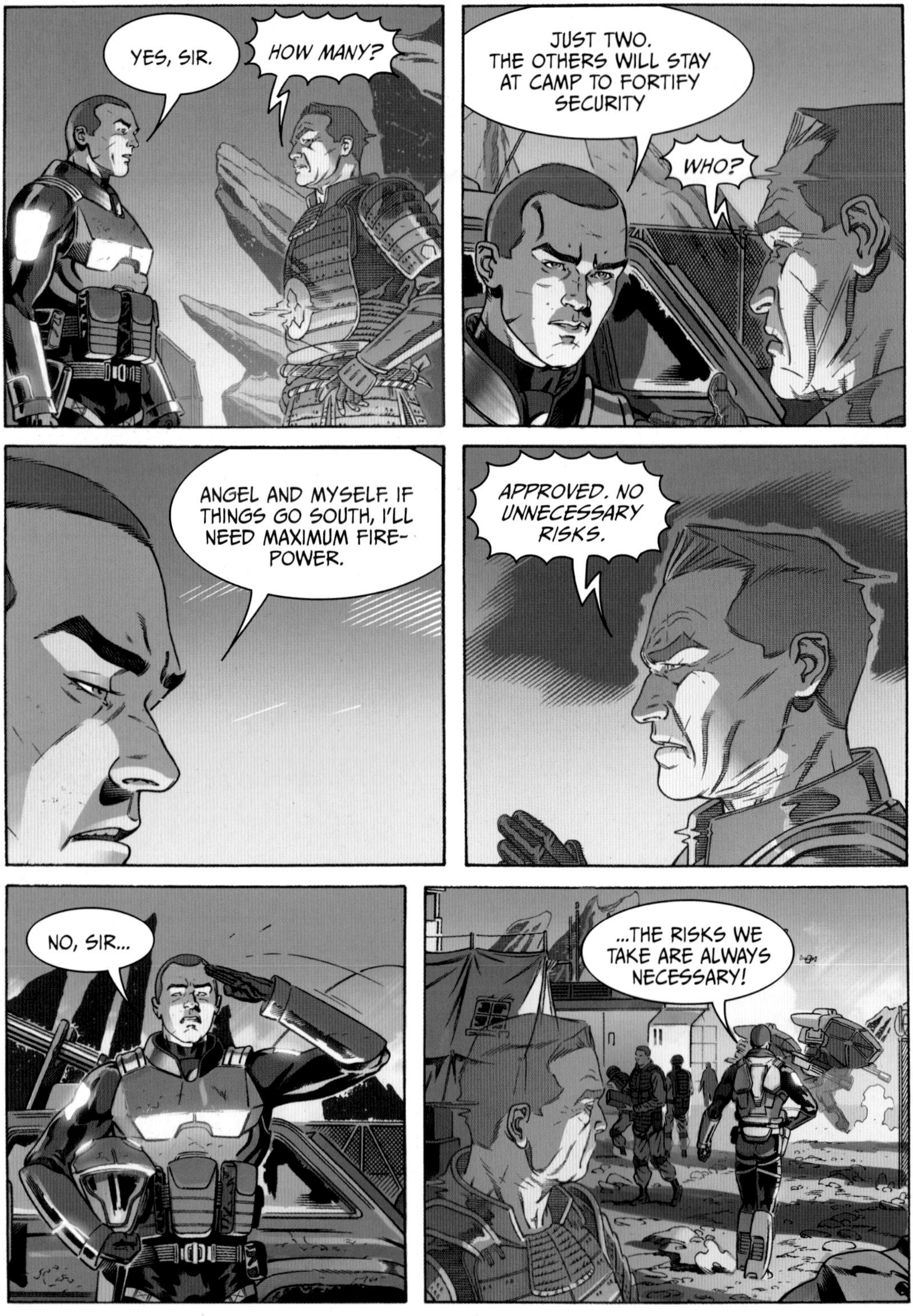
YES, SIR.
HOW MANY?
JUST TWO. THE OTHERS WILL STAY AT CAMP TO FORTIFY SECURITY
WHO?
ANGEL AND MYSELF. IF THINGS GO SOUTH, I'LL NEED MAXIMUM FIRE-POWER.
APPROVED. NO UNNECESSARY RISKS.
NO, SIR...
...THE RISKS WE TAKE ARE ALWAYS NECESSARY!

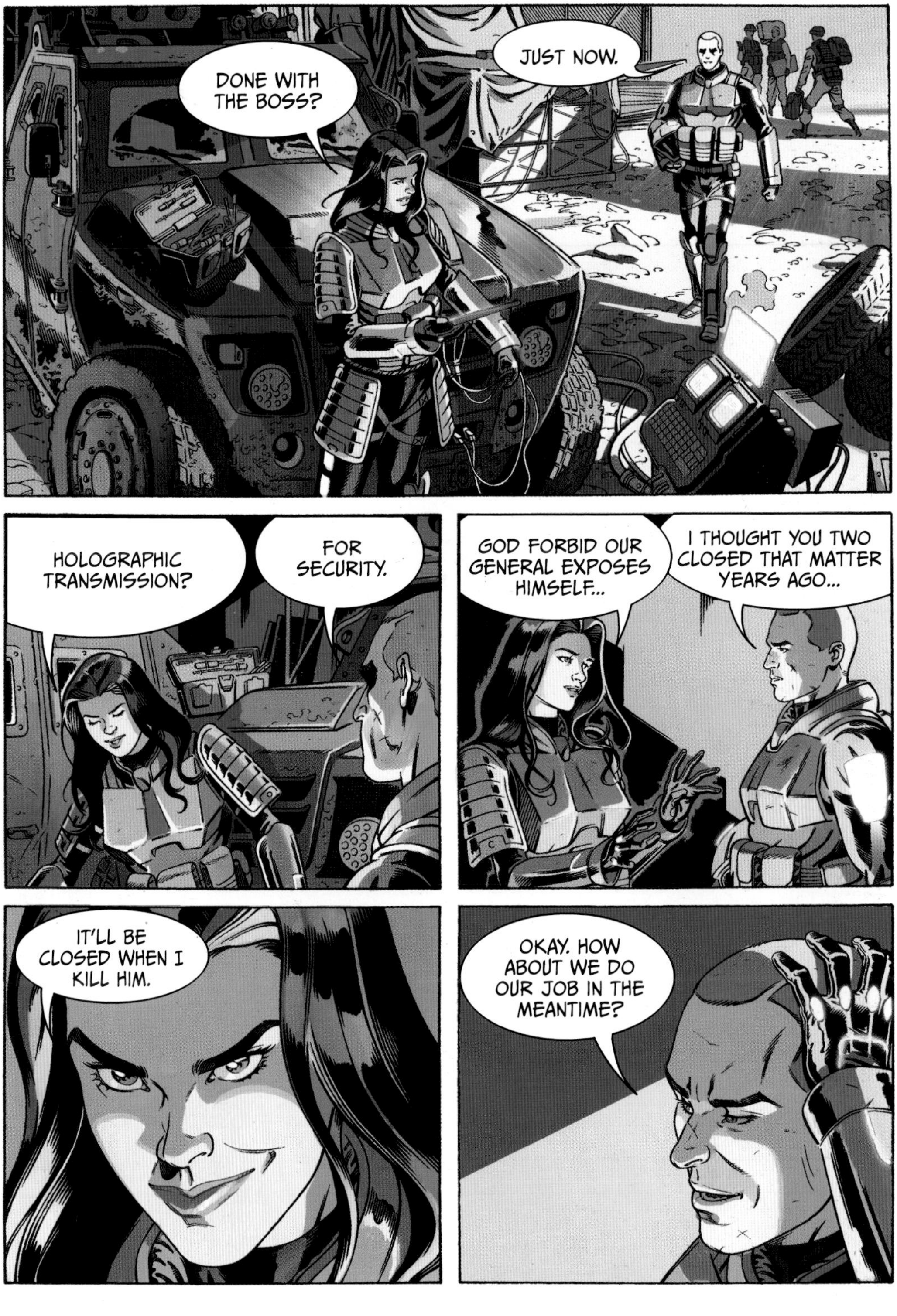
DONE WITH THE BOSS?
JUST NOW.
HOLOGRAPHIC TRANSMISSION?
FOR SECURITY.
GOD FORBID OUR GENERAL EXPOSES HIMSELF...
I THOUGHT YOU TWO CLOSED THAT MATTER YEARS AGO...
IT'LL BE CLOSED WHEN I KILL HIM.
OKAY. HOW ABOUT WE DO OUR JOB IN THE MEANTIME?

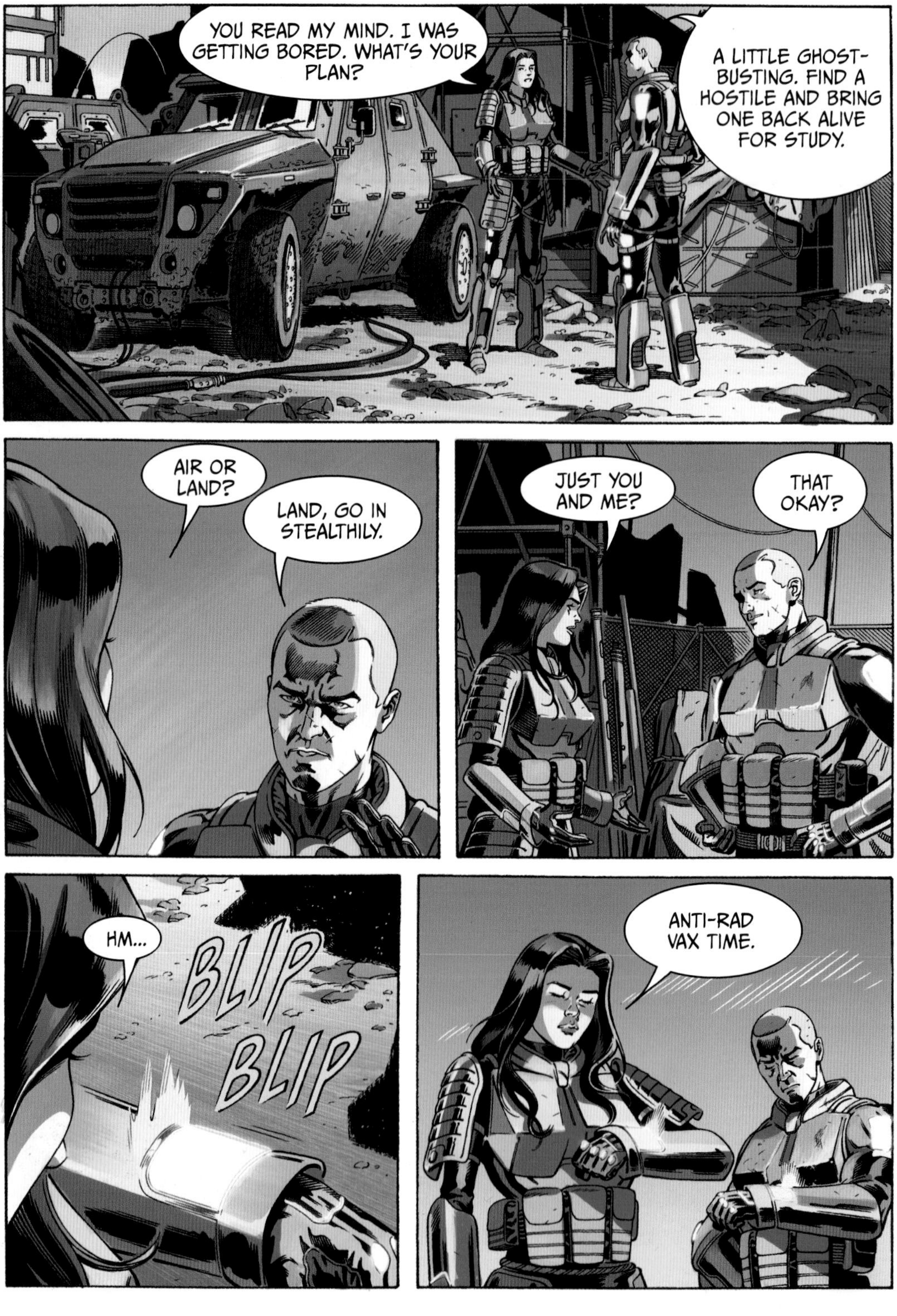
YOU READ MY MIND. I WAS GETTING BORED. WHAT'S YOUR PLAN?
A LITTLE GHOST-BUSTING. FIND A HOSTILE AND BRING ONE BACK ALIVE FOR STUDY.
AIR OR LAND?
LAND, GO IN STEALTHILY.
JUST YOU AND ME?
THAT OKAY?
HM...
BLIP BLIP
ANTI-RAD VAX TIME.

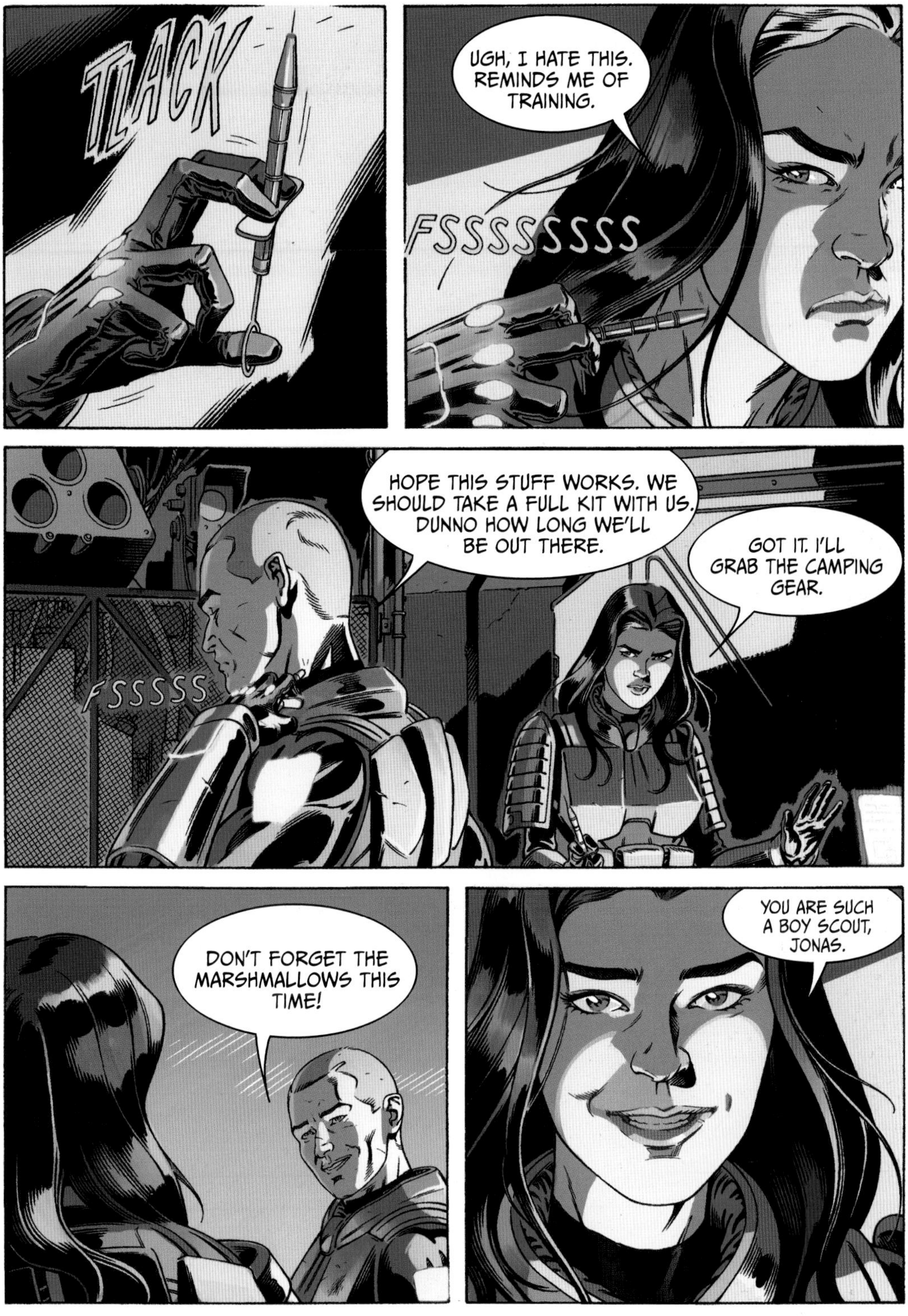
TLACK
UGH, I HATE THIS. REMINDS ME OF TRAINING.
FSSSSSSSS
HOPE THIS STUFF WORKS. WE SHOULD TAKE A FULL KIT WITH US. DUNNO HOW LONG WE'LL BE OUT THERE.
FSSSSS
GOT IT. I'LL GRAB THE CAMPING GEAR.
DON'T FORGET THE MARSHMALLOWS THIS TIME!
YOU ARE SUCH A BOY SCOUT, JONAS.

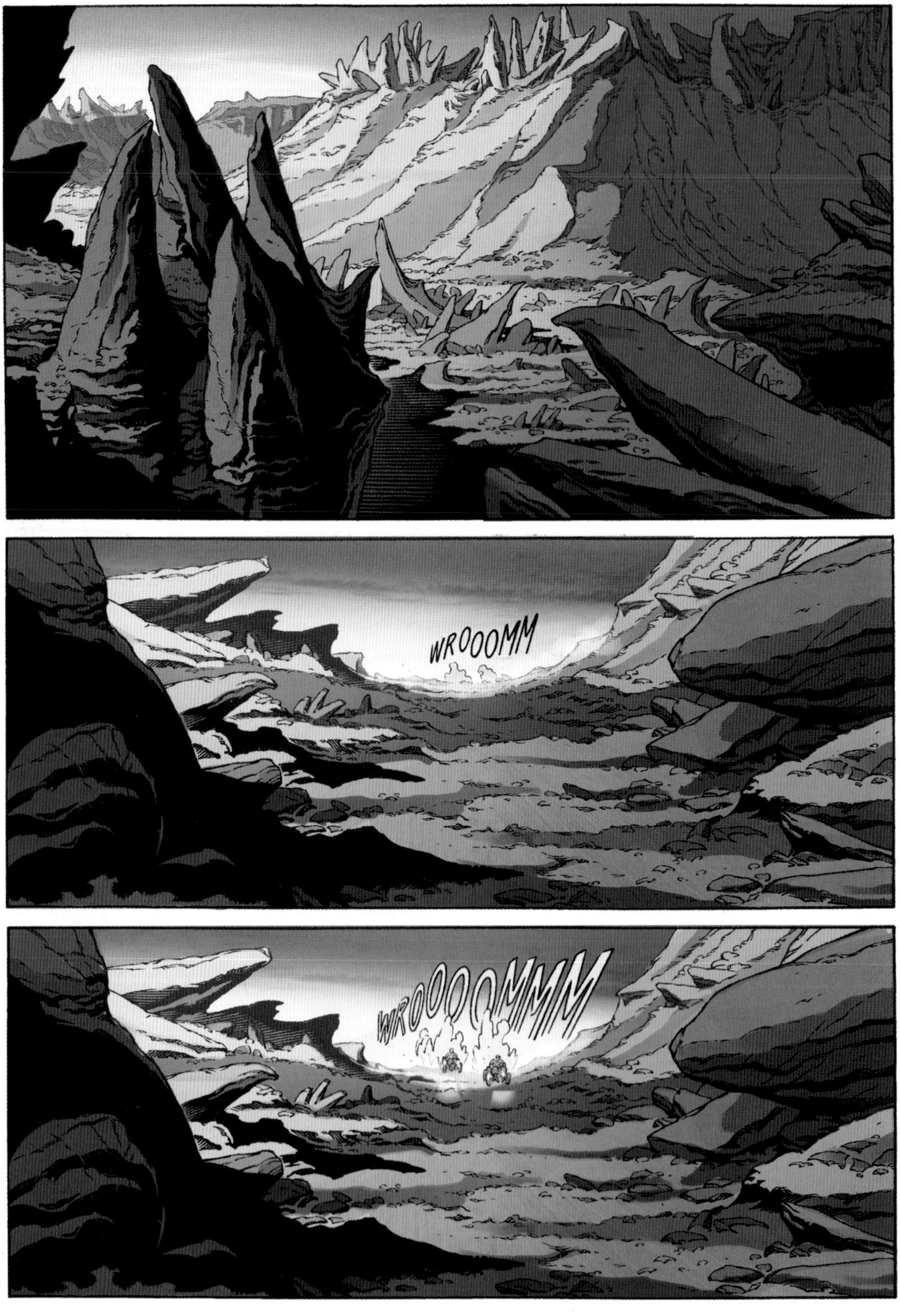
WROOOMM
WROOOOMMM

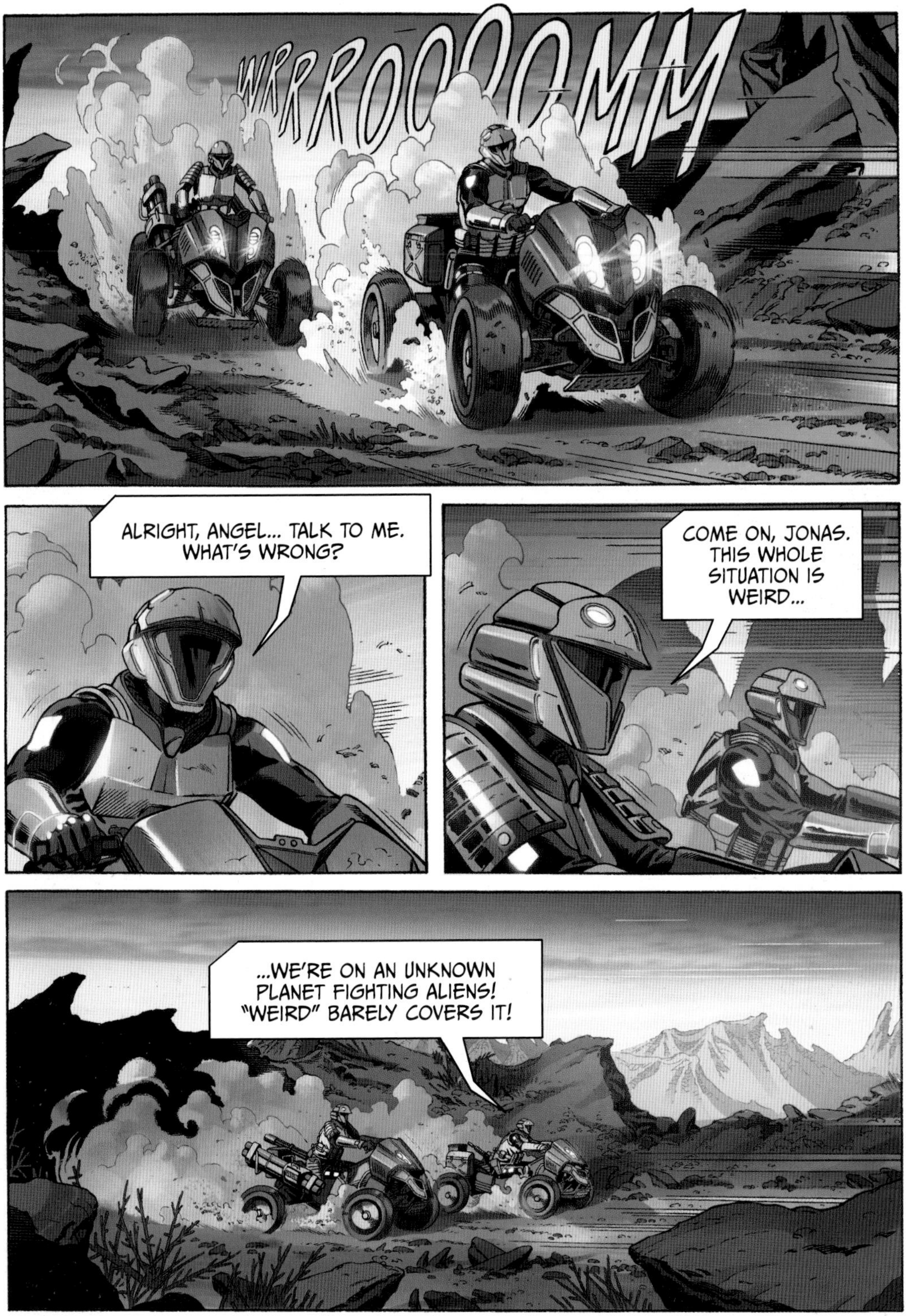
WRRROOOOOMM
ALRIGHT, ANGEL... TALK TO ME. WHAT'S WRONG?
COME ON, JONAS. THIS WHOLE SITUATION IS WEIRD...
...WE'RE ON AN UNKNOWN PLANET FIGHTING ALIENS! "WEIRD" BARELY COVERS IT!

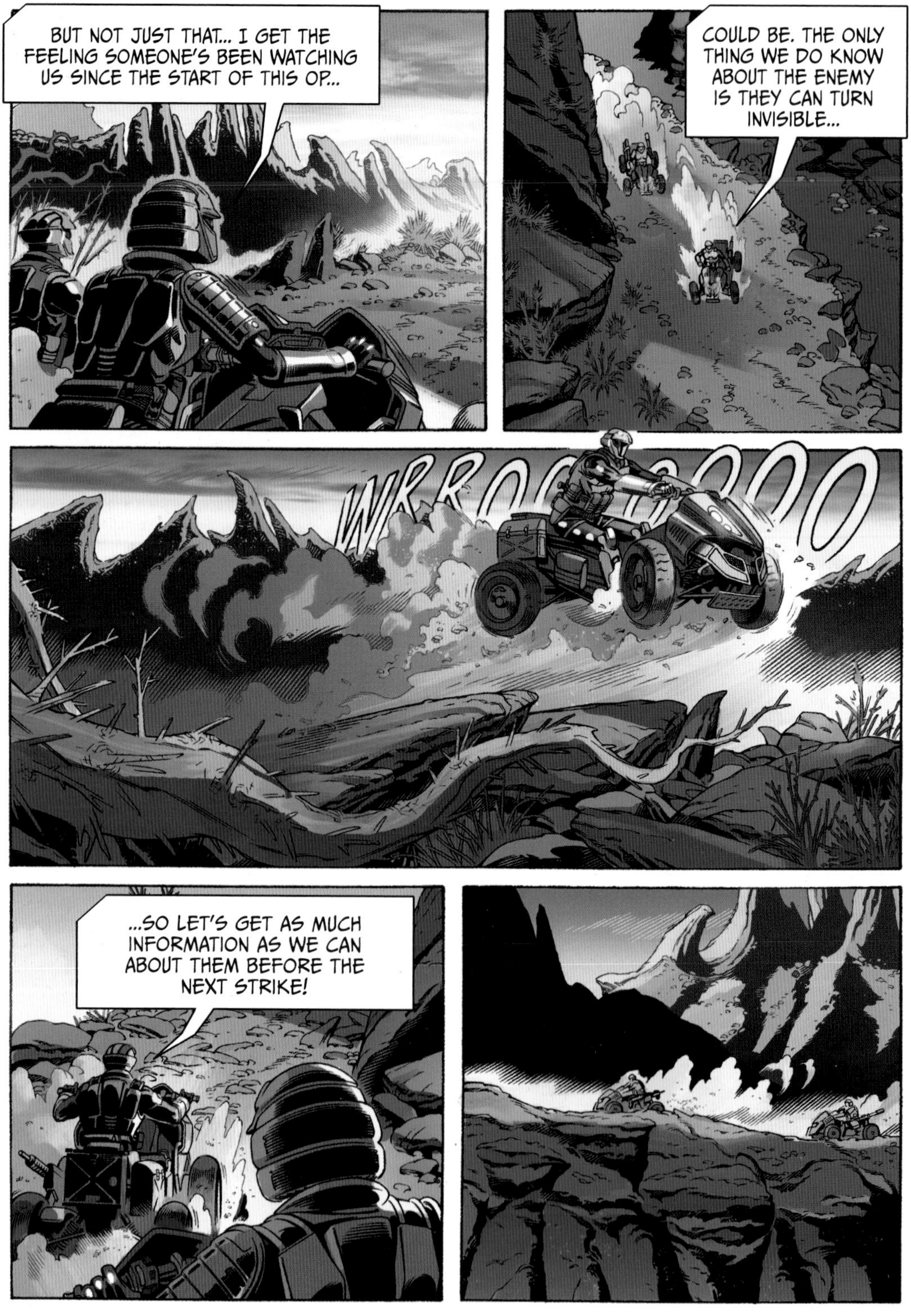
BUT NOT JUST THAT... I GET THE FEELING SOMEONE'S BEEN WATCHING US SINCE THE START OF THIS OP...
COULD BE. THE ONLY THING WE DO KNOW ABOUT THE ENEMY IS THEY CAN TURN INVISIBLE...
...SO LET'S GET AS MUCH INFORMATION AS WE CAN ABOUT THEM BEFORE THE NEXT STRIKE!

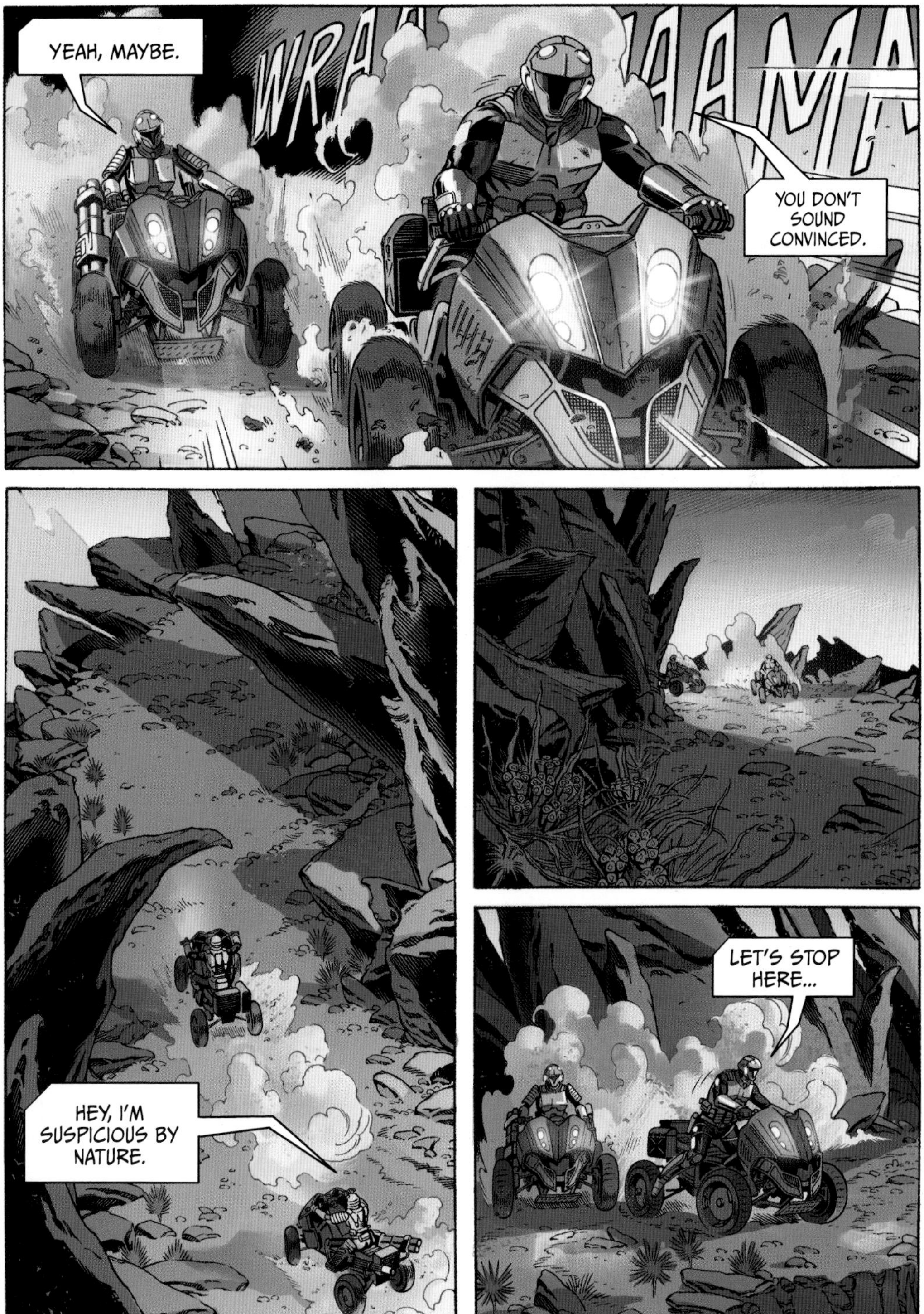
YEAH, MAYBE.
WRAAAAAMM
YOU DON'T SOUND CONVINCED.
HEY, I'M SUSPICIOUS BY NATURE.
LET'S STOP HERE...

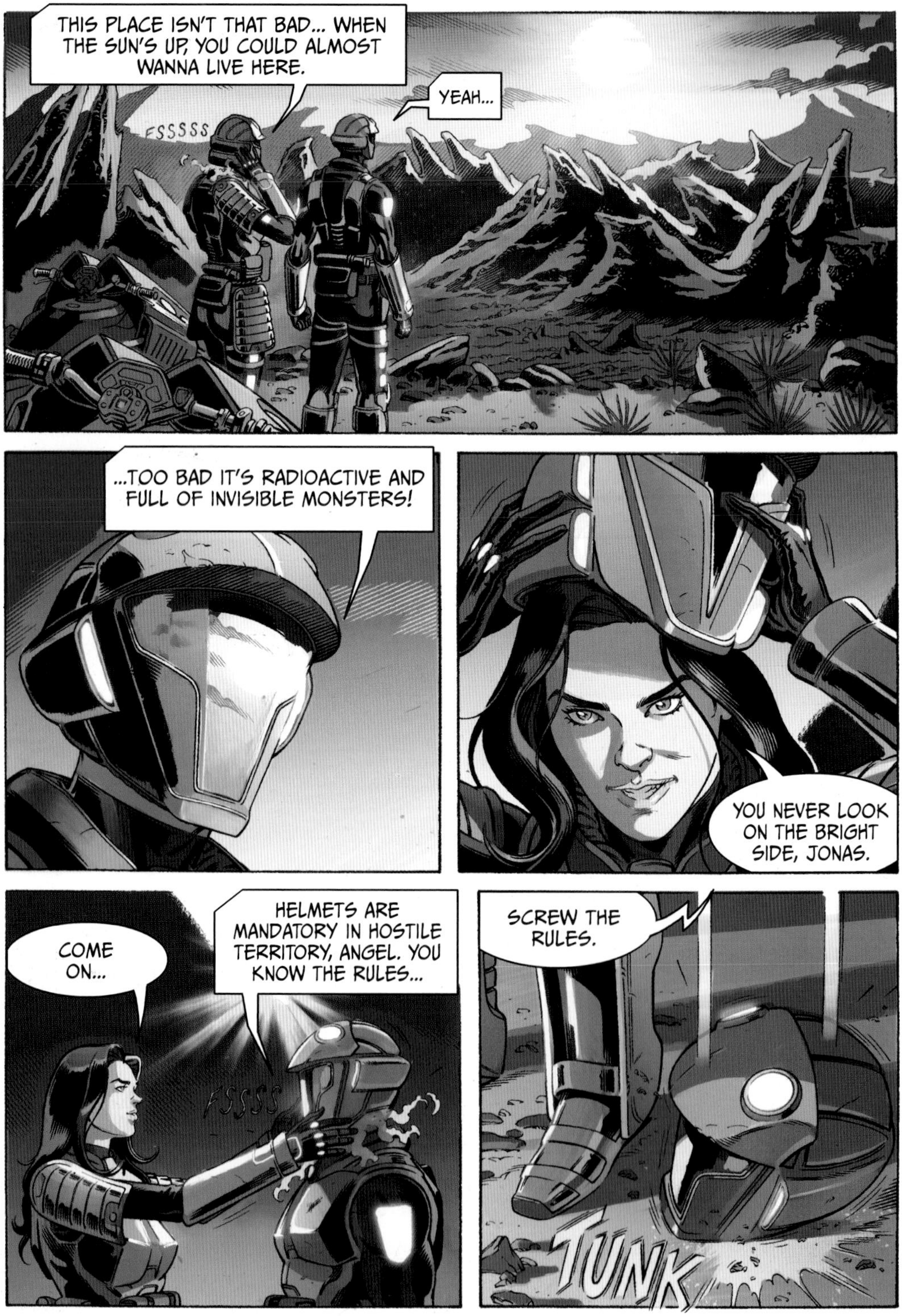

THIS PLACE ISN'T THAT BAD... WHEN THE SUN'S UP, YOU COULD ALMOST WANNA LIVE HERE.
YEAH...
FSSSSS
...TOO BAD IT'S RADIOACTIVE AND FULL OF INVISIBLE MONSTERS!
YOU NEVER LOOK ON THE BRIGHT SIDE, JONAS.
COME ON...
HELMETS ARE MANDATORY IN HOSTILE TERRITORY, ANGEL. YOU KNOW THE RULES...
FSSSS
SCREW THE RULES.
TUNK

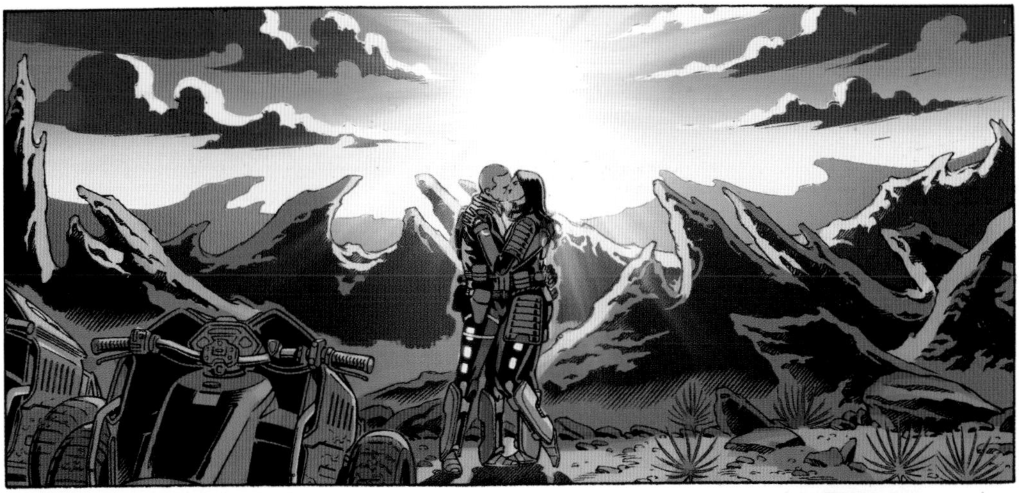

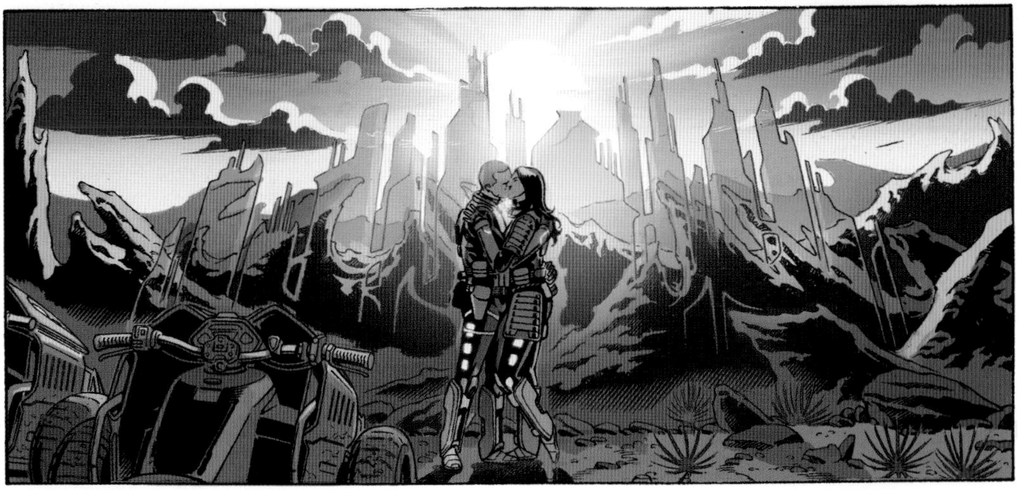

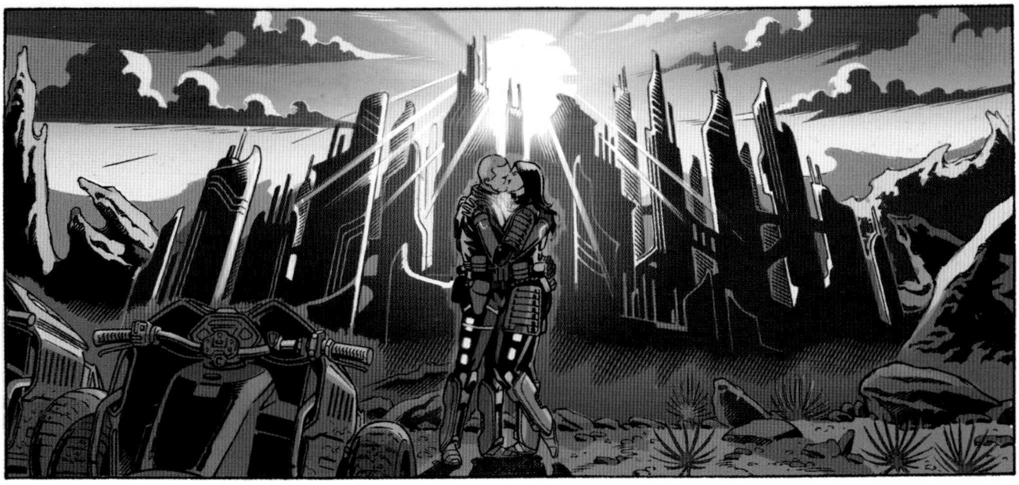

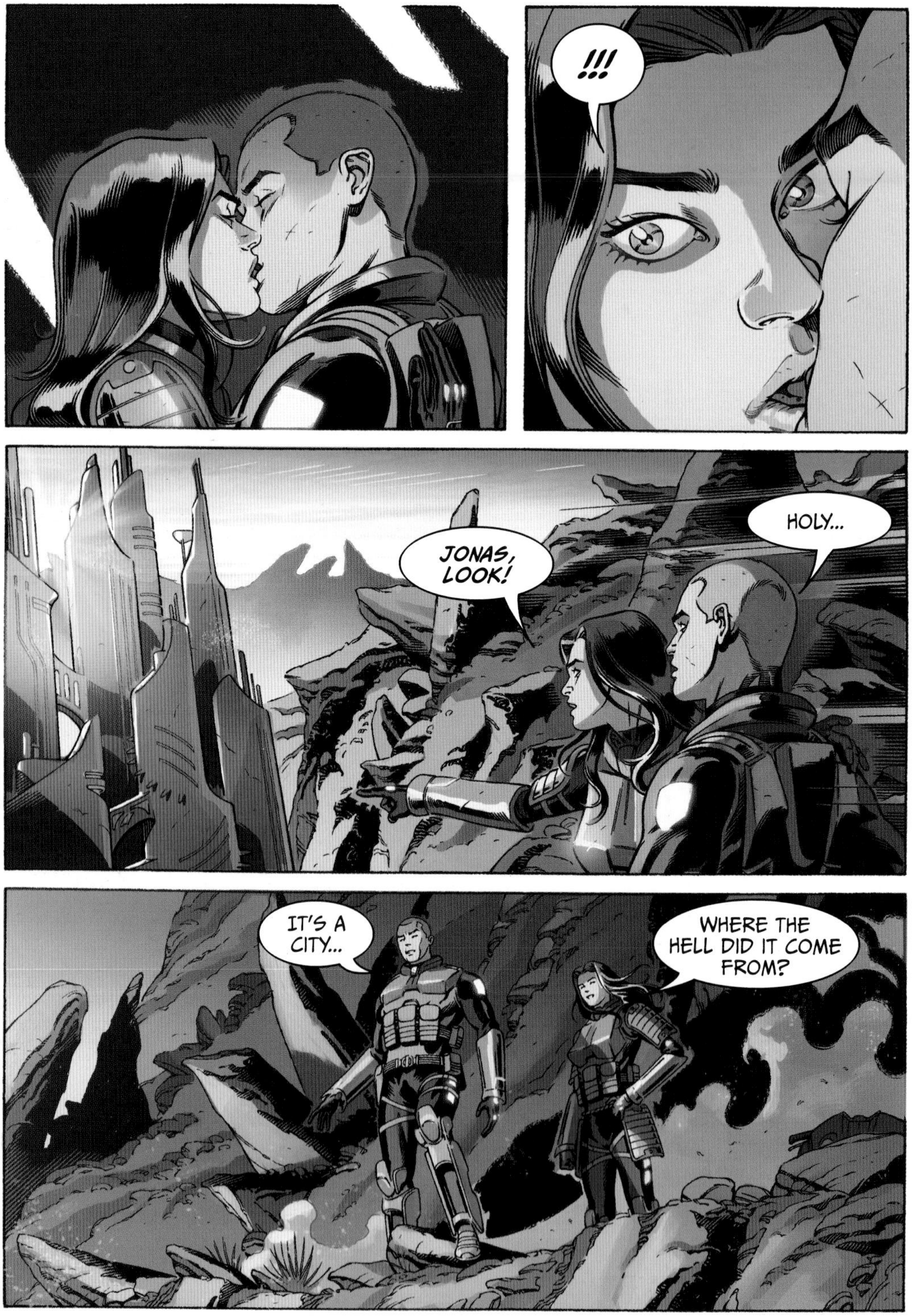
!!!
JONAS, LOOK!
HOLY...
IT'S A CITY...
WHERE THE HELL DID IT COME FROM?

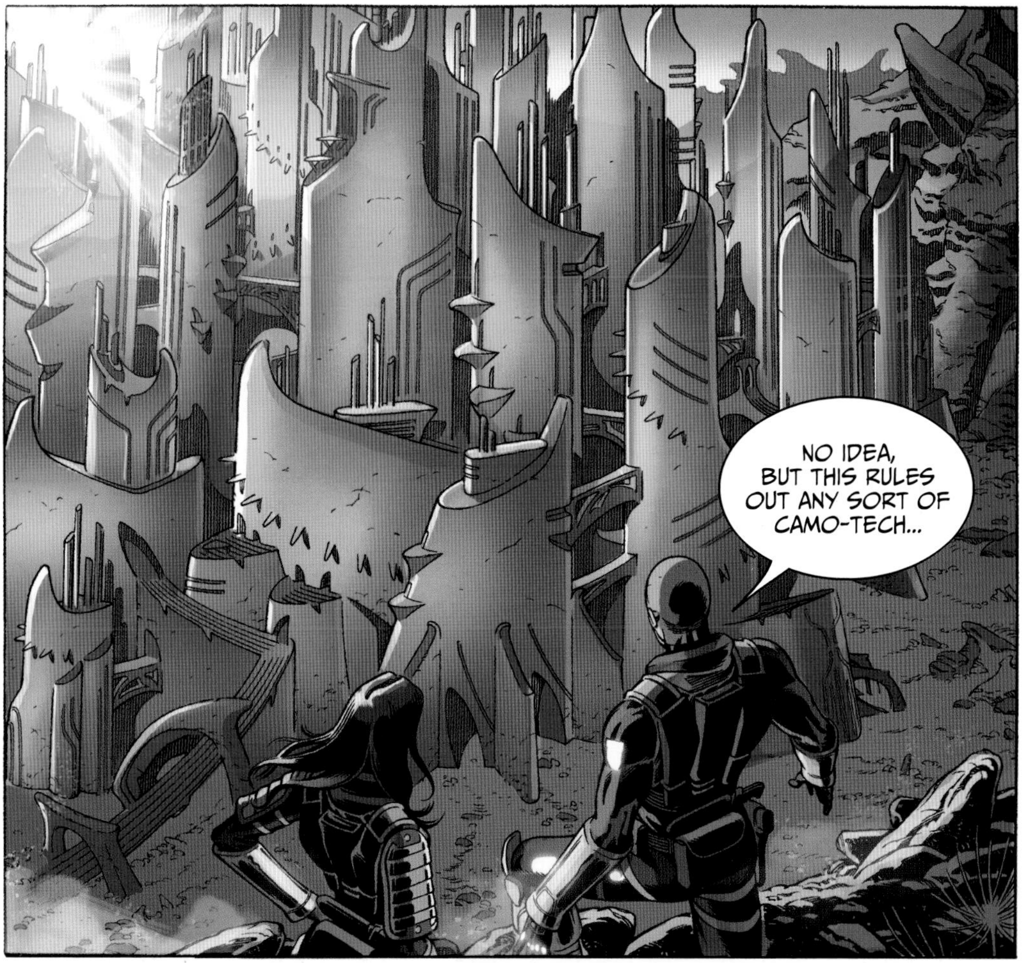
NO IDEA, BUT THIS RULES OUT ANY SORT OF CAMO-TECH...

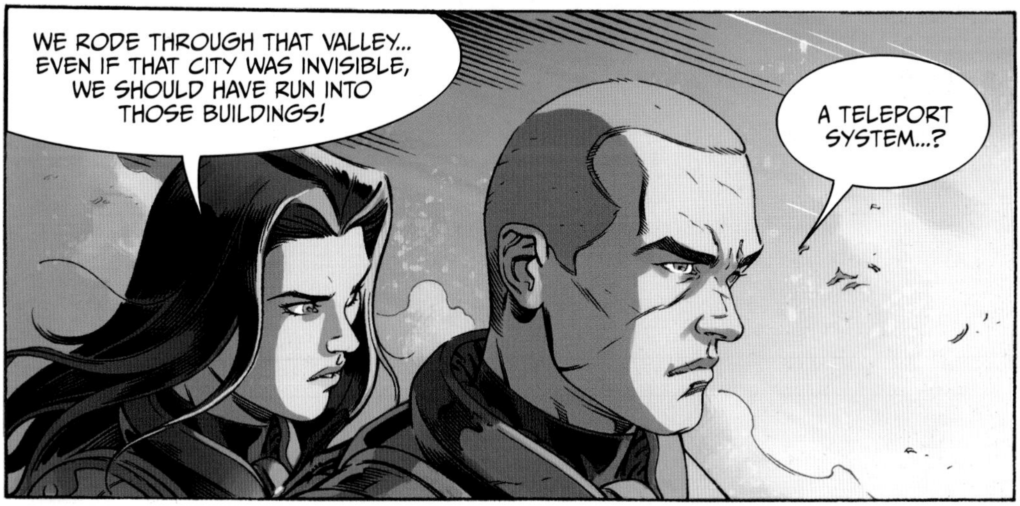
WE RODE THROUGH THAT VALLEY... EVEN IF THAT CITY WAS INVISIBLE, WE SHOULD HAVE RUN INTO THOSE BUILDINGS!
A TELEPORT SYSTEM...?

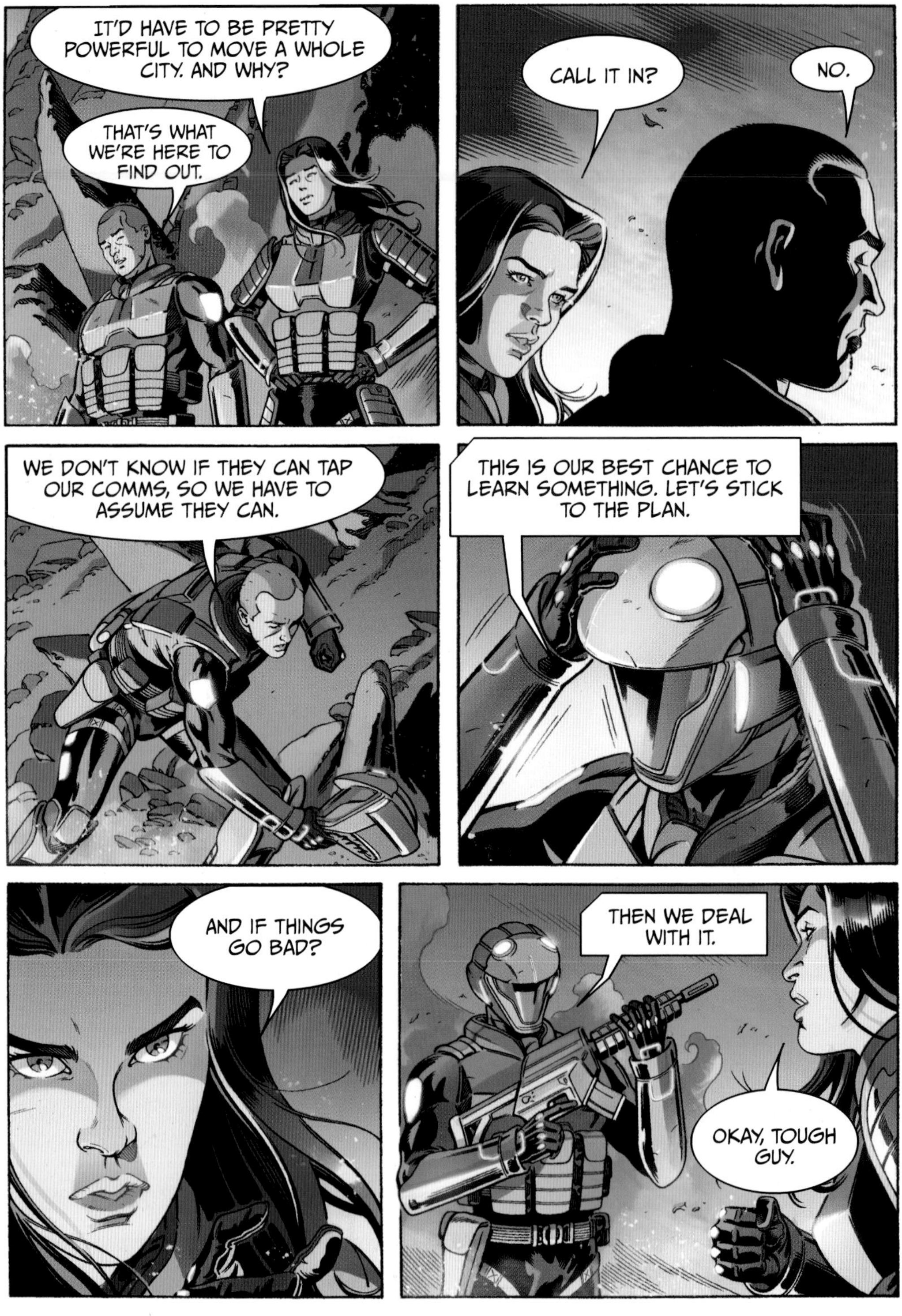
IT'D HAVE TO BE PRETTY POWERFUL TO MOVE A WHOLE CITY. AND WHY?
THAT'S WHAT WE'RE HERE TO FIND OUT.
CALL IT IN?
NO.
WE DON'T KNOW IF THEY CAN TAP OUR COMMS, SO WE HAVE TO ASSUME THEY CAN.
THIS IS OUR BEST CHANCE TO LEARN SOMETHING. LET'S STICK TO THE PLAN.
AND IF THINGS GO BAD?
THEN WE DEAL WITH IT.
OKAY, TOUGH GUY.

THIS IS AN INFILTRATION MISSION -- GET IN, GRAB A HOSTILE, GET OUT, QUICK AND QUIET. GOT IT?

WHO ARE YOU TALKING TO?

A STONE-COLD KILLER.

FLATTERY... BUT IF YOU WANTED SUBTLE, YOU PROBABLY SHOULD HAVE PICKED SOMEONE ELSE.

I FEEL SAFER WITH YOU.

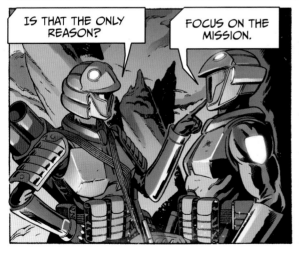

IS THAT THE ONLY REASON?

FOCUS ON THE MISSION.

YES, SIR!

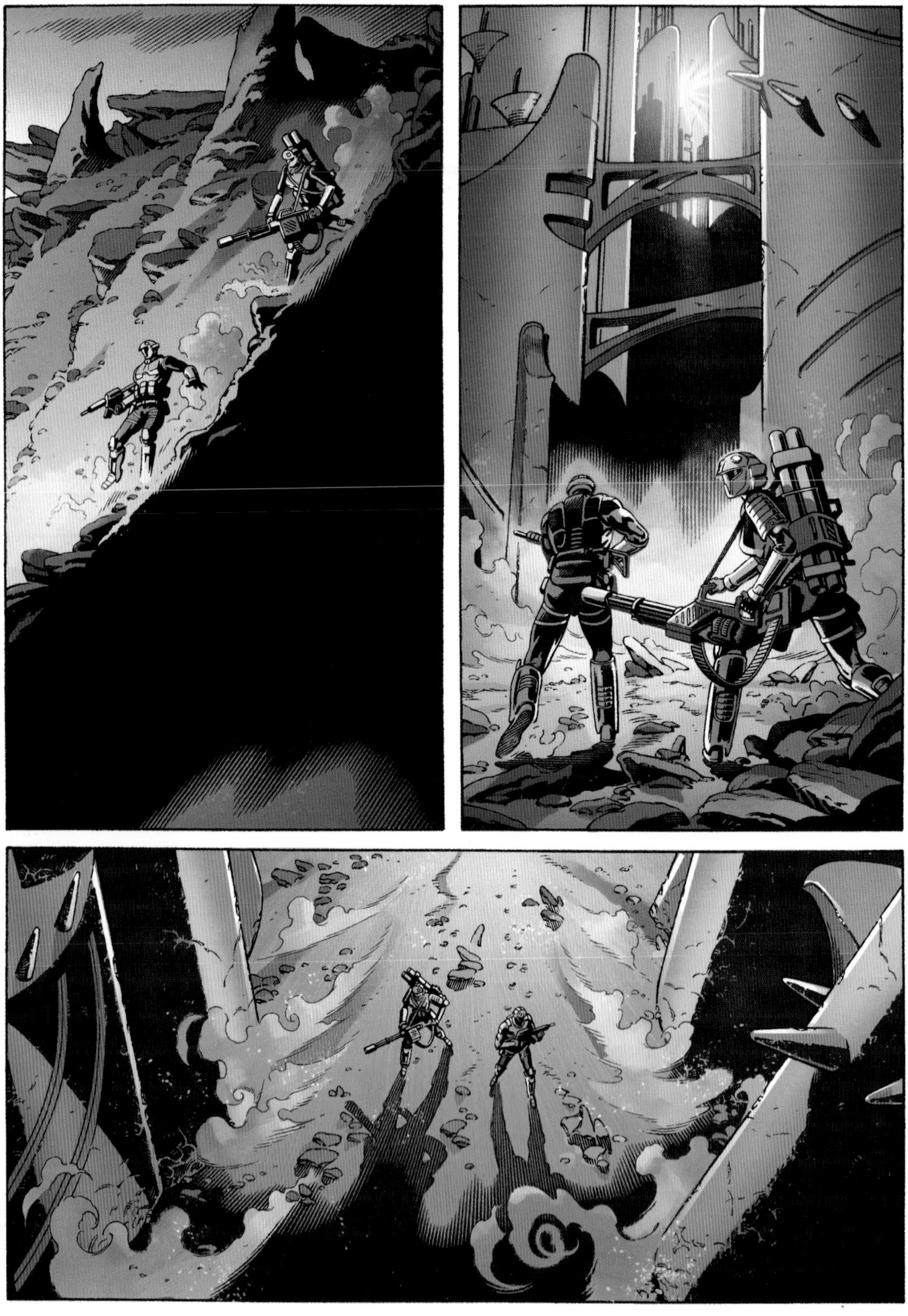

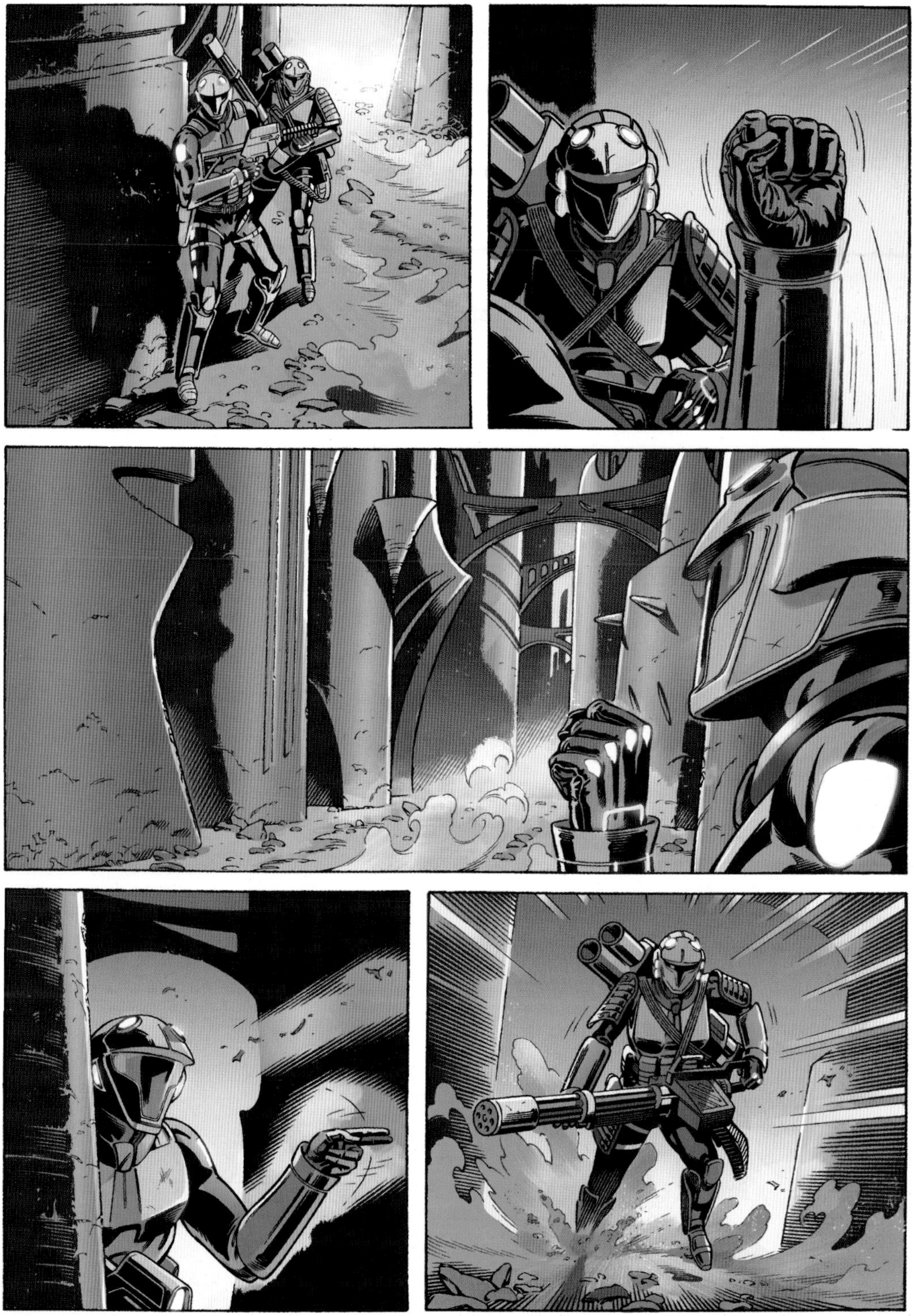

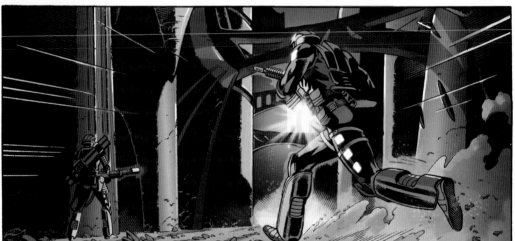

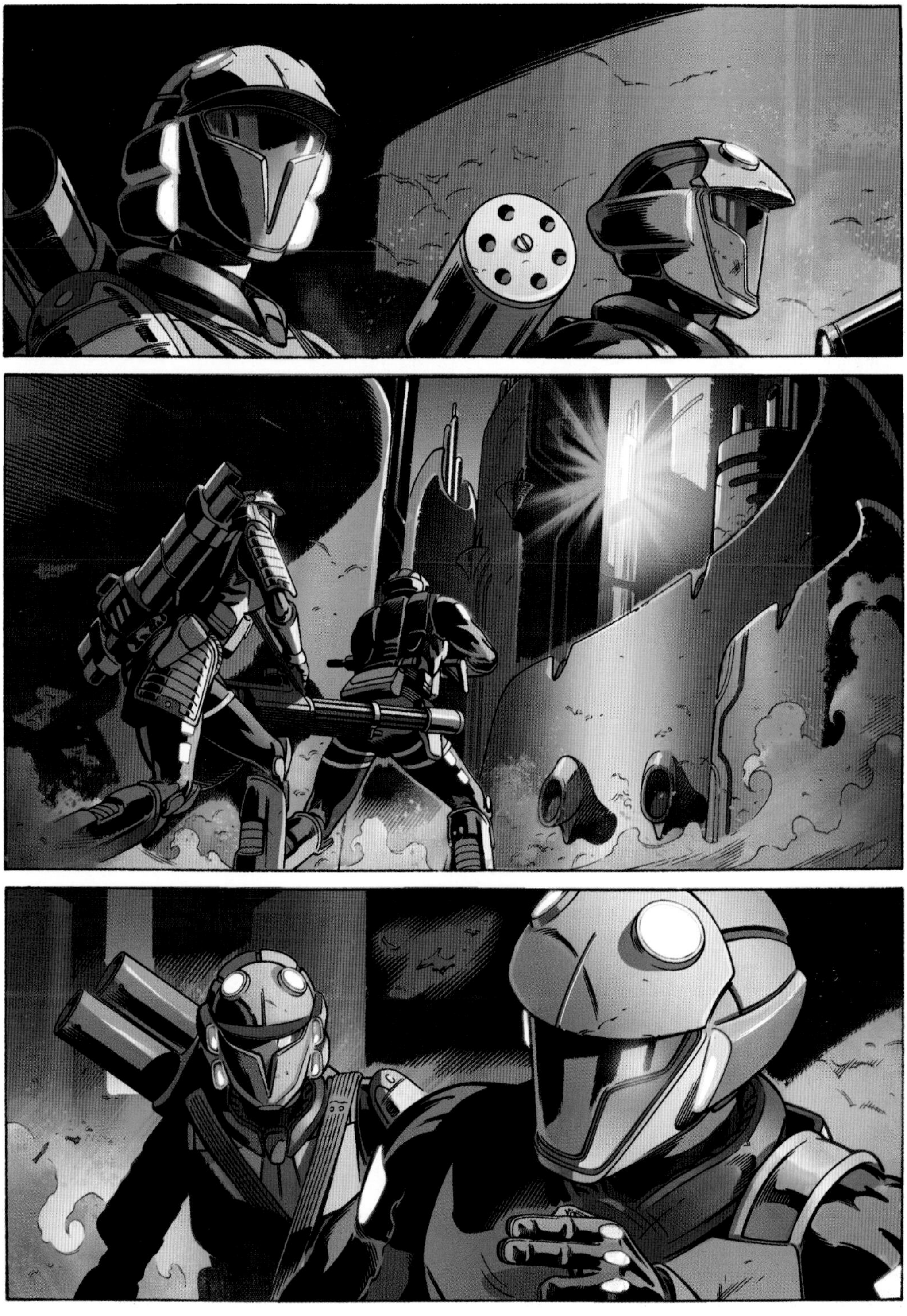

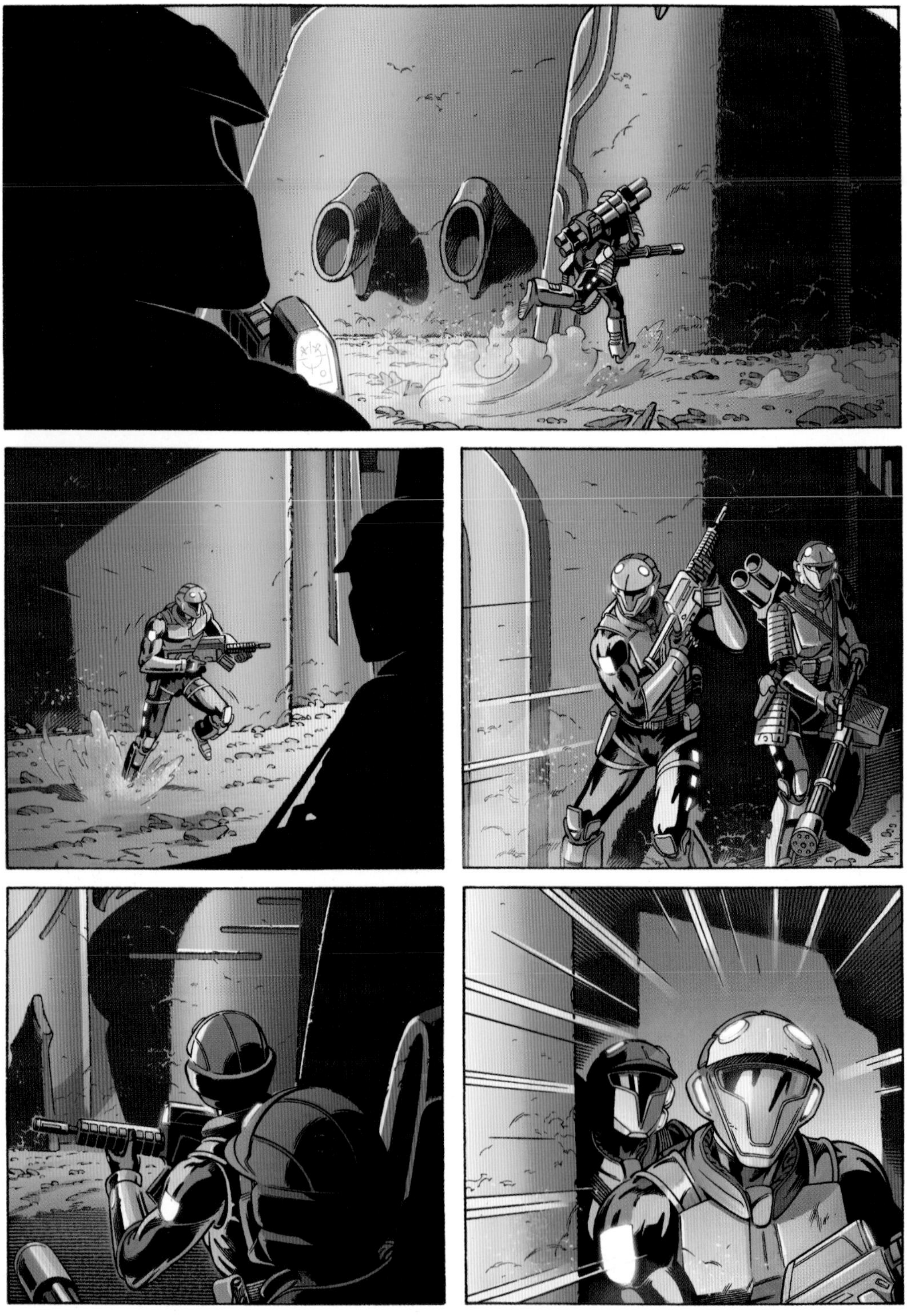

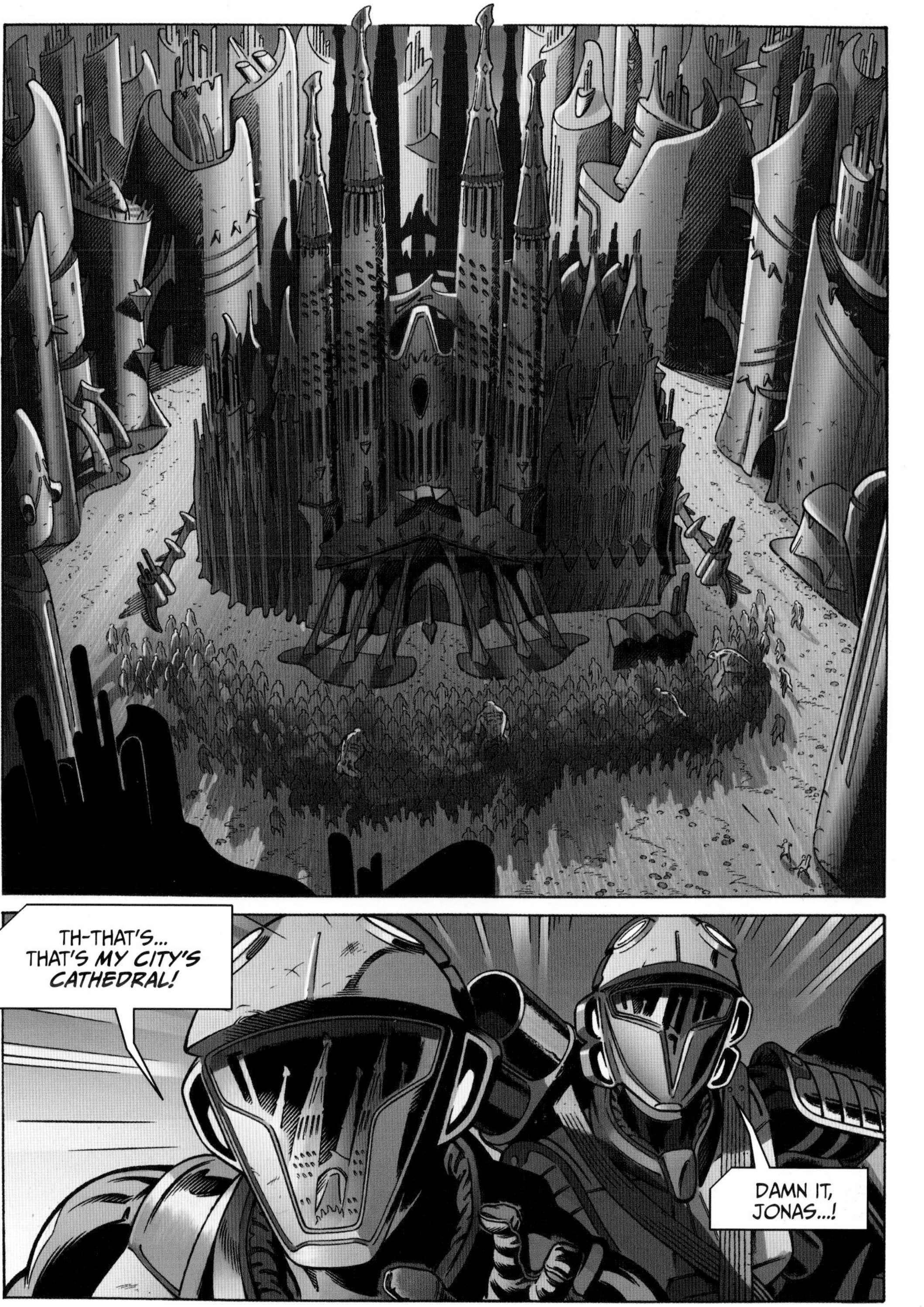
TH-THAT'S... THAT'S *MY CITY'S CATHEDRAL!*
DAMN IT, JONAS...!

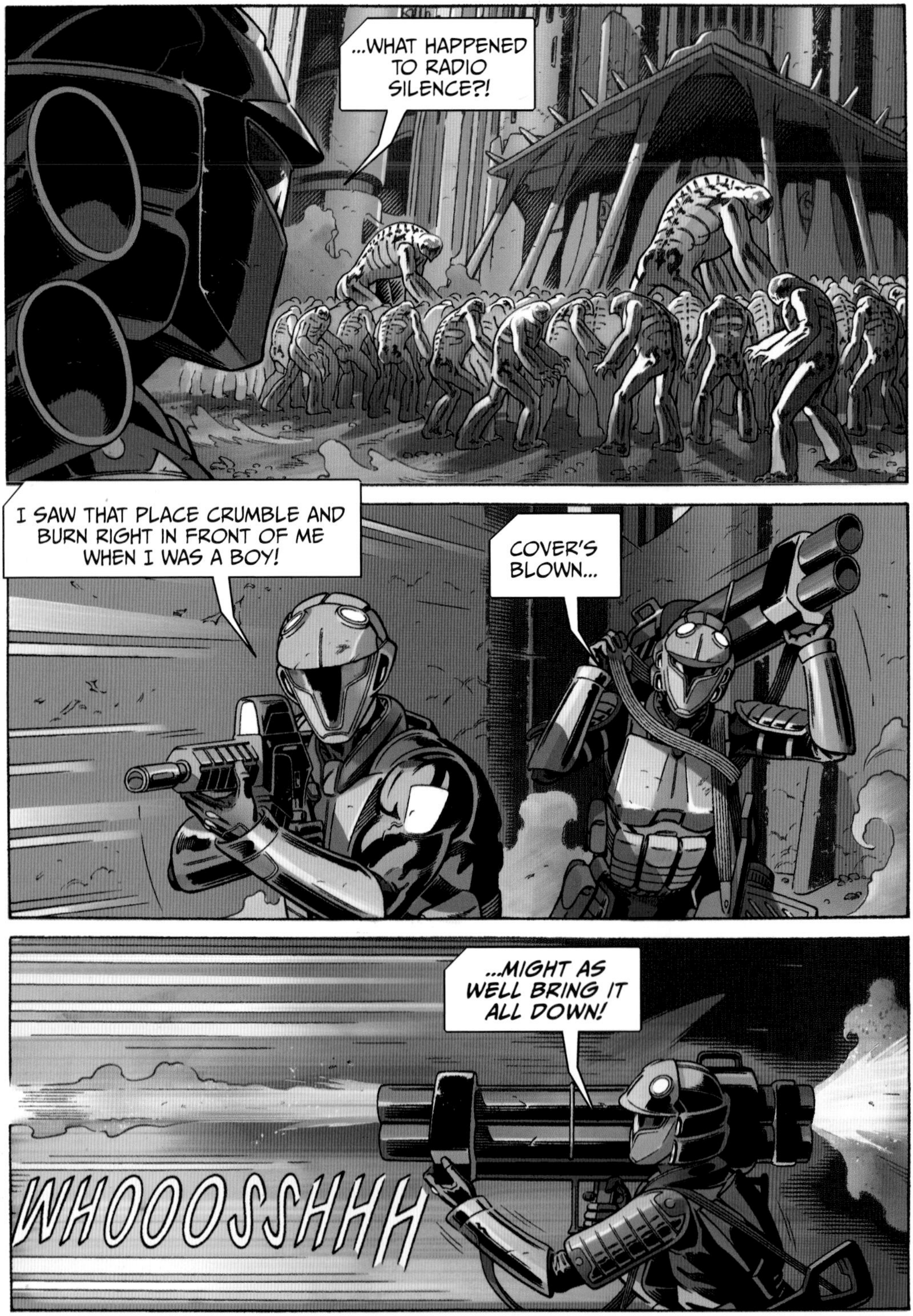
...WHAT HAPPENED TO RADIO SILENCE?!
I SAW THAT PLACE CRUMBLE AND BURN RIGHT IN FRONT OF ME WHEN I WAS A BOY!
COVER'S BLOWN...
...MIGHT AS WELL BRING IT ALL DOWN!
WHOOOSHHH

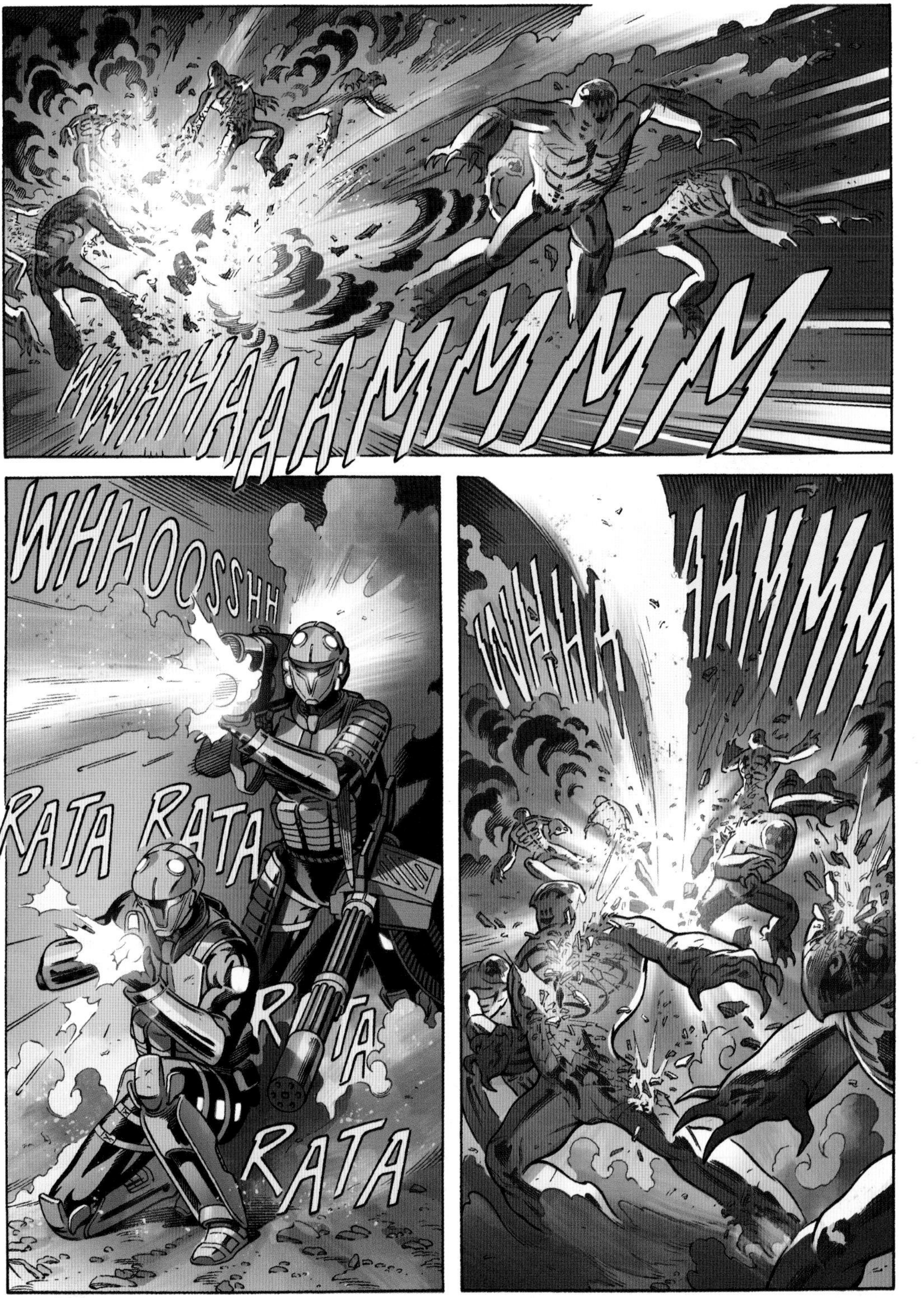
WWHHAAAMMMMM
WHHOOSSHH
RATA RATA
RATA
RATA
WHHAAAMMM

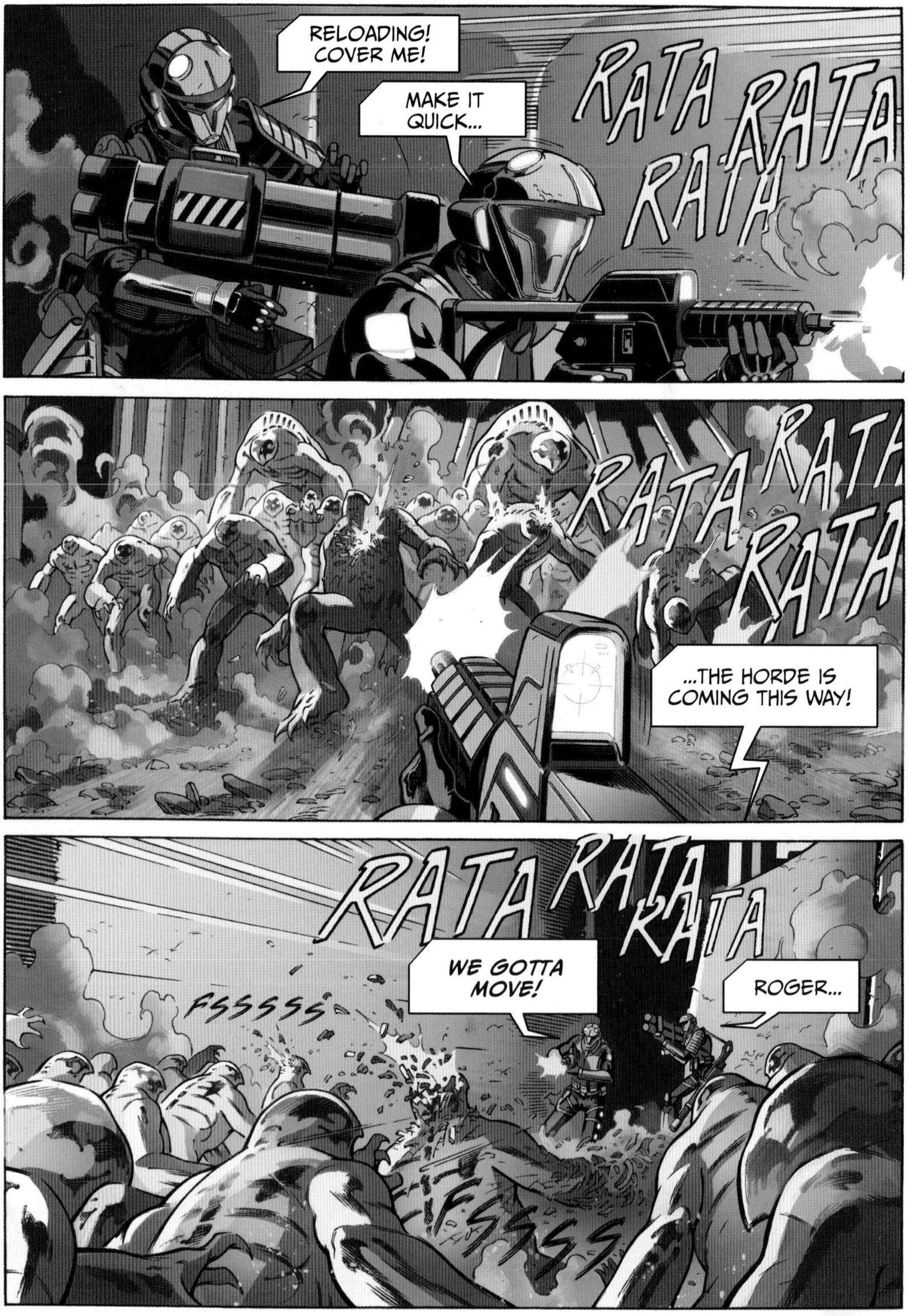
RELOADING! COVER ME!
MAKE IT QUICK...
RATA RATA RATA RATA
RATA RATA RATA RATA
...THE HORDE IS COMING THIS WAY!
RATA RATA RATA RATA
WE GOTTA MOVE!
ROGER...
FSSSSS
FSSSS

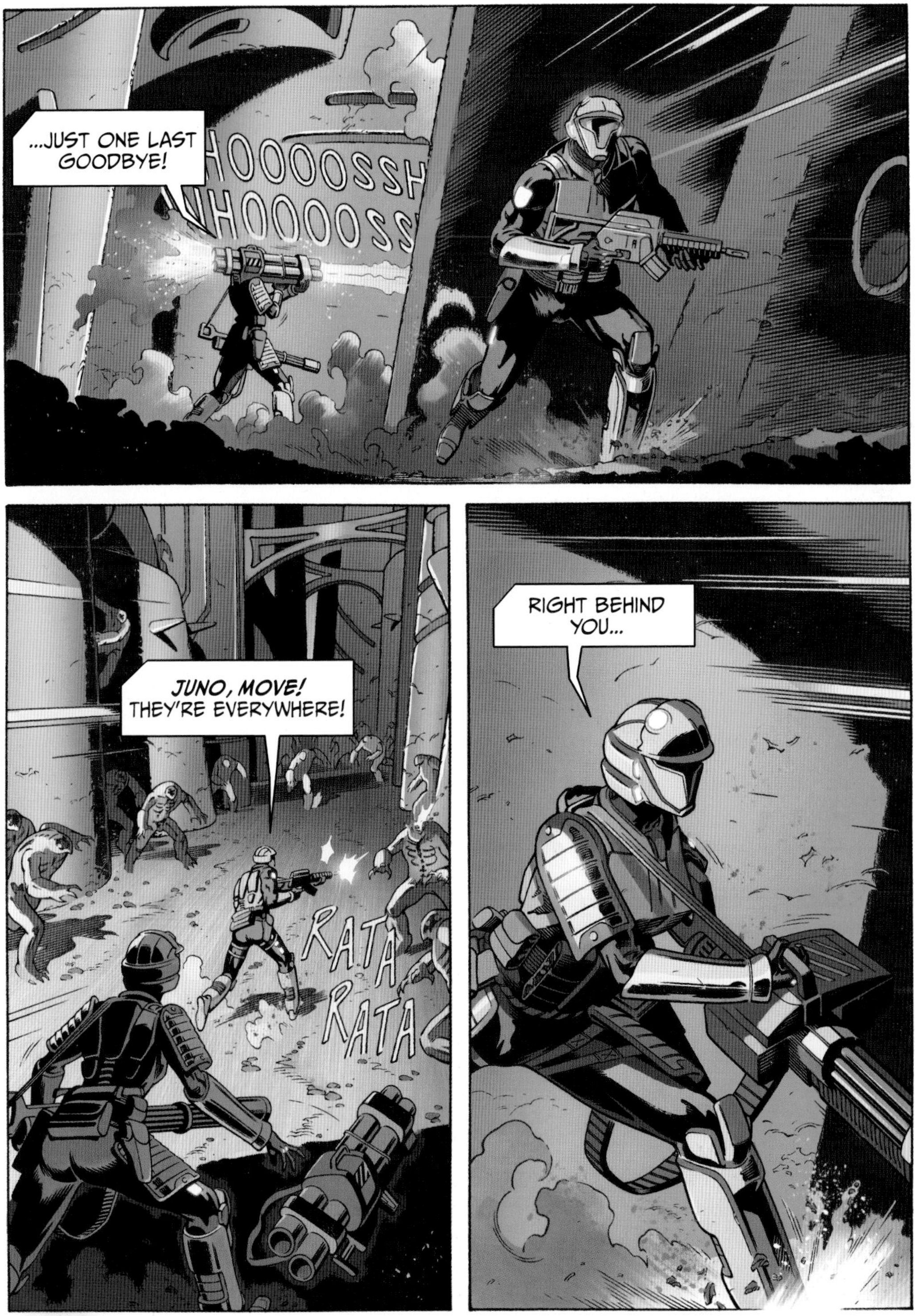
...JUST ONE LAST GOODBYE!
JUNO, MOVE! THEY'RE EVERYWHERE!
RATA RATA
RIGHT BEHIND YOU...

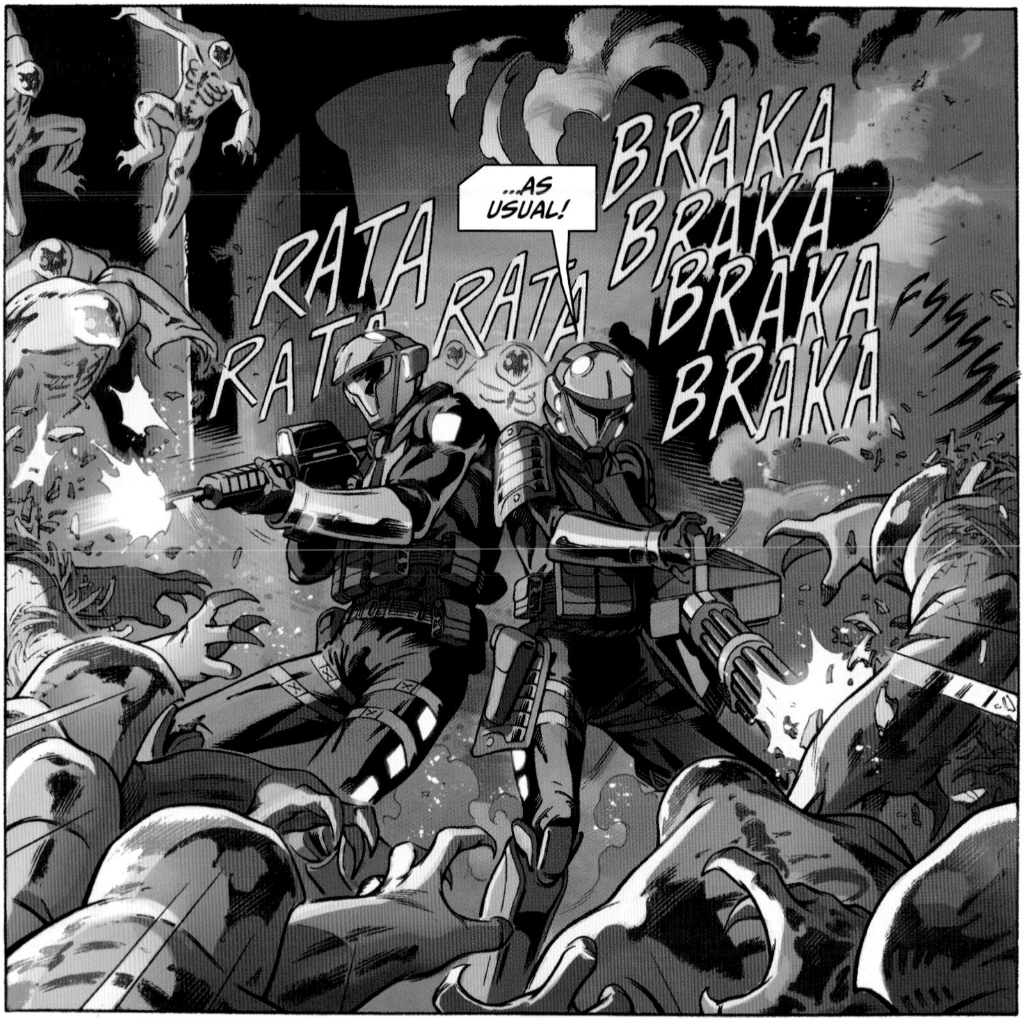
RATA
RATA
RATA
...AS USUAL!
BRAKA
BRAKA
BRAKA
BRAKA
FSSSSS

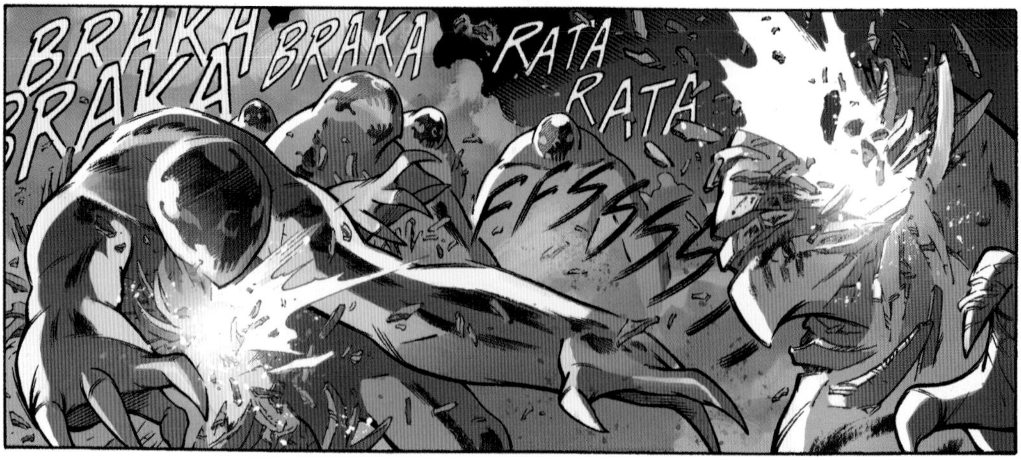
BRAKA
BRAKA
BRAKA
RATA
RATA
FFSSSSS

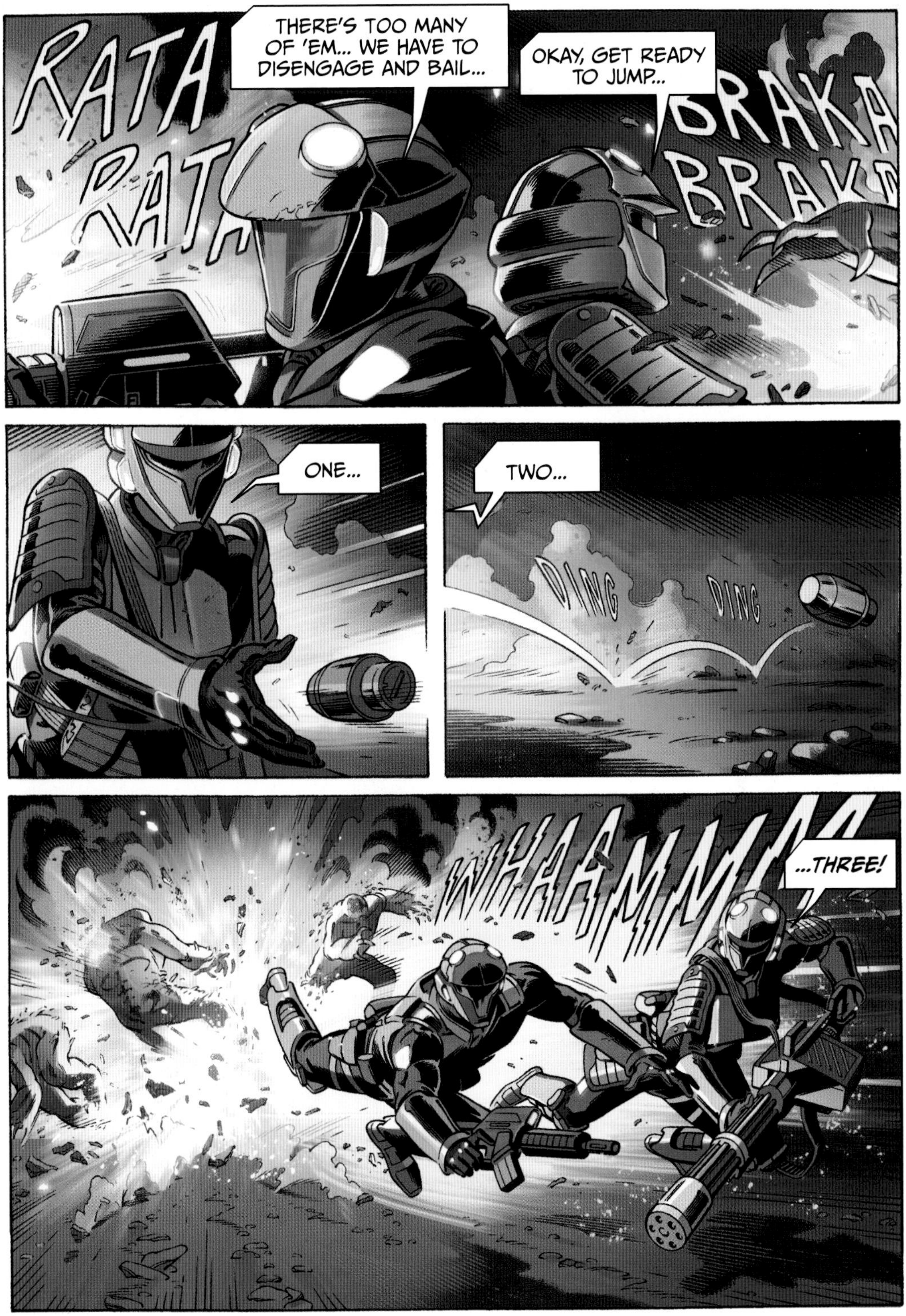
RATA
THERE'S TOO MANY OF 'EM... WE HAVE TO DISENGAGE AND BAIL...
OKAY, GET READY TO JUMP...
DRAKA
ONE...
TWO...
DING
DING
WHAAMM
...THREE!

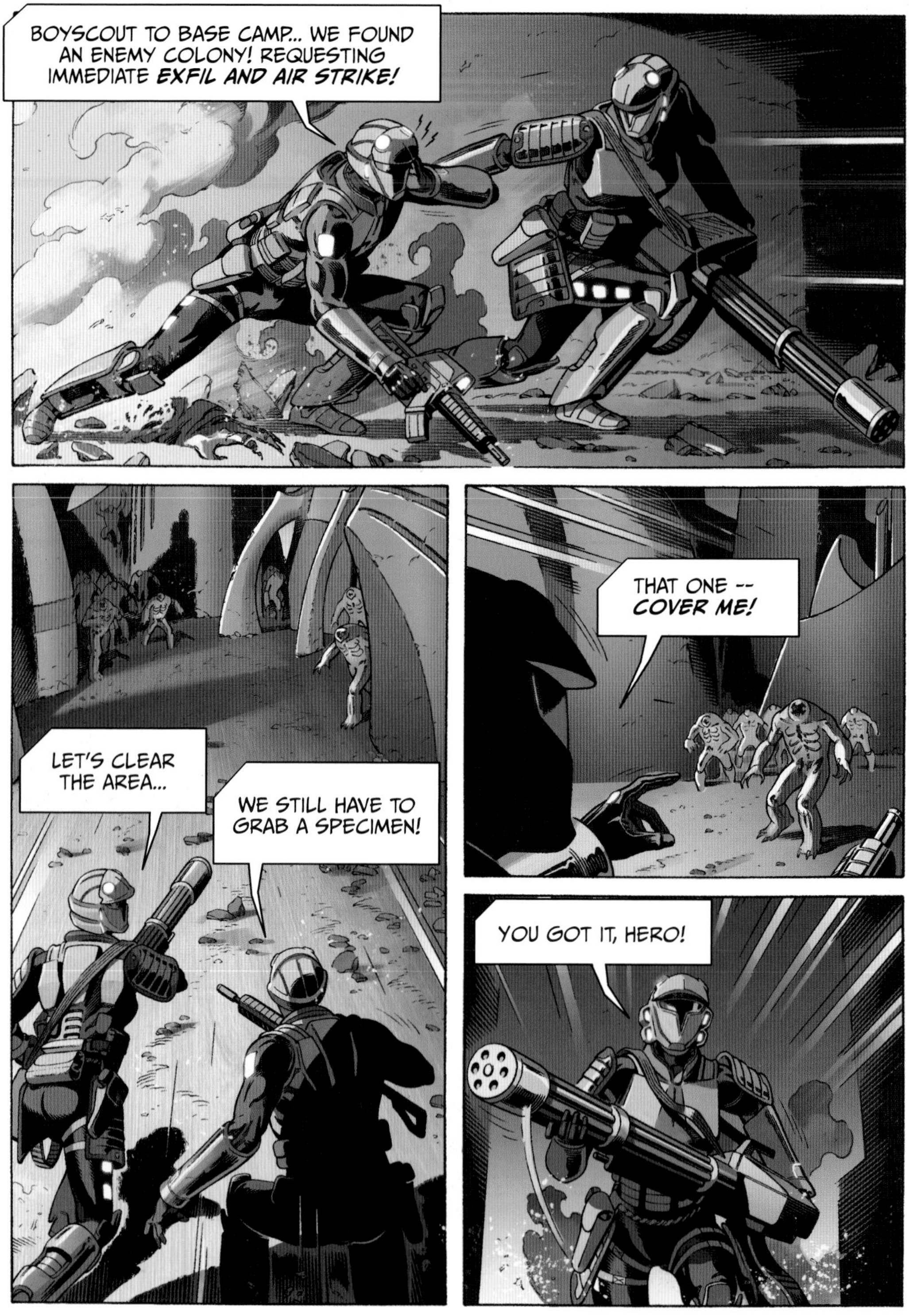
BOYSCOUT TO BASE CAMP... WE FOUND AN ENEMY COLONY! REQUESTING IMMEDIATE EXFIL AND AIR STRIKE!
LET'S CLEAR THE AREA...
WE STILL HAVE TO GRAB A SPECIMEN!
THAT ONE -- COVER ME!
YOU GOT IT, HERO!

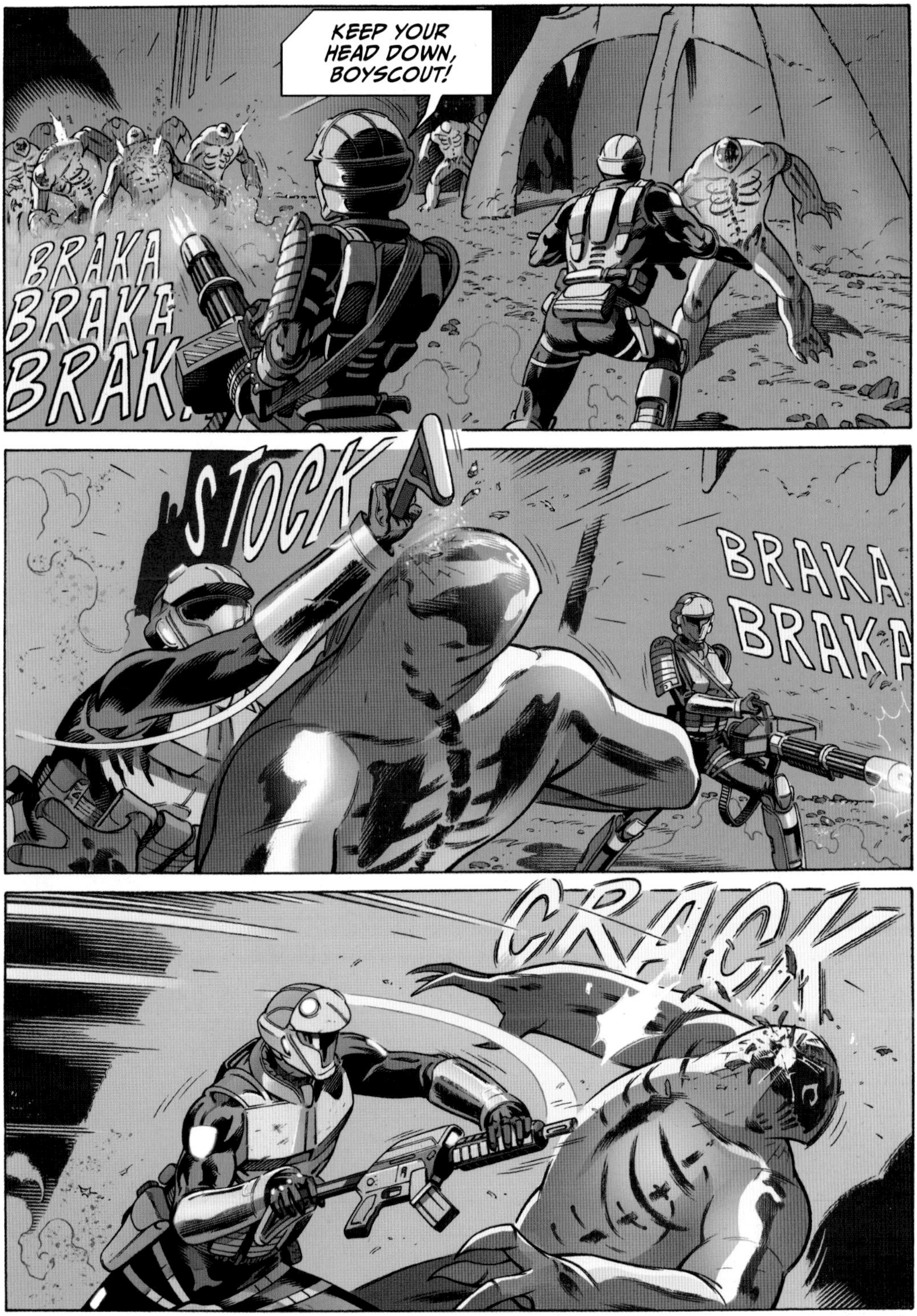
KEEP YOUR HEAD DOWN, BOYSCOUT!
BRAKA
BRAKA
BRAK
STOCK
BRAKA
BRAKA
CRACK

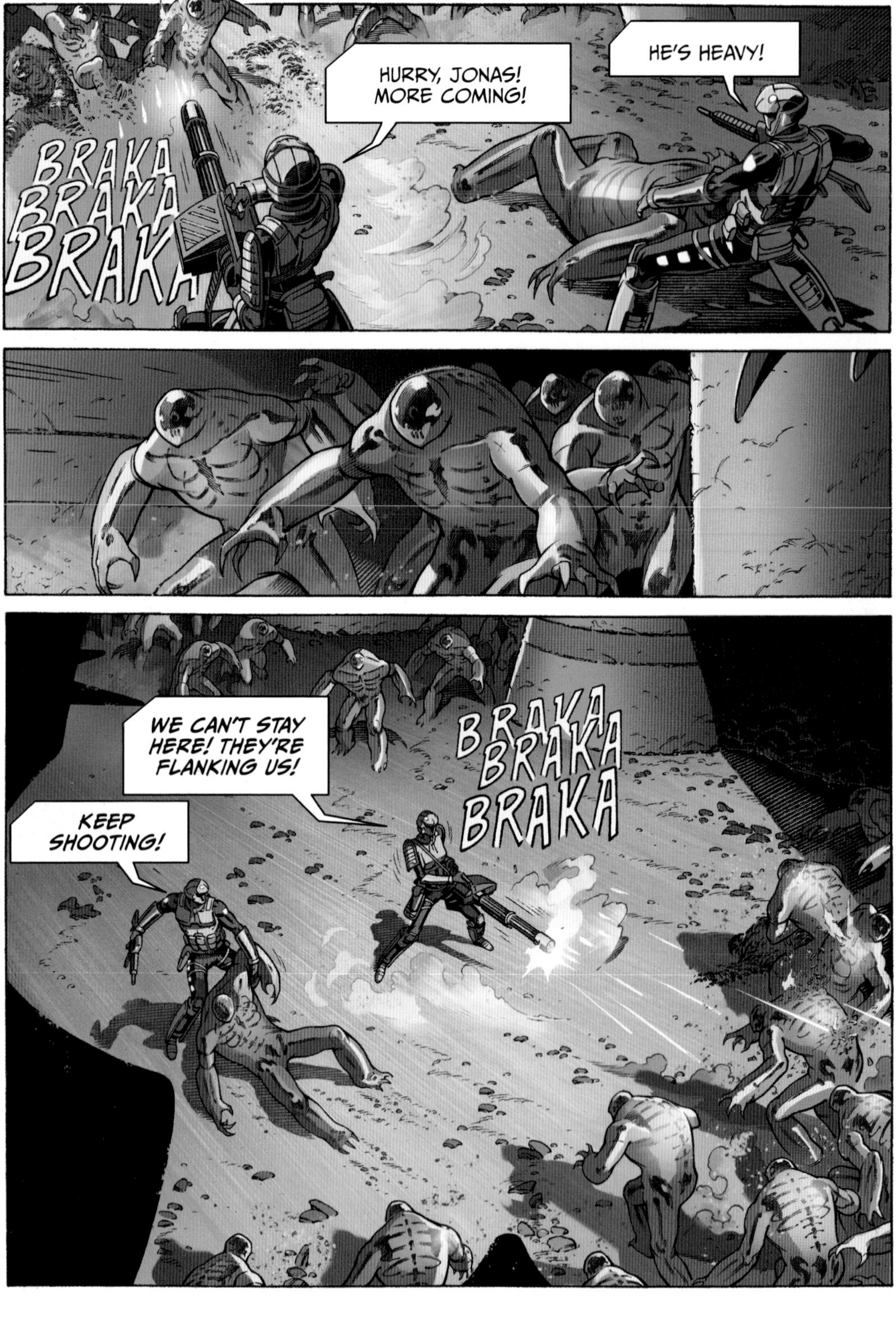
HURRY, JONAS! MORE COMING!
BRAKA BRAKA BRAKA
HE'S HEAVY!
WE CAN'T STAY HERE! THEY'RE FLANKING US!
KEEP SHOOTING!
BRAKA BRAKA BRAKA

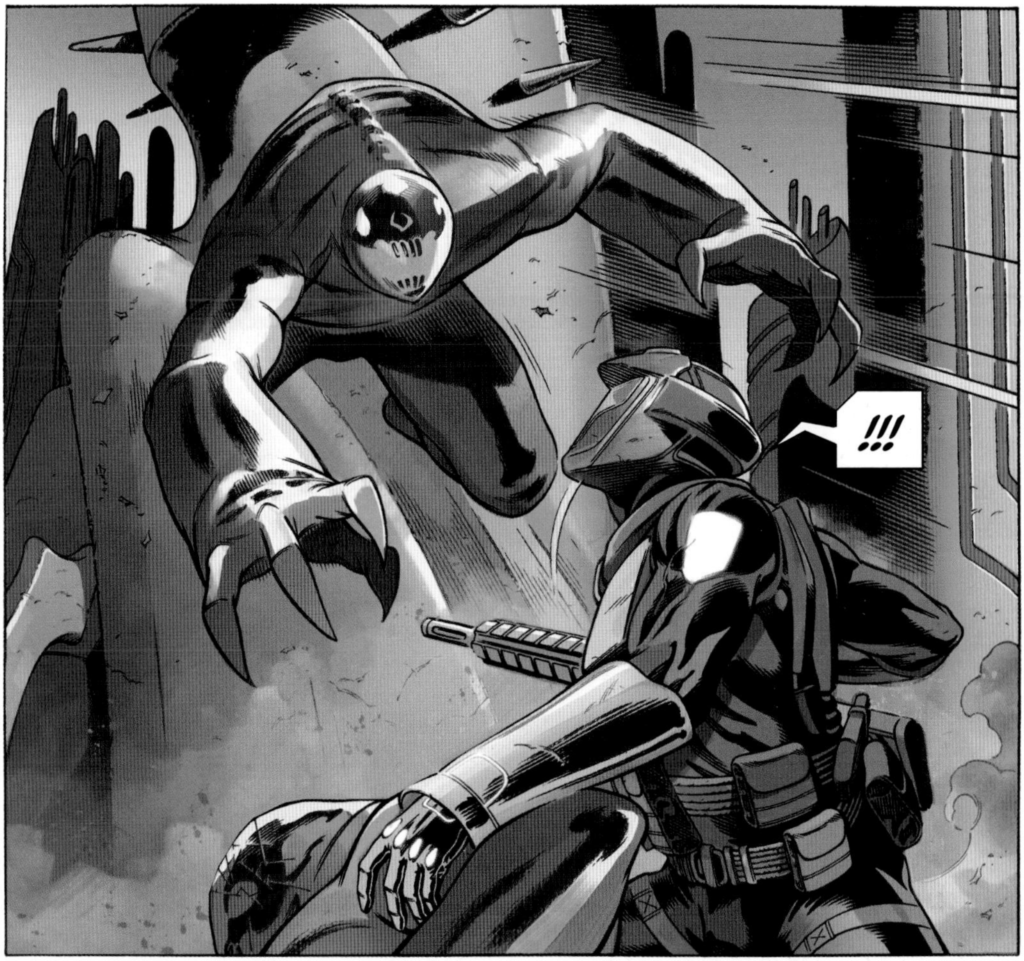
!!!

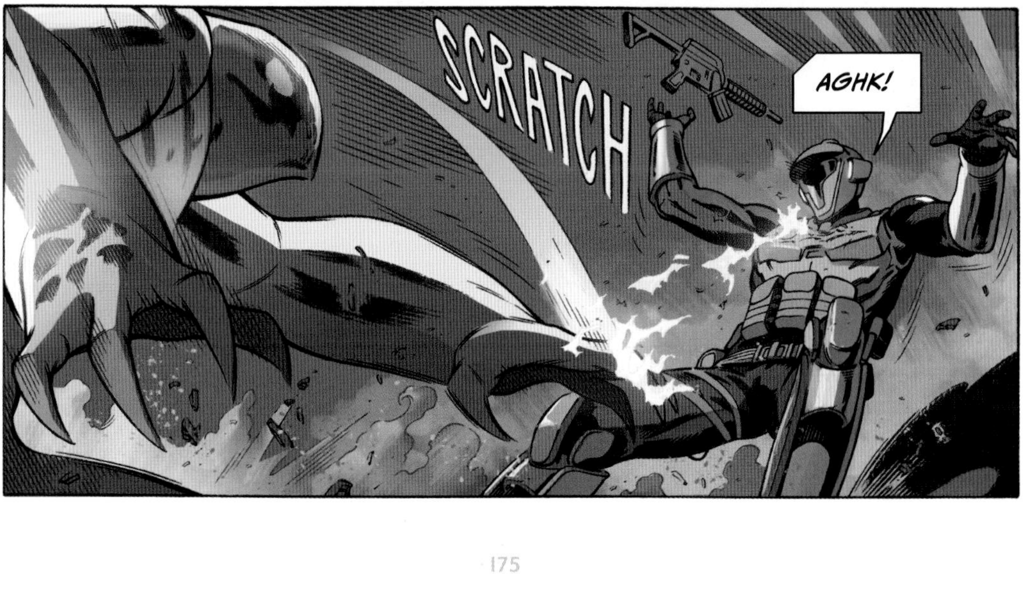
SCRATCH
AGHK!

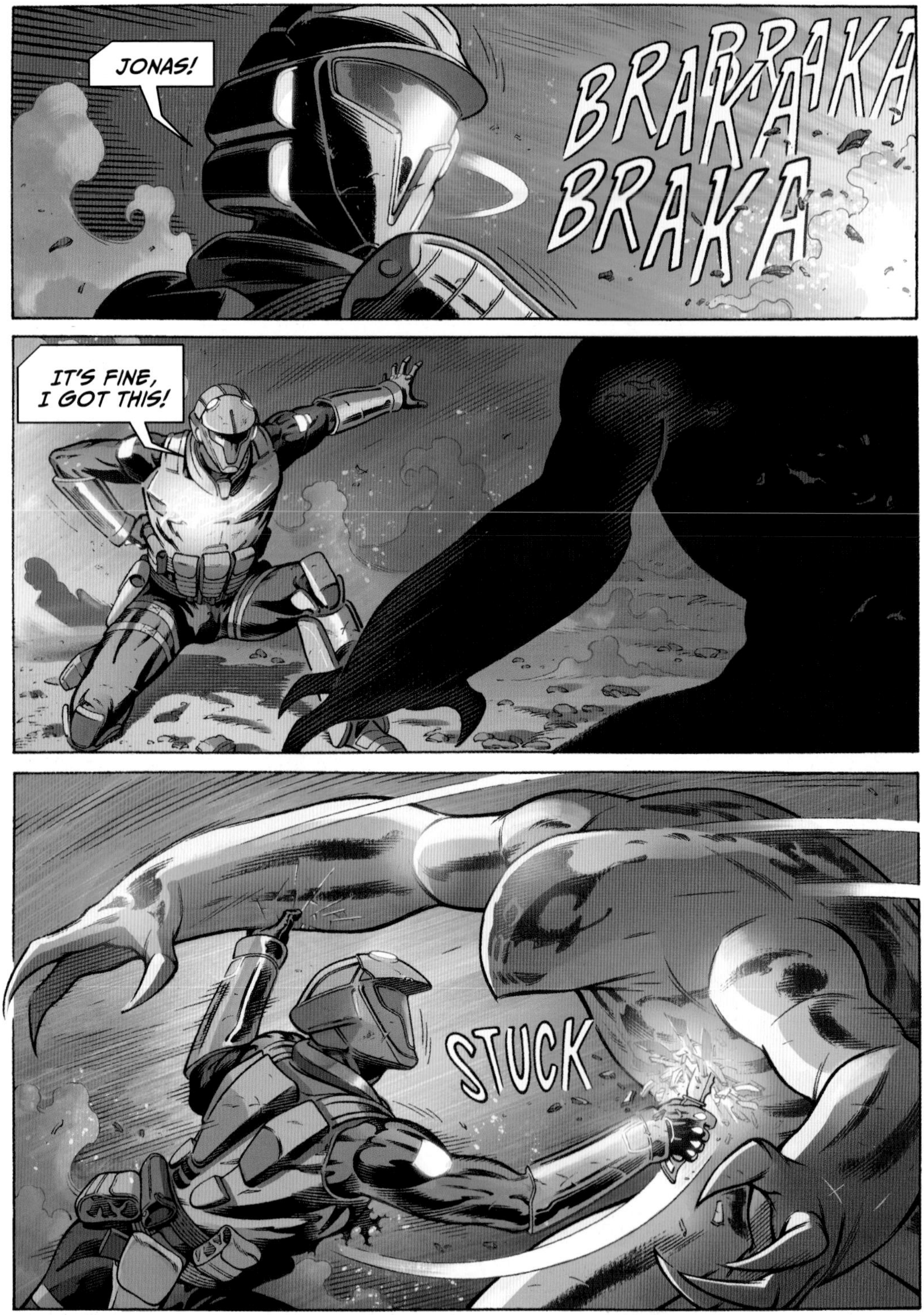
JONAS!
BRAKA BRAKA BRAKA BRAKA
IT'S FINE, I GOT THIS!
STUCK

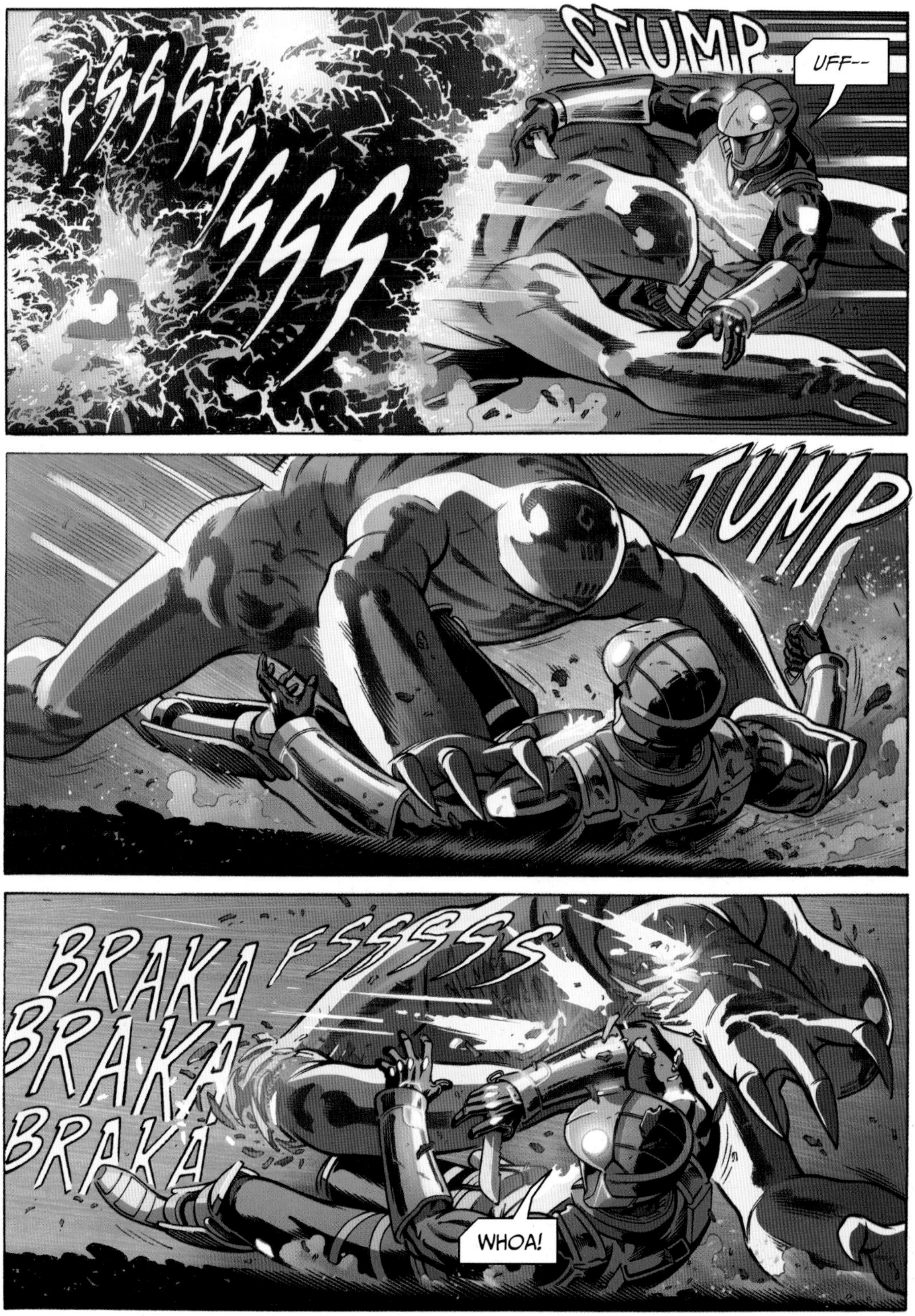
FSSSSSSSS
STUMP
UFF--
TUMP
BRAKA
BRAKA
BRAKA
FSSSSSS
WHOA!

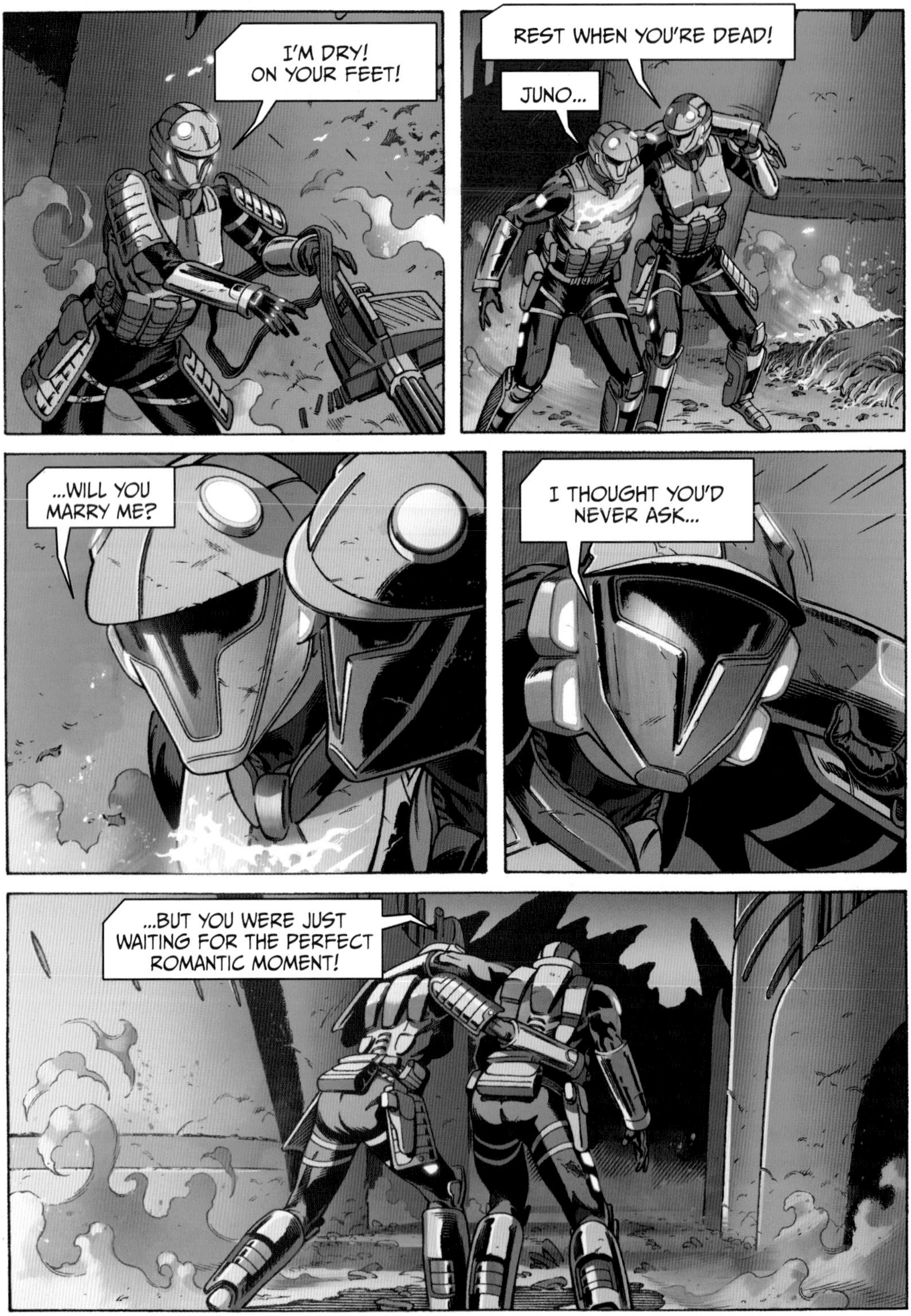
I'M DRY! ON YOUR FEET!
REST WHEN YOU'RE DEAD!
JUNO...
...WILL YOU MARRY ME?
I THOUGHT YOU'D NEVER ASK...
...BUT YOU WERE JUST WAITING FOR THE PERFECT ROMANTIC MOMENT!

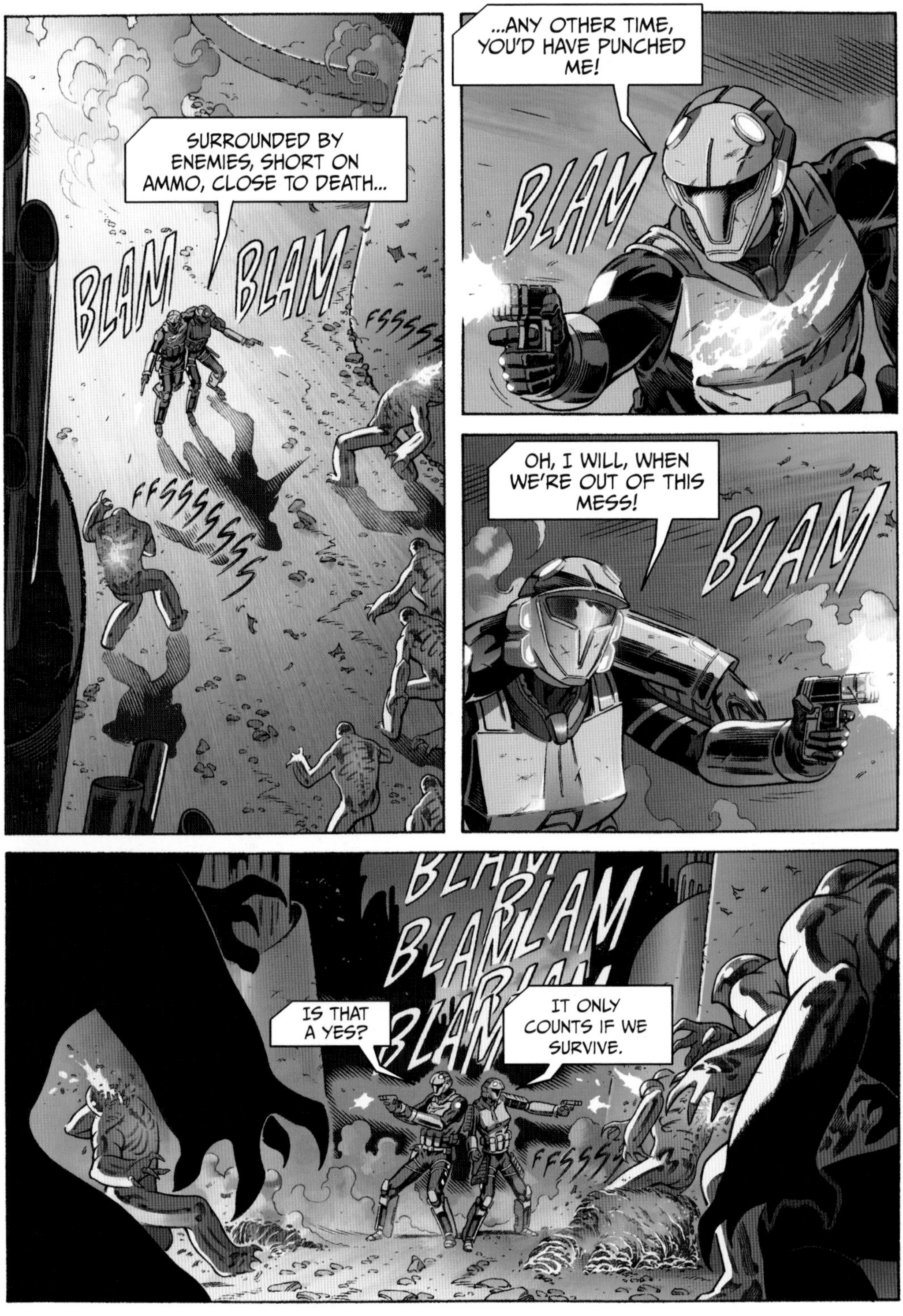
SURROUNDED BY ENEMIES, SHORT ON AMMO, CLOSE TO DEATH...
BLAM BLAM
FFSSSS
FFSSSSSSSSS
...ANY OTHER TIME, YOU'D HAVE PUNCHED ME!
BLAM
OH, I WILL, WHEN WE'RE OUT OF THIS MESS!
BLAM
BLAM
BLAM
IS THAT A YES?
IT ONLY COUNTS IF WE SURVIVE.
FFSSSS

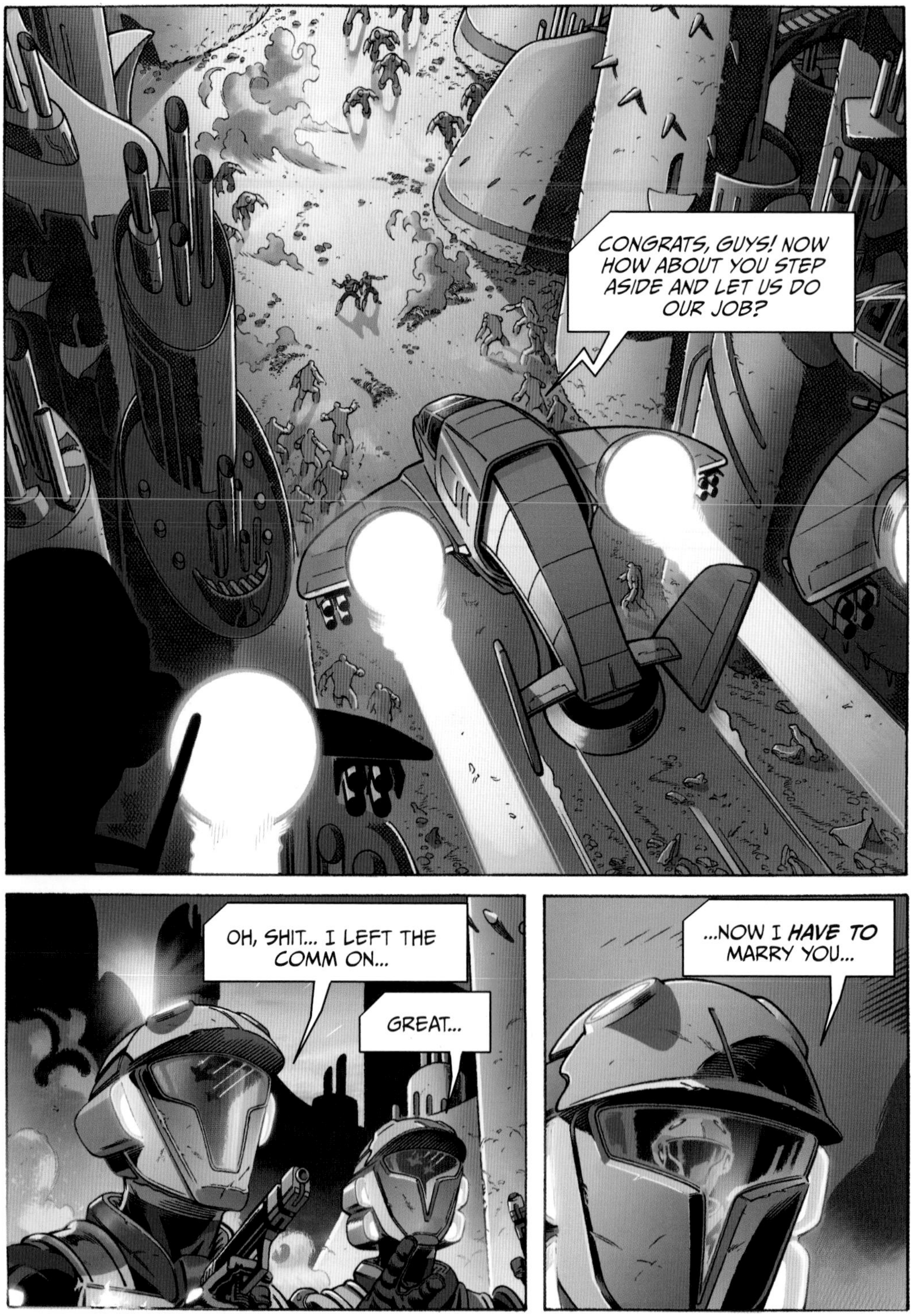
CONGRATS, GUYS! NOW HOW ABOUT YOU STEP ASIDE AND LET US DO OUR JOB?
OH, SHIT... I LEFT THE COMM ON...
GREAT...
...NOW I HAVE TO MARRY YOU...

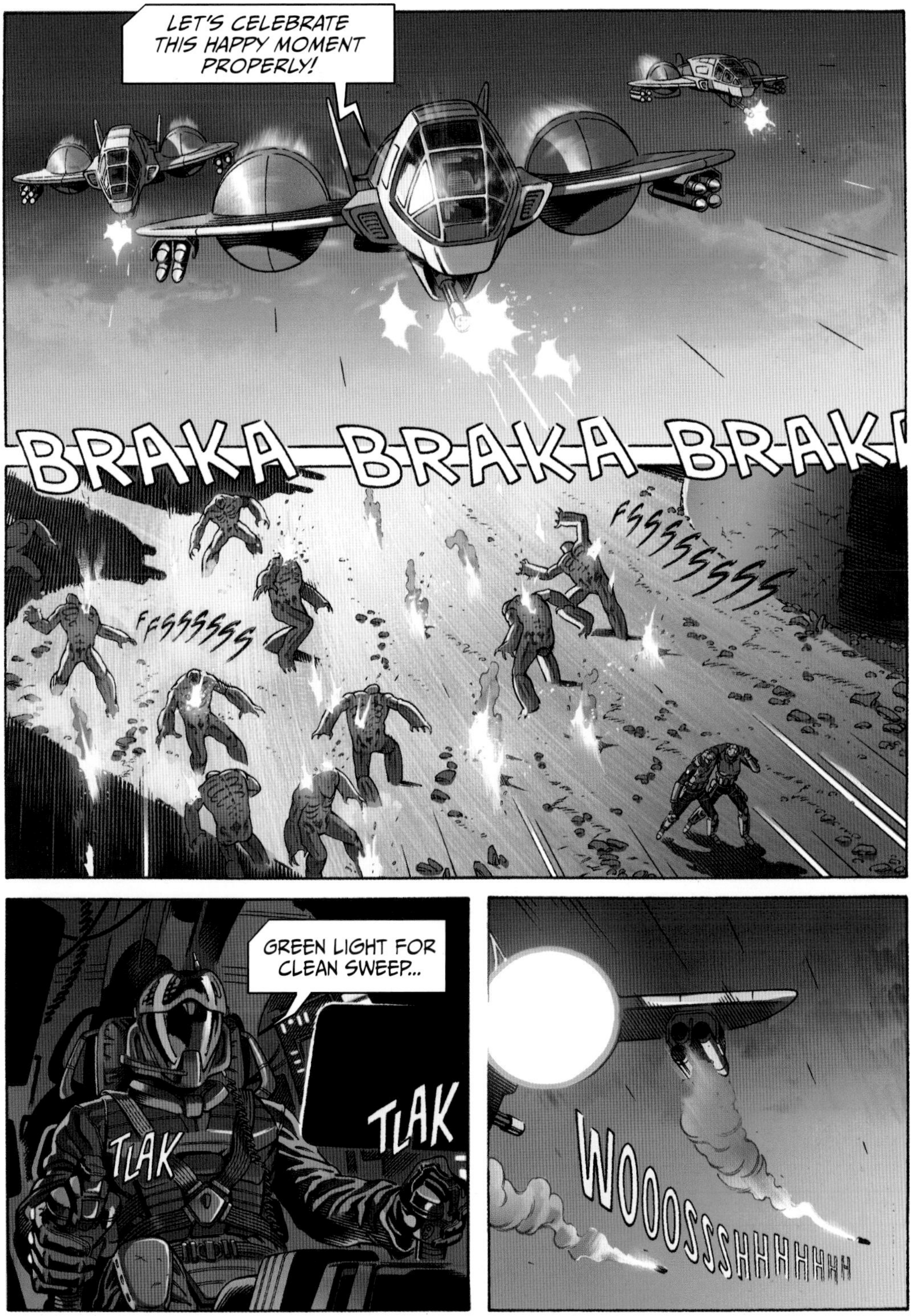
LET'S CELEBRATE THIS HAPPY MOMENT PROPERLY!
BRAKA BRAKA BRAK
FSSSSSSSSS
FSSSSSSS
GREEN LIGHT FOR CLEAN SWEEP...
TLAK
TLAK
WOOOSSSHHHHHHHH

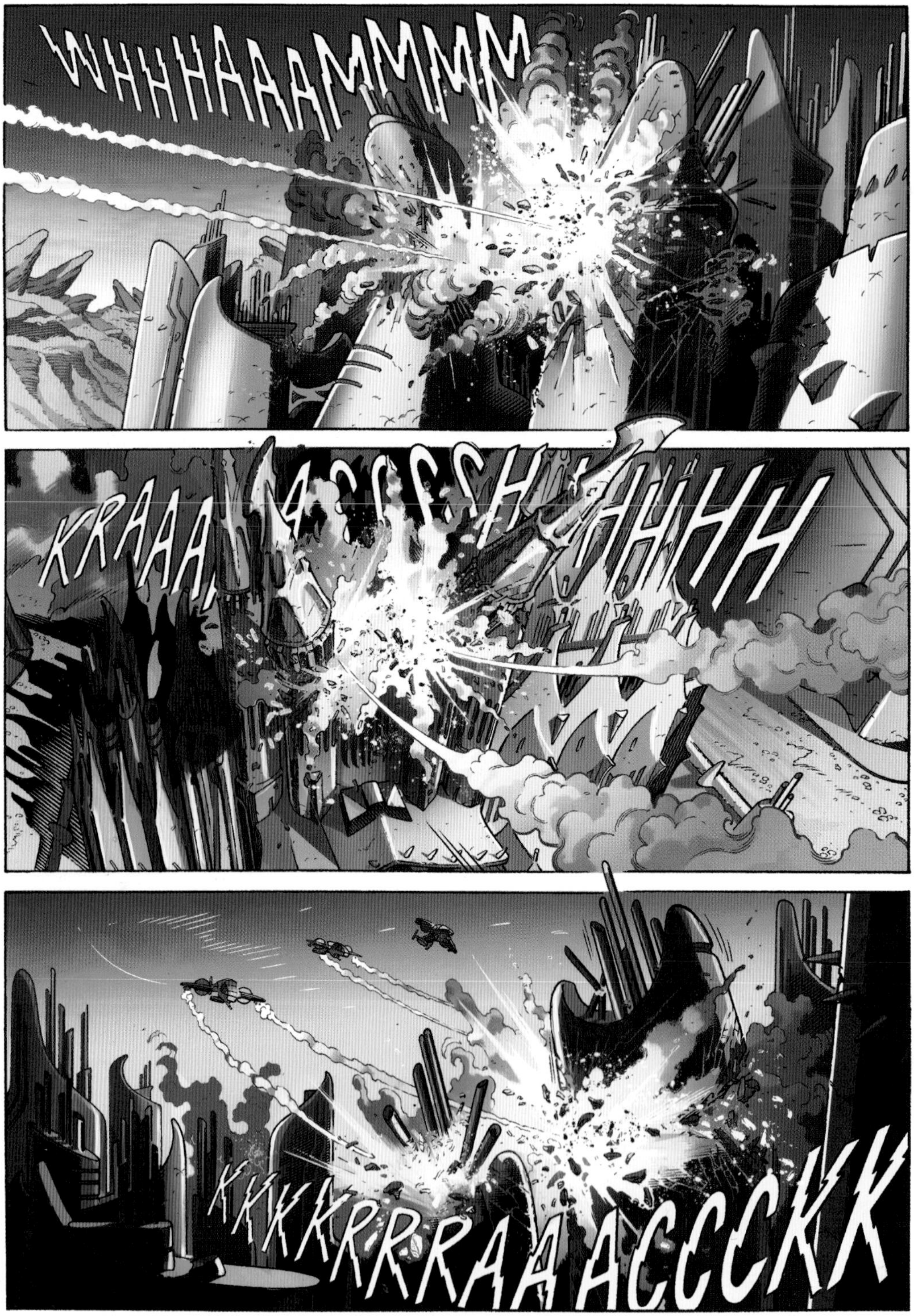
WHHHAAAMMMM
KRAAAACCCSHHHHHH
KKKKRRRAAACCCCKK

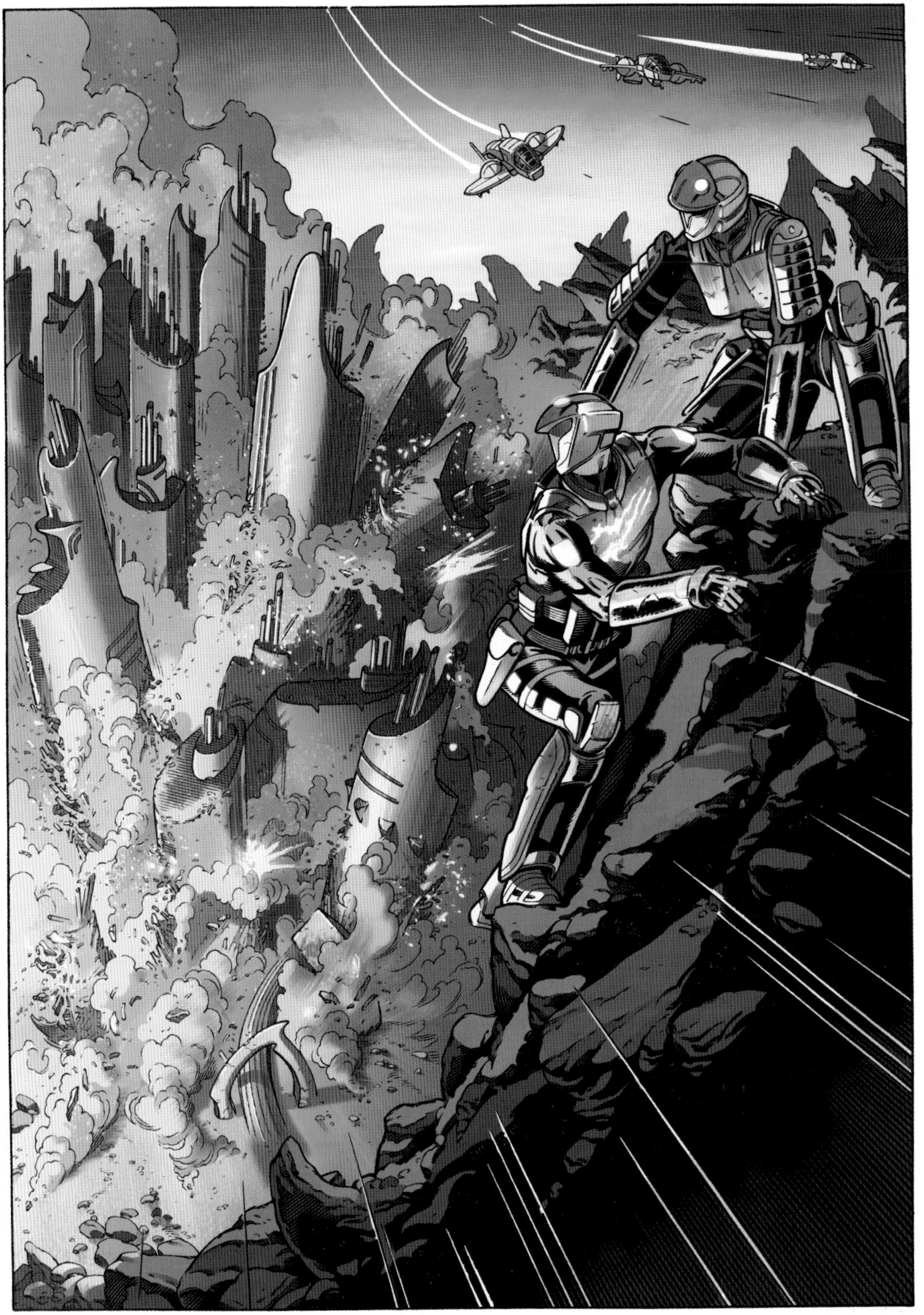

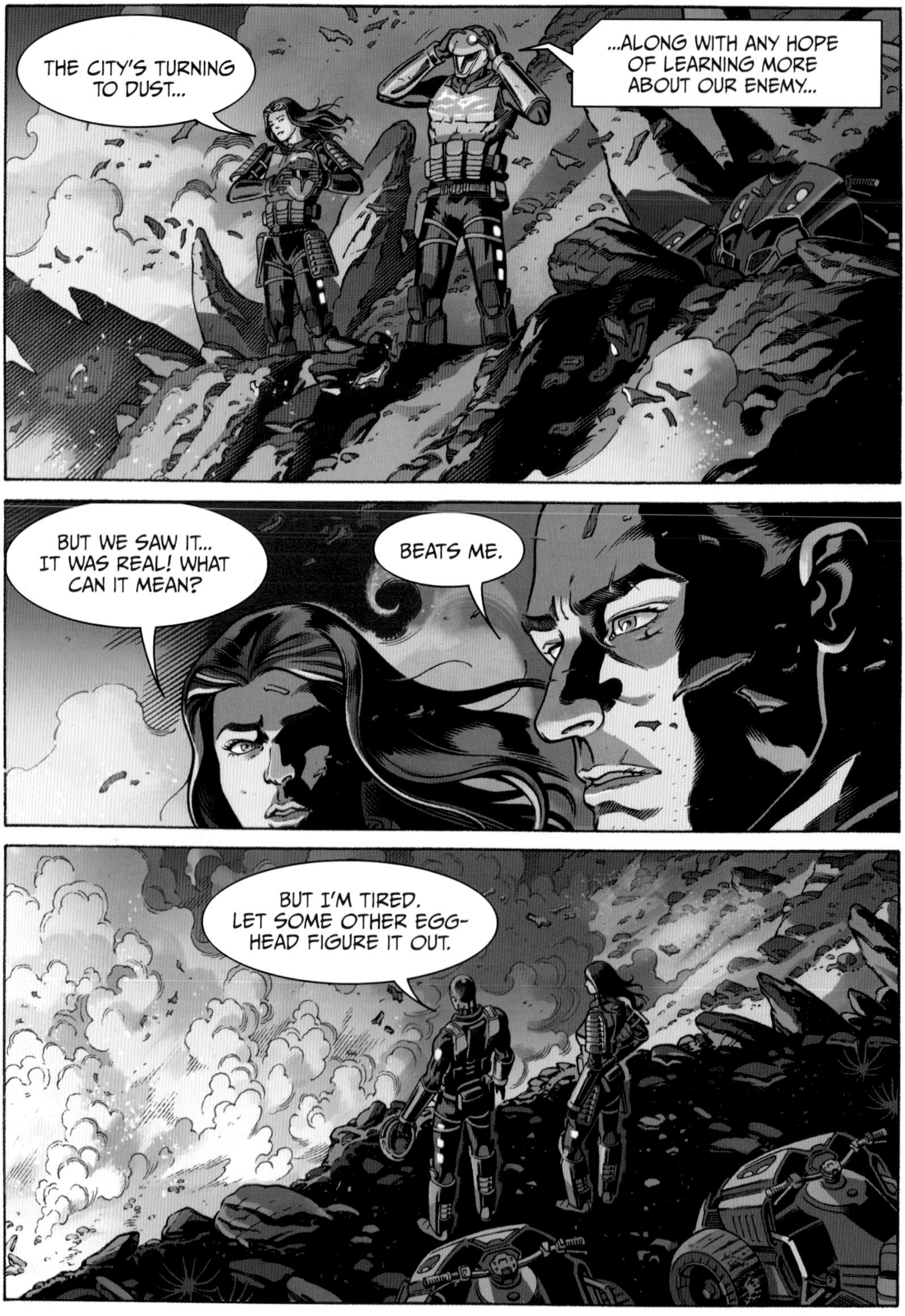
THE CITY'S TURNING TO DUST...
...ALONG WITH ANY HOPE OF LEARNING MORE ABOUT OUR ENEMY...
BUT WE SAW IT... IT WAS REAL! WHAT CAN IT MEAN?
BEATS ME.
BUT I'M TIRED. LET SOME OTHER EGG-HEAD FIGURE IT OUT.

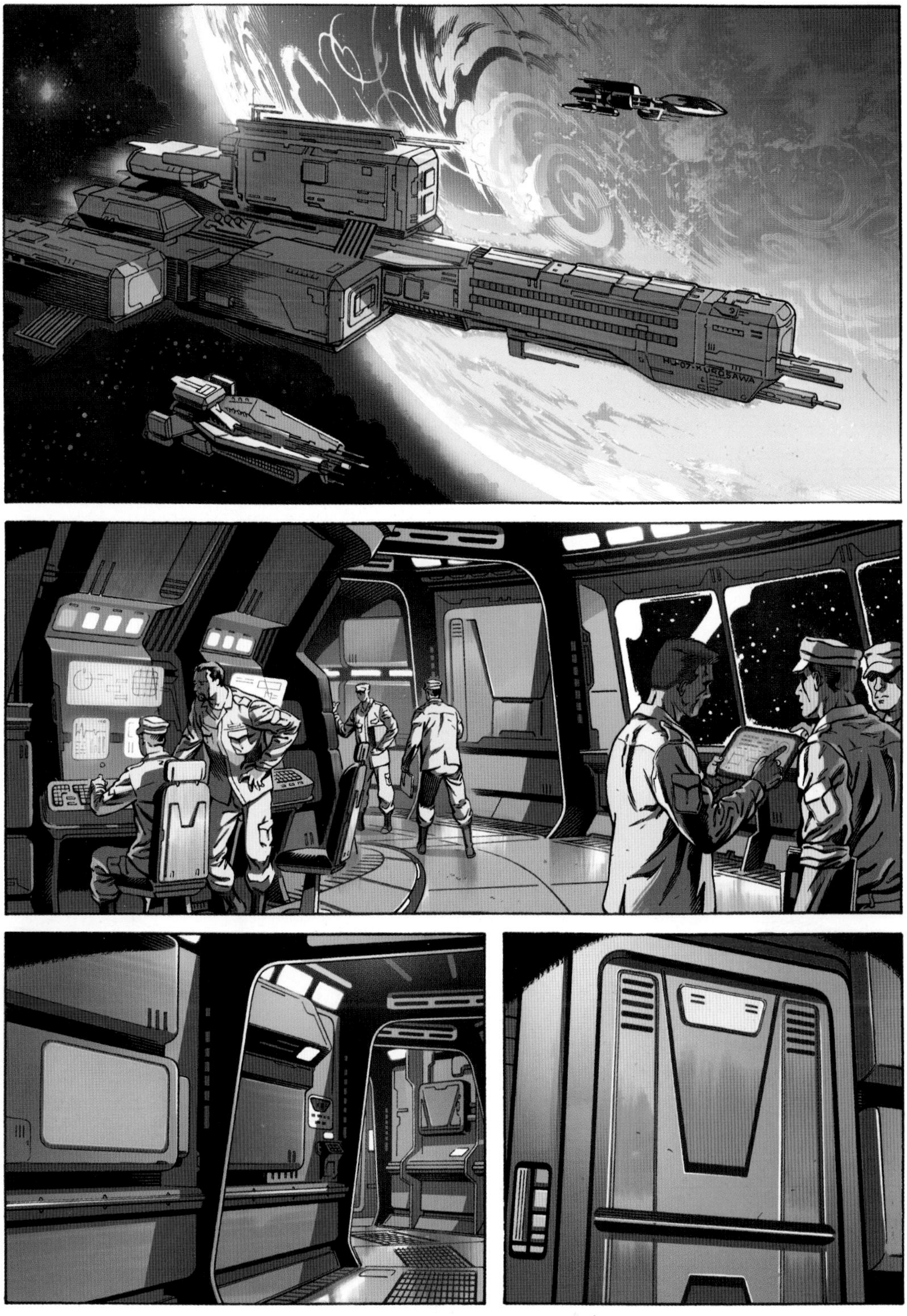
HU-07-KUROSAWA

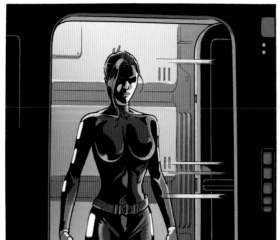

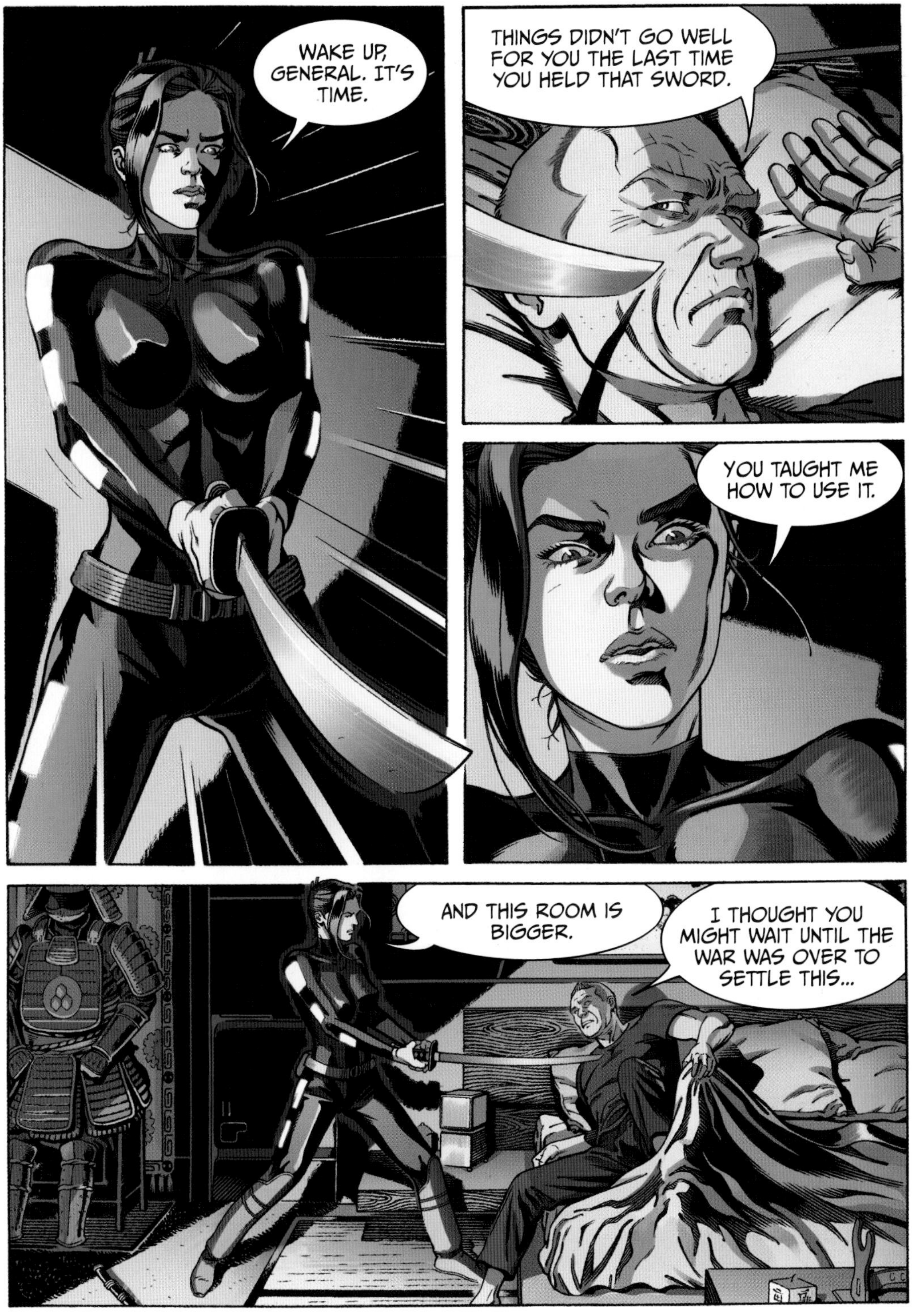
WAKE UP, GENERAL. IT'S TIME.
THINGS DIDN'T GO WELL FOR YOU THE LAST TIME YOU HELD THAT SWORD.
YOU TAUGHT ME HOW TO USE IT.
AND THIS ROOM IS BIGGER.
I THOUGHT YOU MIGHT WAIT UNTIL THE WAR WAS OVER TO SETTLE THIS...

YEAH, WELL, THINGS CHANGED.

HOW?

THIS ENEMY IS NOTHING LIKE WE EXPECTED. THIS WAR COULD LAST FOREVER.

I SEE.

AND JONAS PROPOSED TO ME.

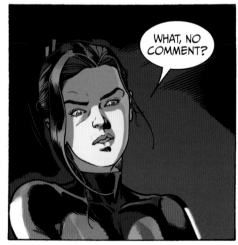

WHAT, NO COMMENT?

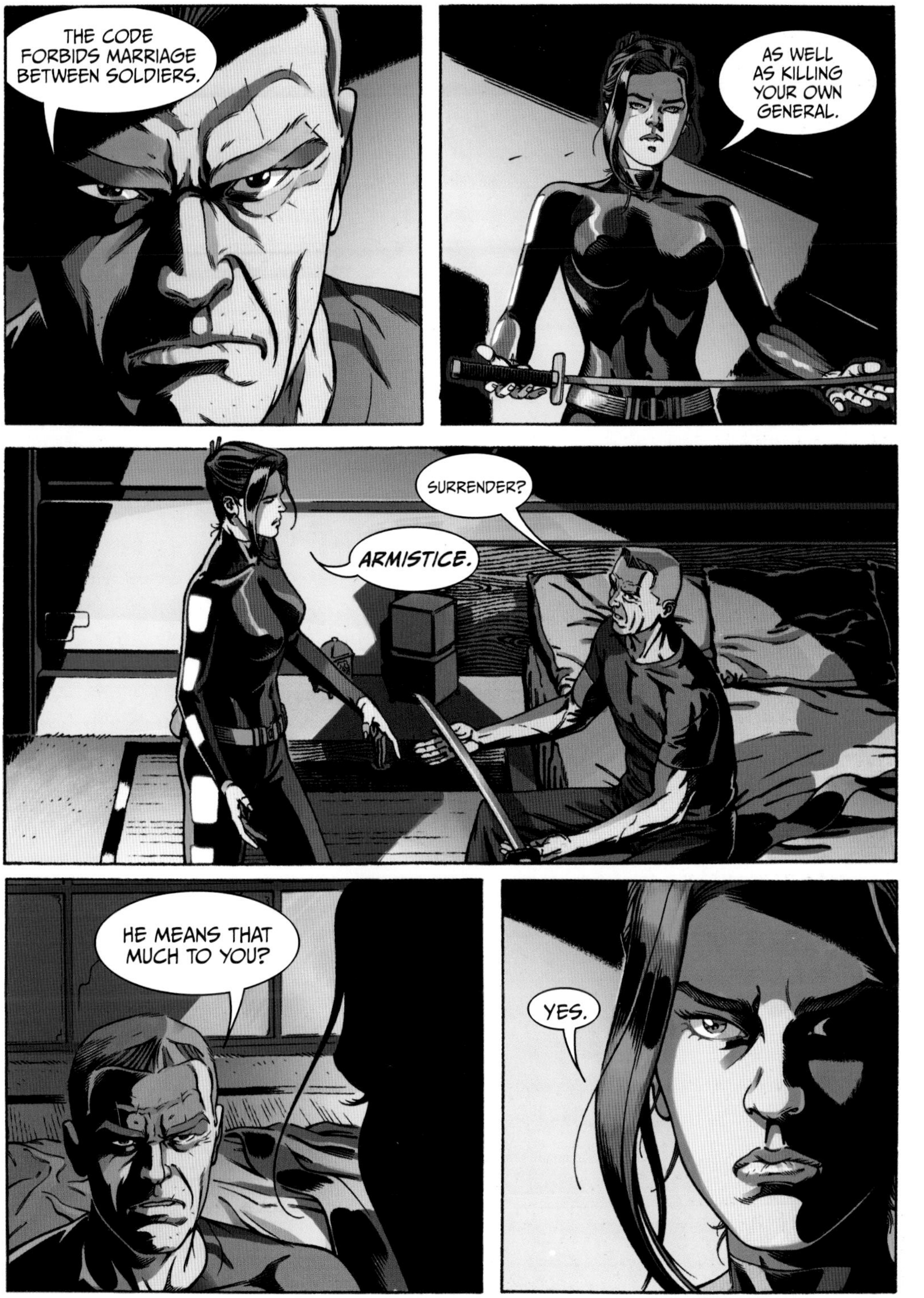
THE CODE FORBIDS MARRIAGE BETWEEN SOLDIERS.
AS WELL AS KILLING YOUR OWN GENERAL.
SURRENDER?
ARMISTICE.
HE MEANS THAT MUCH TO YOU?
YES.

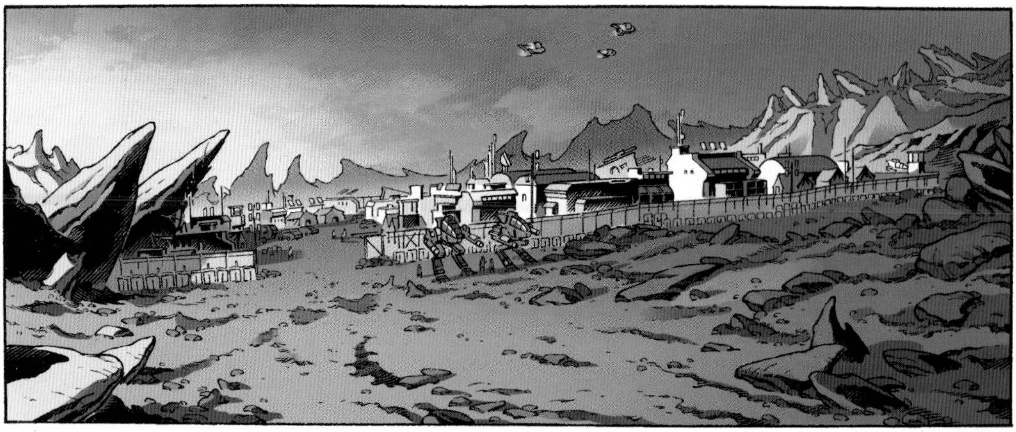

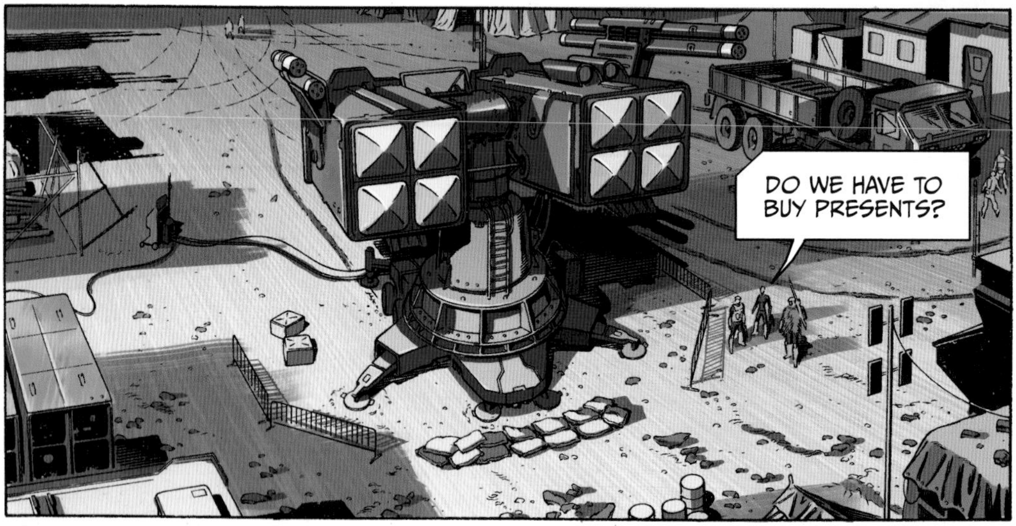
DO WE HAVE TO BUY PRESENTS?

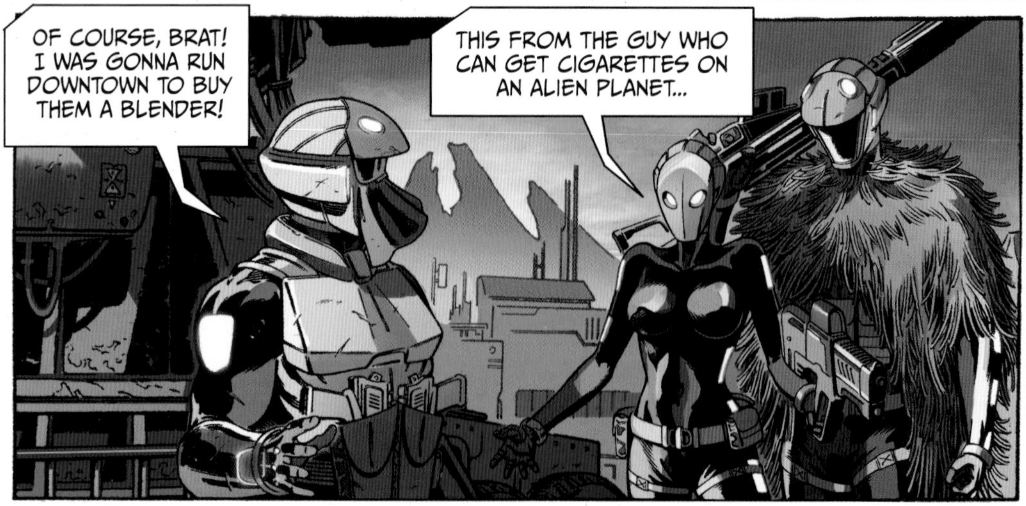
OF COURSE, BRAT! I WAS GONNA RUN DOWNTOWN TO BUY THEM A BLENDER!
THIS FROM THE GUY WHO CAN GET CIGARETTES ON AN ALIEN PLANET...

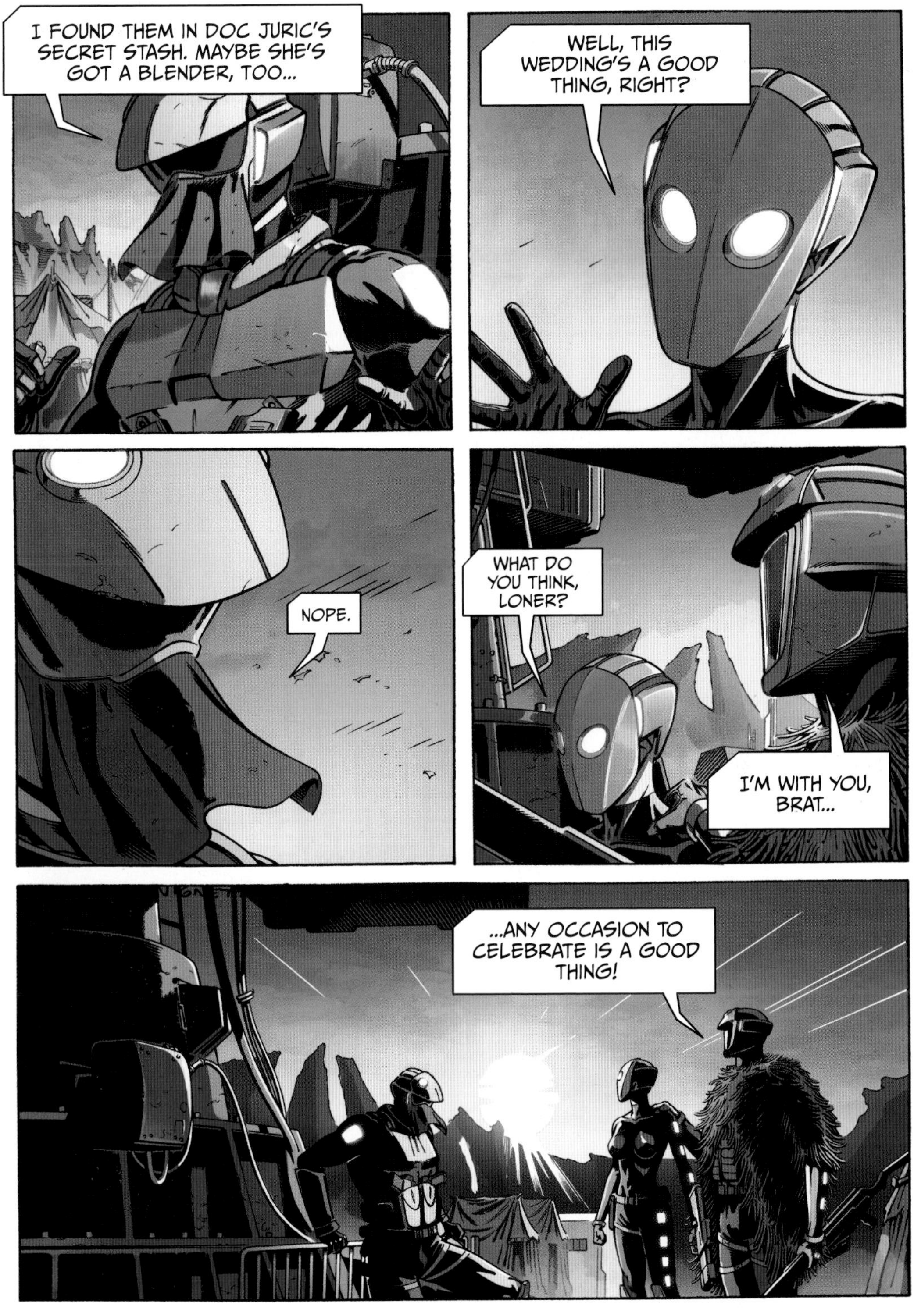
I FOUND THEM IN DOC JURIC'S SECRET STASH. MAYBE SHE'S GOT A BLENDER, TOO...
WELL, THIS WEDDING'S A GOOD THING, RIGHT?
NOPE.
WHAT DO YOU THINK, LONER?
I'M WITH YOU, BRAT...
...ANY OCCASION TO CELEBRATE IS A GOOD THING!

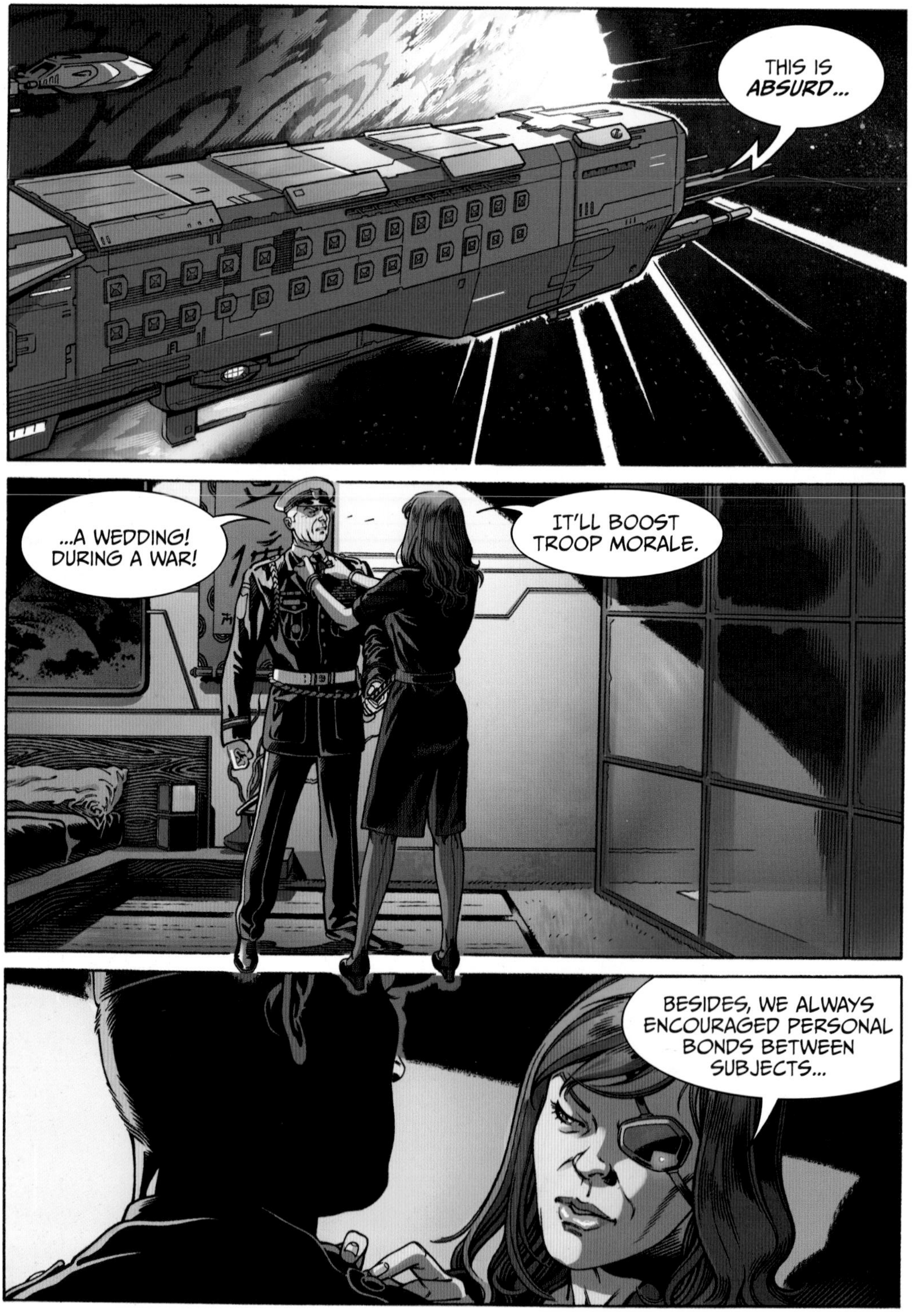
THIS IS ABSURD...
...A WEDDING! DURING A WAR!
IT'LL BOOST TROOP MORALE.
BESIDES, WE ALWAYS ENCOURAGED PERSONAL BONDS BETWEEN SUBJECTS...

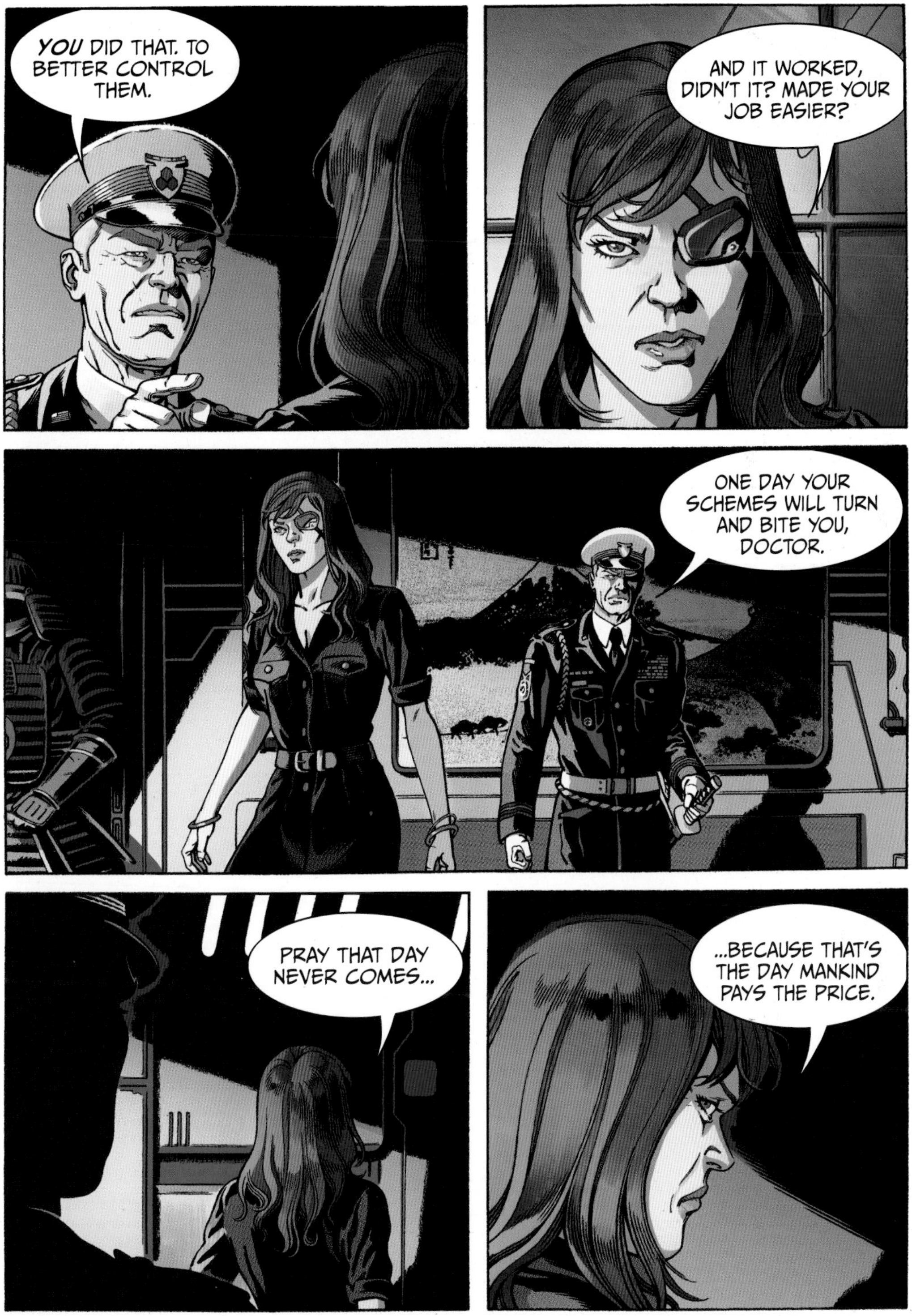
YOU DID THAT. TO BETTER CONTROL THEM.
AND IT WORKED, DIDN'T IT? MADE YOUR JOB EASIER?
ONE DAY YOUR SCHEMES WILL TURN AND BITE YOU, DOCTOR.
PRAY THAT DAY NEVER COMES...
...BECAUSE THAT'S THE DAY MANKIND PAYS THE PRICE.

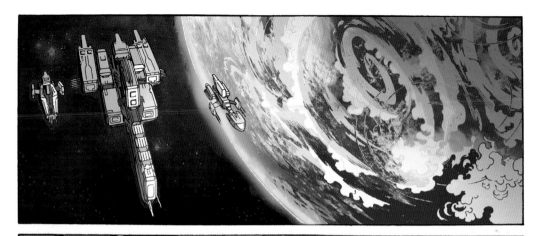

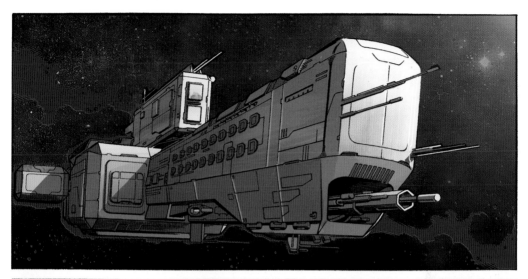

WHAT THE...?!

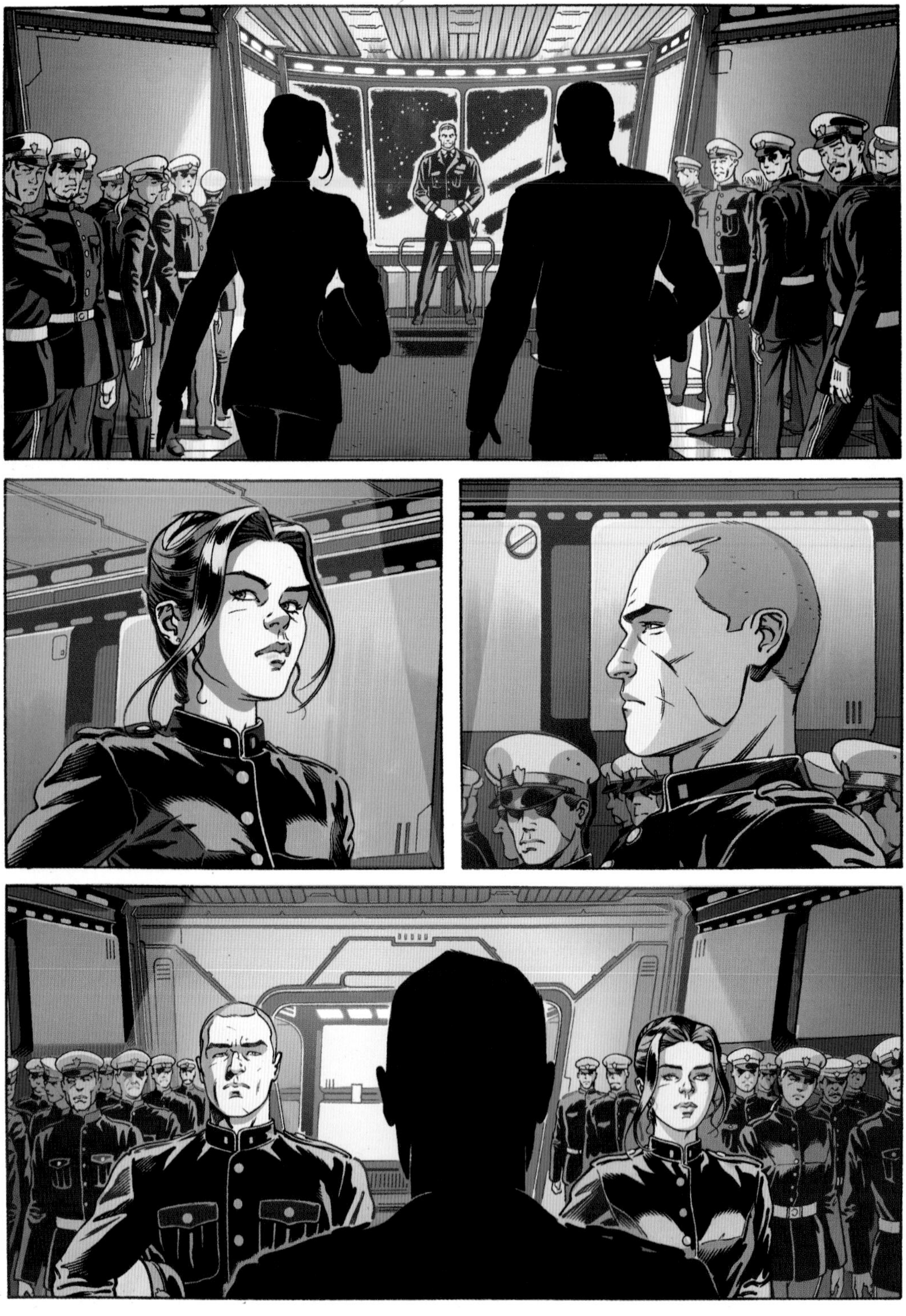

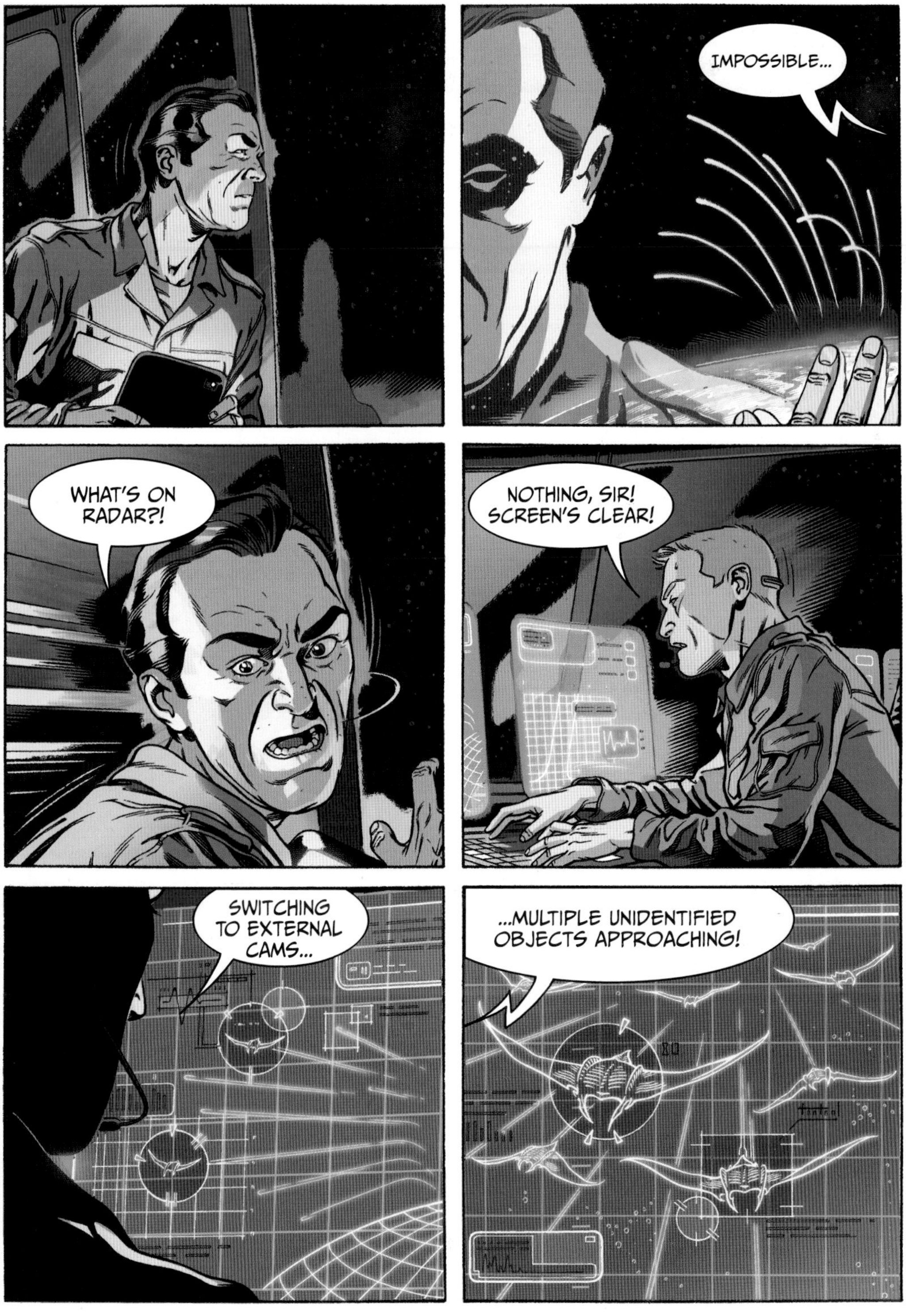
IMPOSSIBLE...
WHAT'S ON RADAR?!
NOTHING, SIR! SCREEN'S CLEAR!
SWITCHING TO EXTERNAL CAMS...
...MULTIPLE UNIDENTIFIED OBJECTS APPROACHING!

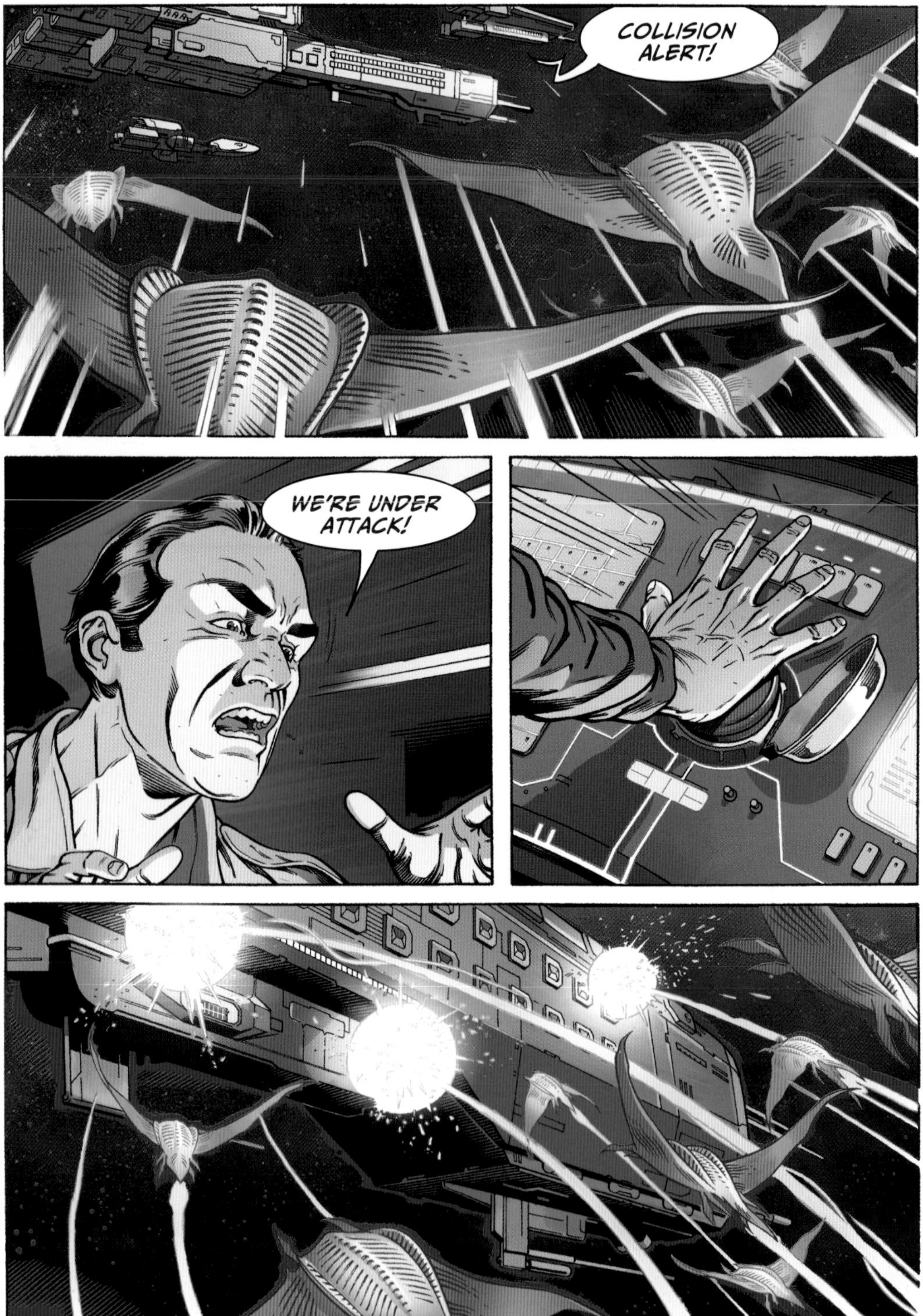
COLLISION ALERT!
WE'RE UNDER ATTACK!

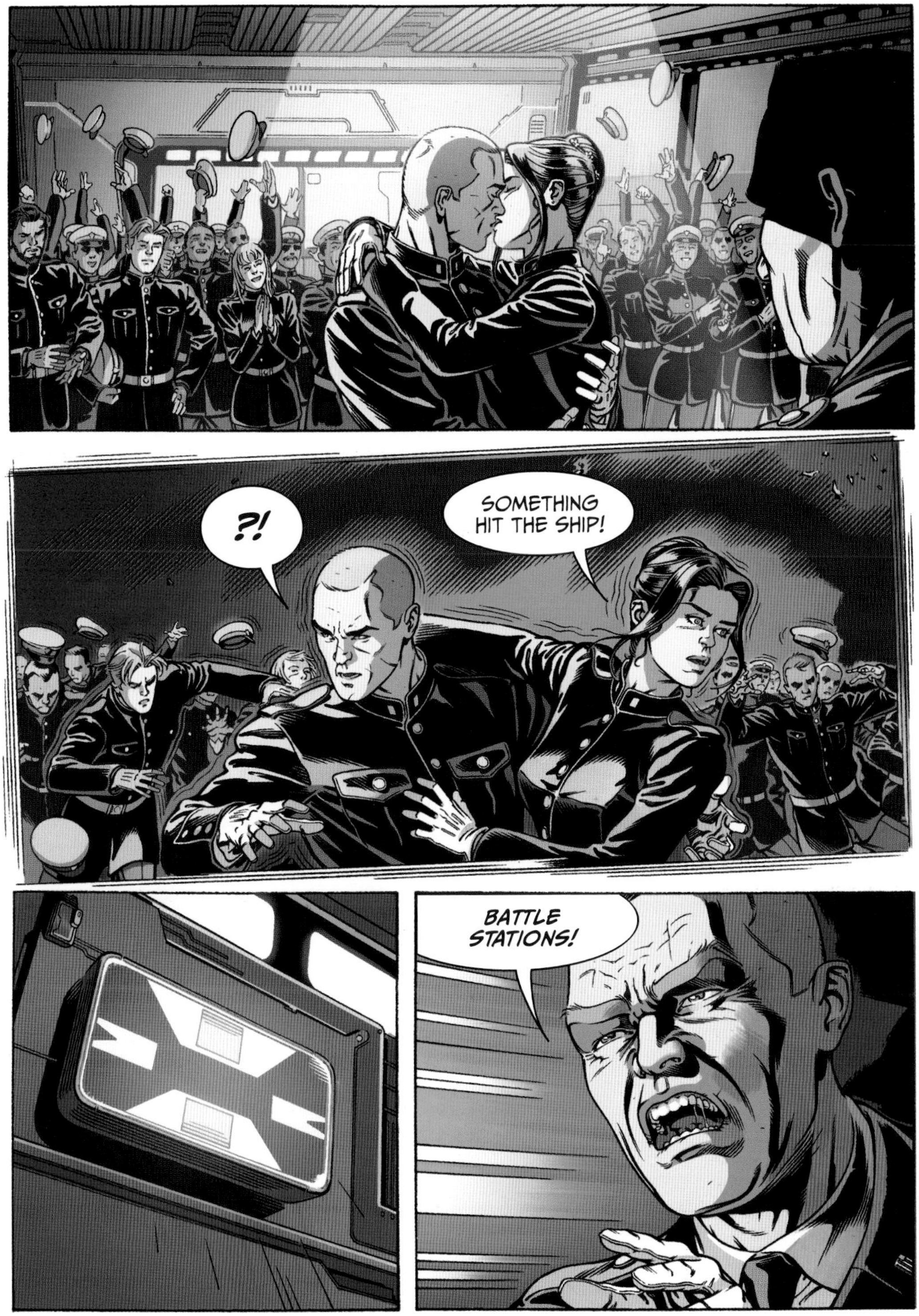
?!
SOMETHING HIT THE SHIP!
BATTLE STATIONS!

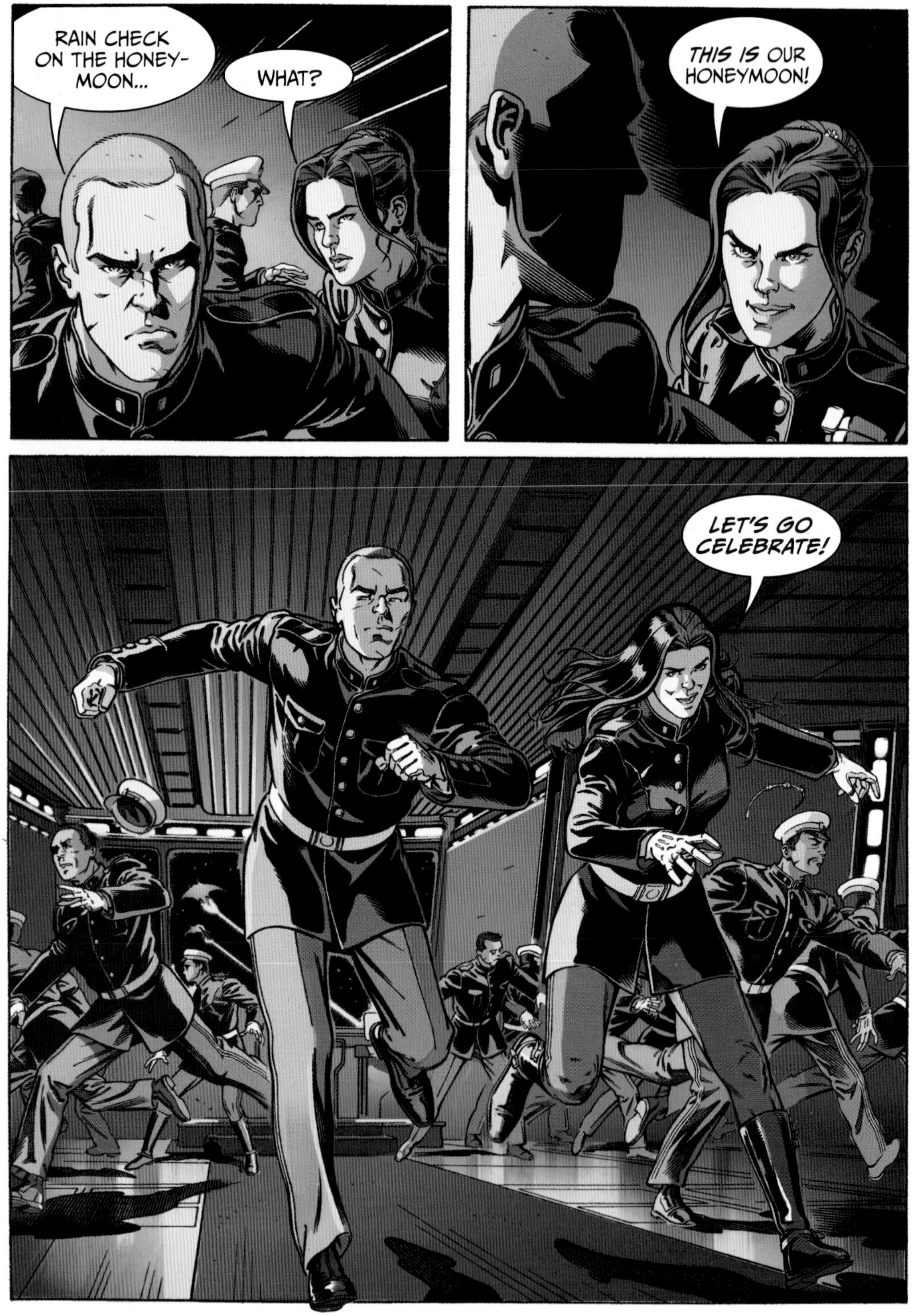
RAIN CHECK ON THE HONEY-MOON...
WHAT?
THIS IS OUR HONEYMOON!
LET'S GO CELEBRATE!

ALESSANDRO BIGNAMINI

ARTIST

When and where were you born? Where do you live now?

I was born in Milan on November 24, 1970, and now I live in Cusano Milanino, Italy.

What sort of artistic education did you have?

I first graduated Hajeck artistic high school in Milan, and then at the Comics School, also in Milan.

Tell us about your previous works, before *Orphans*.

I was published in *Fumo di China* and *Comic Art*, and then I started working with the publisher Universo with stories in *Intrepido* magazine. I've also been working for Sergio Bonelli Editore for twenty years. For almost ten years, I worked with Maurizio Colombo on *Mister No*, creating his "pulp" alter ego Detective Jerry Drake. Since 2005, I have worked on two episodes of *Brad Barron* and the work I am most proud of, *Greystorm*. After that, I drew a brief story for *Dylan Dog* for the *Color Fest #10*, and then started on *Orphans*.

When did you start working on *Orphans*, and when did you finish drawing this chapter?

It was about December 2011. It took me about a year of work, as I had other projects still in progress.

What tools did you use?

I used Fabriano F2 rough paper, whose absorbing property gives me complete control of the line, so I can have shaded effects, crumbled lines, and a more relaxed approach while working on the pencils. To ink, I use Staedler or Rotring fineliners, a brush felt-tip pen, and big markers to fill bigger black parts.

What was the most difficult scene and which one did you have to redraw more times?

The scene I needed to make bigger was redrawing the alien's posture when attacking Boyscout (on page 175). I also had to redraw the kids on the very first pages of the story because they looked a little bit older than what they needed to be.

If you could go back in time, what would you change about this chapter?

When I finish an issue, my first thought is about planning the next work. This way of looking forward helps me avoid the temptation to throw away everything I've drawn and start again from the beginning!

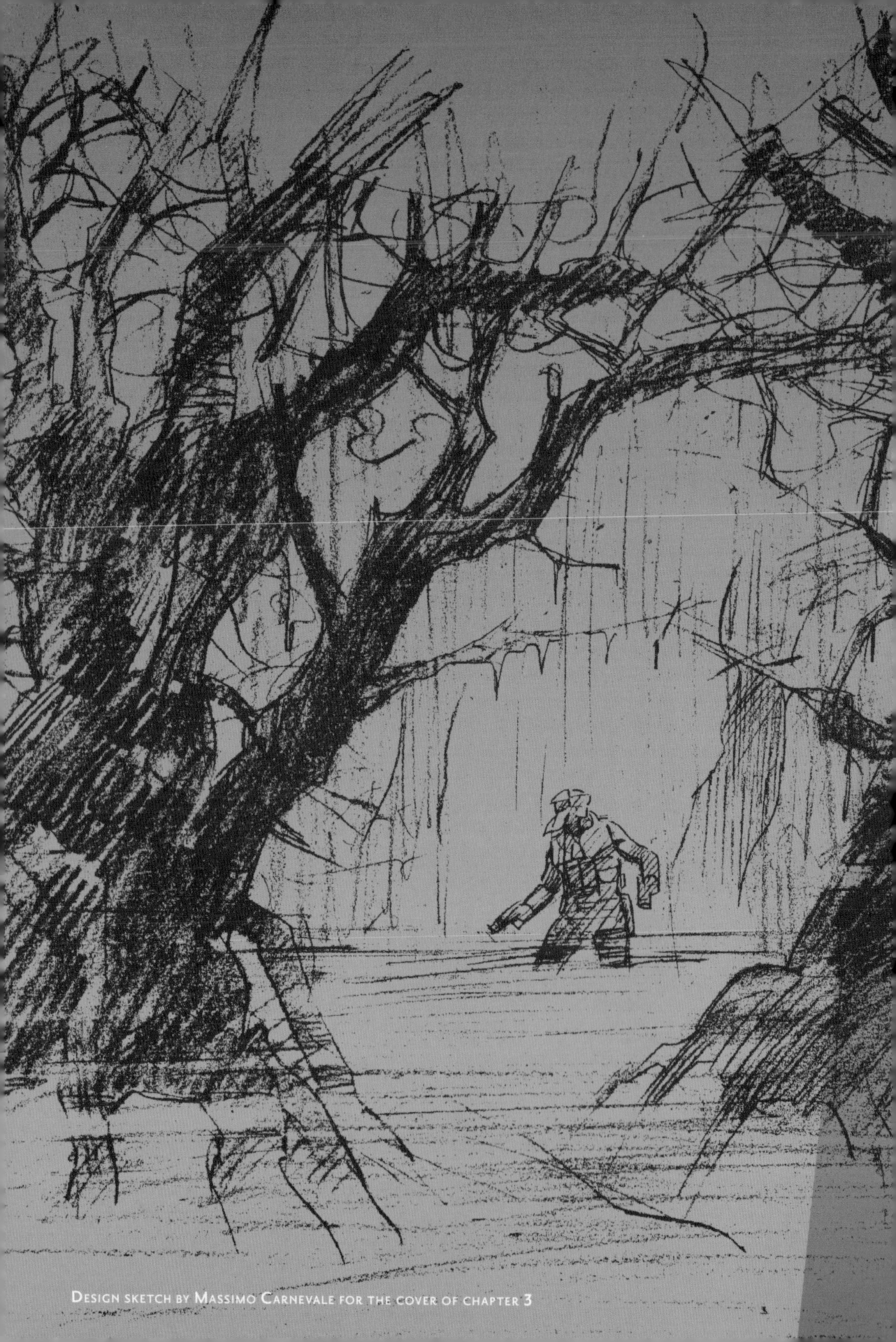

Design sketch by Massimo Carnevale for the cover of chapter 3

FIRST BLOOD

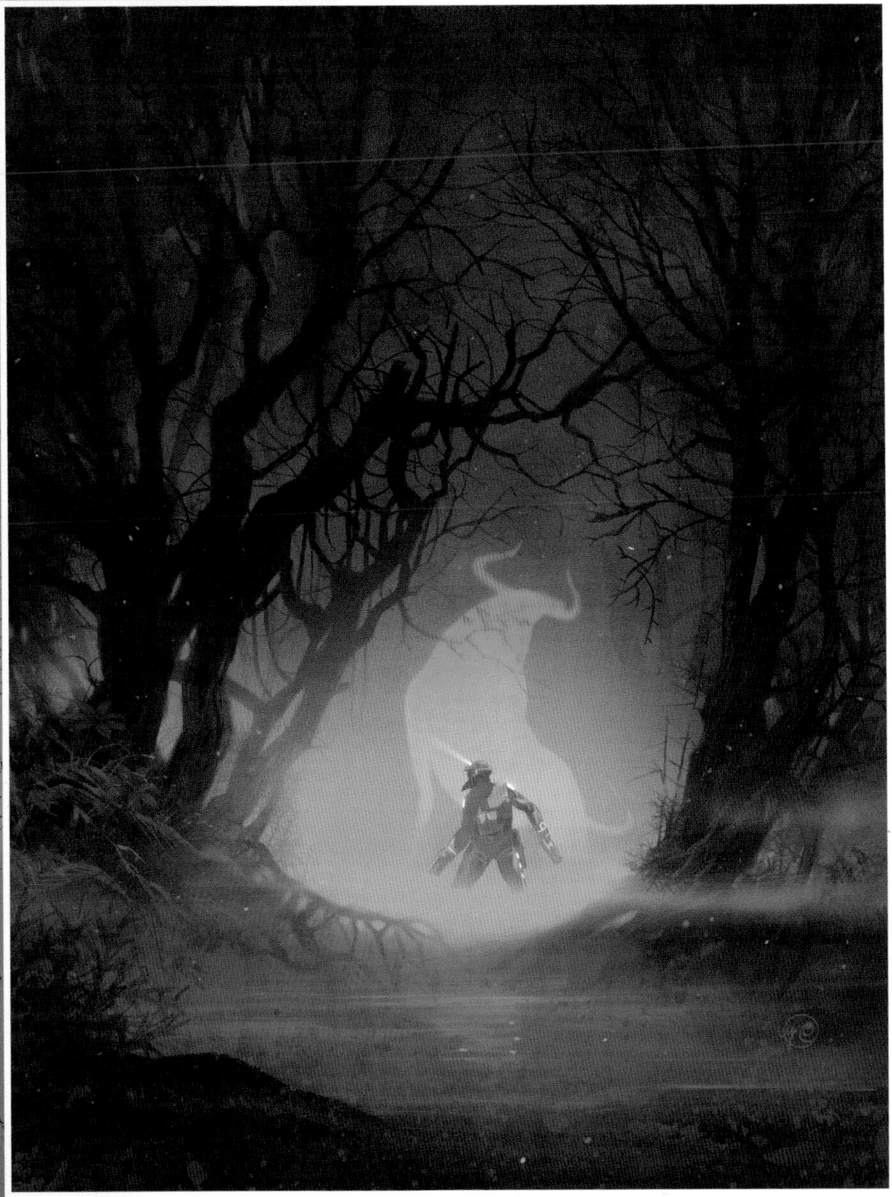

ORPHANS: CHAPTER 3

story: ROBERTO RECCHIONI
art: GIGI CAVENAGO
colors: ARIANNA FLOREAN
cover: MASSIMO CARNEVALE

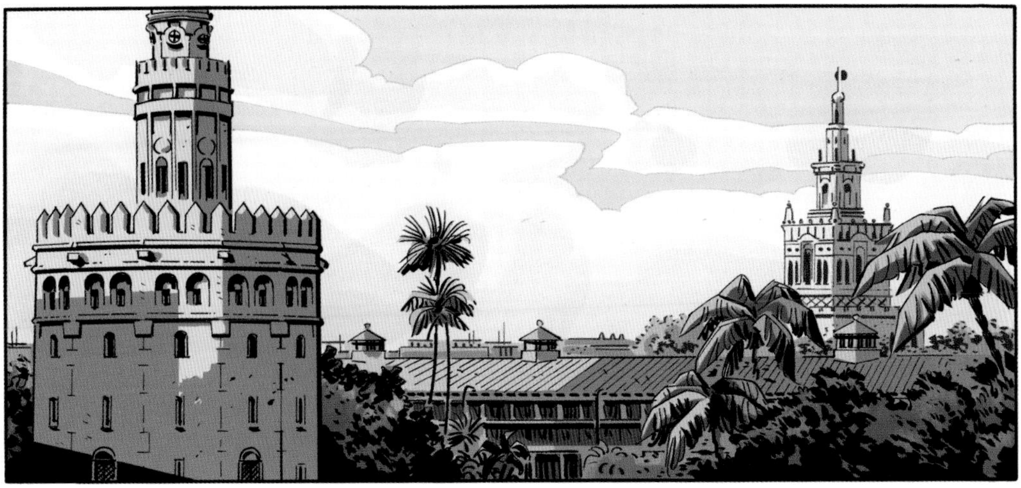

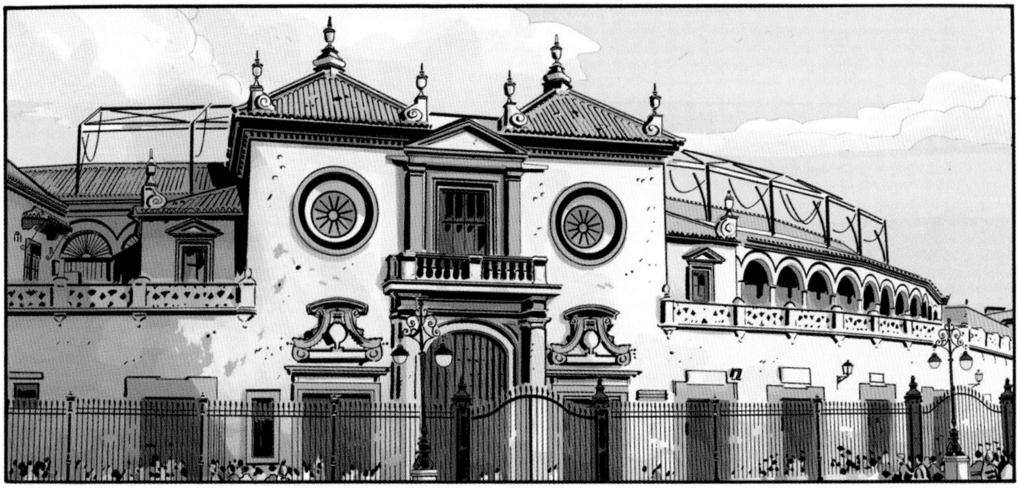

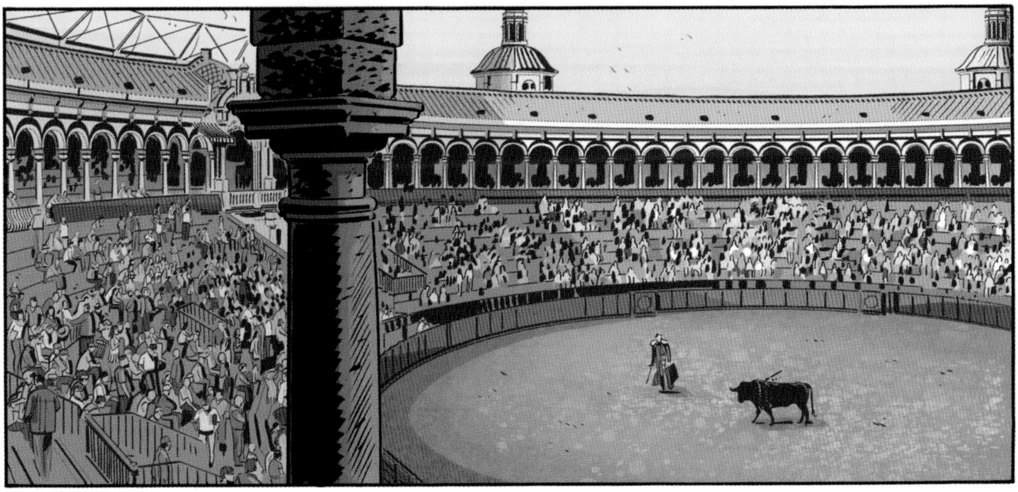

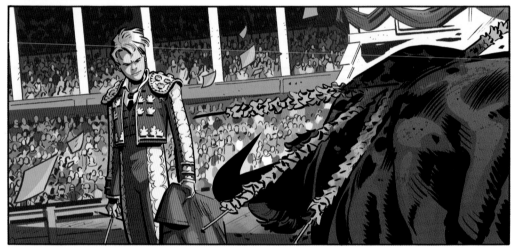

WHEN THE END OF THE WORLD CAME...

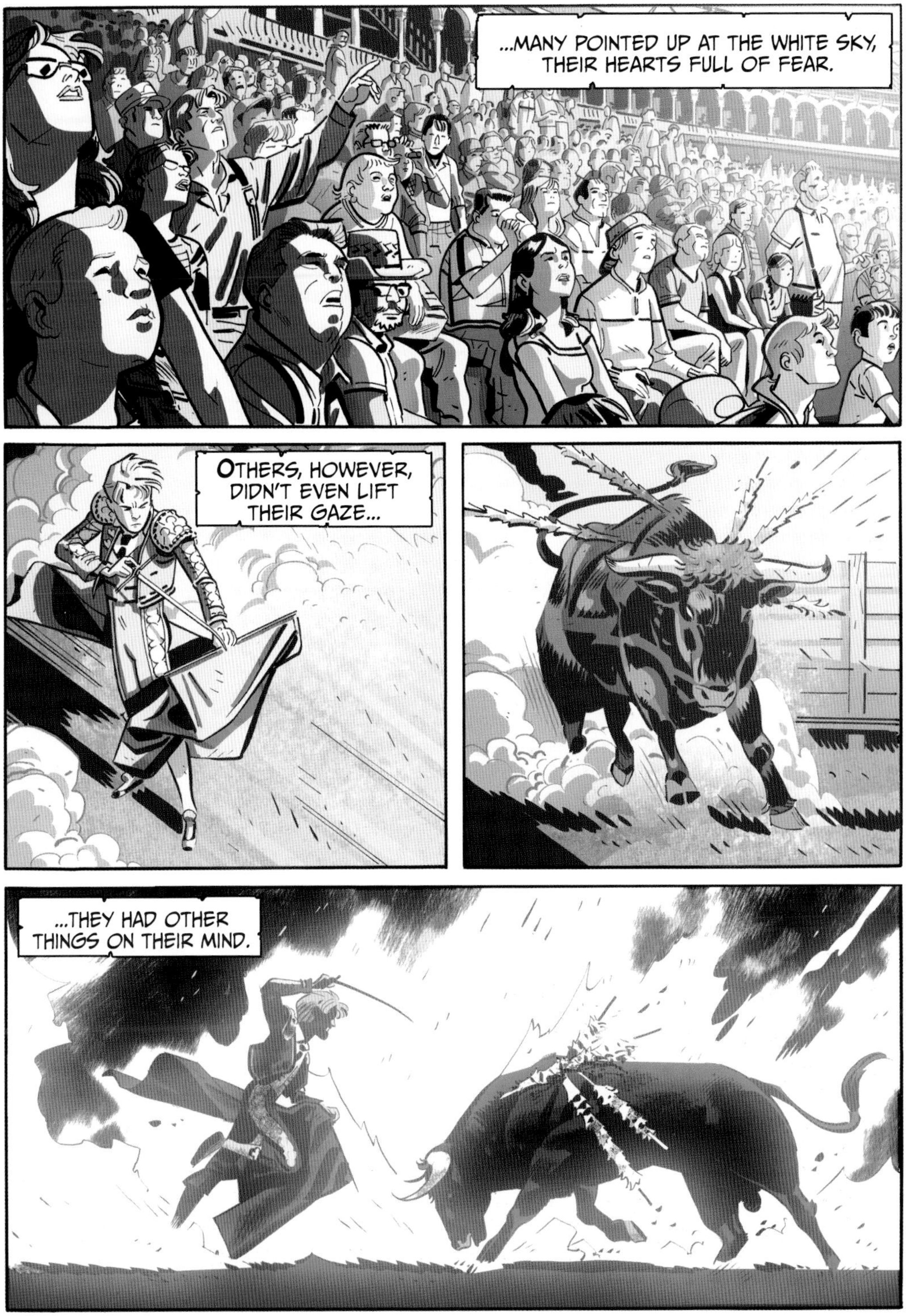
...MANY POINTED UP AT THE WHITE SKY, THEIR HEARTS FULL OF FEAR.
OTHERS, HOWEVER, DIDN'T EVEN LIFT THEIR GAZE...
...THEY HAD OTHER THINGS ON THEIR MIND.

...AT MACH 1, THE AIRCRAFT HAS ALMOST CAUGHT UP WITH THE PRESSURE WAVES PRODUCED BY ITS FORWARD MOTION...

...THIS PRESSURE IS CALLED THE "COMPRESSIBILITY BURBLE," WHICH CAN SIGNIFICANTLY SLOW A VEHICLE...

SO, BY THAT PRINCIPLE, WHICH AERODYNAMIC CHARACTERISTICS DOES AN AIRCRAFT NEED TO EXCEED THE SPEED OF SOUND?

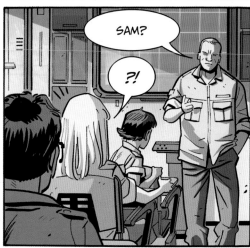

SAM?

?!

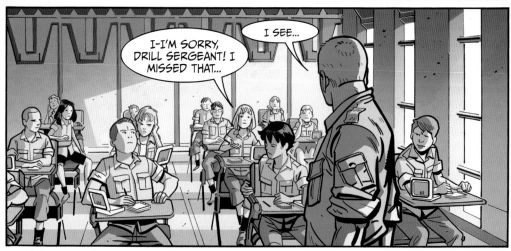

I-I'M SORRY, DRILL SERGEANT! I MISSED THAT...

I SEE...

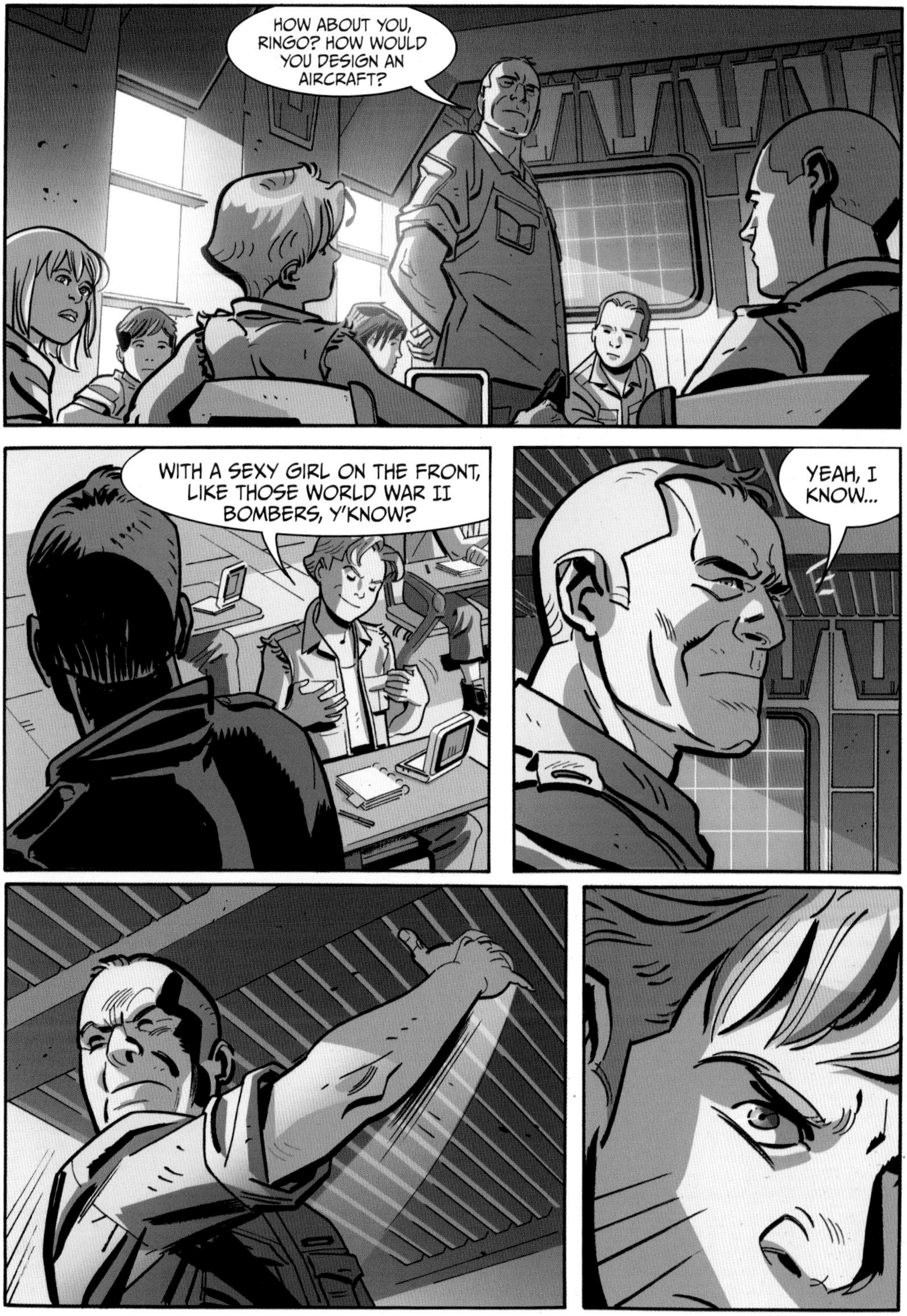
HOW ABOUT YOU, RINGO? HOW WOULD YOU DESIGN AN AIRCRAFT?
WITH A SEXY GIRL ON THE FRONT, LIKE THOSE WORLD WAR II BOMBERS, Y'KNOW?
YEAH, I KNOW...

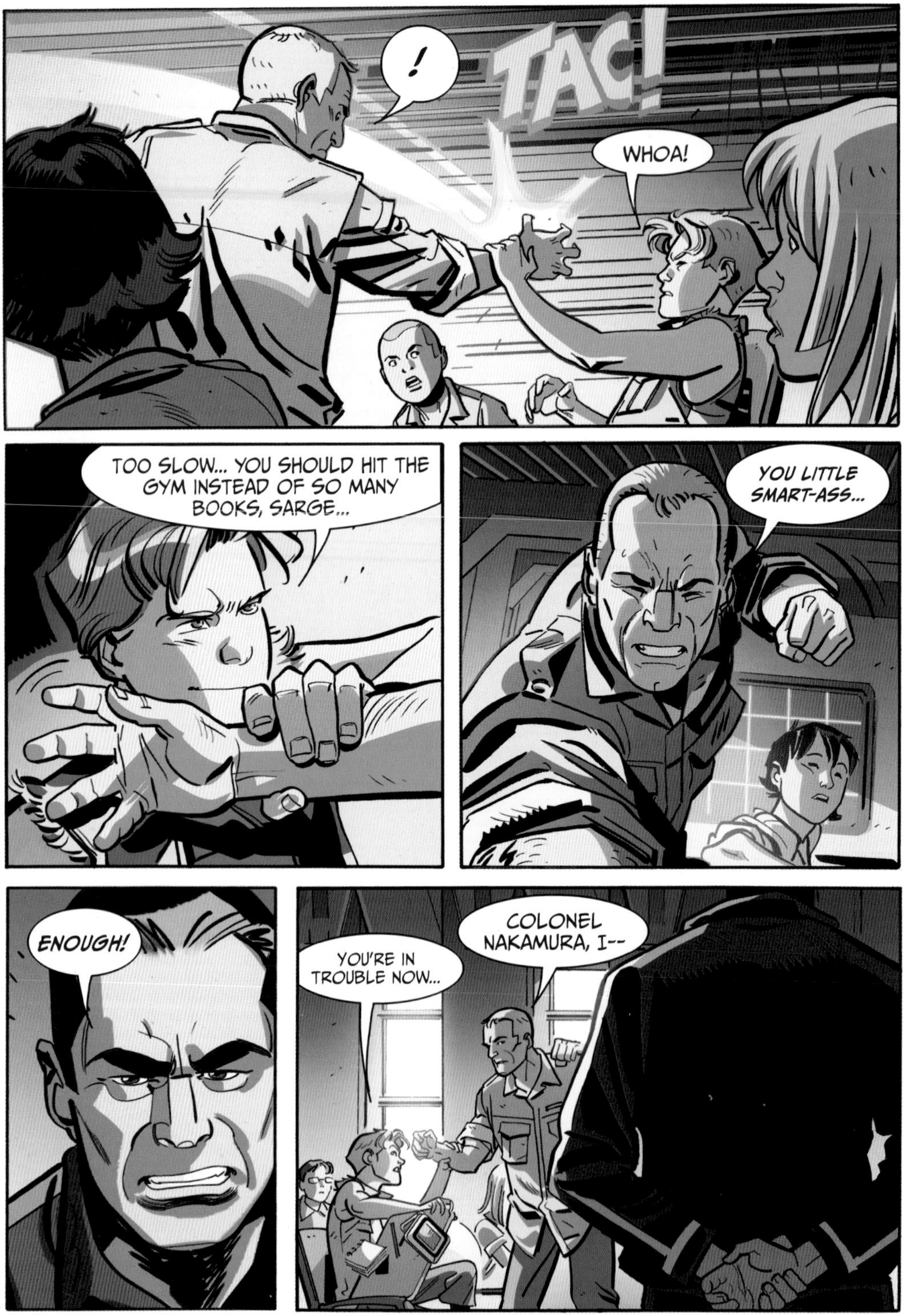
!
TAC!
WHOA!
TOO SLOW... YOU SHOULD HIT THE GYM INSTEAD OF SO MANY BOOKS, SARGE...
YOU LITTLE SMART-ASS...
ENOUGH!
COLONEL NAKAMURA, I--
YOU'RE IN TROUBLE NOW...

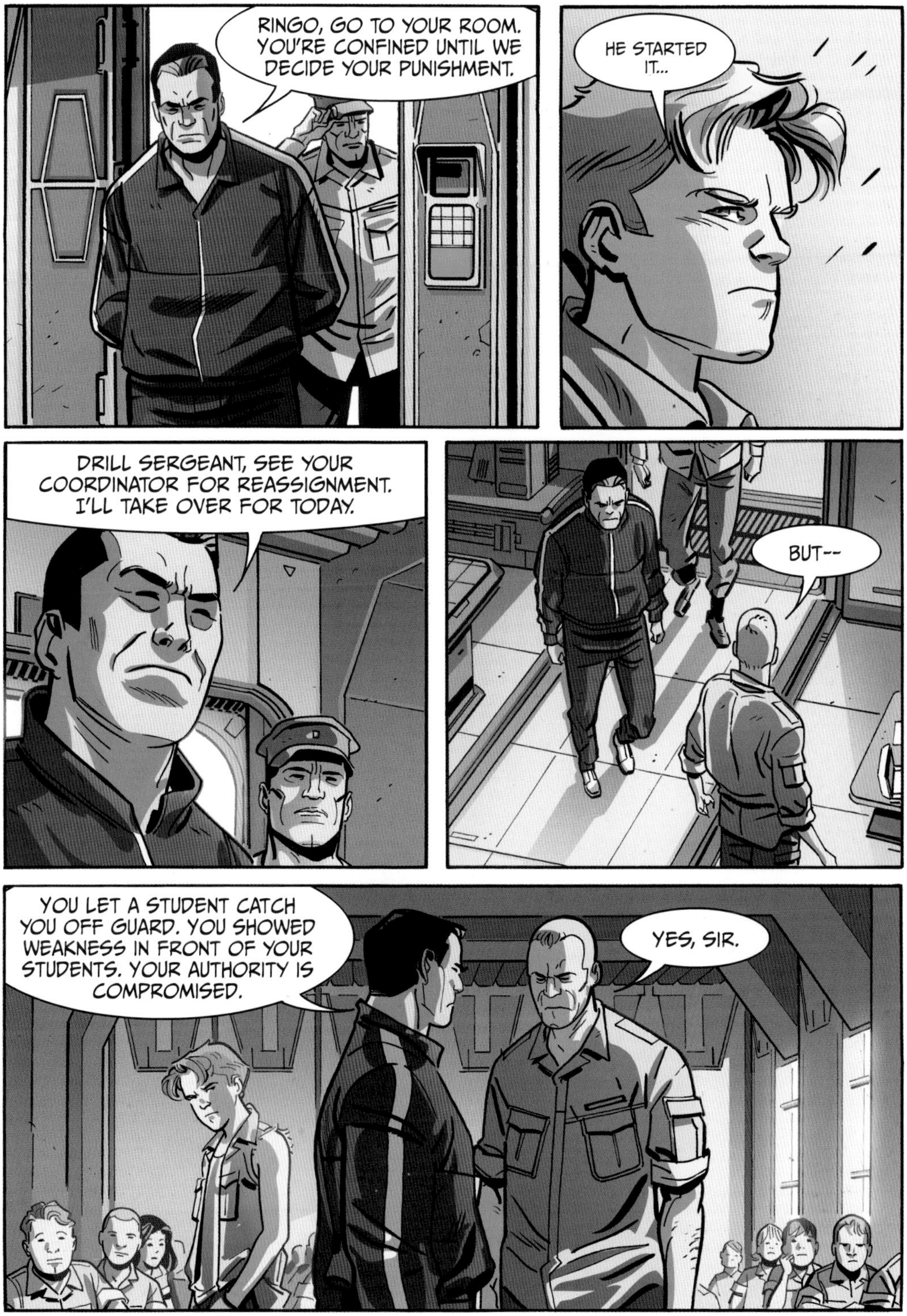
RINGO, GO TO YOUR ROOM. YOU'RE CONFINED UNTIL WE DECIDE YOUR PUNISHMENT.
HE STARTED IT...
DRILL SERGEANT, SEE YOUR COORDINATOR FOR REASSIGNMENT. I'LL TAKE OVER FOR TODAY.
BUT--
YOU LET A STUDENT CATCH YOU OFF GUARD. YOU SHOWED WEAKNESS IN FRONT OF YOUR STUDENTS. YOUR AUTHORITY IS COMPROMISED.
YES, SIR.

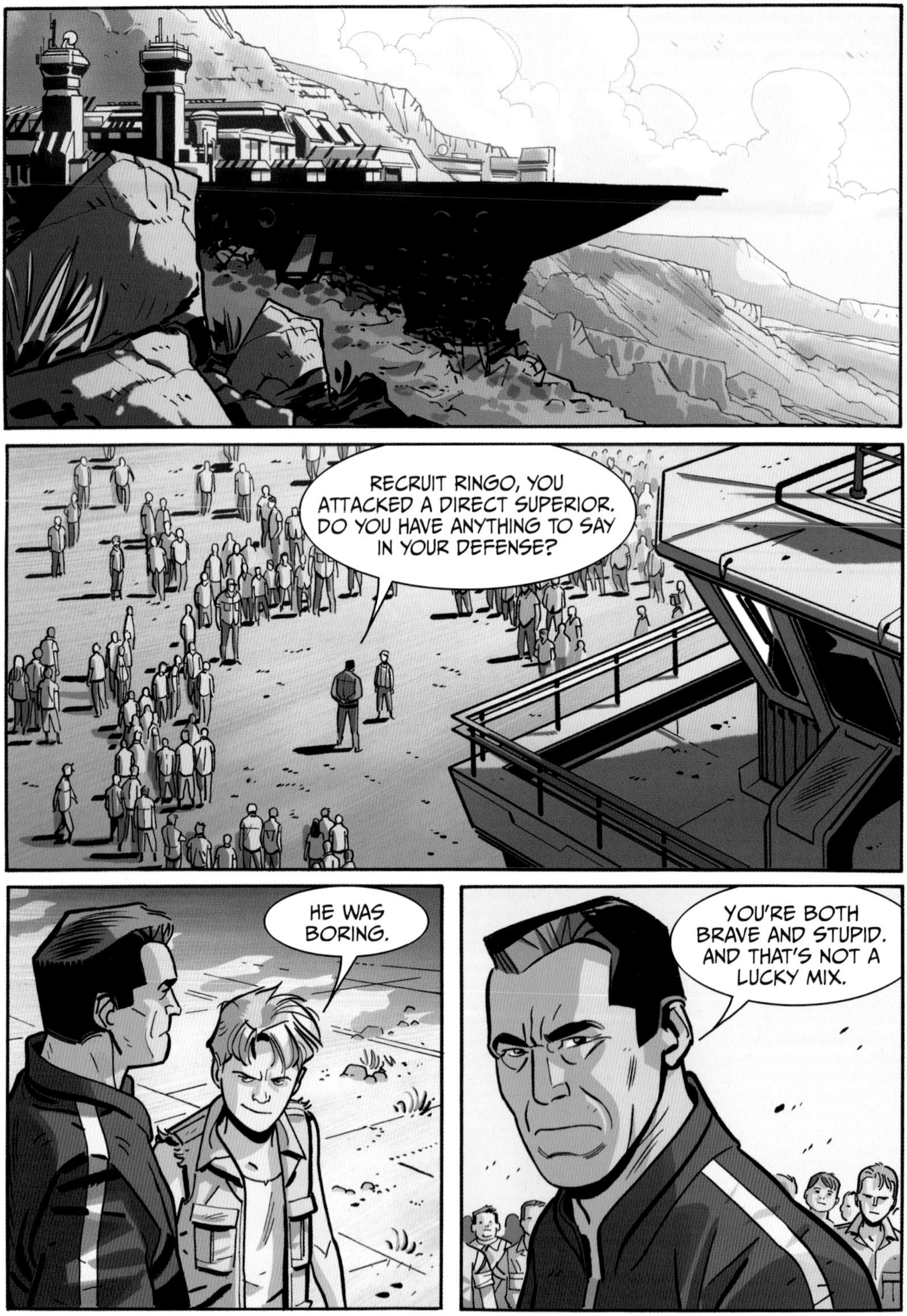
RECRUIT RINGO, YOU ATTACKED A DIRECT SUPERIOR. DO YOU HAVE ANYTHING TO SAY IN YOUR DEFENSE?
HE WAS BORING.
YOU'RE BOTH BRAVE AND STUPID. AND THAT'S NOT A LUCKY MIX.

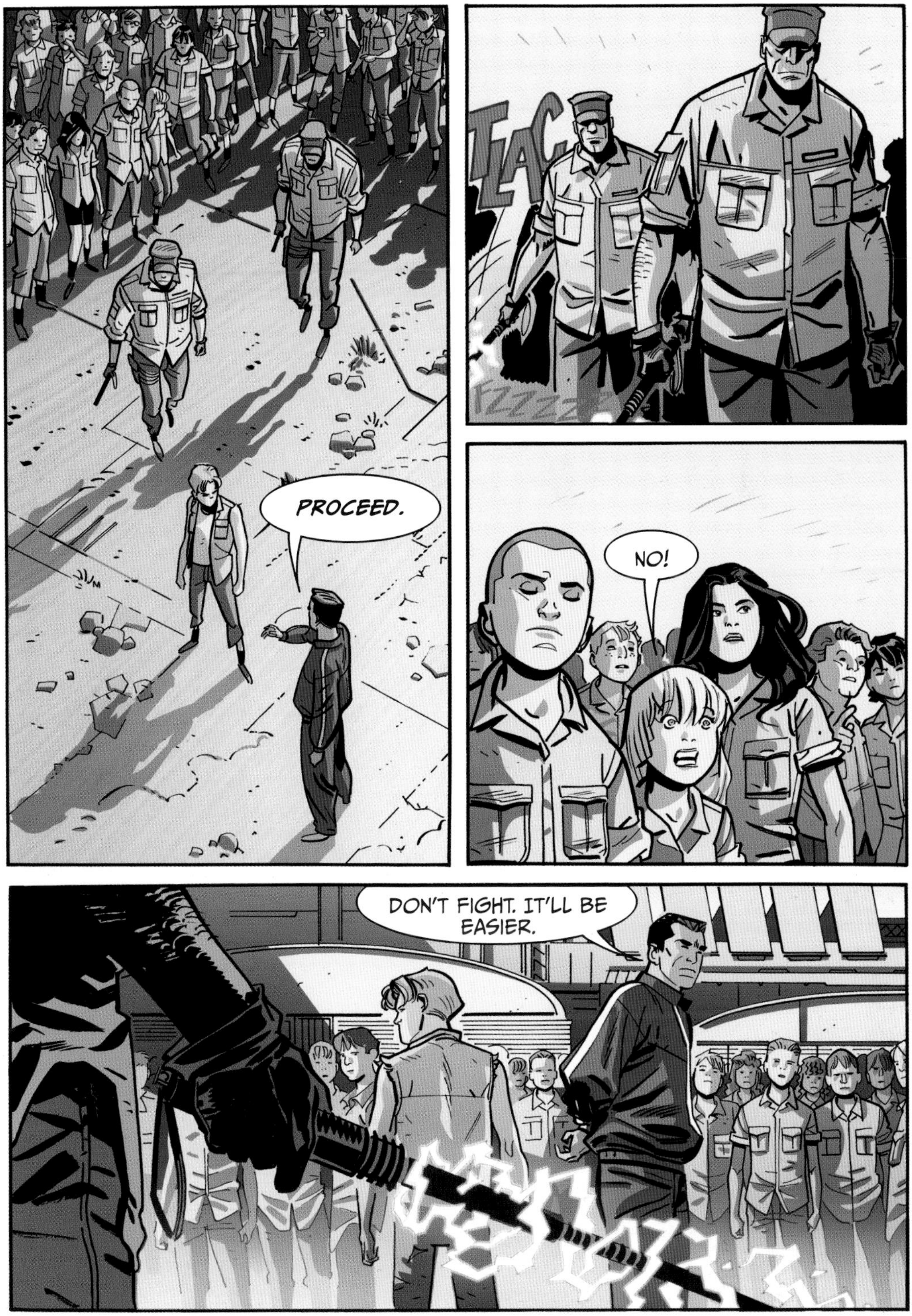
PROCEED.
NO!
DON'T FIGHT. IT'LL BE EASIER.

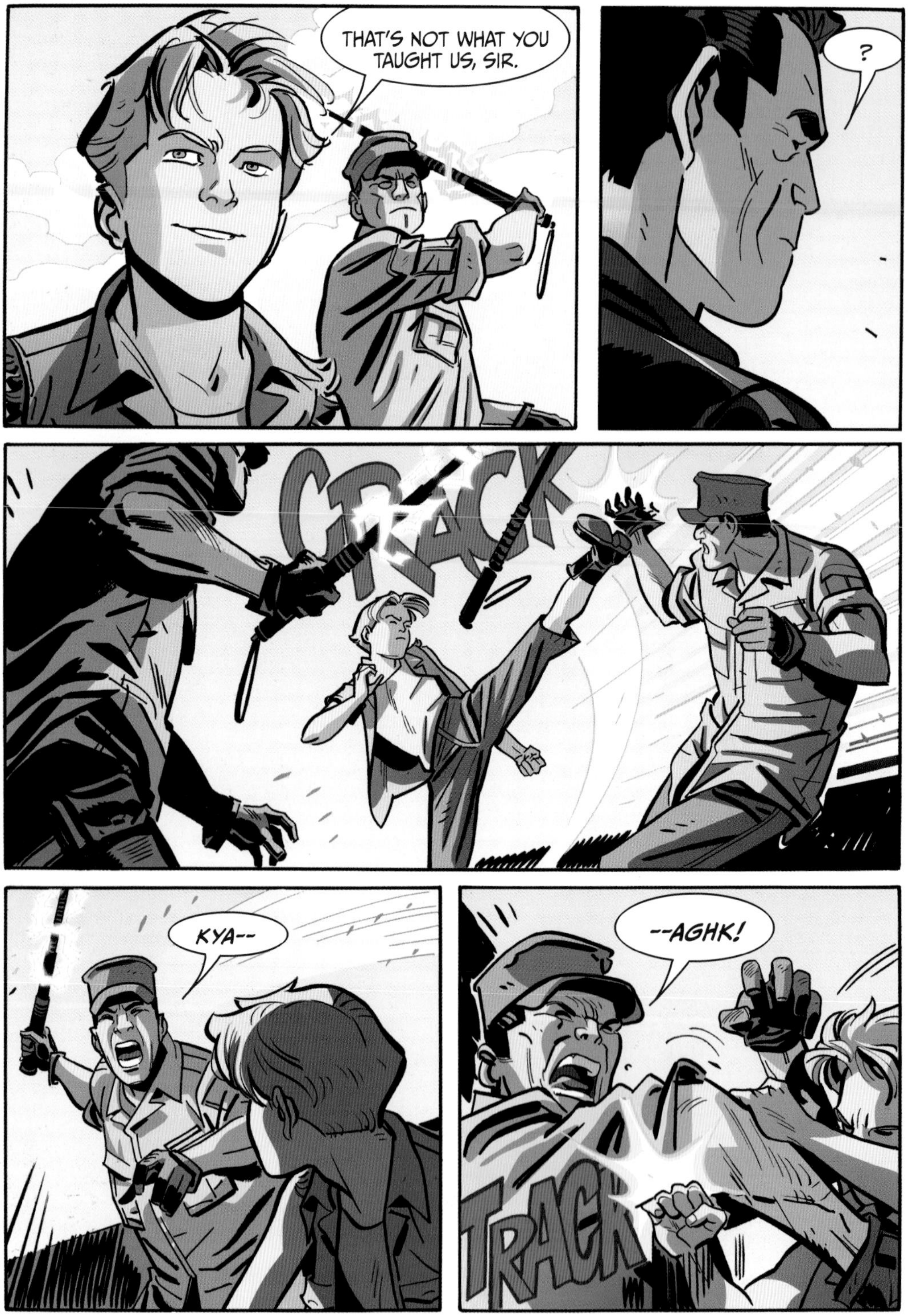
THAT'S NOT WHAT YOU TAUGHT US, SIR.
?
CRACK
KYA--
--AGHK!
TRACK

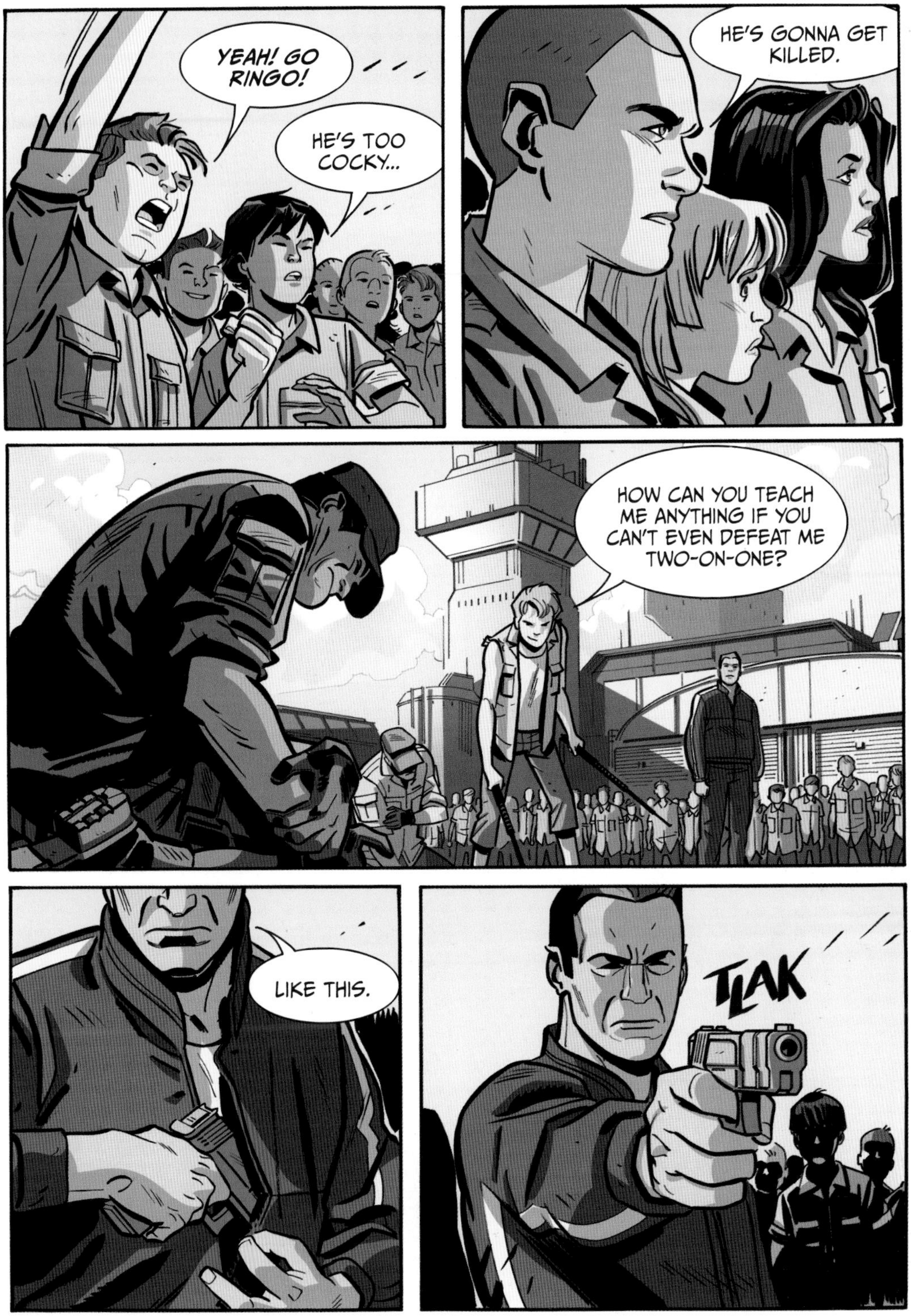
YEAH! GO RINGO!
HE'S TOO COCKY...
HE'S GONNA GET KILLED.
HOW CAN YOU TEACH ME ANYTHING IF YOU CAN'T EVEN DEFEAT ME TWO-ON-ONE?
LIKE THIS.
TLAK

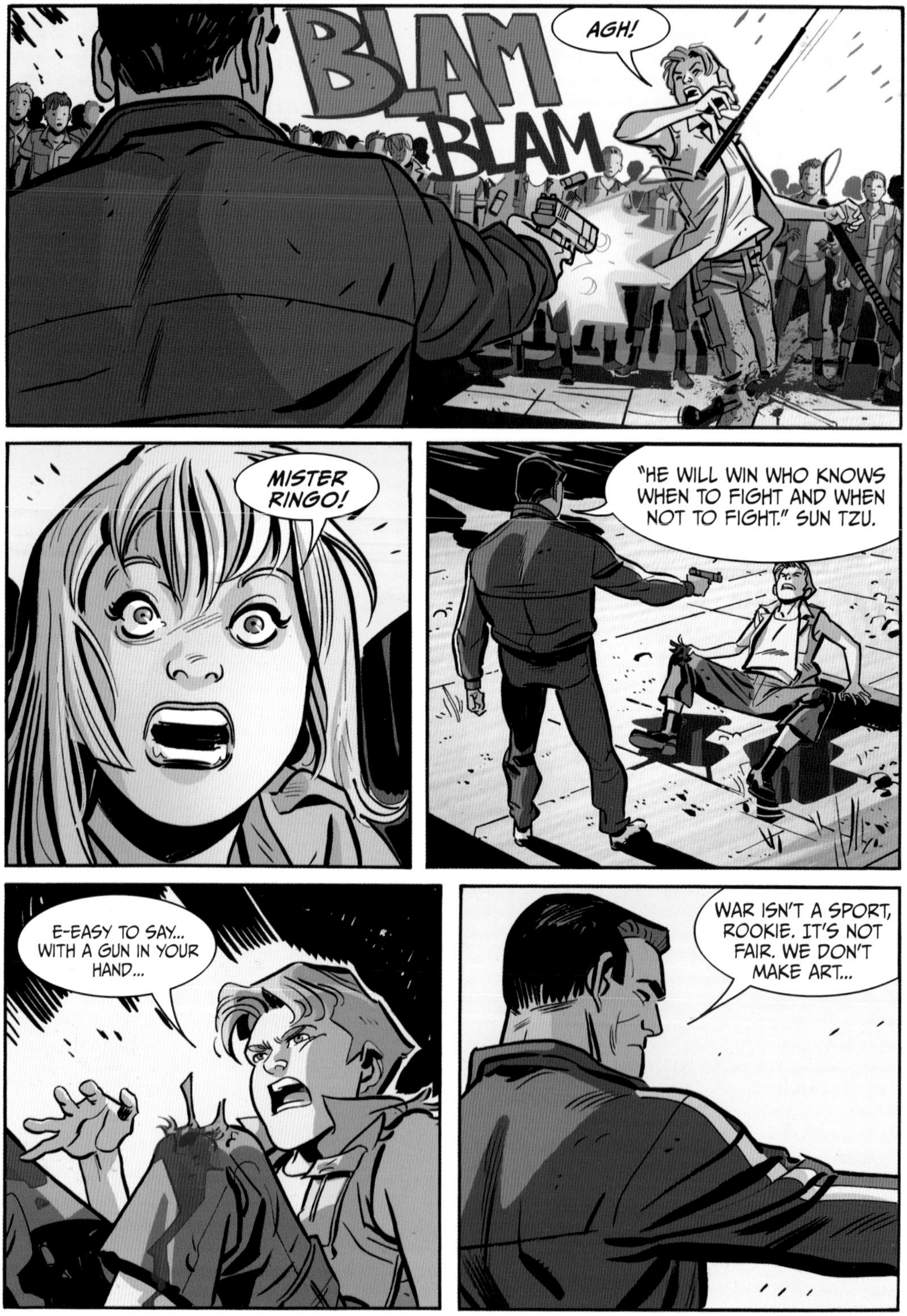
BLAM
BLAM
AGH!
MISTER RINGO!
"HE WILL WIN WHO KNOWS WHEN TO FIGHT AND WHEN NOT TO FIGHT." SUN TZU.
E-EASY TO SAY... WITH A GUN IN YOUR HAND...
WAR ISN'T A SPORT, ROOKIE. IT'S NOT FAIR. WE DON'T MAKE ART...

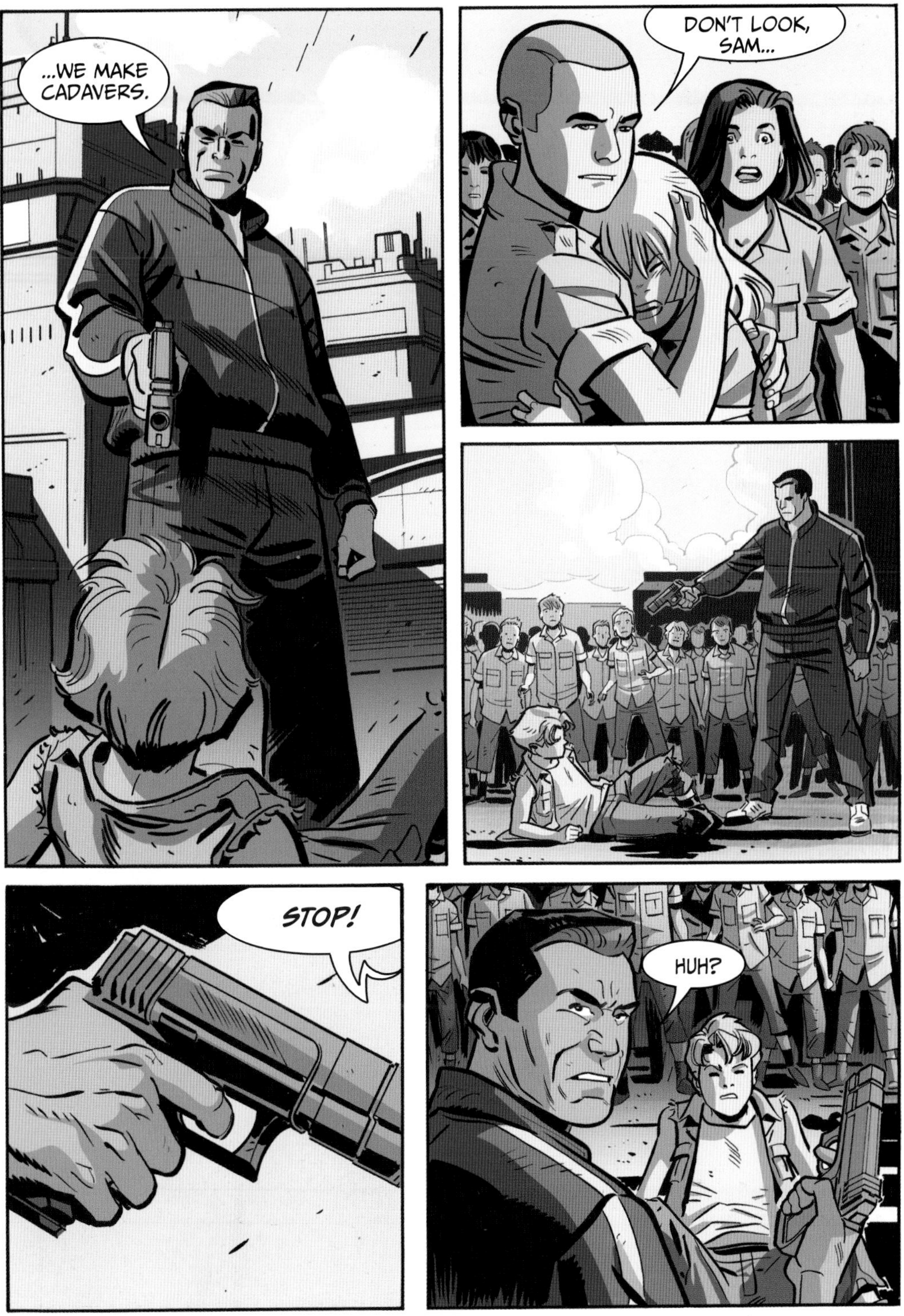
...WE MAKE CADAVERS.
DON'T LOOK, SAM...
STOP!
HUH?

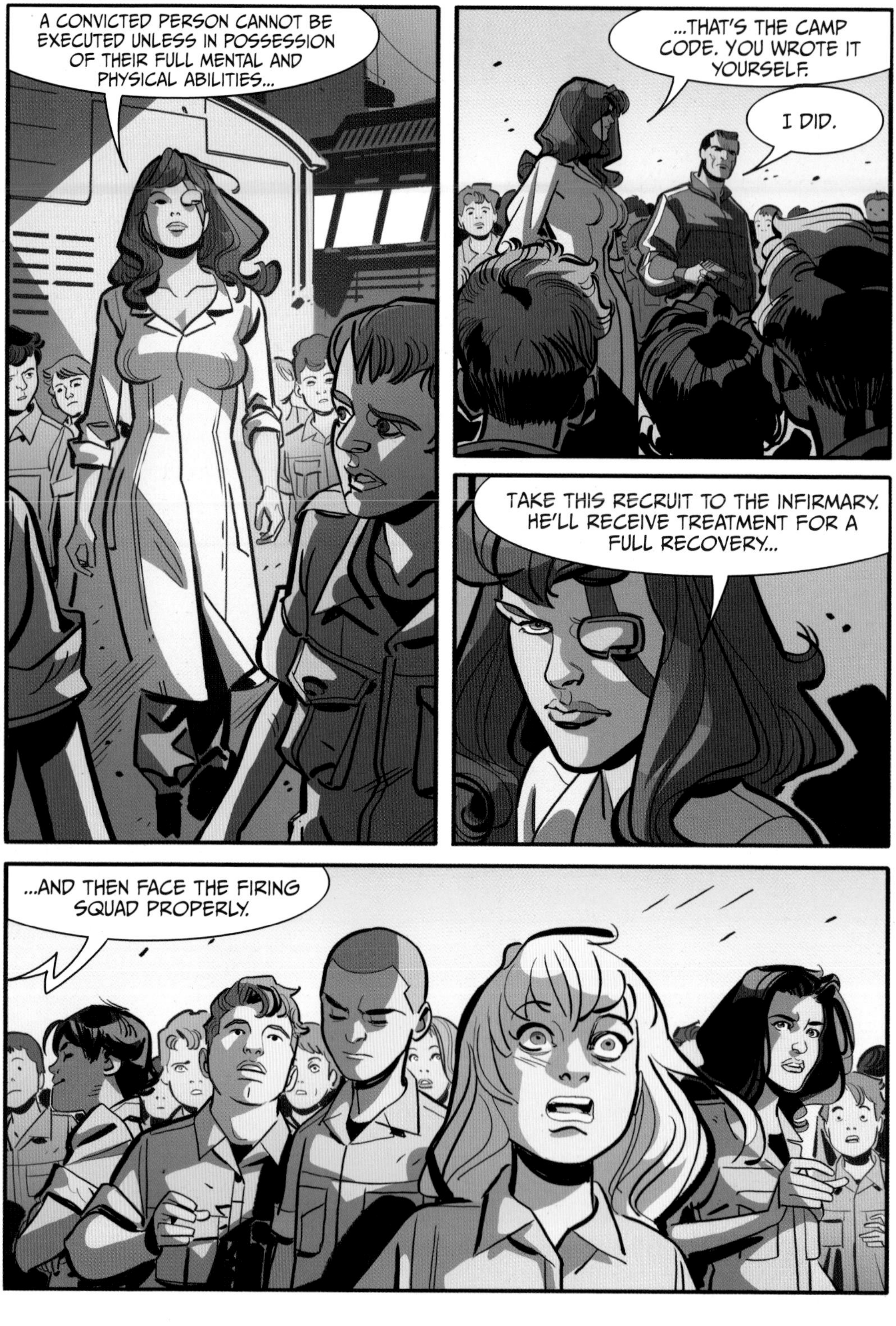
A CONVICTED PERSON CANNOT BE EXECUTED UNLESS IN POSSESSION OF THEIR FULL MENTAL AND PHYSICAL ABILITIES...
...THAT'S THE CAMP CODE. YOU WROTE IT YOURSELF.
I DID.
TAKE THIS RECRUIT TO THE INFIRMARY. HE'LL RECEIVE TREATMENT FOR A FULL RECOVERY...
...AND THEN FACE THE FIRING SQUAD PROPERLY.

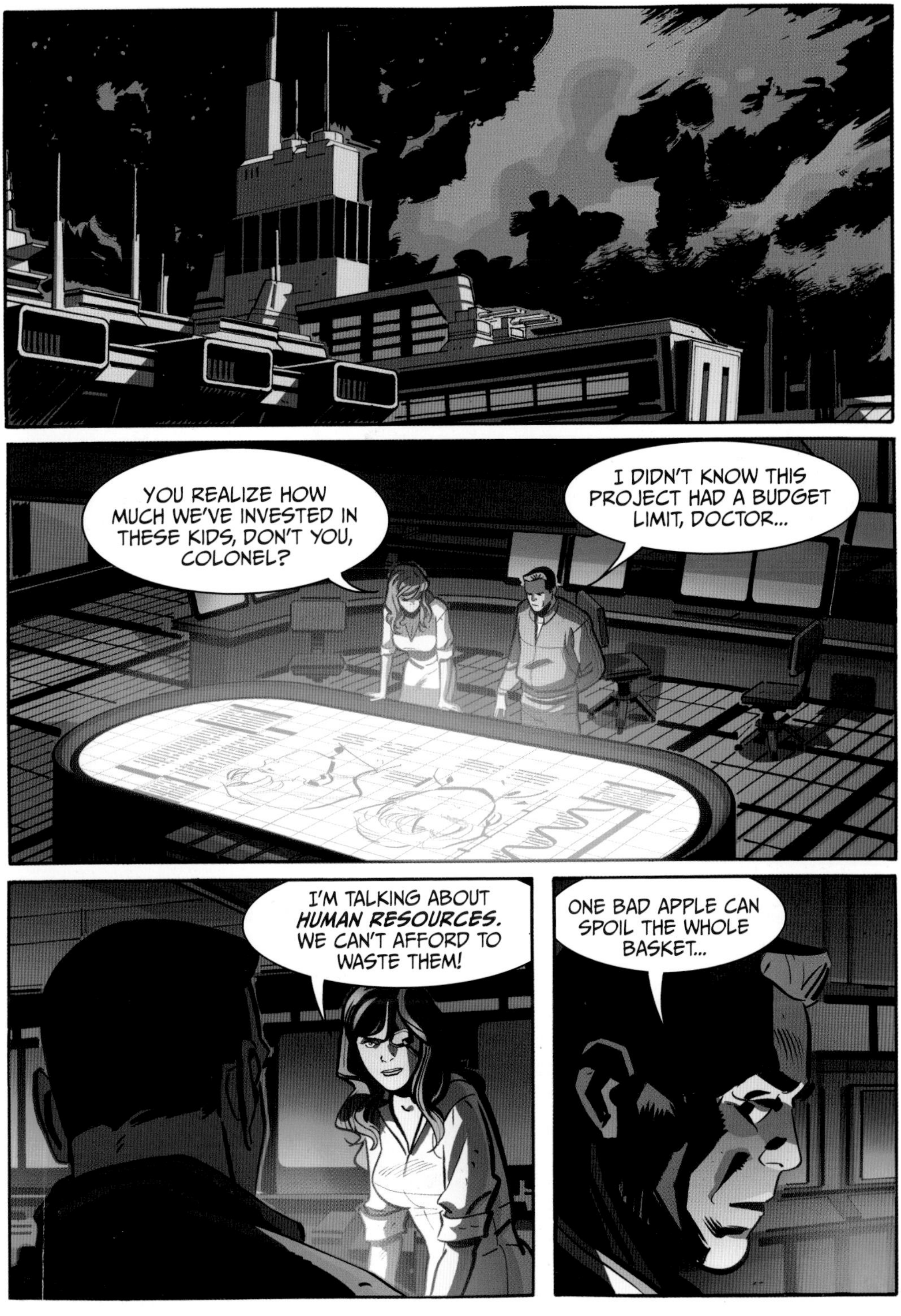
YOU REALIZE HOW MUCH WE'VE INVESTED IN THESE KIDS, DON'T YOU, COLONEL?
I DIDN'T KNOW THIS PROJECT HAD A BUDGET LIMIT, DOCTOR...
I'M TALKING ABOUT *HUMAN RESOURCES.* WE CAN'T AFFORD TO WASTE THEM!
ONE BAD APPLE CAN SPOIL THE WHOLE BASKET...

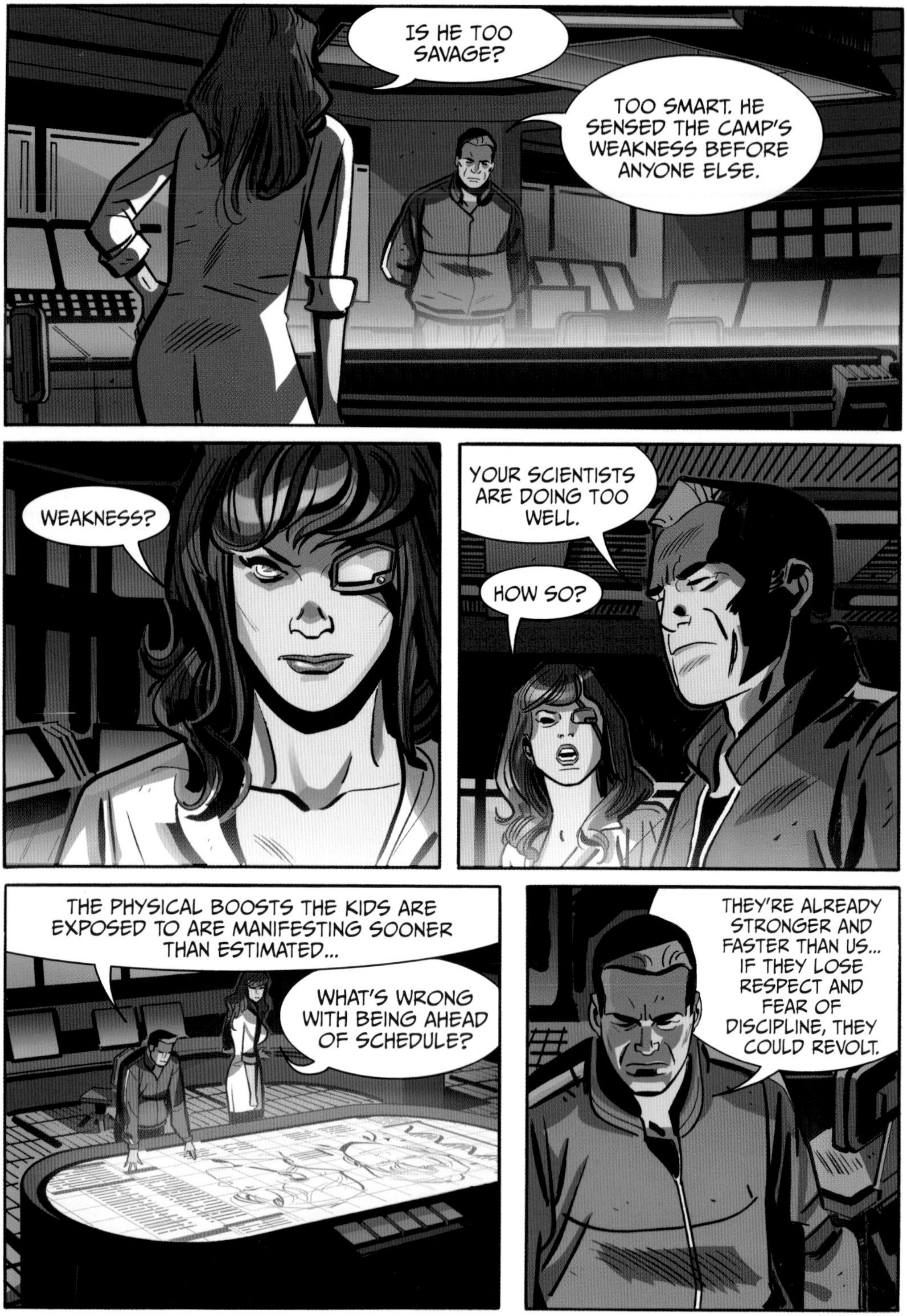
IS HE TOO SAVAGE?
TOO SMART. HE SENSED THE CAMP'S WEAKNESS BEFORE ANYONE ELSE.
WEAKNESS?
YOUR SCIENTISTS ARE DOING TOO WELL.
HOW SO?
THE PHYSICAL BOOSTS THE KIDS ARE EXPOSED TO ARE MANIFESTING SOONER THAN ESTIMATED...
WHAT'S WRONG WITH BEING AHEAD OF SCHEDULE?
THEY'RE ALREADY STRONGER AND FASTER THAN US... IF THEY LOSE RESPECT AND FEAR OF DISCIPLINE, THEY COULD REVOLT.

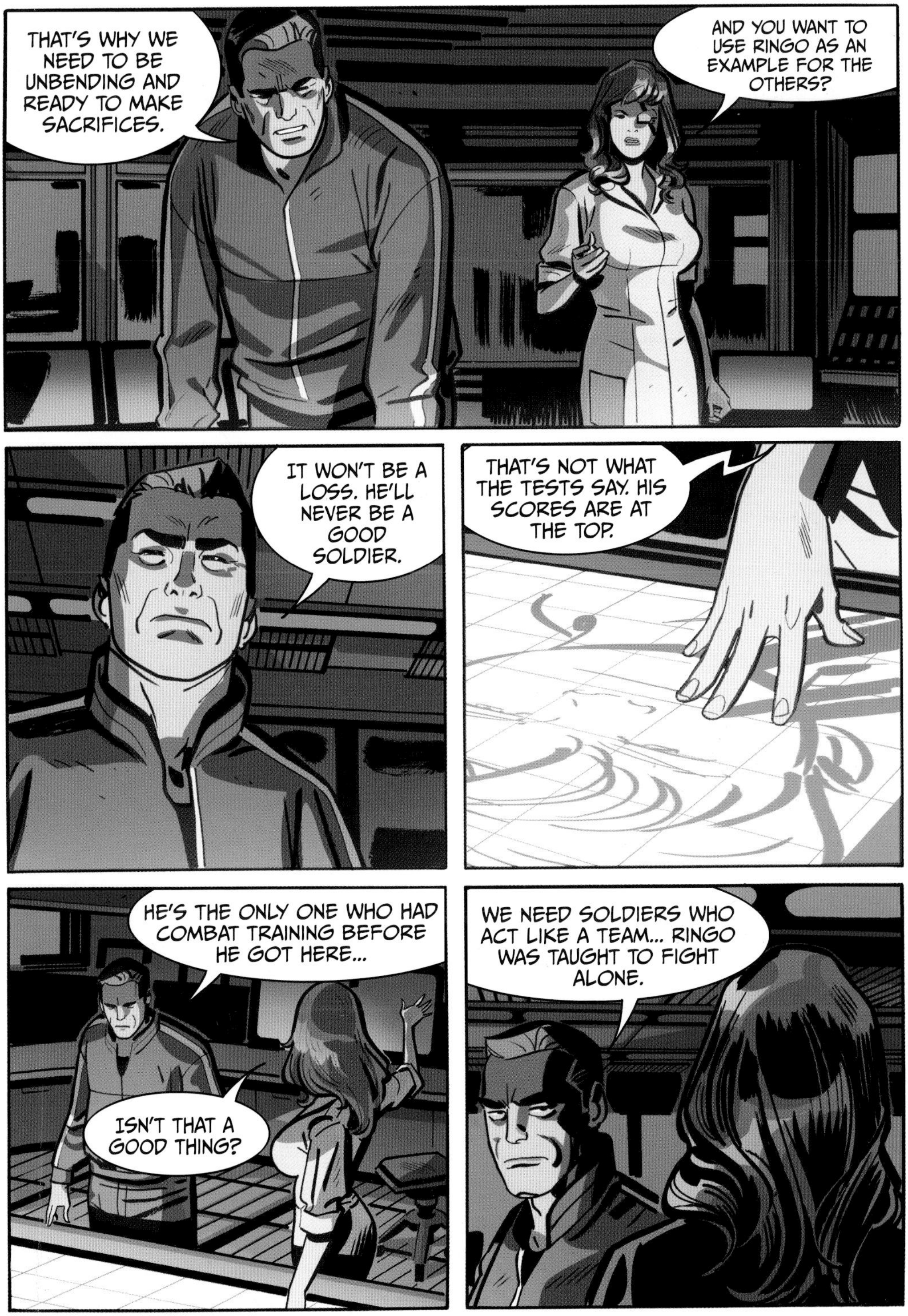
THAT'S WHY WE NEED TO BE UNBENDING AND READY TO MAKE SACRIFICES.
AND YOU WANT TO USE RINGO AS AN EXAMPLE FOR THE OTHERS?
IT WON'T BE A LOSS. HE'LL NEVER BE A GOOD SOLDIER.
THAT'S NOT WHAT THE TESTS SAY. HIS SCORES ARE AT THE TOP.
HE'S THE ONLY ONE WHO HAD COMBAT TRAINING BEFORE HE GOT HERE...
ISN'T THAT A GOOD THING?
WE NEED SOLDIERS WHO ACT LIKE A TEAM... RINGO WAS TAUGHT TO FIGHT ALONE.

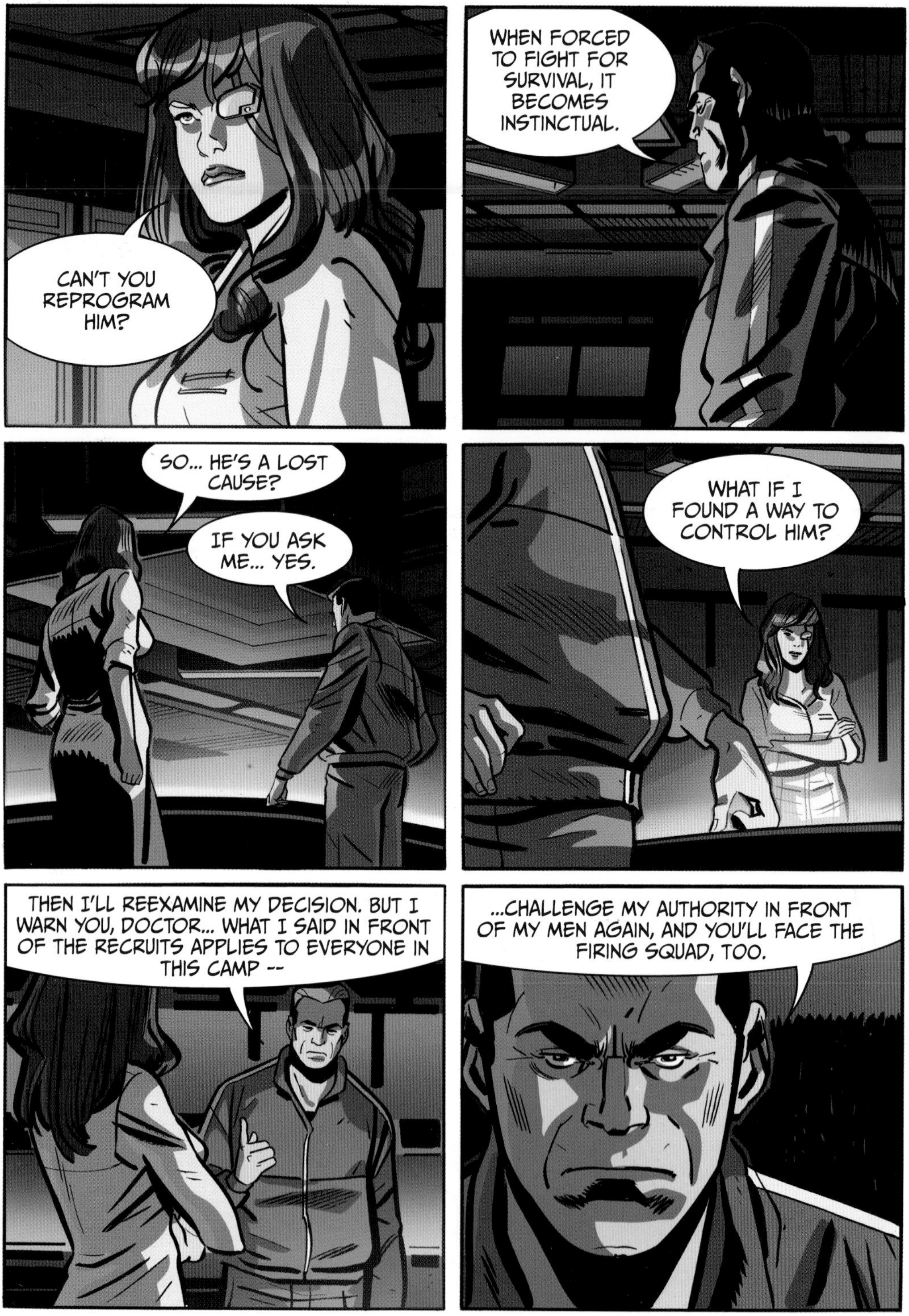
CAN'T YOU REPROGRAM HIM?
WHEN FORCED TO FIGHT FOR SURVIVAL, IT BECOMES INSTINCTUAL.
SO... HE'S A LOST CAUSE?
IF YOU ASK ME... YES.
WHAT IF I FOUND A WAY TO CONTROL HIM?
THEN I'LL REEXAMINE MY DECISION. BUT I WARN YOU, DOCTOR... WHAT I SAID IN FRONT OF THE RECRUITS APPLIES TO EVERYONE IN THIS CAMP --
...CHALLENGE MY AUTHORITY IN FRONT OF MY MEN AGAIN, AND YOU'LL FACE THE FIRING SQUAD, TOO.

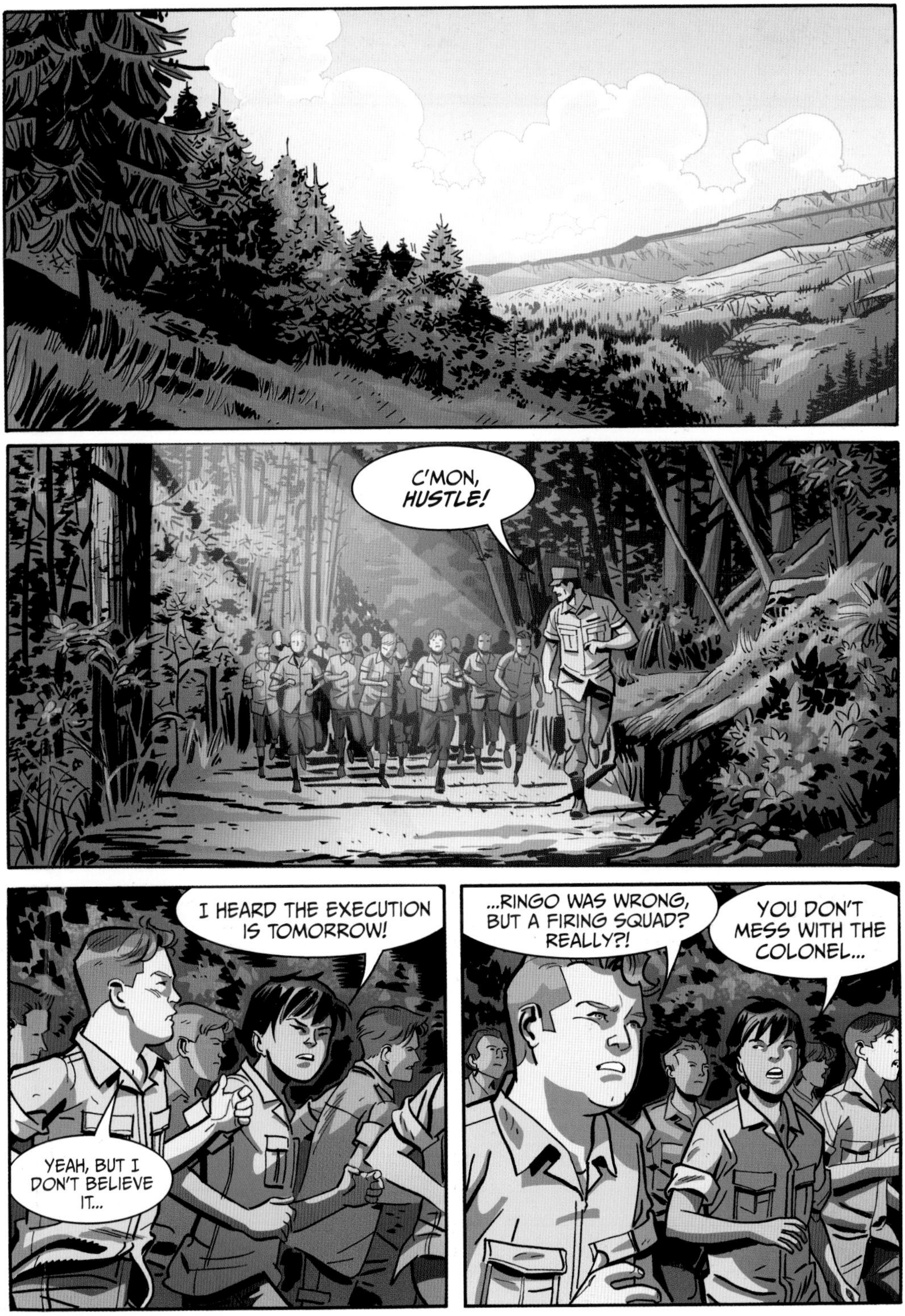
C'MON, *HUSTLE!*
I HEARD THE EXECUTION IS TOMORROW!
YEAH, BUT I DON'T BELIEVE IT...
...RINGO WAS WRONG, BUT A FIRING SQUAD? REALLY?!
YOU DON'T MESS WITH THE COLONEL...

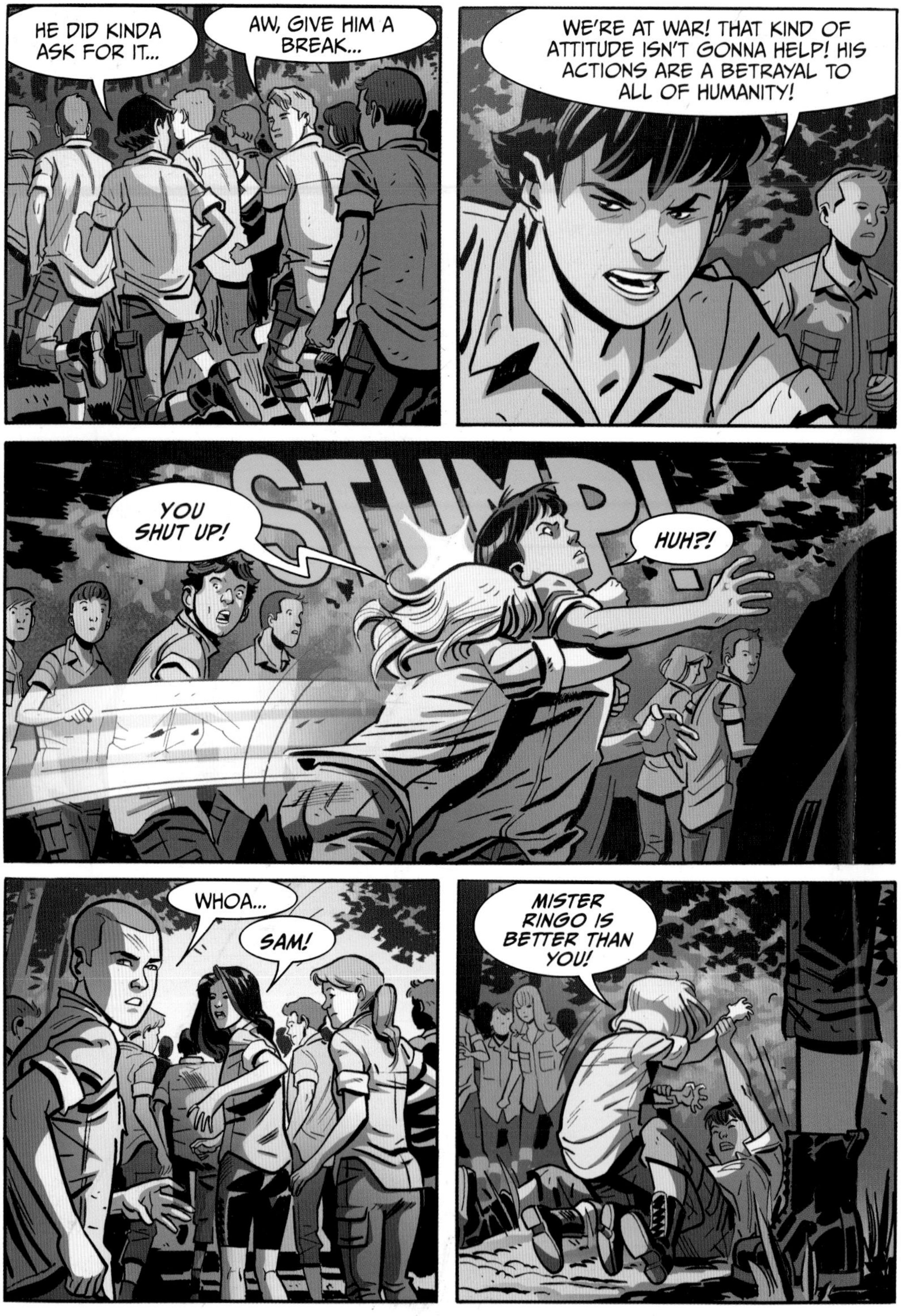
HE DID KINDA ASK FOR IT...
AW, GIVE HIM A BREAK...
WE'RE AT WAR! THAT KIND OF ATTITUDE ISN'T GONNA HELP! HIS ACTIONS ARE A BETRAYAL TO ALL OF HUMANITY!
STUMP!
YOU SHUT UP!
HUH?!
WHOA...
SAM!
MISTER RINGO IS BETTER THAN YOU!

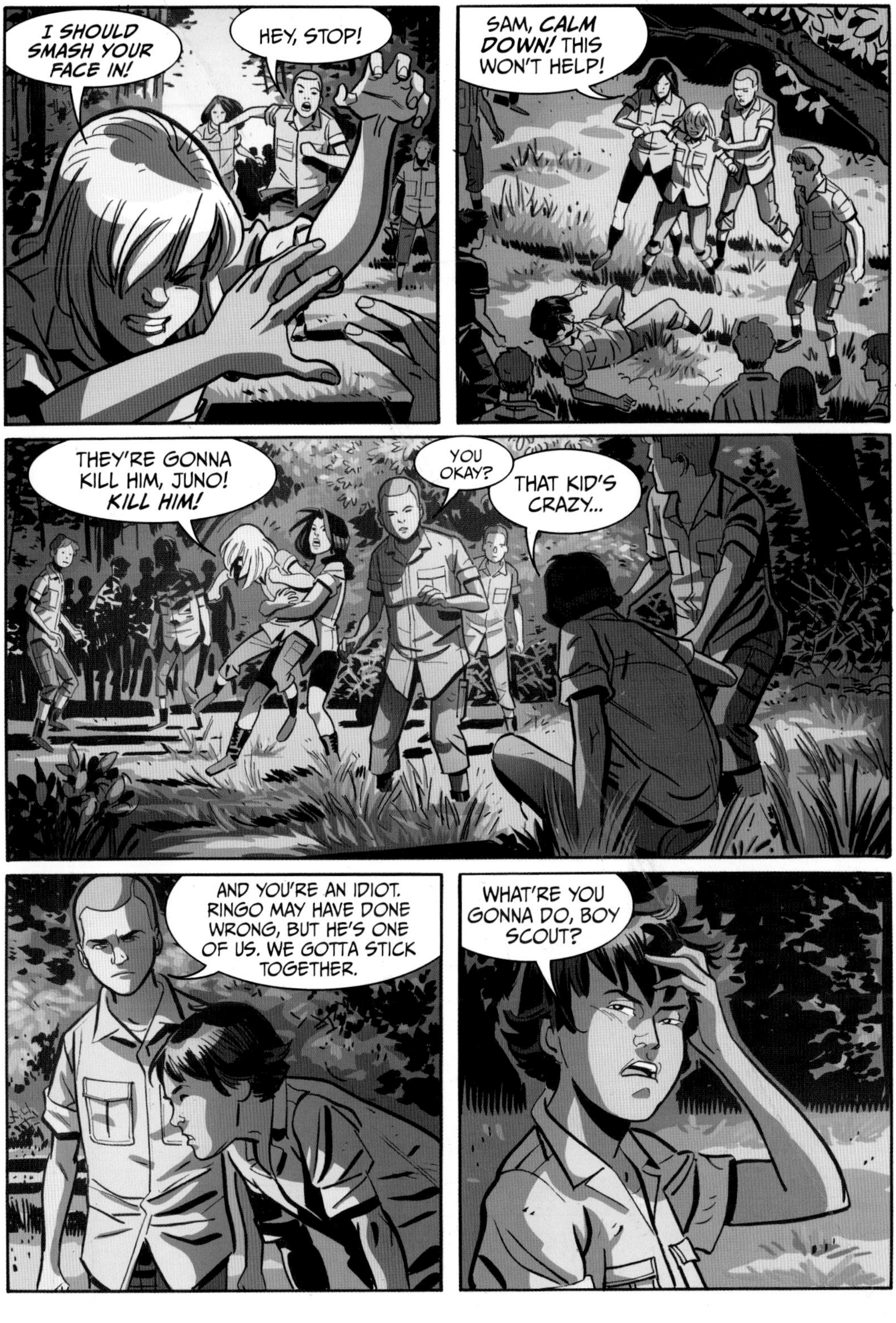
I SHOULD SMASH YOUR FACE IN!
HEY, STOP!
SAM, CALM DOWN! THIS WON'T HELP!
THEY'RE GONNA KILL HIM, JUNO! KILL HIM!
YOU OKAY?
THAT KID'S CRAZY...
AND YOU'RE AN IDIOT. RINGO MAY HAVE DONE WRONG, BUT HE'S ONE OF US. WE GOTTA STICK TOGETHER.
WHAT'RE YOU GONNA DO, BOY SCOUT?

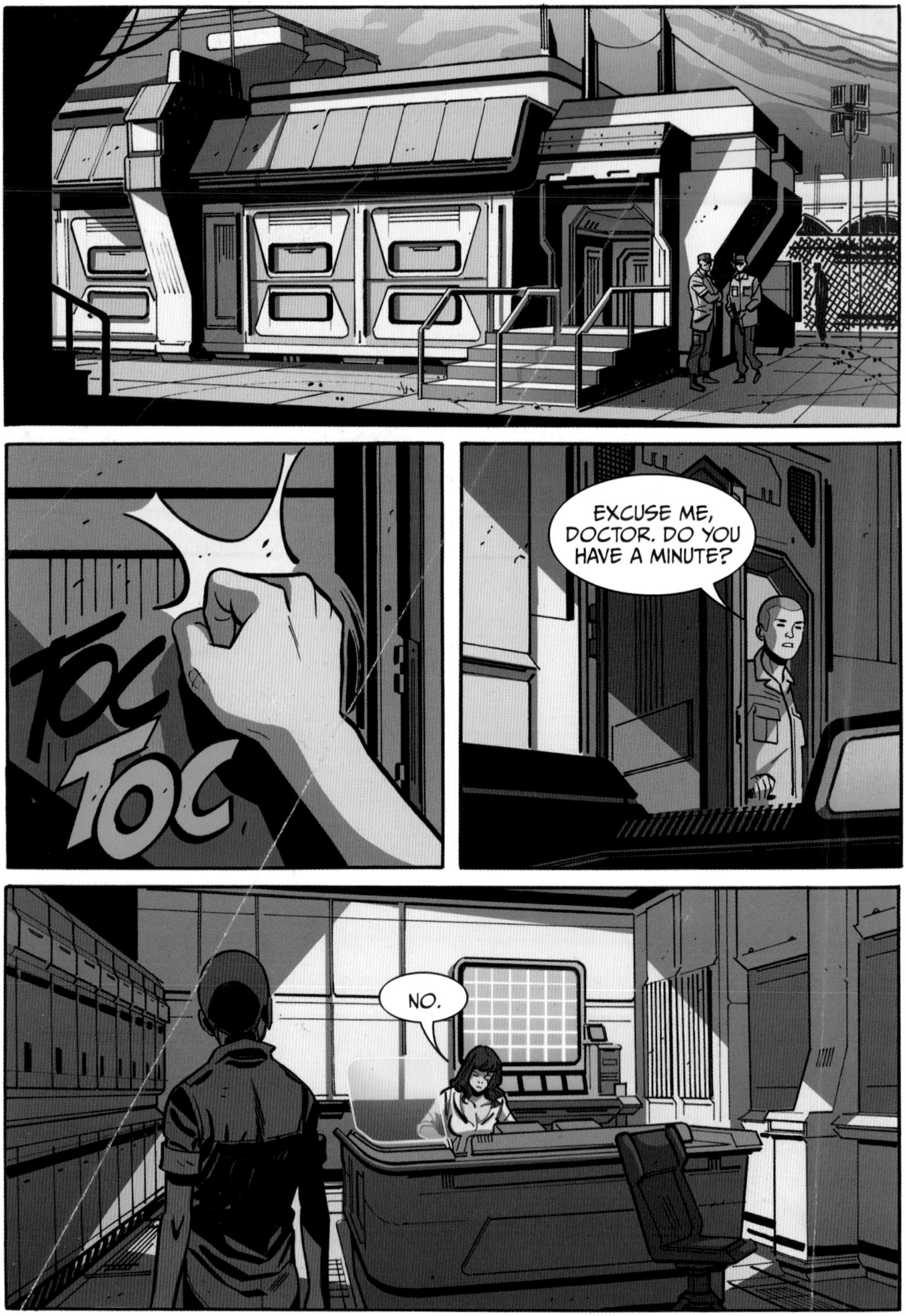
TOC
TOC
EXCUSE ME, DOCTOR. DO YOU HAVE A MINUTE?
NO.

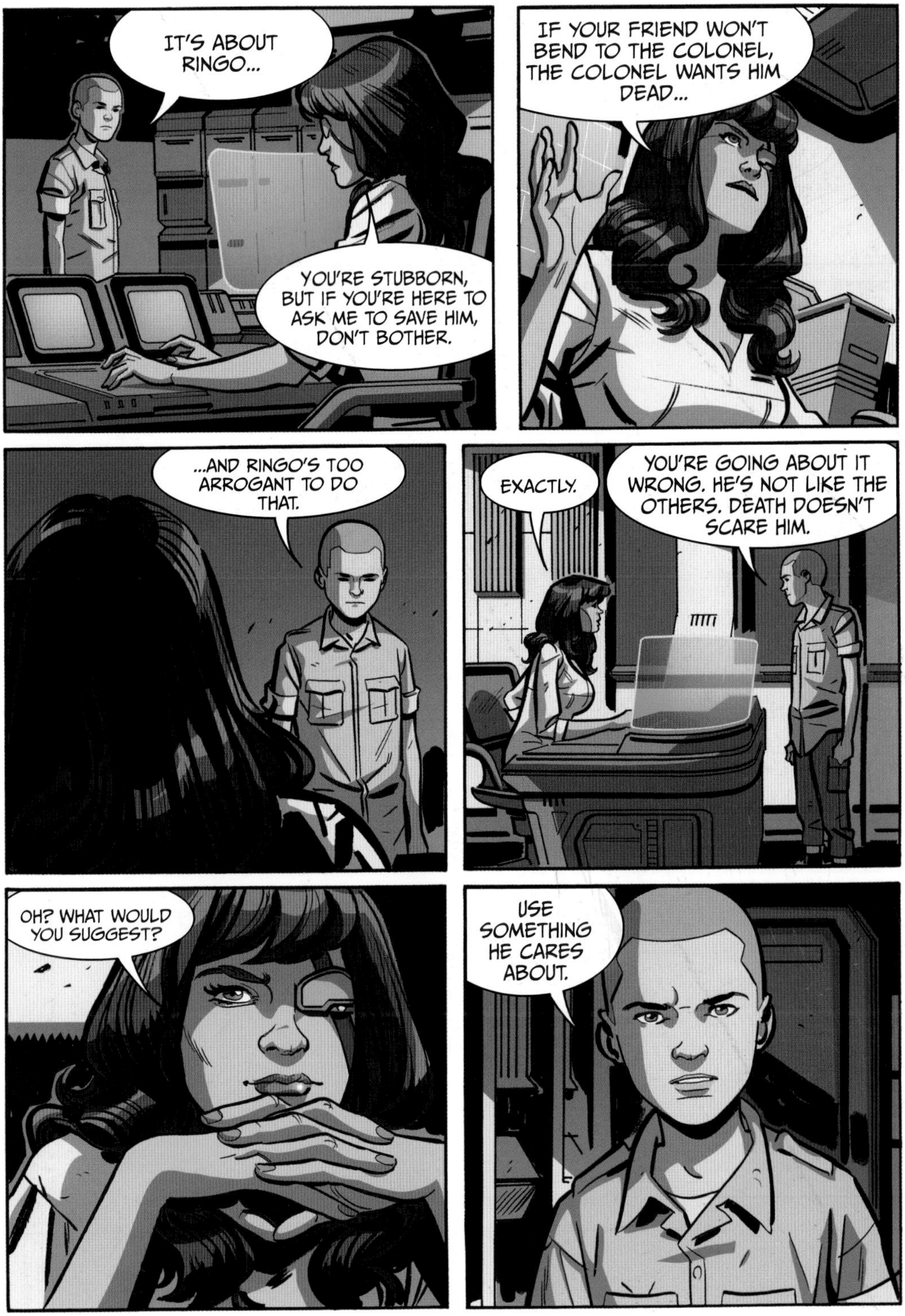
IT'S ABOUT RINGO...
YOU'RE STUBBORN, BUT IF YOU'RE HERE TO ASK ME TO SAVE HIM, DON'T BOTHER.
IF YOUR FRIEND WON'T BEND TO THE COLONEL, THE COLONEL WANTS HIM DEAD...
...AND RINGO'S TOO ARROGANT TO DO THAT.
EXACTLY.
YOU'RE GOING ABOUT IT WRONG. HE'S NOT LIKE THE OTHERS. DEATH DOESN'T SCARE HIM.
OH? WHAT WOULD YOU SUGGEST?
USE SOMETHING HE CARES ABOUT.

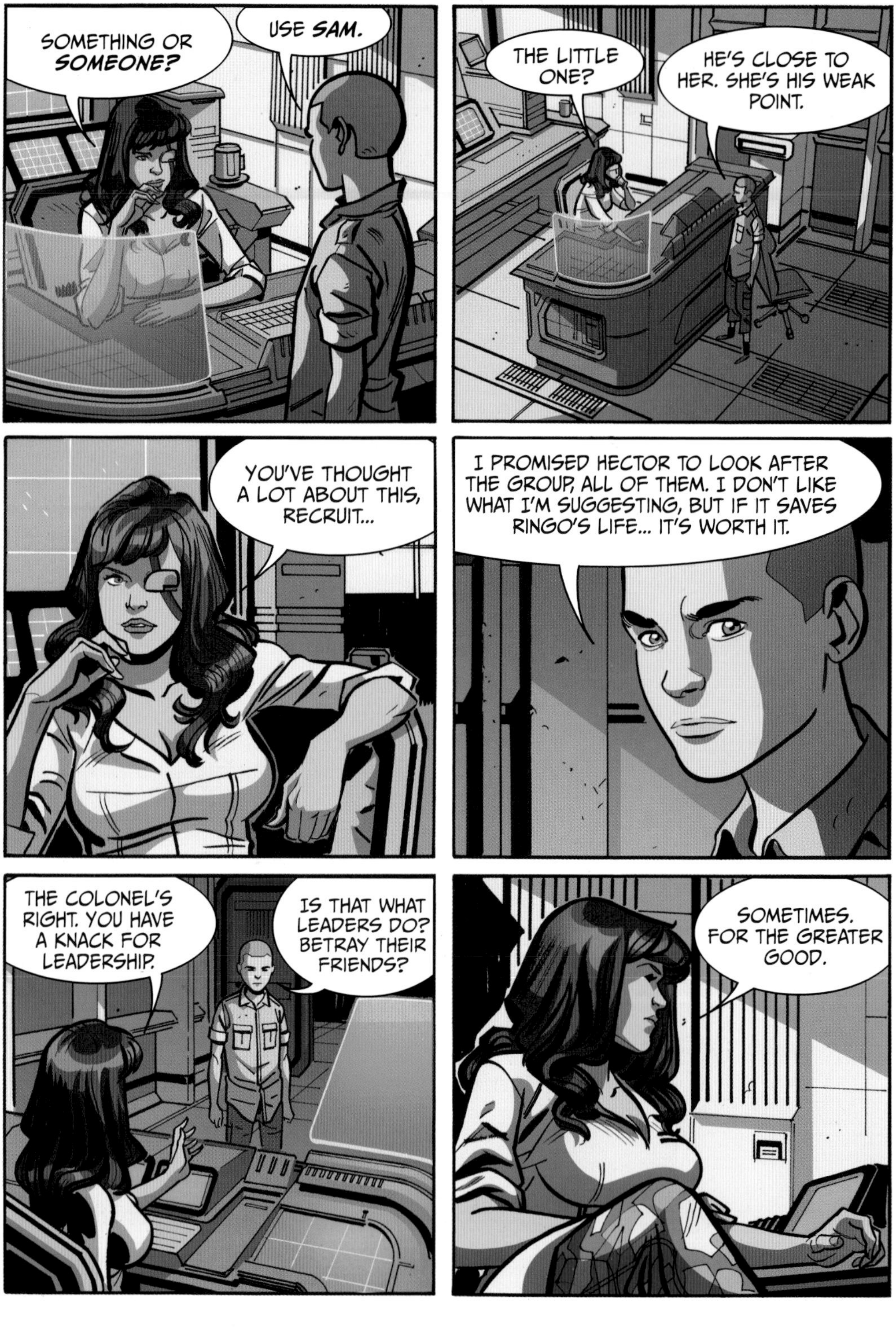
SOMETHING OR SOMEONE?
USE SAM.
THE LITTLE ONE?
HE'S CLOSE TO HER. SHE'S HIS WEAK POINT.
YOU'VE THOUGHT A LOT ABOUT THIS, RECRUIT...
I PROMISED HECTOR TO LOOK AFTER THE GROUP, ALL OF THEM. I DON'T LIKE WHAT I'M SUGGESTING, BUT IF IT SAVES RINGO'S LIFE... IT'S WORTH IT.
THE COLONEL'S RIGHT. YOU HAVE A KNACK FOR LEADERSHIP.
IS THAT WHAT LEADERS DO? BETRAY THEIR FRIENDS?
SOMETIMES. FOR THE GREATER GOOD.

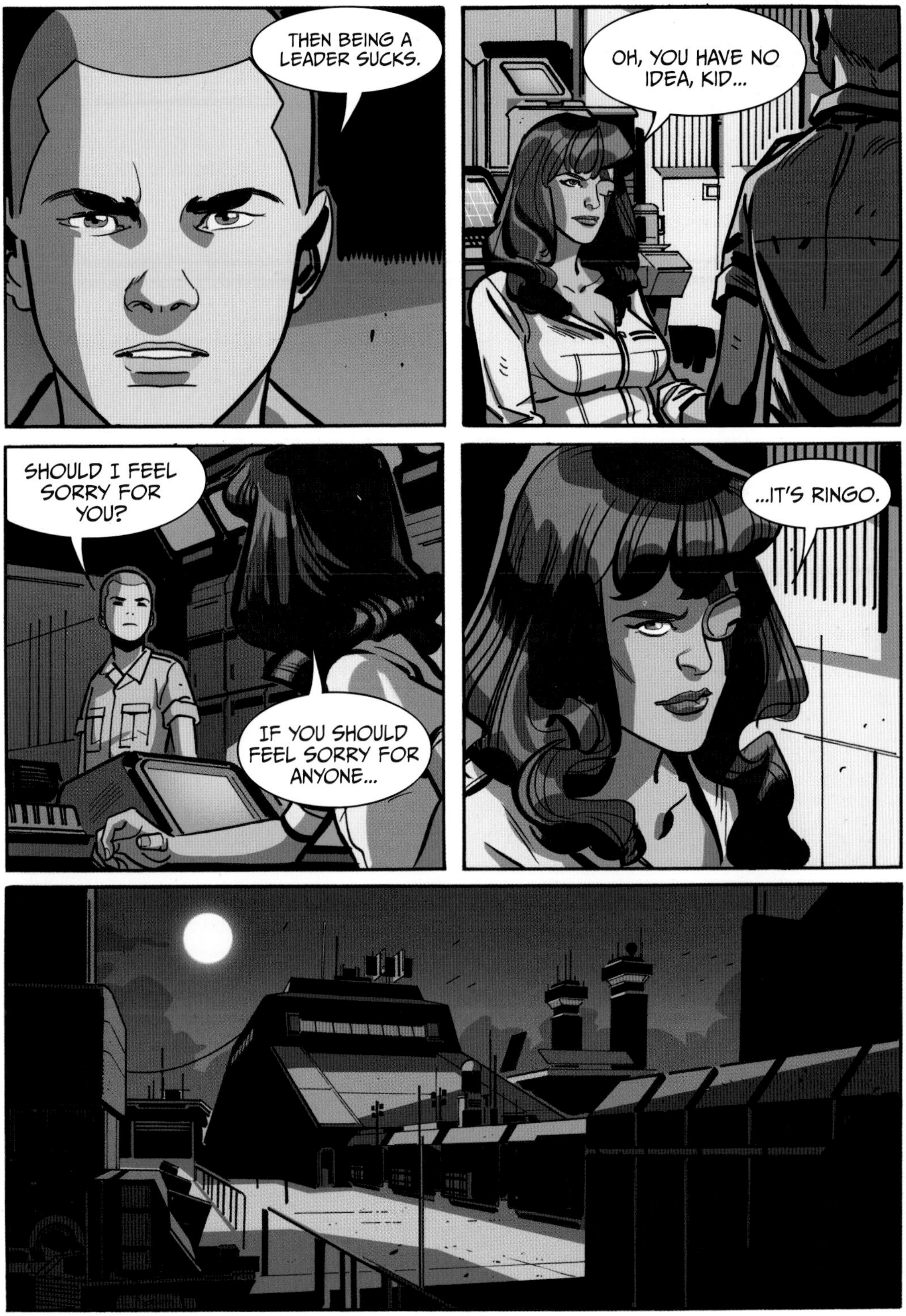
THEN BEING A LEADER SUCKS.
OH, YOU HAVE NO IDEA, KID...
SHOULD I FEEL SORRY FOR YOU?
IF YOU SHOULD FEEL SORRY FOR ANYONE...
...IT'S RINGO.

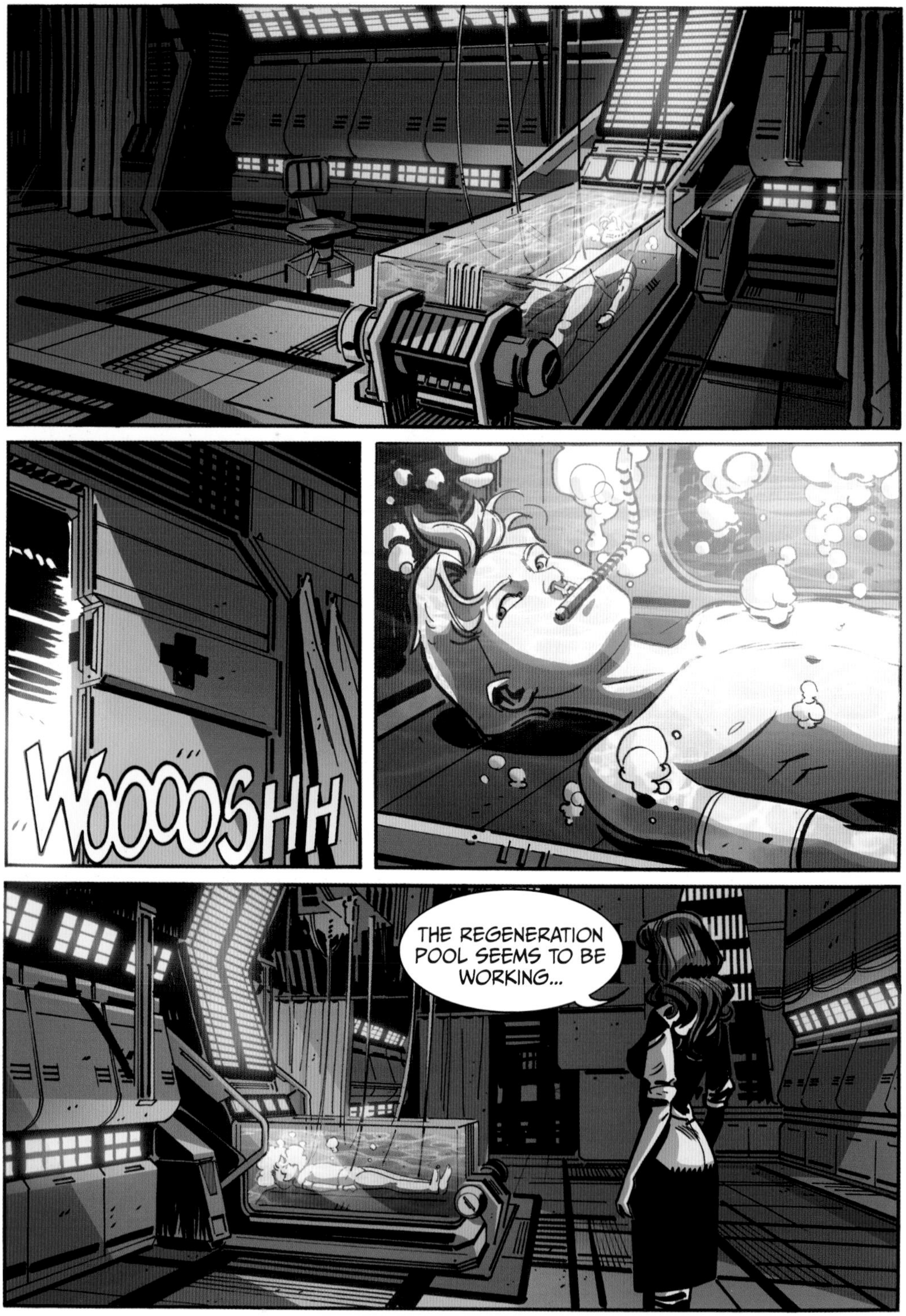
WOOOOSHH
THE REGENERATION POOL SEEMS TO BE WORKING...

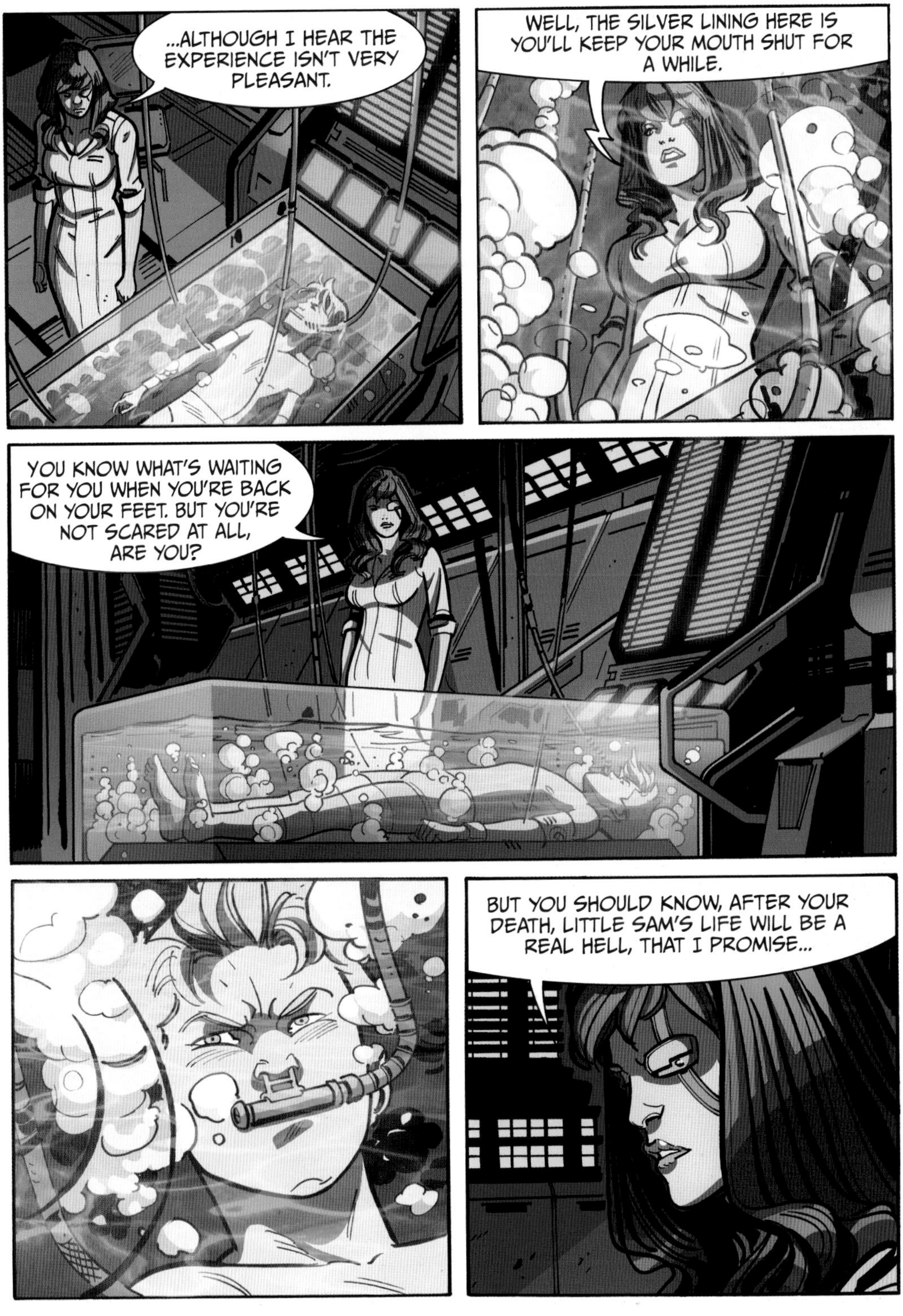
...ALTHOUGH I HEAR THE EXPERIENCE ISN'T VERY PLEASANT.
WELL, THE SILVER LINING HERE IS YOU'LL KEEP YOUR MOUTH SHUT FOR A WHILE.
YOU KNOW WHAT'S WAITING FOR YOU WHEN YOU'RE BACK ON YOUR FEET. BUT YOU'RE NOT SCARED AT ALL, ARE YOU?
BUT YOU SHOULD KNOW, AFTER YOUR DEATH, LITTLE SAM'S LIFE WILL BE A REAL HELL, THAT I PROMISE...

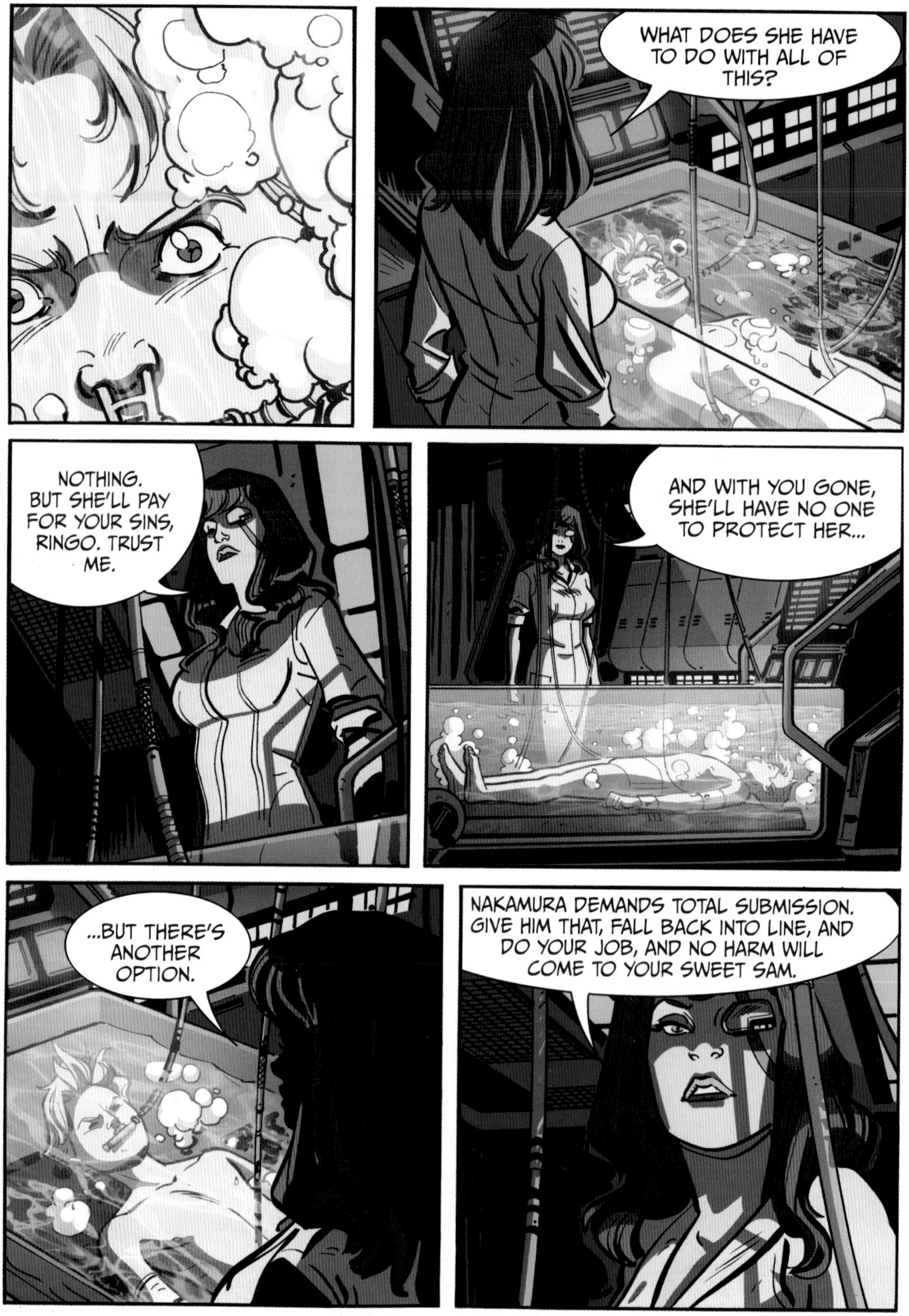
WHAT DOES SHE HAVE TO DO WITH ALL OF THIS?
NOTHING. BUT SHE'LL PAY FOR YOUR SINS, RINGO. TRUST ME.
AND WITH YOU GONE, SHE'LL HAVE NO ONE TO PROTECT HER...
...BUT THERE'S ANOTHER OPTION.
NAKAMURA DEMANDS TOTAL SUBMISSION. GIVE HIM THAT, FALL BACK INTO LINE, AND DO YOUR JOB, AND NO HARM WILL COME TO YOUR SWEET SAM.

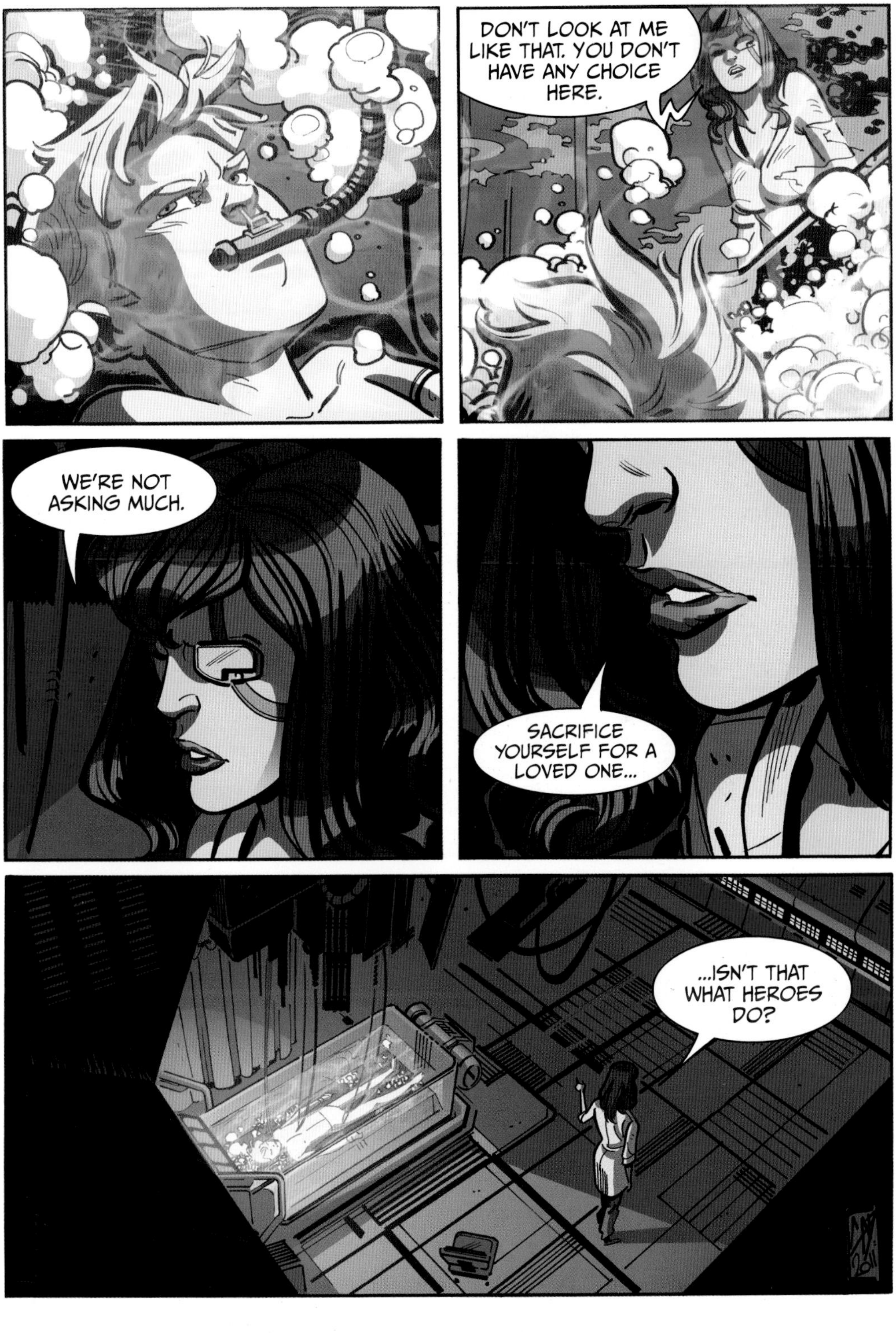
DON'T LOOK AT ME LIKE THAT. YOU DON'T HAVE ANY CHOICE HERE.
WE'RE NOT ASKING MUCH.
SACRIFICE YOURSELF FOR A LOVED ONE...
...ISN'T THAT WHAT HEROES DO?

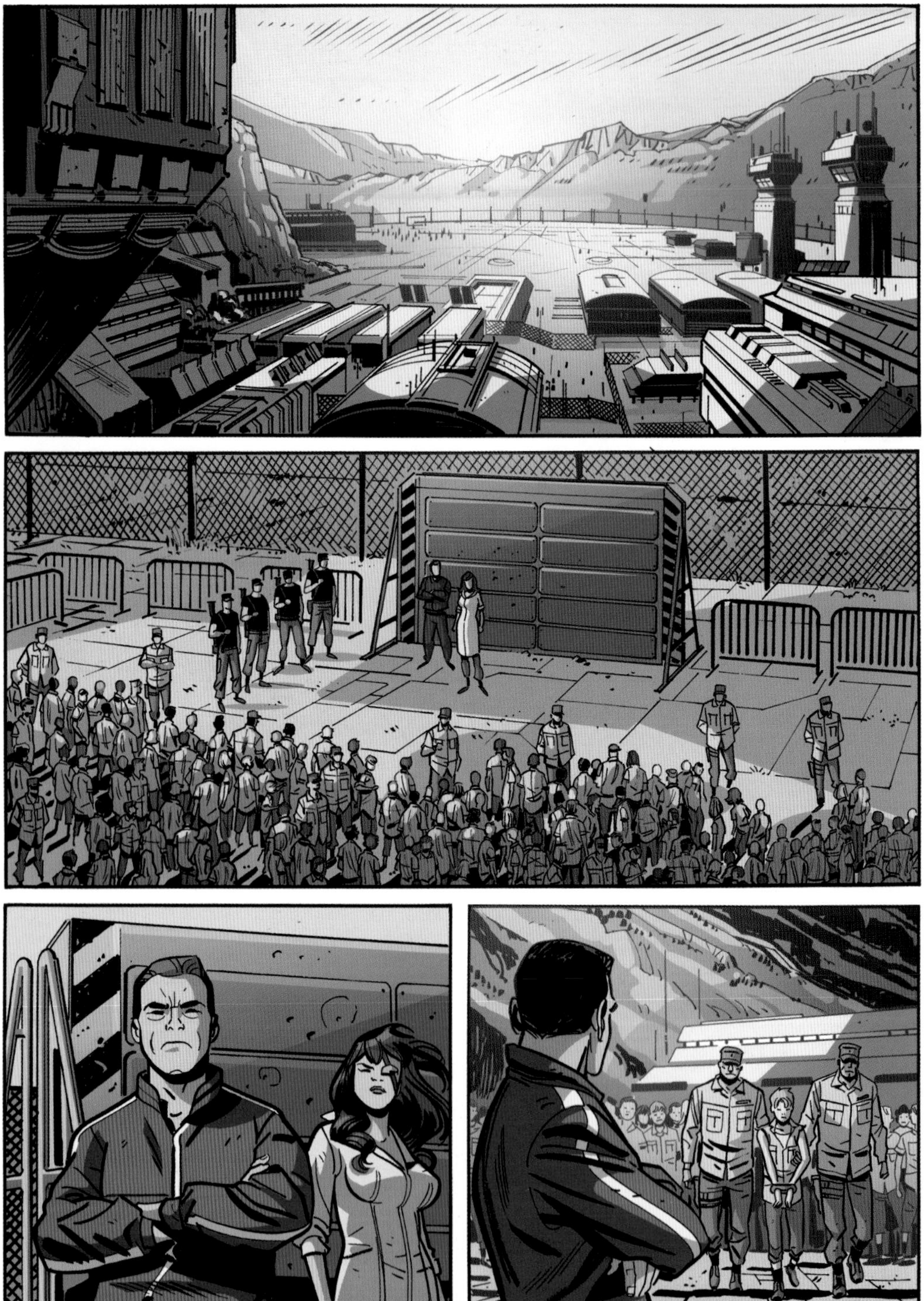

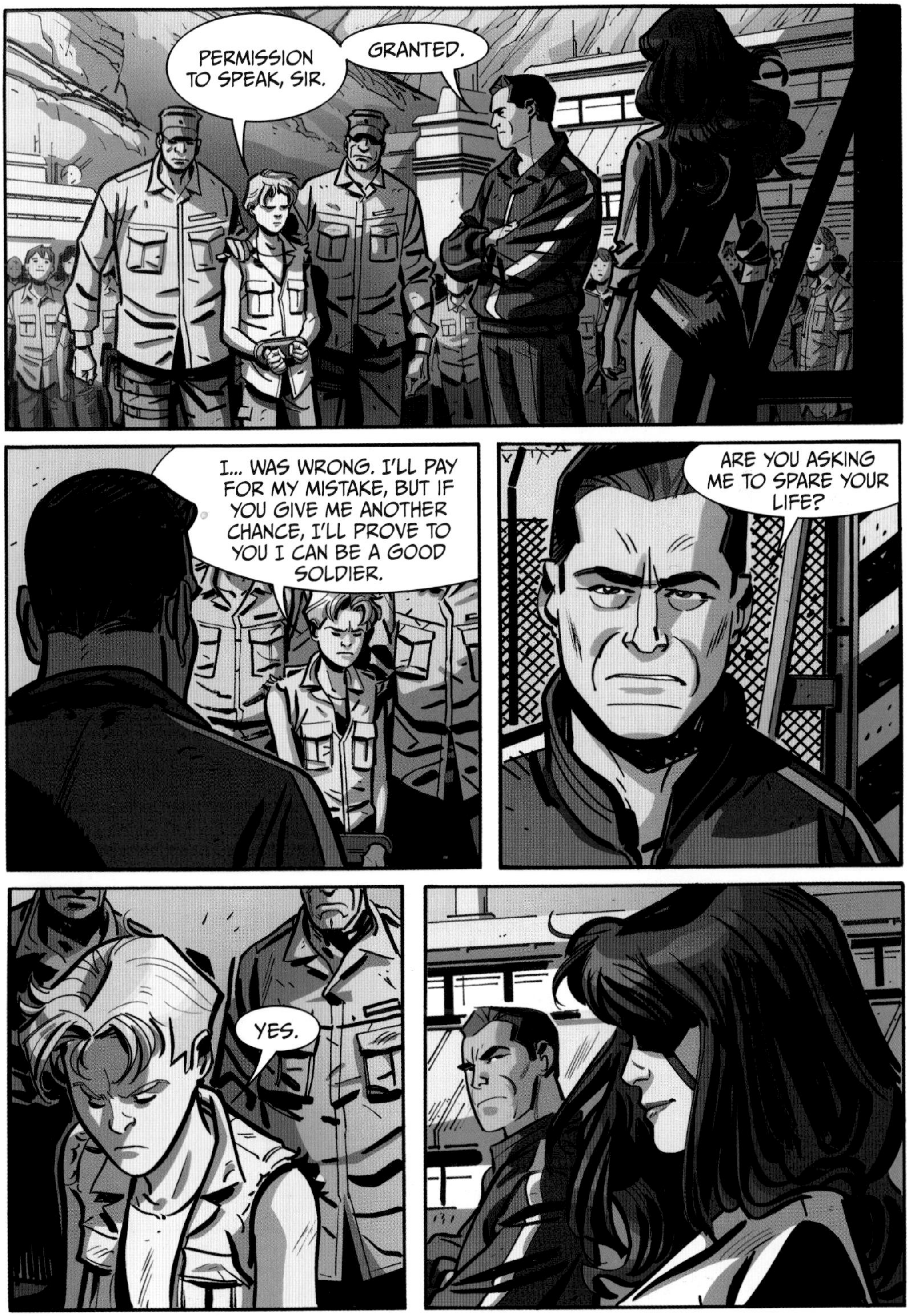
PERMISSION TO SPEAK, SIR.
GRANTED.
I... WAS WRONG. I'LL PAY FOR MY MISTAKE, BUT IF YOU GIVE ME ANOTHER CHANCE, I'LL PROVE TO YOU I CAN BE A GOOD SOLDIER.
ARE YOU ASKING ME TO SPARE YOUR LIFE?
YES.

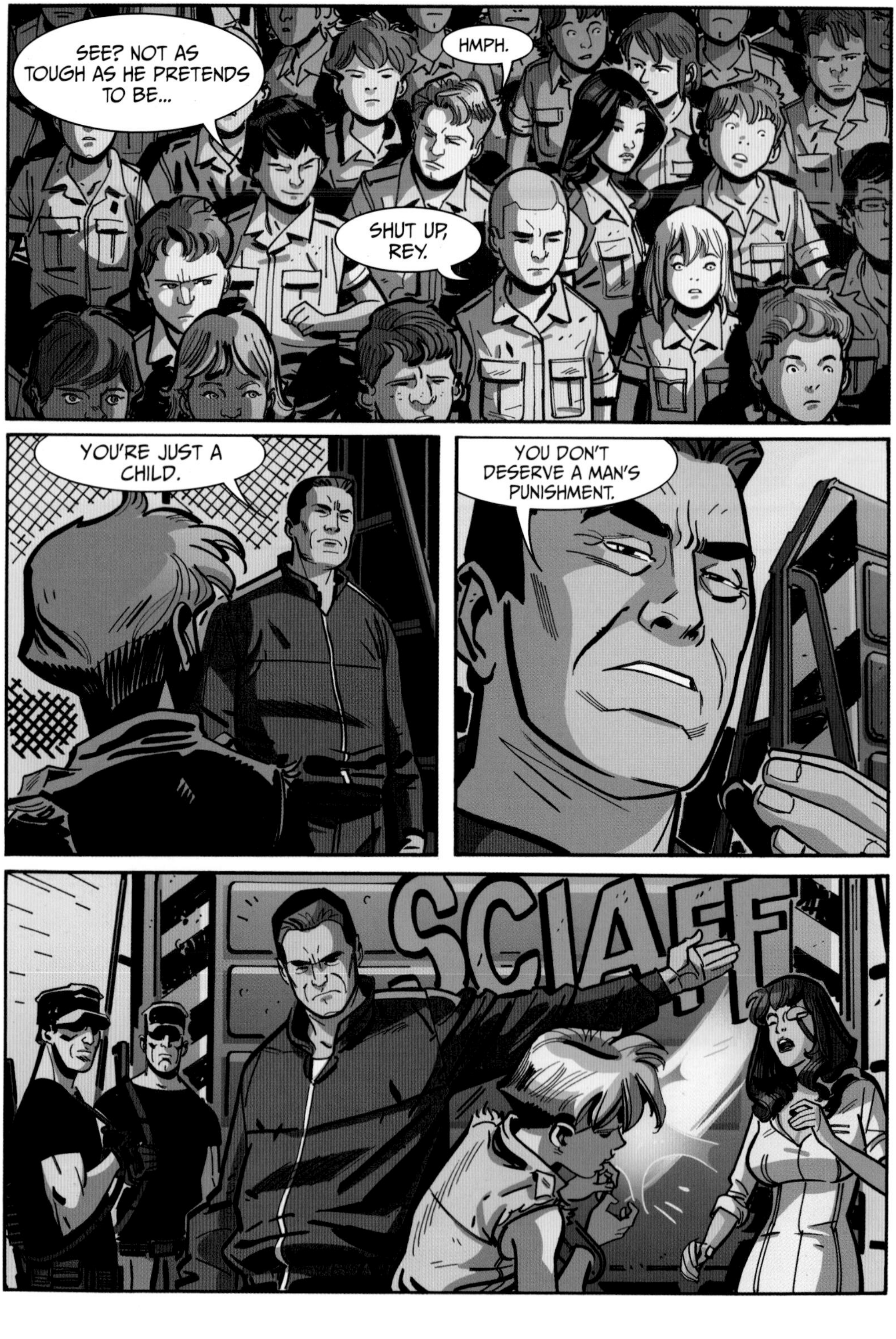
SEE? NOT AS TOUGH AS HE PRETENDS TO BE...
HMPH.
SHUT UP, REY.
YOU'RE JUST A CHILD.
YOU DON'T DESERVE A MAN'S PUNISHMENT.
SCIAFF

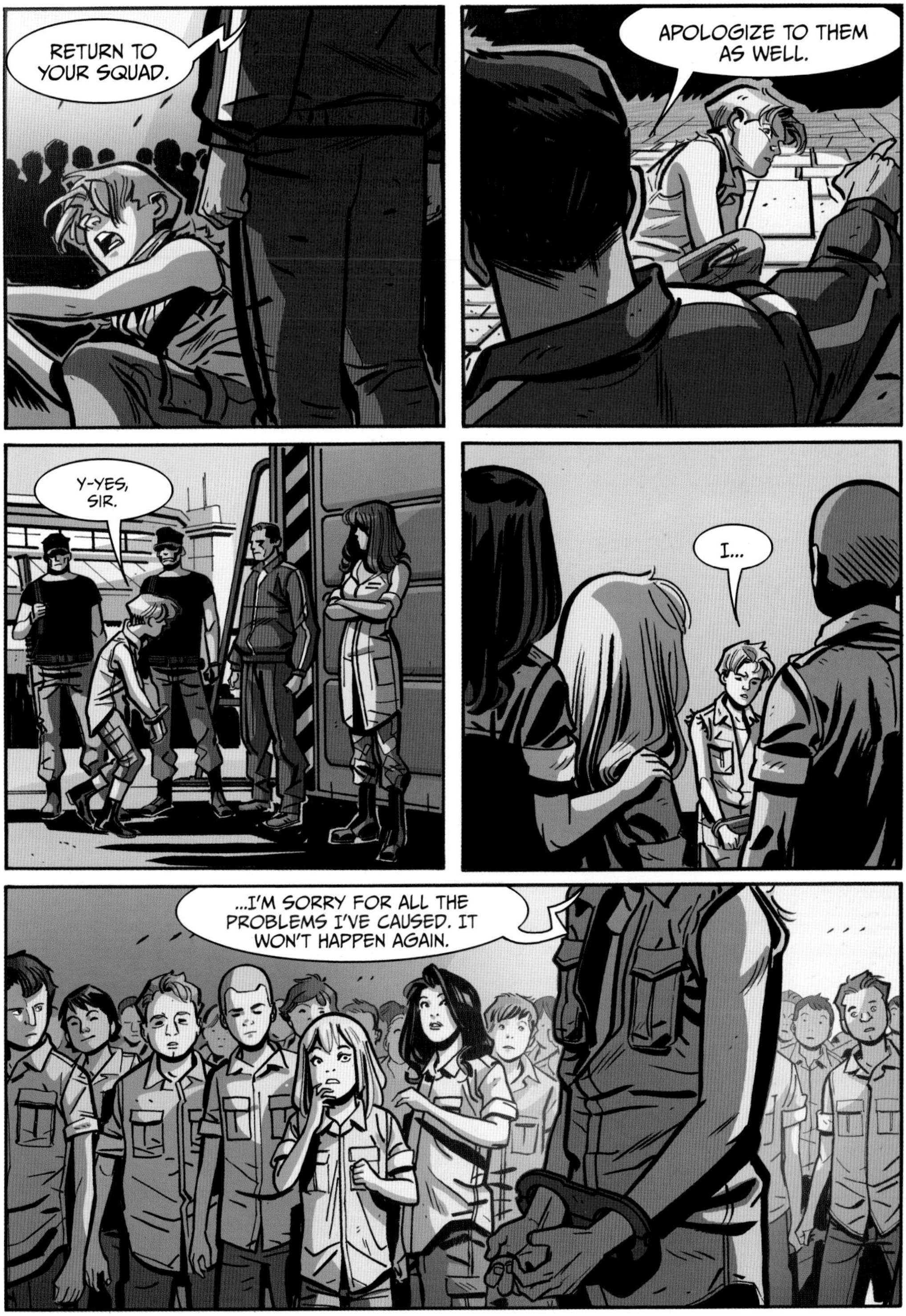
RETURN TO YOUR SQUAD.
APOLOGIZE TO THEM AS WELL.
Y-YES, SIR.
I...
...I'M SORRY FOR ALL THE PROBLEMS I'VE CAUSED. IT WON'T HAPPEN AGAIN.

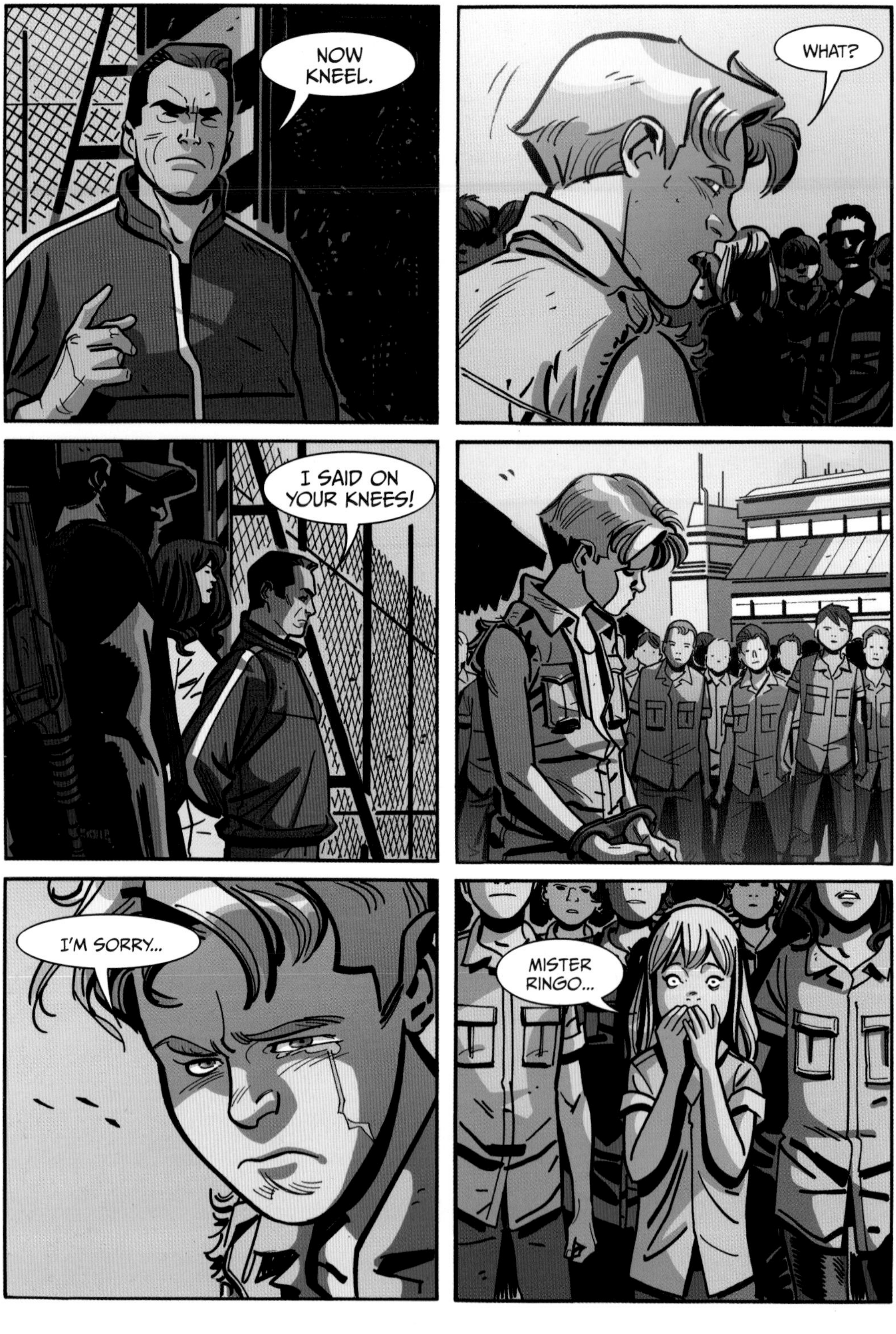
NOW KNEEL.
WHAT?
I SAID ON YOUR KNEES!
I'M SORRY...
MISTER RINGO...

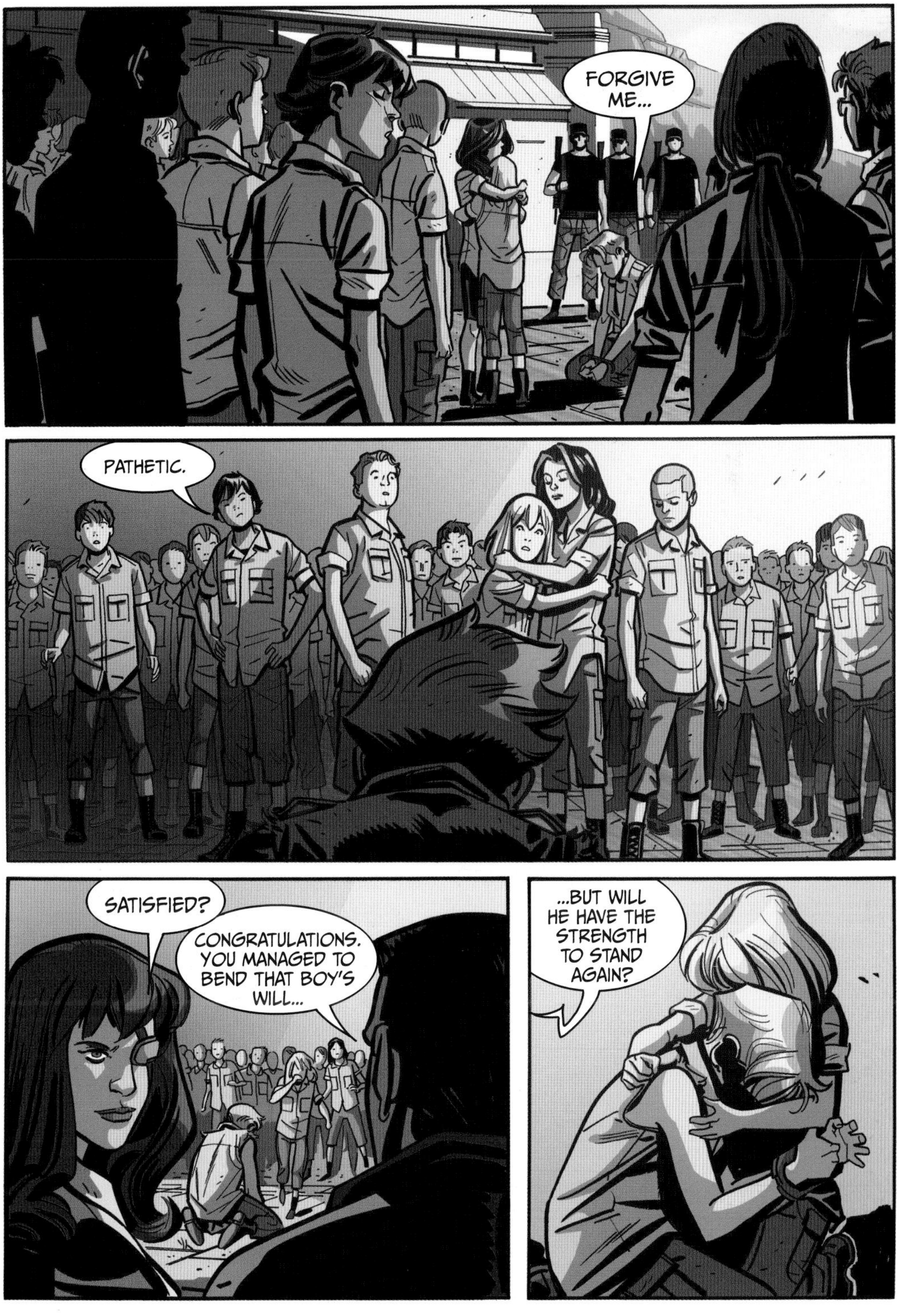
FORGIVE ME...
PATHETIC.
SATISFIED?
CONGRATULATIONS. YOU MANAGED TO BEND THAT BOY'S WILL...
...BUT WILL HE HAVE THE STRENGTH TO STAND AGAIN?

FFFFSSSSSSSSSSSSSSSSS SS

HEY, HEY... THE REBEL WITHOUT A CAUSE...

GLAD NAKAMURA MADE YOU SWALLOW SOME PRIDE. WHO'D YOU THINK YOU WERE OUT THERE?

LEAVE ME ALONE, REY. I'M NOT IN THE MOOD.

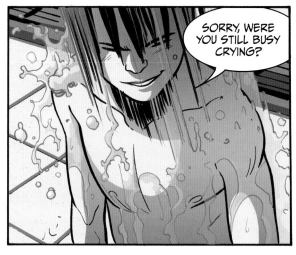

SORRY, WERE YOU STILL BUSY CRYING?

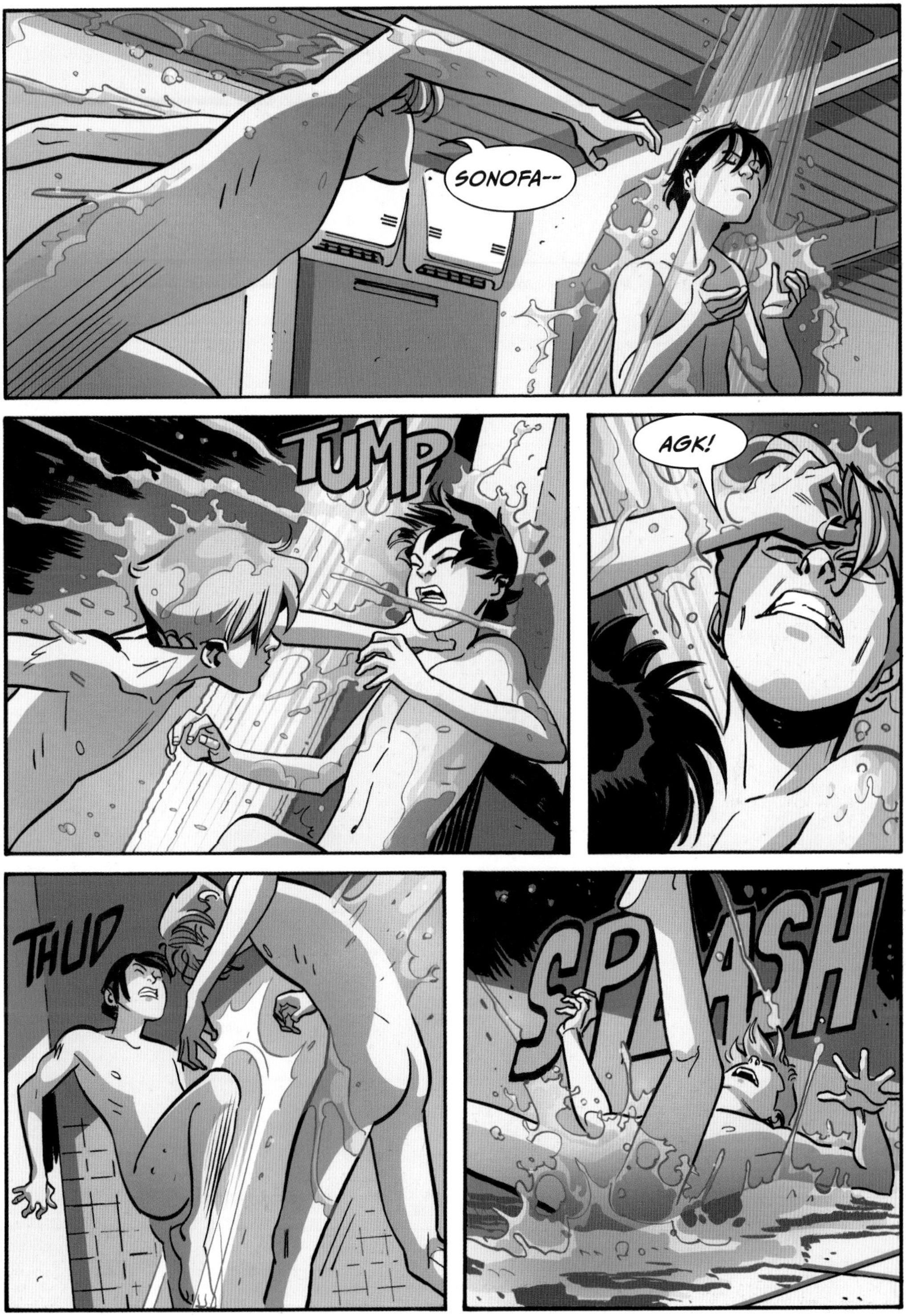
SONOFA--
TUMP
AGK!
THUD
SPLASH

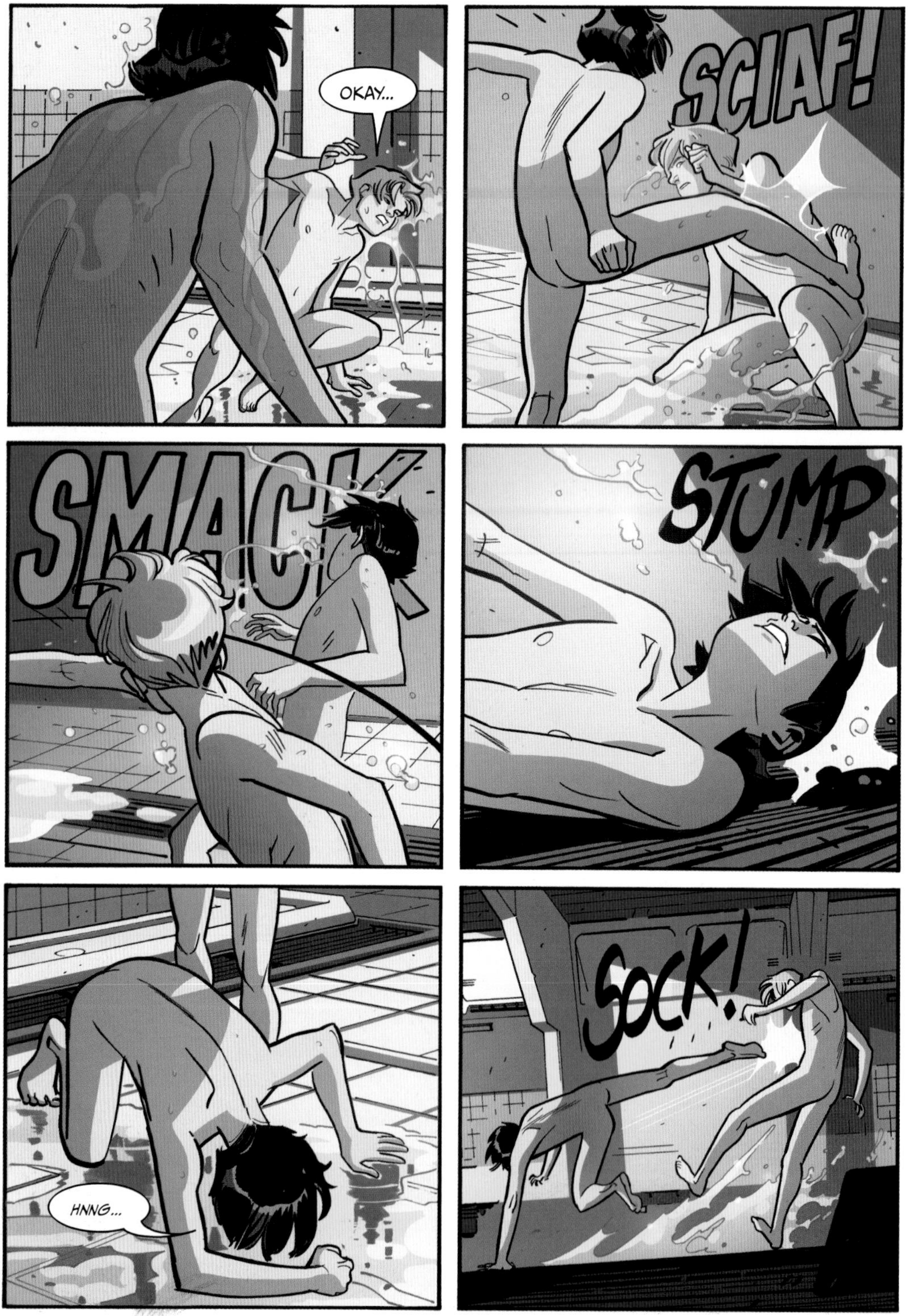
OKAY...
SCIAF!
SMACK
STUMP
HNNG...
SOCK!

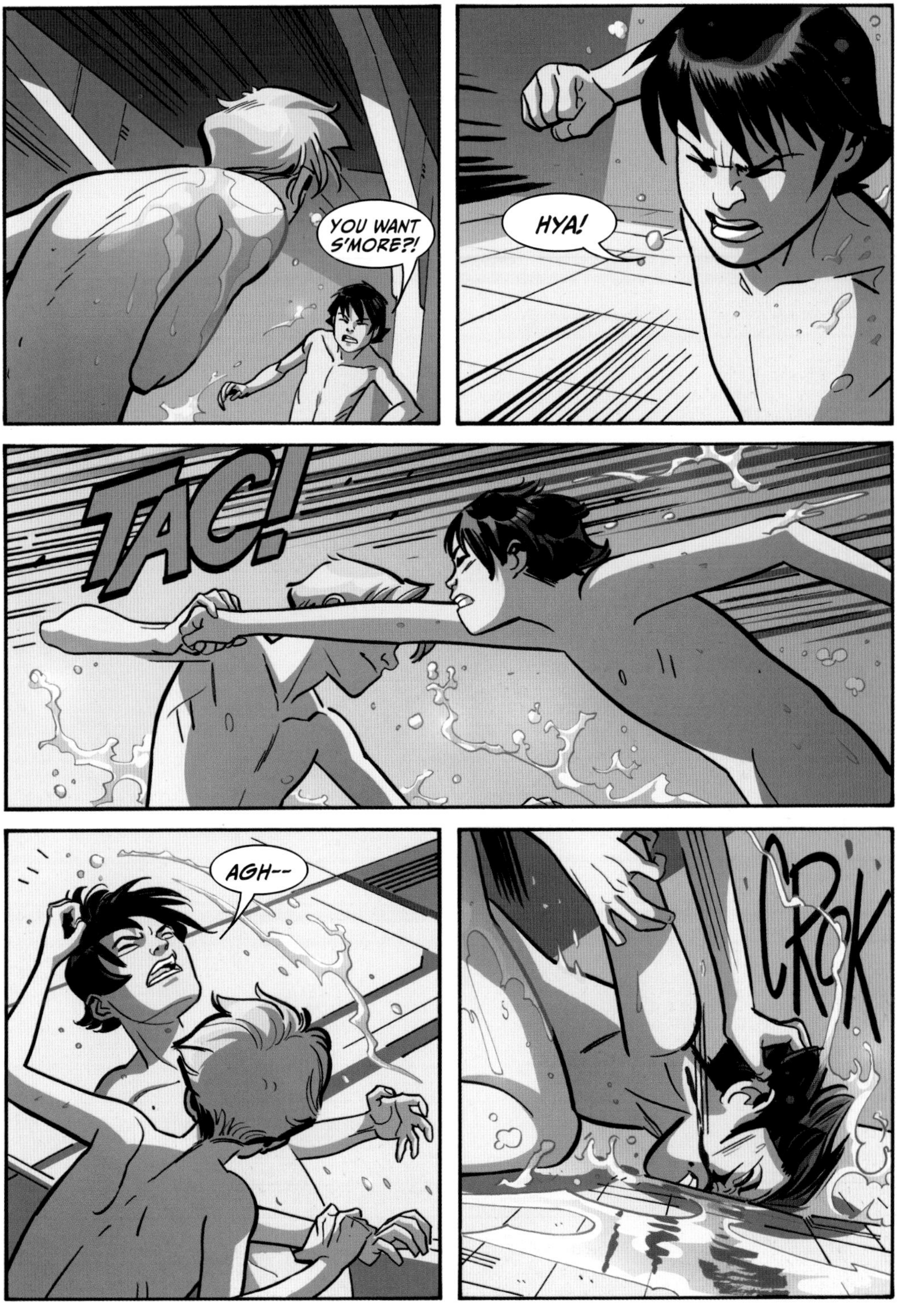
YOU WANT S'MORE?!
HYA!
TAC!
AGH--
CRCK

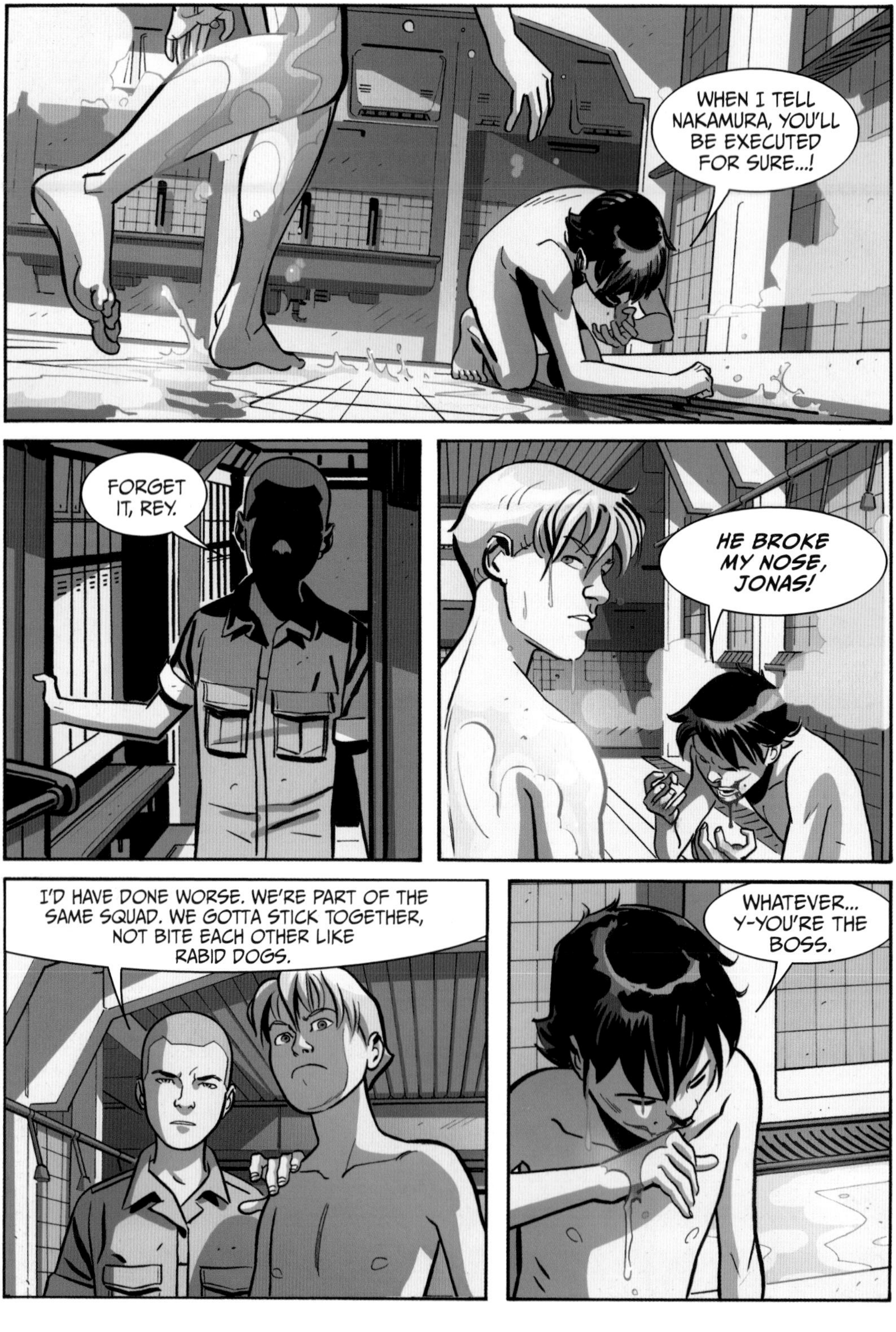
WHEN I TELL NAKAMURA, YOU'LL BE EXECUTED FOR SURE...!
FORGET IT, REY.
HE BROKE MY NOSE, JONAS!
I'D HAVE DONE WORSE. WE'RE PART OF THE SAME SQUAD. WE GOTTA STICK TOGETHER, NOT BITE EACH OTHER LIKE RABID DOGS.
WHATEVER... Y-YOU'RE THE BOSS.

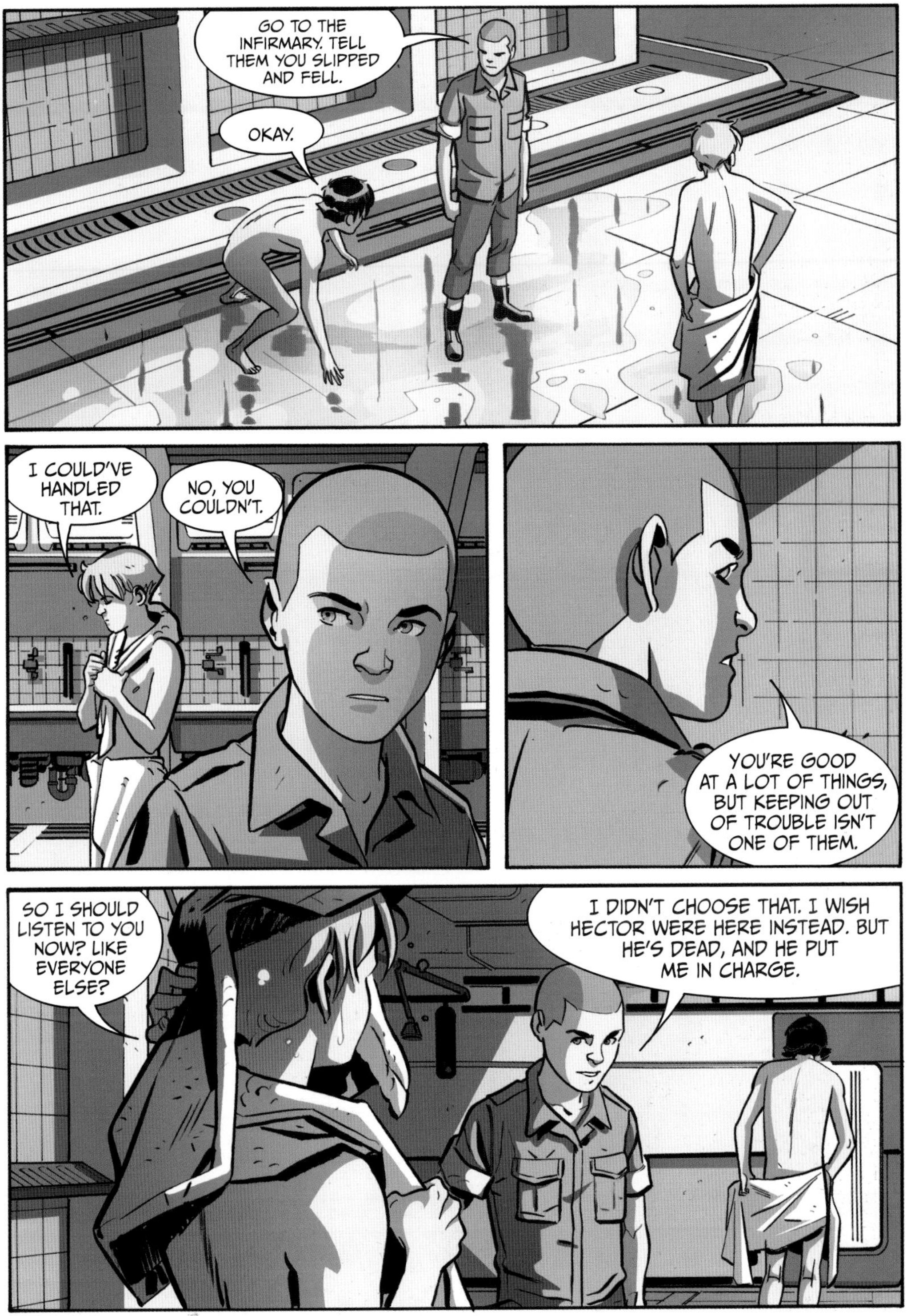
GO TO THE INFIRMARY. TELL THEM YOU SLIPPED AND FELL.
OKAY.
I COULD'VE HANDLED THAT.
NO, YOU COULDN'T.
YOU'RE GOOD AT A LOT OF THINGS, BUT KEEPING OUT OF TROUBLE ISN'T ONE OF THEM.
SO I SHOULD LISTEN TO YOU NOW? LIKE EVERYONE ELSE?
I DIDN'T CHOOSE THAT. I WISH HECTOR WERE HERE INSTEAD. BUT HE'S DEAD, AND HE PUT ME IN CHARGE.

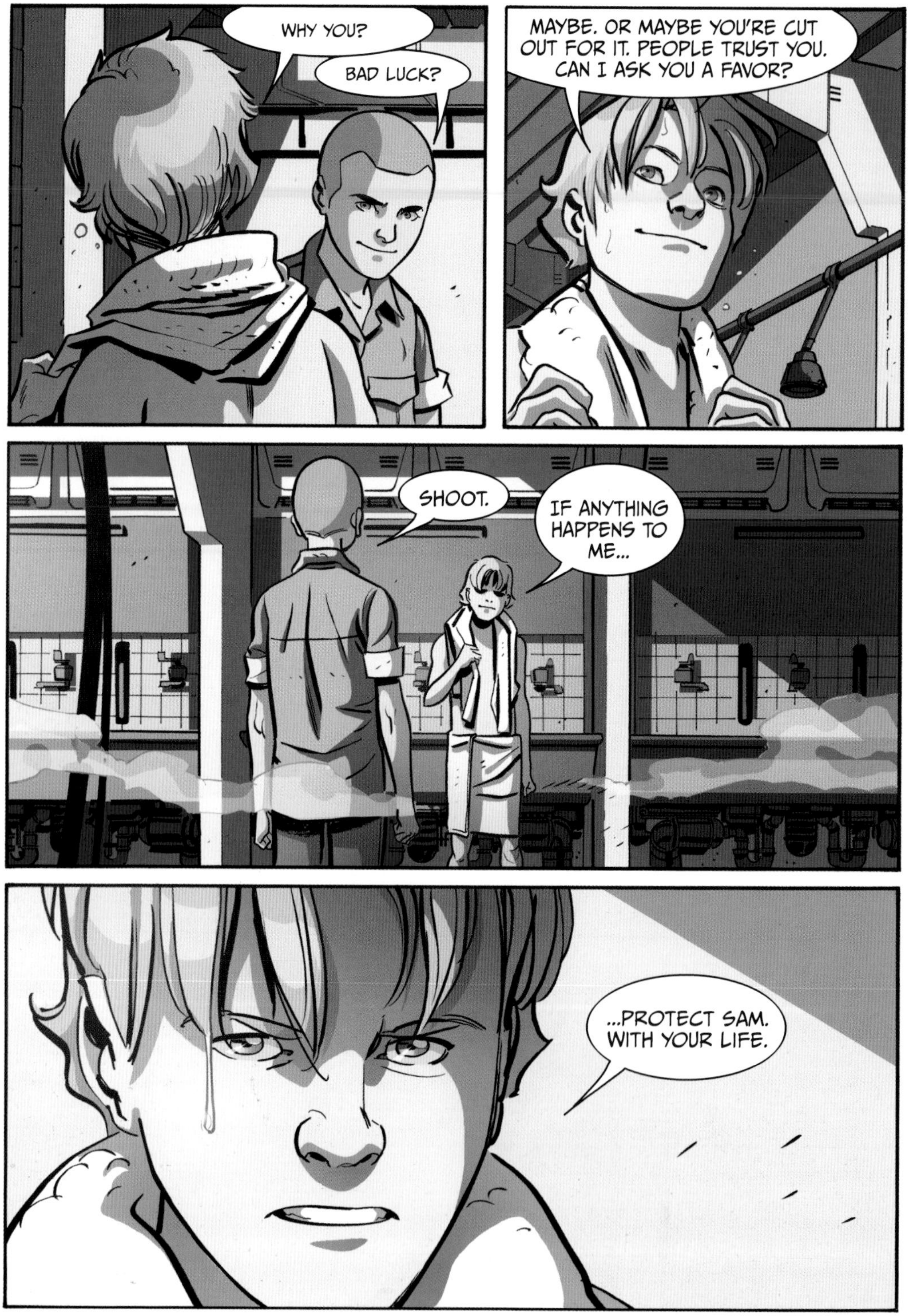
WHY YOU?
BAD LUCK?
MAYBE. OR MAYBE YOU'RE CUT OUT FOR IT. PEOPLE TRUST YOU. CAN I ASK YOU A FAVOR?
SHOOT.
IF ANYTHING HAPPENS TO ME...
...PROTECT SAM. WITH YOUR LIFE.

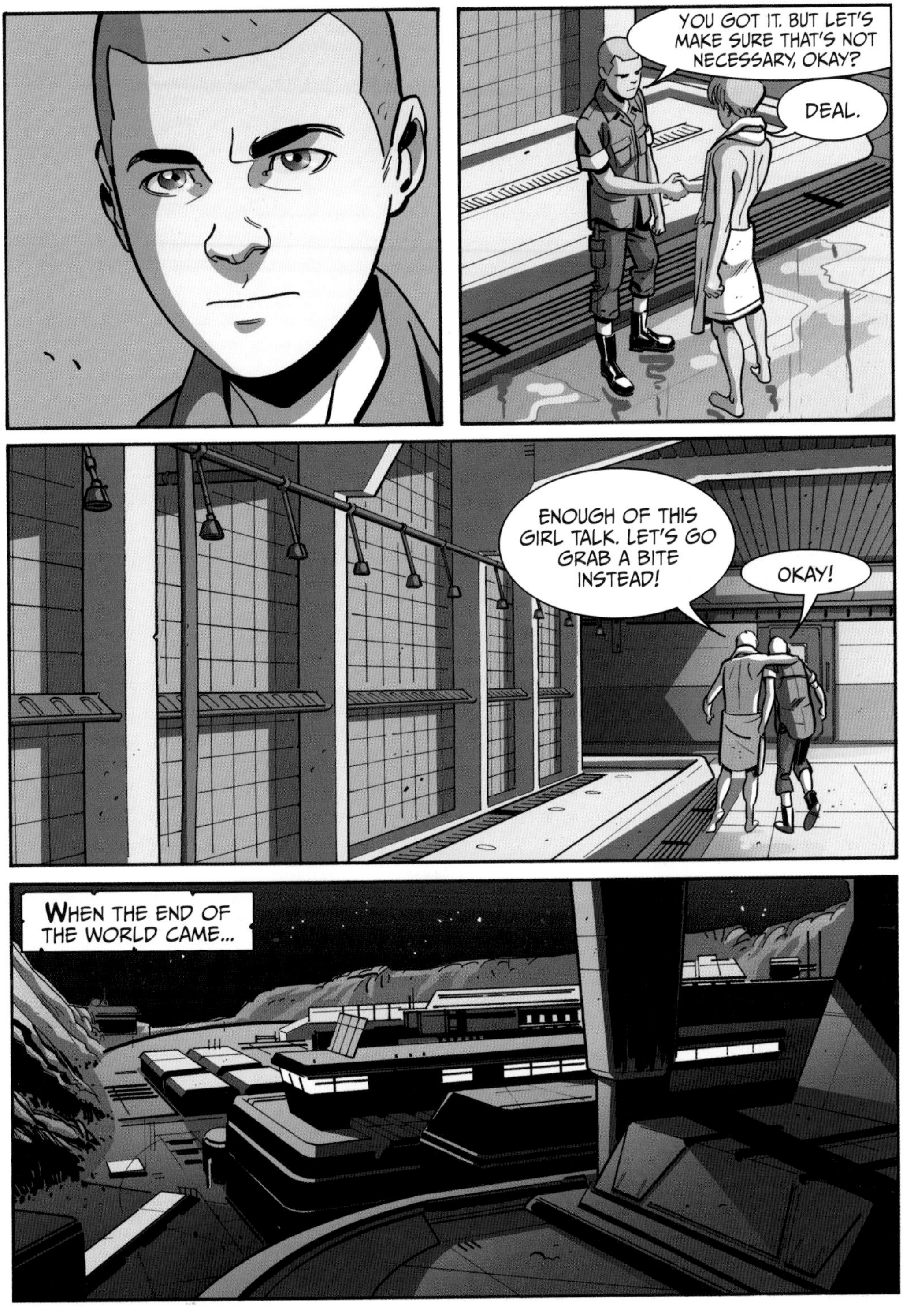
YOU GOT IT. BUT LET'S MAKE SURE THAT'S NOT NECESSARY, OKAY?
DEAL.
ENOUGH OF THIS GIRL TALK. LET'S GO GRAB A BITE INSTEAD!
OKAY!
WHEN THE END OF THE WORLD CAME...

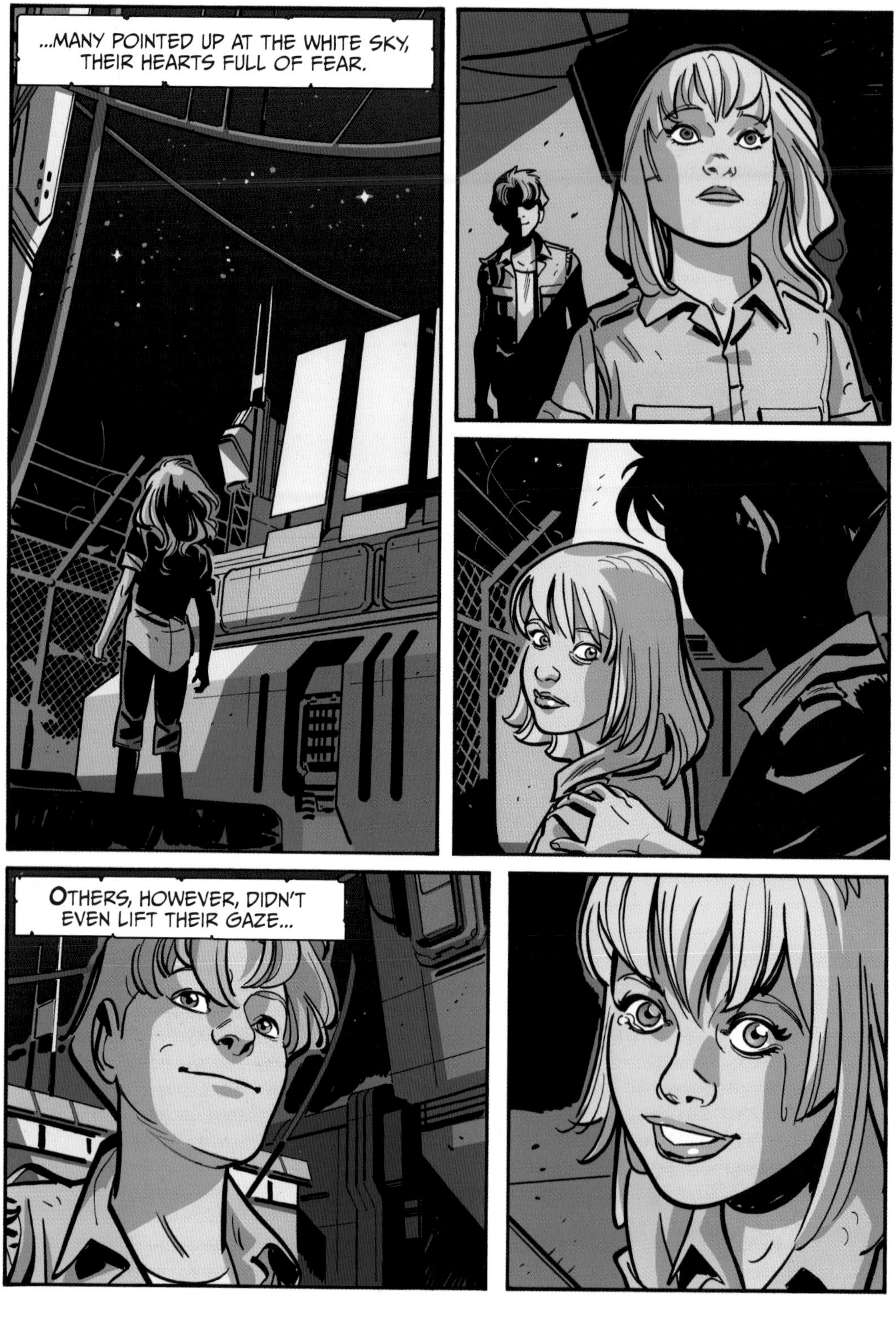
...MANY POINTED UP AT THE WHITE SKY, THEIR HEARTS FULL OF FEAR.
OTHERS, HOWEVER, DIDN'T EVEN LIFT THEIR GAZE...

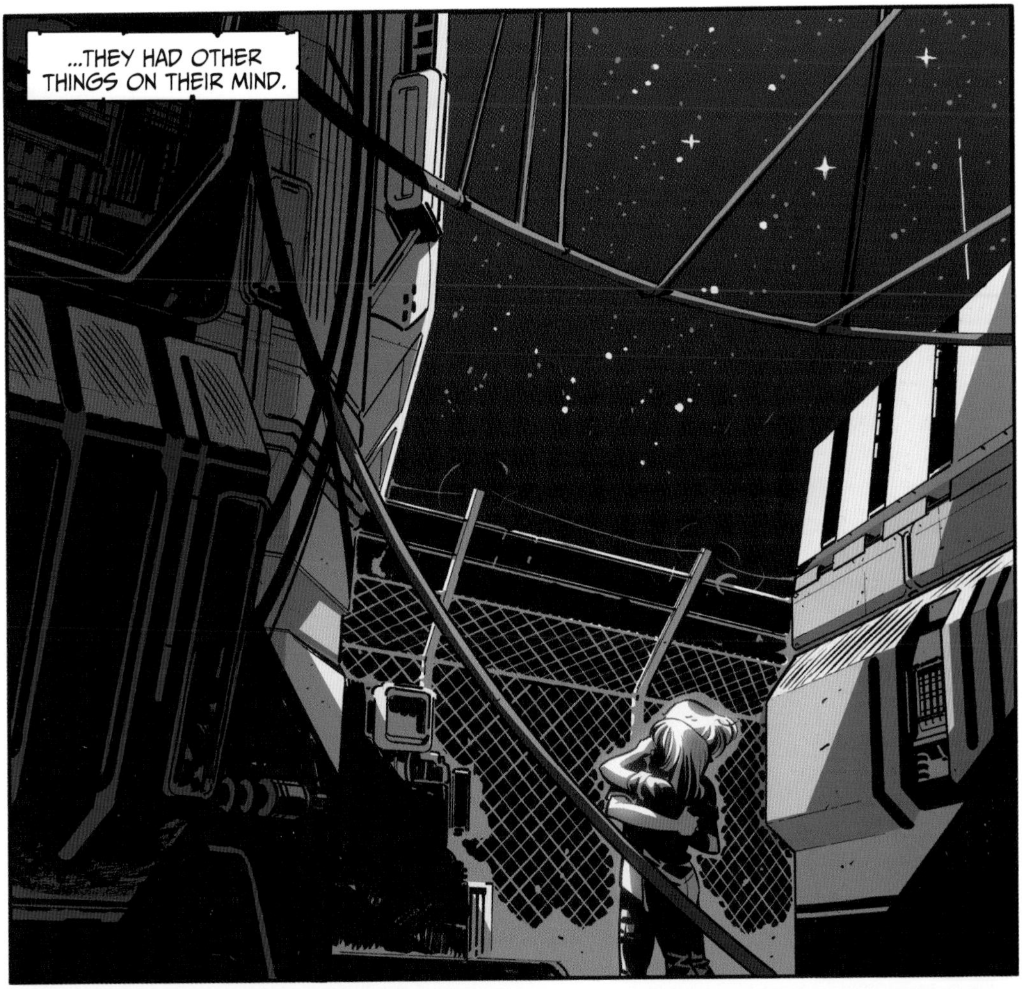
...THEY HAD OTHER THINGS ON THEIR MIND.

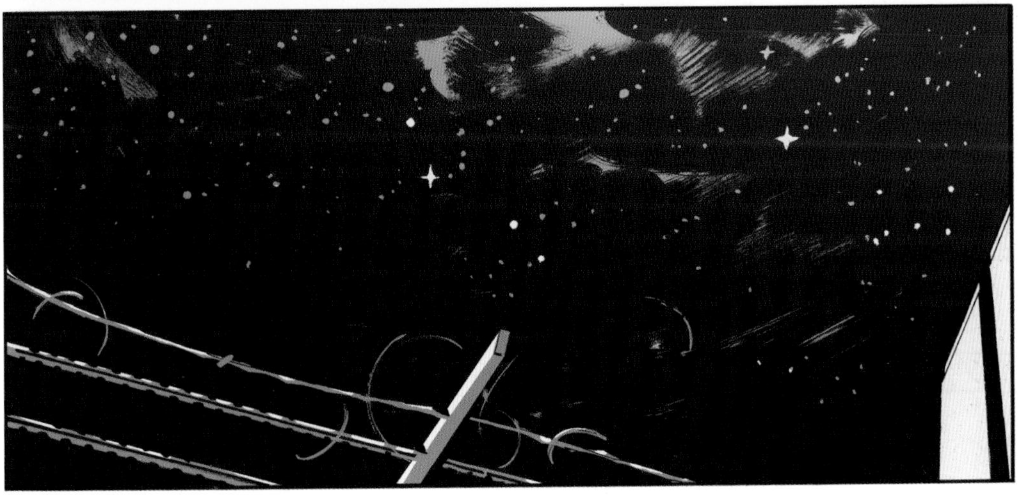

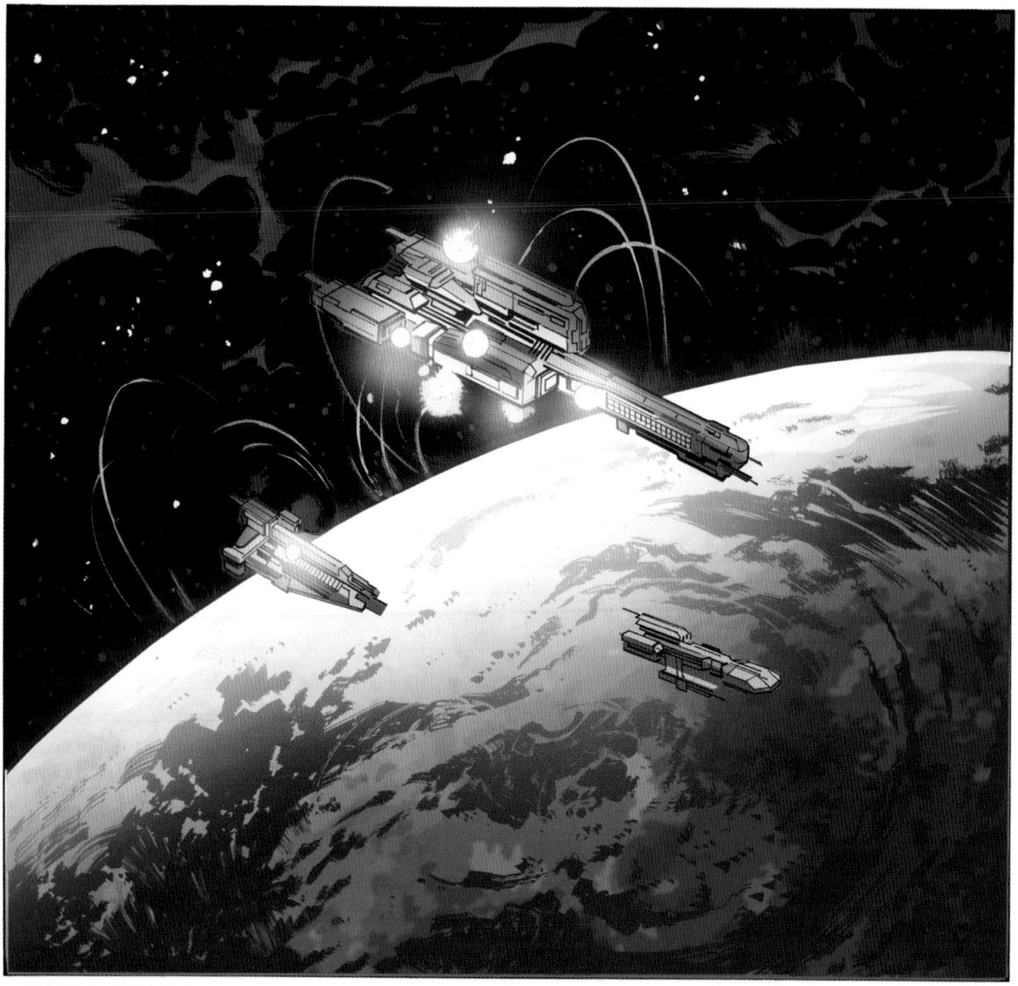

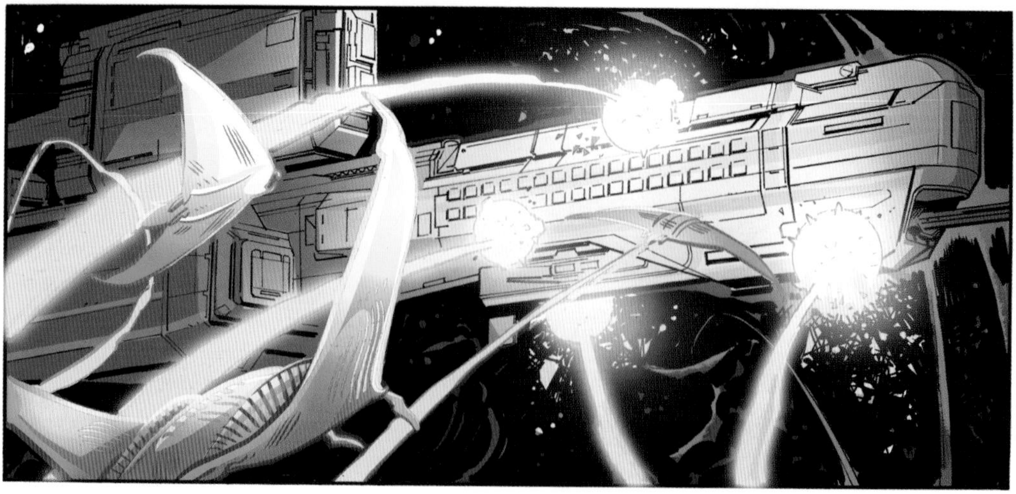

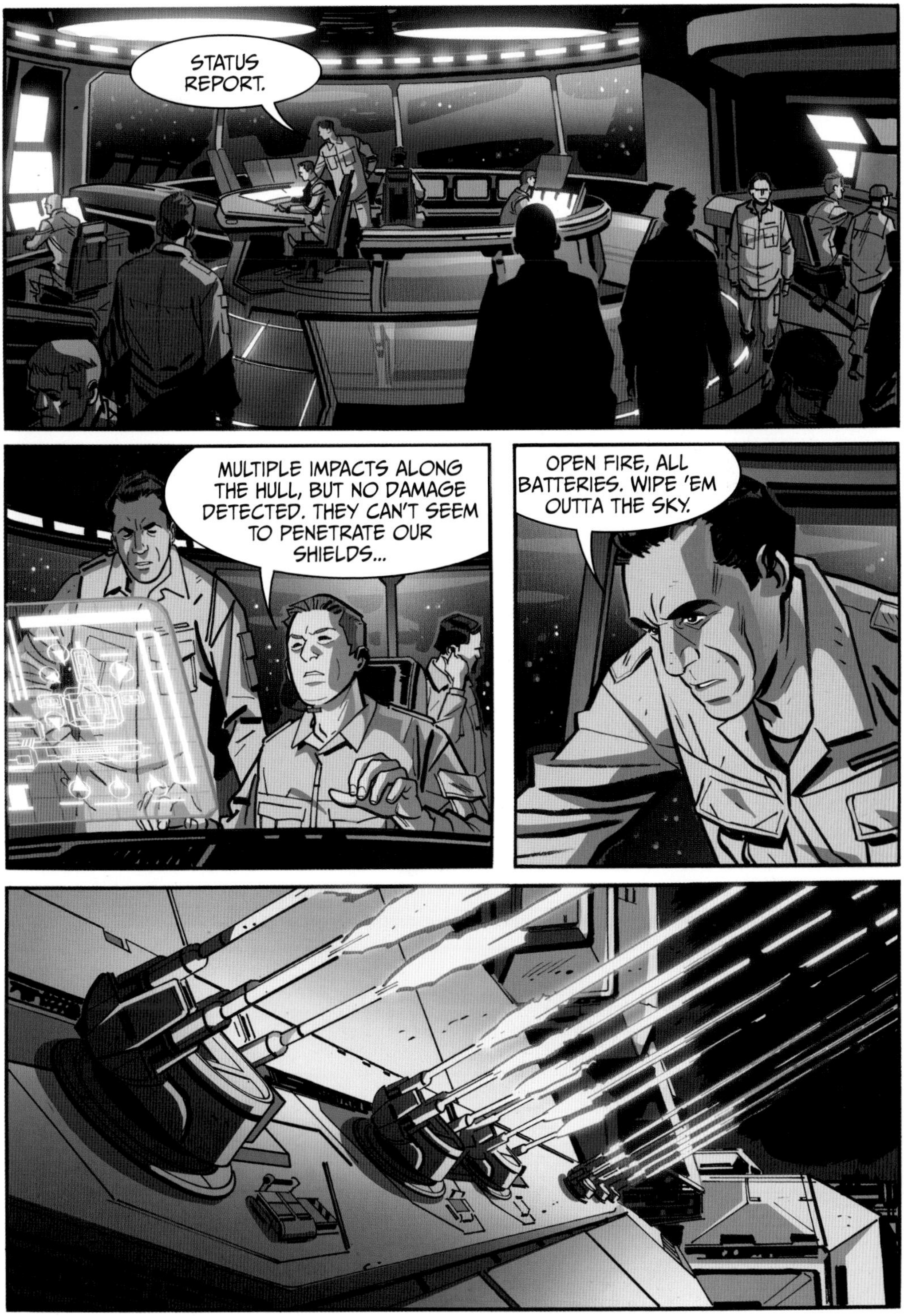
STATUS REPORT.
MULTIPLE IMPACTS ALONG THE HULL, BUT NO DAMAGE DETECTED. THEY CAN'T SEEM TO PENETRATE OUR SHIELDS...
OPEN FIRE, ALL BATTERIES. WIPE 'EM OUTTA THE SKY.

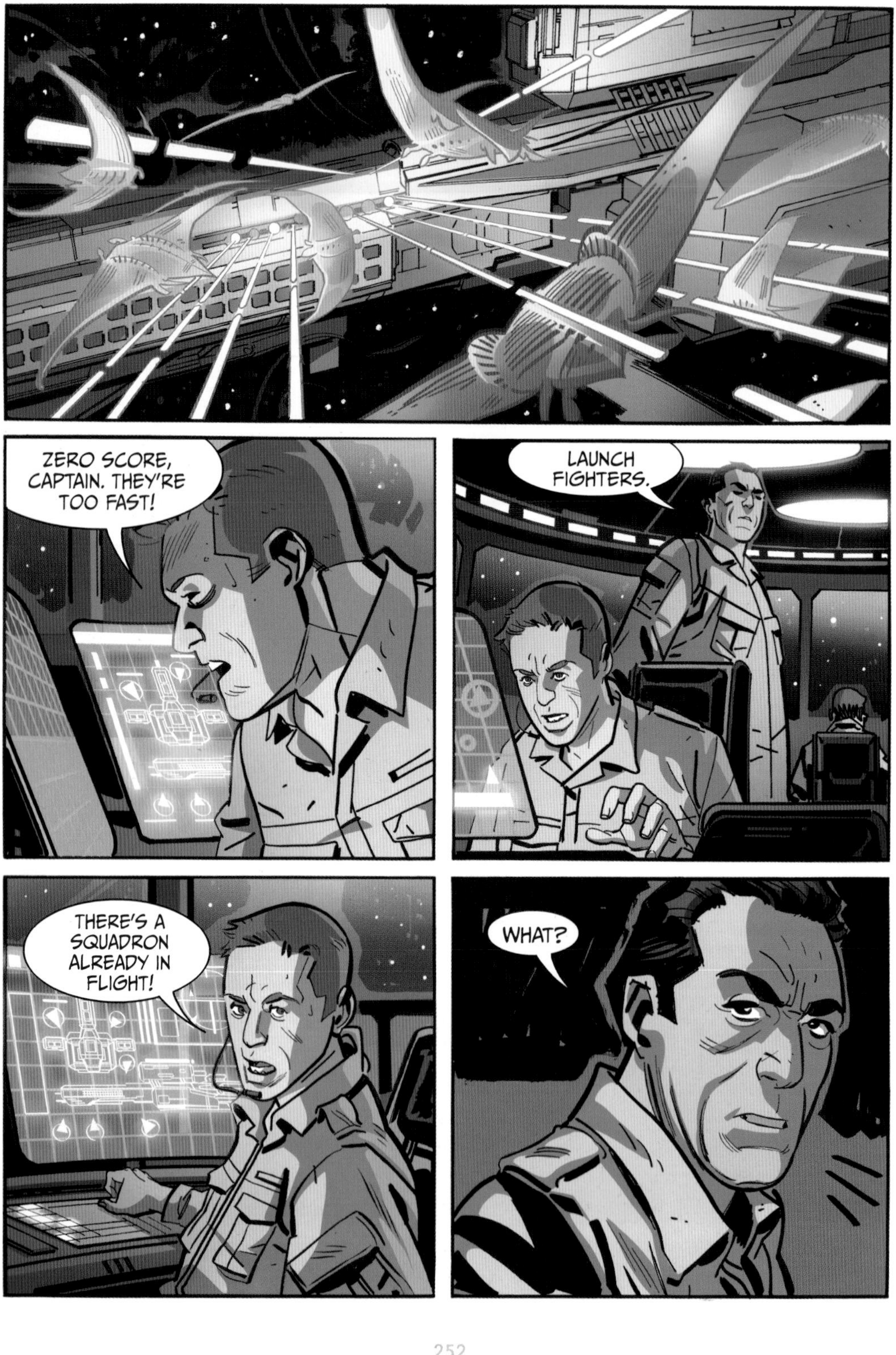
ZERO SCORE, CAPTAIN. THEY'RE TOO FAST!
LAUNCH FIGHTERS.
THERE'S A SQUADRON ALREADY IN FLIGHT!
WHAT?

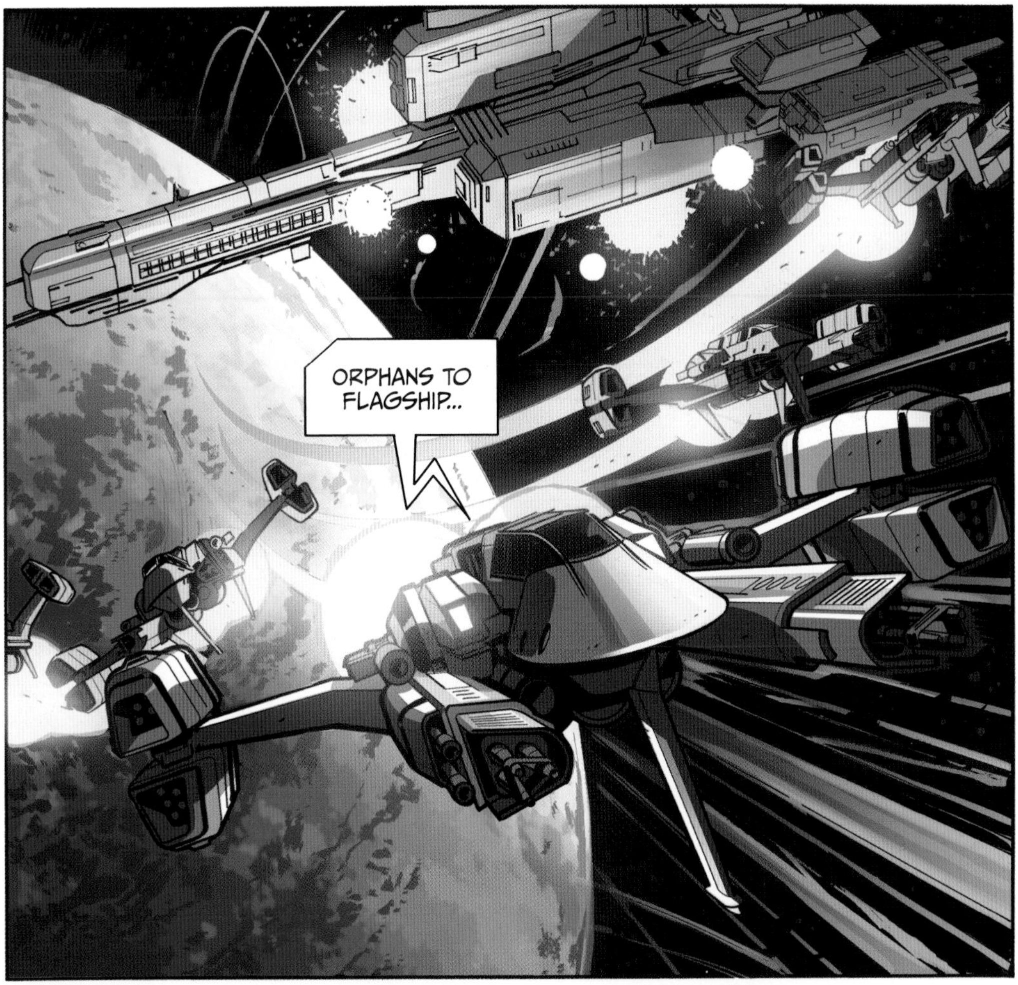
ORPHANS TO FLAGSHIP...

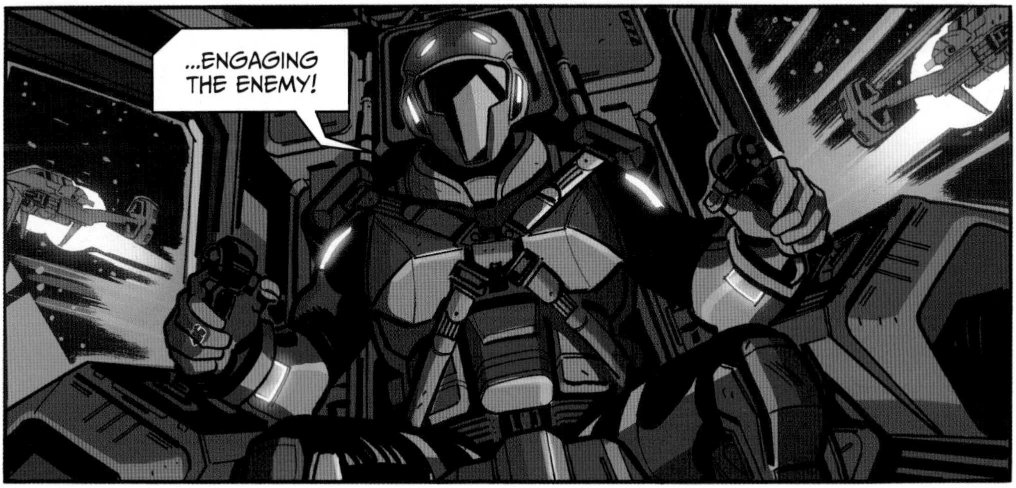
...ENGAGING THE ENEMY!

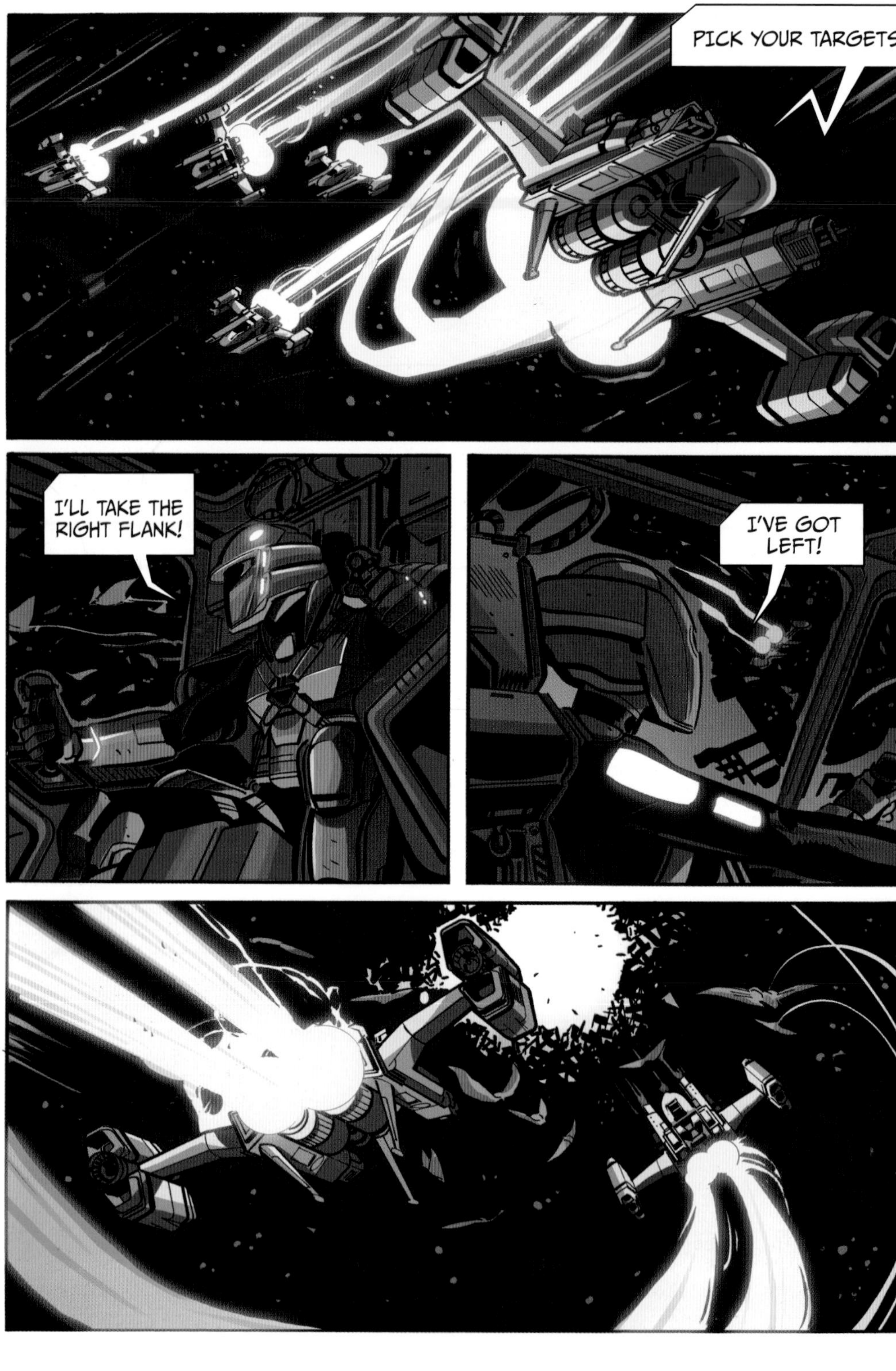
PICK YOUR TARGETS!
I'LL TAKE THE RIGHT FLANK!
I'VE GOT LEFT!

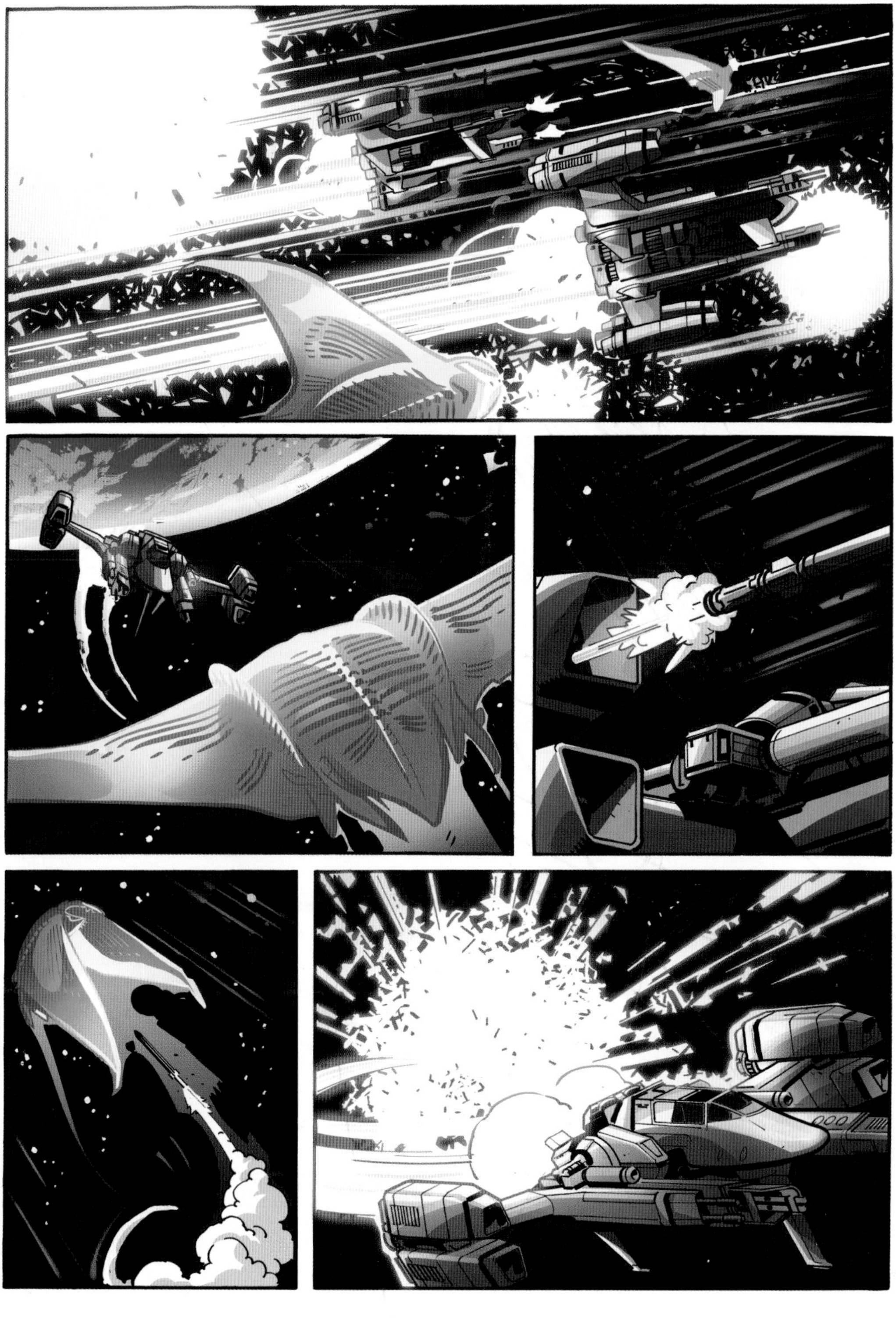

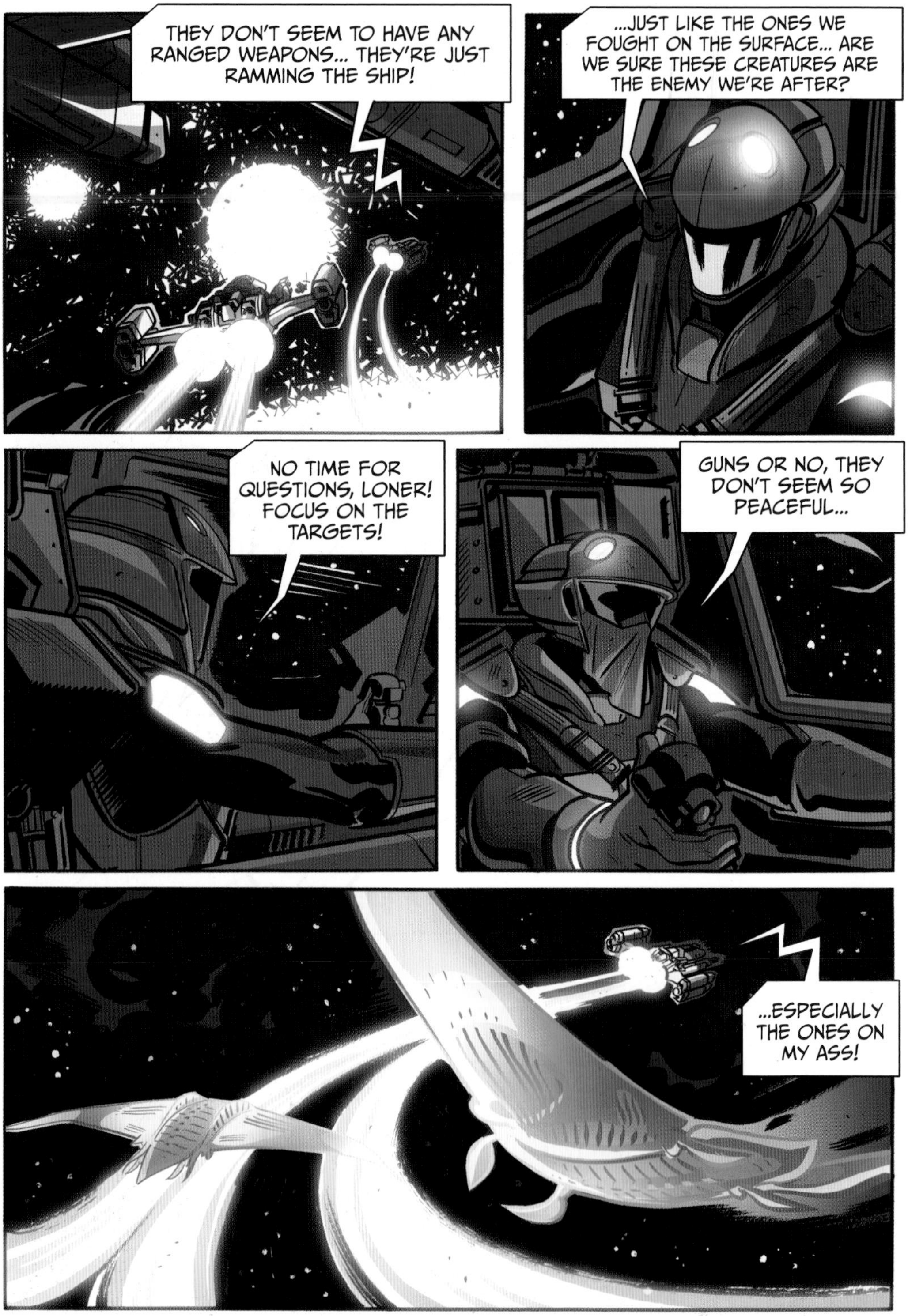
THEY DON'T SEEM TO HAVE ANY RANGED WEAPONS... THEY'RE JUST RAMMING THE SHIP!
...JUST LIKE THE ONES WE FOUGHT ON THE SURFACE... ARE WE SURE THESE CREATURES ARE THE ENEMY WE'RE AFTER?
NO TIME FOR QUESTIONS, LONER! FOCUS ON THE TARGETS!
GUNS OR NO, THEY DON'T SEEM SO PEACEFUL...
...ESPECIALLY THE ONES ON MY ASS!

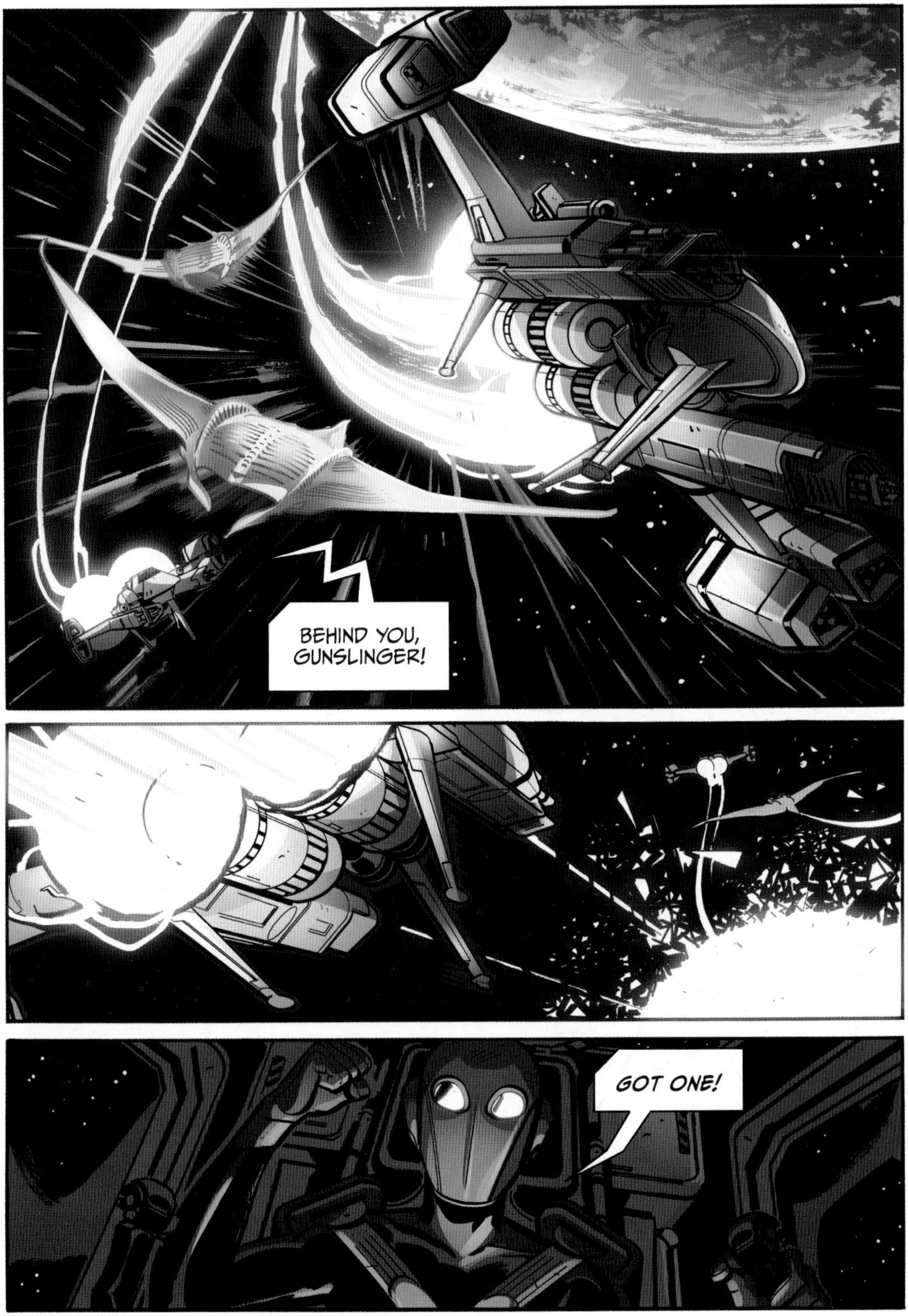
BEHIND YOU, GUNSLINGER!
GOT ONE!

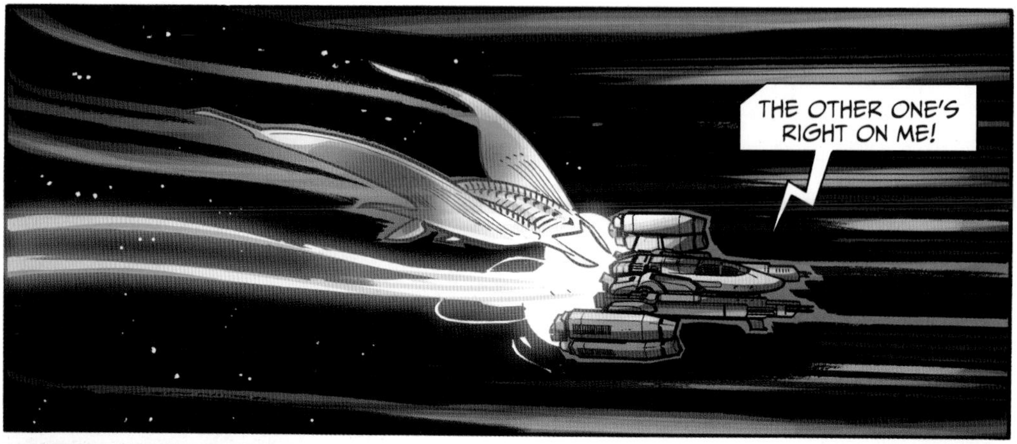
THE OTHER ONE'S RIGHT ON ME!

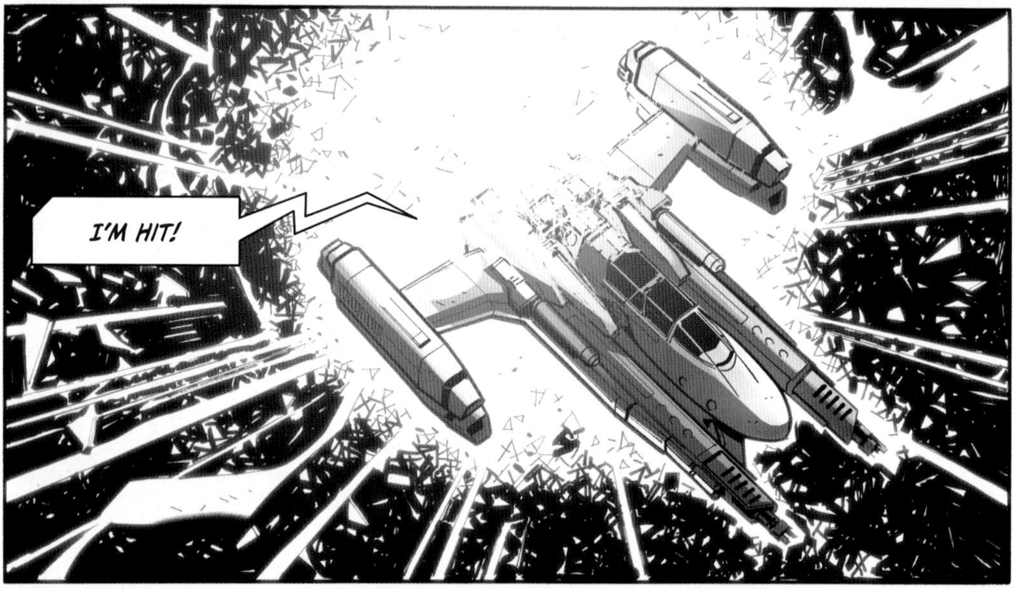
I'M HIT!

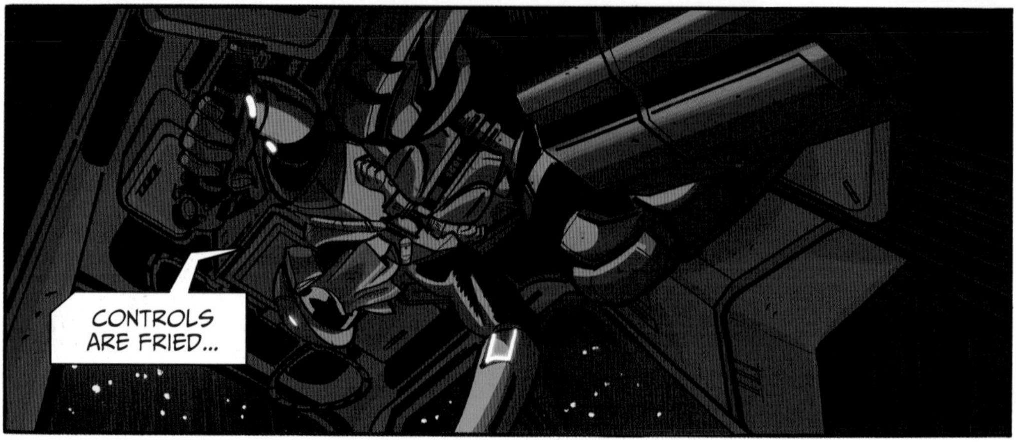
CONTROLS ARE FRIED...

DON'T PANIC, GUNSLINGER! REMEMBER THE DRILL!

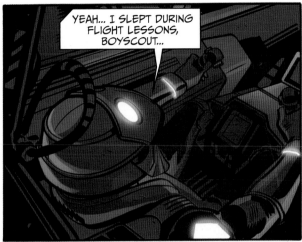

YEAH... I SLEPT DURING FLIGHT LESSONS, BOYSCOUT...

RINGO!

...I'M GOING DOWN!

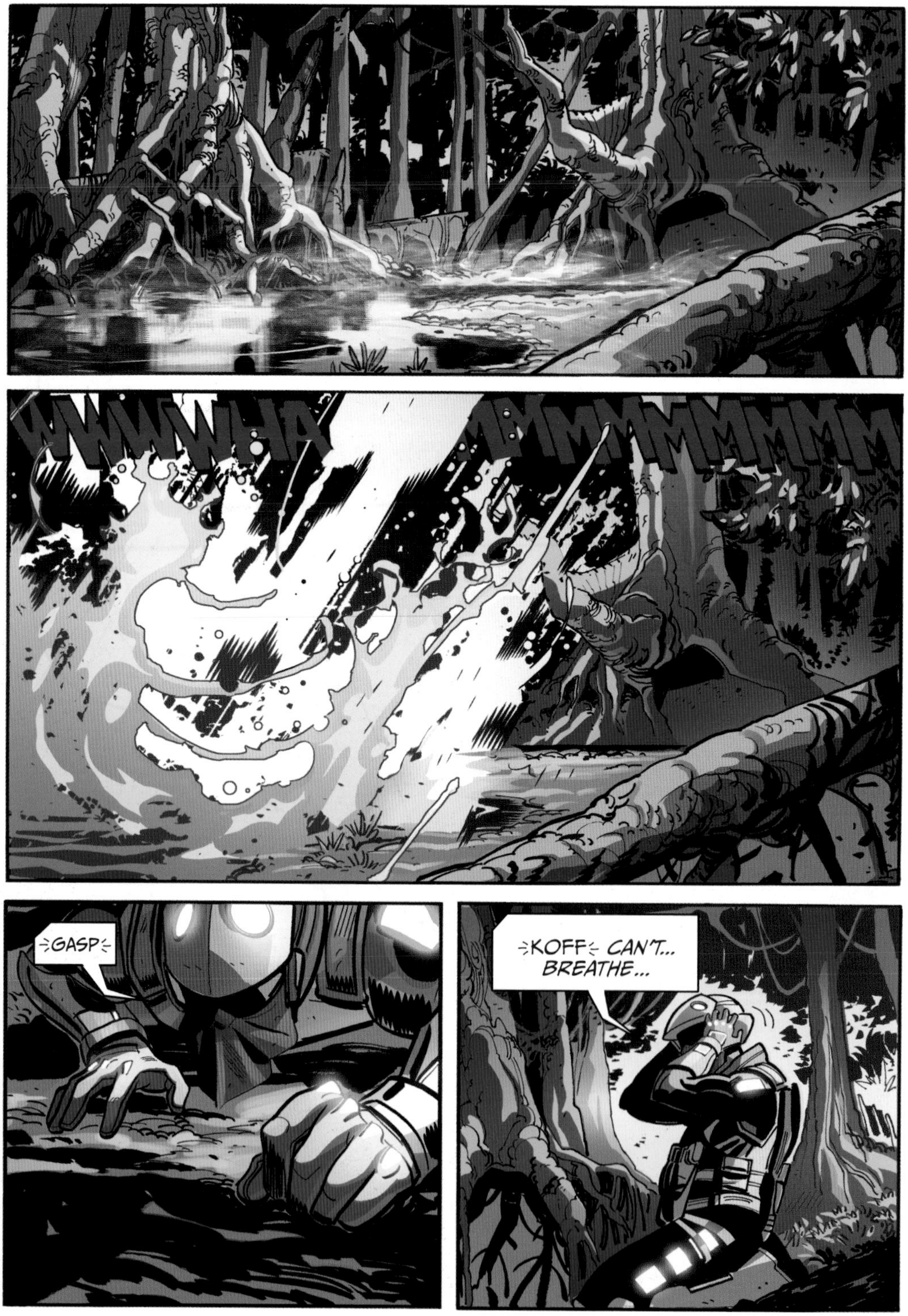
WWWWHAMMMMMMMMMMM
≈GASP≈
≈KOFF≈ CAN'T... BREATHE...

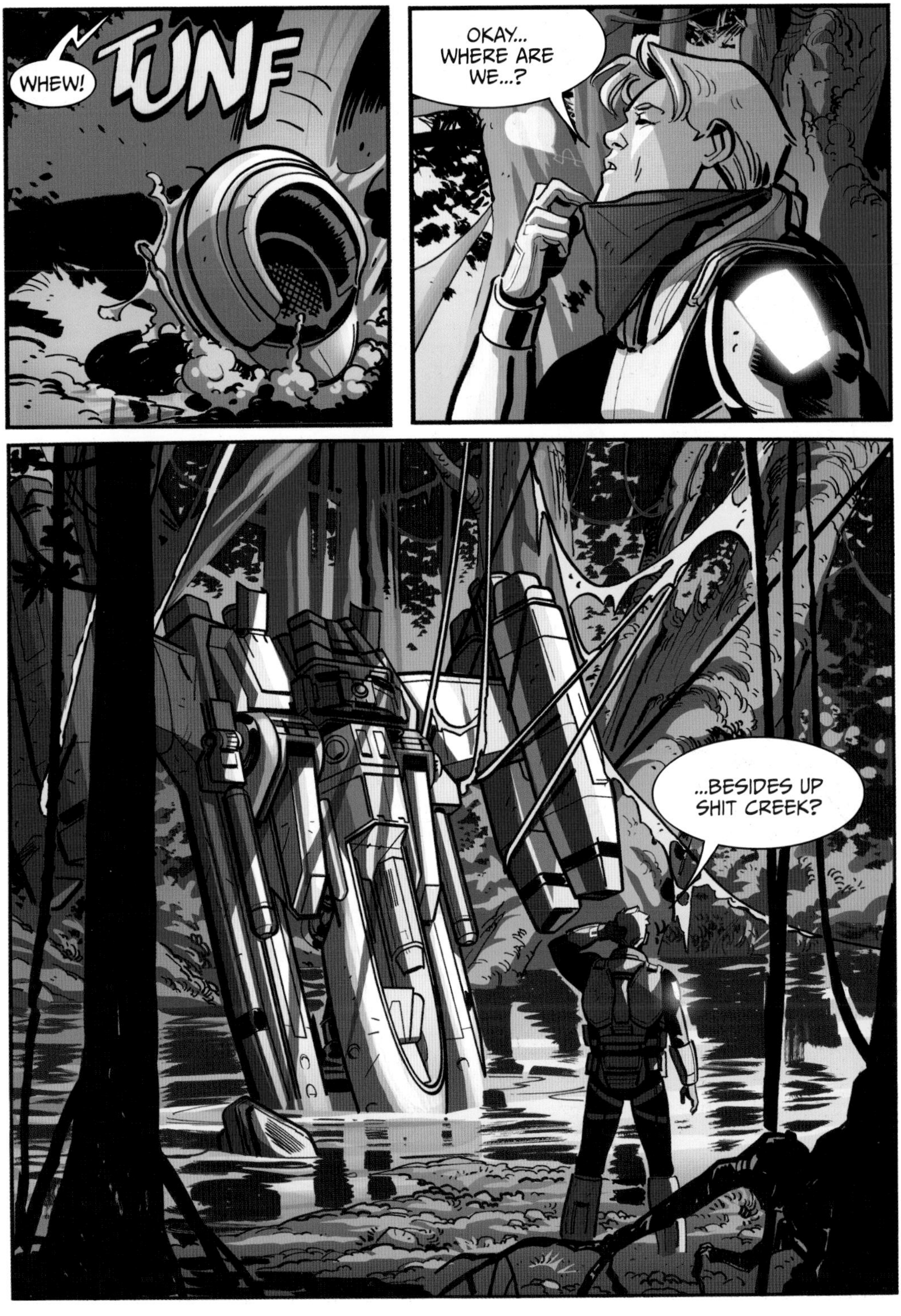
WHEW!
TUNF
OKAY... WHERE ARE WE...?
...BESIDES UP SHIT CREEK?

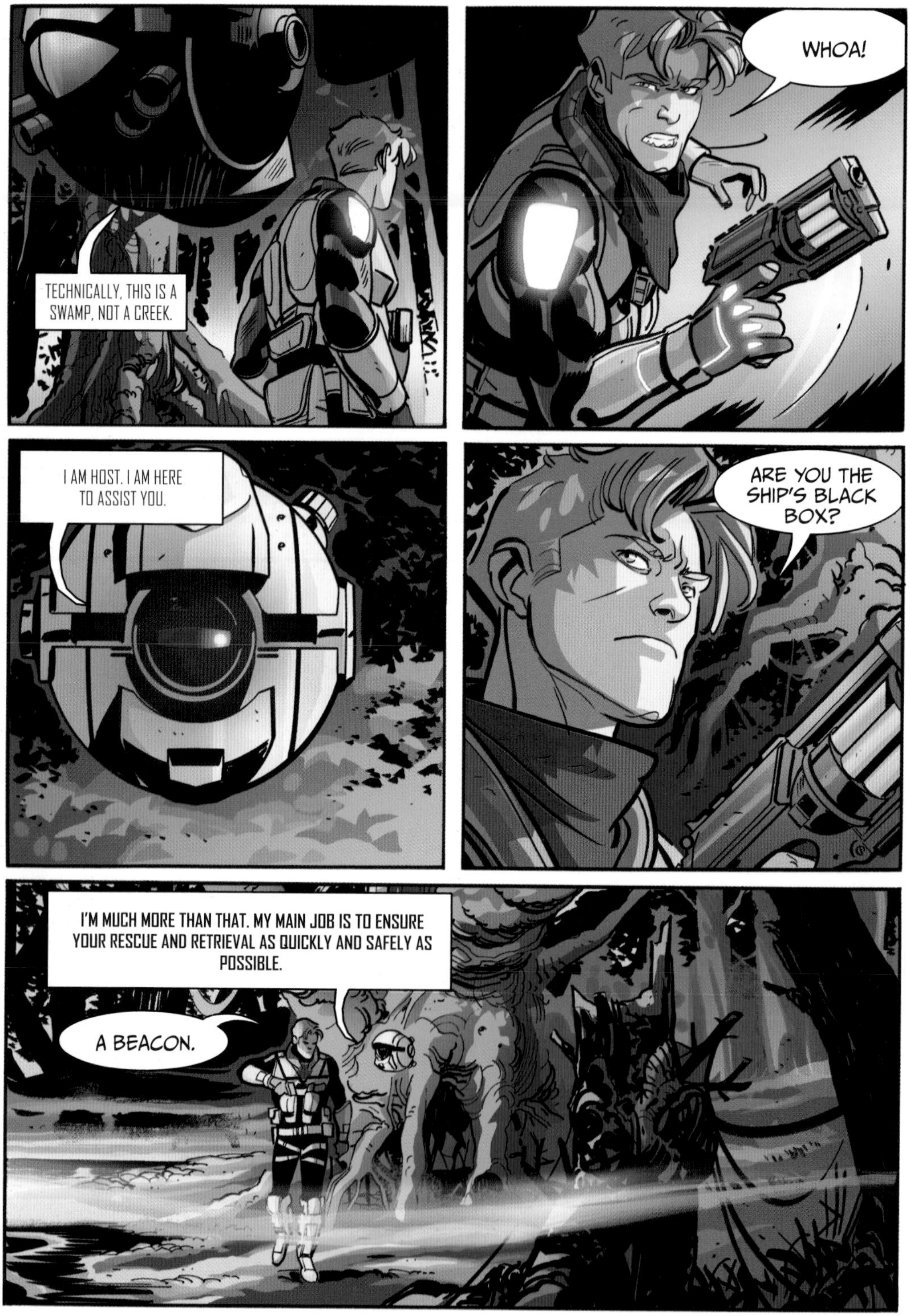
TECHNICALLY, THIS IS A SWAMP, NOT A CREEK.
WHOA!
I AM HOST. I AM HERE TO ASSIST YOU.
ARE YOU THE SHIP'S BLACK BOX?
I'M MUCH MORE THAN THAT. MY MAIN JOB IS TO ENSURE YOUR RESCUE AND RETRIEVAL AS QUICKLY AND SAFELY AS POSSIBLE.
A BEACON.

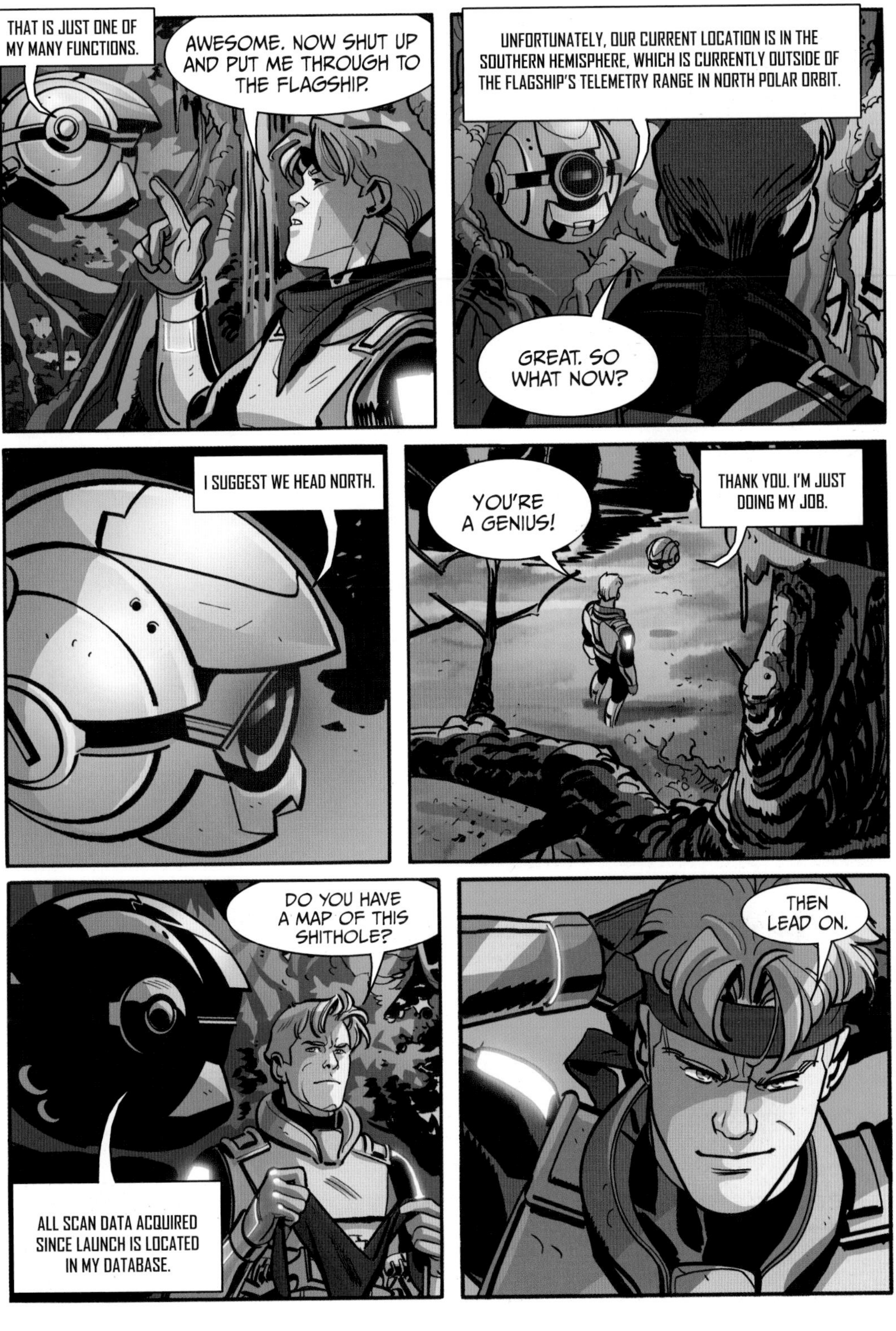
THAT IS JUST ONE OF MY MANY FUNCTIONS.
AWESOME. NOW SHUT UP AND PUT ME THROUGH TO THE FLAGSHIP.
UNFORTUNATELY, OUR CURRENT LOCATION IS IN THE SOUTHERN HEMISPHERE, WHICH IS CURRENTLY OUTSIDE OF THE FLAGSHIP'S TELEMETRY RANGE IN NORTH POLAR ORBIT.
GREAT. SO WHAT NOW?
I SUGGEST WE HEAD NORTH.
YOU'RE A GENIUS!
THANK YOU. I'M JUST DOING MY JOB.
DO YOU HAVE A MAP OF THIS SHITHOLE?
ALL SCAN DATA ACQUIRED SINCE LAUNCH IS LOCATED IN MY DATABASE.
THEN LEAD ON.

BEFORE WE BEGIN, THERE IS A MINOR PROBLEM TO ADDRESS.

SHOOT, BOWLING BALL.

MY NAME IS HOST.

WHATEVER, WHAT'S THE PROBLEM?

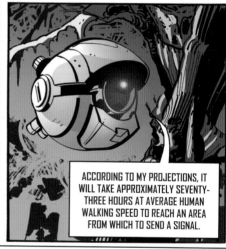

ACCORDING TO MY PROJECTIONS, IT WILL TAKE APPROXIMATELY SEVENTY-THREE HOURS AT AVERAGE HUMAN WALKING SPEED TO REACH AN AREA FROM WHICH TO SEND A SIGNAL.

A GOOD WALK NEVER KILLED ANYONE...

IN THIS CASE, I FEAR IT WILL. YOUR BIOMETRIC DATA INDICATES YOU DID NOT FOLLOW THE VACCINATION PROTOCOL BEFORE LANDING.

THIS WASN'T A PLANNED STOP.

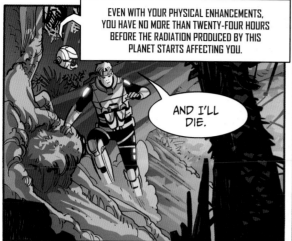

EVEN WITH YOUR PHYSICAL ENHANCEMENTS, YOU HAVE NO MORE THAN TWENTY-FOUR HOURS BEFORE THE RADIATION PRODUCED BY THIS PLANET STARTS AFFECTING YOU.

AND I'LL DIE.

SLOWLY AND PAINFULLY, YES.

GREAT. WE JUST MET AND I HATE YOU ALREADY.

GUESS THERE'S NO TIME TO LOSE, THEN...

FORGIVE ME, WHAT IS YOUR PLAN?

WE RUN!

265

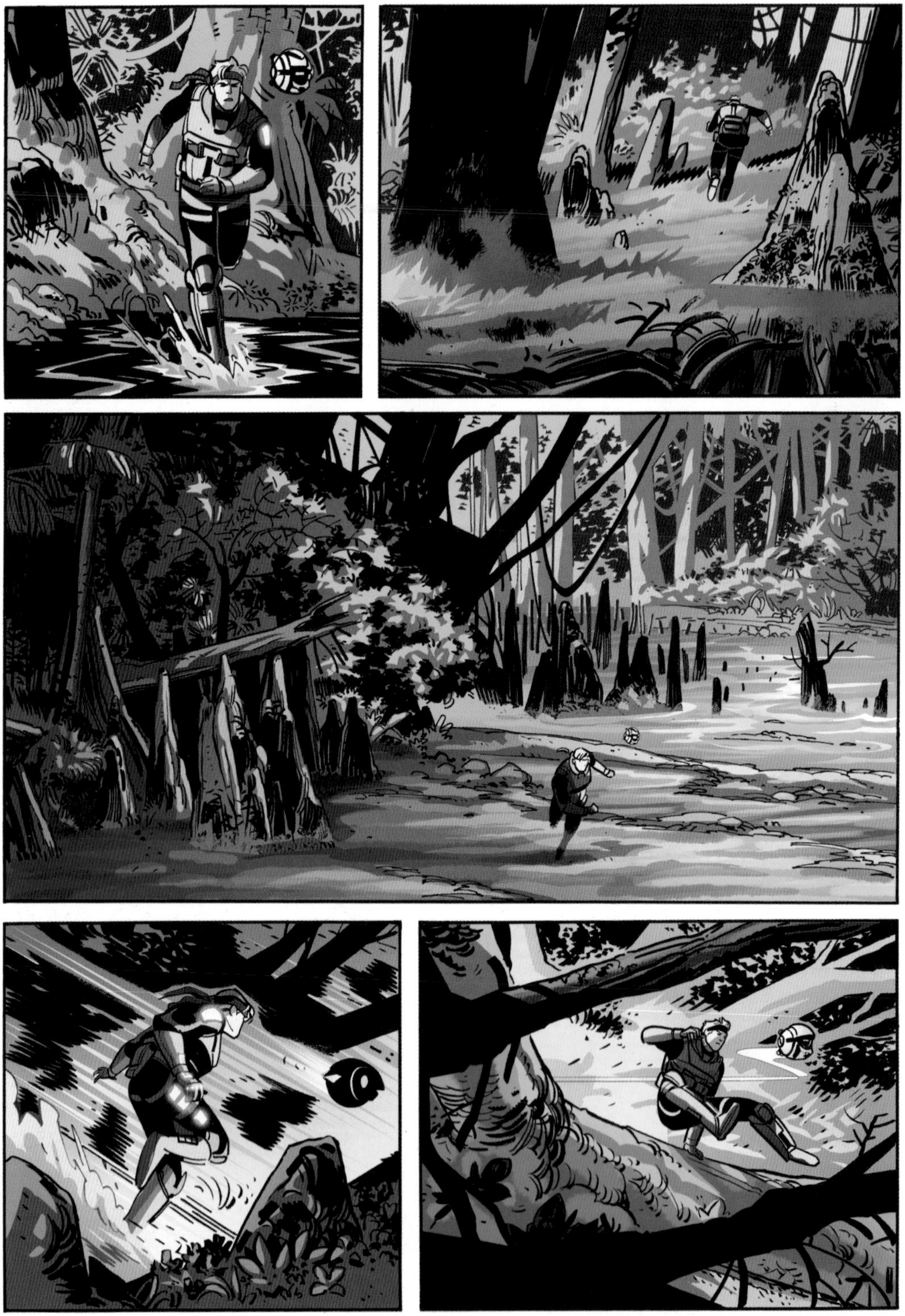

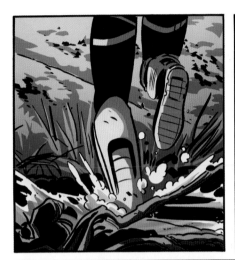

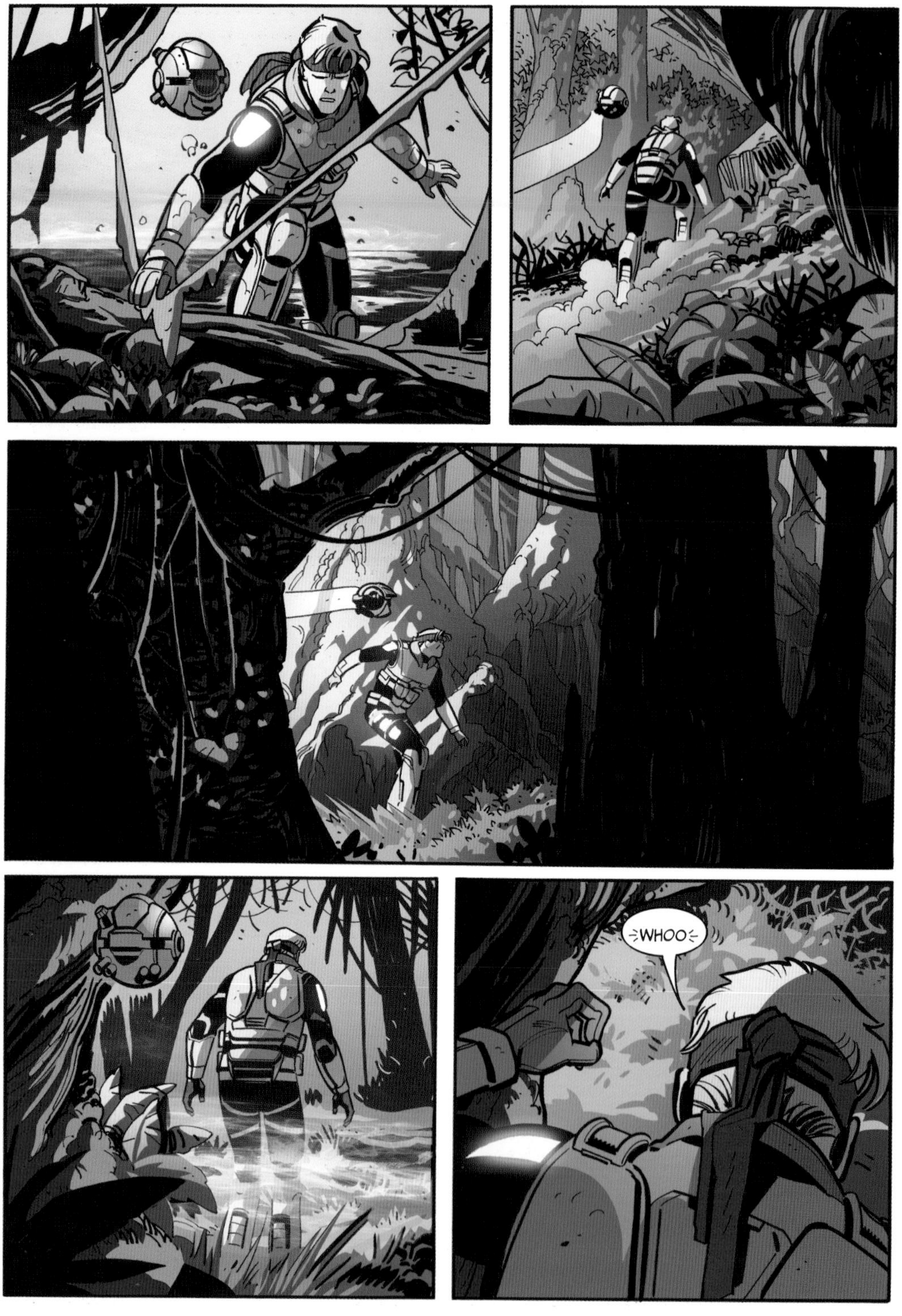
WHOO

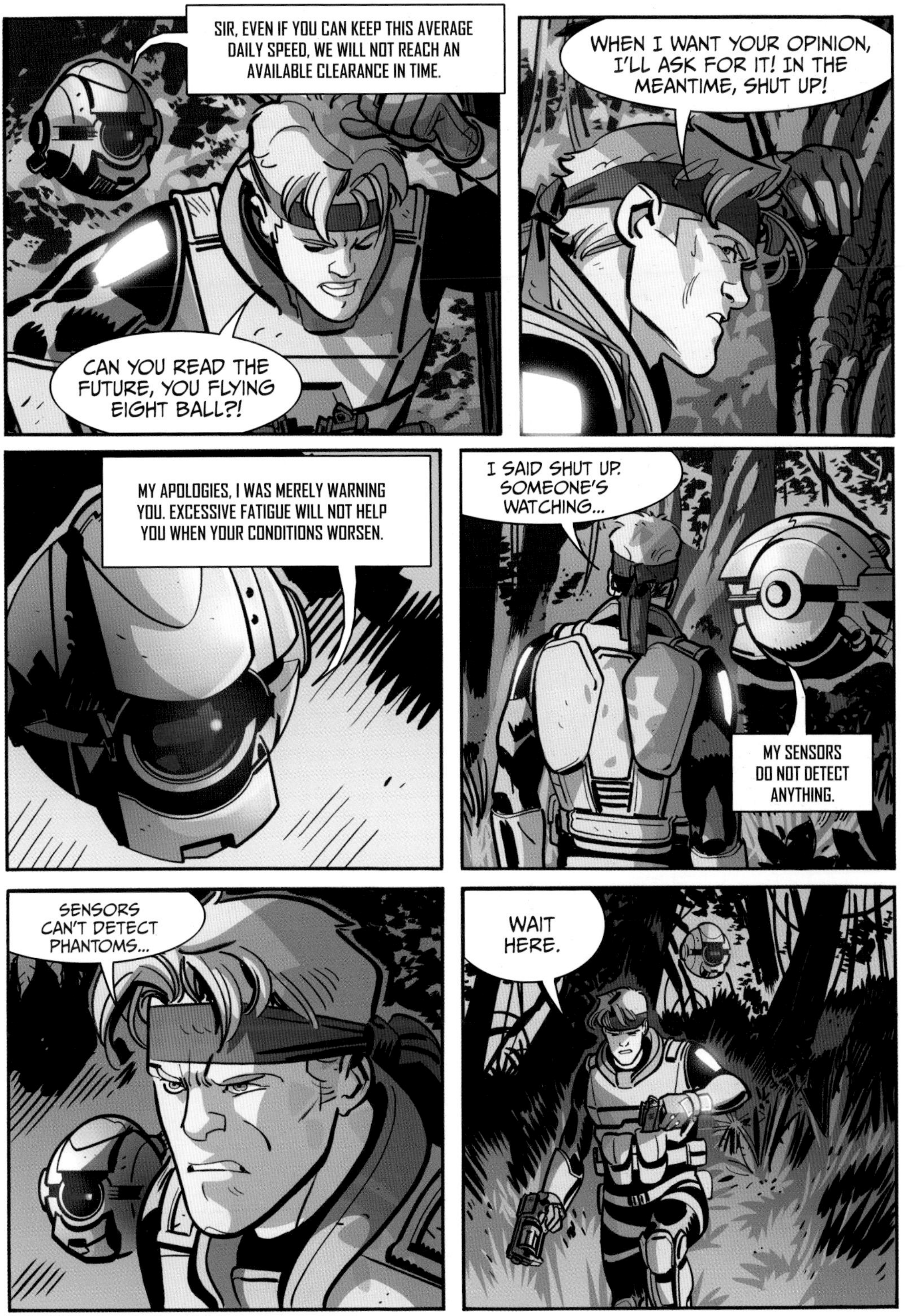
SIR, EVEN IF YOU CAN KEEP THIS AVERAGE DAILY SPEED, WE WILL NOT REACH AN AVAILABLE CLEARANCE IN TIME.
CAN YOU READ THE FUTURE, YOU FLYING EIGHT BALL?!
WHEN I WANT YOUR OPINION, I'LL ASK FOR IT! IN THE MEANTIME, SHUT UP!
MY APOLOGIES, I WAS MERELY WARNING YOU. EXCESSIVE FATIGUE WILL NOT HELP YOU WHEN YOUR CONDITIONS WORSEN.
I SAID SHUT UP. SOMEONE'S WATCHING...
MY SENSORS DO NOT DETECT ANYTHING.
SENSORS CAN'T DETECT PHANTOMS...
WAIT HERE.

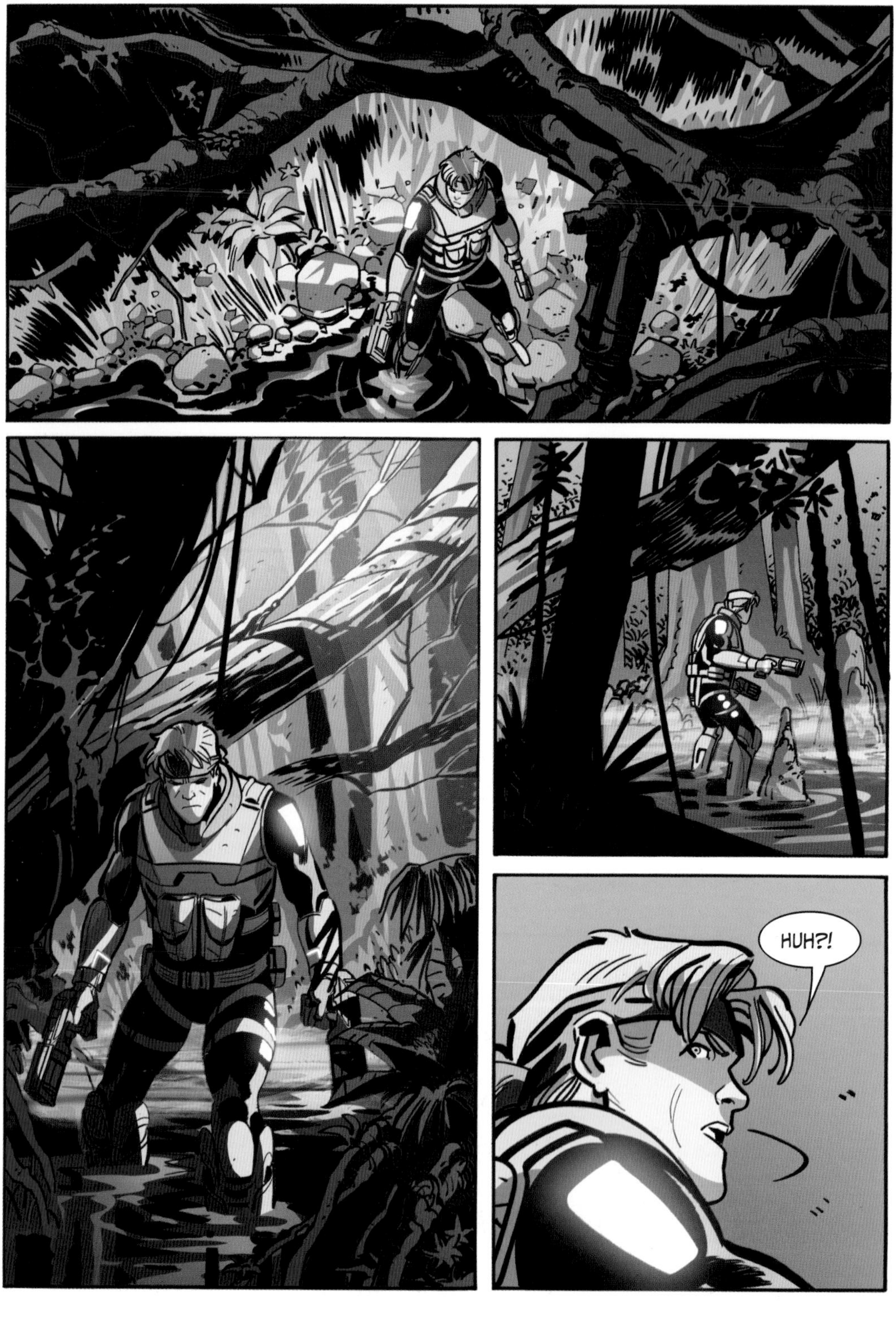
HUH?!

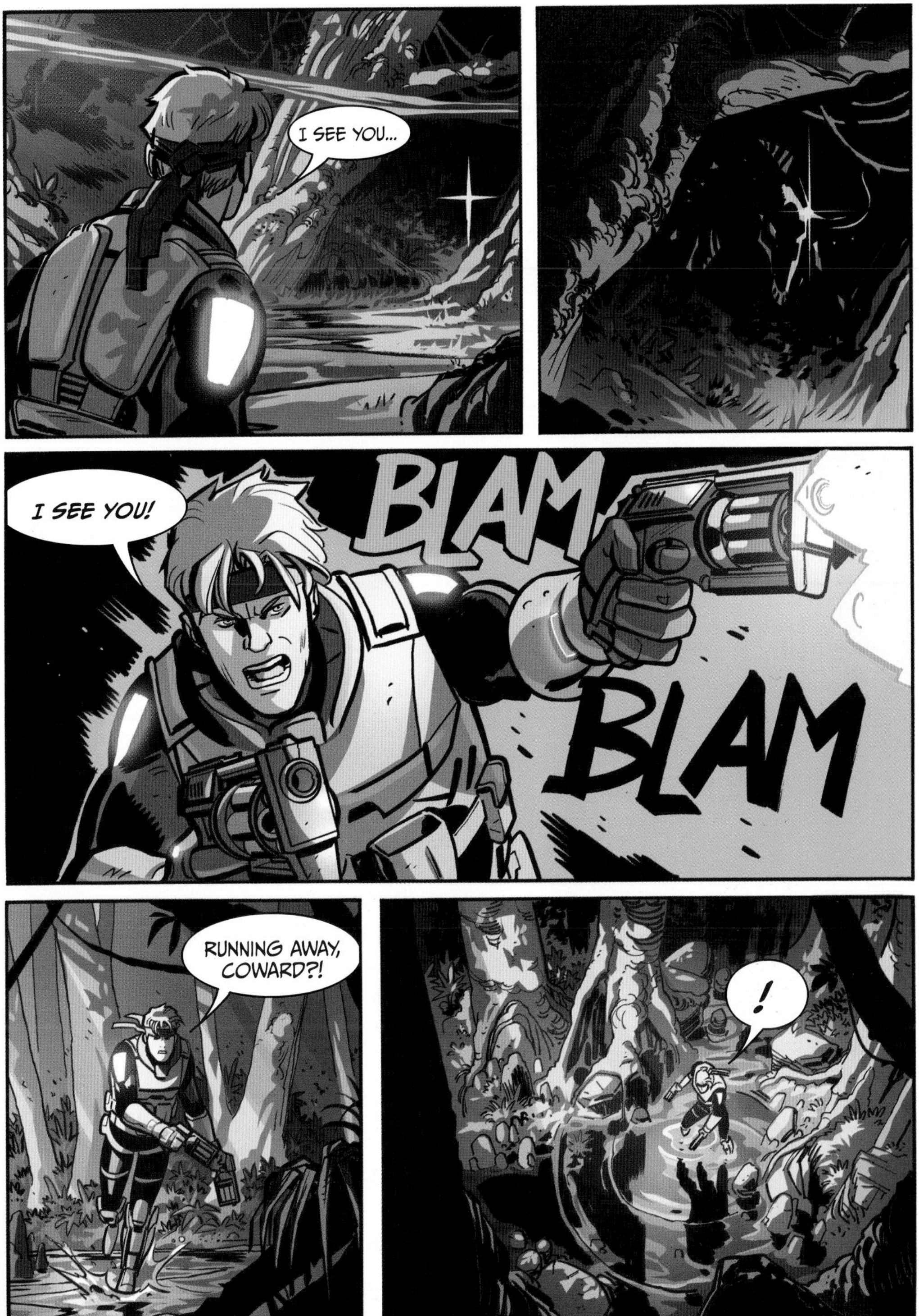
I SEE YOU...
I SEE YOU!
BLAM
BLAM
RUNNING AWAY, COWARD?!
!

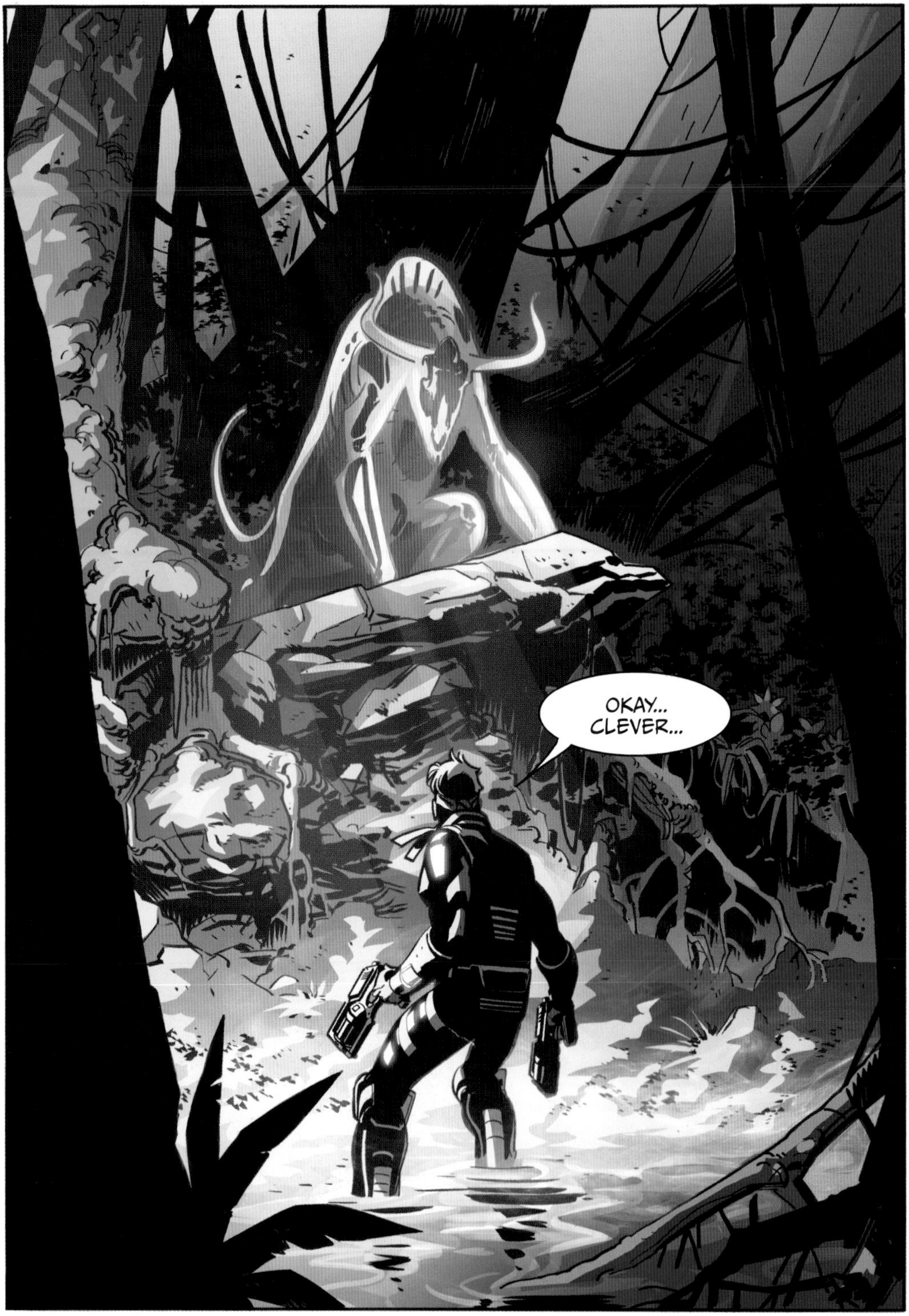
OKAY... CLEVER...

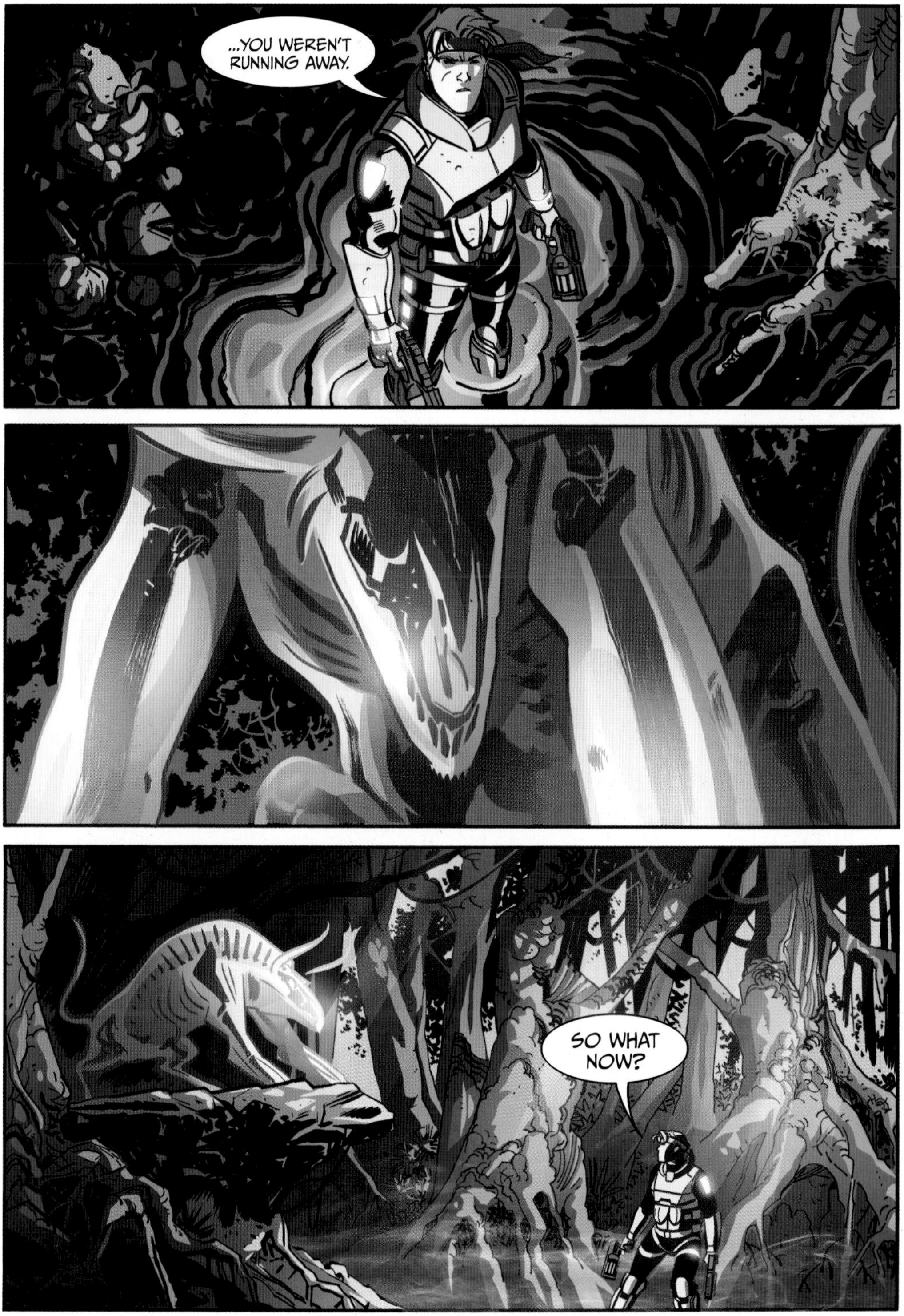
...YOU WEREN'T RUNNING AWAY.
SO WHAT NOW?

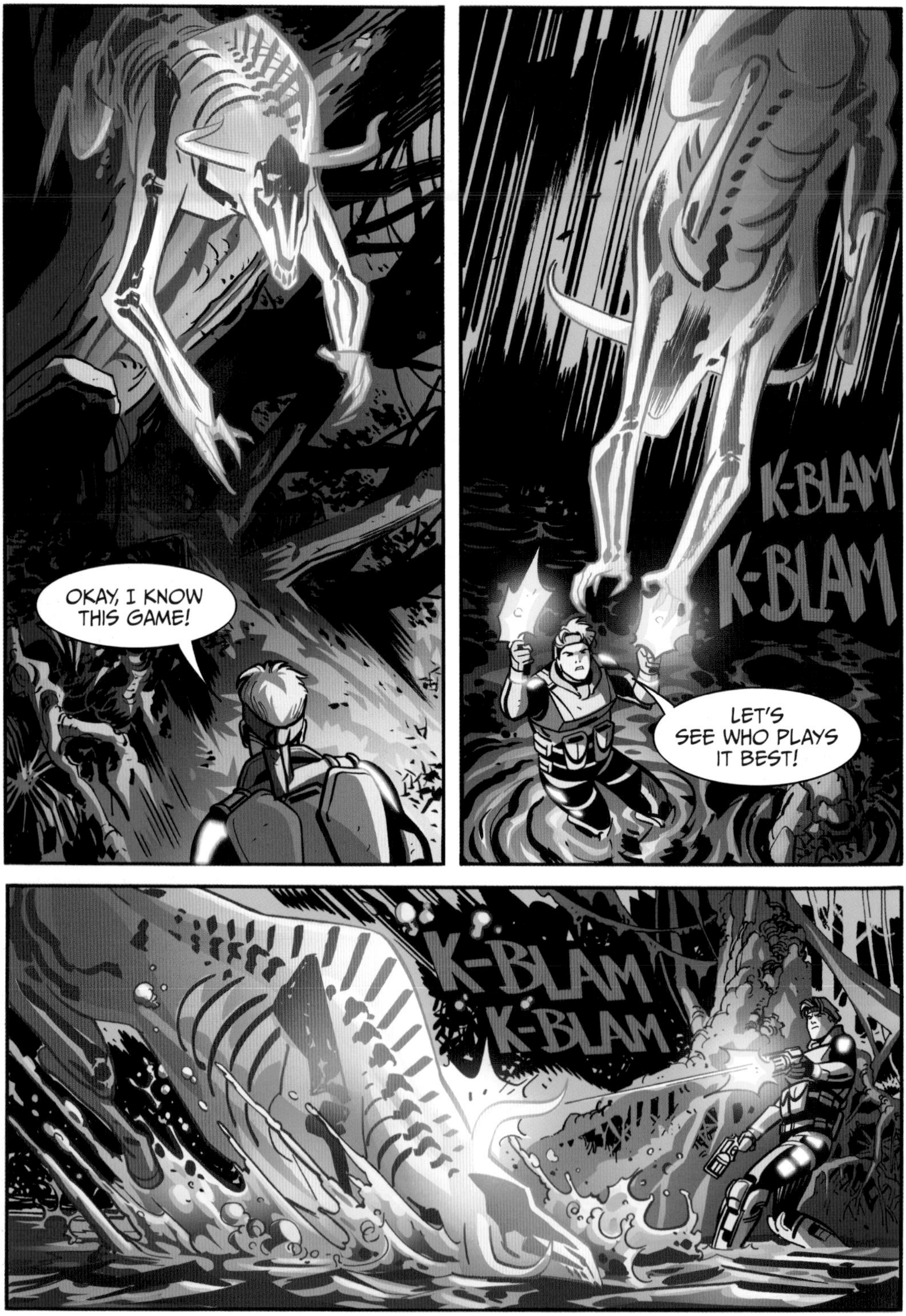
OKAY, I KNOW THIS GAME!
K-BLAM
K-BLAM
LET'S SEE WHO PLAYS IT BEST!
K-BLAM
K-BLAM

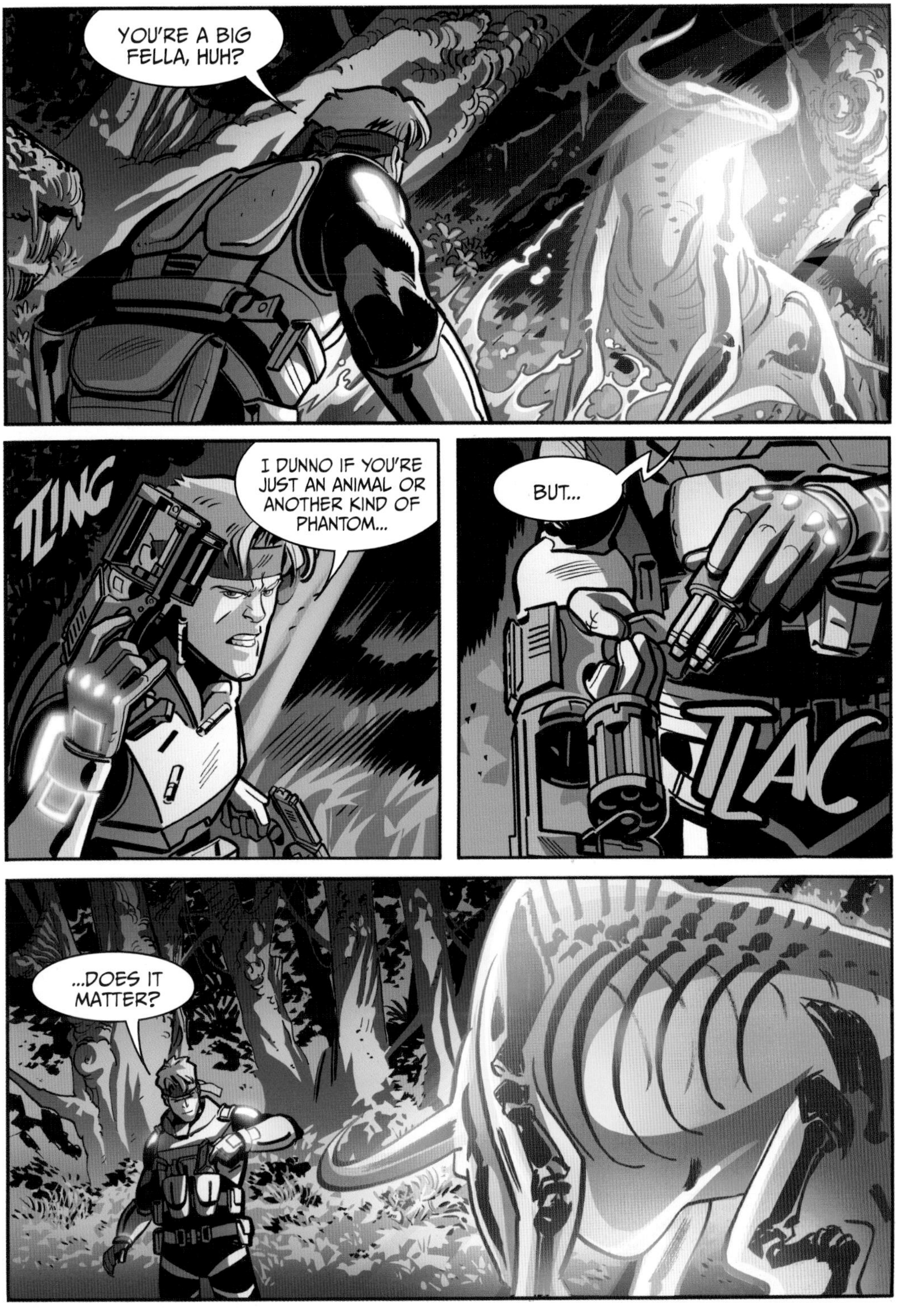
YOU'RE A BIG FELLA, HUH?
TLING
I DUNNO IF YOU'RE JUST AN ANIMAL OR ANOTHER KIND OF PHANTOM...
BUT...
TLAC
...DOES IT MATTER?

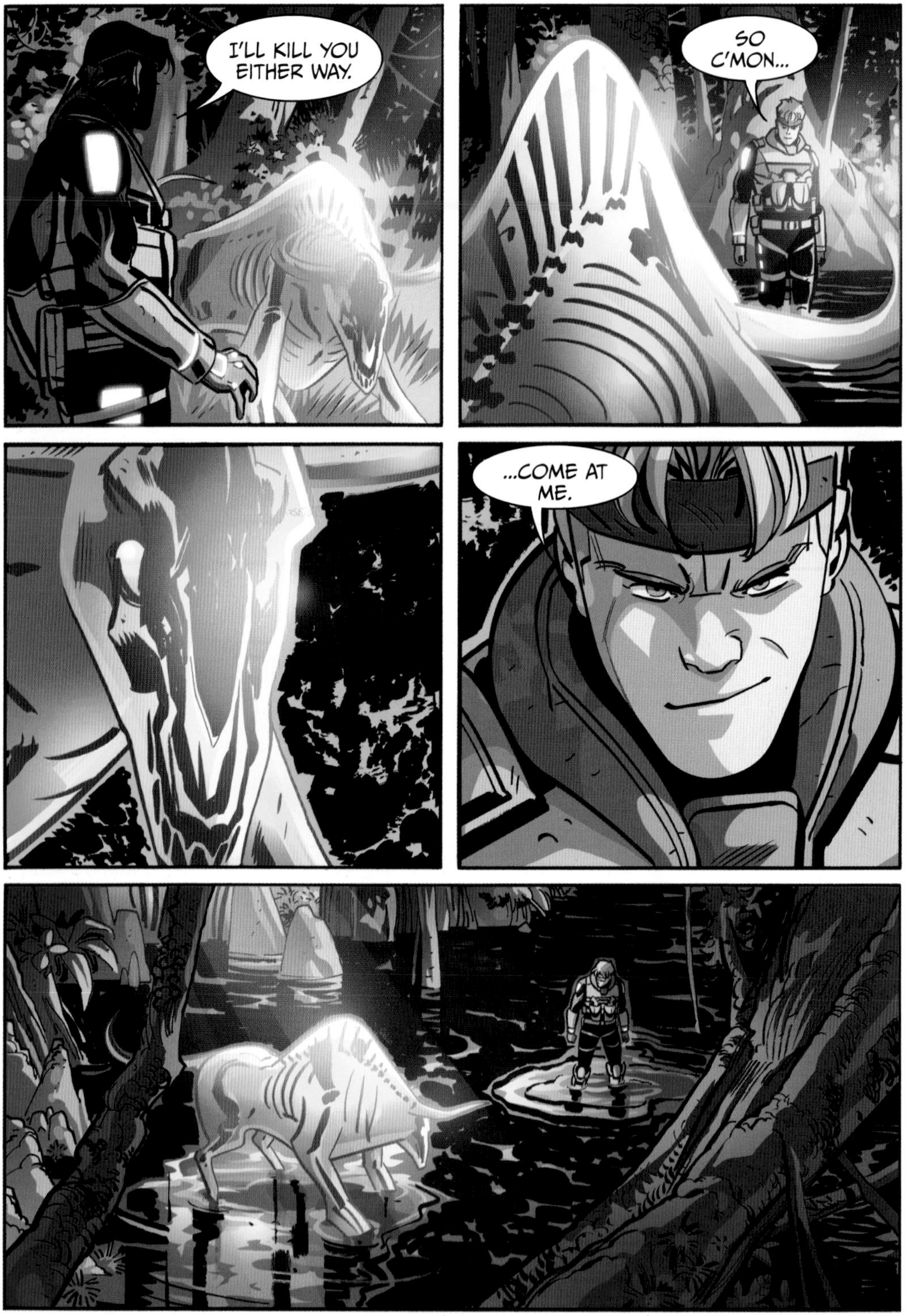
I'LL KILL YOU EITHER WAY.
SO C'MON...
...COME AT ME.

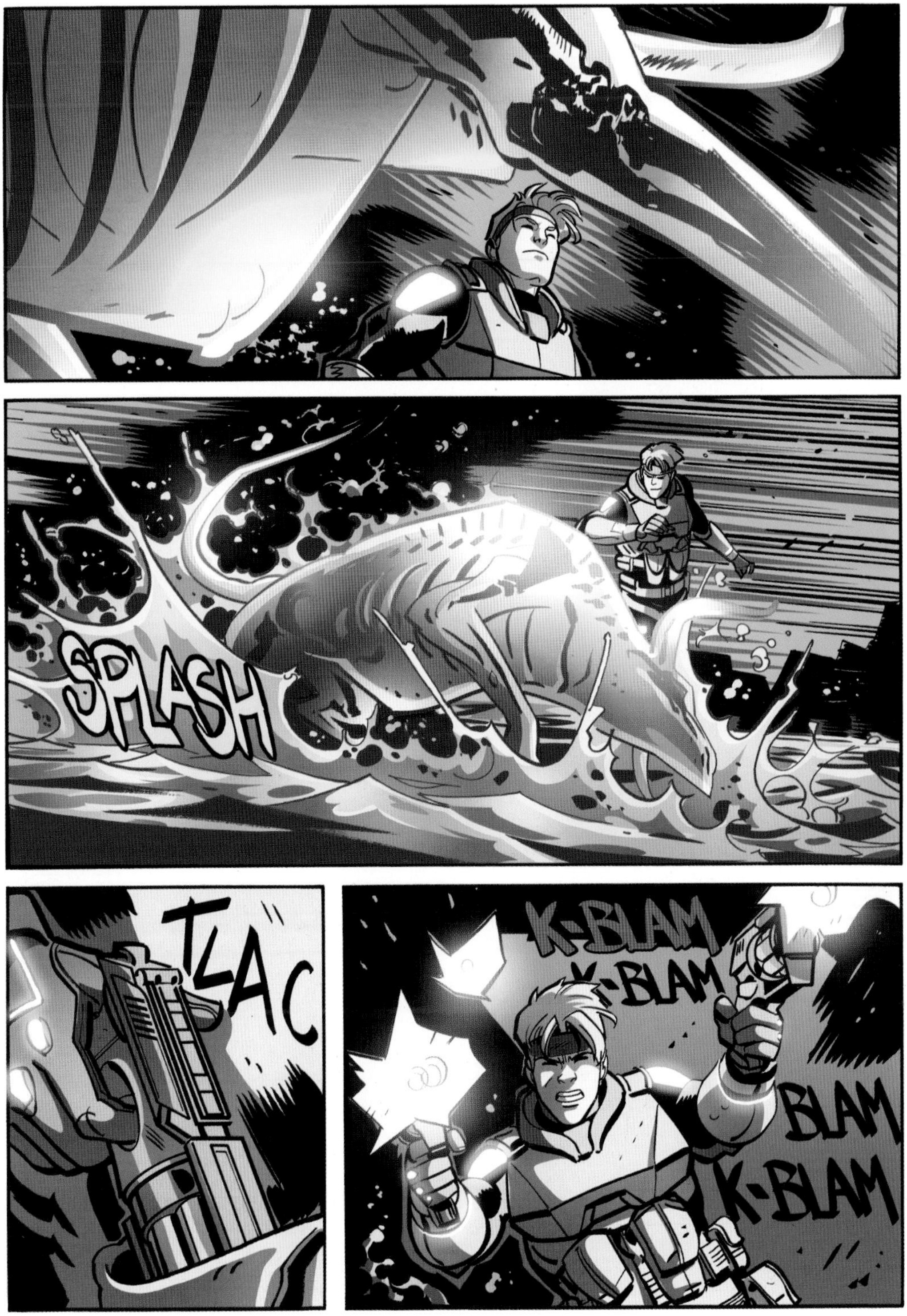
SPLASH
TLAC
K-BLAM
K-BLAM
BLAM
K-BLAM

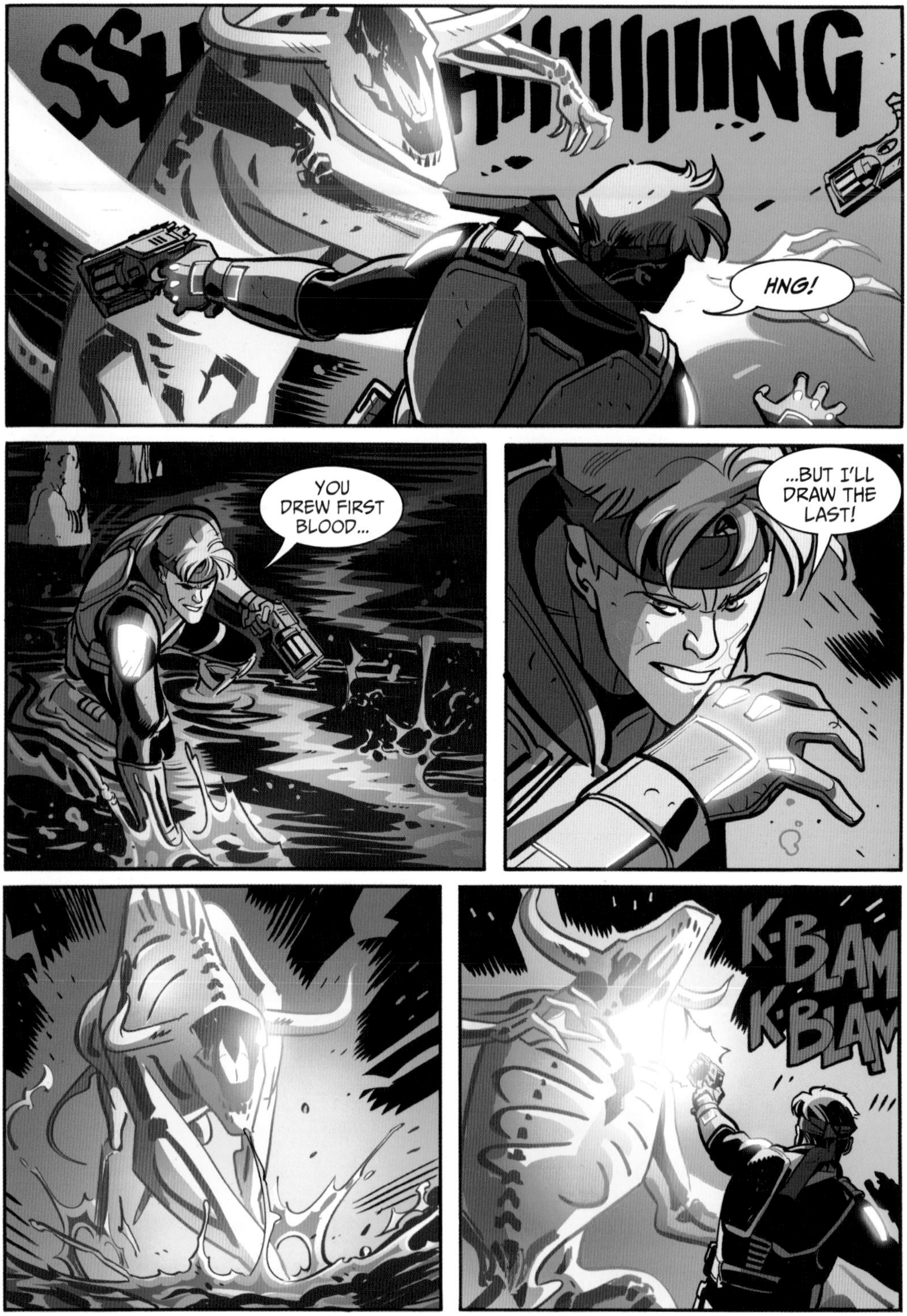
SSHHHHIIIIING
HNG!
YOU DREW FIRST BLOOD...
...BUT I'LL DRAW THE LAST!
K-BLAM
K-BLAM

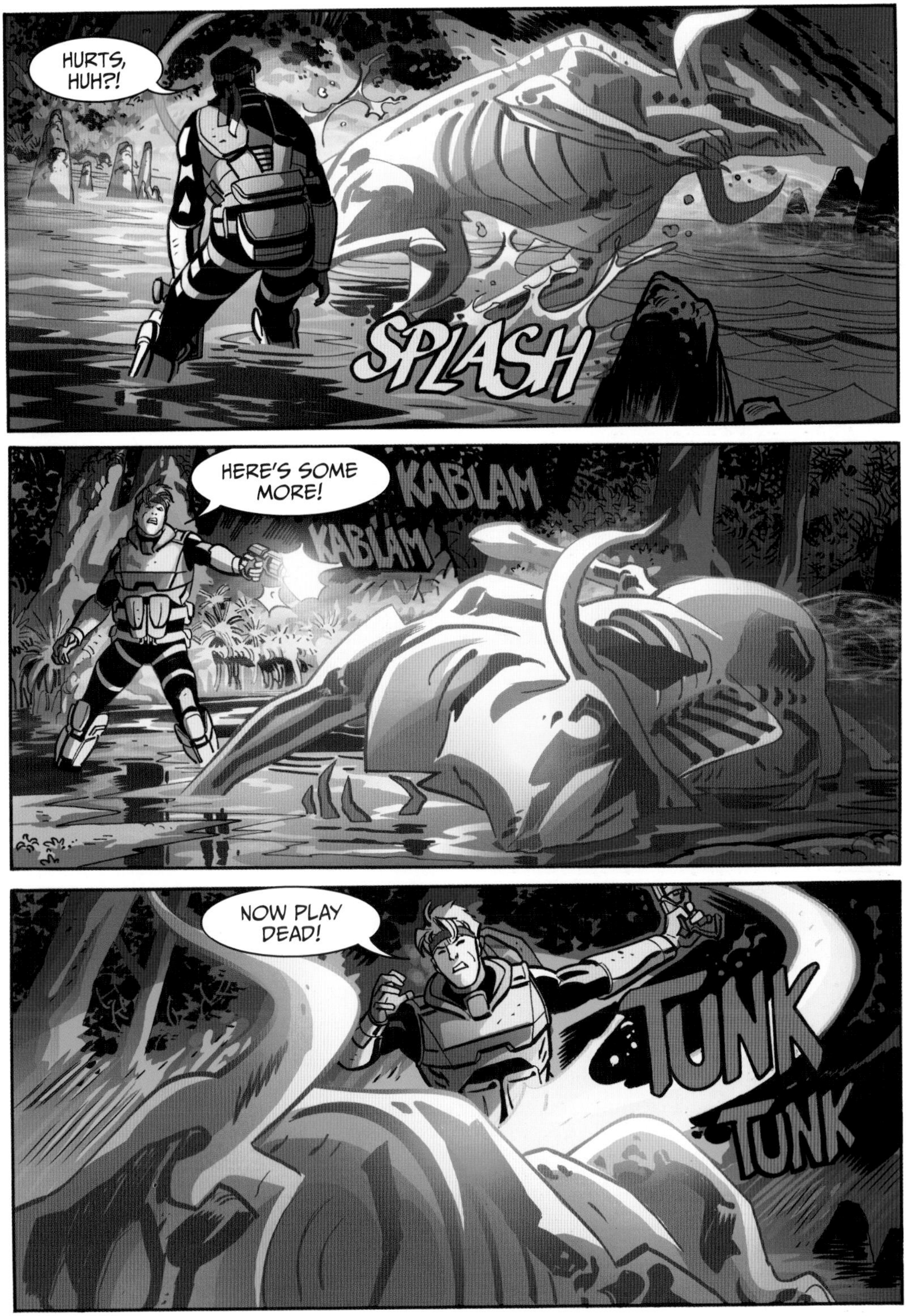
HURTS, HUH?!
SPLASH
HERE'S SOME MORE!
KABLAM
KABLAM
NOW PLAY DEAD!
TUNK
TUNK

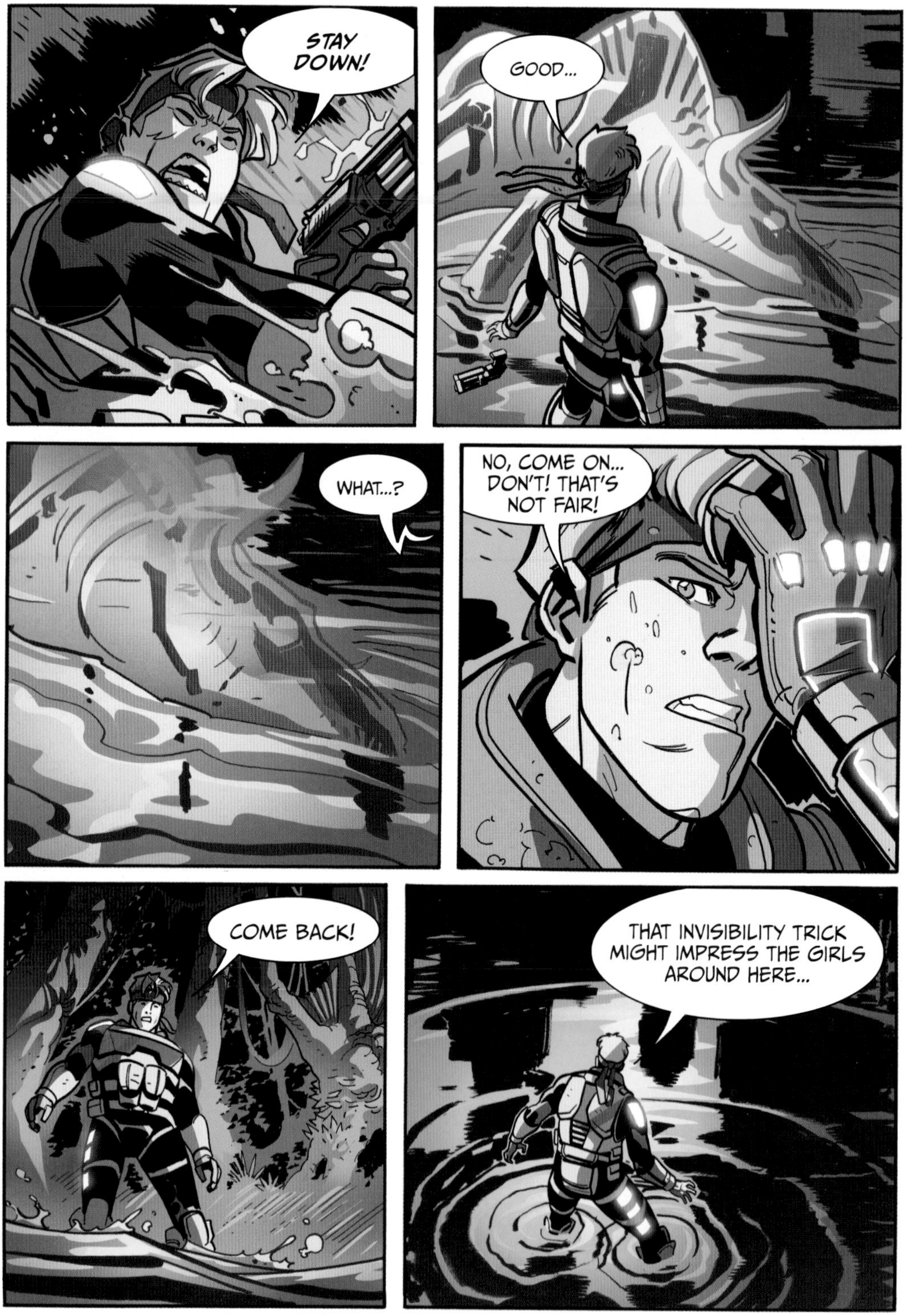
STAY DOWN!
GOOD...
WHAT...?
NO, COME ON... DON'T! THAT'S NOT FAIR!
COME BACK!
THAT INVISIBILITY TRICK MIGHT IMPRESS THE GIRLS AROUND HERE...

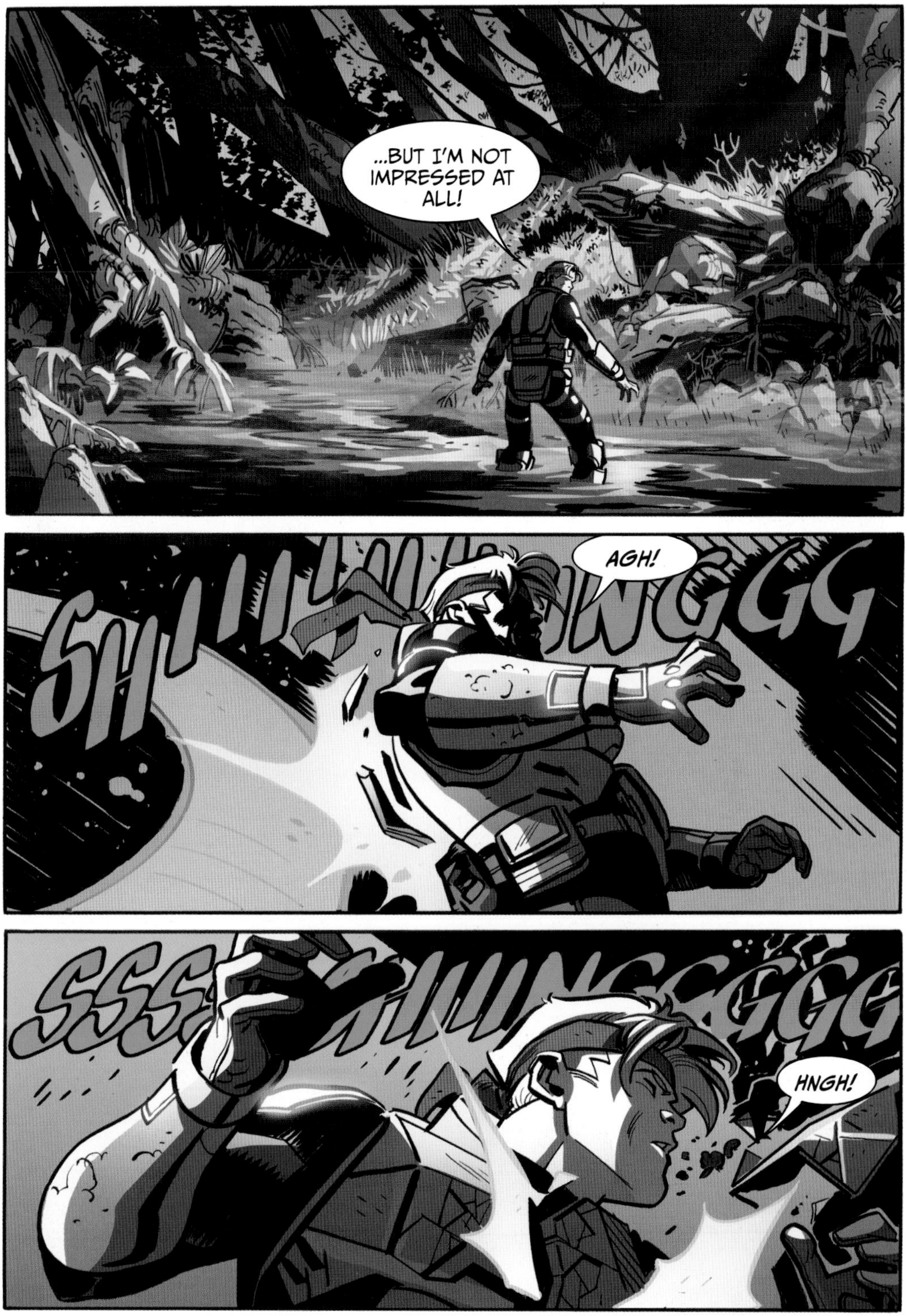
...BUT I'M NOT IMPRESSED AT ALL!
AGH!
HNGH!

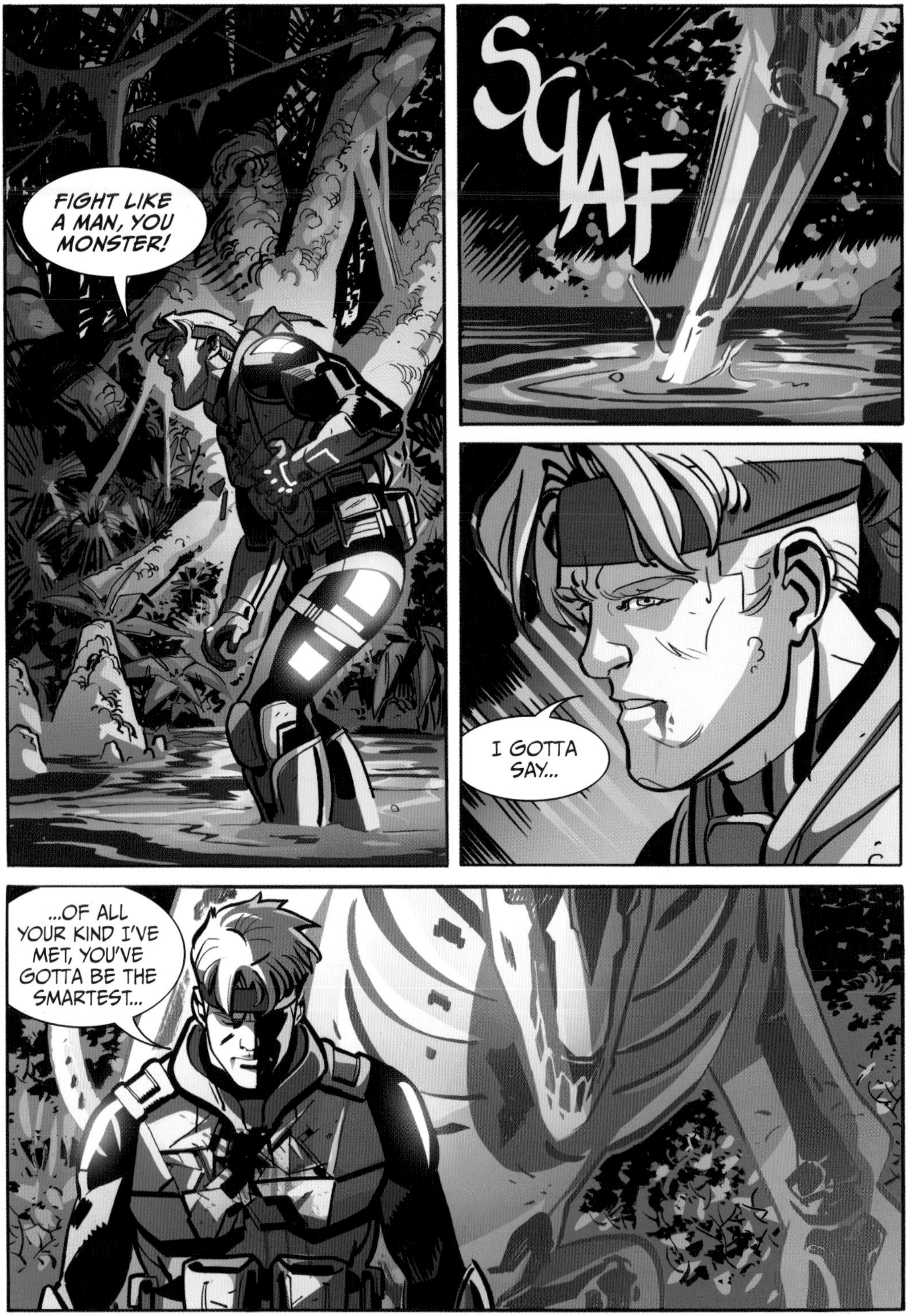
FIGHT LIKE A MAN, YOU MONSTER!
SCHAF
I GOTTA SAY...
...OF ALL YOUR KIND I'VE MET, YOU'VE GOTTA BE THE SMARTEST...

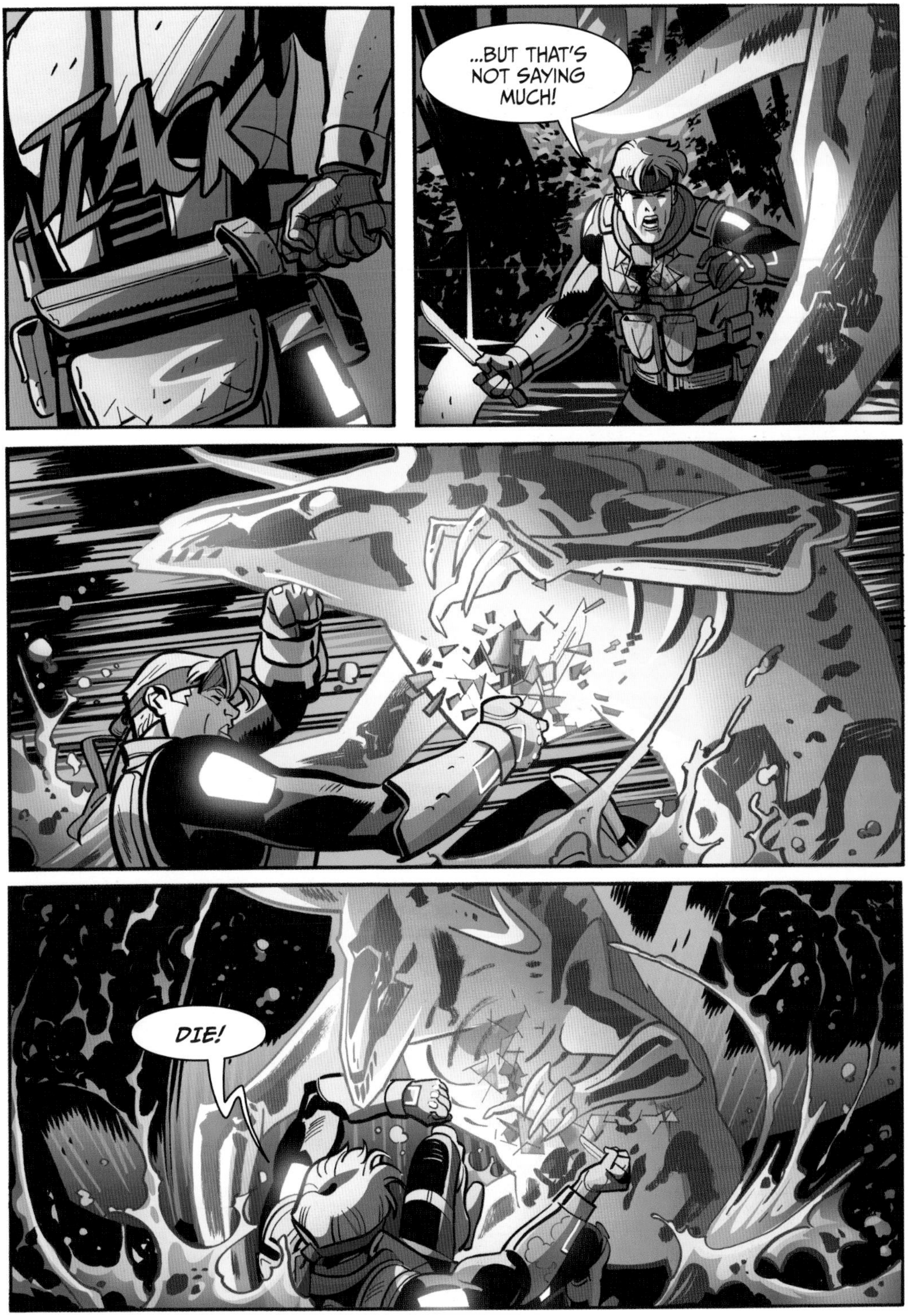
TLACK
...BUT THAT'S NOT SAYING MUCH!
DIE!

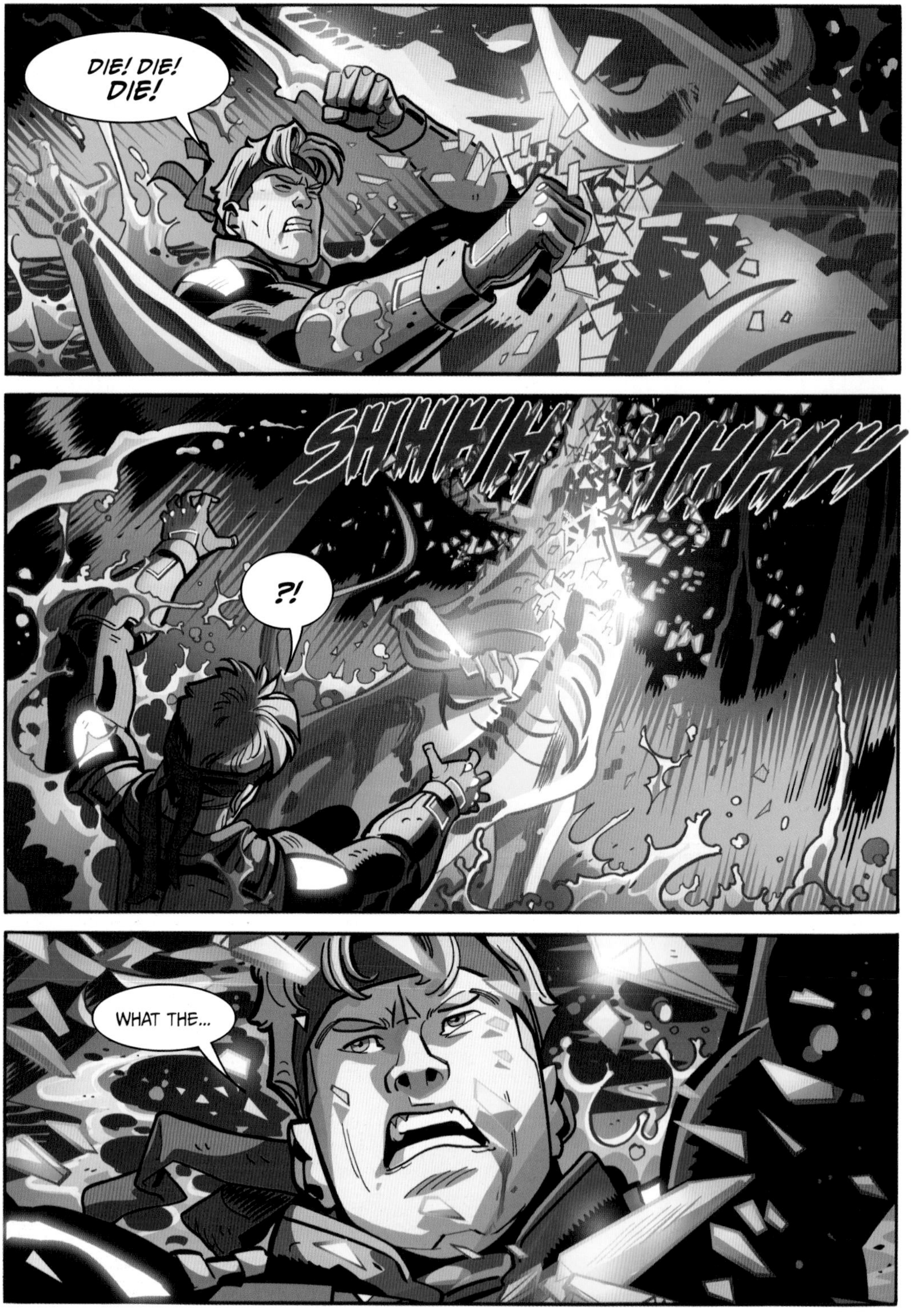
DIE! DIE! DIE!
SHHHHHHHHHH
?!
WHAT THE...

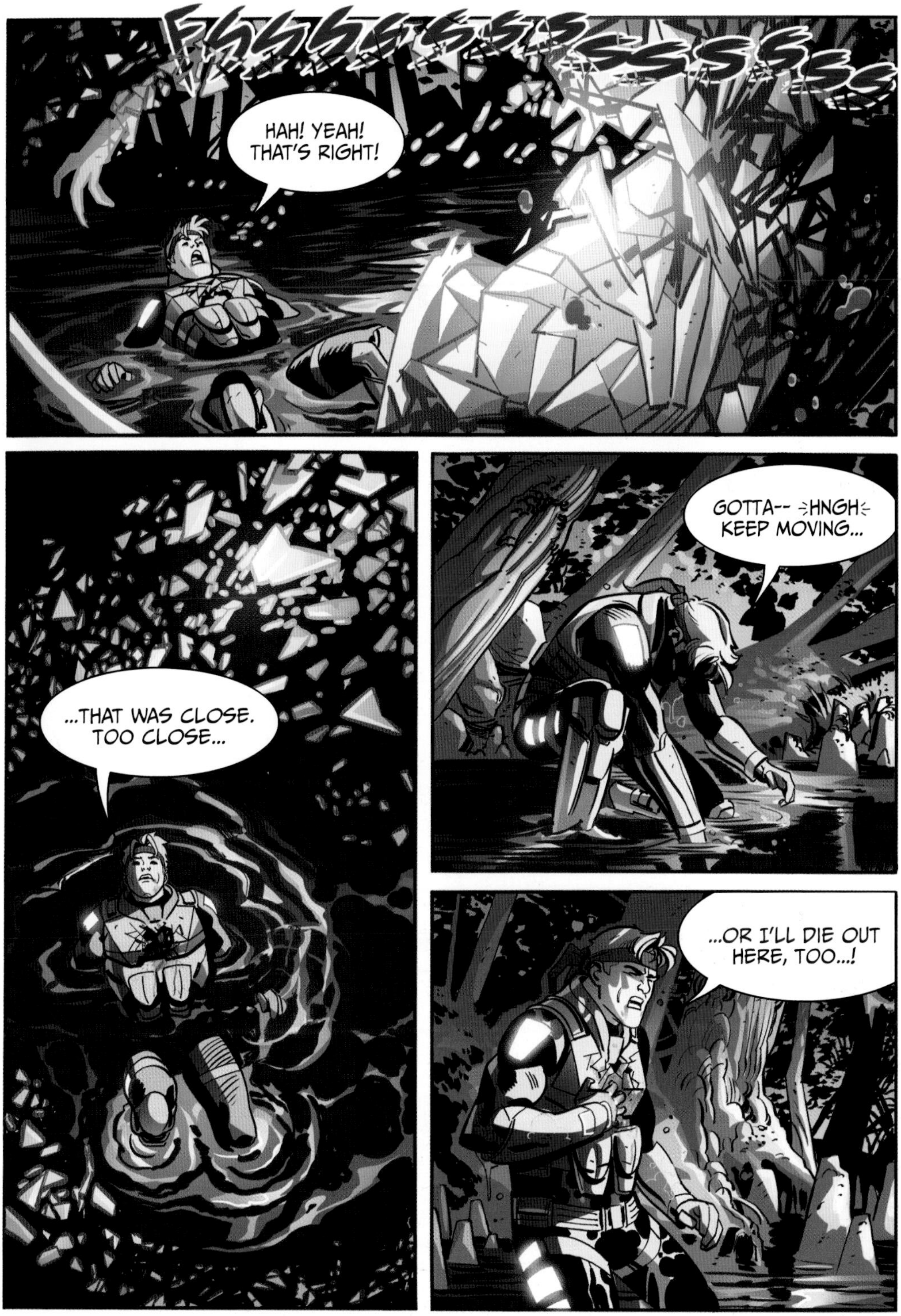
FSSSSSSSSSSSSSSS
HAH! YEAH! THAT'S RIGHT!
...THAT WAS CLOSE. TOO CLOSE...
GOTTA-- HNGH KEEP MOVING...
...OR I'LL DIE OUT HERE, TOO...!

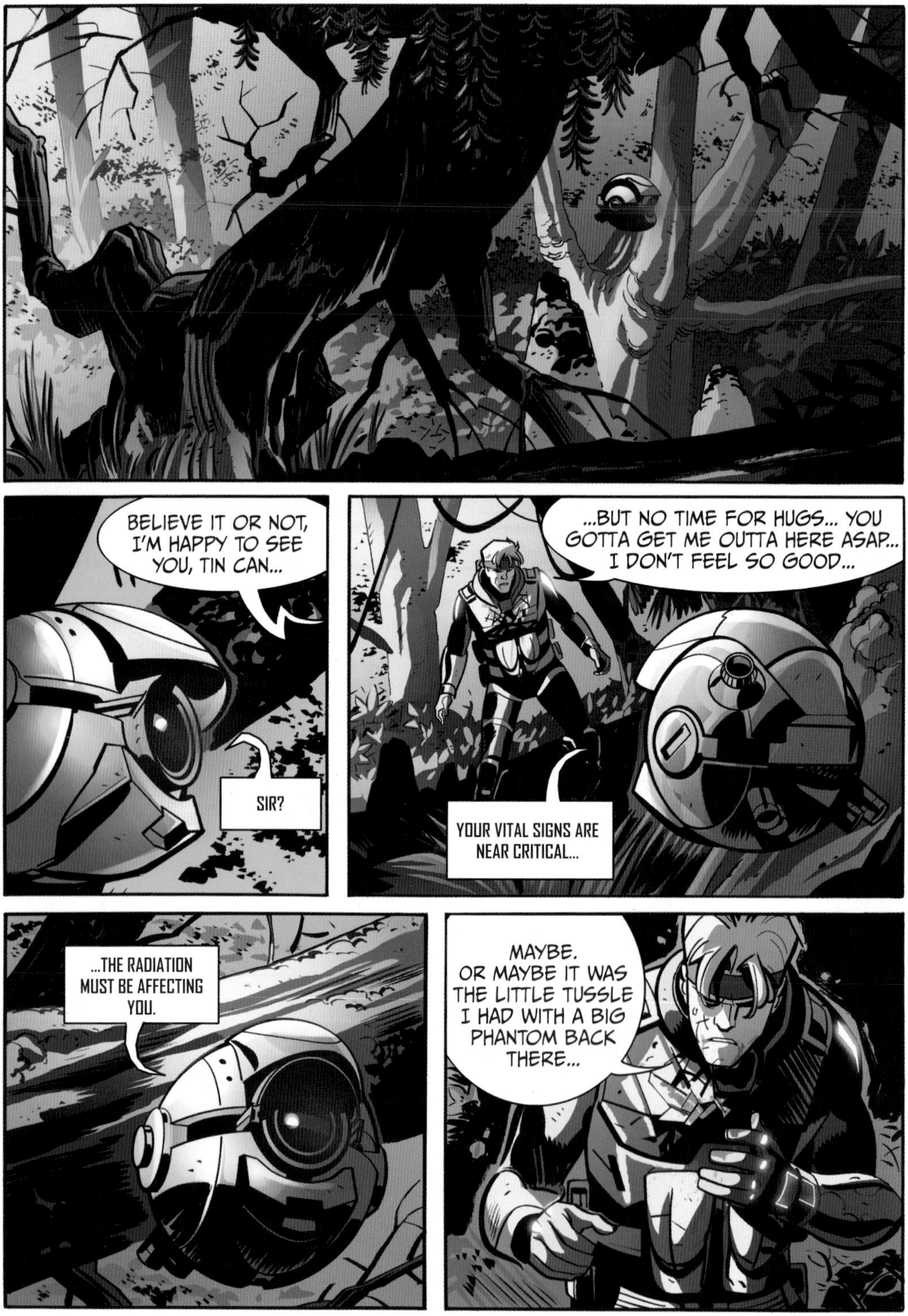
BELIEVE IT OR NOT, I'M HAPPY TO SEE YOU, TIN CAN...
SIR?
...BUT NO TIME FOR HUGS... YOU GOTTA GET ME OUTTA HERE ASAP... I DON'T FEEL SO GOOD...
YOUR VITAL SIGNS ARE NEAR CRITICAL...
...THE RADIATION MUST BE AFFECTING YOU.
MAYBE. OR MAYBE IT WAS THE LITTLE TUSSLE I HAD WITH A BIG PHANTOM BACK THERE...

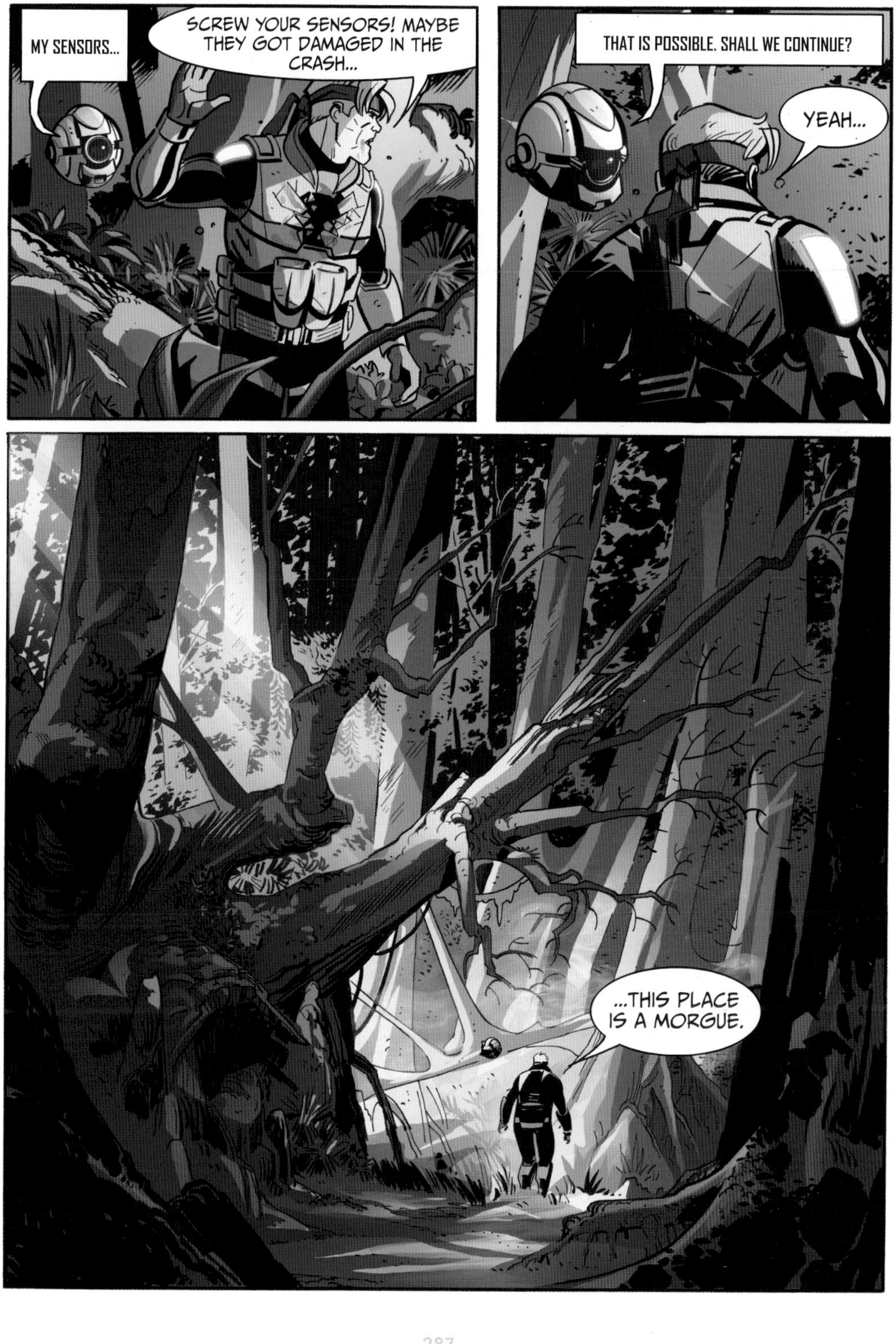
MY SENSORS...
SCREW YOUR SENSORS! MAYBE THEY GOT DAMAGED IN THE CRASH...
THAT IS POSSIBLE. SHALL WE CONTINUE?
YEAH...
...THIS PLACE IS A MORGUE.

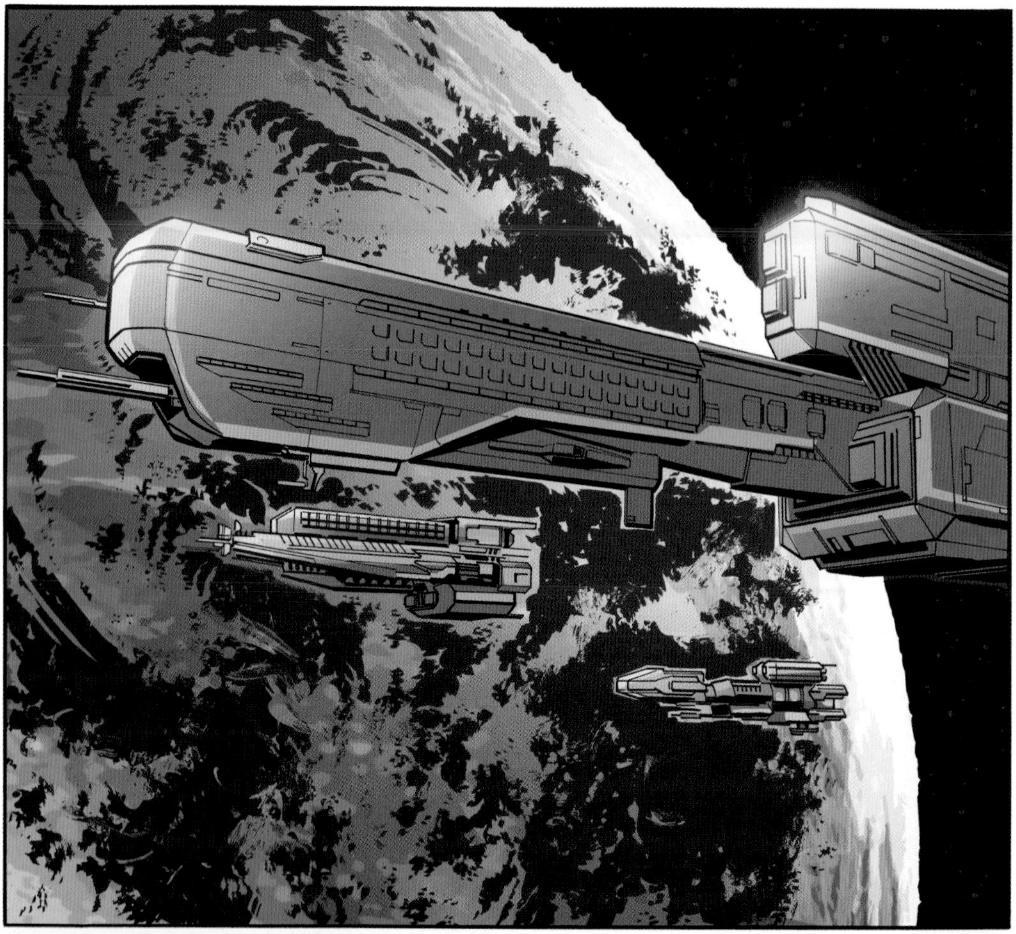

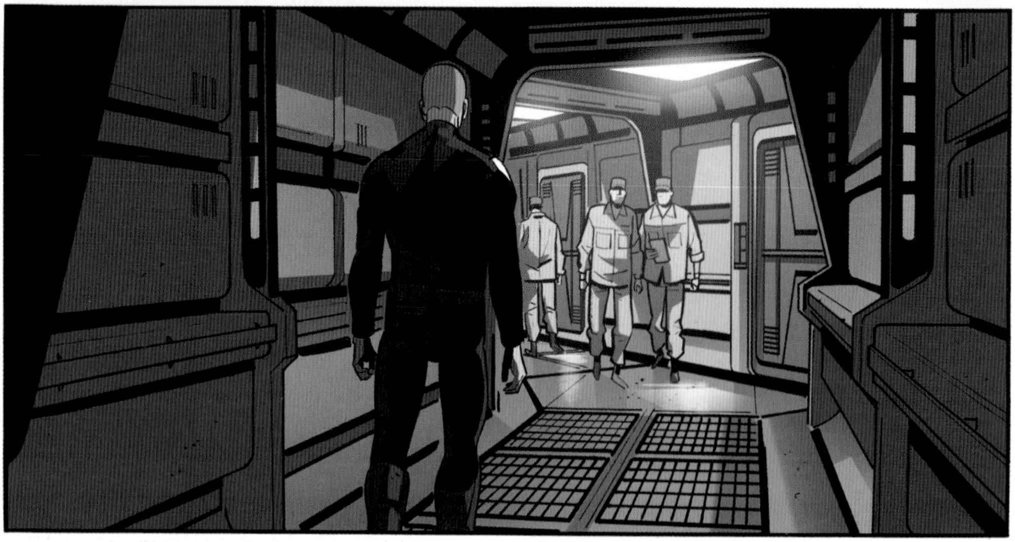

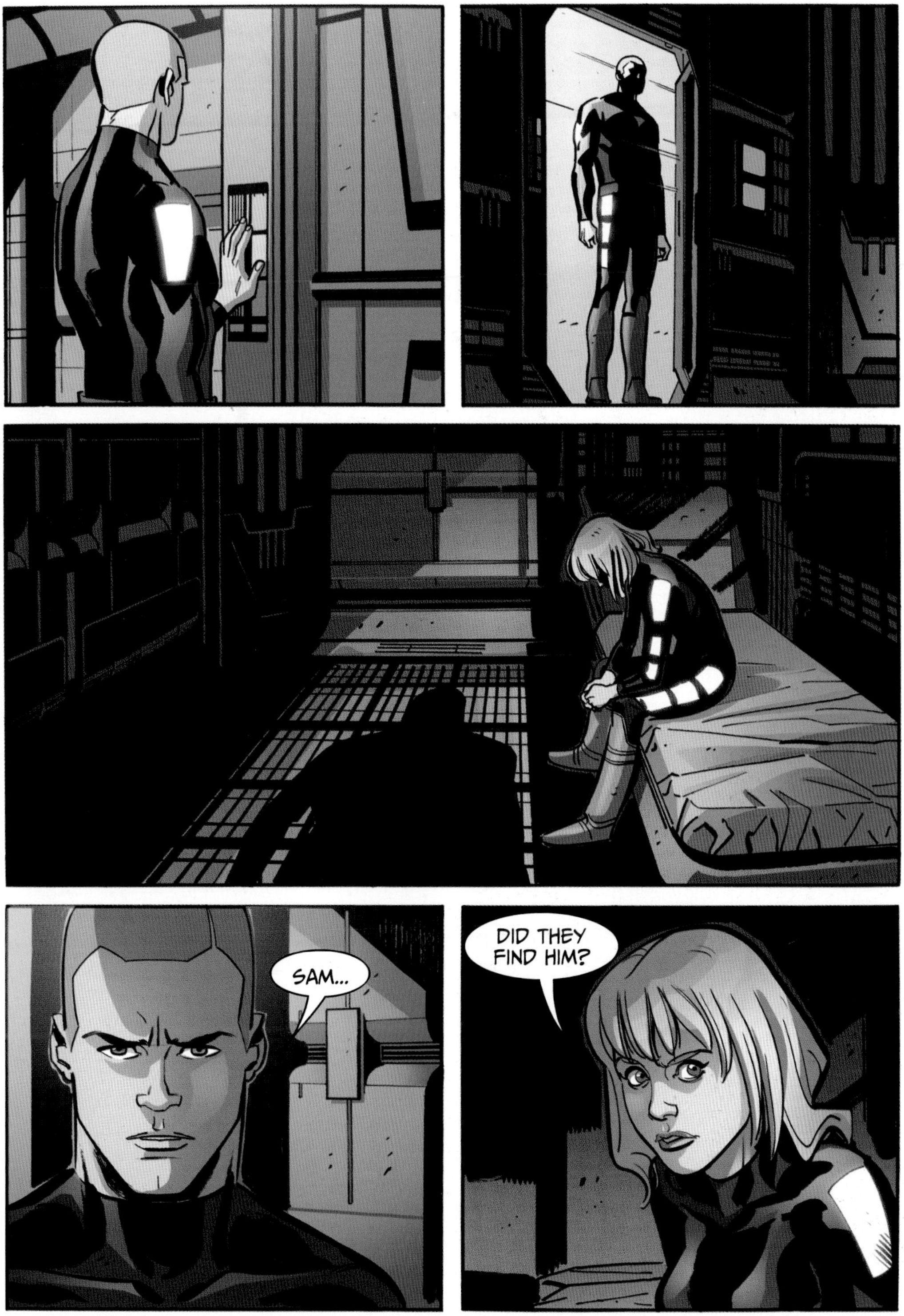
SAM...
DID THEY FIND HIM?

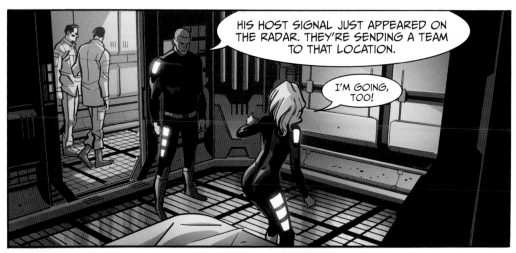

HIS HOST SIGNAL JUST APPEARED ON THE RADAR. THEY'RE SENDING A TEAM TO THAT LOCATION.

I'M GOING, TOO!

IT'S BEEN MORE THAN THREE DAYS SINCE HE CRASHED. THE CHANCES OF HIM SURVIVING ARE SMALL, SAM...

I HAVE TO GO. YOU'D DO THE SAME IF IT WERE JUNO!

YOU'RE RIGHT. I'D DO THE SAME FOR ANY OF YOU. I'M GOING, TOO.

THANK YOU!

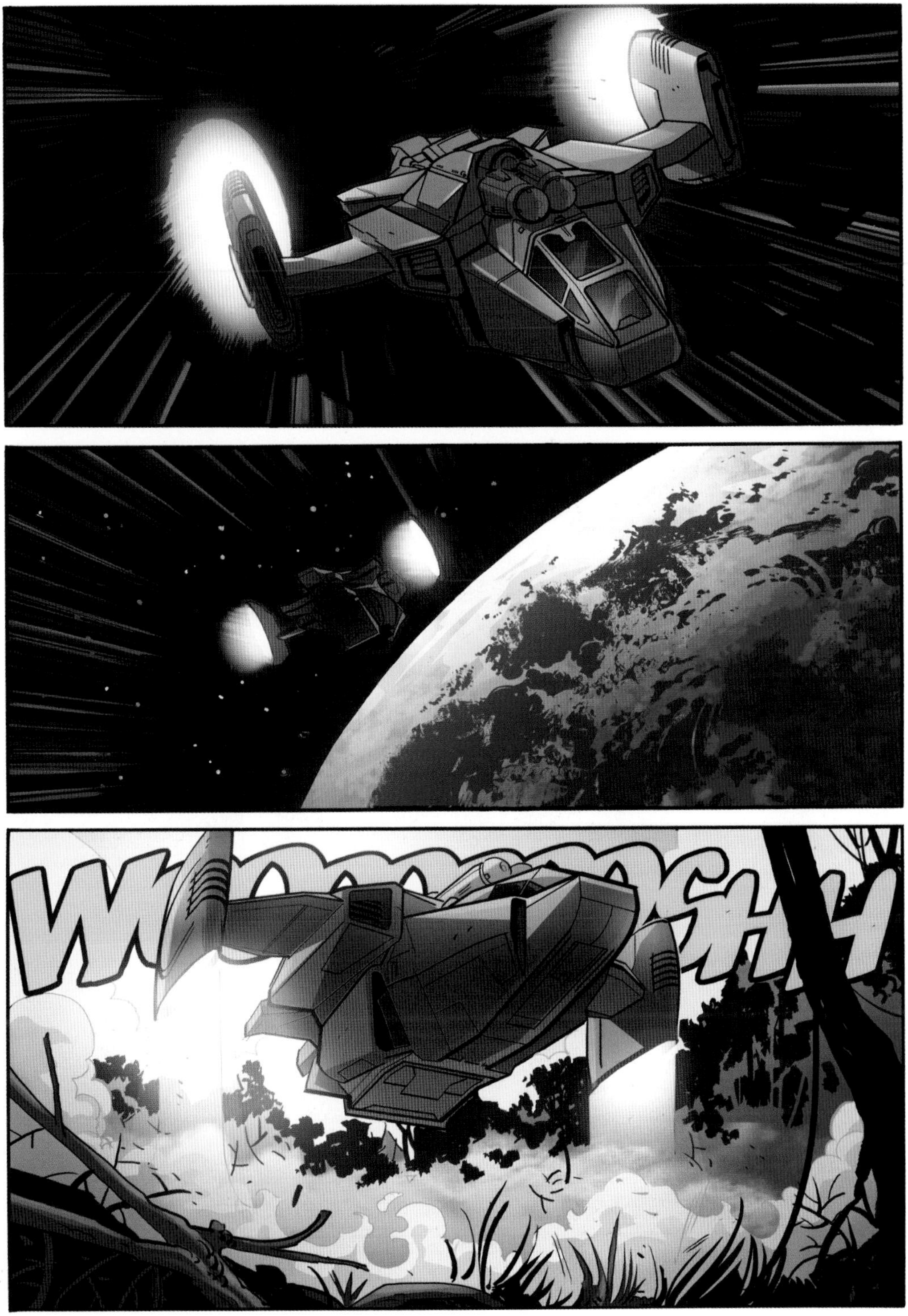

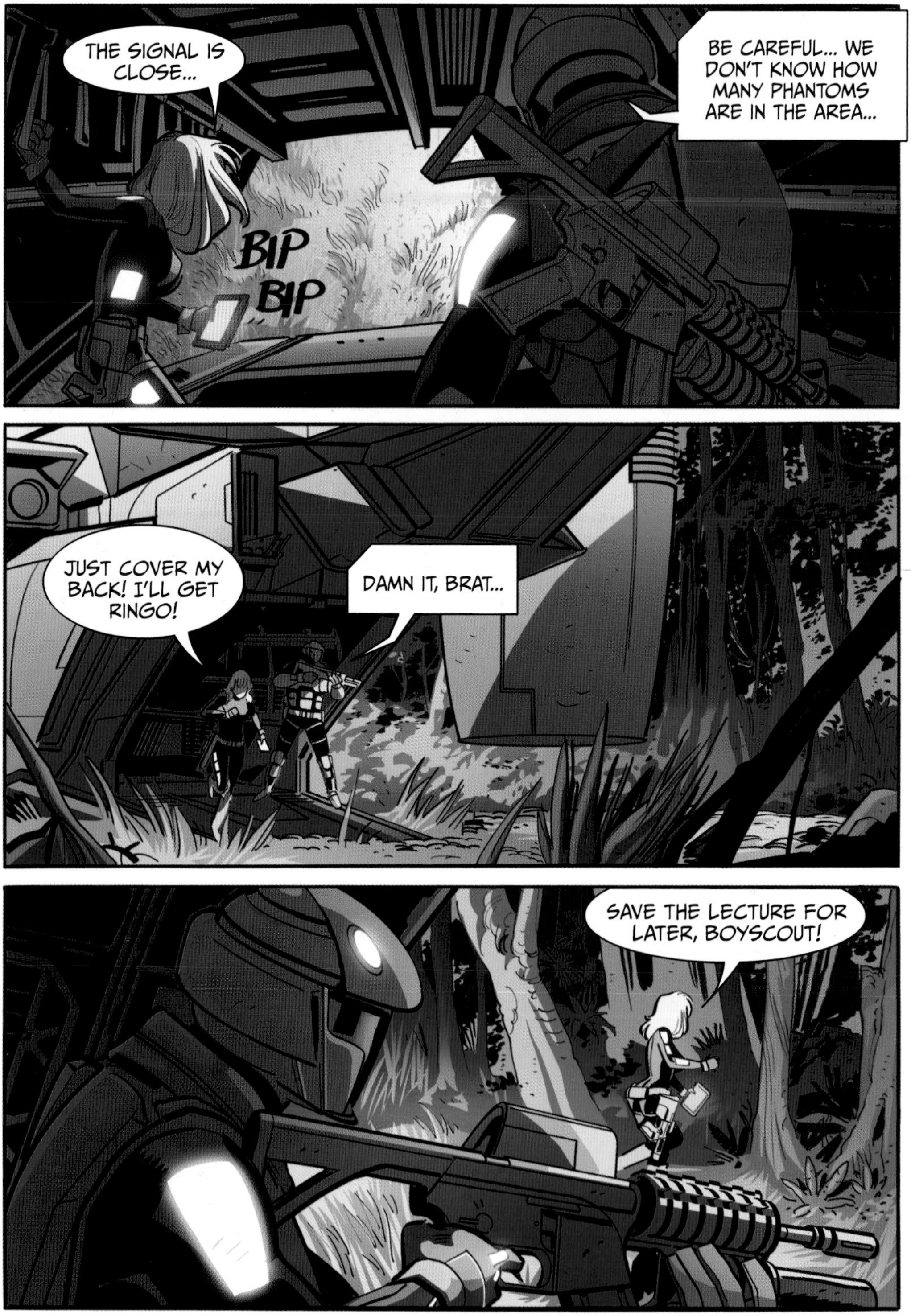
THE SIGNAL IS CLOSE...
BE CAREFUL... WE DON'T KNOW HOW MANY PHANTOMS ARE IN THE AREA...
BIP BIP
JUST COVER MY BACK! I'LL GET RINGO!
DAMN IT, BRAT...
SAVE THE LECTURE FOR LATER, BOYSCOUT!

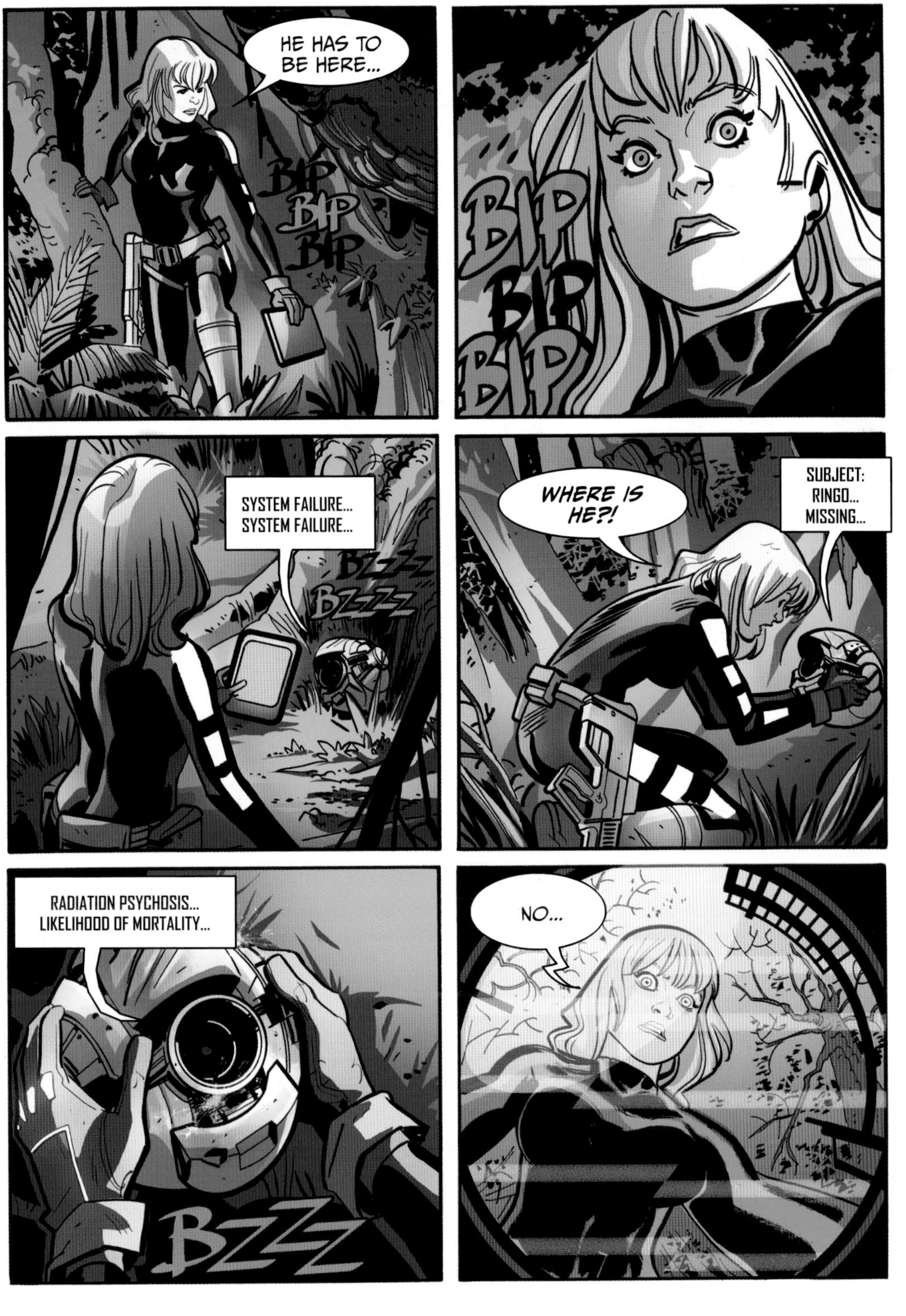
HE HAS TO BE HERE...
BIP BIP BIP
BIP BIP BIP
SYSTEM FAILURE... SYSTEM FAILURE...
BZZZZ BZZZZ
WHERE IS HE?!
SUBJECT: RINGO... MISSING...
RADIATION PSYCHOSIS... LIKELIHOOD OF MORTALITY...
BZZZ
NO...

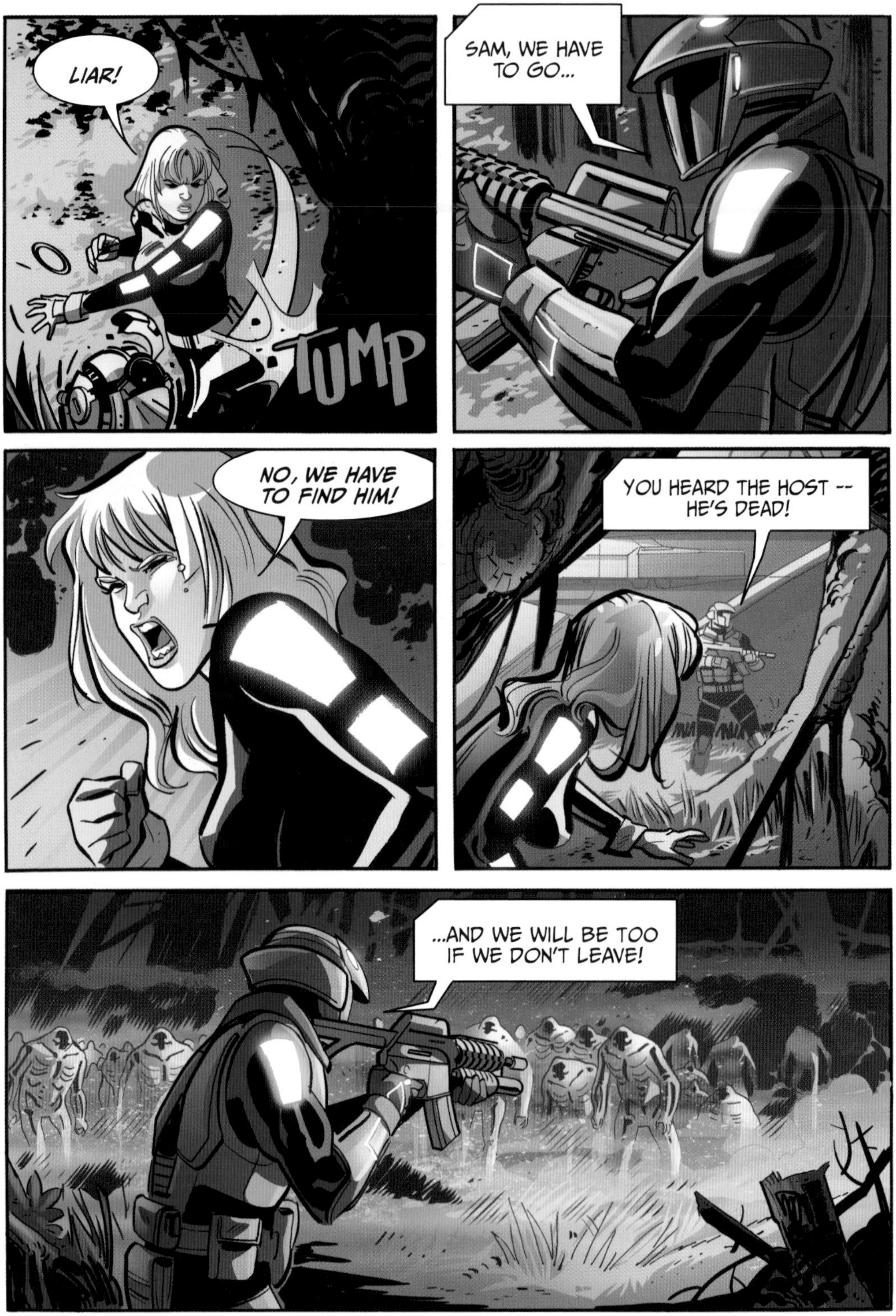
LIAR!
TUMP
SAM, WE HAVE TO GO...
NO, WE HAVE TO FIND HIM!
YOU HEARD THE HOST -- HE'S DEAD!
...AND WE WILL BE TOO IF WE DON'T LEAVE!

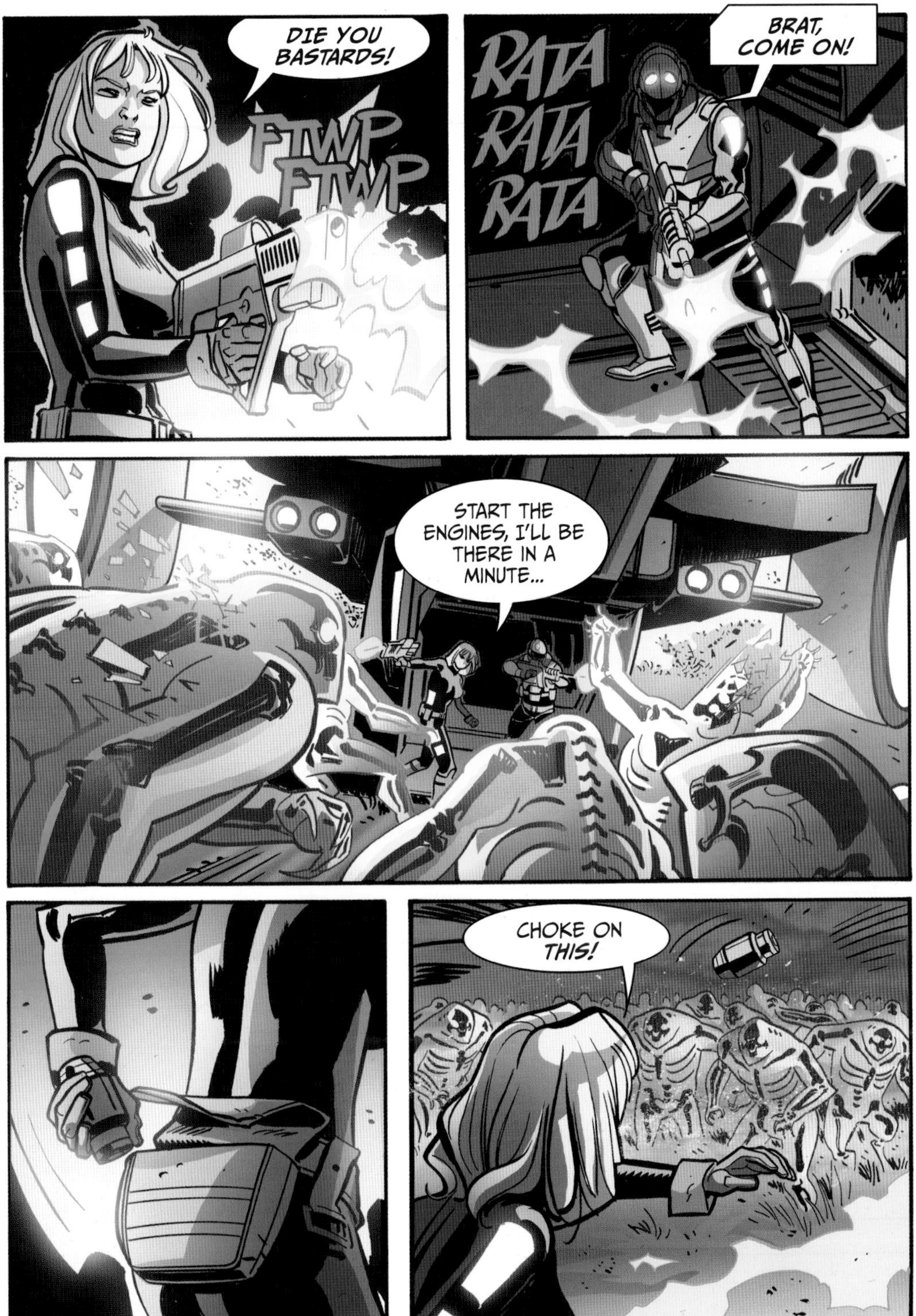
DIE YOU BASTARDS!
FTWP FTWP
RATA RATA RATA
BRAT, COME ON!
START THE ENGINES, I'LL BE THERE IN A MINUTE...
CHOKE ON THIS!

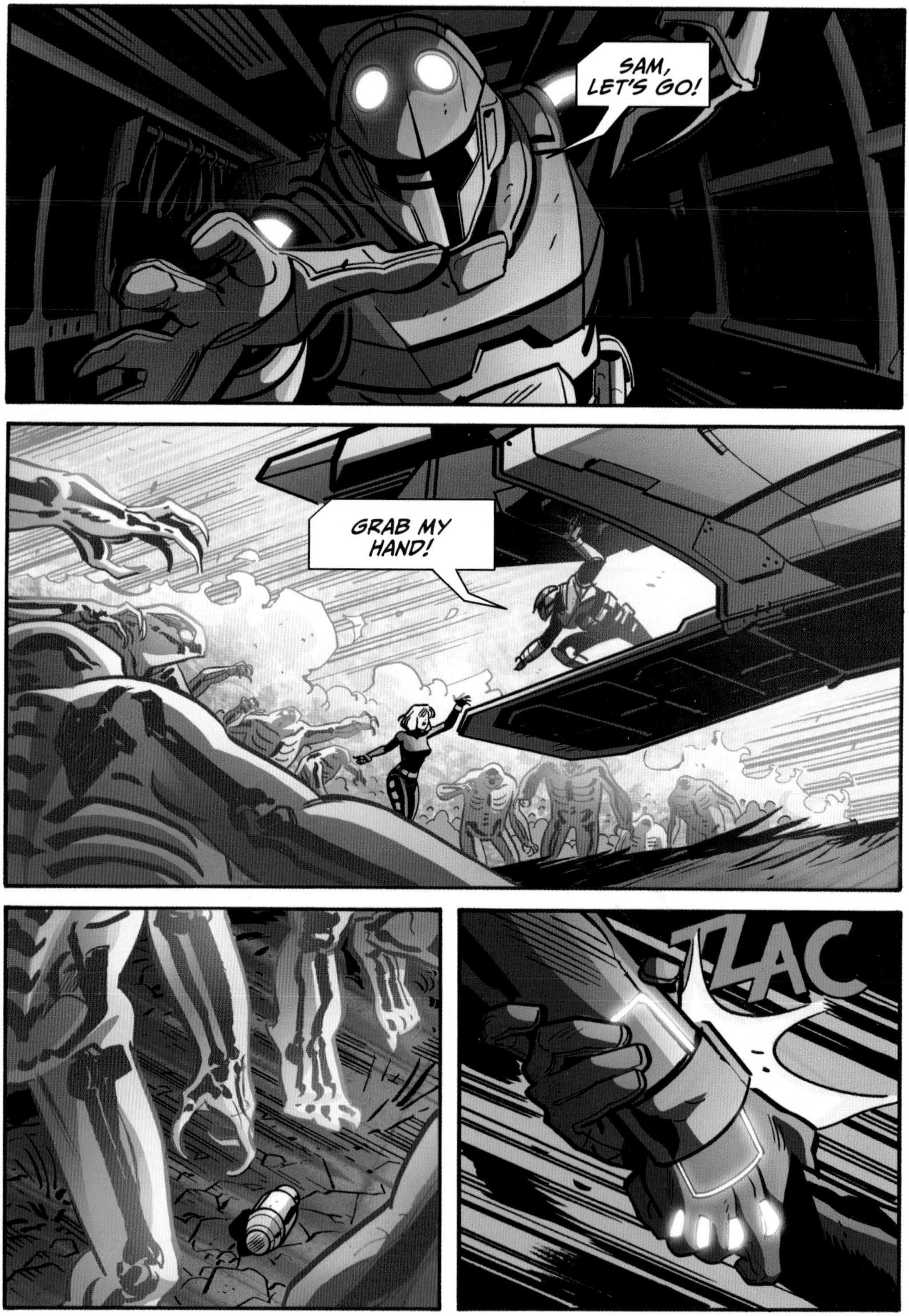
SAM, LET'S GO!
GRAB MY HAND!
TZAC

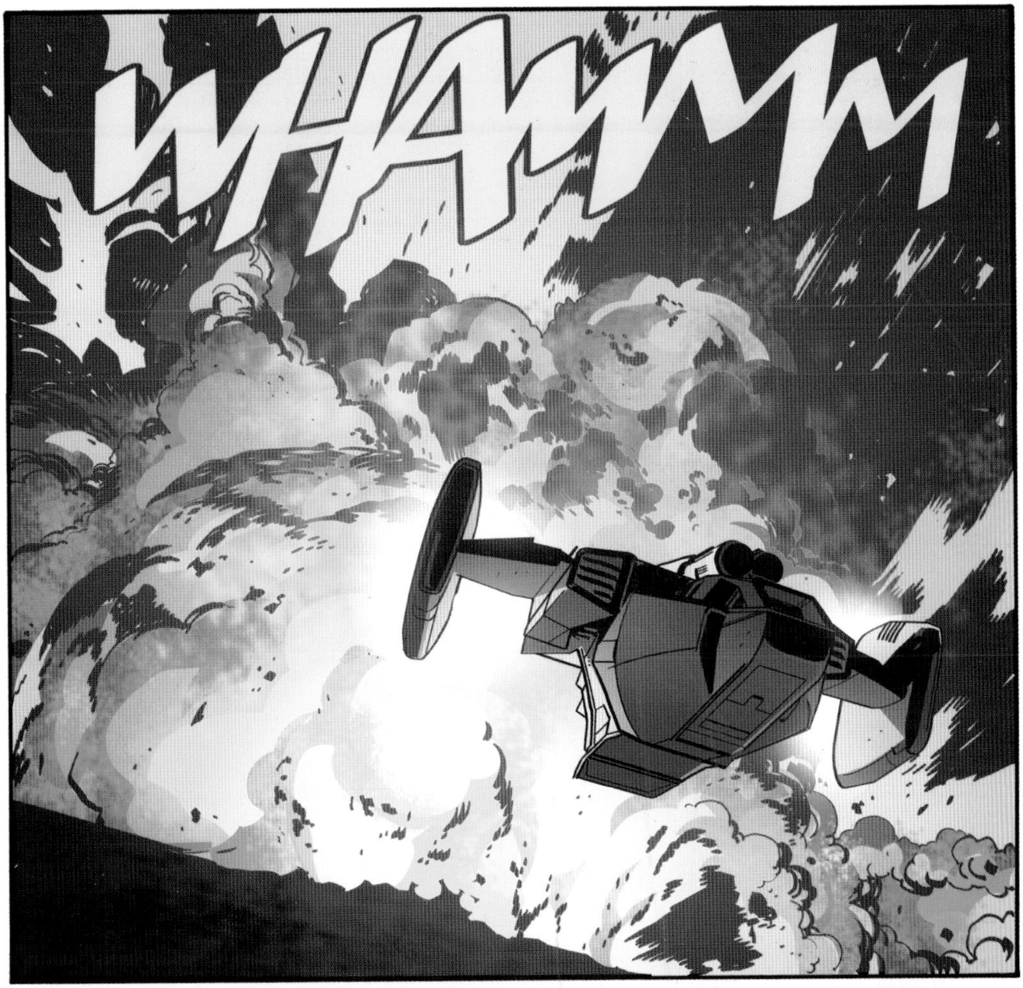
WHAMM

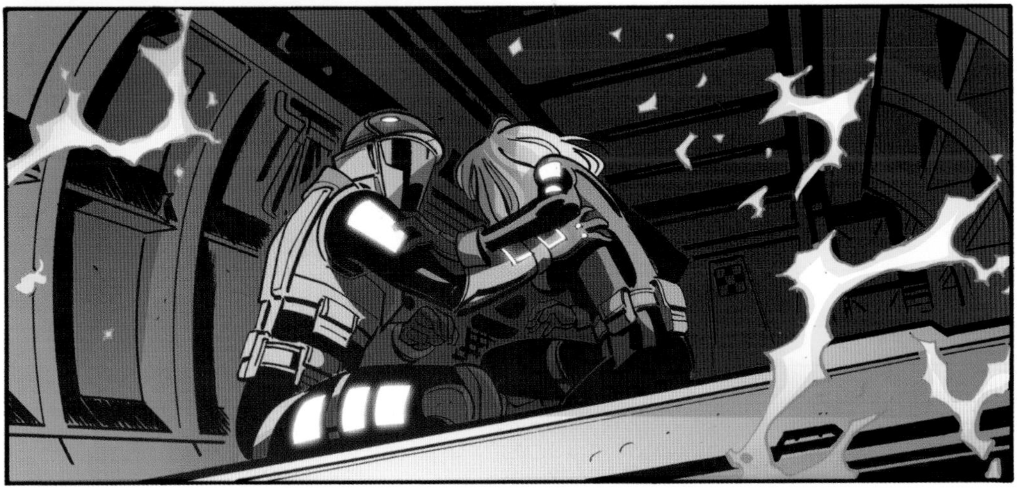

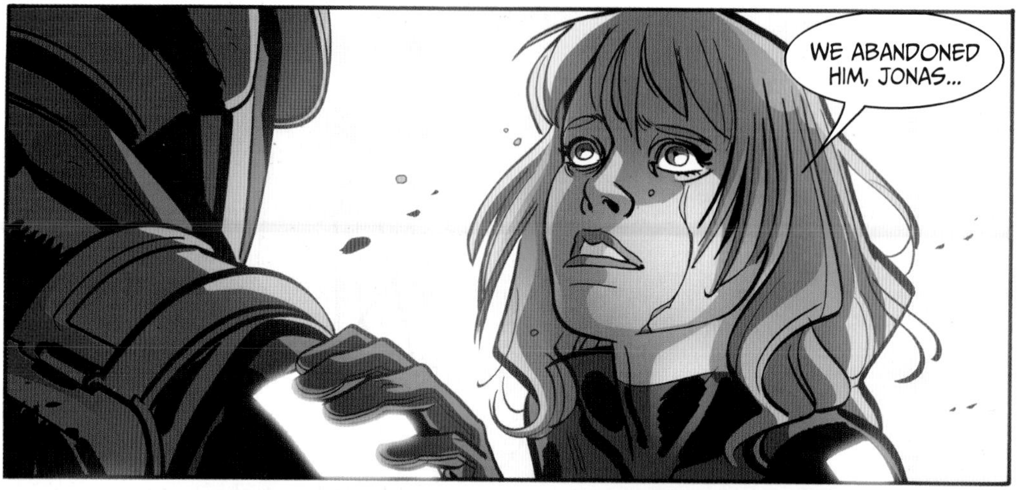
WE ABANDONED HIM, JONAS...

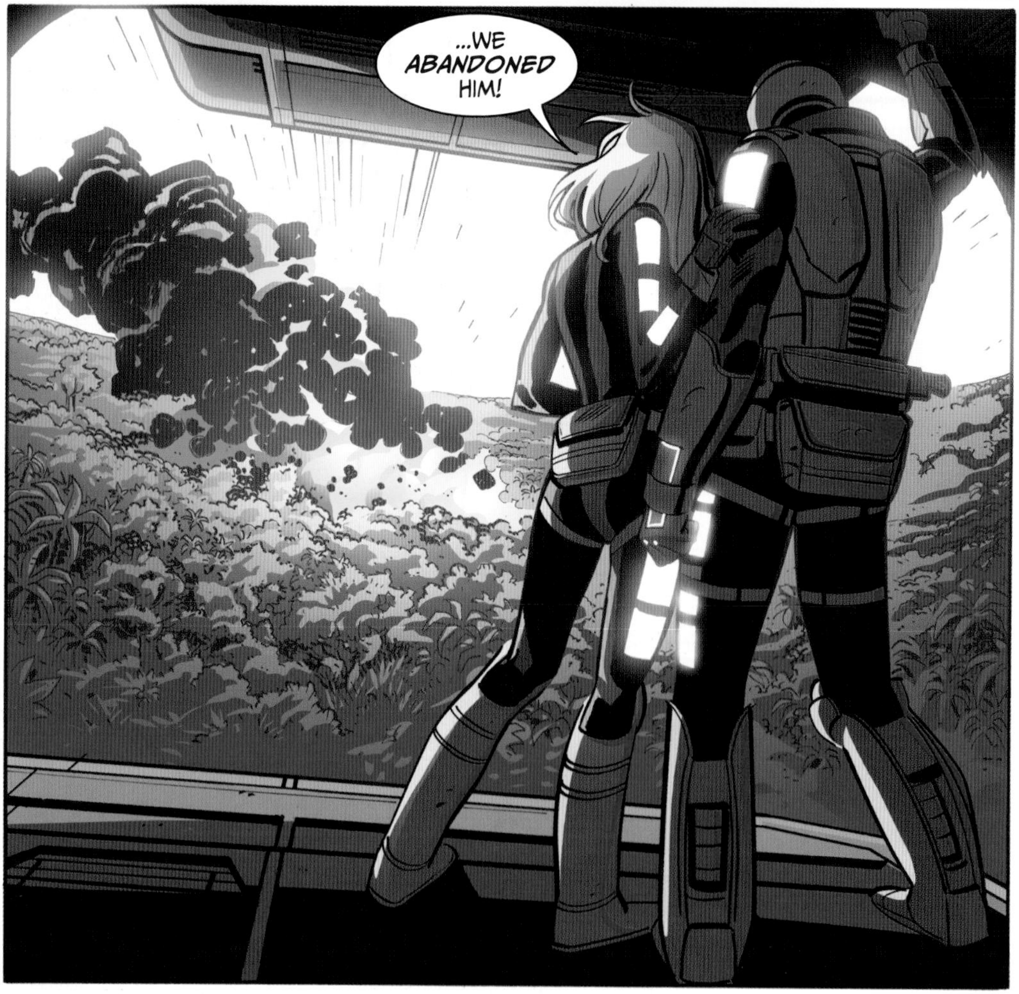
...WE *ABANDONED* HIM!

GIGI CAVENAGO **ARTIST**

When and where were you born? Where do you live now?

I was born in Milan on April 12, 1982. Now I live in Senago, Italy.

What sort of artistic education did you have?

I attended a course in comic design at the Comics School in Milan and studied graphic design at the Rizzoli Institute of Graphic Arts.

Tell us about your previous works, before *Orphans*.

Jonathan Steele, by Memola and Marzia, published by Star Comics, the miniseries *Dr. Voodoo* with Giovanni Gualdoni for Free Books and, last but not least, *Cassidy*, a miniseries by Pasquale Ruju for Sergio Bonelli Editore.

When did you start working on *Orphans*, and when did you finish drawing this chapter?

It was about January 2010 when I received my very first treatment. My first studies and drawings came a year later. In that lapse of time, I worked on my second and last issue of *Cassidy* and I contributed a little to the *Orphans Property Bible*.

What tools did you use?

I alternated between digital and traditional drawing. Basically, I always work with Winsor & Newton paintbrushes and Staedler pigment liners, but sometimes I like to use different types of calligraphic brush felt-tip pens, which help give an incisive and modulated line to my design. When I use Photoshop, I follow the same principles as inking by hand, and I choose brushes that can provide the same result (if not better) as the real ones I have on my working table.

What was the most difficult scene and which one did you have to redraw more times?

The scene I had to redraw more times is the fight between Ringo and the Phantom Bull. In three or four pages, I had been a bit too loose.

If you could go back in time, what would you change about this chapter?

If I could redraw the entire chapter now, I'd change it almost completely, especially the first thirty pages. There are many little details, on some faces in particular, but you learn from your mistakes. In the following issues I took care of my shortcomings.

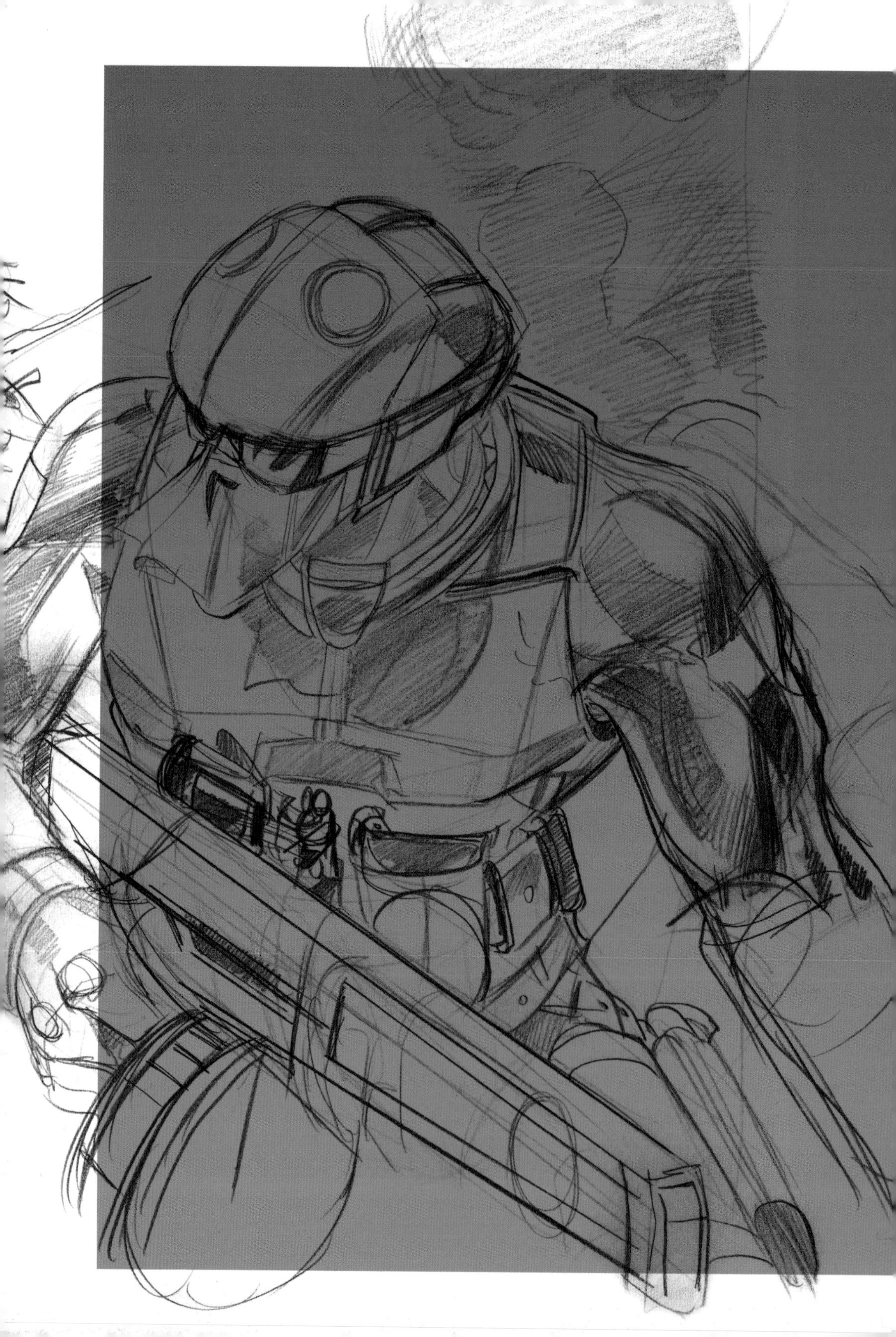

ORPHANS

EXTRAS

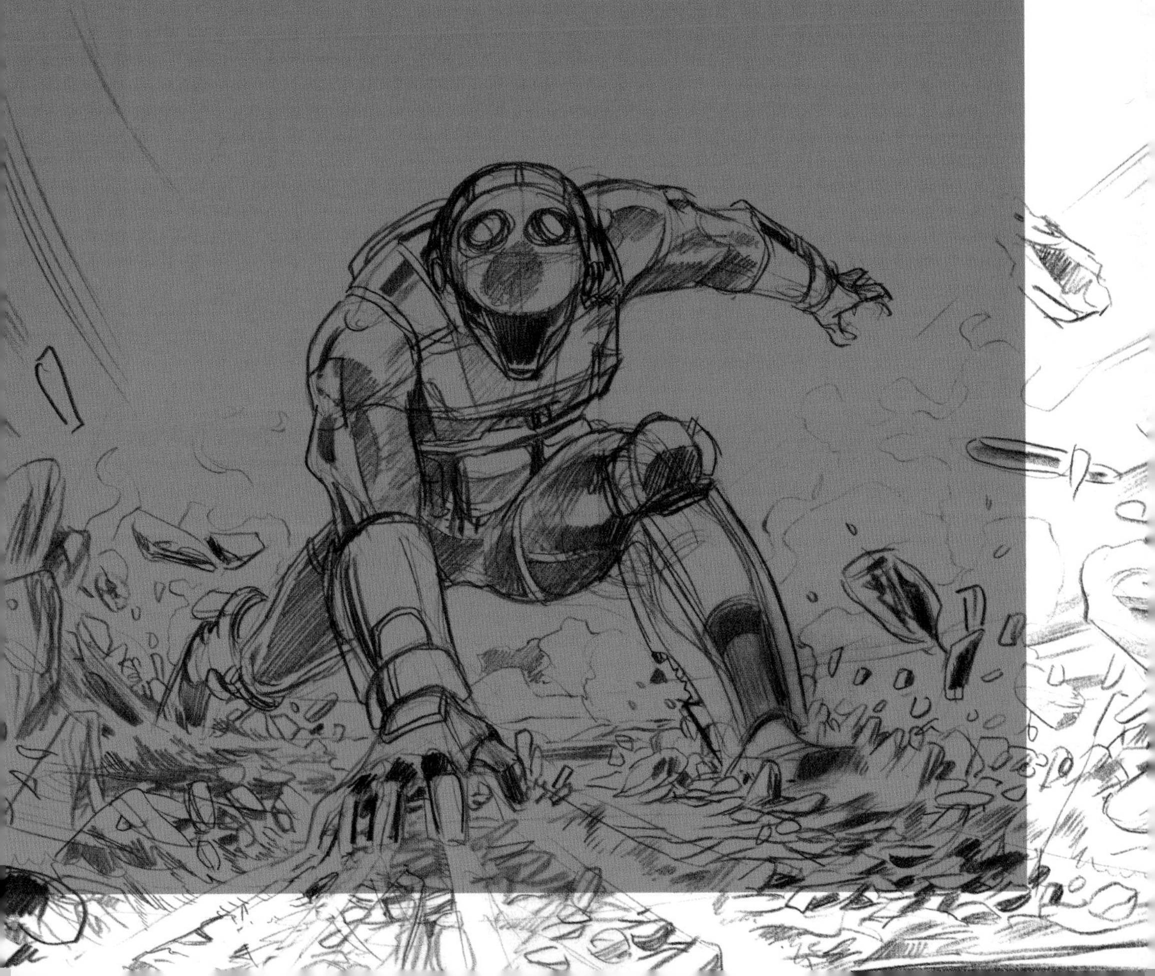

SIGNING A CONTRACT FOR A SERIES IMPOSSIBLE TO REALIZE MEANS YOU HAVE TO MAKE IT POSSIBLE, NO MATTER HOW HARD IT'S GOING TO BE.

– Roberto Recchioni

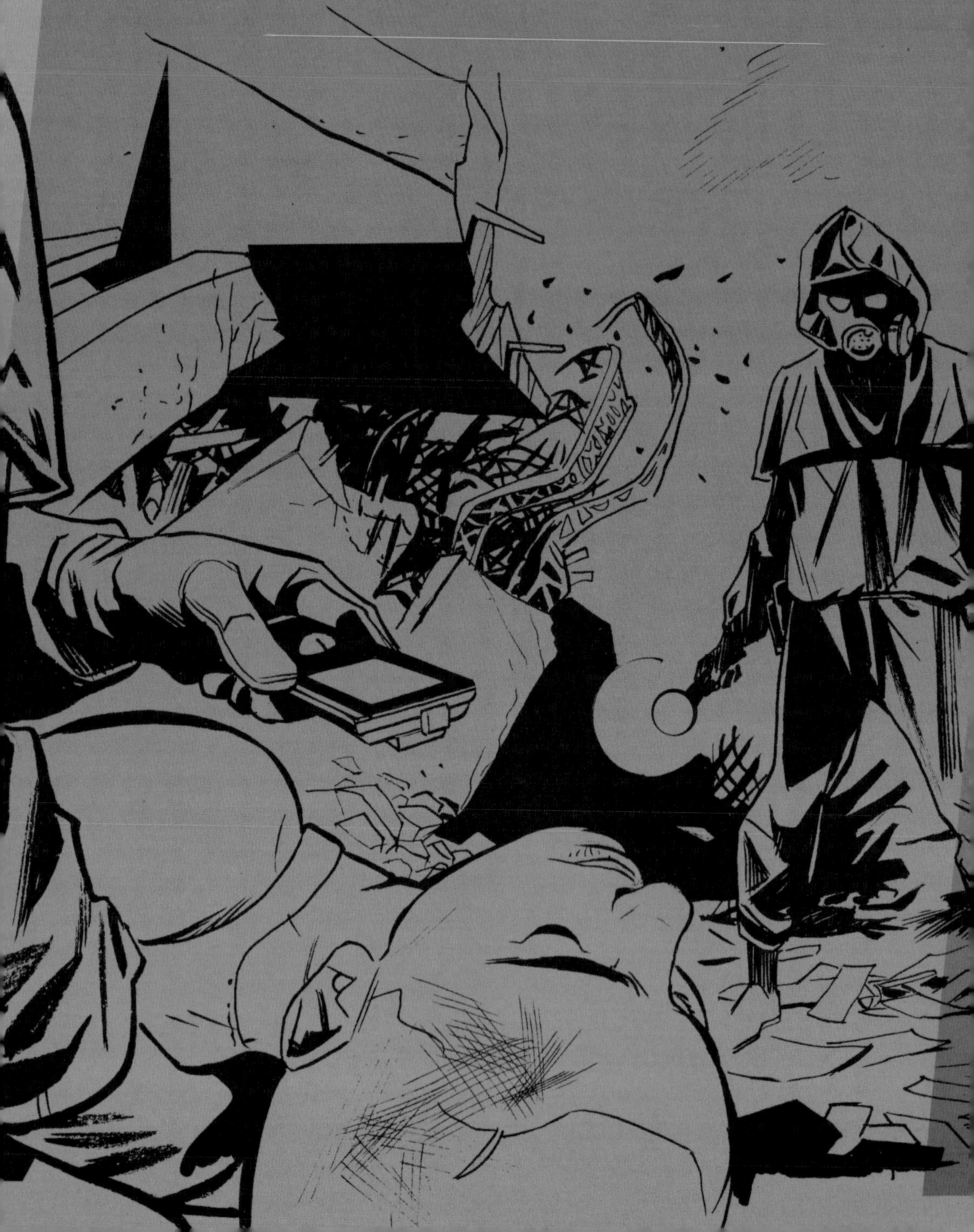

BORN ORPHANS

When did you first think about *Orphans*? How long have you been actively working on it?

Roberto Recchioni: *Four years ago. No, five. They say time flies when you have fun; truth is, it passes much faster when you rush headlong into something. In the last five years,* Orphans *has been a commitment that ran parallel to our private lives and other work at first, but then took over entirely.*

Emiliano Mammucari: *We started in the Summer of 2009. The idea to create a series together was sort of a game for us, and our way of working always kept things kind of playful… even when the project took an amount of work no series has demanded before.*

Did you ever think that the project wouldn't come true, and why? And at what point did you feel that nothing could stop this idea and its creation?

RR: *Yes and no. Yes, because it's normal for such complex, difficult, and lengthy projects to end up overwhelming you, bringing up lots of fears and doubts. But also no, because failure wasn't an option. Signing a contract for a series impossible to realize means you have to make it possible, no matter how hard it's going to be.*

EM: *We had many problems, because creating an entire color series forced us to reinvent a production model. But I had no doubt that, one*

PREVIOUS THREE PAGES: STUDIES BY EMILIANO MAMMUCARI

way or another, we would succeed in bringing *Orphans* to publication. Roberto and I have in common an extremely concrete approach to creativity: it's easy to pull something out of thin air, to dream. To create, to look at your idea coming true... it gives you an almost physical pleasure.

From a graphic point of view, our main difficulty was to find a stylistic identity for the series. We didn't want a "classic" Bonelli series, but we didn't want a series that resembled American comic books either. So we worked on the language, disassembling and reassembling every aspect, from direction to sound effects. Then came the color. When the publisher proposed to make it a full-color series, we said "yes" on the condition that we would work on it. The problem was that we hadn't realized that in Italy, we didn't have an "idea of color" that was fit for our series yet.

A LOT HAS BEEN SAID ABOUT THE EVIDENT NARRATIVE AND VISUAL INFLUENCES, WHICH YOU HAVE SOMETIMES CONFIRMED. ARE THERE ANY OTHER INFLUENCES THAT HAVE NOT BEEN CAUGHT SO CLEARLY BUT THAT YOU CONSIDER IMPORTANT FOR THE REAL IDENTITY OF THE WORK?

RR: Let me stop you there. If there was such an important influence as to define the identity of this work, then that means that I failed. The meaning of a piece of work can't be defined by something external to the work itself, otherwise we'd just have a derivative product without any dignity of its own. In *Orphans*, we notice its many influences, both from a narrative and a visual point of view, but they're just that: fascinations, references, archetypes, elements extrapolated from their context and put into a different one, sabotaged, modeled in new and, hopefully, significant ways. So, to answer your question, I'd say no. I hope that what we've captured is what belongs to the comic and emerges from it organically.

EM: Our references and fascinations are all very clear – I mean... they're everything we love! Curiously, the main characters ended up looking like people that somehow lived the *Orphans* adventure with us, both physically and in temper. Sometimes, I feel I'm a boy scout

CURIOUSLY, THE MAIN CHARACTERS ENDED UP LOOKING LIKE PEOPLE THAT SOMEHOW LIVED THE *ORPHANS* ADVENTURE WITH US, BOTH PHYSICALLY AND IN TEMPER. IT'S A WAY LIKE ANY OTHER OF GIVING THE CHARACTERS A BREATH OF LIFE.

– EMILIANO MAMMUCARI

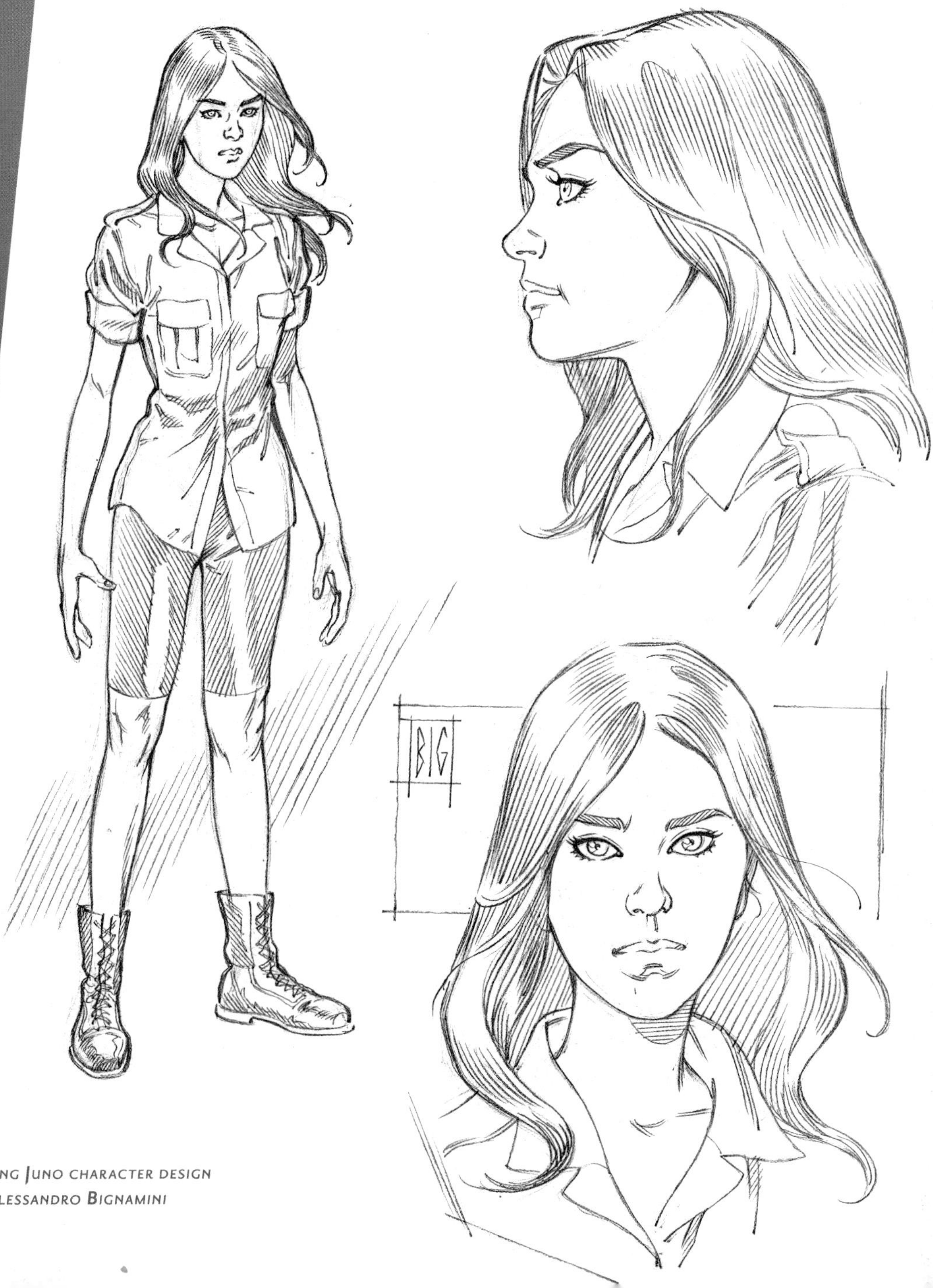

YOUNG JUNO CHARACTER DESIGN BY ALESSANDRO BIGNAMINI

WE CHOSE AN EXTREMELY SIMPLE DESIGN, WHICH GAVE EVERYTHING A MINIMAL AND ELEGANT LOOK.

– ROBERTO RECCHIONI

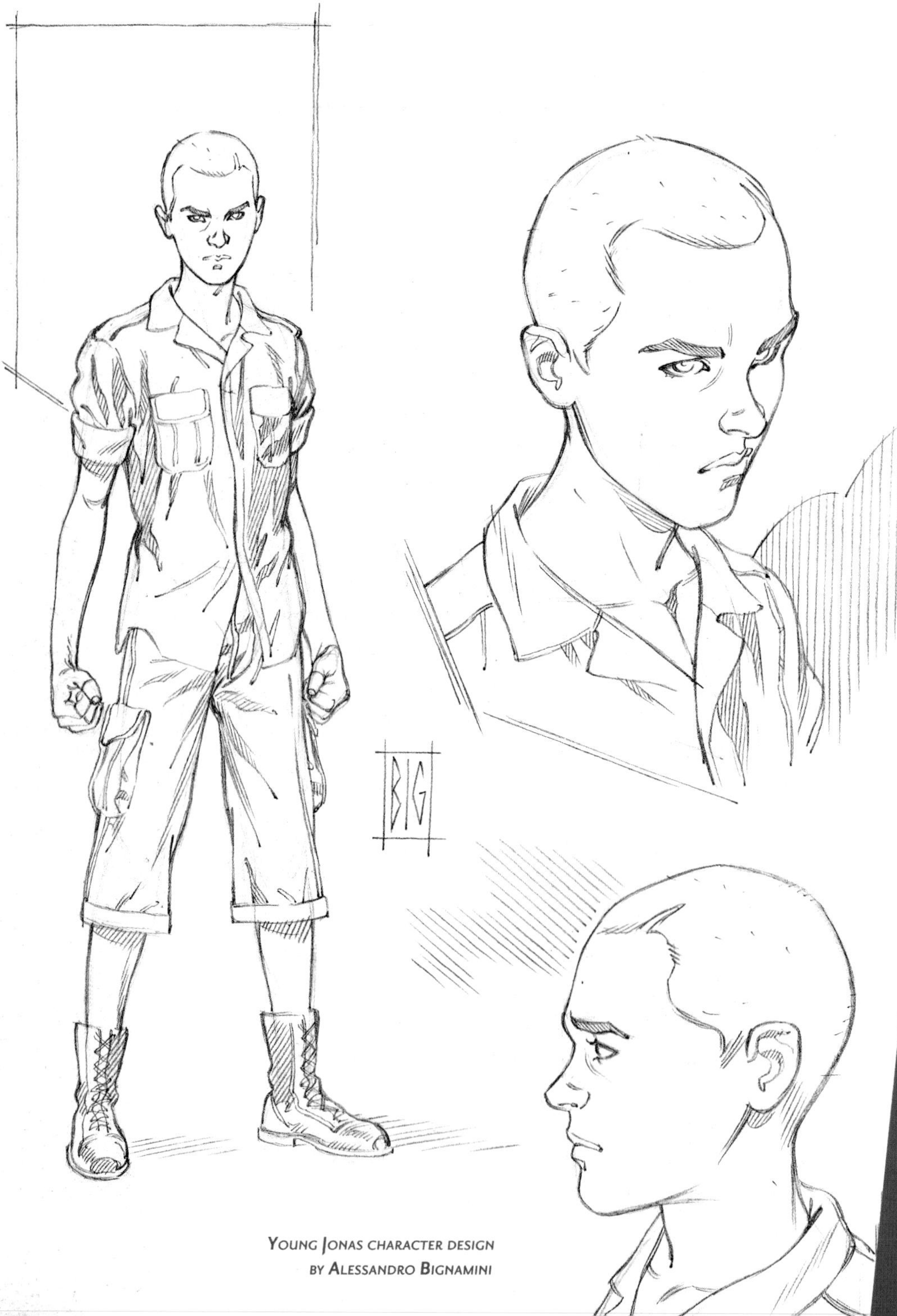
BIG

YOUNG JONAS CHARACTER DESIGN
BY ALESSANDRO BIGNAMINI

like Jonas, and Roberto is noisy and impetulant like Ringo. It's a way like any other of giving the characters a breath of life.

HOW MANY OF YOUR STYLISTIC AND VISUAL CHOICES CAME OUT OF YOUR NARRATIVE DESIRE AND HOW MANY, IN THE END, WERE THE RESULT OF COMPROMISES WITH THE PUBLISHER'S OBSERVATIONS AND THE NEED TO REPEAT, MONTH AFTER MONTH (USING DIFFERENT ARTISTS), PREARRANGED SETS AND STRUCTURES?

RR: The publisher made no command whatsoever, but we had to take production needs into account. You can create the most complex and original design, but then you not only have to draw it for almost 1,200 pages, but also have different people draw it, always keeping it consistent. And then you have to have it colored consistently. So, initially we opted for extremely essential designs, which gave everything a minimal and elegant look. The visual aspect influenced the writing as well. Everything was so clean and minimal that I went back to check what I had written and polished it as much as I could.

EM: Most of the boundaries we set and the choices we made were dictated by the will to create a comic book that could reach new readers. Making ourselves understood was the real challenge. Especially with a story as complex and unusual as *Orphans*. In a word, we tried to make a punk comic, wrapped in reassuring classical elements.

CAN YOU TELL US ABOUT THE CREATIVE PROCESS OF THE SERIES' PLOT, CHARACTERS, SETTINGS, AND VISUAL STYLES (WEAPONS, ARMOR, VEHICLES)? IS THERE SOMETHING YOU INITIALLY CARED FOR THAT DIDN'T SURVIVE THE EVOLUTION OF THE STORY?

RR: The relationship between Emiliano and myself was based on a constant exchange: the visual aspect and the writing influenced each other. There isn't any visual element in *Orphans* that we haven't thoroughly discussed, trying to understand whether it was what we needed and if it fit everything else. We scrapped many beautiful ideas, even powerful ones, that simply weren't useful for the story and would have taken too much room (and pages) to describe. Personally, I'm *still bitter about leaving behind the idea of leg pads resembling those of hockey goaltenders. (It's an inside joke between Emiliano and me: at a certain point I set my heart on this absurd plan and forced Emiliano to humor me until I got over it.)*

EM: *Most of our ideas were born by miming them; that is to say we jumped on Roberto's couch and pretended to shoot. Or we just watched and drew stuff together. Our biggest problem was the helmets: any shape we drew, any way we altered them, there was always someone who had already done it. After all, they're just a round object with a visor. I've lost count of all the helmets we designed...*

WHEN YOU HEARD ABOUT THE AUDIENCE'S FIRST REACTIONS, WAS THERE ANYTHING YOU WOULD'VE CHANGED? ANY MISUNDERSTANDING WITH YOUR READERS THAT MADE YOU ESPECIALLY AMUSED OR WORRIED?

RR: *From a narrative point of view, the first issues of the series took many risks. More specifically, the series looks completely "masked," as it pretends to be some sort of shoot-'em-up with monolithic characters quoting bad lines from 1980s action films. But we wanted to create a contrast with what would follow (let's say from the third chapter on) and convey a strong sense of discovery and growth. But, as I said, it was a risk. Obviously, some readers decided that Orphans was exactly as it seemed from issue #1 and it wasn't worth following. Luckily, they were a minority, and those who stuck with us found out there was much more behind it.*

EM: *We put so much thought into the pages that no, I wouldn't change anything at all. About the criticism, with the advent of social networks, you have to get used to people talking on gut instincts. A reproach that I found funny was about chapter two: it came from an animal rights supporter scolding us for having a bunny killed – and I quote – "... without showing the children eat it." It's curious to see what people feel uncomfortable about, in a comic series where children are trained to kill.*

Pose studies
by Gigi Cavenago

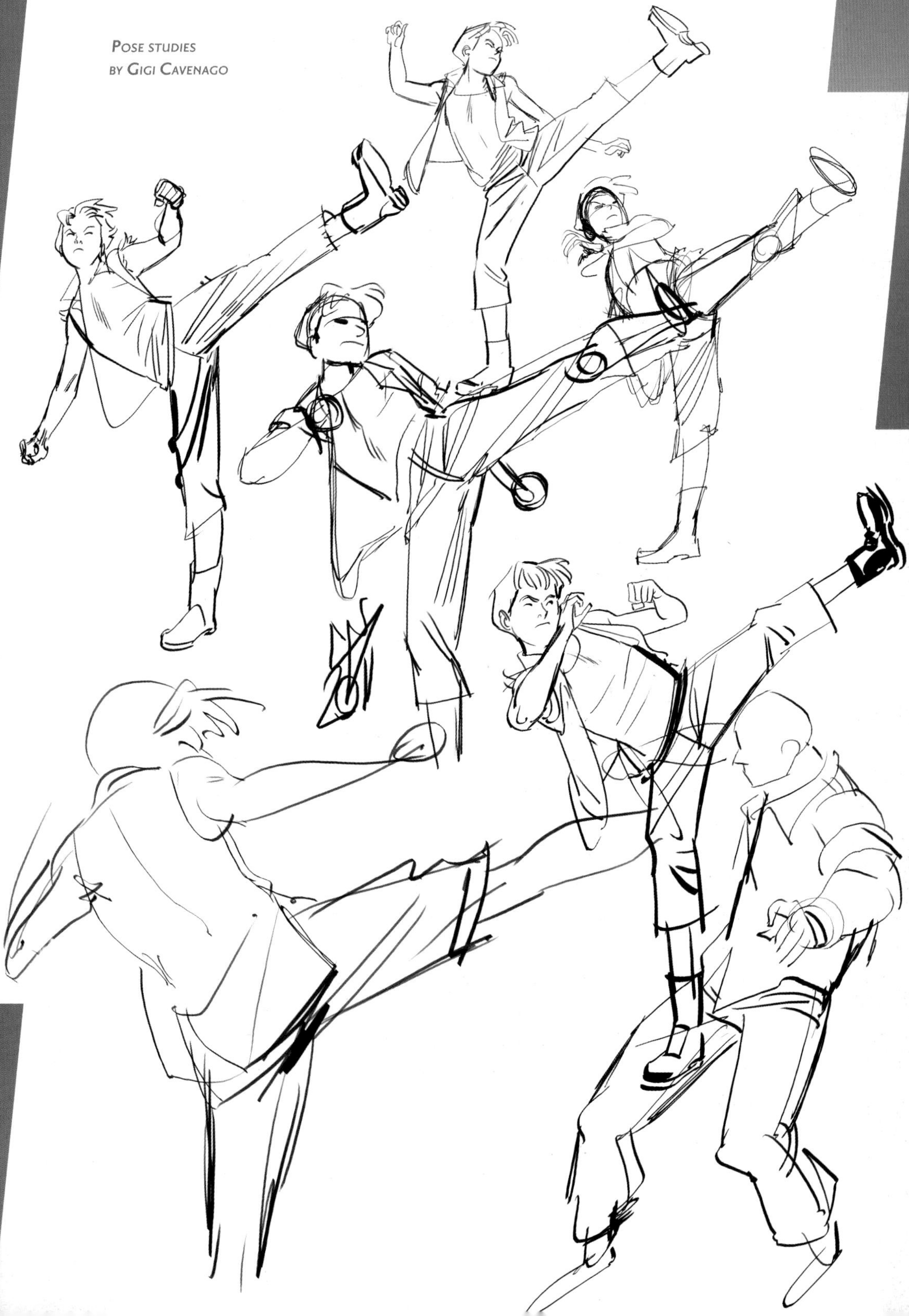

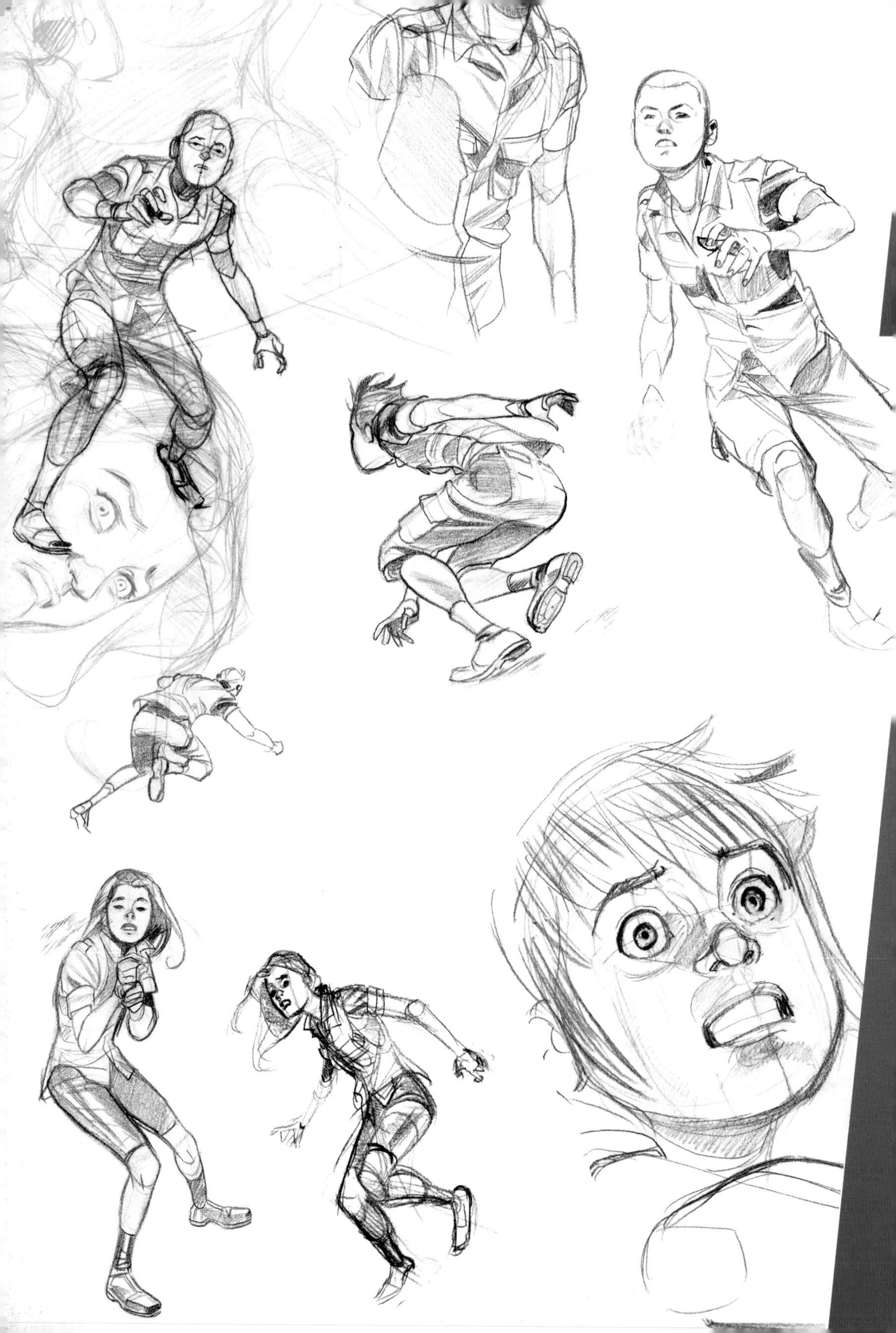

MAKING OURSELVES UNDERSTOOD WAS THE REAL
CHALLENGE. ESPECIALLY WITH SUCH A COMPLEX AND
UNUSUAL STORY.
– EMILIANO MAMMUCARI

THESE TWO PAGES: STUDIES
BY EMILIANO MAMMUCARI

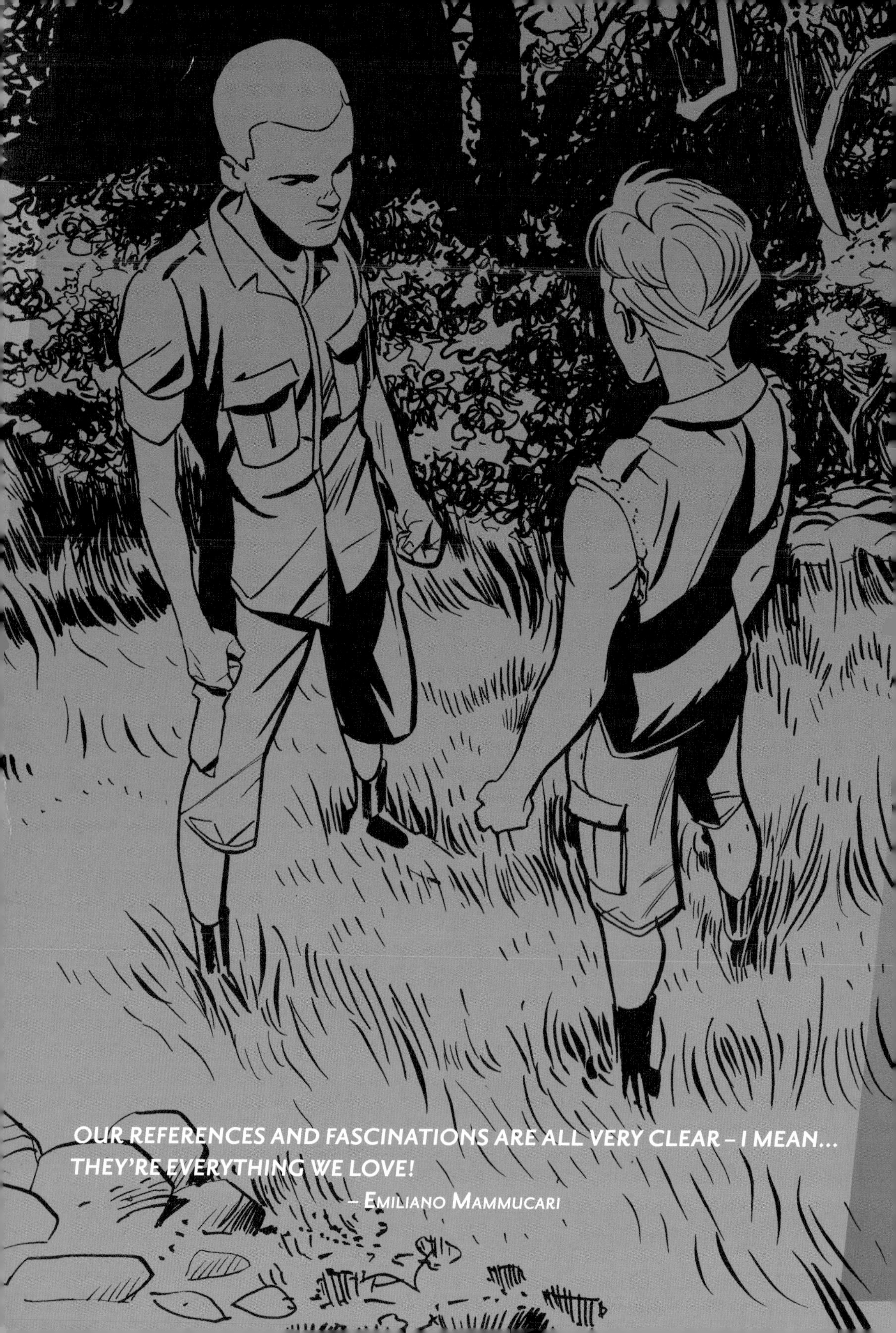

OUR REFERENCES AND FASCINATIONS ARE ALL VERY CLEAR – I MEAN... THEY'RE EVERYTHING WE LOVE!

– Emiliano Mammucari

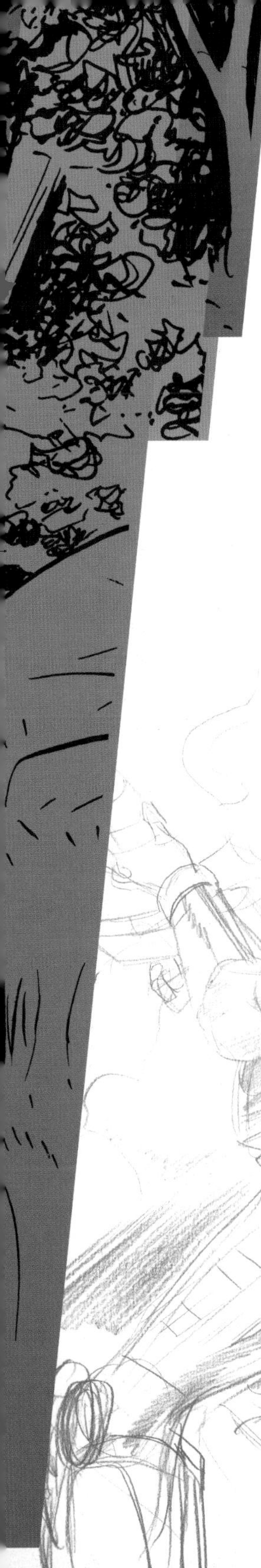

CHARACTERS

In *Orphans,* the characters are shown in two timelines: as kids and as adults. It was a real challenge for the artists to combine the characters' features with their individual drawing styles.

THESE TWO PAGES: STUDIES BY EMILIANO MAMMUCARI

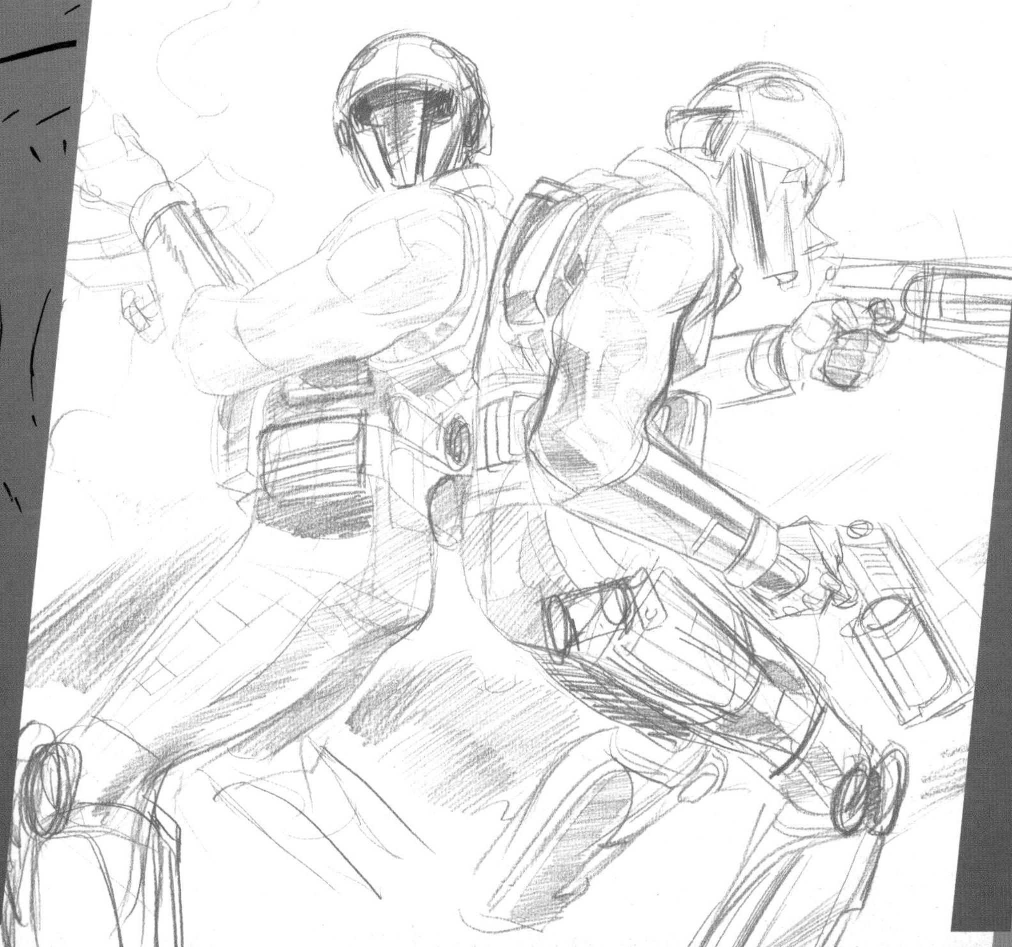

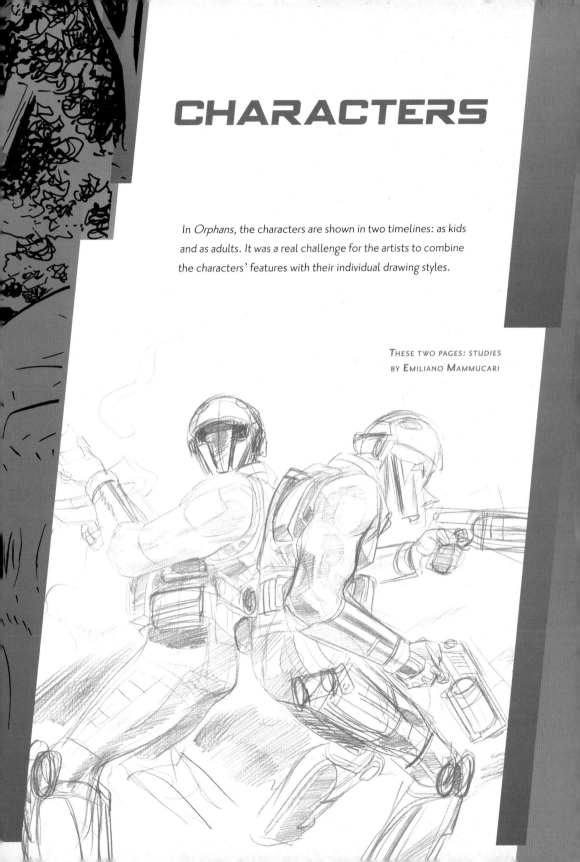

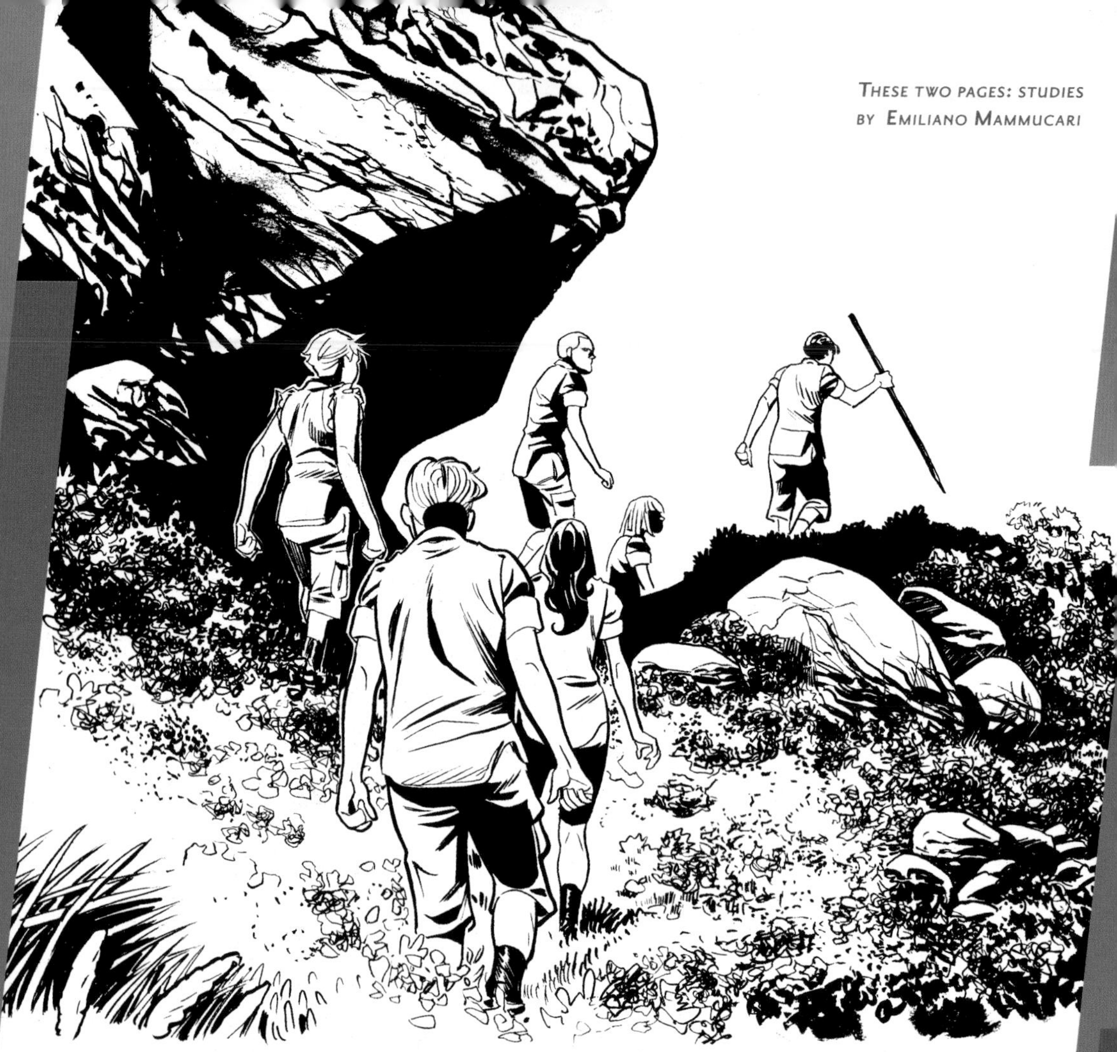

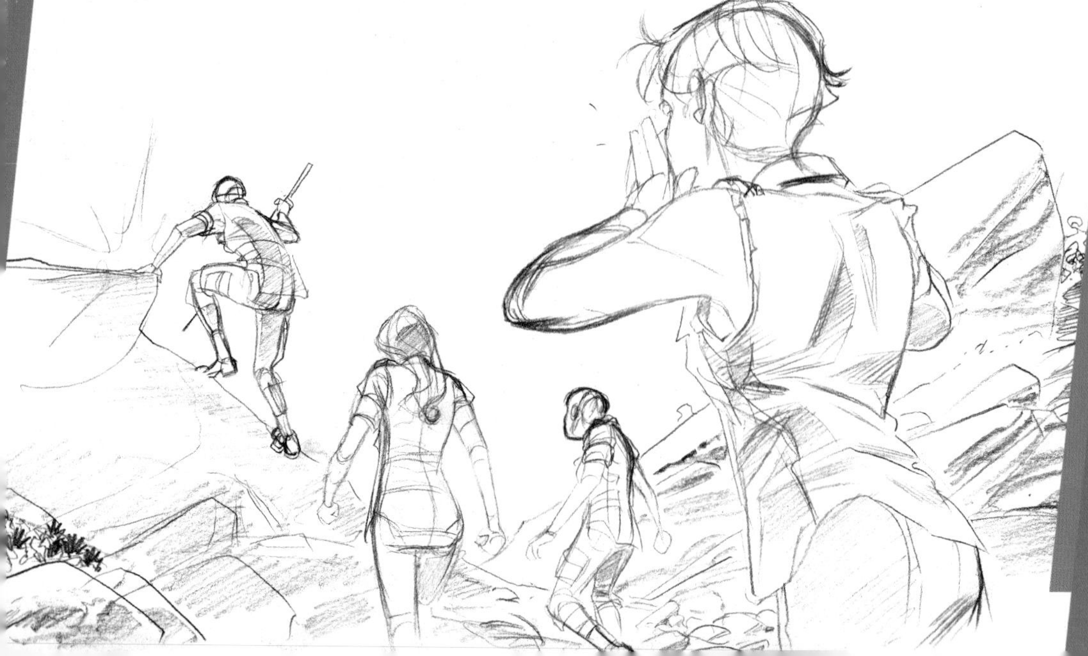

These two pages: studies by Emiliano Mammucari

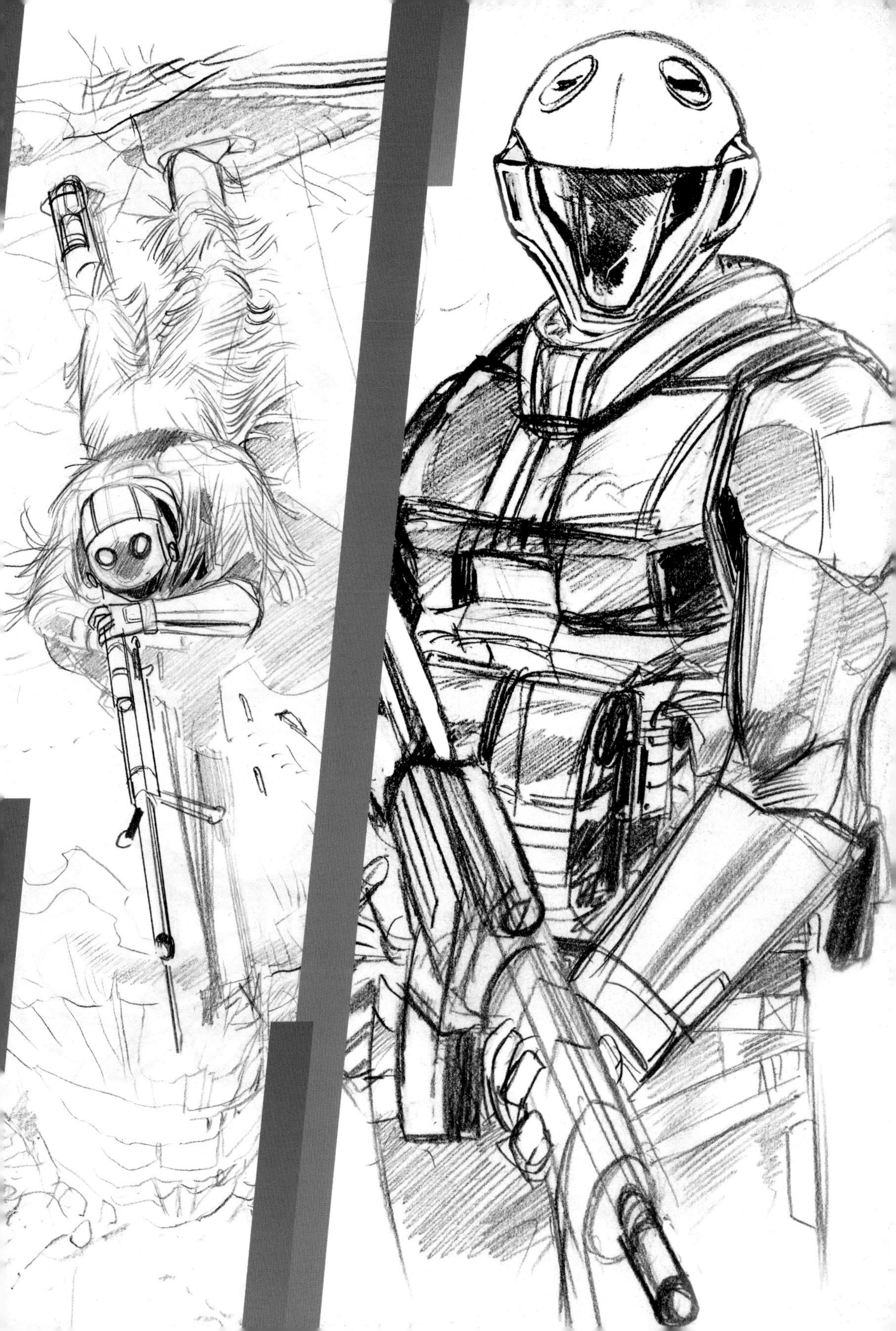

ALESSANDRO BIGNAMINI: Emiliano's great preliminary work provided a real technical handbook for all of us artists, both in clarity and richness of images. I didn't have to make very many studies to better understand the elements contained in my chapter, just a few sketches of Juno, Jonas, and their suits, to be more at ease while drawing. Apart from that, as I often do, I started directly from the page, drawing inspiration from the photographic material collected in advance.

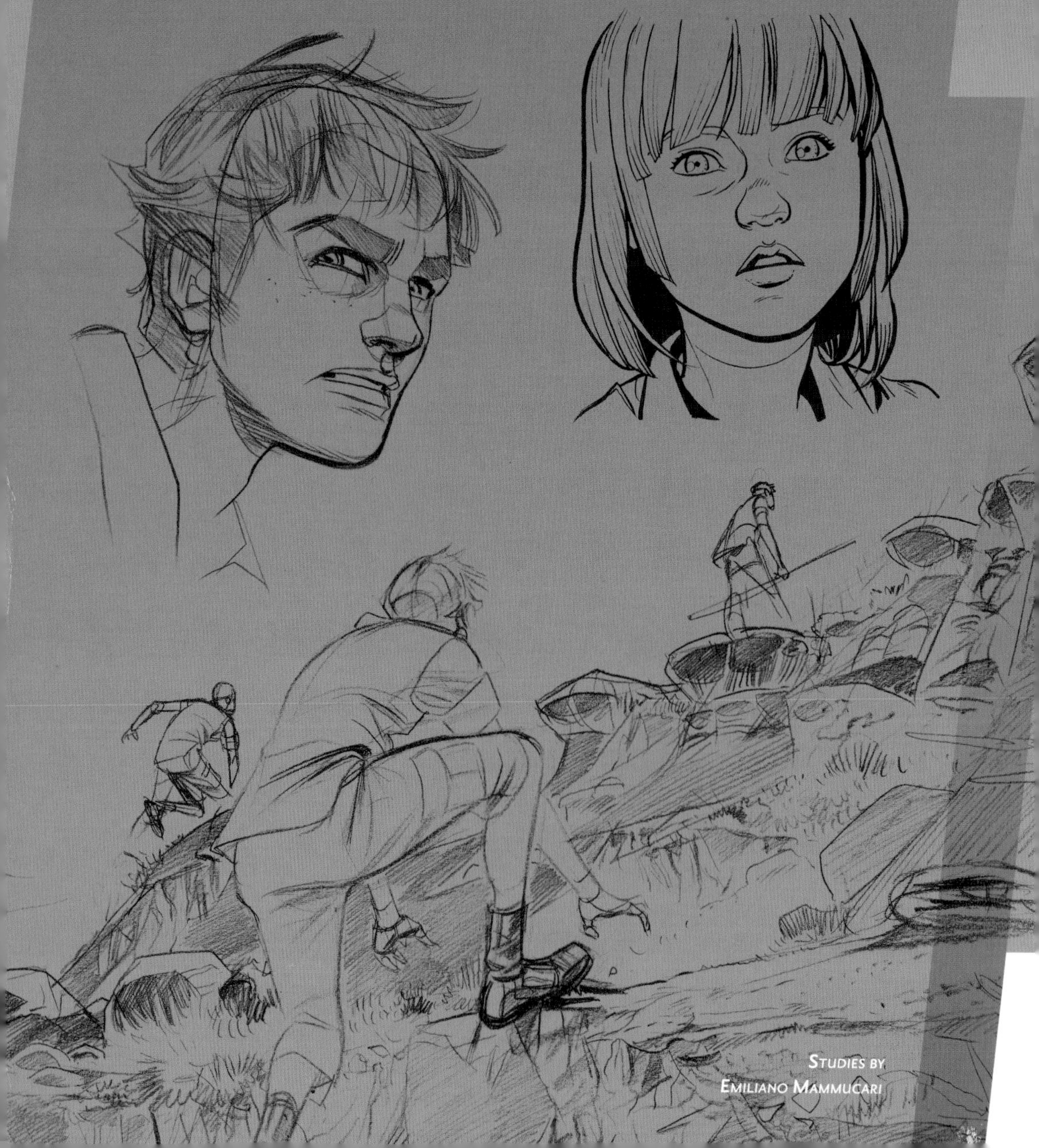

STUDIES BY
EMILIANO MAMMUCARI

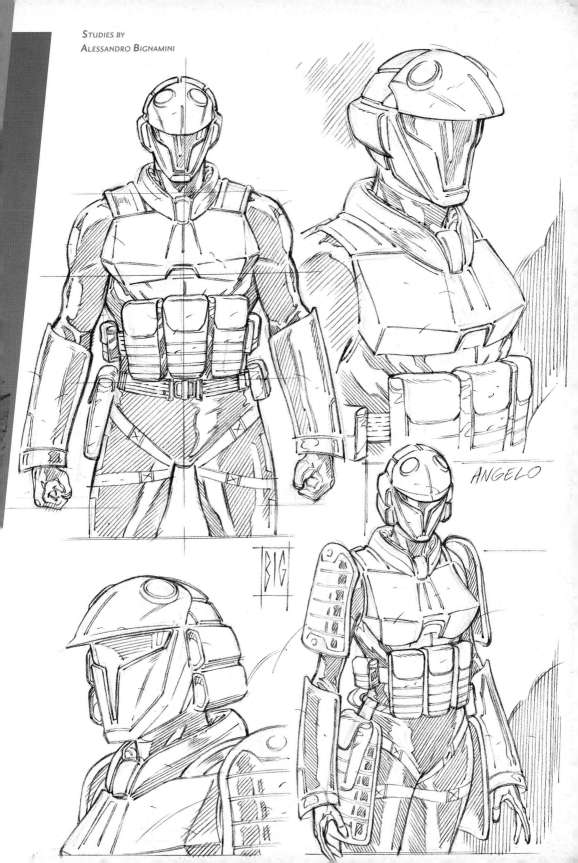

STUDIES BY
ALESSANDRO BIGNAMINI

ANGELO

BIG

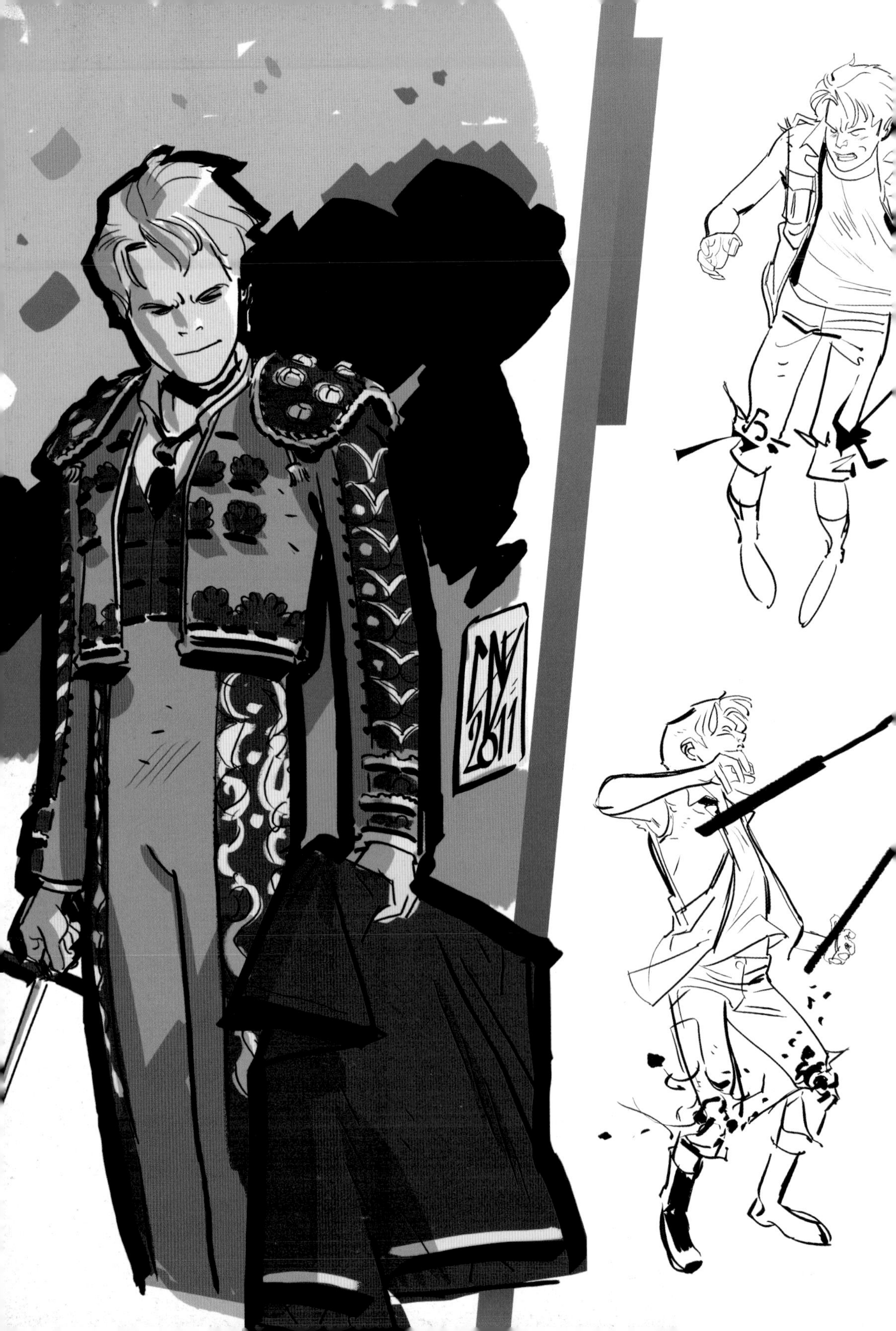

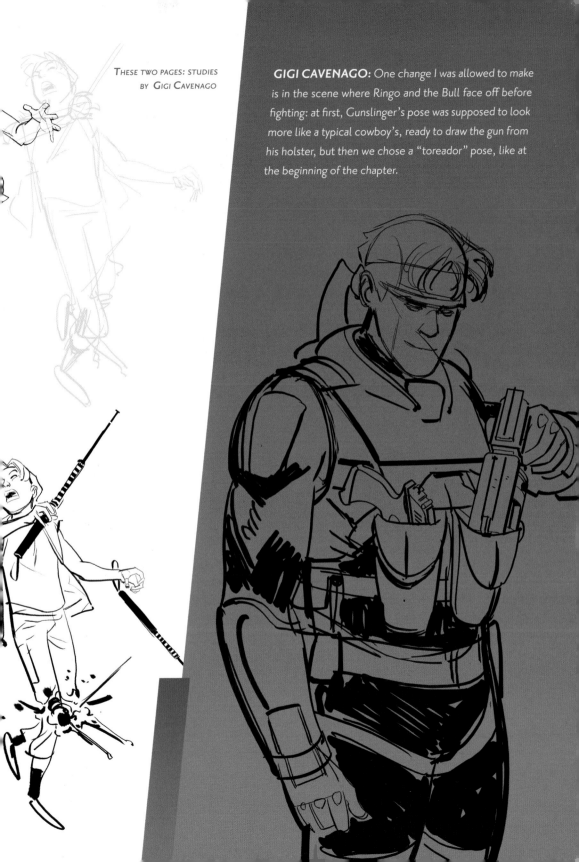

These two pages: studies by Gigi Cavenago

GIGI CAVENAGO: One change I was allowed to make is in the scene where Ringo and the Bull face off before fighting: at first, Gunslinger's pose was supposed to look more like a typical cowboy's, ready to draw the gun from his holster, but then we chose a "toreador" pose, like at the beginning of the chapter.

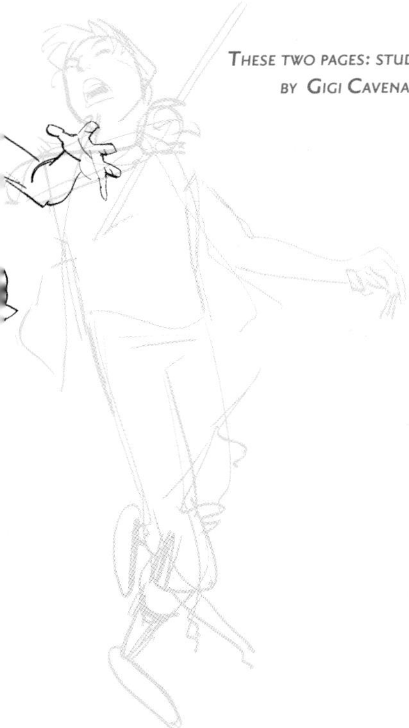

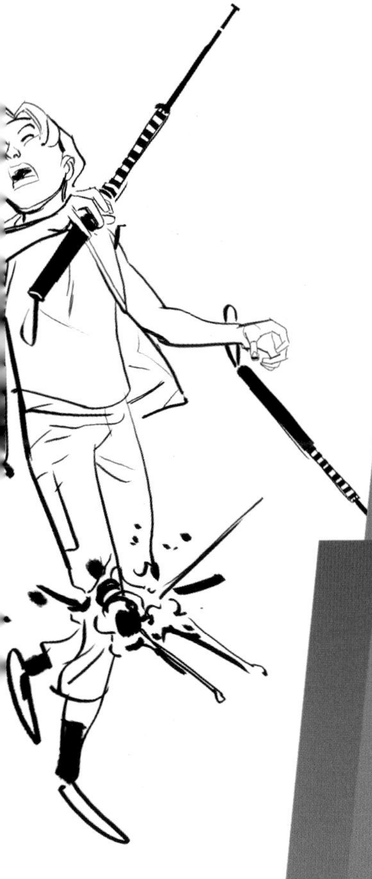

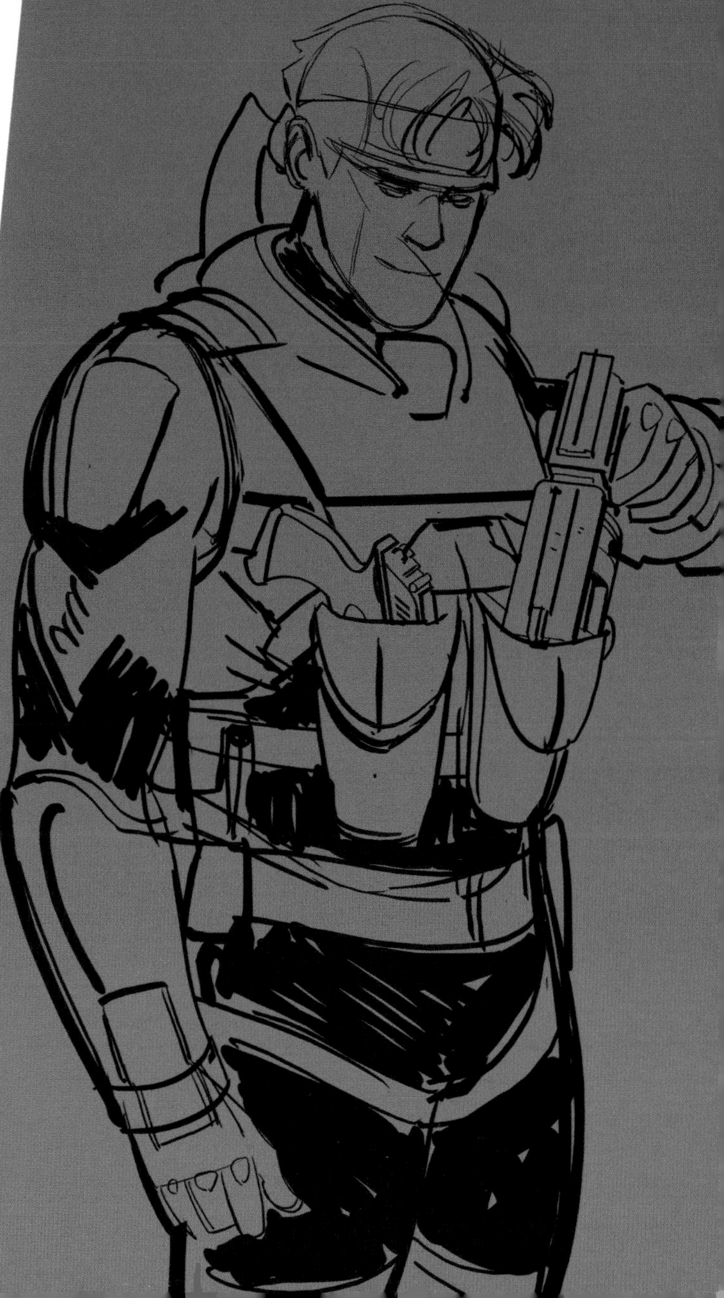

GIGI CAVENAGO: *Working with Roberto and Emiliano wasn't a problem at all. At first, they supervised a lot, especially with the character designs and the first pages. Emiliano and I were always in touch, especially when we had to create a new location or when I had some difficulties defining some characters. I still have to thank him for insisting I redraw a few horrible close-ups! But when I began settling down and felt more confident, I moved more freely. Roberto was always there, too, in each phase of the project, giving me suggestions about the visual aspects of the series, and of course on all the matters concerning direction.*

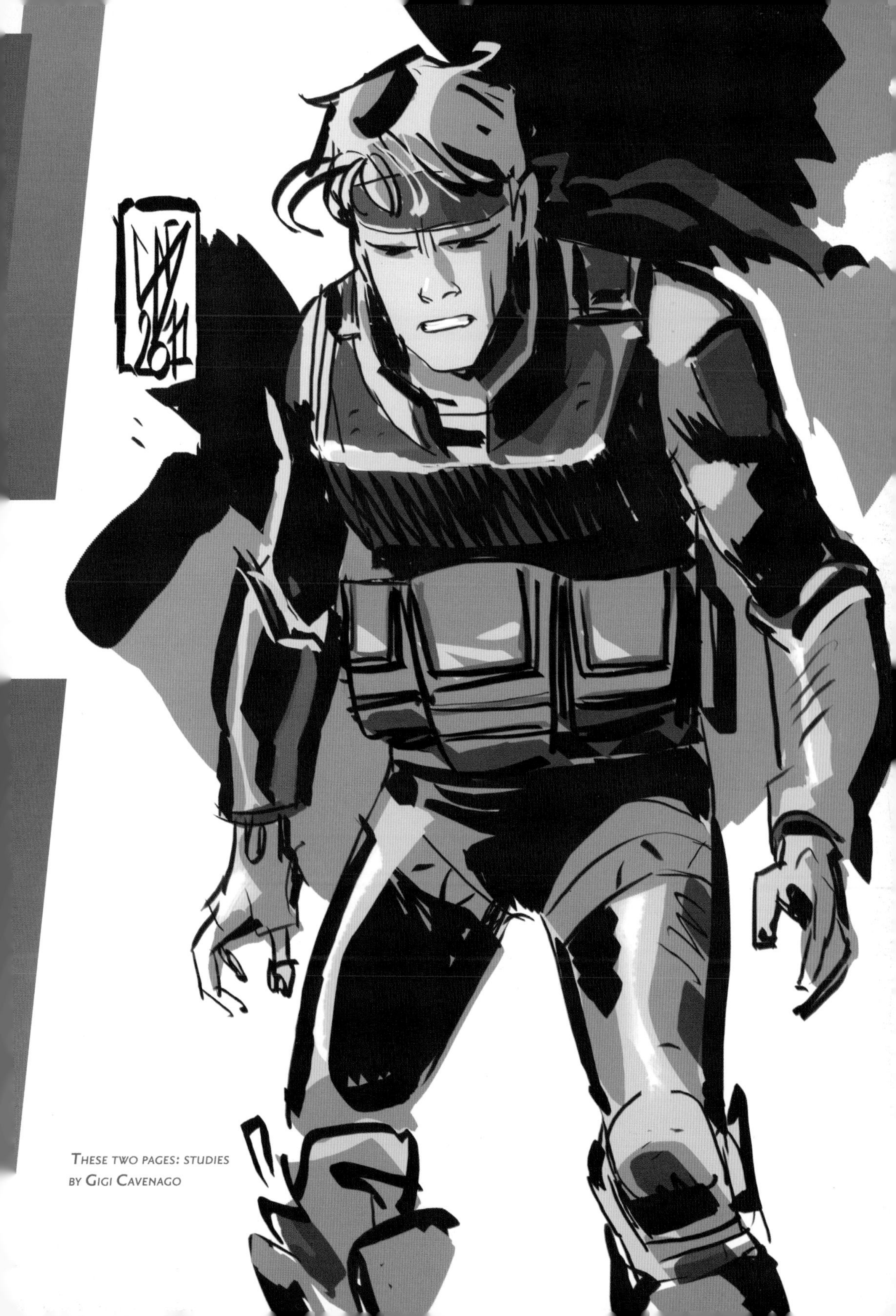

These two pages: studies by Gigi Cavenago

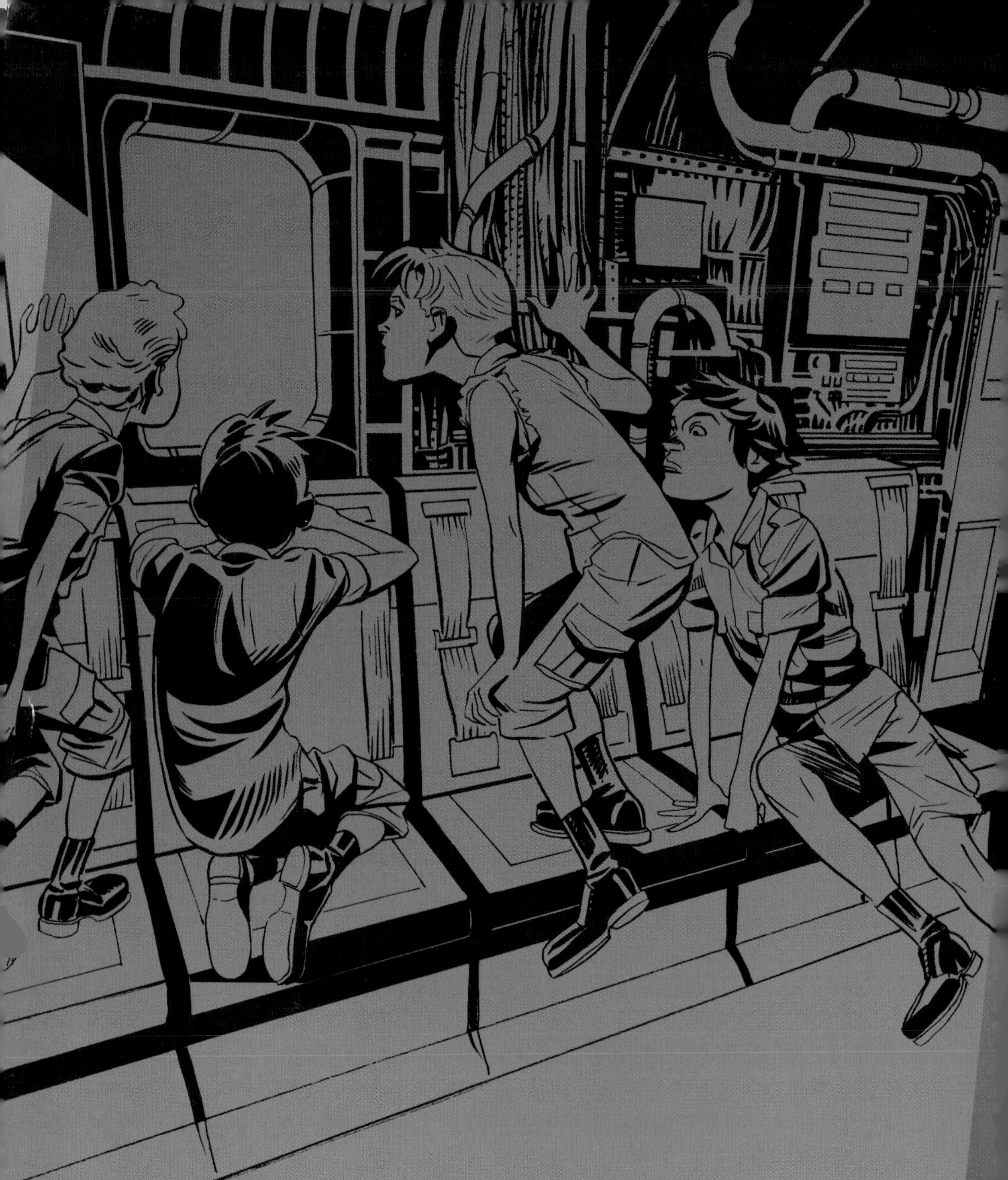

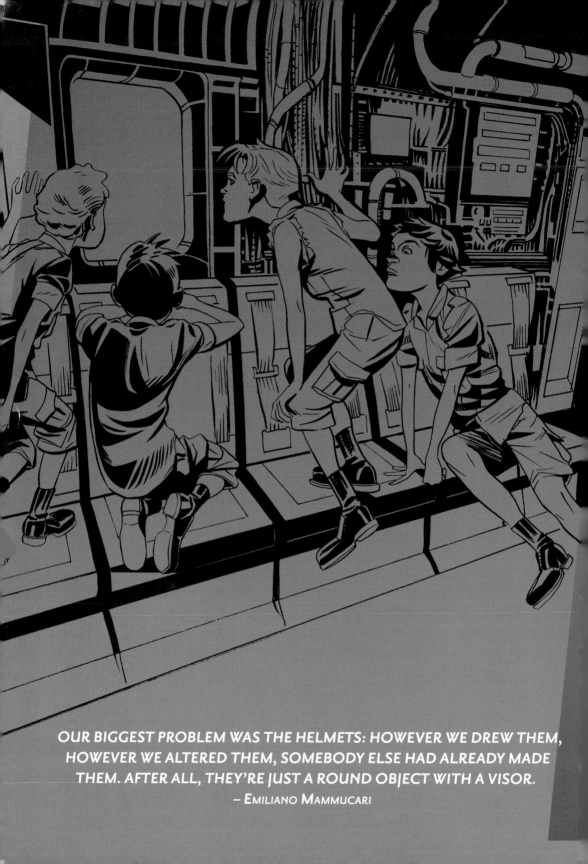

OUR BIGGEST PROBLEM WAS THE HELMETS: HOWEVER WE DREW THEM, HOWEVER WE ALTERED THEM, SOMEBODY ELSE HAD ALREADY MADE THEM. AFTER ALL, THEY'RE JUST A ROUND OBJECT WITH A VISOR.

– EMILIANO MAMMUCARI

TECHNOLOGY

GIGI CAVENAGO: The Wolfhounds (the ships flown by the Orphans) were created using Google Sketchup. I had a general shape in mind, but the creative process was different from usual: I downloaded dozens of 3-D models, from Apache helicopters to Gundam, then I took them all apart and put them back together until I created different space ship models to provide Roberto and Emiliano a wide choice.

ABOVE: SPACESHIP STUDY BY GIGI CAVENAGO
PREVIOUS PAGE: SKETCH BY EMILIANO MAMMUCARI

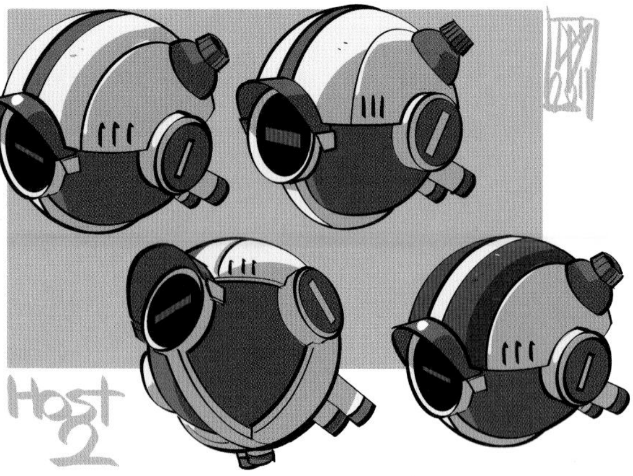
Host 2

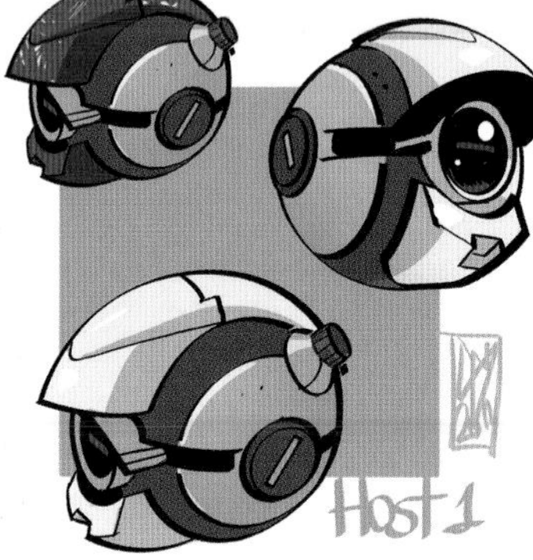
Host 1

Studies by
Gigi Cavenago

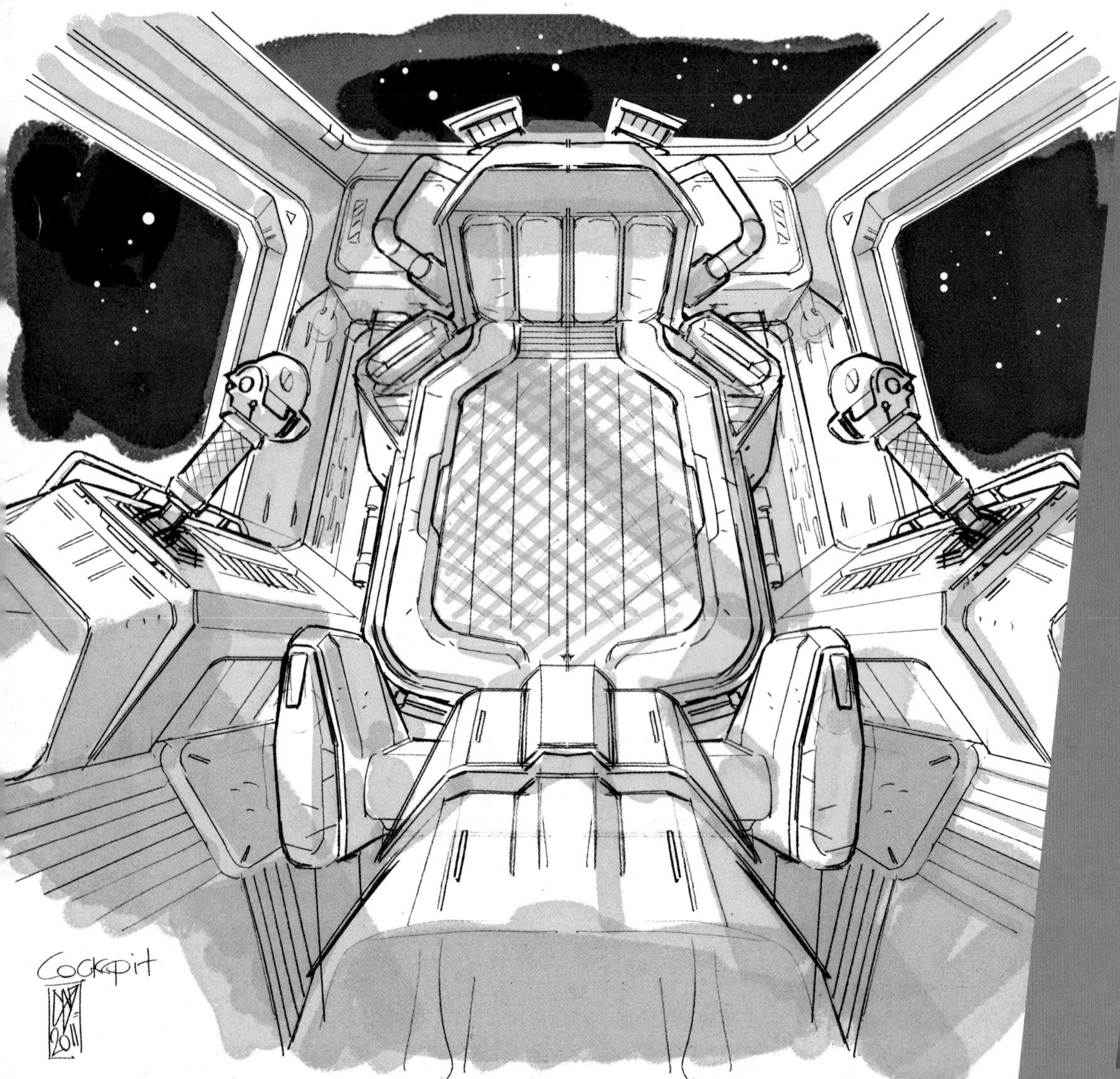
Cockpit
2011

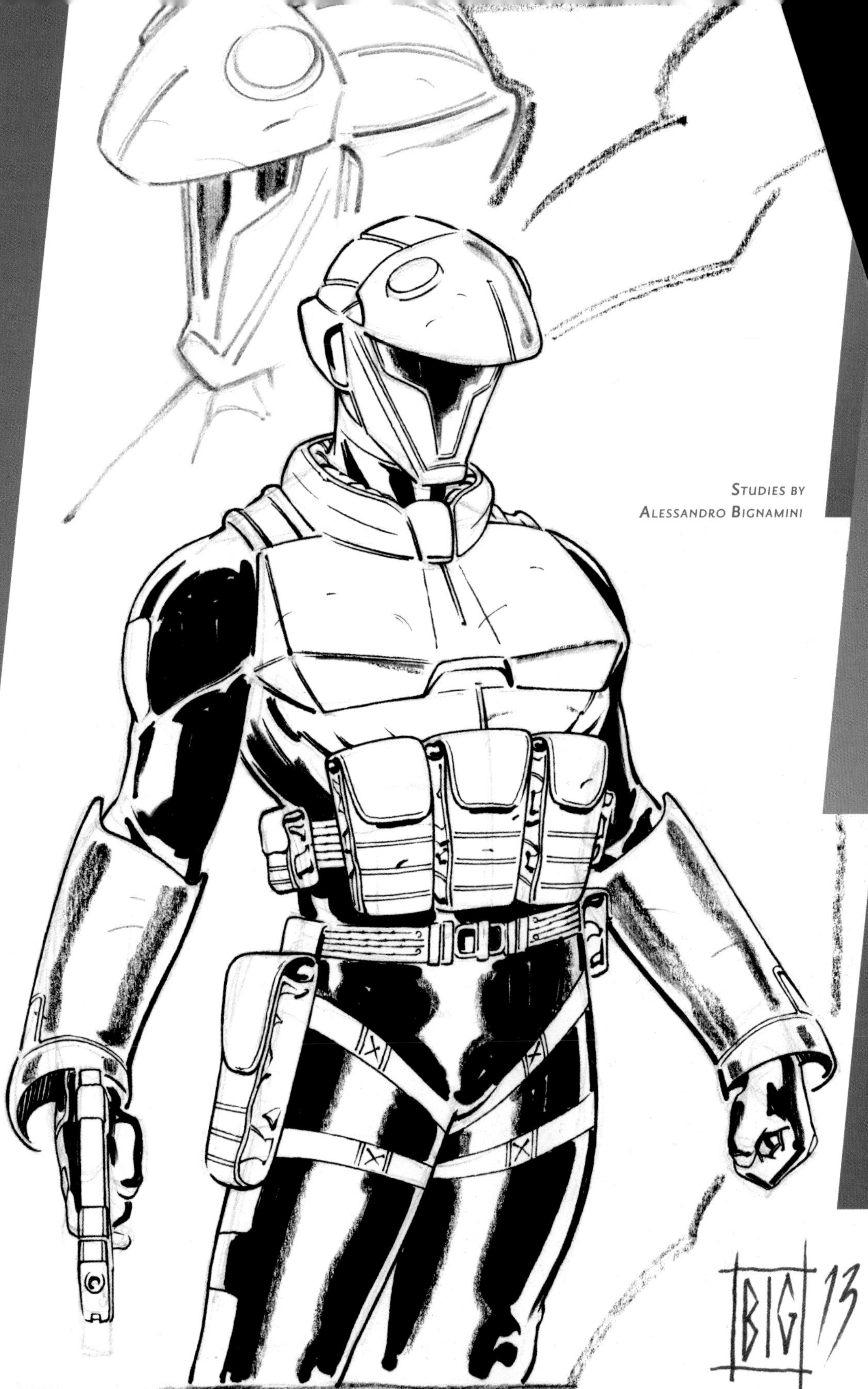
BIG 13

STUDIES BY
ALESSANDRO BIGNAMINI

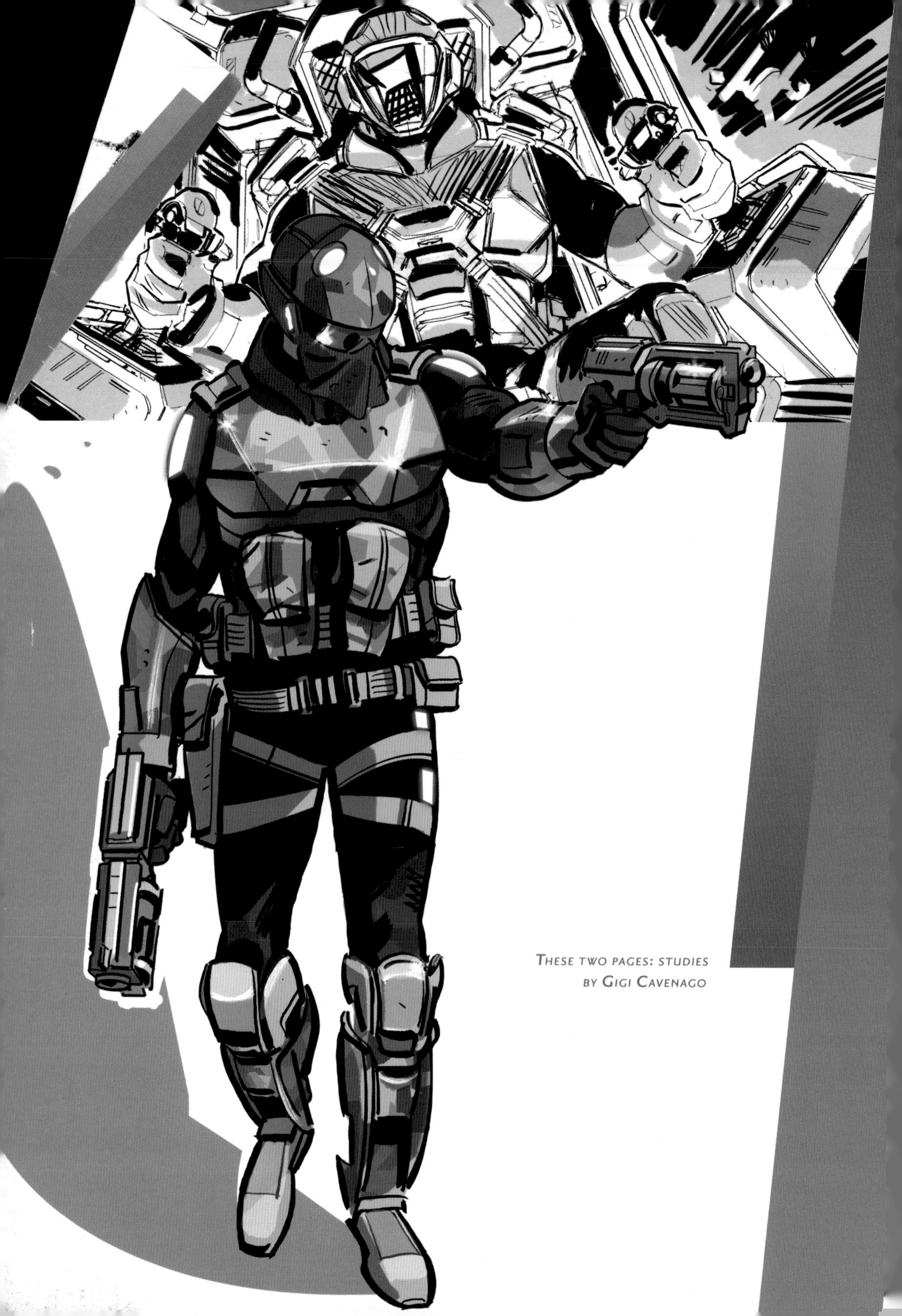

These two pages: studies by Gigi Cavenago

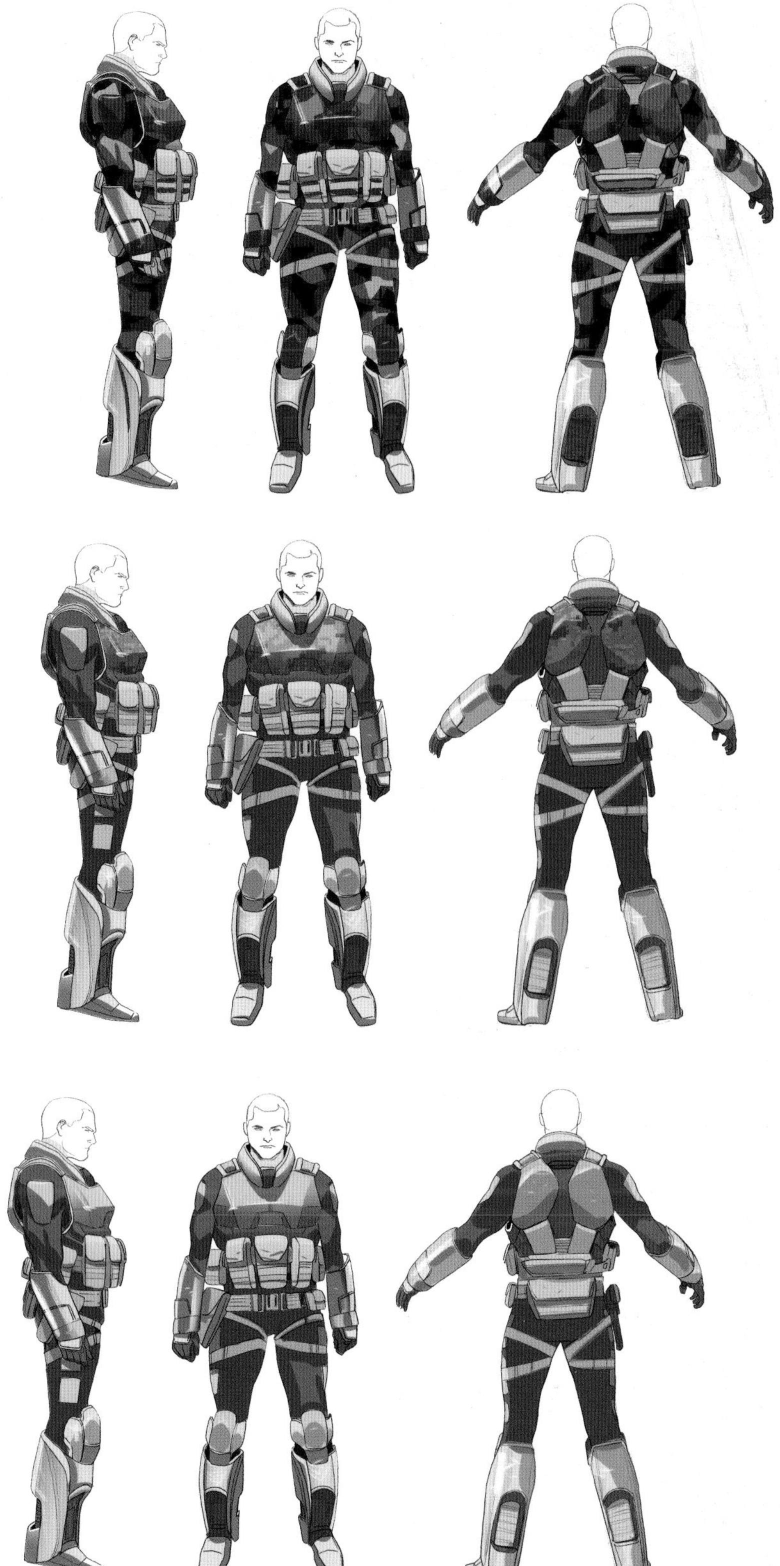

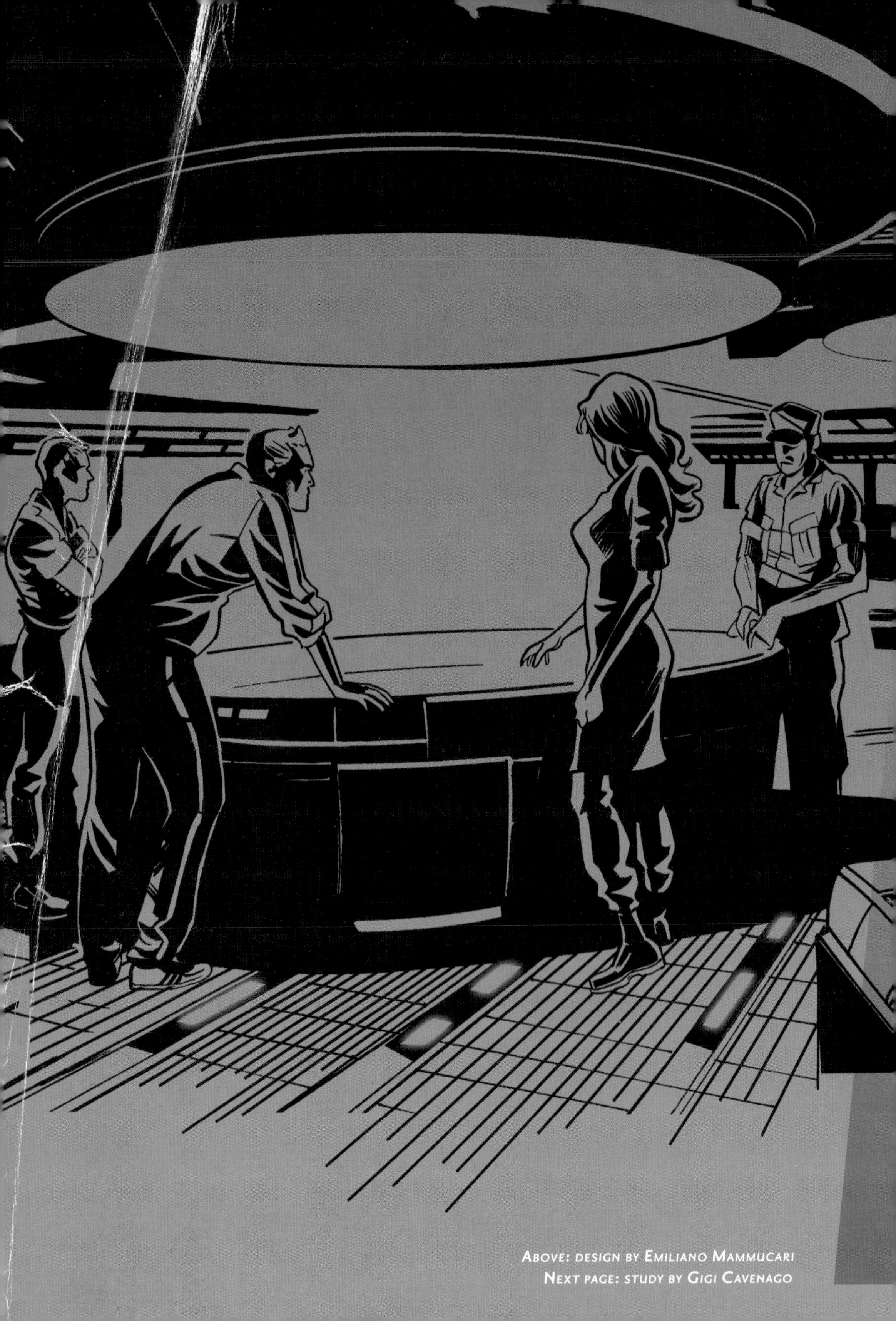

Above: design by Emiliano Mammucari
Next page: study by Gigi Cavenago

LOCATIONS

EMILIANO MAMMUCARI: *I spent a lot of time working on Ridgeback Camp. The first version was a normal training camp, like many others, but during the creative phase we realized that it had to be something more. Ridgeback Camp had to be another character, a visual metaphor of what we call home. So I thought to make it a bit more unreal, with a space divided between two platforms in the mountains, to give it some personality.*

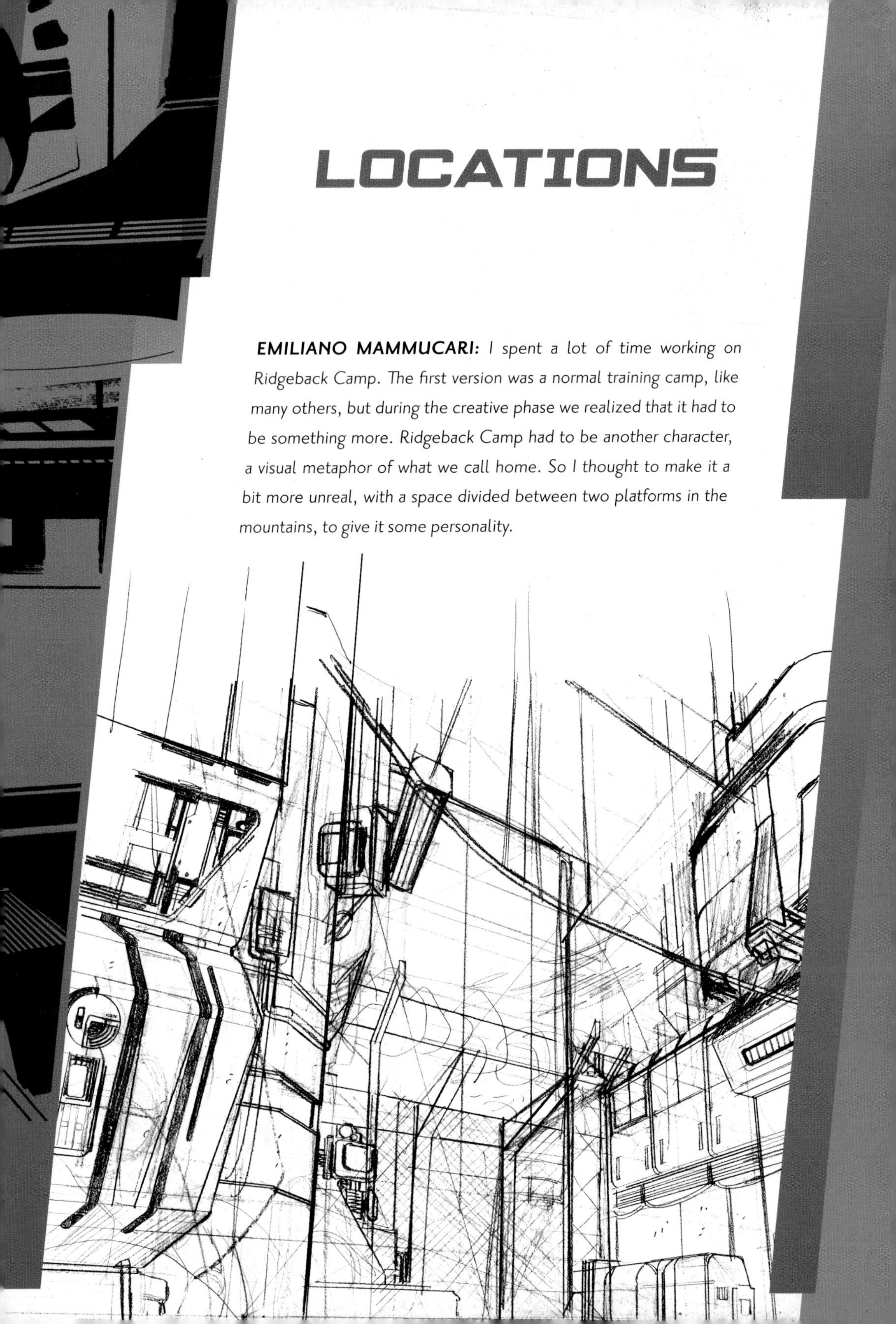

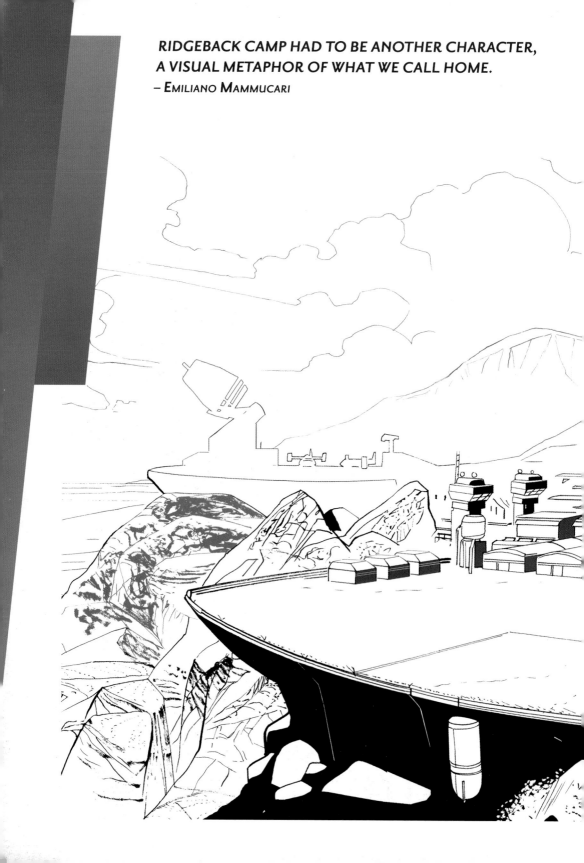

RIDGEBACK CAMP HAD TO BE ANOTHER CHARACTER, A VISUAL METAPHOR OF WHAT WE CALL HOME.

– Emiliano Mammucari

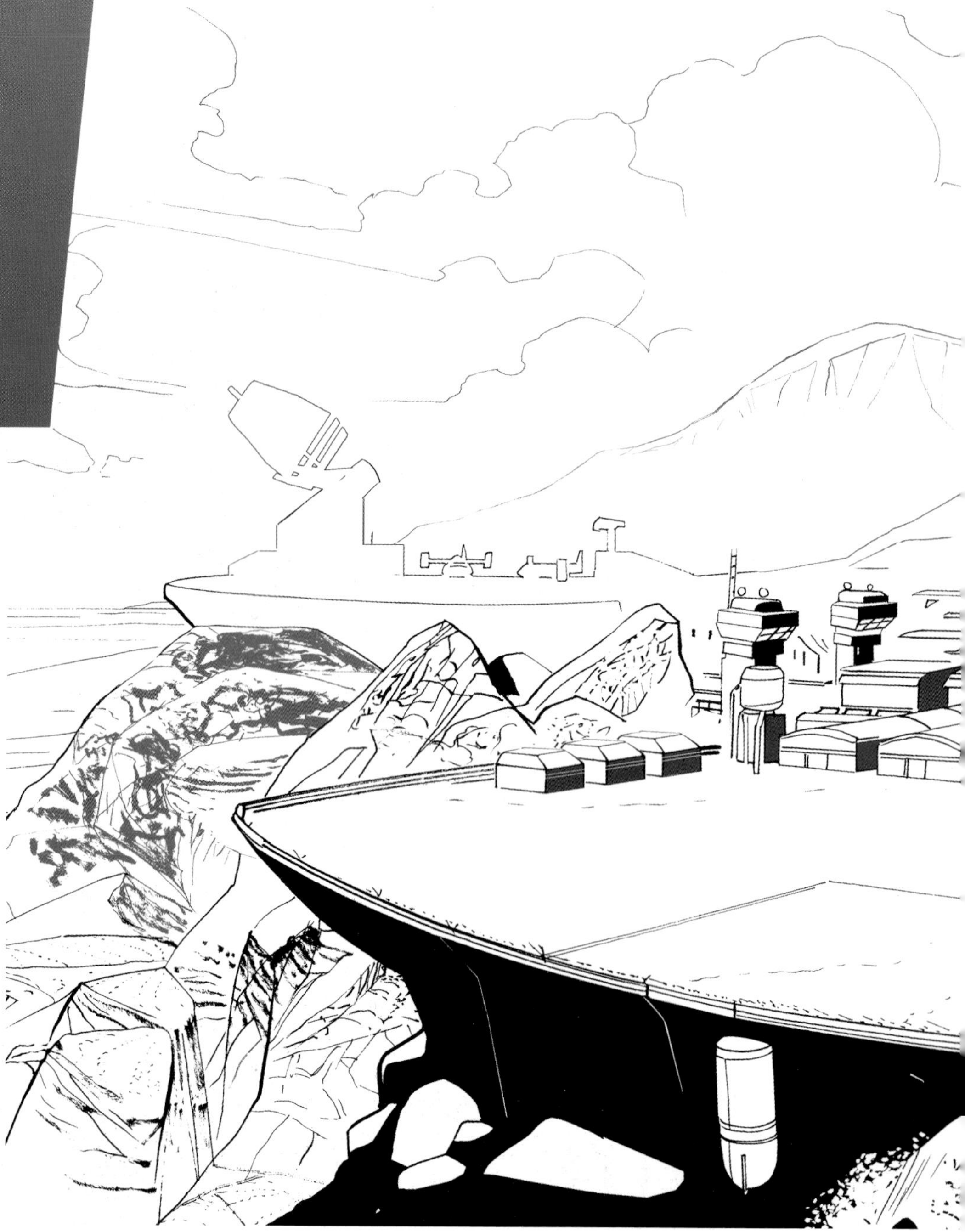

Final version of the Ridgeback training camp created by
Emiliano Mammucari

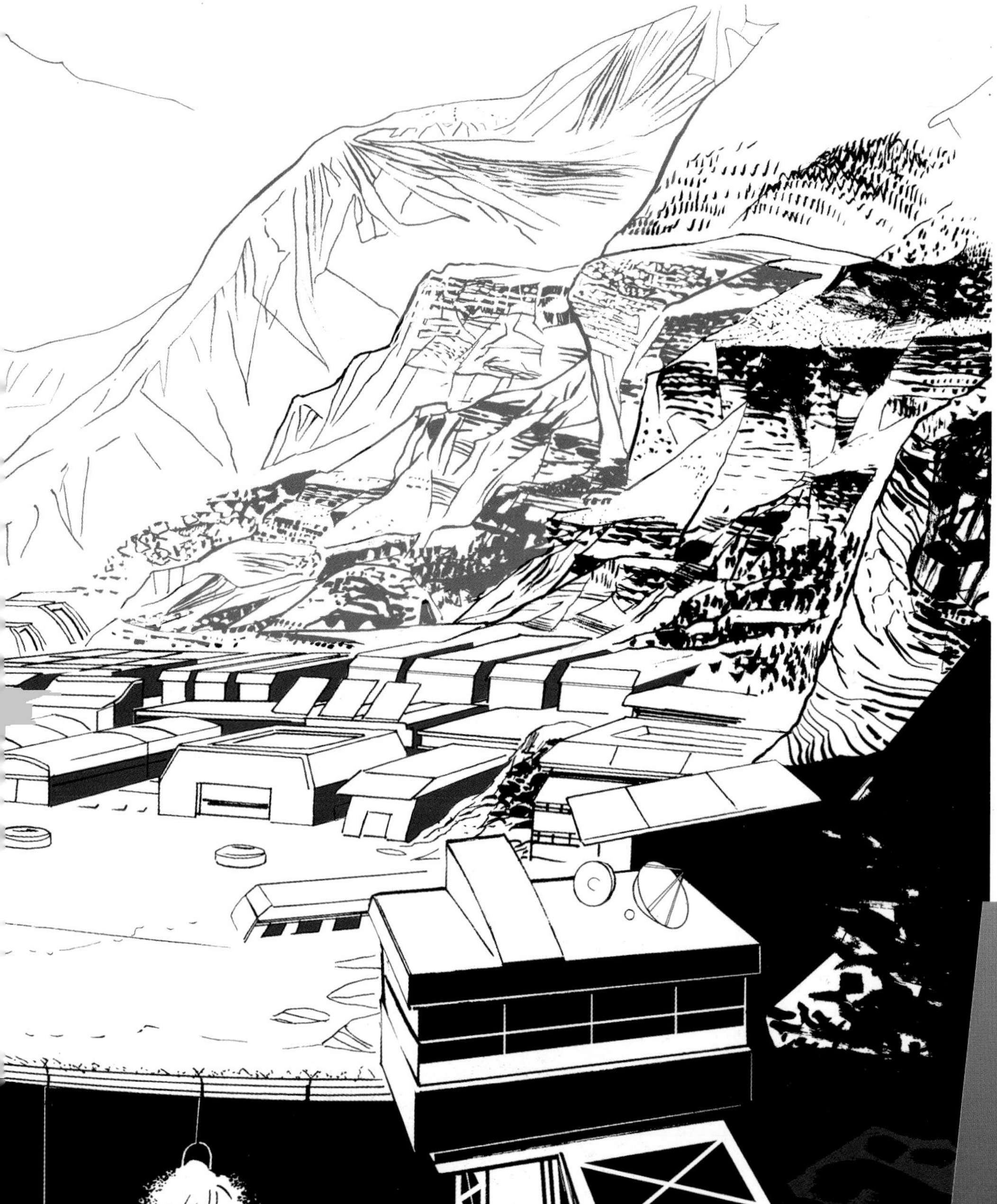

GIGI CAVENAGO: *The various locations in Ridgeback Camp were pretty tough to draw: when I started drawing the issue we hadn't decided on all of the architecture yet. Actually, in chapter one, there were about thirty pages in which the training camp didn't appear that much. So I had to recreate new locations in line with what Emiliano had already shown: the classroom, Juric's office, the infirmary, the showers, the spaceship decks with the Orphans' cabins... luckily, I could alternate all this with the scenes set in the swamp.*

BELOW: A SKETCH BY EMILIANO MAMMUCARI
NEXT PAGE AND FOLLOWING TWO PAGES: STUDIES BY GIGI CAVENAGO

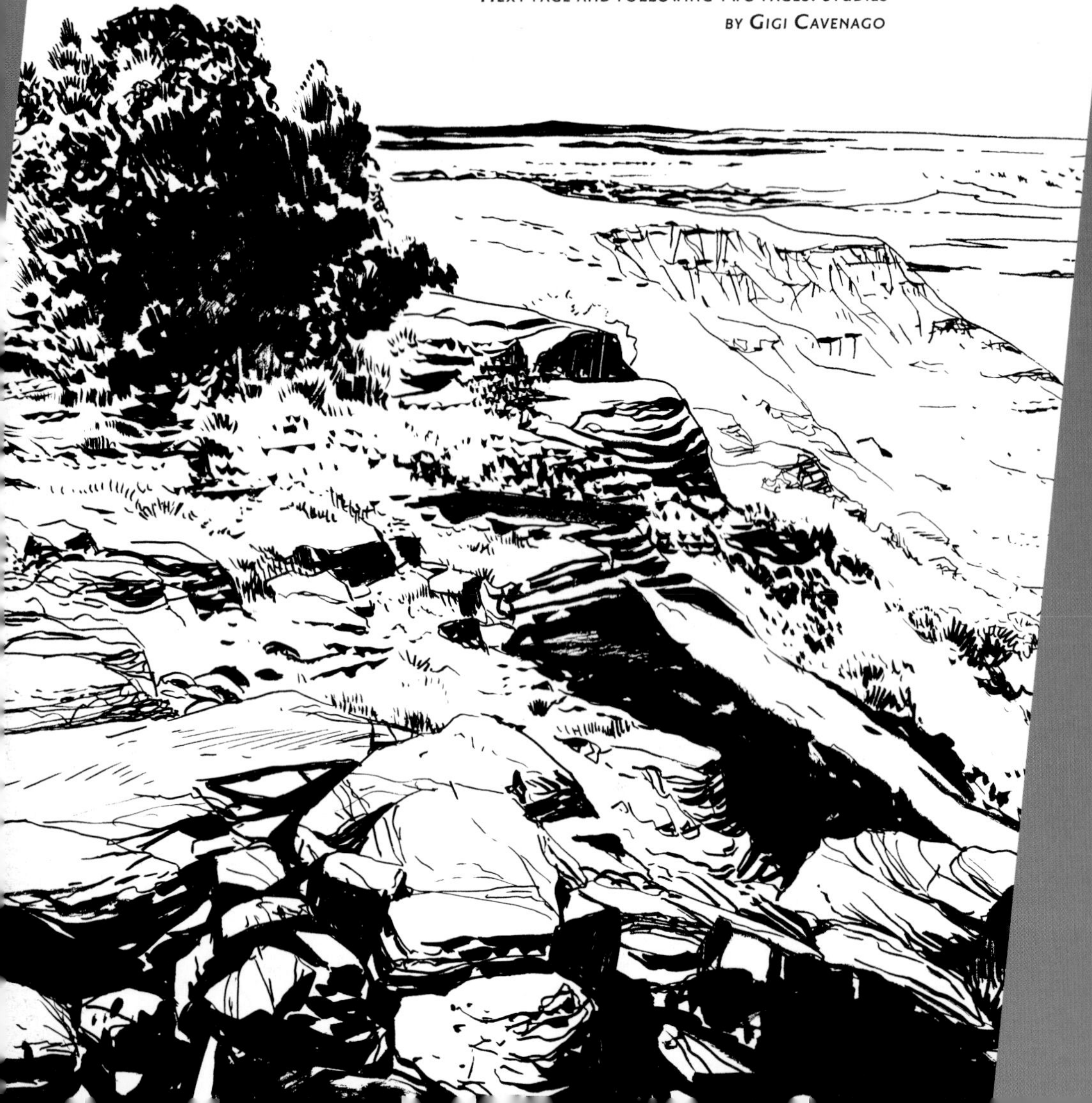

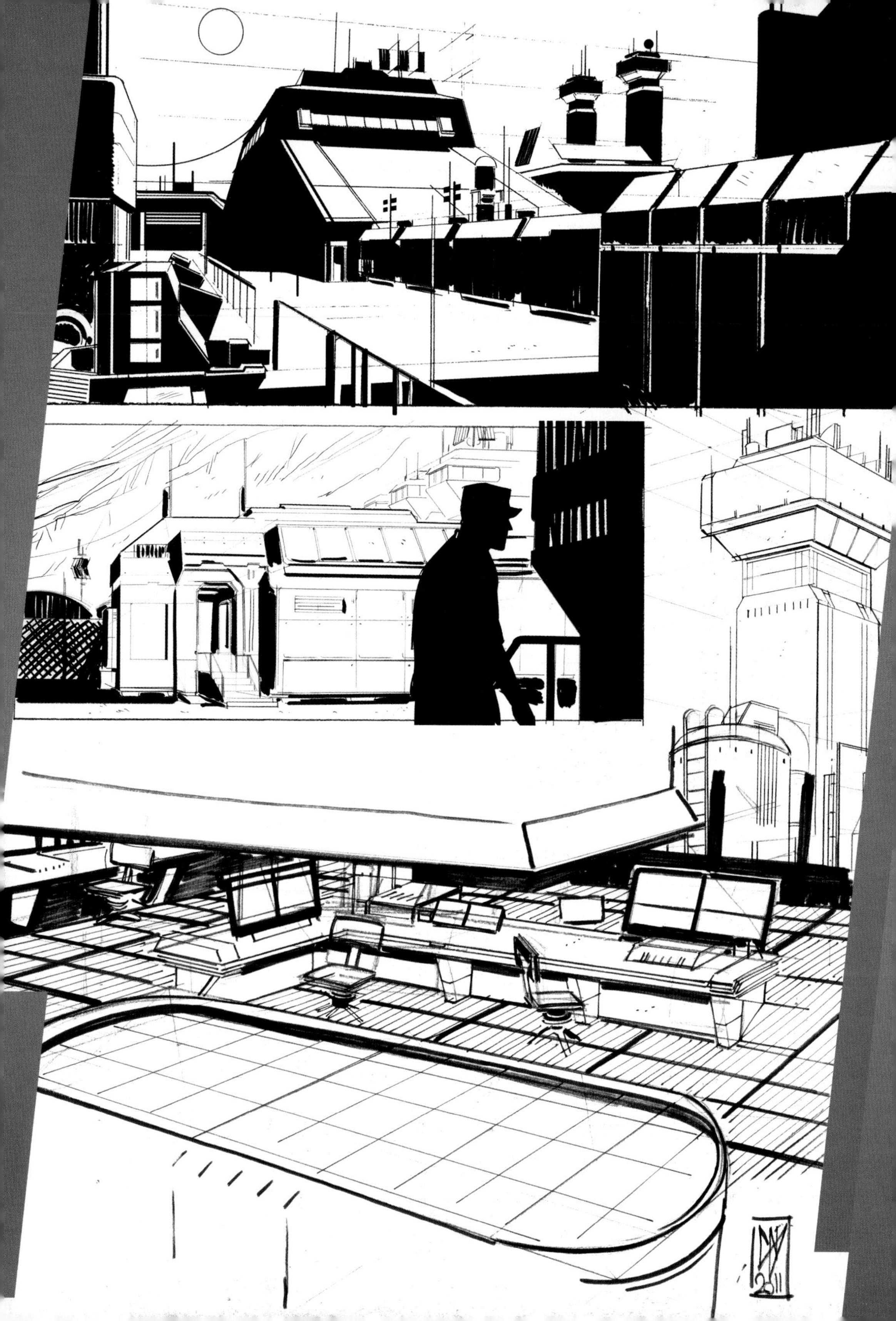
2011

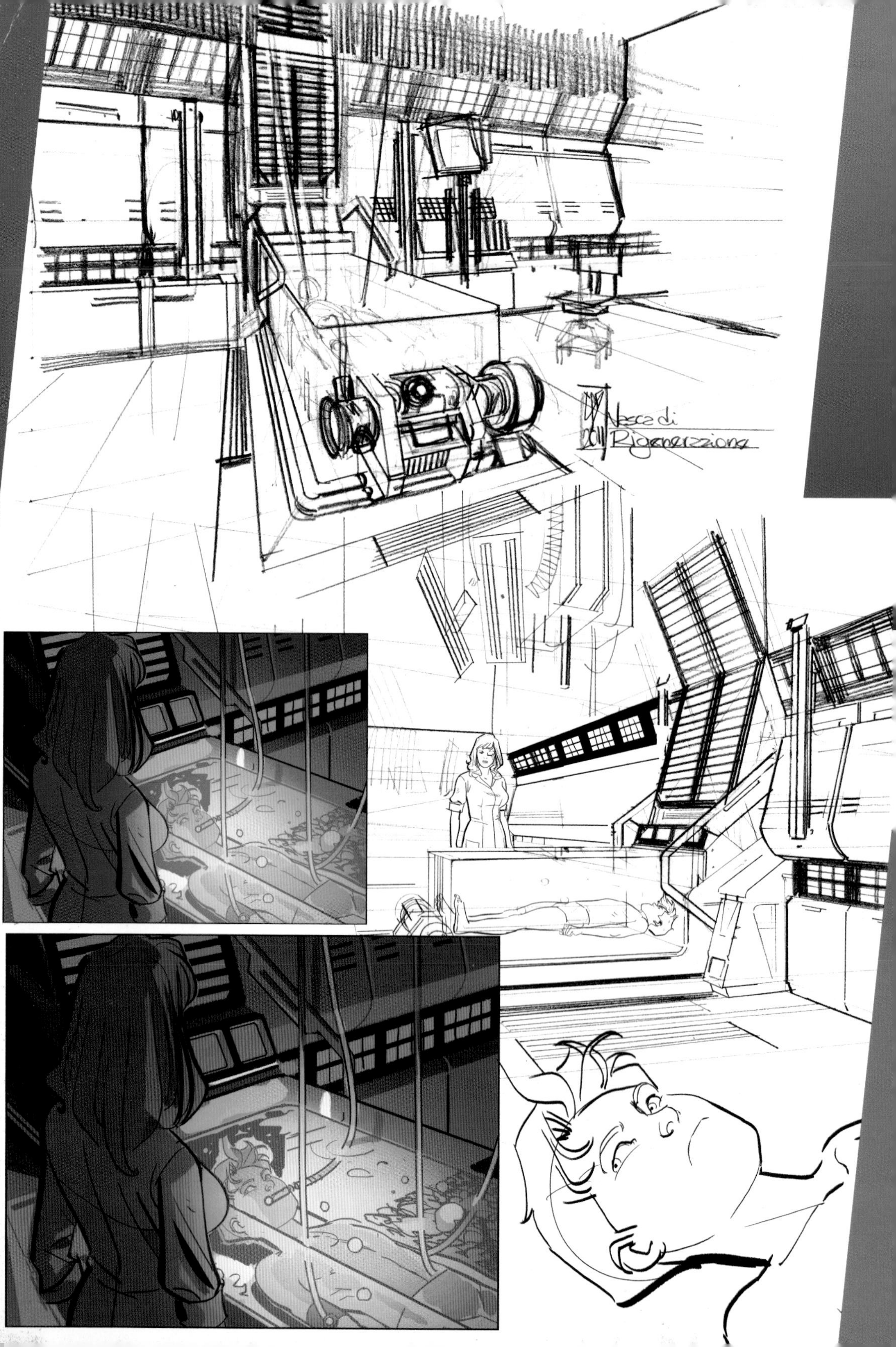
Vasca di
2011

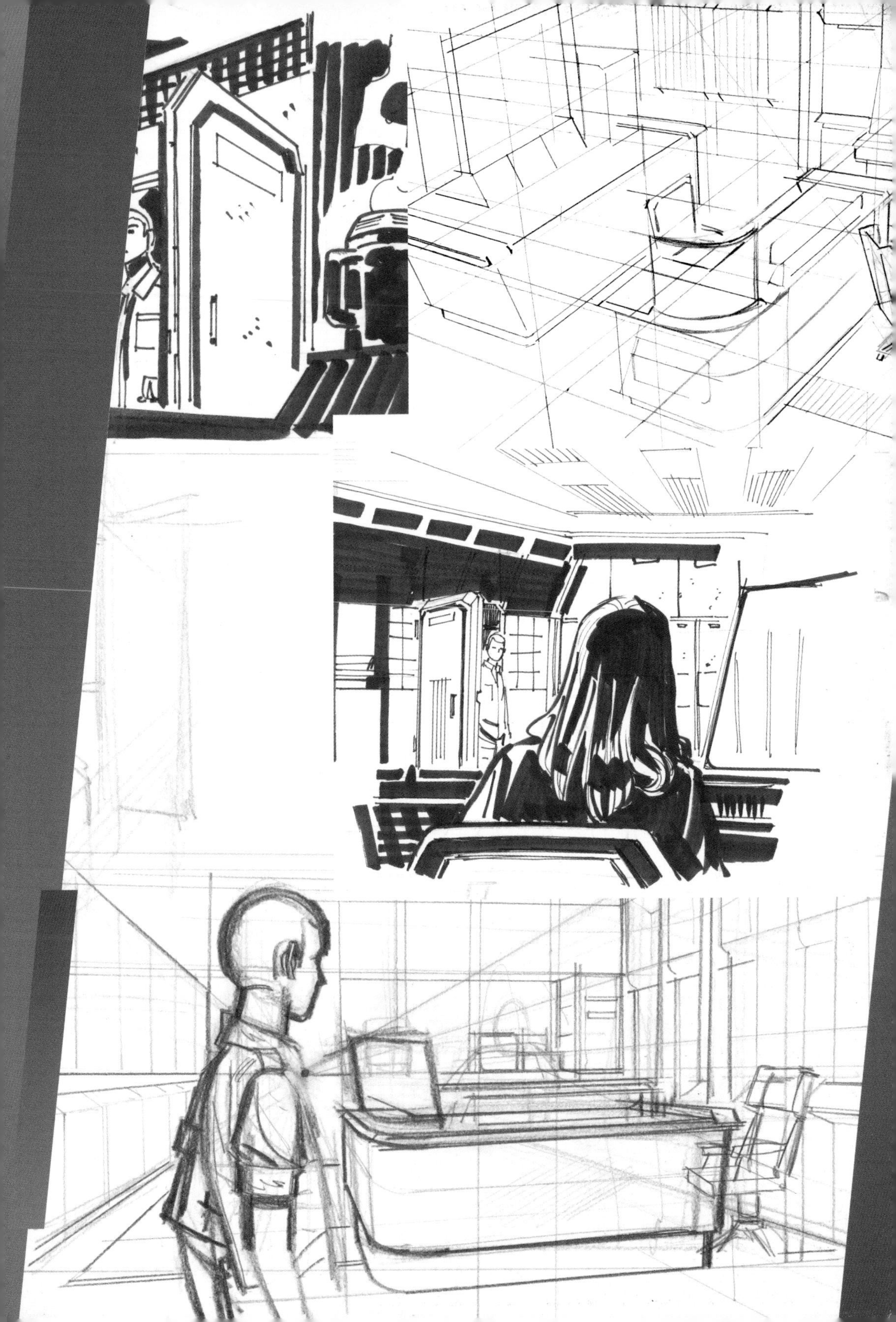

ALIENS

GIGI CAVENAGO: In the beginning, I lent a hand in the creation of the Property Bible, especially the part concerning the phantoms' appearance. Roberto and Emiliano's instructions were very precise and I could even count on some pencil sketches by Werther Dell'Edera. My job was to provide the final look. I had to work on many "species," and the hardest part was to imagine how each one of them moved. The most interesting one was the phantom mammoth, which initially was supposed to move like a charging elephant. Then we decided to give it two big upper limbs, like those of a gorilla, so that it could swipe soldiers away in a single gesture.

ABOVE: STUDY BY EMILIANO MAMMUCARI
PREVIOUS PAGE: STUDY BY GIGI CAVENAGO

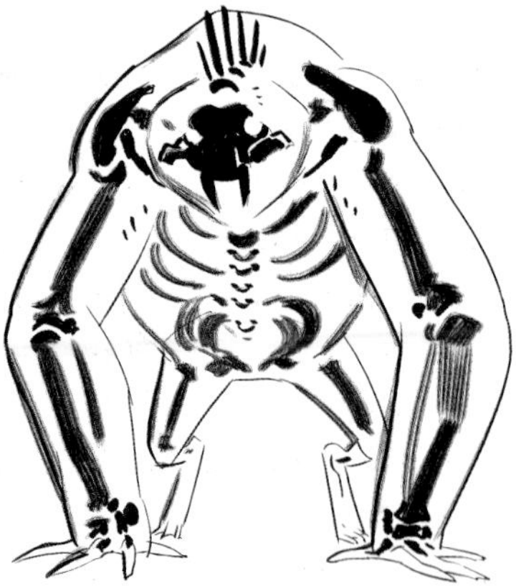

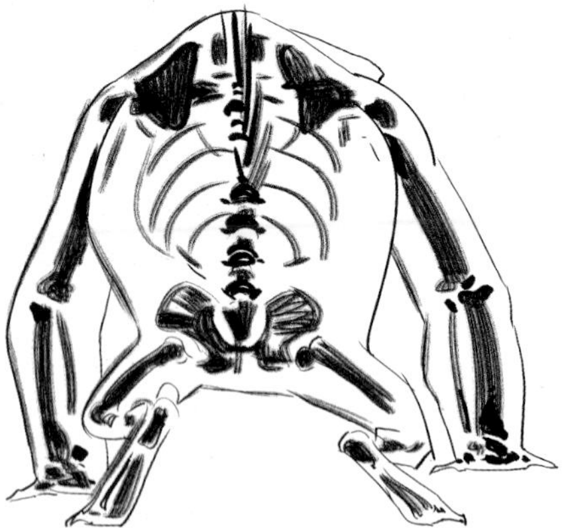

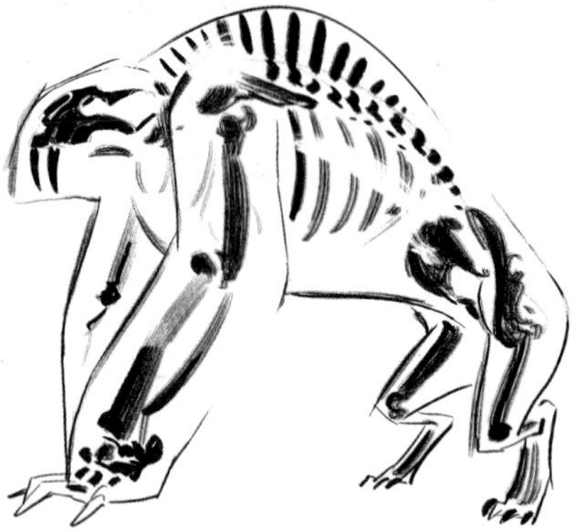

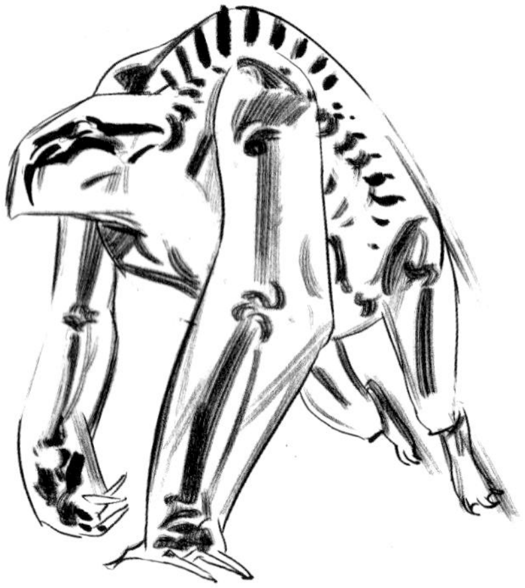

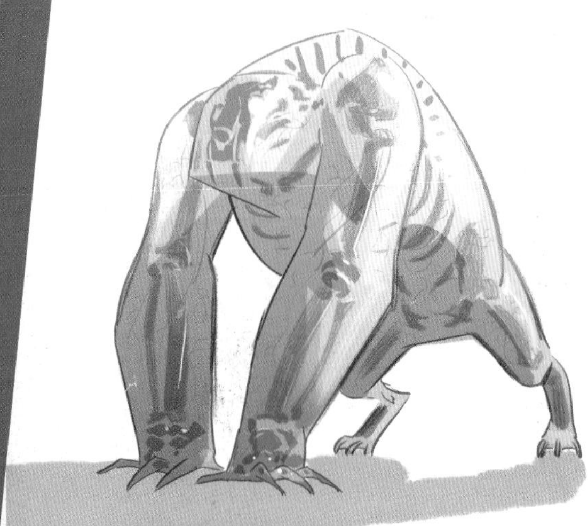

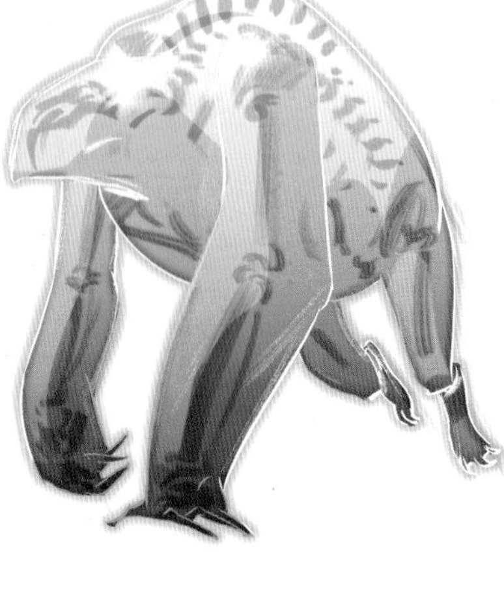

GIGI CAVENAGO: *The skeleton is a collage of different animals: I realized one of the first studies by assembling many photos of different kinds of skeletons in Photoshop – the arms of a gorilla, the spine of a bison, the hind legs of a tiger. The phantom mammoth's skull is also that of a tiger – a sabertooth, to be precise: since the phantoms are silent creatures (they don't growl or roar), I needed their faces to convey a sense of menace. The humanoid phantom's skull, instead, was inspired by a certain kind of fish. I deliberately avoided skulls that would look too human, both because they wouldn't have seemed like aliens anymore and the result would have been too grotesque and unpractical.*

About the other creatures, I can say that the devilfish was the easiest one to realize and the explosive chickens were the funniest (stay tuned for those). There were also phantom bats, but eventually we decided to leave them behind and never show them in action.

THESE TWO PAGES: STUDIES BY GIGI CAVENAGO

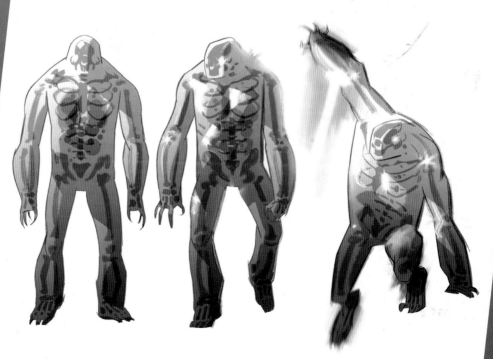

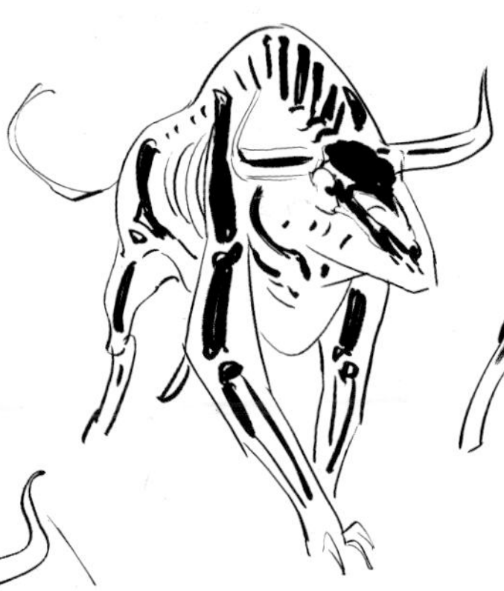
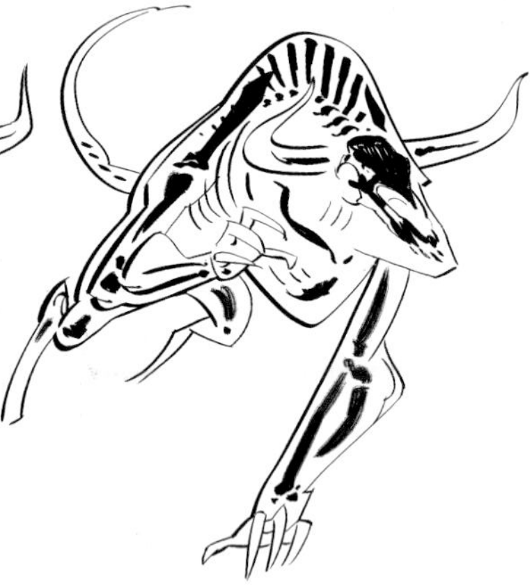
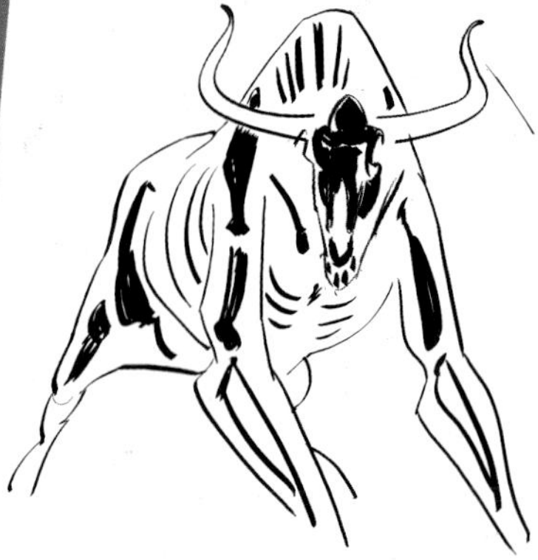
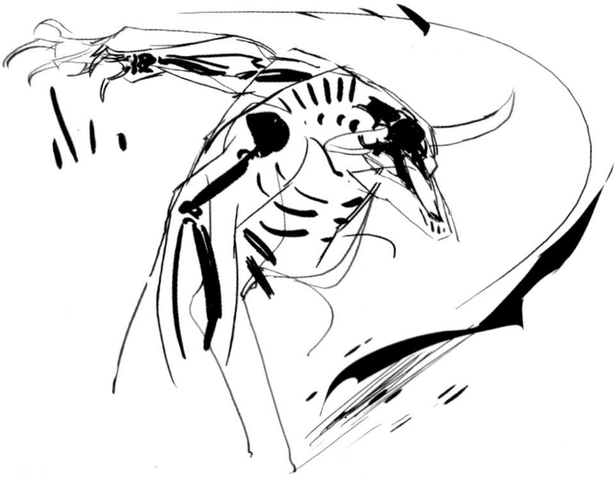
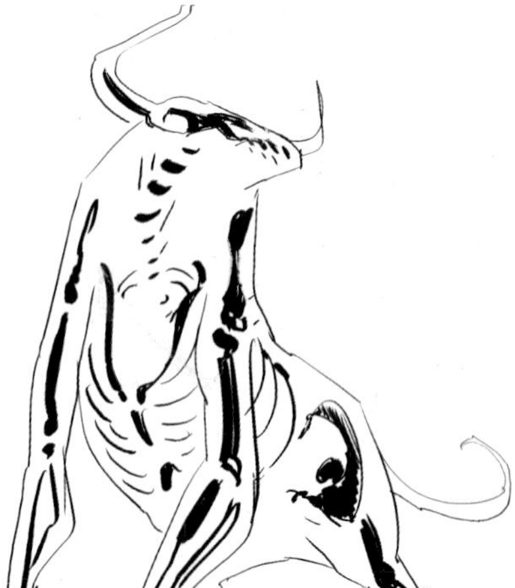
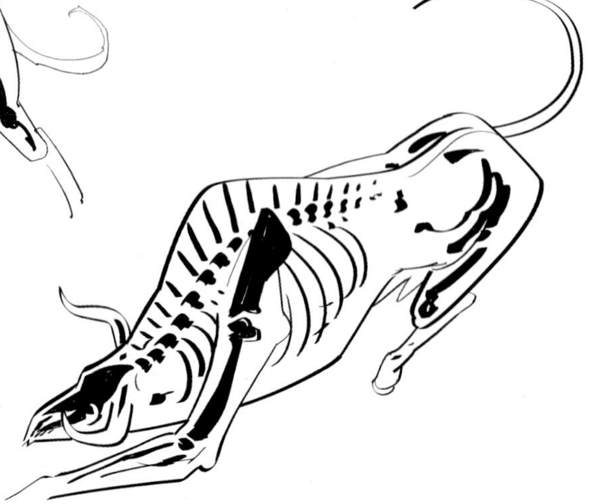

Studies by
Gigi Cavenago

Study by
Emiliano Mammucari

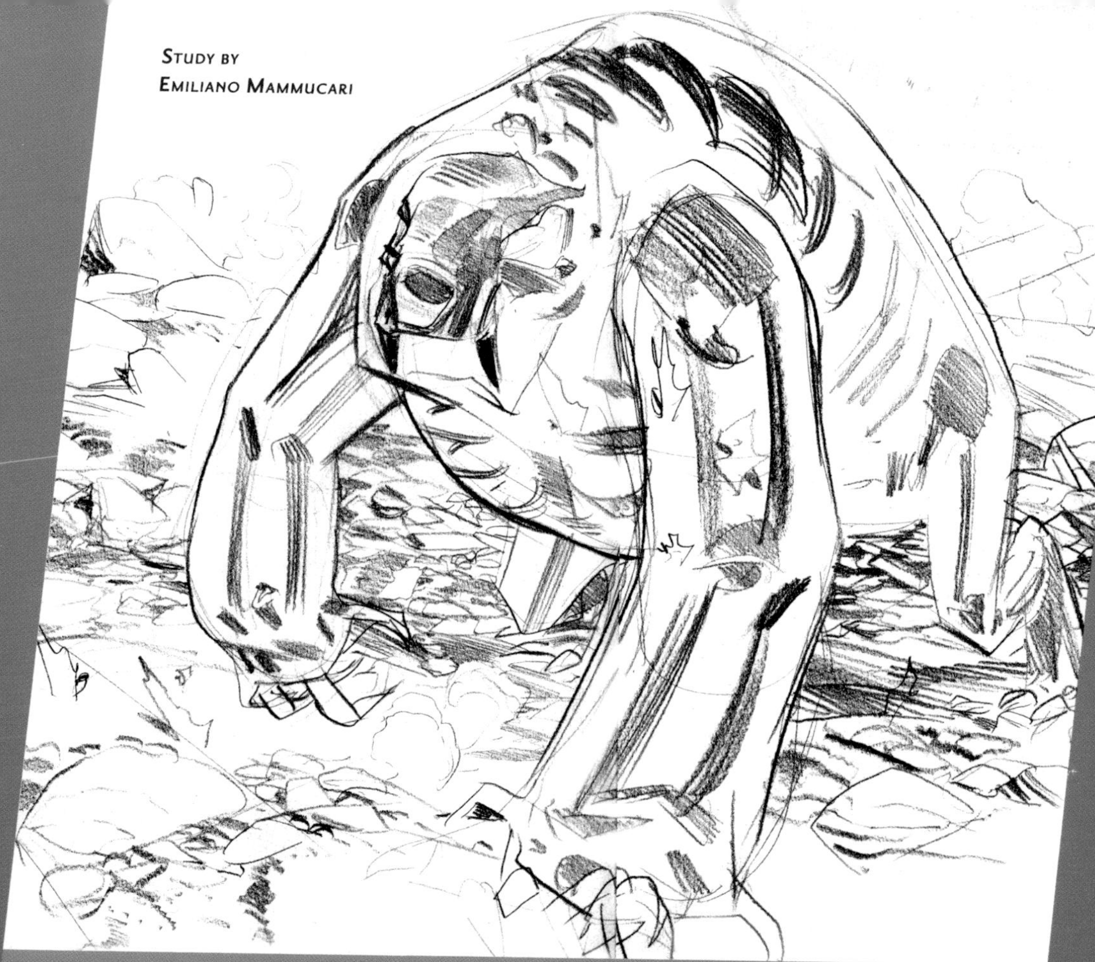

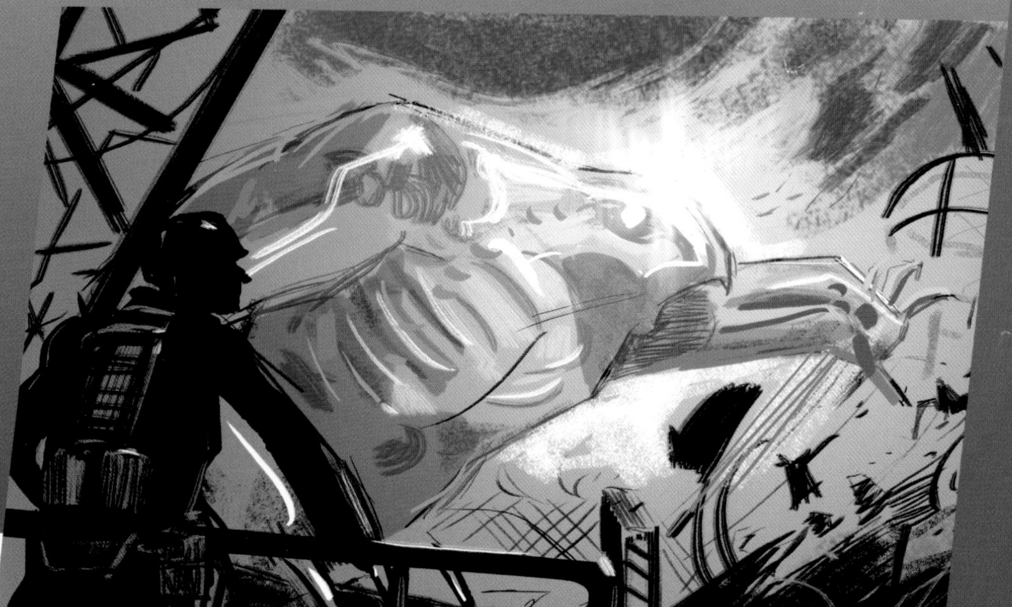

Illustration by Gigi Cavenago

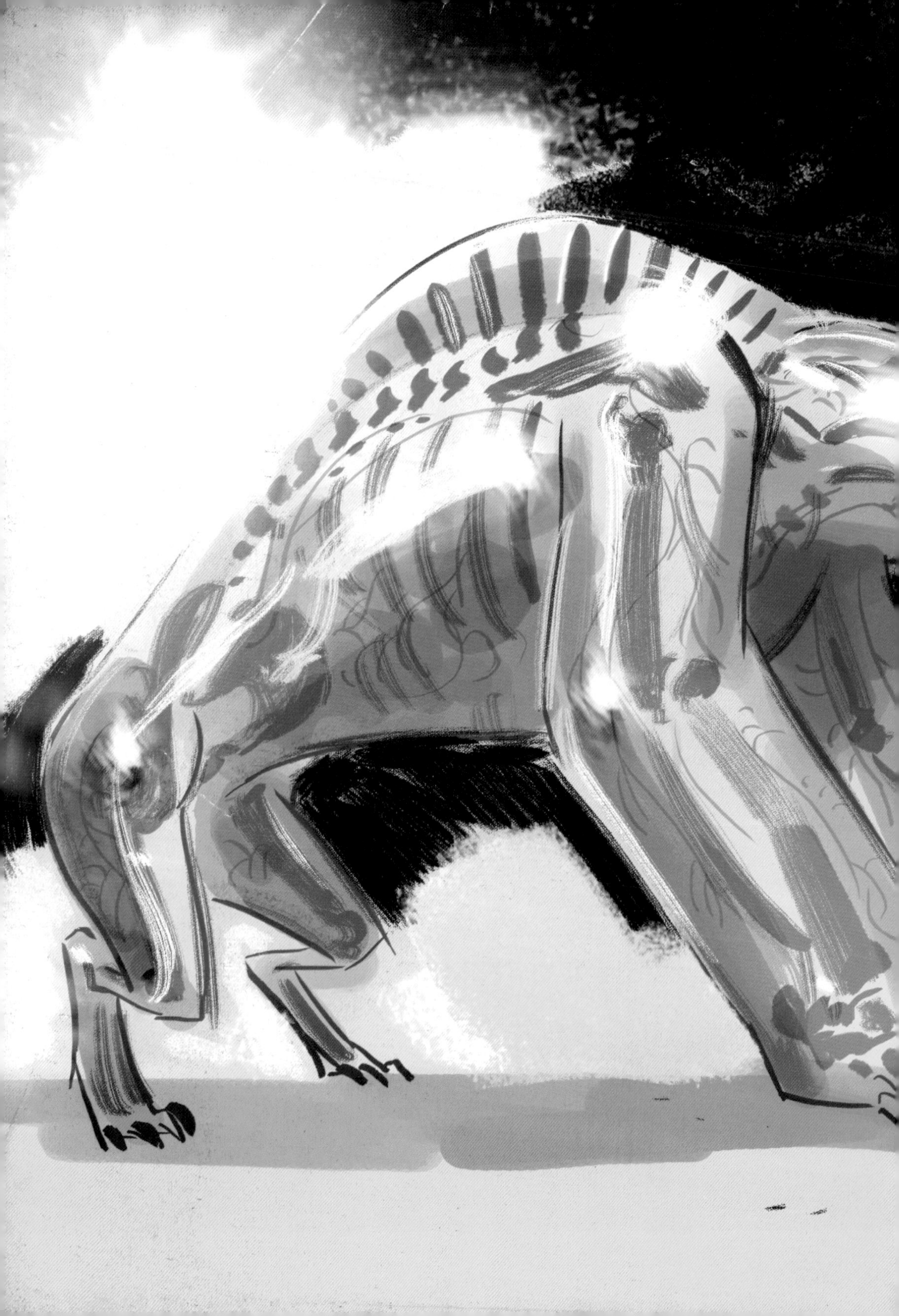

Previous page: illustration by Gigi Cavenago
Below: study by Emiliano Mammucari

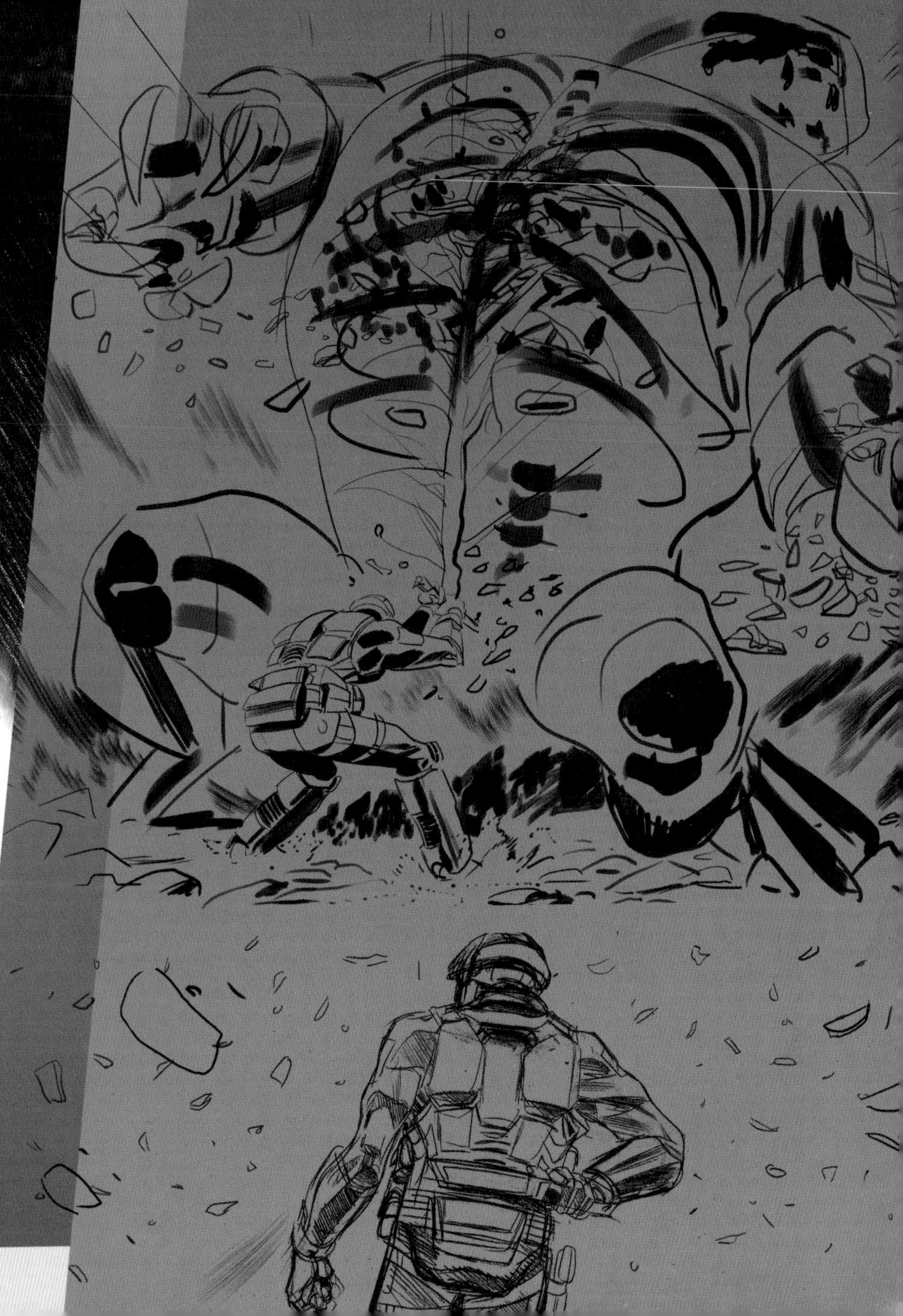

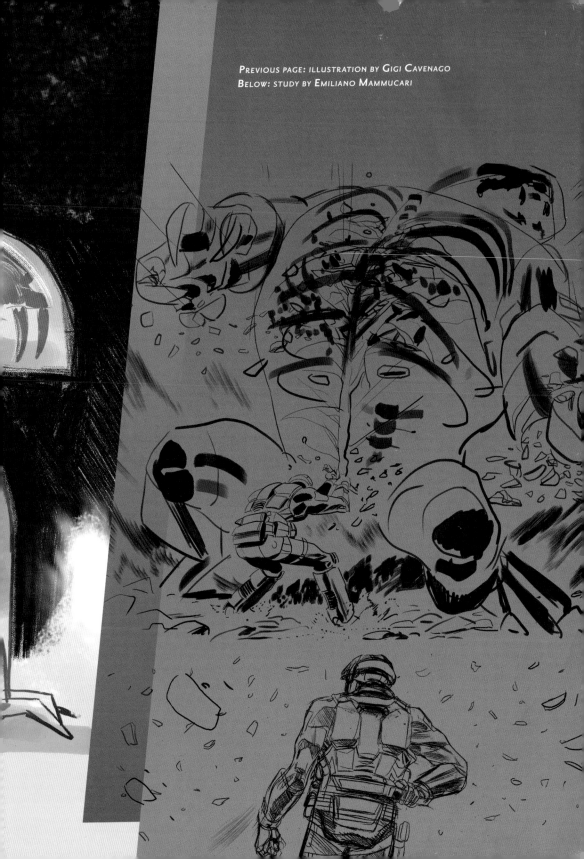

*I'LL CHECK MY EMAIL AND THERE IT IS...
A BEAUTIFUL COVER IS THERE JUST WAITING FOR ME.*

– Roberto Recchioni

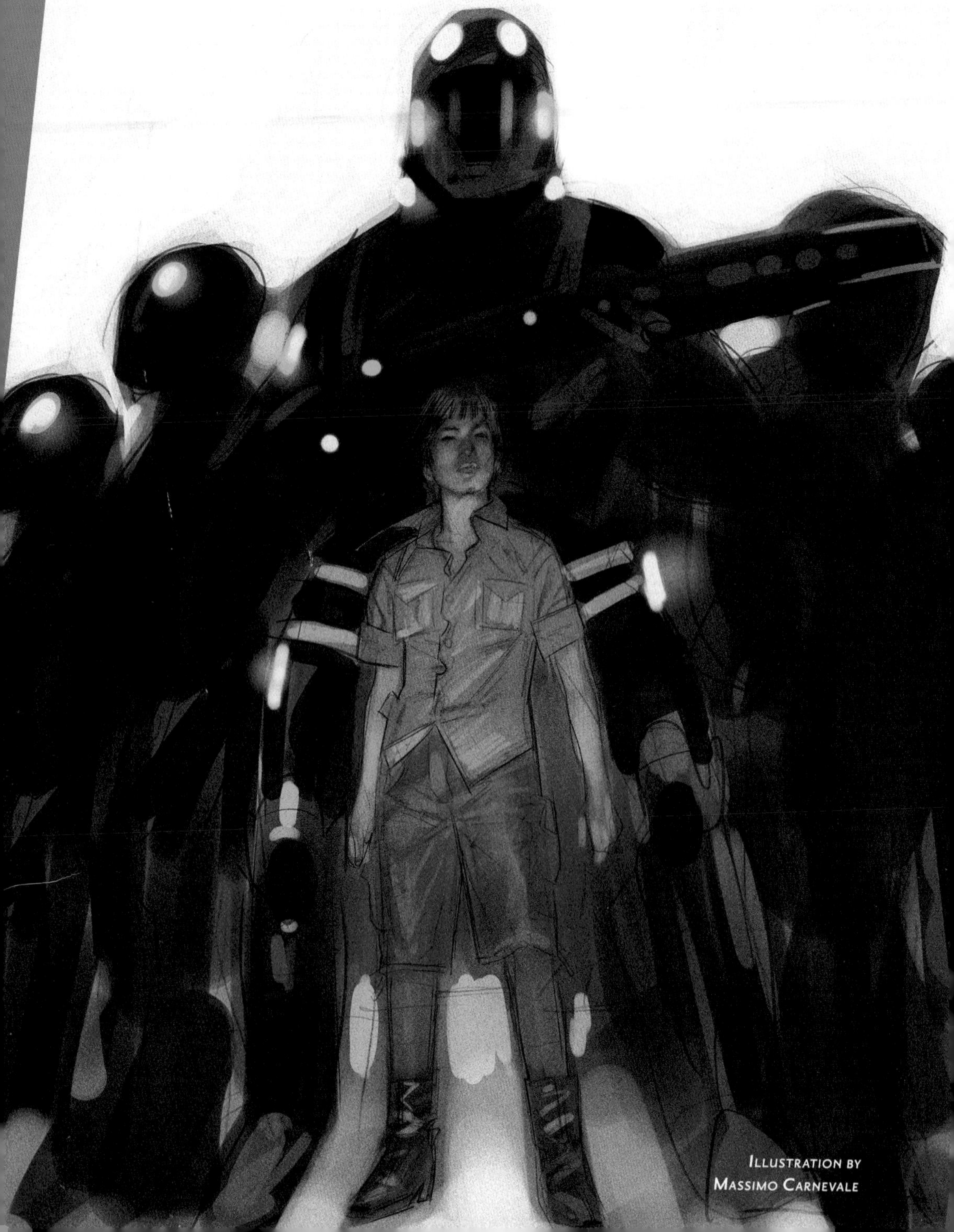

Illustration by
Massimo Carnevale

COVERS

ROBERTO RECCHIONI: Working on the creative process with Massimo Carnevale (cover artist of season one) is always a big deal. Trust me, I've designed about a hundred covers with him. It usually goes this way: first, we talk about the general mood and approach of the series; then, month after month, I tell him which elements should be pointed out according to the issue. When I talk about "elements," I mean actual things (like an alien city in the middle of a desert) as well as emotional things. We need a sad cover? A romantic one? Maybe an anxious one? Best-case scenario, we have time and Massimo sends me a few sketches with different solutions, and together (along with Emiliano and the editorial staff) we consider which is the best one to bet on. Worst-case scenario, it goes something like this:

- Hi, Massimo... you remember you have to draw this month's cover, right?
- Who are you? Who gave you my number?
- Roberto, Roberto Recchioni... we're friends, remember? We've done lots of things together...
- Like what?
- John Doe... Garrett... Detective Dante... Mater Morbi...
- Hmm... yeah... sort of... what do you want?
- This month's *Orphans* Cover.
- I sent it in last week.
- No, that one was for last month's issue...
- What, you need another one?
- Yeah, you know, it's a monthly series...
- All right. Hold on... okay, check your email.

And as it usually happens, I'll check my email and there it is... a beautiful cover is there just waiting for me.

THE ACRYLIC COLORING STAGES IN THE PRODUCTION OF THE COVER TO CHAPTER TWO BY MASSIMO CARNEVALE
NEXT PAGE: SKETCH FOR THE SAME COVER

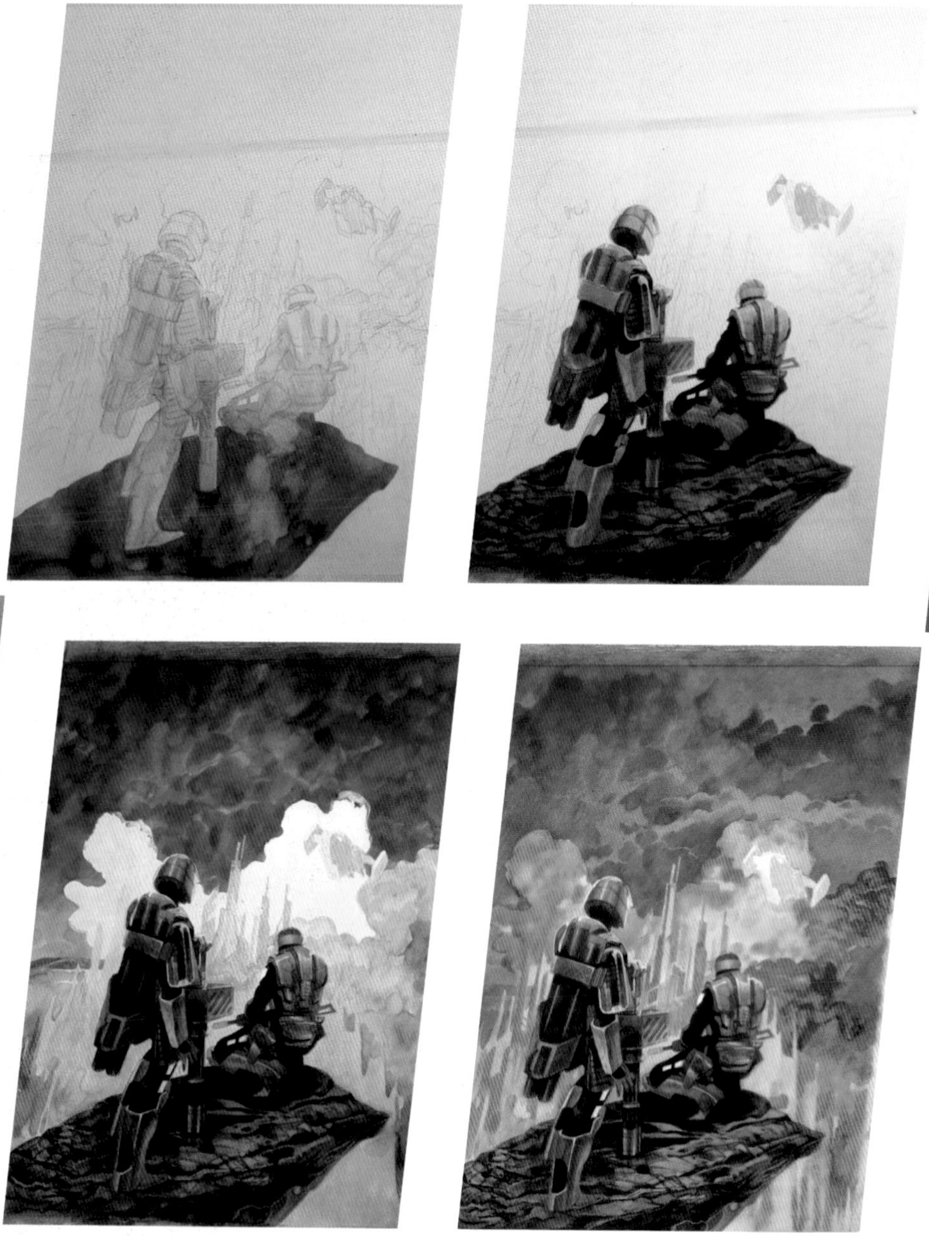

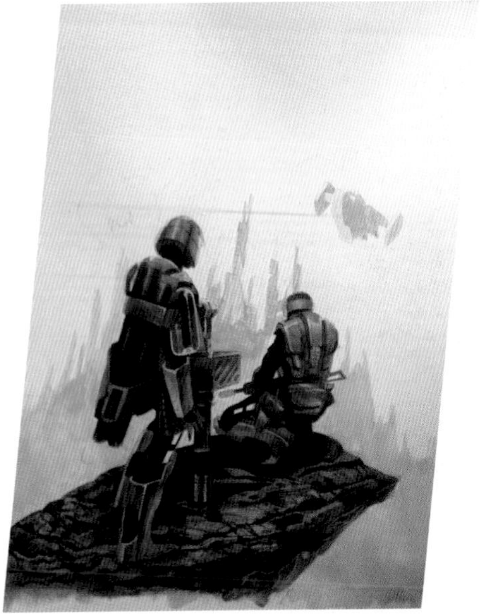

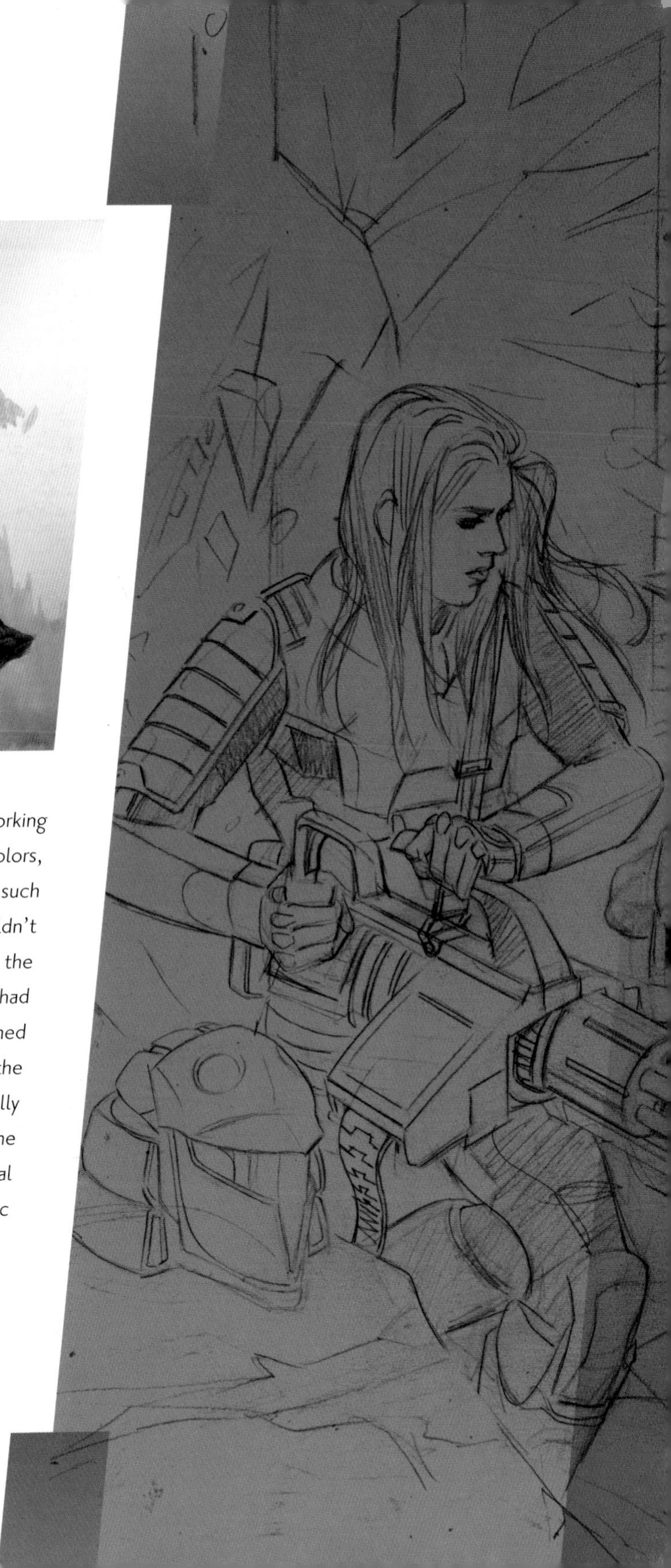

Massimo Carnevale started working on the covers using acrylic colors, but when he realized that such a traditional technique couldn't convey the modern mood of the series, he scanned the work he had done up to that point and polished the work digitally. Satisfied with the result, he started working digitally from the very beginning, finding the right balance between a pictorial style and the potential of a graphic tablet.

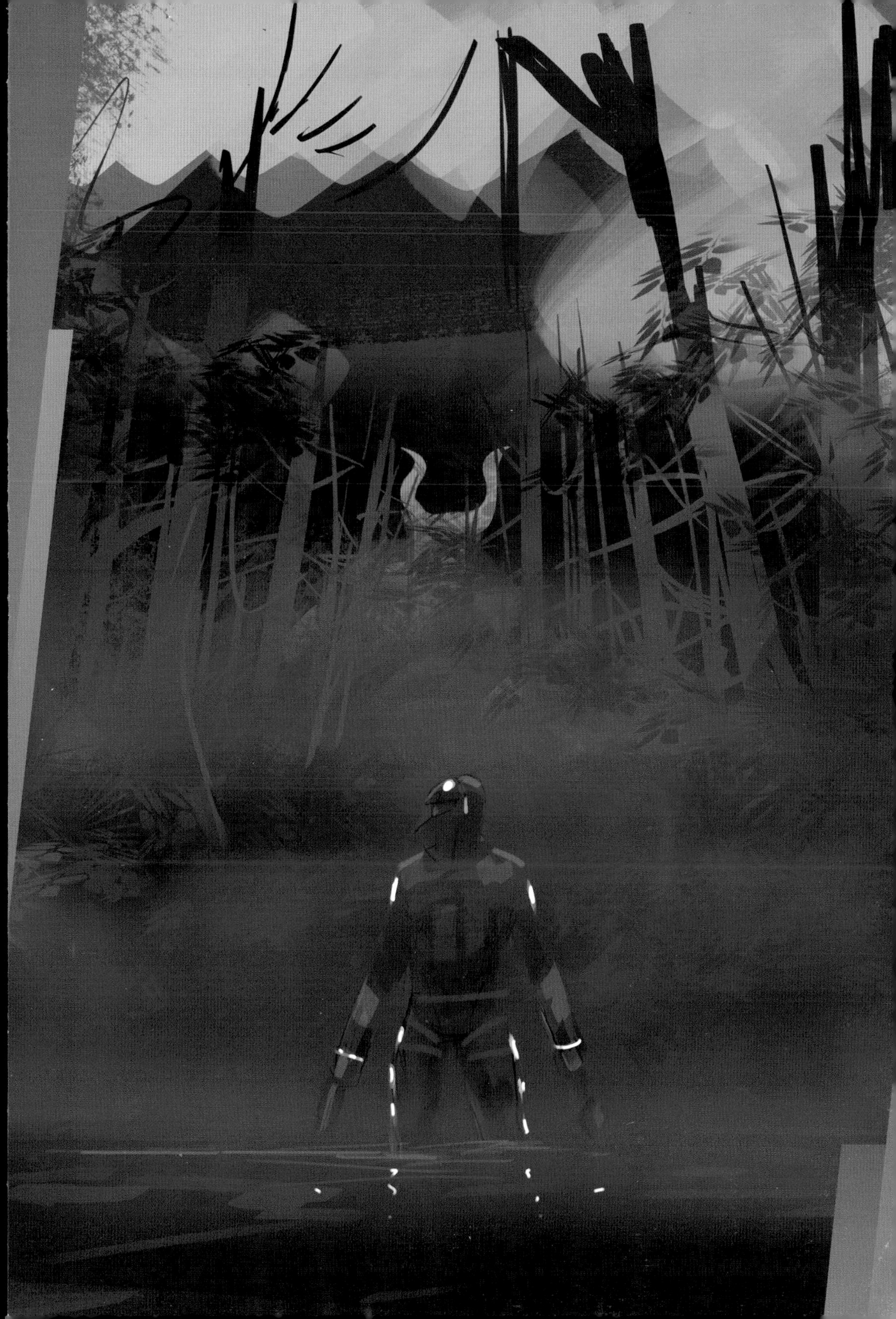

Illustration by Alessandro Bignamini
Colors by Annalisa Leoni

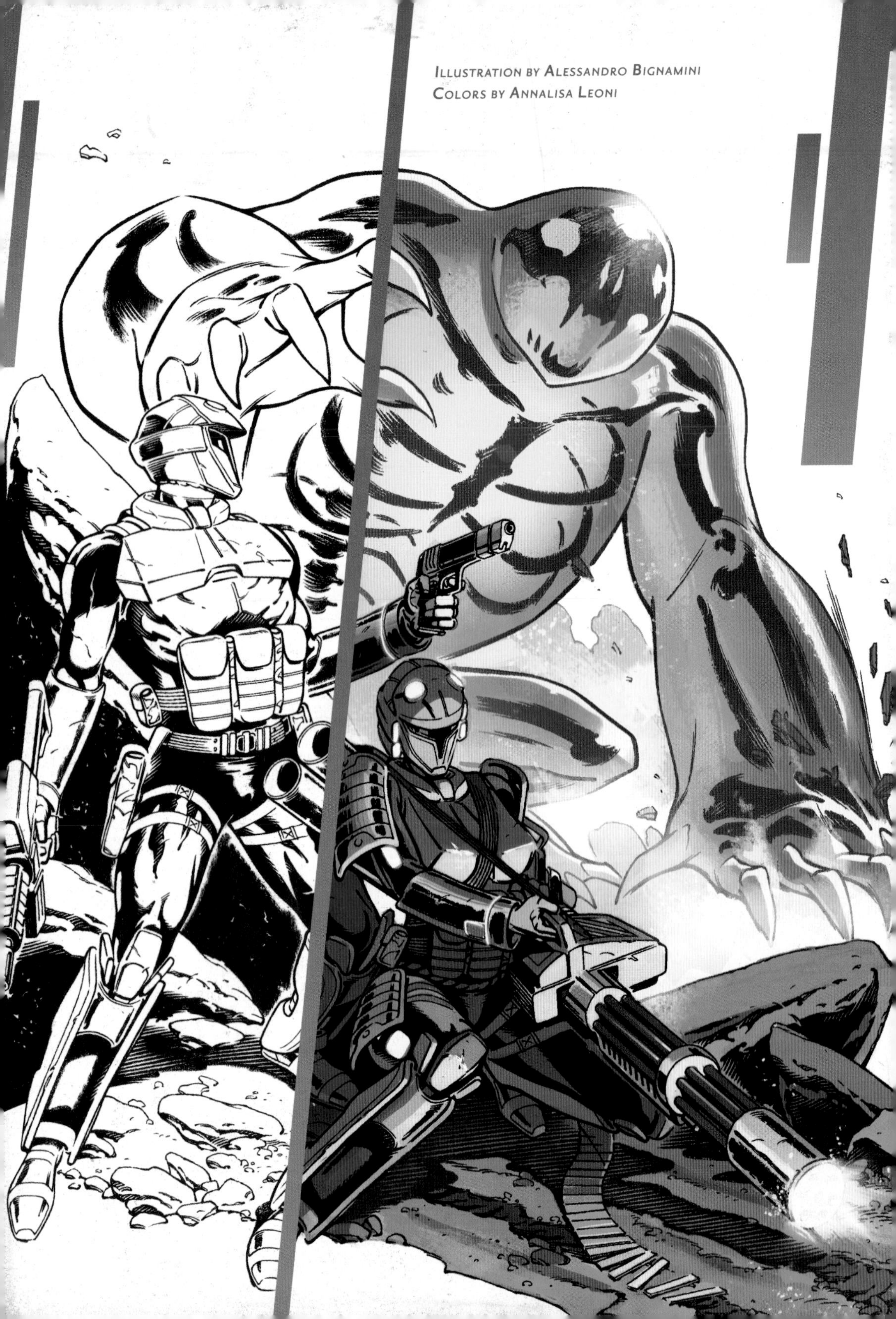

In the next volume...

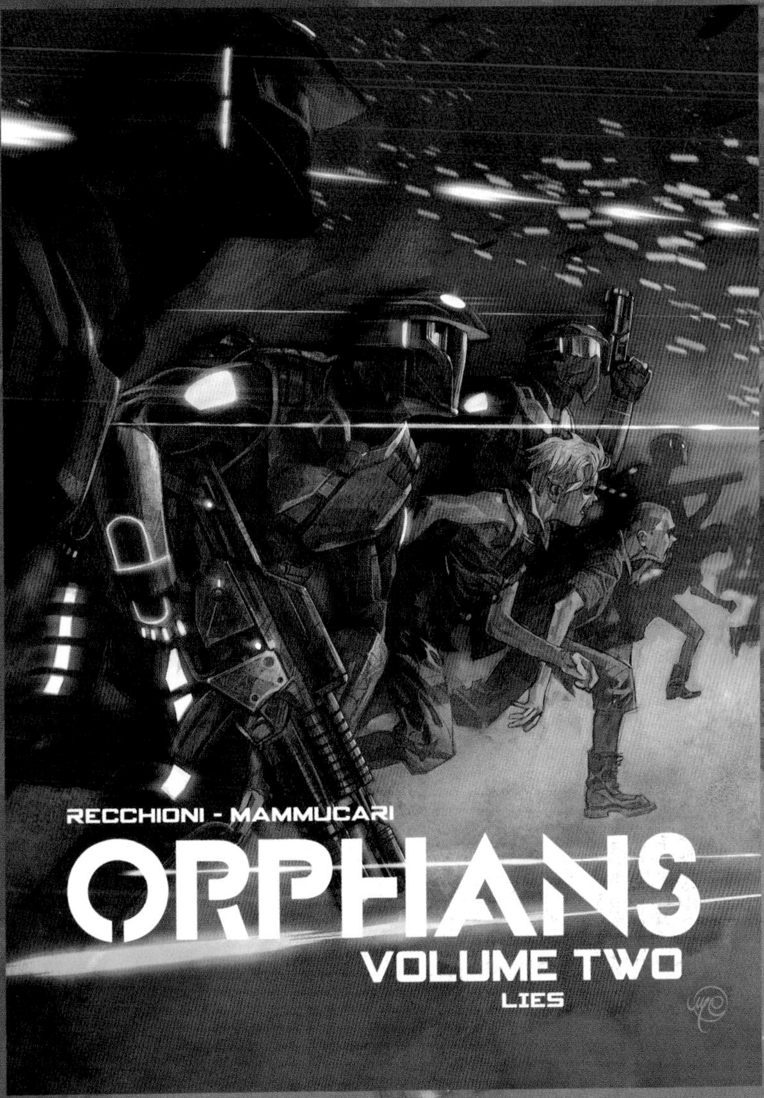
RECCHIONI - MAMMUCARI
ORPHANS
VOLUME TWO
LIES